WASHINGTON SUMMIT PUBLISHERS
2015

The Long Crusade

Profiles in Education Reform, 1967-2014

RAYMOND WOLTERS

© 2015 by Raymond Wolters
All rights reserved.

No part of this publication may be reproduced, distributed, or transmitted in any form or by any means, including photocopying, recording, or other electronic or mechanical methods, or by any information storage and retrieval system, without prior written permission from the publisher, except for brief quotations embodied in critical reviews and certain other non-commercial uses permitted by copyright law. For permission requests, contact the publisher.

Washington Summit Publishers
P.O. Box 100563
Arlington, VA, 22210

email : Info@WashSummit.com
web: www.WashSummit.com

Cataloging-in-Publication Data is on file with the Library of Congress

  ISBN: 978-1-59368-041-1
eISBN: 978-1-59368-040-4

Printed in the United States of America
10 9 8 7 6 5 4 3 2 1
First Edition

Contents

ix	Preface
1	Introduction

13	***Neo-Progressives***
15	Jonathan Kozol
73	Howard Gardner and the Theory of Multiple Intelligences
123	Theodore R. Sizer and the Coalition of Essential Schools

183	***Back To Basics***
185	Chris Whittle and the Edison Schools
213	Robert Slavin and Success for All
241	E. D. Hirsch and Core Knowledge

281	***Teach For America and its Progeny***
283	Wendy Kopp and Teach for America
333	Kopp's Kids: KIPP, DFER, and Michelle
413	Recent Trends in School Reform

469	***Contrarian Views of School Reform***
471	Diane Ravitch
513	The Race Realists
549	Robert Weissberg

569	Conclusion
579	Index
595	About the Author

Other Books by Raymond Wolters

Negroes and the Great Depression (1970)
The New Negro on Campus (1975)
The Burden of Brown (1984)
Right Turn (1996)
Du Bois and His Rivals (2002)
Race and Education, 1954-2007 (2009).

To Mary

Preface

It is customary for authors to say they could not have written a book without the support of family, friends, and colleagues. That certainly is the case in this instance, for my health declined as I worked on this book. In 2005 I was diagnosed with idiopathic pulmonary fibrosis, but for a few years I hardly noticed any effects. It was not until 2010, when I made plans to interview the leading school reformers, that I felt a shortness of breath. Not long after that, I needed increasing amounts of oxygen from what became my *vade mecum*, an oxygen tank. I then scrapped my plans to go on the road for interviews and instead did the only thing I could do at the time. I read a lot. I discovered a trove of new information on the Web, where I began most days reading the entries of blogger Steve Sailer. Sailer's writing introduced me to a number of other writers who, like Sailer, made a case for "race realism" and for the importance of "human biodiversity." I was especially impressed with the work of Napoleon Chagnon, Gregory Cochran, Henry Harpending, and Nicholas Wade.

I am grateful for the support and assistance I received during my illness. I am especially indebted to the anonymous donor of a lung that I received as a transplant at the Duke University Medical Center, which is one of only a very few places that will do lung transplants for patients who are over the age of 65. Without this new lung, this book would not have been completed. While I was hospitalized, the Delaware chapter of the American Association of University Professors (AAUP) helped me obtain a semester of medical leave from the University of Delaware. Afterwards, my department chairman, John Hurt, arranged for a reduced teaching load for one semester.

When I was in North Carolina awaiting the transplant, David Brook showed my wife and me around art galleries in Durham and Raleigh, and David F. Allmendinger, a former colleague who had moved to Chapel Hill after retiring from the University of Delaware, invited us for meals in Cary and Chapel Hill. A score or more of my colleagues at Delaware also sent me notes and email messages that I deeply appreciated. In terms of moral support, special thanks go to Peter Pettus. I had not known Peter prior to my giving a talk in Charlotte, North Carolina in 2011, a talk that eventually morphed into one of the chapters in this book. Peter liked the talk so much that we began to exchange emails and, as my health deteriorated, Peter read the entire manuscript and repeatedly assured me of the importance of publishing this book. I cannot overstate the importance of this moral support in seeing me through to publication.

I am also grateful to my Delaware colleague Robert L. Hampel for reading and commenting on every chapter of this book and to David Brook, Charles W. Eagles, Edward P. Johanningsmeier, Gerard Mangone, Gerald Martin, Paul D. Moreno, Diane Ravitch, and J. Samuel Walker for comments on specific portions of the manuscript. An earlier version of Chapter 9 first appeared as an article in the Summer 2010 issue of *The Occidental Quarterly*, and an earlier version of Chapter 12 was published in the November 2010 issue of *American Renaissance*. I am indebted to Kevin MacDonald and Jared Taylor, the editors of those journals, for valuable suggestions.

I am indebted as well to three people at Washington Summit Publishers: to Richard B. Spencer, the director of the press, for assessing the manuscript, for handling contractual matters, and for producing this book; to editor F. Roger Devlin for improving my prose and bringing consistency to the footnotes; and to Bill Regnery for supporting the press.

Preface

My greatest debt is to my wife, Mary Wolters. Mary graduated from the University of California, Berkeley, with a major in mathematics and a Phi Beta Kappa key. She taught high-school math for almost 30 years while also taking care of our home and our three sons. For more than 50 years, she has been a tremendous source of love and, now especially, support. In 1984, I dedicated an earlier book, *The Burden of Brown*, "To Mary." A second dedication was in order.

The Long Crusade

Introduction

This book discusses the lives and ideas of several of America's best-known school reformers. The first three chapters deal with men who are generally known as neo-progressives: Jonathan Kozol, Howard Gardner, and Theodore Sizer. The next three chapters deal with educators who favor back-to-basics approaches: Chris Whittle, Robert Slavin, and E. D. Hirsch. Chapters Seven, Eight, and Nine deal with Teach for America and its progeny. And three final chapters deal with writers who are skeptical about school reform: Diane Ravitch, John Derbyshire, and Robert Weissberg.

These profiles focus on the last 40 years of school reform, but these reforms occurred following an era of school desegregation and at a time when the ethnic composition of the United States was changing markedly. These two developments are summarized in this Introduction, for they provide the context for the modern era of school reform.

Many people initially resisted the major school reform of the 1950s—the desegregation the Supreme Court called for in its landmark decision of 1954, *Brown v. Topeka Board of Education*. By the end of the 1960s, however, the great majority of Americans accepted this policy. The turnabout occurred because both the Supreme Court and the U. S. Congress made it clear that desegregation required only that public schools should not discriminate racially. In several decisions between 1954 and 1968, the Supreme Court handed down rulings (and upheld lower-court decisions) that forbade the exclusion of children from public schools solely on the grounds of race. But the Supreme Court and the lower federal courts did not insist that compulsory *inclusion* must begin. The courts held that the proper remedy for compulsory separation was to end such separation. They made no demand that enrollments at individual schools be balanced to achieve approximately the same proportions that existed in a larger region or state. Congress endorsed this approach in the Civil Rights Act of 1964, which defined *desegregation* both positively and negatively:

> 'Desegregation' means the assignment of students to public schools and within such schools without regard to their race, color, religion, or national origin, but 'desegregation' shall not mean the assignment of students to public schools in order to overcome racial imbalance.[1]

By the late 1960s, the great majority of America's public school students were being assigned on a racially non-discriminatory basis. This was usually accomplished in one of two ways. Public school students were either assigned to schools close to their homes or allowed to attend whatever school they chose. By assigning students by neighborhood rather than race or by allowing them to choose their school, school districts satisfied the requirements of *Brown* and the Civil Rights Act. Yet neither policy achieved a racial mix in school enrollments that approximated the demographic proportions in the larger region. Enrollments in neighborhood schools turned out to be either mostly White or mostly Black, because most Whites and Blacks lived in neighborhoods that were inhabited predominantly by people of their own race. Enrollment in choice schools was also skewed because most students did not wish to attend a school in which their race would be a minority.

---

1 *Brown v. Board of Education*, 347 US 485 (1954); *Brown v. Board of Education*, 349 US 294 (1955); *Cooper v. Aaron*, 358 US 1 (1958); *Brown v. Board of Education*, 139 F. Supp (1955); *Briggs v. Elliott*, 132 F. Supp (1955); *Evans v. Buchanan*, 207 F. Supp 820 (1963); Public Law 88-352 (1964).

Introduction

Assignment on non-racial bases had no sooner been attained than the Supreme Court changed the meaning of desegregation. In *Green v. New Kent County* (1968), and in subsequent rulings in the 1970s, the Court held that school districts must take affirmative steps to achieve the maximum feasible amount of racial balance in student enrollments. In these decisions, the Court re-defined *desegregation* to mean precisely what the Civil Rights Act of 1964 said it did *not* mean: "the assignment of students to public schools in order to overcome racial imbalance." Commenting on this inversion, then-Justice William H. Rehnquist noted that it was "one thing . . . to require that a genuinely 'dual' system be disestablished," in the sense that the assignment of a child to a particular school is not made to depend on race. It was "quite obviously something else . . . to require that school boards affirmatively undertake to achieve racial mixing in schools where such mixing is not achieved in sufficient degree by neutrally drawn boundary lines."[2]

Green and its progeny led to busing for racial balance—a major school reform of the 1970s and 1980s. The social science rationale for this policy stressed the importance of a student's peers. Reformers said that youngsters were more likely to consider schoolwork important if their peers were serious about their studies, and middle-class youths were more likely to appreciate the importance of academic work. Since most White students were from the middle class and most Blacks were not, it seemed to follow that students should be assigned to create schools with enough middle-class youngsters to create a peer culture that favored education and a substantial number of lower-class students who could benefit from being exposed to such peers.

This point of view eventually became the conventional wisdom of most liberal academics. Over the course of several decades, thousands

---

2 *Green v. New Kent County*, 391 US 430 (1968); *Swann v. Charlotte Mecklenburg*, 402 US 1 (1971); *Columbus v. Penick*, 443 US 449 (1979); *Keyes v. School District No. 1*, 413 US 189 (1973) 257-58.

of professors signed statements claiming research had established that the academic achievement of Black students improved, and that of Whites did not decline, if students attended schools where the enrollments were racially balanced and predominantly White. In one Supreme Court case in 2006, 553 social scientists signed a statement that assured the Supreme Court that this sort of racially balanced integration improved "critical thinking skills" and boosted the "achievement level of African-American students." Beyond that, the 553 said racially balanced integration also "promotes cross-cultural understanding," "reduces racial prejudice," and increases the likelihood "that individuals . . . will work more productively with individuals of other races."[3]

By 2006, however, there was a mountain of evidence that contradicted these assertions. Chief Justice John G. Roberts understated the truth when he wrote that there was no consensus among the most knowledgeable scholars when it came to "whether racial diversity in schools in fact has a marked impact on test scores . . . or achieves intangible socialization benefits." If the best research on these topics were summarized candidly, the bottom line would be that the negative effects of integration often outweighed the positive.[4]

Many parents never accepted the policy of court-ordered integration. Forced busing gave rise to flight, initially among Whites and eventually among middle-class Blacks as well. The leading authority on the subject, sociologist James S. Coleman, calculated that after a tipping point had been reached, an increase of 5 percent in the average White child's Black classmates caused an additional 10 percent of White families to leave. Thus the nation faced "an insoluble dilemma." There would be no racially balanced integration

---

3   Brief of 553 Social Scientists, *Parents Involved v. Seattle*, U. S. Supreme Court, 2006.

4   *Parents Involved v. Seattle*, 127 S. Ct. 2378 (2007) 2755.

Introduction

without court-ordered busing, but such busing had the overall effect of defeating integration. The official push for school integration was offset by the actions of families who moved away from areas where there was a large enrollment of Black students to areas where there was less racial mixing.[5]

Many reformers, nevertheless, persisted with demands for racially balanced integration. In 1984, Jennifer Hochschild, a professor at Princeton, called for "democracy" to give way to "liberalism." Since most parents would not voluntarily send their children to racially balanced schools, courts should insist that they do so. Quoting John Dewey, Hochschild maintained, "what the best and wisest parent wants for his child, that must the community want for all its children." If most Americans would not choose to have racially balanced schools, "they must permit elites to make that choice for them."[6]

Other school reformers agreed. James Liebman, a Columbia law professor who worked on several school integration cases for the National Association for the Advancement of Colored People (NAACP), explained that one goal was to withdraw control from parents and to give children "a wider range of choices about the persons with whom they might associate and the values they might adopt as they approach adulthood." A principal purpose was to deny parents the right to send their children to schools that would reinforce "the 'personal features' and values those parents have chosen as their own." Liebman urged the government to protect the "autonomy" of children from the "tyranny" of parents. The state should make sure

---

5   James S. Coleman, "Recent Trend in School Integration," paper delivered to the American Educational Research Association (2 April 1975); Raymond Wolters, *Race and Education, 1954-2007* (Columbia: University of Missouri Press, 2008) 228-233.

6   Jennifer Hochschild, *The New American Dilemma: Liberal Democracy and School Desegregation* (New Haven: Yale University Press, 1984) 129, 124, 145, vii, 203.

that children were exposed to "a broader range of value options than their parents could hope to provide." According to Liebman, "family life" was too often "marked by exclusiveness, suspicion and jealousy as to those without."[7]

Although Blacks were assured that they would benefit from racially balanced integration, many African-American parents also had reservations about court-ordered busing. According to a Gallup poll of 1981, half the Black population in the United States believed this policy "caused more difficulties than it is worth." In another poll, 75 percent of African-Americans agreed with the assertion, "the schools work so hard to achieve integration that they end up neglecting their most important goal—teaching kids."[8]

Public opinion in the Black community might have been different if either desegregation or integration had led to improved achievement. But despite desegregation, the performance of Black students on standardized tests, when compared with the performance of White students, remained about where it had been in the 1950s. The evidence with respect to integration was not as conclusive since, due to White flight, integration often turned out to be a short-lived transitional phase. However, there were some communities where integration persisted for a generation or more. When that happened, Black and Hispanic students enjoyed the advantage of learning side-by-side with White students. But this did not change the academic

---

7   James S. Liebman, "Desegregating Politics: 'All-Out' School Desegregation Explained," *Columbia Law Review* 90 (October 1990) 1639, 1650; Liebman, "Implementing *Brown* in the Nineties," *Virginia Law Review* (April 1990) 365.

8   *New York Times* (2 March 1981); Greg Winter, "Long after *Brown*, Sides Switch," *New York Times* (16 May 2004) summarizing the results of a poll by Public Agenda, a nonpartisan research group. Pollster Samuel Lubell reported that about 50 percent of African-Americans were opposed to busing for racial balance. See Ben. J. Wattenberg, *The Real America* (Garden City: Doubleday, 1974) 252.

Introduction

outcomes. A familiar pattern persisted, with about 85 percent of the Black students (and 75 percent of the Hispanics) scoring below the White average.[9]

Eventually, the Supreme Court adjusted its jurisprudence. The Court came to recognize that, as Justice Lewis Powell put it, many parents regarded busing for racial balance as an interference with "the concept of community" and with the "liberty to direct the upbringing and education of children under their control." The legal tide first turned against court-ordered busing in 1974, when the Supreme Court set up roadblocks that stopped courts from requiring busing between most predominantly Black inner cities and their predominantly White suburbs. The Court followed up in the 1990s with three decisions that provided a road map for school districts that wished to be released from court orders in those places where courts had already required busing for integration. Then, in 2007, the Supreme Court ruled that local communities could not assign students by race to promote balanced integration, even if the communities wished to do so.[10]

In significant part, the modern era of school reform stemmed from the persistence of racial and ethnic achievement gaps and the demise of court-ordered busing. Because racial and ethnic differences in academic achievement proved to be impervious to amelioration through either desegregation or racial balancing, many educators embraced other varieties of school reform as alternative ways to uplift Black and Hispanic students. They had no choice. Because of the

---

9 Abigail Thernstrom and Stephan Thernstrom, *No Excuses* (New York: Simon & Schuster, 2003) 12 and *passim*; John U. Ogbu, *Black American Students in an Affluent Suburb* (Mahwah, NJ: Lawrence Erlbaum Associates, 2003).

10 *Milliken v. Bradley*, 418 US 717 (1974); *Keyes v. School District No. 1*, 413 US 189 (1973); *Oklahoma City v. Dowell*, 111 S.Ct. 630 (1991); *Freeman v. Pitts*, 60 USLW 4286 (1992); *Missouri v. Jenkins*, 63 USLW (1995); *Parents Involved v. Seattle*, 127 S.Ct. 2378 (2007).

Supreme Court's rulings, reformers could no longer regard getting the correct mix of students as the key to ensuring that no group would lag behind. Other approaches had to be tried.

Most reformers were well-intentioned. They wanted to help weak students. And they sought to promote the national interest as well. By 2010, Blacks and Hispanics made up 40 percent of all children under 18, and demographers predicted that these minorities would become a majority of all American children by as soon as 2023. Many analysts, therefore, warned that the American economy would falter if the educational performance of African-American and Hispanic youths did not improve. The U. S. had "a tremendous stake in investing in the education of young Latinos and African-Americans," said Stephen Klineberg, a sociologist at Rice University. "The gap in achievement has to be narrowed if there's any serious hope for American competitiveness in the global economy."[11]

In recent years, school reformers have experimented with a number of plans. Some school districts increased their spending markedly. Others provided more services, reformed the curriculum, reduced class size, and employed more minority teachers to serve as role models. Some confronted teachers' unions, abolished tenure for teachers, and instituted merit pay. In recent years, there has been an emphasis on school choice and accountability. School choice was manifest in proposals for vouchers, tax credits, magnet schools, and

---

11   Stephen Klineberg, quoted by Ronald Brownstein, "The Gray and the Brown," *National Journal* (24 July 2010). Also see Brownstein, "King's Echo: Why Equal Opportunity is Now a Competitiveness Issue," *National Journal* (26 August 2011); and Brownstein, "Bound Together: Why America Must Bridge the Widening Divide Between the Brown and the Gray," *National Journal* (9 September 2011). For a critique that says Brownstein is "blissfully ignorant of all the social science research, whether in race differences in academic potential or on the disastrous consequences of multiculturalism," see Kevin MacDonald, "The Republican Party Is Doomed," *TheOccidentalObserver.net* (14 September 2011).

Introduction

charter schools. Accountability was manifest in the establishment of state educational standards and in the testing associated with the federal No Child Left Behind program.

When I began this book, I recognized that different students take to different approaches, and for that reason I sympathized with reformers who wished to give students a greater range of choices. I also thought schools should be accountable for ensuring that students learned the fundamentals of reading and arithmetic. As I learned more about school reform, however, I developed mixed feelings. I still favor school choice and accountability, but some limitations and weaknesses of progressive education have become apparent, as have some problems associated with standardized testing and "back to basics" direct instruction. Teach for America, and the movement it spawned, has also had some surprising consequences. Some of its graduates have transitioned from their initial emphasis on helping hard-pressed schools to blaming teachers and their unions for the shortcomings of low-achieving students. They say racial and ethnic achievement gaps could be closed if only there were better teachers, and that the best way to get good teachers is to fire the teachers whose students make low scores on standardized tests, to hire replacements on probationary contracts, and to keep only those teachers who excel in raising the test scores of their students.

As this book goes to press, "blaming the teachers" has become the fashion in school reform. Writing in the *New York Times*, Nicholas D. Kristof explained, "We all understand intuitively the difference a great teacher makes." And now, Kristof wrote, there is research to support this intuition. "One Los Angeles study found that having a teacher from the 25 percent most effective group of teachers for four years in a row would be enough to eliminate the black-white achievement gap." Another study reported that good teachers, "even kindergarten teachers, increase their students' earnings many years later.... A teacher better than 93 percent of other teachers would add

$640,000 to lifetime pay of a class of 20, the study found."[12]

Ivy League researchers have chimed in. At a conference at Columbia University in 2010, Doug Staiger, a professor at Dartmouth, and Jonah Rockoff, a professor at Columbia, described a simulation exercise that built on prior findings about the way teachers can affect student scores and the fraction of new teachers who can boost scores substantially. After checking and rechecking their analyses, Staiger and Rockoff concluded that to get the very best teachers about 80 percent of new teachers should be fired after two years' probation. If 2.8 million of the nation's 3.5 million teachers were fired, they concluded, the achievement gaps could be closed and prosperity enhanced.[13]

The research and rationale of these reformers will be discussed in the body of this book. For this introduction, it should suffice to say that skepticism is warranted. I believe that modern school reformers, when they exalt the importance of firing so many "bad teachers," are as extreme in their approach as were their pro-busing precursors—the earlier generation of school reformers who insisted that "democracy" should give way to "liberalism" and that the government should protect the "autonomy" of children from the "tyranny" of their parents.

This account is structured so that readers will understand that I take exception to aspects of both neo-progressivism and back-to-basics, and that I have mixed feelings about Teach for America and its progeny. Readers will further understand that I am less critical of "the contrarians"—the skeptical educators and writers who are discussed in the final chapters of this book. Like the skeptics, I question the "narrative of crisis"—the idea that the entire system of American education is mired in failure. On the contrary, I believe that most

---

12 Nicholas D. Kristof, "Pay Teachers More," *New York Times* (12 May 2001).

13 Columbia professor Ray Fisman summarized this research in "Clean Out Your Desk," Slate.com (11 August 2010).

Introduction

teachers and students are doing well. Of course, many students are not doing as well as they could or should, and this is especially true of Black and Hispanic students. But there is no system-wide crisis. In fact, as will be noted, most American students are already doing as well as students anywhere in the world.

In writing this account of modern American education, I have tried to be objective and even-handed, not polemical. The current fashion is for books on public policy to present an argument, but I do not think there is a "silver bullet" that will solve our educational problems. Beyond that, I am an historian, not a reformer, and I have written a narrative rather than a lawyer's brief. My intent is to provide readers with enough information—including information that some education writers consider taboo—to draw their own conclusions as well as to understand my views.

Part I

Neo-Progressives

I

Jonathan Kozol

In some ways, Jonathan Kozol was a lonely and isolated individual critic of America's schools. But as the nation's best-selling education writer, he enjoyed enormous influence. Indeed, Kozol's prescription for public education—his calls for teachers to have more empathy for minority students, for taxpayers to provide more money for inner-city schools, for curriculum planners to design less prescriptive courses of study, and for the nation to integrate students from the mostly Black cities with students from predominantly White suburbs—came to represent the mainstream of liberal school reform in the 1970s and early 1980s. Even after the Supreme Court of the 1990s ruled against busing for integration, other courts cited Kozol's book *Savage Inequalities* (1991) as part of their rationale for ordering additional spending for public schools that enrolled disproportionate numbers of disadvantaged students.

Kozol's prominence began in 1967, when his account of a year he spent teaching in a Boston elementary school received a National Book Award. The title and subtitle summed up his message: *Death at an Early Age: The Destruction of the Hearts and Minds of Negro Children in the Boston Public Schools*. The book enjoyed phenomenal success, with sales eventually amounting to more than two million copies. According to one Boston journalist, *Death at an Early Age* also "stirred more controversy in this city than perhaps any title published since Boston stopped banning books."[1]

---

1   Jonathan Kozol, *Death at an Early Age: The Destruction of the Hearts and Minds of Negro Children in the Boston Public Schools* (Boston: Houghton

Born into a well-to-do family in Massachusetts, Kozol attended a private prep school and then flourished at Harvard. As s young man, he resigned a Rhodes scholarship at Oxfrd and went to Paris to become a novelist. When that did not work out, he returned to Boston and became a teacher in a mostly-Black public school. Since most of Kozol's pupils came from impoverished families, the school received extra funds from the federal government. With this money, the school was able to provide Kozol's fourth-grade class with special teachers for art, reading, and mathematics as well as a regular teacher (Kozol). As Kozol told the story, however, this was not an advantage, for the special teachers (and most other teachers at the school) were racist White authoritarians.

Death at an Early Age began by introducing Stephen, "an indescribably mild and unmalicious" eight-year-old Black boy who was beaten occasionally at his foster home and also at school, where teachers talked about the way to use a rattan cane on children. "When you do it, you want to snap it abruptly or else you are not going to get the kind of effect you want." When Kozol asked if it was within the rules to strike a child, he was told: "Don't worry about the law. You just make damn sure no one's watching." Some teachers used the cane to maintain order in unruly classes, but Kozol also observed instances where there were "unmistakable" signs of "sadism." There were moments "when the visible glint of gratification becomes undeniable in the White teacher's eyes."[2]

The damage from the blows was slight when compared with the psychic harm that Stephen suffered "at the hands of the art teacher . . . a lady no longer very young who had some rather fixed values and opinions about children and about teaching." In Kozol's telling,

---

Miflin Company, 1967); Mark Feeney, "The Gentlest Angry Man," *Boston Globe* (17 May 2000).

2   *Ibid.*, 1-2, 16-17.

Stephen was a "fine artist" who made "delightful drawings" in which he "elaborated, amended, fiddled with, and frequently added to . . . pictures which he had copied out of comic books." But the art teacher would have none of this. "Garbage!" she said to the entire class. "Junk! He gives me garbage and junk. And garbage is one thing I will not have." Although enrollment at the school had changed from mostly White to 60-percent Black, the art teacher insisted that students must imitate what had been done before, "and the neatest and most accurate reproductions of the original drawings would be the ones that would win the highest approval." On one occasion, the art teacher told the Black students, "These are the kinds of pictures that the children who came to this school used to do here. You children couldn't do it."[3]

Another memorable instance occurred when the mother of one young girl told the school that her daughter would "finish off this year but would not be back again." Having ascertained that both Kozol and the art teacher were Jewish, as were the mother and daughter, the mother then said, "familiarly and, somehow, knowingly and intimately," that she did not want her daughter to be where there were "so many colored." The art teacher immediately sympathized. "It's not moving away from Negro people," she said. "It is just wanting to live where there are more Jews." The art teacher further said she thought about the Jewish children when she planned her art classes. "It is this remnant which I cannot help having at heart." She did not wish "to deny any Negro child but rather only 'to save this Jewish remnant.'" The art teacher also drew "an unfavorable comparison between the kinds of homes the Negro people kept in Roxbury and the homes of the Jews who had lived in these blocks only about ten or fifteen years before." She said the homes in the area "had been beautiful once when the Jewish people lived there, but now had been allowed to go to pieces through lack of proper maintenance and appropriate care."[4]

---

3   Ibid., 1-4, 153.

4   Ibid., 148-153.

Kozol was aghast. He thought it unconscionable that the art teacher would speak this way. And he became even more troubled when he sensed that the reading teacher, a White Christian woman, also favored children "whose parents were most like herself." Although the reading teacher insisted that she harbored no racial prejudice and professed an "all-enveloping love" for the Black children she was teaching, she went out of her way only for White children—making arrangements for one poor White student to attend a summer camp and for the parents of another to visit the teacher's home, but "not once . . . offer[ing] to do anything of that sort for any child who was Negro." The reading teacher also told Kozol that she would be "shocked" if he "fell in love with a Negro girl" and would feel "terribly sad" if he married one.[5]

Other teachers were not only racially conscious but deeply prejudiced. One pointed at the children in the playground and said: "Those are the animals, and this is the zoo." Another told Kozol that teaching disadvantaged Black children was a hopeless cause. The chairman of the school committee declared, "We have no inferior education in our schools. What we have been getting is an inferior type of student." Whether they considered the students disadvantaged or inferior, most teachers thought the school had been given an impossible task. Sometimes "a frank distaste for Negro children was stated bluntly and forthrightly." In one instance a teacher blurted out, "Christ, I'm prejudiced. I'll admit it. Look at my hand. . . . I just barely grazed one of them out there on his forehead and I got all this junk on me. Look at it—I've got to go and wash it."[6]

Kozol also complained that for a while his class had to share an auditorium with another fourth grade, with a choir, and with a group

---

5   Ibid., 147, 65, 22-23.

6   *Time* (10 November 1967), 56; William O'Connor, quoted by Nat Hentoff, "The Most Deadly Sin," *New Yorker* 44 (6 March 1968) 166; Jonathan Kozol, "Department of Lower Learning," *The New Republic* 156 (20 May 1967) 33.

that was rehearsing for a Christmas play. Yet the emphasis in *Death at an Early Age* was not on any inadequacy in facilities or funds. As *Time* magazine noted in its review of the book, the main charge was that "a powerful anti-Negro prejudice permeates the entire Boston school system." This was evident not only in the teachers' attitudes but also in curricular materials. "The school system was still using textbooks of an openly racist nature," Kozol wrote, books that "contained such information as ... 'most Southern people treated their slaves kindly' ... [and] 'the white men who have entered Africa are teaching the natives how to live.'" Nevertheless, Kozol was rebuked when he supplemented these books with other readings about Black people and race relations. "I wouldn't mind using them," the reading teacher said of the supplementary readings, "if these were all Negro children in your room. But it would not be fair to the white children.... We do not have all Negroes. If we did, it would be different."[7]

Kozol was also criticized for driving one Black student home from school, for arranging a museum trip for another Black student, and for visiting some Black parents in their homes. Yet he felt certain there would have been no similar censure if the students or parents had been White. A school supervisor informed Kozol, "You are here to keep order and to teach these children, not to be a pal.... You're here to instruct them and keep them orderly, not to be a big brother." Kozol was told that "any friendly relationship with a student outside the classroom would make teaching him impossible or, at the least, substantially more difficult."[8]

Because *Death at an Early Age* was a tale of pervasive callousness and cruelty, some readers found Kozol's descriptions unbelievable. The superintendent of Boston's public schools angrily denied the

---

7   *Time* (10 November 1967), 56; Jonathan Kozol, "Department of Lower Learning," 34; Kozol, *Death at an Early Age*, 83.

8   Jonathan Kozol, *Death at an Early Age*, 111-112.

allegation that Black pupils were whipped with rattan canes. And specific teachers could not respond, since they were not identified in the book. While stating that the "attitudes . . . [and] viewpoints ascribed to the faculty . . . in this book accurately reflect the author's experience," Kozol acknowledged that his characters did "not have counterparts in real life" and were "described . . . in a manner which will not identify real people." *Time* magazine noted that Kozol was "not really trying to be fair" but rather "to assault and appall his readers, to jar them from . . . complacen[cy]"⁹

In this he succeeded. While admitting that Kozol's description of White teachers were "stereotyped and totally negative " (and that he offered "no unsympathetic sketch of a Negro adult or child"), Elizabeth M. Eddy, the reviewer for the *Harvard Educational Review*, concluded, "For me, Kozol's account rings true." Writing in the *New York Review of Books*, John Holt admitted that Kozol's account was so "grotesque" that he felt compelled to ask, "Are these horrors true? Have indignation and resentment made Kozol exaggerate or distort what really happened? Is he a credible witness?" Nevertheless, Holt concluded that there was "no doubt" that Kozol was telling the truth. The Dean of Harvard's Graduate School of Education, Theodore Sizer, went further and was reported as saying, "Kozol's recital of the ills of the Boston schools could be duplicated in many other big U. S. school systems."¹⁰

Kozol's portrayal of racist White teachers was so unsparing that some Black readers must have been tempted to give up on integration and establish their own schools, with Black teachers and an Afrocentric curriculum. That is what Blacks of the late-1960s did in

---

9   *New York Times* (27 October 1967); Jonathan Kozol, *Death at an Early Age*, ix; *Time* (8 February 1988) 74.

10   *Harvard Educational Review* 38 (1968) 367-370; *New York Review of Books* (21 December 1967) 5-9; *Time* (10 November 1967), 56.

many areas—in Atlanta, in Ocean Hill-Brownsville, in Hyde County, North Carolina, and elsewhere. Kozol, however, recommended racially balanced integration as the best policy. He condemned Boston's policy of assigning children to the nearest neighborhood public school, because this policy made it impossible to achieve proportional integration at each school, and he later wrote with satisfaction that "*Death at an Early Age* appears to have had some effect in heightening the pressure that led in time to the court-ordered integration of the Boston schools." In *The Shame of the Nation*, a book published in 2005, Kozol reiterated his support for racially balanced integration.[11]

Kozol's insistence on integration may have been inconsistent in 1965. It was less so in 2005, for by then the education of teachers had been substantially reformed, and many of the changes were in the direction that Kozol had implicitly recommended. After *Death at an Early Age*, the next generation of teachers was steeped in the importance of caring for minority students and cultivating their self-esteem. The journalist Rita Kramer emphasized this point after spending the academic year 1988-89 visiting schools of education throughout the United States, sitting in on classes, talking with faculty and students, and visiting the schools where education students did their practice teaching.

Kramer found that Kozol's book (along with the works of other like-minded education writers) "permeated the ed school world." At Columbia Teacher's College, the professors talked about "things like feeling, warmth, [and] empathy more than . . . about

---

11 See Kevin M. Kruse, *White Flight: Atlanta and the Making of Modern American Conservatism* (Princeton: Princeton University Press, 2005); Jerald E. Podair, *The Strike that Changed New York: Blacks, Whites, and the Ocean Hill-Brownsville Crisis* (New Haven: Yale University Press, 2002); David S. Cecelski, *Along Freedom Road* (Chapel Hill: University of North Carolina Press, 1994); Jonathan Kozol, "The Crippling Inheritance," *New York Times* (3 March 1985).

skills, training, discipline." At the State University of New York in Plattsburgh, prospective teachers were told that students needed "a warm, caring, supportive environment, role models and mentors." At Michigan State University, the emphasis was "on the low-achieving problem student" and the teacher's task was defined as "changing their attitudes towards themselves." At California State University in Long Beach, prospective teachers were told their job was not to provide students with information "but to be sensitive to their need for positive reinforcement, for self-esteem." At one education school after another, the emphasis was on promoting the self-confidence of students, on inculcating positive self-images, on encouraging respect for others from all cultural backgrounds. Rather than stress the importance of transmitting academic knowledge, the schools of education were training teachers to work with students "in egalitarian ways, respecting diversity, and integrating everyone for the future of our country."[12]

In addition to demanding that teachers develop empathy and sensitivity, Kozol tried to instill in his students a critical sensibility. Although his fourth grade textbook attributed the success of George Washington to Washington's character, looks, and style, Kozol emphasized the importance of Washington's wealth and connections. "George Washington was not really a very handsome man," Kozol told the students. "He did not really have much of a sense of humor and people even said that he was rather short-tempered." This was too much for the reading teacher. She did not often become angry, but she considered Kozol's lesson on Washington "out of the question," saying, "We are not going to start teaching cynicism here in the Fourth Grade."[13]

---

12 Rita Kramer, *Ed School Follies* (New York: The Free Press, 1991), 8, 25, 31, 84, 135, 75. John I. Goodland has written a number of scholarly books that reinforce some—not all—of Kramer's points. In particular, see Goodlad, *A Place Called School* (New York: McGraw-Hill, 1984).

13 Jonathan Kozol, *Death at an Early Age*, 74-75.

Late in the school year, the authorities fired Kozol. Because Kozol repeatedly departed from a list of approved readings, the authorities claimed he lacked "the personal discipline to abide by rules and regulations" and therefore was "unsuited for the highly responsible profession of teaching." The final incident that precipitated Kozol's dismissal involved his reading of a poem by Langston Hughes, "Ballad of the Landlord."[14]

Landlord, landlord,
My roof has sprung a leak.
Don't you 'member I told you about it
Way last week?

Landlord, landlord,
These steps is broken down.
When you come up yourself
It's a wonder you don't fall down.

Ten bucks you say I owe you?
Ten bucks you say is due?
Well, that's ten bucks more'n I'll pay you
Till you fix this house up new.

What? You gonna get eviction orders?
You gonna cut off my heat?
You gonna take my furniture and
Throw it in the street?

Um-huh! You talking high and mighty.
Talk on—till you get through.
You ain't gonna be able to say a word
If I land my fist on you.

Police! Police!
Come and get this man!
He's trying to ruin the government
And overturn the land!

---

14 *Ibid.*, 225-227, 231-232.

Copper's whistle!
Patrol bell!
Arrest.

Precinct station.
Iron cell.
Headlines in press:

MAN THREATENS LANDLORD
TENANT HELD NO BAIL
JUDGE GIVES NEGRO 90 DAYS IN COUNTY JAIL

When the newspapers in Boston published the story—HARVARD MAN FIRED FOR TEACHING LANGSTON HUGHES—the public school authorities seemed to be narrow-minded, if not villainous, and Kozol emerged as a sympathetic victim. Before long, influential powers in the education world were acclaiming the young teacher as a witness to injustice. The Ford, Rockefeller and Guggenheim foundations gave Kozol generous grants, and *Death at an Early Age* became required reading at many American colleges and schools of education.[15]

As Kozol's fame and influence grew, the young author became increasingly radical. In *Death at an Early Age*, he had briefly criticized Boston's White teachers for trying to instill "their own code of values in the hearts and minds of [Black] children." But in his next books Kozol became more emphatic in stressing this point. In *Free Schools* (1972), he accused teachers of cultural imperialism, of treating Black communities as "internal colonies," and he described Black children as "colonized children." In *The Night is Dark and I am Far From Home* (1975), Kozol maintained that the teacher's proper role was to subvert the prevailing beliefs that had made America so racist and uncaring.[16]

---

15   Sol Stern, "America's Most Influential—and Wrongest—School Reformer," *City Journal* (Winter 2000).

16   Jonathan Kozol, *Death at an Early Age*, 175, 207; Kozol, *Free Schools* (Boston:

In the past, Kozol lamented, teachers had stressed the importance of following orders. In Boston and in many other cities they had taught students to recite, "Every day, in every way, it is our duty to obey."[17] The emphasis on obedience infuriated Kozol. After declaring himself "in strongest possible opposition to the present social order of the U.S.," he urged teachers to "say no" to the system. In a book published in 1981, *On Being a Teacher*, Kozol urged teachers to engage in what he called "disobedience instruction." To combat "state indoctrination," they should refuse to lead the Pledge of Allegiance." To prevent an excessive love of country, they should depict the history of the United States not as "a heroic westward drive" but rather as "murder and exploitation of the only native residents of North America." Children should learn that Abraham Lincoln was "profoundly racist" and that Martin Luther King said that America was "the greatest purveyor of violence in the world." To discredit docility, teachers should condemn the ordinary people who followed orders "into Watergate to steal, into My Lai to kill." They should also discuss the mass murderer Adolf Eichmann, whose "own preparation for obedient behavior was received in the German public schools, which resembled our own in aiming to promote 'good Germans,' or 'good citizens,' as we in the United States would say."[18]

Kozol candidly confessed that he was "not opposed to the idea of adult 'imposition' on the minds of children." He was "convinced that there is no way ... to overcome such imposition." All education was "either for freedom or domestication." The problem with American

---

Houghton Miflin Company, 1972), 48-49; Kozol, *The Night is Dark and I am Far From Home* (Boston: Houghton Miflin Company, 1975).

17 Jonathan Kozol, *The Night is Dark and I am Far From Home*, 16.

18 *Ibid.*, 2, 16; Jonathan Kozol, *On Being a Teacher* (New York: Continuum, 1981) 4, 25, 79ff, 59, 23-24; Jonathan Leaf, "The Learning Disabled Education Expert," *Weekly Standard* 13 (31 December 2007/7 January 2008), 25.

schooling, as Kozol came to see it, was that most school districts adhered to a policy that the state of Arizona stated boldly: that the goal of education was to "augment a child's love of country ... [and] appreciation of traditional values." Kozol, on the other hand, wanted to destroy such loyalty. He insisted that schools should not "augment a child's love of country," but instead try to "create a new social order." Kozol urged teachers to "articulately rebel." "The place to jam the gears of an unjust machine is where we stand."[19]

Kozol was only one of many education writers who insisted that the school curriculum should be reformed to teach "social justice." Another was Maxine Greene, a professor at Columbia University's Teachers College, who instructed future teachers about their responsibility to improve American society by developing a "transformative" vision of social justice and democracy in their classrooms. "They should portray homelessness as a consequence of the private dealings of landlords, an arms buildup as a consequence of corporate decisions, racial exclusion as a consequence of a private property-holder's choice."[20]

All this was music to the ears of Bill Ayers, a radical activist and friend of Jonathan Kozol. In the 1970s, Ayers and his partner Bernadine Dohrn spent several years on the lam from the law, as fugitives who had planted bombs as part of the Weather Underground opposition to the war in Vietnam. Thanks to a lack of witnesses and procedural complexities, Ayers never went to trial or jail. Reflecting on his case with writers Peter Collier and David Horowitz, Ayers exulted: "Guilty as hell, free as a bird—America is a great country."[21]

---

19 Jonathan Kozol, *The Night is Dark and I am Far From Home*, 1-2; Kozol, *On Being a Teacher*, 85, 73.

20 Sol Stern, "The Ed School's Latest—and Worst—Humbug," *City Journal* (Summer 2006).

21 *Ibid.*

In 1984, Ayers enrolled in one of Professor Greene's classes at Teachers College, where he heard how the "'oppressive hegemony' of the capitalist order 'reproduces itself' through the traditional practice of public schooling." As journalist Sol Stern noted, this was "critical pedagogy's fancy way of saying that the evil corporations exercised thought control through the schools." After earning a doctorate in education, Ayers received an academic appointment and eventually became Distinguished Professor of Education and Senior University Scholar at the University of Illinois at Chicago. One of his books, on the importance of teaching for social justice, eventually became a best-seller that was assigned as required reading in education schools throughout the country.[22]

Ayers and Greene were by no means representative of all professors of education. But they were symptoms of a trend that was developing. Throughout the country, some professors were preparing their teachers-in-training to cure a sick society. At Austin Peay State University, prospective teachers were told of the need "to reform society through the schools." Students at Eastern Michigan University were told that education functioned either to reinforce the existing order or to transform it. The teacher-training program at Marquette University proclaimed its "commitment to social justice" and to using schools "to transcend the negative effects of the dominant culture." Marquette even required all education degree candidates to express a "desire to work for social justice, particularly in an urban environment."[23]

So it went. The purpose of one course at Humboldt State University was stated in the syllabus: "It is not an option for history teachers to teach social justice and social responsibility; it is a mandate." At the Claremont Graduate University, prospective

---

22 Ibid.

23 Rita Kramer, *Ed School Follies*, 51, 96; Sol Stern, "The Ed Schools' Latest … Humbug."

teachers were required to commit to social justice, and also were screened to make sure they had this essential "disposition." Kozol recommended that the deans of colleges of education should evaluate the dispositions of prospective teachers "by spend[ing] a weekend with each person." "If [the dean] can't stand them," Kozol said, "don't inflict them on school children."[24]

Some students resisted the indoctrination, saying that they had been denied the chance to become teachers because their dispositions were deemed politically incorrect. Students at Brooklyn College and Washington State University, for example, complained that they had been denied the opportunity after they "ran afoul of their ed schools' social justice disposition requirements." The complaints further alleged that their teacher-training programs placed more emphasis on the need for liberal policies to achieve social justice than on the importance of giving instruction in academic subjects.[25]

Some prospective teachers went to court with their complaints. In 2002, Stephen M. Head sued the trustees of the California State University system on First Amendment grounds. Head, a 50-year old Silicon Valley software engineer, wanted to switch careers and become a high-school math teacher. To that end, he enrolled in the Teacher Credential Program at San Jose State University. The syllabus in one of the required courses proclaimed the purpose of "preparing teachers to ... promote social justice" and "articulate rationales for ... integrating ... feminist education throughout the secondary education curriculum." The syllabus further encouraged students to develop "sensitivity to the diversity ... in California [and to] understand diversity as including

---

24 Rita Kramer, *Ed School Follies*, 51, 96; Katherine Kersten, "At U, Future Teachers May Be Reeducated," *Minneapolis-St. Paul Star Tribune* (22 November 2009).

25 Sol Stern, "The Ed Schools' Latest ... Humbug"; Rita Kramer, *Ed School Follies*, 37-38.

sexual orientation." One of the handouts encouraged prospective teachers to support "cultural pluralism and alternative life styles . . . and . . . power equity among groups."[26]

Head attended all the classes and turned in his written assignments on time. But when Head mentioned that there were critics of the multicultural approach to education, the professor said Head was "unfit to teach" because he lacked the correct "disposition." The professor proceeded to give Head an "F" for the course, and Head sued on constitutional grounds. He said the First Amendment forbade public officials from requiring him to "espouse liberal views." He said that, in violation of the Constitution, San Jose's college of education had ordained feminism and multiculturalism as a secular religion. In 2006, however, U.S. District Judge William Alsup ruled against Head's claims.

Freed from constitutional restraints, some colleges moved toward imposing a new orthodoxy. After surveying the application criteria at 20 of America's most selective schools, Glenn Ricketts and Peter Wood reported in 2009 that "'diversity' essay questions" were being shaped to promote the multicultural ideology. Thus Yale asked applicants to explain how their "personal perspective and life experiences" would add "to the diversity in a college community." And Berkeley required applicants for all graduate programs to provide personal statements that included information on how they had "overcome barriers to access opportunities in higher education," how they had "come to understand the barriers faced by others," and "evidence of [their] academic service to advance equitable access to higher education for women, racial minorities, and individuals from other groups that have been historically underrepresented." At the University of Southern California, one administrator candidly

---

26 *Stephen M. Head v. Board of Trustees, California State University.* Case C05-05328-WHA (2006).

acknowledged that the school of education was using admission essays to weed out "people with unsuitable views."[27]

In 2010, the National Association of Scholars (NAS) published an account of one graduate student's experience at a prominent school of education. The NAS explained that this school, which was not named to protect the student, pushed the "progressive" line that attributed racial and ethnic achievement gaps to "social injustice, institutionalized racism, white prejudice and other societal ills." The school disparaged but tolerated "the conservative view . . . that parents and teachers of low-performing students are the cause of the gap by failing to give the students the correct cultural values." But the school would not abide the suggestion that academic shortcomings might be influenced by deficiencies in inherent cognitive ability. When the head of the school became aware that the student held this opinion, he insisted that "someone with [these] views could not be given the imprimatur of this university."[28]

Students at the University of Minnesota had a similar experience. There a faculty task group on teacher education proposed to make race, class, and gender politics the "overarching framework for all education courses at the university." To that end, prospective teachers were required to prepare an "autoethnography" that described their own prejudices and stereotypes. The goal was to ensure that "future teachers will be able to discuss their own histories and current thinking drawing on notions of white privilege, hegemonic masculinity, heteronormativity and internalized oppression."[29]

---

27 Yale statement at the Common Application Online (CAO), quoted by Glenn Ricketts and Peter Wood, Diversi-Oaths: Creedal Admissions in the American University (30 November 2009) at NAS.org; Berkeley Statement, quoted by Rickets and Weed, *ibid.*; Statement regarding USC quoted in "Achievement Gap Politics," NAS.org (7 May 2010).

28 "Achievement Gap Politics," NAS.org (7 May 2010).

29 Katherine Kersten, "At U, Future Teachers May Be Reeducated."

In order to gain the recommendation for licensure required by the Minnesota Board of Teaching, the university's college of education also proposed to require its students to repudiate the idea that hardworking people of every color and creed could get ahead on their own merits. Instead, future teachers were expected to recognize that, as "a result of dissimilarities in power and influence," there were fundamental injustices at the heart of American society. According to Minnesota's college of education, these injustices were largely responsible for the poor academic performance of non-Asian minority students.[30]

Of course, not all education professors were as extreme as those in the North Star State, and even there—after the proposed program of indoctrination received negative publicity in the national press—the University of Minnesota eventually turned to more subtle methods of inculcating political correctness. In general, education faculties, like other faculties in the humanities and social science, simply hired far more liberal professors than conservatives, and then allowed politically correct perspective to seep into the corps of prospective teachers.

However the new political perspective was disseminated, advocates of teaching-for-social-justice received a boost when the Bill and Melinda Gates Foundation embraced their cause. With the ability to give American educators more than $1billion every year, the Gates Foundation loomed so large that historian Diane Ravitch has called Gates "the nation's superintendent of schools" because "he can support whatever he wants, based on any theory or philosophy that appeals to him." As it happened, Gates chose to finance social justice schools such as the School for Democracy and Leadership in Brooklyn and the Leadership Institute in the Bronx. When asked about this, New York City's school chancellor, Joel Klein, saw no

---

30 *Ibid.* After publication of this exposé the University of Minnesota backed away from enforcing this proposal, but individual professors remained free to proceed as they wished.

problem, saying, "Giving schools 'leadership' or 'social justice' themes is fine with me." Then Klein added a qualification: "as long as the teachers and principals do not bring politics and ideologies into our classrooms." This, however, is precisely what social justice teachers had been trained to do.[31]

The apparent transformation of teacher training helps to explain Jonathan Kozol's change of mind. In 1967, when *Death at an Early Age* was published, Kozol had been unsparing in his criticism of public school teachers; by the 1990s, however, he was no longer finding fault with teachers. "Public school teachers are my favorite people," he now insisted, "especially those who teach little people, elementary school. I get so upset when I hear people disparaging these wonderful people."[32]

A more mundane consideration should also be mentioned. When asked, "Who are your readers," Kozol answered: "My typical readers are simply decent mainstream American people—not only liberals. They are ordinary citizens, including many religious people who are profoundly troubled by [social injustice].... If only liberals read my books, they wouldn't be best sellers." When questioners persisted, Kozol conceded that teachers made up a disproportionate share of his audience. On book tours, he would speak to "crowds of 1500 people... in cities like Chicago and Los Angeles and Seattle and New York City... and two thirds of them are teachers." Few things pleased Kozol more than hearing someone say that he or she had become a teacher "in the first place" after reading one of Kozol's books or hearing one of his talks "when I was in college."[33]

---

31 Diane Ravitch, "Bill Gates: The Nation's Superintendent of Schools," *Los Angeles Times* (30 July 2006); Sol Stern, "The Ed Schools' Latest... Humbug."

32 Jonathan Kozol, quoted by Peter Rose, "Kozol Says Re-segregation Shaming America," *San Diego Union-Tribune* (17 November 2005).

33 *St. Louis Post Dispatch* (2 October 2005); *Fairness and Accuracy in Reporting* (March 2006); *Herald News*, Passaic County, New Jersey (25 May 2005); *Omaha World-Herald* (5 November 2005).

Attributing motives necessarily involves speculation. Whatever the reason for Kozol's change of heart, the fact is indisputable. This erstwhile critic of public school teachers eventually became a leading defender of the established order in public education. The "later Kozol" found fault with those who proposed to reform the public schools by using charter schools and vouchers to encourage competition and choice. He opposed plans to hold teachers "accountable" by rewarding (or discharging) those whose students performed well (or poorly) on standardized tests. Instead, Kozol insisted that public schools were sound, save in three respects—the necessity for more money, the importance of more racial integration, and the need for freedom from excessive reliance on government-mandated standardized tests.

Kozol's support for the education establishment was understandable. As Robert L. Hampel has noted in his history of American high schools, there was enormous change after the mid-1960s. One survey indicated that in 1965 high school principals ranked "development of positive self-concept and good human relations" seventh of eight educational goals. Twelve years later, "the same objective was second of ten." Other surveys reported that there was more informality in classrooms and greater candor about sexuality. Hampel reported that the period of greatest change was "short and stormy," but "after the late 1960s, liberals felt more at home in public schools than did conservatives." "The major changes . . . promoted equity and equality for the disadvantaged. [...] Instead of foisting middle-class white Protestant values on a captive audience, high schools began to respect pluralism more than ever before."[34]

David F. Labaree, a professor at Stanford, concurred. "For American education schools," he wrote in 2004, "the progressive vision has become canonical." Almost everywhere, the colleges of

---

34 Robert L. Hampel, *The Last Little Citadel* (Boston: Houghton Miflin Company, 1986) 137-138, 140.

education were committed to "cooperation over competition . . . democratic decision-making, social equality . . . multiculturalism, and internationalism." The National Council for Accreditation of Teacher Education (NCATE) accepted the premise that "schooling cannot be expected to succeed without greater equity, diversity and social justice . . . and thus teacher training must be infused with right-minded social and political values."[35]

Professor Labaree offered some qualifications. He noted that the ascendancy of liberal pedagogy was not entirely new, since progressive views had been influential in colleges of education for several decades. And he maintained that, despite the prevalence of progressive ideology in the colleges, most teachers turned out to be quite traditional when it came to teaching their own classes. After examining the data on teaching practices, another Stanford professor, Larry Cuban, concluded that the impact of progressivism on the classroom was modest. John Goodlad, dean of the Graduate School of Education at UCLA, similarly concluded that progressivism had scant impact on the actual practice in schools. In most classrooms, Goodlad reported, teachers were still presenting academic information and students were generally engaged in "listening to teachers, writing answers to questions, and taking tests and quizzes." When faced with the everyday problems of teaching and managing students, most teachers decided there was no alternative to the long-established practices of traditional education.[36]

For Cuban and Goodlad, the persistence of traditional approaches was bad news. They would have been happier if progressivism had conquered not only the colleges of education but

---

35 David F. Labaree, *The Trouble with Ed Schools* (New Haven: Yale University Press, 2004) 131, 136, 142, 141 (quoting with approval from a statement by Professor J. E. Stone).

36 John I. Goodlad, *A Place Called School*, 123-124.

also had been implemented in the everyday practice of those who taught in the nation's elementary schools and high schools. Labaree, on the other hand, was pleased to know that not all the aspects of progressive education had been widely implemented. "If our progressive rhetoric were faithfully put into practice," Labaree wrote, "the impact on teaching might well be negative in significant ways."[37]

Perhaps Jonathan Kozol was too easily satisfied—seduced by progressive rhetoric into believing that the nation's public-school teachers had been reformed according to his pattern. Perhaps Professor Labaree was too optimistic in concluding that progressive education had not damaged the schools because the college professors did not have the power to implement their vision. Perhaps both men were correct in their assessments, but only to a degree.

In 1988 Kozol departed from his focus on education and published a book about homeless families, *Rachel and Her Children*. He followed with two more books about disadvantaged people who lived in Mott Haven, one of the poorest areas in a South Bronx congressional district that by some measures was the poorest congressional district in the United States. *Amazing Grace* (1995) described a world where jobs were scarce, where many mothers were infected with AIDS, and where a large portion of the men were either in prison or addicted to drugs. *Ordinary Resurrections* (2000) described a surprisingly resilient group of poor children whom Kozol met at an after school program in Mott Haven. A young Hispanic boy, Elio, and a young Black girl, Pineapple, were especially memorable kids. In some of his earlier books, Kozol had downplayed anecdotes, but when he wrote about the children of Mott Haven, he said, it was "the moments of digression that I recall with most interest." Thus Kozol recounted one girl's explanation of how she made pancakes for her mother's boyfriend. "You pour it on the pan and then it's cooking on the pan

---

37 David F. Labaree, *The Trouble with Ed Schools*, 193.

and then you look at it until it gets a little brown and then you start to see little bubbles." He recalled another instance when a small boy teasingly urged Kozol to receive communion at an Episcopal Mass. "'Try it. You'll like it,' the boy whispered."[38]

Kozol's focus on children was part of a strategy. Like many left-liberal activists, Kozol believed that poverty stemmed from injustice and should be combated by income redistribution, racial preference programs, and more government spending for schools and welfare. He understood, however, that others attributed poverty to drug abuse, out-of-wedlock births, crime, indifference to education, and chronic welfare dependency. He also understood that it would be harder to "blame the victim" and reject public spending if he shifted the focus to innocent children. After all, the children had done nothing wrong. They had committed no crime. Many were too young to have committed any offense.

"When I write a book," Kozol has said, "I am not simply trying to sort out points that will be interesting to other intellectuals. I need my books to have results. . . . I write to change the world." By presenting poor children as good, innocent, and wise, Kozol hoped to discredit the idea that inner-city children were different from other children, "with a set of problems or . . . 'pathologies' so complicated, so alarming, so profound that they aren't 'children' in the sense in which most of us use that world but that they're really 'premature adults,' perhaps precocious criminals, 'predators.'"[39]

---

38 Jonathan Kozol, *Rachel and Her Children* (New York: Crown Publishers, 1989). Kozol, *Amazing Grace* (New York: Crown Publishers, 1995); Kozol, *Ordinary Resurrections: Children in the Years of Hope* (New York: Crown Publishers, 2000); Ethan Bronner, "What's Still Wrong with Kids Today," *New York Times* (11 June 2000); Mark Feeney, "The Gentlest Angry Man."

39 Jonathan Kozol, *Illiterate America* (Garden City: Anchor Press/Doubleday, 1985) xvi. Kozol elaborated on this theme in a *Fire in the Ashes* (New York: Crown Publishers, 2012), a book that provided updated accounts of how

Kozol knew that evidence could be cited to support a negative appraisal of young children from the inner cities. People who had read *Death at an Early Age* sometimes asked whether Kozol knew what had happened to the children he described. "What happened to Stephen? Angelina? Frederick? Did they somehow manage to survive?" Before they were 30, Stephen was in prison, serving a 20-year term for murdering a man who was confined to a wheelchair; Frederick was a wealthy pimp who also dealt drugs; and Angelina was an illiterate mother with three children, still living in the neighborhood where Kozol first met her when she was eight-years-old.[40]

Nevertheless, Kozol did not regard disadvantaged children as a breed apart, "and the more time that I spend with inner-city children, the less credible and less legitimate these large distinctions seem." If many of these children eventually dropped out of school and gravitated toward drugs or crime, it was through no fault of their own or of their families. It was because an oppressive American society had "robbed these children . . . of childhood." Inner-city children had been "denied the . . . happiness and care" that other children of the middle- and upper-classes had received.[41]

As Kozol saw it, many inner-city children eventually turned to drugs and crime and antisocial behavior because they had come to think that they did not matter to society. They grew up on the poor side of town, but they noticed how much better living conditions were in the wealthy districts of their cities. Beyond that, they recognized

---

some of the protagonists of *Ordinary Resurrections* were faring as young adults. Some were doing all right while others were mired in pathology and poverty. Yet however the children had turned out, Kozol described their lives with compelling empathy.

40 Jonathan Kozol, *Illiterate America*, Ibid.

41 Jonathan Kozol, "The Hopeful Years: Children of the South Bronx," *Christian Century* 117 (10 May 2000) 536.

that life in the suburbs differed from life in the cities. Kozol quoted an inner-city youth as saying,

> You can understand things better when you go among the wealthy. You look around you ... and you take a deep breath at the sight of all those beautiful surroundings. Then you come back home and see that these are things you do not have.... People on the outside may think that we don't know what it is like for other students, but we *visit* other schools and we have eyes and we have brains. You cannot hide the differences. You see it and compare.[42]

Other writers had noticed that young students, those who were still in elementary school, seemed to do fairly well in inner-city schools. In *Slums and Suburbs* (1961), James B. Conant praised the elementary schools of the inner cities, but noted that many Black students, at about age 12, lost interest in school. "At that time the 'street' takes over. In terms of schoolwork, progress ceases; indeed many pupils begin to go backward in their studies!" In accounting for this turn for the worse, James S. Coleman, in *Equality of Educational Opportunity* (1966), also emphasized how important the influence of peer groups could be.[43]

Rather than blame the influence of peers (or families), Kozol pointed an accusing finger at inequality. As he saw it, the disparity in school spending was poisoning the children of America's inner cities. Elementary students were too young to understand that they had been "set apart." They had "not yet [been] soiled by the knowledge that their nation does not love them." But teenagers recognized that there was "no will in this society to bring [them] back into the mainstream." Because taxpayers spent less for inner-city schools than for schools in

---

[42] Jonathan Kozol, *Savage Inequalities* (New York: Crown Publishers, 1991) 104, 179, 181.

[43] James B. Conant, *Slums and Suburbs* (New York: McGraw Hill, 1961) 23, 22, 21, 12, 8, 17-18; James S. Coleman, *Equality of Educational Opportunity* (Washington: Government Printing Office, 1966).

some of the wealthy suburbs, one student declared, "They teach you how much you are hated." When the *Wall Street Journal* noted that spending for inner-city schools had increased substantially, Kozol answered, "What the *Journal* does not add is that per-pupil spending grew at the same rate in the [wealthy] suburbs ... thereby preventing any catch-up." According to Kozol, the recognition of inequality was largely responsible for turning Stephen, a protagonist in *Death at an Early Age*, from a "shy child" into "a kind of monster."[44]

Some readers did not clearly understand Kozol's message. The editors of the *St. Louis Post Dispatch*, for example, mistakenly said that Kozol was not arguing that less should be spent on the education of students in the well-to-do districts but only that more should be invested in the education of poor children. But S. Keith Graham, of the *Atlanta Journal and Constitution*, got the point: Kozol was arguing that relative spending mattered, "that the disparity of funding between schools ... is a key problem."[45]

To set things aright, Kozol urged Americans to give poor children "something so spectacular, so wonderful and special" that they "might be able somehow to soar above the hopelessness, the clouds of smoke and sense of degradation all around them." He wanted to "pour vast amounts of money, ingenuity and talent into public education" for the urban poor.[46]

---

44 Lois Lewis, "Ordinary Resurrection: An E-Interview with Jonathan Kozol," at EducationWorld.com; Jonathan Kozol, *Savage Inequalities*, 195, 133; unidentified student, quoted in Barbara Roche, "Savage Inequalities," *Commonweal* 119 (10 April 1992) 22.

45 *St. Louis Post Dispatch* (17 February 1992); S. Keith Graham, "If You Only Read One Book on Education, This Is It," *Atlanta Journal and Constitution* (29 September 1991); Jonathan Kozol, quoted by Pius Kamau, "The Essential Ingredient in Children's Education," *Denver Post* (27 October 2005); Kozol, quoted by Gordon W. E. Nore, "U.S. Schools Still Separate and Unequal, Says Author," *The Ottawa Citizen* (14 September 1991).

46 Jonathan Kozol, quoted by Andrew Hacker, "Why the Rich Get Smarter,"

Early in his career, Kozol had made the case on pragmatic grounds, saying, "Every dollar you invest in Head Start will save $6 later on in higher productivity or in lower prison cost." But he later came to regard such calculations as "obscene," saying, "I'm ashamed that I made such arguments. Why not invest in them because they're babies and deserve to have some joy in life?" Kozol urged Americans to increase spending on public education in the inner cities, "not to produce better test scores," although better scores would be welcome. Nor was the reason to fashion a more suitable work force, though Kozol would not object if the youngsters eventually found good jobs. "The reason is because children deserve decent living conditions, and because their school environments are under public control, it is up to the public to provide for them." "Surely there is enough for everyone within this country," Kozol wrote. "It is a tragedy that these good things are not more widely shared. All our children ought to be allowed a stake in the enormous riches of America. Whether they were born to poor white Appalachians or to wealthy Texans, to poor black people in the Bronx or to rich people in Manhasset or Winnetka, they are all quite wonderful and innocent when they are small."[47]

Kozol's rationale was theological. If innocent children were equal in the sight of God, a just society should provide equal educational opportunities. And to do this, schools for disadvantaged children needed more than equal funds. "Equity does not mean equal funds for unequal needs," Kozol said. "If we budgeted education in accord with the real needs of children, . . . [inner-city] children . . . would be

---

New York Times (6 October 1991); Kozol, quoted by Nicholas Lemann, "Public Education: Still Separate, Still Unequal," *Washington Post* (20 October 1991).

47 "Falling behind: An Interview with Jonathan Kozol," *Christian Century* (10 May 2000) 541-544; "An Interview with Jonathan Kozol," *Educational Theory* 43 (Winter 1993) 55-70; Nel Noddings, "For All Its Children," *Educational Theory* 43 (Winter 1993) 15-22; Kozol, "How We Fail the Children," *St. Petersburg Times* (13 October 1991).

getting considerably more than the suburbs and possibly even a little bit more than the poor white rural districts, because . . . poverty in the inner city is more oppressive even than the bitter poverty in rural areas.'" If funds were allocated according to the real needs of children, . . . New York City would get $15,000 [per pupil] a year," and the wealthiest suburbs could "get by on $7,000."[48]

With these thoughts in mind, in 1991 Kozol published his most influential book, *Savage Inequalities*. In this book, he described how inner-city schools in five American cities differed from the best urban and suburban schools in funding, in amenities provided, and in educational standards achieved. He did so by comparing and contrasting some of the worst schools in Camden, Chicago, East St. Louis, New York, and Washington with the best schools in the wealthiest nearby suburbs, and by comparing and contrasting ordinary urban schools with more elite urban magnet schools and with specialty schools like the Bronx School of Science. In Kozol's account, the ordinary urban schools were in bad repair, with overcrowded classrooms and such a shortage of faculty that in Chicago, to mention but one example, about 18,000 students were assigned each day to classes that had no teacher.[49]

Despite Kozol's vivid descriptions, *Savage Inequalities* failed to impress many social scientists. People who were familiar with the research on education based their discussions on sociologist James S. Coleman's landmark report of 1966, *Equality of Educational Opportunity*, which had presented detailed information on 4,000 schools and test results from 570,000 students and 60,000 teachers.

---

48 "*Savage Inequalities*: An Interview with Jonathan Kozol," *Christian Century* (10 May 2000) 541-544; "An Interview with Jonathan Kozol," 57-58; Laurel Shaper Walters, "Author Criticizes Rich-Poor Gap in US," *Christian Science Monitor* (21 October 1991).

49 Jonathan Kozol, *Savage Inequalities*, 54. Kozol also discussed, more briefly, conditions in San Antonio, Texas.

At the outset of his research, Coleman had predicted, "the study will show the difference in the quality of schools that the average Negro child and the average white child are exposed to." Speaking to a reporter, Coleman had said: "You know yourself that the difference is going to be striking. And even though everybody knows there is a lot of difference between suburban and inner-city schools, once the statistics are there in black and white, they will have a lot more impact." Yet to Coleman's surprise, when the data were assembled, they indicated that by 1966 there was substantial *equality* in facilities and other measurable resources at majority-Black and majority-White schools. Although there were regional variations, with schools in the South less generously funded than schools in other sections, neither race suffered when it came to average expenditure per student, the size of the classes, the formal training of teachers, and many other factors.[50]

Equally surprising, the Coleman report also indicated that the students' academic achievement, as measured by test scores, would not have changed much, even if the distribution of resources had been different. The average of academic scores varied from school to school, with students from middle- and upper-class-families usually doing better than students from poor families. But after controlling for the students' socioeconomic background, there was no correlation between average achievement and the facilities, amenities, or programs the schools provided. Resources and teachers mattered less than the family background, the motivation, and the intelligence (IQ) of the students.

Over the years, other scholars confirmed Coleman's findings. In addition, between 1970 and 2000, per pupil spending on America's public schools nearly doubled (in constant dollars), and the trend was toward a more egalitarian distribution of funds. By 1990, the districts in which Black and other minority students made up a majority of

---

50 Frederick Mosteller and Daniel P. Moynihan, *On Equality of Educational Opportunity* (New York: Random House, 1972) 8.

the enrollment spent more per pupil than those with hardly any minority students. Kozol had contrasted the poor, largely minority schools of Camden, Chicago, and the Bronx with the affluent, largely White schools of Princeton, New Trier, and Manhasset. But these comparisons conveyed a distorted impression of the national pattern. Even in 1991, when *Savage Inequalities* was published, the expenditure per student in East St, Louis, the most impoverished of the inner cities Kozol described, was greater than the state-wide average in Illinois, though it was less than the expenditure in some of the state's top spending districts. And the situation in East St. Louis was not atypical. As University of Virginia law professor James E. Ryan has noted, "it is generally not true that predominantly minority districts are 'underfunded,' if one defines that term in relation to the statewide average." "[M]inority districts are more likely than not to spend above the state average."[51]

Several studies also indicated that even massive spending did not necessarily improve the quality of education for African-American and Hispanic students. One of the most careful of these studies, *Complex Justice* (2008), by Joshua M. Dunn, told the story of court-ordered "desegregation" in Kansas City, Missouri. By order of U.S. District Judge Russell Clark, the taxpayers of Missouri spent some $2 billion to upgrade the predominantly Black schools of Kansas City. As a result, the city's educational facilities were unparalleled. Central High School had "a computer for every pupil, a six-lane indoor track, a natatorium

---

51 Frederick Mosteller and Daniel P. Moynihan, *On Equality of Educational Opportunity*; Christopher Jencks, *Inequality: A Reassessment of the Effect of Family and Schooling in America* (New York: Basic Books, 1972); Eric Hanushek, "Spending on Schools," in Terry Moe, ed., *A Primer on America's Schools* (Stanford: Hoover institution, 2001); Richard Rothstein and K. H. Miles, *Where's the Money Gone? Changes in the Level and Composition of Educational Spending* (Washington: Economic Policy Institute, 1995); Abigail and Stephan Thernstrom, *No Excuses*, chapter 8; Jonathan Kozol, *Savage Inequalities*, 37; James E. Ryan, "The Influence of Race in School Finance Reform," *Michigan Law Review* 98 (November 1999) 436, 439.

with an underwater viewing room, and an Olympic-quality gymnastics center." A few miles away, the Paseo Academy of Fine and Performing Arts had "every amenity a drama or music teacher could imagine." At Southwest High there was a model United Nations, where students' comments were simultaneously translated into foreign languages. Nor were these schools exceptional. "Pick almost any public school in Kansas City," Dunn wrote, "and you will find that it is housed in a state-of-the-art facility or in completely renovated buildings with additions like climate-controlled art galleries, greenhouses, and petting zoos." In the 1990s Kansas City's expenditure per student, when adjusted for the cost of living, was the highest of any city in the United States and almost three times the expense in some of Missouri's predominantly White districts. In the end, however, the expenditure of Kansas City "failed . . . to improve student achievement." On standardized exams, the average scores of Kansas City's predominantly African-American students actually declined.[52]

The story was much the same in the largely Black public schools of Cambridge, Massachusetts. By 2003 the annual expenditure per student amounted to a surprisingly large $17,000, but there was little to show for the expense, if one judged by the results of the Massachusetts Comprehensive Assessment Test. So it went also in almost all-Black-and-Hispanic Camden, New Jersey, which by the year 2000 spent more per pupil (and also had more computers and teachers per student) than the upscale, predominantly White nearby town of Princeton. Once again, however, researchers reported that "gains to students . . . have been quite limited." So it went, again, in Hartford, Connecticut, where test scores did not improve after authorities set per-pupil expenditures in the city above the level in the nearby suburbs and 50 percent higher than the national average. Eventually, even civil-rights activists admitted, "successful school

---

52 Joshua M. Dunn, *Complex Justice: The Case of Missouri v. Jenkins* (Chapel Hill: University of North Carolina Press, 2008) 1, 6, 113, 126 and *passim*.

finance reform did not make a significant difference in the academic achievement of Hartford students." Evidence such as this led Professor Ryan to conclude, "simply equalizing expenditures, even at a relatively high level, may not be sufficient to improve the academic achievement of low-income students."[53]

Kozol did not mention a single case study where academic achievement improved after a school district spent a lot more money. In fact, he rarely mentioned case studies or the work of any researchers. "I simply don't read boring think tank reports," Kozol acknowledged. He joked that none of his recommendations were "research based." He said it was better to fashion policy on the basis of the comments of students and their teachers, and he gave the impression that he regarded most scholarly works as disingenuous rationalizations—as well-crafted arguments "to justify why the immense resources which the nation does in fact possess should go not to the child in the greatest need but to the child of the powerful and well born."[54]

Conservative critics took exception. Abigail Thernstrom disparaged Kozol's work as "faith-based writing" with "little grounding in actual evidence." Douglas J. Besharov agreed, saying that "the weight of authority" was against Kozol's ideas. Charles Murray accused Kozol of "self-righteousness," and Chester Finn dismissed Kozol's books as "tear-jerking accounts of how poor kids get cheated by the tightwad public schools and the miserable, selfish, capitalist society of the United States."[55]

---

53   Abigail Thernstrom and Stephan Thernstrom, *No Excuses*, 165; James E. Ryan, "Schools, Race, and Money," *Yale Law Journal* 109 (1999); Ryan, "Sheff, Segregation, and School Finance Litigation," *New York University Law Review* 74 (May 1999) 540, 538, 533.

54   Nicholas Lemann, "Public Education: Still Separate, Still Unequal"; James D. Anderson, "Power, Privilege, and Public Education," *Educational Theory* 43 (Winter 1993) 4.

55   Abigail Thernstrom, "Lessons Not Learned," *Wall Street Journal* (29 September 2005); Douglas J. Besharov, quoted by Mark Feeney, "The

Some liberals recognized that 25 years of educational research had established that spending levels had little effect on success in school. Others resorted to psychology in their efforts to account for Kozol's preoccupation with school funding. In the *Washington Post*, reporter Jay Mathews described Kozol as "an intense loner," and *New York Times* education editor Ethan Bronner noted that Kozol had spent several years living alone with his dog in rural Massachusetts. According to Bronner, this isolation had led Kozol to regard poor, inner-city children as a surrogate family, "a surprising source of human contact and comfort."[56]

Yet Kozol also found support in influential quarters. *Savage Inequalities* impressed the editors of *Publishers Weekly* so favorably that this book-trade journal forsook the $30,000 it usually received for a front-page advertisement and instead ran a cover editorial urging the nation's leaders to read Kozol's book. Kozol was delighted when then-Senator Al Gore stood with him in Washington on the day *Savage Inequalities* was published, and he was especially pleased when Bill Clinton quoted from *Savage Inequalities* during his 1992 presidential campaign. Kozol acknowledged, "There are few things that a writer could ever hope for as deeply as to see the day that a man who is about to become President of the United States would actually [endorse] something he has written."[57]

Within four years, *Savage Inequalities* sold more than 300,000 copies, and Kozol was pleased to know that the book was "being read

---

Gentlest Angry Man"; Charles Murray, "Grading the Schools," *Wall Street Journal* (3 September 1985); Chester Finn, "Ordinary Resurrection," *First Things* (August 2000) 67.

56 Jay Matthews, "A Liberal Dose of Reality," *Washington Post* (25 November 1995); Ethan Bronner, What's Still Wrong with Kids Today," *New York Times* (11 June 2000).

57 *New York Times* (19 September 1992); "*Savage Inequalities*: An Interview with Jonathan Kozol," 66.

most widely in colleges, and an awful lot of college professors have their students write essays on it." One graduate of the University of Maryland reported that he had been required to read *Savage Inequalities* "in no less than three separate classes." Kozol was even more pleased when he learned that *Savage Inequalities* had breathed new life into efforts to replace property taxes as the basis for financing schools. *Savage Inequalities* achieved even "more than I had hoped for," he acknowledged.[58]

Property taxes have been defended as essential for maintaining local control of public education. But the value of property varies from district to district, and this disparity ensures that financing via property taxes leads to unequal funding of public schools. Since many urban areas are studded with banks, factories, and corporations, this method of financing does not necessarily disadvantage city schools. In fact, as has been noted, the expenditures per student in urban areas generally exceeded the statewide averages. But local financing ensured that there would be inequalities and, as also noted, Kozol thought that inequality gave rise to a corrosive attitude that eventually poisoned many youths. For Kozol, inequality had to be abolished. As he saw it, "The state, by requiring attendance but refusing to require equity, effectively requires inequality." He therefore demanded that states replace property taxes and instead use steeply graduated income taxes to finance public schools.[59]

Within a few years after the publication of *Savage Inequalities*, civil-rights lawyers filed several lawsuits, and several judges ordered the implementation of Kozol's approach. In these lawsuits, the lawyers argued that the equal protection clauses that most state constitutions contained should be interpreted to require equal spending for public education. In some cases, this argument fell on deaf ears. In 18 of

---

58 "*Savage Inequalities*: An Interview with Jonathan Kozol," 56; Jeff Barrus, letter to *Salon.com* (27 September 2005).

59 "*Savage Inequalities*: An Interview with Jonathan Kozol," 69-70; Jonathan Kozol, quoted by Dennis Kelly, "Exposing Segregation, '90s Style," *USA Today* (20 September 1991).

the first 36 cases decided by state supreme courts, the courts decided against the civil-rights lawyers. Nevertheless, in states as far flung as Connecticut, Kentucky, New York, and Texas, state supreme courts required school districts throughout the state to spend approximately the same amount per student or required, as in New Jersey, that the expenditure per pupil in poor districts should exceed the statewide average and match the amount spent in the wealthiest districts.

After the victories in several equalization lawsuits, and emboldened especially by their triumph in New Jersey, civil-rights lawyers proceeded with demands for still more funding. In addition to equal protection clauses, many state constitutions also contained provisions that required the state to provide an "adequate public education," a "thorough and efficient system of free schools," or "an educational program of high quality." Such statements had previously been considered vague generalizations, but in the 1990s civil rights lawyers persuaded several judges to interpret this language to mean that states must move beyond equalization and provide the extra funds that were required to make public education "adequate" or "sufficient" for students who had suffered the disadvantages associated with living in poverty. Kozol recommended that the extra money be used for school repairs, pre-school programs, reducing class size, and ensuring that the poorest districts could pay their teachers well.[60]

Kozol was "very much in favor of these court suits." He was personally involved in some cases and directly or indirectly supported many others. He acknowledged, "issues of money ... are so important

---

60 There is a large and growing literature on this subject. See Peter Schraag, *Final Test* (New York: New Press, 2003); and James S. Liebman and Charles F. Sabel, "A Public Laboratory Dewey Barely Imagined," *New York University Review of Law and Social Change* 28 (2003) 184-304. The quotations are from the constitutions of Georgia, New Jersey and Virginia. For Kozol's recommendations as to how the money should be spent, see McGrory, "Rescuing Kids 'Programmed to Fail,'" *Washington Post* (29 September 1991).

to me." He candidly conceded, "no matter what devices are contrived to bring about equality, it is clear that they require money-transfer, and the largest source of money is the portion of the population that possesses the *most* money. When wealthy districts indicate they see the hand of Robin Hood in this, they are clear sighted and correct." One of Kozol's friendly reviewers, Nel Noddings of Stanford University, made this point in blunt language. Upon hearing that some wealthy people had questioned whether more money would solve educational problems in the inner cities, Professor Noddings blurted, "If money is not important, we'll appropriate a good chunk of yours!" Noddings went on to say, "the well-to-do have resources that should allow them to maintain satisfactory levels of education even in the face of great losses in public funding."[61]

Ironically, the success of the "equity" and "adequacy" litigation had one unintended effect. It undermined Black support for integration. For some time, many Blacks had harbored reservations. Some took exception to what they considered the condescending implications. To assume that African-Americans could not learn unless White students were present in the classroom seemed to suggest that there was something wrong with Blacks. According to Malcolm X, "what the integrationists . . . are saying . . . is that the whites are so much superior that just their presence in the black classroom balances it out." Supreme Court Justice Clarence Thomas also criticized people who assumed "that blacks cannot succeed without the benefit of the company of whites"; that "blacks, when left on their own, cannot achieve." The Black economist Glenn Loury made the same point in pithy language: "We need better schools, not racial condescension."[62]

---

61 *Savage Inequalities*: An Interview with Jonathan Kozol," 57; Kozol, *Savage Inequalities*, 223; Nel Noddings, "For All Its Children," 18-19.

62 George Breitman, ed., *Malcolm X: By Any Means Necessary* (New York: Pathfinder Press, 1970) 17; *Missouri v. Jenkins*, 63 USLW 4486 (1995), 4498-4500; Glenn C. Loury, "Integration Has Had Its Day," *New York Times* (23 April 1995).

These reservations increased after the success of the equity and adequacy lawsuits. With urban schools adequately funded, more Blacks came to think that racially balanced mixing was not necessary, that urban, minority schools could succeed if they received sufficient resources. As the legal scholar Robert A. Garda has explained, "With the hope that all schools will be sufficiently funded to yield adequate educational outcomes, parents have little reason to demand integration." In 1994, a Gallup poll reported that 64 percent of African-Americans chose "increased funding" as the best way to help minorities, while only 25 percent favored "integration." Sixty-four percent also said they would choose local schools over integrated schools outside their community. A dismayed Kozol acknowledged, "legal battles over school funding as well intentioned as they may be . . . can be counterproductive to the more meaningful goal of racial integration."[63]

For Kozol, adequate funding and integration were not separate issues. "They're not two issues for me," he said. "They're the same issue." In *Savage Inequalities*, Kozol mentioned "the remarkable degree of racial [imbalance] that persisted almost everywhere." Kozol expressed doubt about whether increased funding, by itself, would be enough to improve education in the inner cities. He lamented that inner city students were "cut off and disconnected from the outside [White] world." He acknowledged that "greater input" might amount to "very little more than moving around the same old furniture within the house."[64]

Despite Kozol's continuing concern for integration, the emphasis in *Savage Inequalities* was on money. Kozol took particular

---

63 Robert A. Garda, Jr., "Coming Full Circle: The Journey from Separate but Equal to Separate and Unequal Schools," *Duke Journal of Constitutional Law and Public Policy* 2 (2007) 54; Jonathan Kozol, quoted by Amy Stuart Wells, "The Shame of the Nation," *Educational Studies* 40 (August 2006) 82. Despite reservations, Kozol has written, "I have done my best for more than 15 years to rally the support of friends and colleagues for these . . . cases." Kozol, *The Shame of the Nation*, 257.

64 Jonathan Kozol, *Savage Inequalities*, 2, 70, 4.

exception when U.S. Secretary of Education William Bennett said, "You will not buy your way to better performance." Kozol also decried a *Wall Street Journal* editorial that said, "The evidence can scarcely be clearer. . . . Money doesn't buy better education." He was especially dismayed when White high school students in suburban Rye, New York, told him that extra spending in the inner cities would not make much difference because poor children "still would lack the motivation" and "would probably fail in any case because of other problems."[65]

In his next major work on education, Kozol again shifted his emphasis. In *The Shame of the Nation* (2005), he continued to maintain that inner-city schools suffered from inadequate funding. But two additional points came to the fore: the need for racial integration and for progressive approaches to teaching.

When he visited inner-city schools, Kozol reported, he often did not see a single White child in the classrooms. Typically, there would be "a high school in which there are 4,000 kids, all black and Latino except for maybe 10 whites and 15 Asian kids." Principals and teachers would say, "this is a diverse population," but Kozol insisted, "no, these are apartheid schools." "Segregated education is what we have." "If you took a photograph it would look exactly like those dated photographs of Mississippi 50 years ago."[66]

Kozol saw little difference between *de facto* and *de jure* segregation. He knew that inner-city schools were predominantly Black or Hispanic because they were located in neighborhoods that were predominantly Black or Hispanic. He knew that a growing number of minority students were attending schools in predominantly White suburbs. He knew that assigning all students, regardless of race, to the nearest public

---

65 Ibid., 8, 133, 126.

66 Jonathan Kozol, quoted by Richard Halicks, "School Resegregation," *Atlanta Journal-Constitution* (18 September 2005).

school differed from the policy that had existed in many states before *Brown v. Board of Education* (1954), when government authorities in some states had assigned students on the basis of race to keep the races apart. Nevertheless, looking at enrollment statistics, such as those from one area in New York City where only 26 of 11,000 public school students were White, Kozol commented, "two-tenths of one percentage point now mark the difference between legally enforced apartheid in the South of 1954 and socially and economically enforced apartheid in this New York City neighborhood."[67]

Kozol was opposed to severely imbalanced enrollments, regardless of the reason for the imbalance. He explained that his purpose in writing *The Shame of the Nation* was "to inspire Americans to look very hard at the virtually complete apartheid in increasing numbers of our school districts." He wanted to spark a new civil-rights movement, calling for "an enormous national upheaval, a genuine mobilization of decent American people, especially young people." On speaking tours to promote *The Shame of the Nation*, Kozol pleaded for "another passionate political upheaval in this country." He urged his audiences to do whatever was needed to achieve racially balanced integration. He wanted "an all-out struggle . . . an onslaught on apartheid schooling." If it takes 'new turmoil to bring that about,' . . . if it takes people marching in the streets and other forms of adamant disruption of the governing civilities . . . these are prices we should be prepared to pay." At the end of his talks, Kozol would pass around sign-up sheets "for people in the audience who don't want to simply sit there and have a one-time evening of moral indignation but want to do something about it. If there [are] 1,500 people in the audience, typically 500, 600, 700 sign up. And they add comments like, 'When do we start?' By 'start,' they mean, when do we start mobilizing to change this?"[68]

---

67 Jonathan Kozol, quoted by Leslie Balcacci, "Our Schools Are Still Segregated," *Chicago Sun-Times* (18 September 2005).

68 Jonathan Kozol, quoted by Nick Anderson, "School Segregation is Back,"

Despite the brave talk and sign-up sheets, many Black people were ambivalent about racially-balanced integration. And the great majority of Whites were opposed to the busing that would be required to achieve any such balance.

There were many reasons for the Black ambivalence. One pertained to academic achievement. During the 1970s and 1980s, when court-ordered integration had been in fashion, there had been a narrowing of the racial gap in some test scores. However, most of the narrowing was a result of improvement among the very weakest students, and the trend in academic achievement was similar for all Black students, regardless of whether they attended schools that were mostly White or almost entirely Black. Since the test scores of Black students in racially concentrated inner-city schools improved as much as those of Blacks who were attending integrated schools, integration did not seem to be a key variable. In the 1990s, moreover, the racial gap in test scores widened and, as had been the case with the achievement gains of the previous decades, the retrogression occurred among both integrated and concentrated Black students.[69]

Kozol himself did no research on academic achievement. He conveyed the impression that, as journalist Linda Shaw noted, "the educational challenges of many low-income, minority children would disappear if they just attend integrated schools." But he did not provide an analysis of the question. Instead, Kozol endorsed and repeatedly quoted from the work of Gary Orfield, a Harvard sociologist who resurrected a thesis that James S. Coleman had developed in the 1960s. Orfield said that Black youngsters learned

---

Washington Post (17 October 2005); Kozol, quoted by Saran Karnasiewicz, "Apartheid America," *Synthesis/Regeneration* 39 (Winter 2006); Kozol, *The Shame of the Nation*, 263; "Our Media Refuse to Name This Reality," *Fairness and Accuracy in Reporting* (March 2006); Kozol, quoted by Sarah Karnasiewicz, "Apartheid America," *Salon.com* (22 September 2005).

69 David J. Armor, *Forced Justice: School Desegregation and the Law* (New York: Oxford University Press, 1995) *passim*.

more, and Whites did not suffer, when students attended racially balanced, predominantly White schools. Orfield said that students learned from one another and that a child's peer group was of key importance in influencing attitudes toward academic achievement. According to Orfield, "all of the research, starting with the Coleman Report of the late 1960s, shows that low socioeconomic students get some measurable benefit from being in schools that are predominantly middle class, and race is an additional factor." "From an educational standpoint," Black youngsters did better when they attended "schools that have middle-class norms and middle-class expectations."[70]

After proposing this thesis in the 1960s, however, Coleman later came to think that integration did *not* improve the schoolwork of lower-class Black children. Most of the Blacks who attended integrated southern schools in the early 1960s, and who had provided the basis for Coleman's initial conclusions, were well-motivated volunteers who enrolled under freedom-of-choice plans. They were superior students from families who considered education important. It had been simply "wishful thinking," Coleman later confessed, to believe that similar academic improvement would result from the massive integration of Blacks under mandatory court orders.[71]

In the end, Coleman concluded that the most that could be said for large-scale integration was that academic scores usually did not decline. The worst, and a result that Coleman acknowledged after reading some careful studies, was that the academic scores of White students declined in the wake of court-ordered integration. Coleman's initial hypothesis had been that lower-class Black students would

---

70 Linda Shaw, "Segregation Endures in Seattle," *Seattle Times* (26 September 2005); Nathan Glazer, "Separate and Unequal," *New York Times* (25 September 2005); Gary Orfield, quoted in *Boston Globe* (26 December 1991); Jonathan Kozol, *The Shame of the Nation*, 19-20, 280 and *passim*.

71 James S. Coleman, quoted in *National Observer* (7 June 1975) 1.

gain from a greater exposure to middle-class norms. But if lower-class students gained from a redistribution of what is sometimes called "social capital," it followed that middle-class students sometimes suffered from exposure to a peer group that did not value academic achievement highly (or perhaps not at all).[72]

After Coleman, an army of social scientists studied these questions. In 1982, the National Institute of Education convened a panel of seven social scientists that reviewed 157 studies of the matter, but only one of the seven scholars concluded that integration boosted the achievement of Blacks substantially. In its final report, the panel concluded, "on average desegregation did not cause an increase in achievement in mathematics" but did give a small boost ("estimated to be between two to six weeks [of a school year]") to reading levels. Eleven years later, another review of yet another 250 studies similarly concluded, "Research suggests that desegregation has had some positive impact on the reading skills of African-American youngsters. The effect is not large. . . . Such is not the case with mathematical skills, which seem generally unaffected by desegregation." In 2003, after the relation between racial mix and educational achievement had been studied by still more social scientists, Abigail Thernstrom and Stephan Thernstrom reported that there was "no scholarly consensus that a school's racial mix has a clear effect on how much children learn." The best book on the subject, *Forced Justice* (1995) by David Armor, indicated that, after controlling for the relevant variables, Blacks who remained in predominantly Black schools did just as well on standardized tests as those who attended desegregated or integrated schools.[73]

---

72 James S. Coleman, "School Desegregation and City-Suburban Relations," 1978 paper in "Court-Ordered Busing," *Hearings before the Subcommittee on Separation of Powers*, Senate Judiciary Committee, 97th Congress, 1st Session (1981) 454-59.

73 National Institute of Education, *School Desegregation and Black Achievement* (Washington: Government Printing Office, 1984); Janet Ward Schofield,

Meanwhile, public opinion polls reported that more than 80 percent of Whites opposed busing for integration. As has been mentioned in the introduction to this book, some of the best evidence came from the research of James S. Coleman, who, after analyzing data from 20 large school districts, reported that the more Blacks enrolled in a school, the greater the "White flight." After a tipping point had been reached, an increase of 5 percent in the average White child's Black classmates prompted an additional 10 percent of Whites families to leave. Thus, integrationists faced an insoluble dilemma. There would be no racially balanced integration without court-ordered busing, but such busing had the overall effect of defeating integration. The official push for school integration was offset by the actions of White families who moved away from areas where there was a large enrollment of Black students to areas where there was less racial mixing.[74]

Scholars differed in accounting for the White flight. In 1975, Coleman pointed to "the degree of disorder and the degree to which schools...have failed to control lower-class black children." According to Coleman, it was "quite understandable" for middle-class families "not to want to send their children to schools where 90 percent of the time is spent not on instruction but on discipline." Twenty-eight years later, Abigail Thernstrom and Stephan Thernstrom similarly noted, "a wealth of evidence indicates that African-American children—and especially black boys—are far more likely than others to break school rules, disrupting their own and their classmates' education." Teachers

---

"Review of Research on School Desegregation Impact," in J. A. Banks and C. A. McGee Banks eds., *Handbook of Research on Multicultural Education* (New York: McMillan, 1995) 597, 610; Abigail Thernstrom and Stephen Thernstrom, *No Excuses*, 179-180; David J. Armor, *Forced Justice*, passim.

74 Jonathan Kozol, *The Shame of the Nation*, 229; James S. Coleman et al., *Recent Trends in School Integration* (American Educational Research Association, 1979); Raymond Wolters, *Race and Education, 1954-2007* "(Columbia: University of Missouri Press, 2008) 229.

in integrated areas also complained about "having to move at a slower pace ... [and] having to water down the curriculum, causing brighter children to be held back."[75]

Kozol, on the other hand, attributed White flight to exaggerated fears and "racist suppositions." Because of segregation, most Whites never encountered the delightful Black and Hispanic children Kozol wrote about in his books. When children attended racially imbalanced schools, he opined, "They come to accept segregation. Their sweetness and openness is replaced by awareness of racism and the fear and distrust that come with it." Kozol thought this would change if Black and White students attended racially balanced schools. The students would "get to know each other far too well not to be drawn to one another, finally, as friends."[76]

Some social scientists agreed with Kozol. After interviewing students who had graduated from racially balanced schools, Amy Stuart Wells of Columbia University reported that "cross racial friendships" were more common than racial tension. Wells' interviewees said they were "more open-minded and less fearful of other races than peers who went to segregated schools." They said they were "more comfortable with people of other racial backgrounds than those who lack an integrated K-12 experience." Gary Orfield also reported that students "who've been in interracial backgrounds deeply appreciate it. They believe that they're better able to understand each other. They believe that they've learned about each other's culture.

---

75 James S. Coleman, quoted in *National Observer* (7 June 1975) 1; Abigail Thernstrom and Stephen Thernstrom, *No Excuses*, 138; Stephen J. Caldas, Carl L. Bankston III, and Judith S. Cain, "Social Capital, Academic Capital, and the 'Harm and Benefit' Thesis," in Stephen J. Caldas and Carl L. Bankston, *The End of Desegregation?* (New York: Nova Science Publishers, 2003), 135-137.

76 Jonathan Kozol, *The Shame of the Nation*, 233, 234; Kozol, quoted by Leslie Baldacci, "Our Schools Are Still Segregated."

They're comfortable working together; they look forward to living in the society that we're going to have, which is going to be half non-white in the middle of [the 21st] century."[77]

On this point, however, there was a great deal of evidence to the contrary. Several scholars reported that, as often as not, racial mixing led to increased tension and hostility. After reviewing the data from 120 studies, Nancy St. John, a committed integrationist, concluded, "positive findings are less common than negative findings." Another scholar, Walter G. Stephan, reported that integration led Black students to have slightly more favorable attitudes toward Whites, but the reverse was true for Whites. One journalist, Steve Sailer, offered a "one point plan" for "preventing kid prejudice": "Don't let your children get beaten up by underclass minorities." After alluding to Black misbehavior, Sailer urged Whites to "do what wealthy liberals do with their own offspring: insulate."

> Move to an expensive suburb where the schools have good students, or finagle your children into a magnet program or homeschool them, or pay for private tuition. Do what it takes so that the minorities they come in contact with are predominantly middle class.... Don't worry about being duplicitous.... Put your children's welfare first.[78]

Opinions differ as to the quality of the research on integrated education. But there is no doubt that the evidence is subject to conflicting interpretations. As Chief Justice John G. Roberts noted

---

77 Amicus Brief of Amy Stuart Wells et al., *Parents Involved v. Seattle School District*, U.S. Supreme Court, 2006; CNN Sunday Morning (19 January 19 2003) (transcript 011903CN.V46).

78 Nancy St. John, *School Desegregation: Outcomes for Children* (New York: John Wiley and Sons, 1975) 67-68; Walter G. Stephan, "The Effects of School Desegregation," in M. Saks, ed., *Advances in Applied Social Psychology* (Hillsdale, J. J. Erlbaum Associates, 1986); Steve Sailer, "Preventing Kid Prejudice: The Sailer (One Point) Plan," VDARE.com (6 February 2005).

in 2007, there has been much disagreement over "whether racial diversity in schools in fact has a marked impact on test scores . . . or achieves intangible socialization benefits." University of Virginia law professor James E. Ryan has summarized the situation. In one lawsuit after another those who favor the policy of racial balance called upon "experts who paint a . . . positive picture of the benefits of integration." In response, "those challenging the plans hire experts who testify and present studies showing that the social and academic gains from integration are limited at best." Ryan himself strongly favored racially balanced integration but nonetheless conceded, "The evidence regarding the benefits of school desegregation is not sufficiently clear to dislodge any but the most weakly held beliefs. . . ."[79]

Eventually the Supreme Court took account of the inconclusive social science and the public opposition to busing for racial balance. Beginning in 1974, the Court restricted the amount of busing that could be required, and in the 1990s the Court established a process that allowed school districts to be freed from busing programs that lower federal courts had imposed. Kozol considered the Court's decisions "devastating." He said the Court had "ripped the guts out of and trampled on the legacy of *Brown v. Board of Education.*"[80]

Kozol was mistaken. In truth, the Supreme Court, in cases decided in the 1990s and in 2007, returned to the original understanding of *Brown*. The implementation order in *Brown* had been worded to condemn "discrimination," not "racial imbalance." The Court said that *Brown* stood for "the fundamental principle" that there should be no "racial discrimination in public education,"

---

79 *Parents Involved v. Seattle*, 127 S.Ct. 2738 (2007), 2755-56; James E. Ryan, "The Limited Influence of Social Science Evidence in Modern Desegregation Cases," *North Carolina Law Review* 81 (May 2003) 1689-91, 1660, 1664.

80 Nancy G. Nagel and Sara Guest, "An Interview with Jonathan Kozol," *Democracy and Education* 17:1, 3; Kozol, quoted by Kristie McClanahan, "Learning Curve," *Riverfront Times* (5 October 2003).

and the defendant school districts were ordered to proceed "with all deliberate speed" toward establishing schools that would be "free of racial discrimination." For more than a decade after *Brown*, desegregation was understood to mean the disestablishment of segregation. The Court declared that the government should not discriminate on the basis of race, but there was nothing in *Brown* or in the extensive notes of the justices and their clerks to indicate the Court wished to achieve racially balanced enrollments. The Court insisted that public schools must be desegregated, in the sense that no student could be denied admittance solely on the basis of race. It did not require that, in order to be considered "desegregated," authorities must assign students by race so that the proportions of Blacks and Whites at individual schools would be approximately the same as the proportions of Blacks and Whites in the larger community.[81]

Later, the Court changed its policy. In its *Green, Swann*, and *Keyes* decisions of 1968, 1971, and 1973, the Court obliged school districts to assign students by race to achieve more racial mixing than could be achieved by racially neutral policies. Then, in its *Milliken* decision of 1974, and in its *Dowell, Freeman*, and *Jenkins* opinions of 1991, 1992, and 1995, the Court returned to the policy that *Brown* had established. In 2007, in *Parents Involved v. Seattle*, the Court affirmed, "History will be heard. The way to stop discrimination on the basis of race is to stop discrimination on the basis of race."[82]

---

81 These points are developed at length in my book *Race and Education, 1954-2007*. The quotations are from *Brown v. Board of Education*, 349 US 294 (1955). Also see *Cooper v. Aaron*, 358 US 1 (1958).

82 *Green v. New Kent County*, 391 US 430 (1968); *Swann v. Charlotte-Mecklenburg*, 402 US 1 (1971); *Keyes v. School District No. 1*, 413 US 189 (1973); *Milliken v. Bradley*, 418 US 717 (1974); *Oklahoma City v. Dowell*, 111 S.Ct. 630 (1991); *Freeman v. Pitts*, 60 USLW 4286 (1992); *Missouri v. Jenkins*, 63 USLW 4486 (1995); *Parents Involved v. Seattle*, 127 S.Ct. 2738 (2007) 2767, 2768.

In eventually upholding the principle that the Constitution required a policy of racial nondiscrimination rather than one of racially balanced integration, the Supreme Court fashioned a settlement that accorded with American pluralism. Most Americans condemned unfair discrimination, but they also nurtured a sense (consciously or subconsciously) of racial identity, pride, and community. Most Whites favored a system of segmented development in which Blacks and Whites voluntarily chose to live in communities that were predominantly of their own race. Nor were Whites alone in this respect. Marcus Garvey and Malcolm X also spoke in favor of racial communities, and W.E.B. DuBois once recommended that Negroes and Caucasians should live "side by side in peace and mutual happiness," with each group making its own "peculiar contribution to the culture of their common country." Supreme Court justice Clarence Thomas explained that "the Constitution does not prevent individuals from choosing to live together, to work together, or to send their children to school together, so long as the state does not interfere on the basis of race."[83]

Kozol was opposed to mere desegregation. If he had his way, the government would have required proportional mixing. "I want to see the abolition of apartheid," he declared in 2005.

> I've believed for 40 years and I still believe today that segregated schools are never equal to schools serving the mainstream of society. They never were in the century just past; they never will be in the century ahead. Segregated education is the oldest failed experiment in U.S. social history.[84]

But Kozol understood the temper of his times. Most White parents regarded busing for integration as an unwarranted interference with their right to direct the upbringing of their children. They wanted to be free from state impositions that affected such a personal matter.

---

83 *Missouri v. Jenkins* 515 US 70 (1995) 121.

84 Jonathan Kozol, quoted by Richard Halicks, "School Resegregation."

Many Blacks also celebrated their own distinctiveness and sought to maintain and foster their own sense of racial identity, community, and pride. With new waves of immigration, a pluralist mindset also became increasingly popular with other minority groups. By the turn of the 21st century, "multiculturalism" and "diasporic consciousness" were in fashion. The concept of America as "a national community" had lost its sway and, as Harvard scholar Samuel P. Huntington noted, "racial, ethnic, cultural, and other subnational identities" came to the fore.[85]

Kozol continued to believe that school enrollments should be balanced racially and ethnically. But he recognized that, in the new climate of opinion, there would be no massive busing programs. Once again, he shifted his emphasis. In *The Shame of the Cities* and in a companion work of 2007, *Letters to a Young Teacher*, Kozol wrote in opposition to standardized testing and in support of progressive education. He also expressed strong opposition to the idea that parents should be allowed to decide what sort of school was best for their children.[86]

Kozol's harshest criticism was aimed at standardized testing. The federal government's No Child Left Behind Act of 2001 (NCLB) tried to improve education by focusing on the low-achieving students who were most likely to be "left behind." The legislation required public schools to test students in reading and math. It also required the schools to report the average scores of students by race, ethnicity, disability, and level of family income; and if any of the subgroups failed to make "adequate yearly progress," the school would face penalties that increased with each passing year.

---

85 Samuel P. Huntington, *Who Are We: The Challenges to America's National Identity* (New York: Simon & Schuster, 2004) 143 and *passim*.

86 Jonathan Kozol, *Letters to a Young Teacher* (New York: Crown Publishers, 2007).

As it happened, teachers in middle-class schools did not have to spend much time preparing for the NCLB tests because most of their students learned the basics as a matter of course. However, for fear of the penalties that NCLB imposed, most teachers of non-Asian minority students had to reduce the time allotted for instruction in subjects that were not tested. In inner-city schools, Kozol said, students had to spend "at least a quarter of the year" preparing for basic tests.[87]

Kozol acknowledged that this approach led to better test scores, but also noted that sacrifices had been made. Because of NCLB's "relentless and obsessive" emphasis on "the basics," inner-city children learned less about art, music, and history. And that was not all. In order to provide extra time for test preparation, many schools no longer allowed kindergarten children to have nap time. Some went "to the extreme of taking recess from their children," and others closed their playgrounds, "so that no time can be wasted on activities that will not raise [test] scores." Because of NCLB, the principals and superintendents in inner-city schools no longer spoke about "the sense of fun that children have, or ought to have, in public school." NCLB turned inner-city schools "into places not of learning but of robot-like memorization and military style discipline." The teachers became "drill sergeants" and the students "examination soldiers."[88]

Kozol also believed the testing gains were ephemeral. He said he would not have opposed the new emphases if these approaches actually improved the students' ability to read and compute. "The trouble is, they do not work except for the lowest-scoring children in a

---

87 Jonathan Kozol, quoted by Dudley Barlow, "Resources for Educators," *Education Digest* 72 (November 2007) 79.

88 Jonathan Kozol, *Letters to a Young Teacher*, 112-114, 99; Kozol, quoted by John Wilkens, "Separate and Unequal," *San Diego Union-Tribune* (11 September 2005).

class, and, even then, the gains that they achieve sustain themselves for only a brief period of time. These are testing gains, not learning gains." The gains were an artifact of "nonstop drilling for exams." If the gains were real, they would have persisted into high school, but only half the youths in many inner cities ever became high-school seniors and these students were, on average, reading and computing "at the level of the average white seventh-grader." When people said that direct instruction and test preparation were working, they were "telling a terrible lie to the parents of poor children." When testing advocates said "poor and minority students are achieving at dramatically higher levels today than they were two decades ago," as Michael J. Petrilli did in 2011, they were referring to elementary students, not teenagers.[89]

In the meantime, the negative effects were enduring. For years, many teachers had departed from inner-city schools as soon as they acquired enough seniority to qualify for transfers. Many observers attributed this to the difficulties that middle-class White teachers had with lower-class Black and Hispanic students. But Kozol had a different explanation. He told of teachers who telephoned "in the evenings, on the verge of tears, to tell me of the maddening frustration that they feel at being forced" to place so much emphasis on preparing their students for standardized tests. Many of the best teachers, especially young teachers who had been recruited "from the nation's most respected colleges and universities," were "throwing up their hands and giving up their jobs within three years." They were doing so because they could not abide "the miserable drill-and-kill curriculum of robotic 'teaching to the test.'" They resented the condescending implication that teachers were "mediocre drones" who could not be trusted to assess the progress of students whom they saw day-in and day-out. They resented those who said that teachers, as well as the

---

[89] Jonathan Kozol, quoted by Dudley Barlow, "Resources for Educators"; Kozol, quoted by Richard Halicks, "School Resegregation"; Michael J. Petrilli, quoted in "Jeb Bush and Florida's Education Success," posted at EdReform.blogspot.com (30 September 2011).

students in predominantly Black and Hispanic schools, should be judged by the students' progress on elementary tests.[90]

According to Kozol, these teachers also recognized that "the mania of obsessive testing" was "profoundly racist." He quoted one "high spirited, superbly educated" young teacher as saying,

> I didn't study all these years in order to turn black babies into mindless little robots, denied the normal breadth of learning, all the arts and sciences, all the joy in reading literary classics, all the spontaneity and power to ask interesting questions.[91]

As Kozol saw it, segregation had "returned to public education with a vengeance." Modern America was providing two sorts of public education, "one for the affluent and one for the poor." In schools where the great majority of students were either Whites or Asians, students were offered a broad education and exposure to "critical thinking." Meanwhile, youths in predominantly Black or Hispanic communities were being trained for subordinate jobs. It was "not just that we have apartheid schools," Kozol declared. "We also have a separate curriculum for those schools."

> The children of the suburbs learn to think and to interrogate reality; the inner-city kids meanwhile are trained for nonreflective acquiescence. One race and social class is educated for the exploration of ideas and ... future economic power; the other is prepared for intellectual subordination.

It was a "profoundly racist agenda,"—one that Kozol urged teachers to subvert by developing "a coherent oppositional mentality." In 2006, when he was 70 years old, Kozol formed an organization that aimed to stop the standardized testing associated with NCLB. He

---

90 Jonathan Kozol, "Why I Am Fasting: An Explanation to My Friends," originally published at *Huffington Post* (10 September 2007).

91 Ibid.

described "the murderous impact of the NCLB legislation," and urged educators "to resist the testing mania and directly challenge Congress, possibly by a march on Washington, at the time when NCLB comes up for reauthorization in 2007."[92]

To gain publicity and support for this cause, Kozol embarked on a lengthy partial fast. On the 67th day of the fast, he explained that he had been "taking only small amounts of mostly liquid foods each day, and, when I have stomach pains, other forms of nourishment at times, a stipulation that my doctor insisted on in order to avert the risk of doing long term damage to my heart."[93]

What should be said by way of final assessment? Because Kozol supported disadvantaged schoolchildren so passionately, critics initially cut him a lot of slack. Even those who recognized that spending more money was not likely to fix education in the inner cities assumed that Kozol was not doing children any harm. Since his heart was in the right place, he was admired as widely as he was read.

Kozol came in for criticism, however, when he organized an opposition to NCLB and standardized testing. One critic was Whitney Tilson, a hedge-fund manager and a leader of a group called Democrats for Education Reform. Tilson initially thought Kozol was

---

92 Jonathan Kozol, quoted in "Convention Collage," *Reading Today* 23 (June/July 2006) 164; Kozol, quoted by Richard Halicks, "School Resegregation."

93 Jonathan Kozol, statement on "CBS, The Early Show: Hosted by Tracy Smith and Hannah Storm," *CBS Worldwide* (26 December 2005); Kozol, *Letters to a Young Teacher*, 121, 205; Kozol, "Falling Behind," *Religion-Online*, 1990; Kozol "Why I am Fasting."

"misguided." But after Kozol declared war on testing, Tilson regarded him as "a dangerous crackpot who will cause this country's most vulnerable children immeasurable harm." "Doesn't Kozol realize," Tilson asked, "that while NCLB may have some warts and needs to be tweaked, it's the best thing that's ever happened to disadvantaged children? For the first time, school systems can no longer sweep these children under the rug and are FINALLY being measured, which is the first requirement of accountability." As Tilson saw it, "it's precisely BECAUSE kids who haven't had many advantages are so far behind that testing is NECESSARY. Without testing, how is anyone to know how far behind they are? [Without testing,] how can a hue and cry be raised, how can we get extra help for those kids?"[94]

Other critics chimed in. Abigail Thernstrom wrote that Kozol, while acknowledging that inner-city students needed to learn "essential skills," nevertheless strongly opposed the policies that were designed to help them catch up with their higher-performing peers. Instead, Kozol stressed the need for schools that exuded "warmth and playfulness and informality and cheerful camaraderie among the teachers and their children." After noting that Kozol was "still widely read in ed schools and by activist teachers," journalist Sol Stern opined that, to the degree teachers subscribed to Kozol's views, they would "limit the life chances of inner-city children."[95]

Another criticism focused on Kozol's opposition to "choice." Many parents wished to have a choice when it came to the schooling of their children, and by 2010 about one-fifth of America's students attended choice schools of one sort of another. More than half of these

---

94 Whitney Tilson, "My Critique of Jonathan Kozol," EdReform.blogspot.com (2 March 2007).

95 Abigail Thernstrom, "Lessons Not Learned," *Wall Street Journal* (29 September 2005); Sol Stern, "Savage Exaggerations," *Education Next* 6 (Summer 2006) 6.

choice students were enrolled in private schools or were schooled at home. The others were enrolled in "magnet" or "charter" schools that were funded by taxpayers. The magnet schools had originally expanded in the 1980s as a way to maximize racial mixing without producing White flight. The charter schools came into vogue in the 1990s and were especially popular in many inner cities. Because the regular public schools in many urban areas were problematical, a disproportionately large number of Black families have patronized charter schools. In fact, by 2003, the Black proportion of the nation's charter-school students was almost twice as large (33 percent) as the Black proportion of overall student enrollment (17 percent). In some cities, about one-third of the Black students chose to enroll in charter schools.[96]

---

96 Beginning with Minnesota in 1991, many states passed laws that provided public funds for charter schools. These schools were given a great degree of independence in return for accepting accountability for the performance of their students. In particular, many charter schools were allowed to hire teachers who were neither licensed by the state nor members of a union. If charter students did not do will on standardized tests, however, the charter supposedly would be revoked.

Charter proponents borrowed arguments from market economics. If parents and students had more choices, the proponents said, students who previously had no alternative but to attend disorderly schools with low test scores would be the principal beneficiaries. Charter proponents also criticized the concept that one size fits all—the idea that the interests of diverse students could be accommodated in large comprehensive schools. Education reformer Chester E. Finn summed up this point: "The charter idea recognizes that people differ along countless dimensions.... [It] assumes that schools should differ from each other so that the diverse needs of a pluralistic society can be met.... The reason to encourage schools to be different is so that all youngsters, not just those who blossom under the 'one best system,' will have the kinds of education that enable them to learn." [Chester E. Finn, Bruno V. Manno and Greg Vanourek, *Charter schools in Action* (2000) 70-71.]

In addition, proponents hoped that in time the success of charter schools would lead to changes in the broader public school system. "You have to have a West Berlin for East Berlin to fall," one charter proponent said, "and what we're really doing here is building West Berlin." Chris Whittle, quoted by Jonathan Kozol, "Whittle and the Privateers," *Nation* (21 September 1992) 274.] As will be noted in chapters 8 and 9, charter schools eventually became

It is not likely that the United States will return to the situation that prevailed in the 1950s, when the vast majority of parents sent their children to whatever school those in authority chose. Nevertheless, Kozol was strongly opposed to any arrangement that made it easier for students to attend either private schools or publicly-funded charter schools. He thought that vouchers—scholarships from the government that could be used at private schools—were "the single worst, most dangerous idea to have entered education discourse in my adult life."[97]

Kozol recognized that many parents thought the private and charter schools were better than the regular public schools. But Kozol said that these parents, when they removed their children from the regular public schools, increased the likelihood that the regular school would be a bad school. "Here's the thing," he said. "It's a triumph of the individual self-interest over civic virtue." Americans who patronized private and religious schools tended to think, "What's wrong with a nice Catholic school or a Lutheran or a Montessori School?" "There's nothing wrong inherently," Kozol answered. "But ... once you let this genie out of the bottle, you can't restrict it to the kind of schools that seem benign."[98]

In addition, Kozol personally did not regard Catholic schools favorably. Too often, he said, the Catholic curriculum was rigid and discipline-bound and obsessed with tests and drills. He considered it shameful that in some cities taxpayers had provided vouchers that could be used at Catholic schools. And he showed little sympathy for Catholic parents who wanted schools that provide grounding in the

---

    especially popular with people who blamed the teachers' unions for the shortcomings of non-Asian minority students.

97 Lisa Kaiser, "An Interview with Educator and Activist Jonathan Kozol," *ExpressMilwaukee.com* (4 March 2009).

98 *Ibid.*

basics of their faith and family traditions as well as the fundamentals of reading, writing, and arithmetic. He doubted the products of Catholic education would later become either independent thinkers or adults who appreciated and tolerated the opinions of secular people.

Kozol also opposed school choice because he thought most poor African-American parents were not well enough informed to choose a good school for their children. He noted that in many cities these parents had vouchers for healthcare and groceries. Every hospital in Boston, for example, was already obliged to accept any holder of Medicaid, but the poor Black people of Roxbury habitually crowded into the waiting room of Boston City Hospital, "the slum hospital," instead of going to "the beautiful white hospitals on the other side of town." Something similar had happened with food stamps. Although the coupons amounted to vouchers that could be used at almost any grocery store, most of Boston's poor Black people did not buy their groceries "at a beautiful shop over in Cambridge near Harvard University" but instead purchased "spoiled meat at inflated prices in the ghetto."[99]

Kozol further complained that the inner-city children who enrolled in charter schools were likely to have parents who were especially savvy and sophisticated. He believed that if these parents removed their children from regular public schools, the regular students—those whose parents were not savvy and sophisticated—would be "left behind." "We are looking at a social Darwinist scenario," Kozol wrote, "a triage operation that will filter all the fortunate and leave the rest in schools where children of the 'better' parents do not need to see them." Rather than trust parents to make well-informed decisions for their children, Kozol thought it better for enlightened people (like Kozol himself) to make decisions for other people's children.[100]

---

99 Larry Hayes, "A Simple Matter of Humanity: An Interview with Jonathan Kozol," *Phi Delta Kappan* 74 (December 1992) 334.

100 "Falling Behind: An Interview with Jonathan Kozol"; Kozol, *Letters to a*

Jonathan Kozol

Writing in *The Weekly Standard*, playwright Jonathan Leaf called attention to the arrogance behind "Kozol's relentless campaigns . . . against charter schools." And Whitney Tilson noted that many Catholic and charter schools were "achieving some degree of success (in some cases, a very high degree of success) with students who, if these schools didn't exist, would mostly be going absolutely nowhere." So, Tilson asked,

> Can someone explain to me why it's in our city's best interest to let these [Catholic and charter] schools fail . . . when we're utterly wasting $10,000-$12,000 per student per year miseducating comparable students at nearby [regular public] schools? This strikes me as the definition of madness! Yeah, yeah, yeah, I know the reasons—separation of church and state, skimming the best students from the public schools, etc.—but I keep coming back to this question: What do I tell the mother who's trying to get a decent education for her son and keep him away from gangs, yet can only afford to live in a neighborhood in which the local public school has for decades failed to provide an education and is rife with gangs?"[101]

Young Teacher, chapter 11; Kozol, "Whittle and the Privateers," 274; John Dewey, *The School and Society* (Chicago: University of Chicago Press, 1990 [reprint of original edition of 1900]) 7.

101 Jonathan Leaf, "The Learning Disabled Education Expert"; Statement of Whitney Tilson, EdReform.blogspot.com (28 February 2006).

2

Howard Gardner and the Theory of Multiple Intelligences

Comprehending the thought of Howard Gardner is essential to understanding another dimension of the contemporary progressive approach to school reform. A neuro-psychologist and professor of education at Harvard University, Gardner is best known for his theory of multiple intelligences, which he developed in *Frames of Mind* (1983). Since then, Gardner has enjoyed tremendous popularity and influence in the world of teachers, school administrators, and professors of education, although many researchers in the field of psychology and some scholars of education continue to question the validity of his underlying theory.

Ever since the development of the Stanford-Binet IQ tests early in the twentieth century, most psychologists have focused on two varieties of intelligence—linguistic and logical. Most psychologists also thought of intelligence as a general aptitude, a sort of brain power that could be measured by tests the way body temperature could be measured by thermometer. In doing so, they followed the lead of Charles Spearman, an English psychologist who first noted that a person's performance on a test of verbal ability predicted his or her score on a test of mathematical aptitude, and vice versa. Spearman reasoned that therefore there must be some deeper, general ability. Thereafter, most American researchers also concluded that there existed a general factor of intelligence, which they symbolized with a lower case *g*. Although there was much debate about the extent to which *g* was innate or influenced by culture, most psychologists believed in *g* and worked to develop better ways of measuring it. Indeed, as Gardner wrote, many psychologists believed that "intelligence testing was psychology's greatest achievement, its chief claim to social utility."[1]

Gardner, however, thought the prevailing views were mistaken. IQ tests measured linguistic facility (the talent for understanding and manipulating language) and logical ability (comprehending and applying abstract concepts). But Gardner insisted these were but two of seven varieties of intelligence. In addition to aptitudes for language and logic, there was a musical intelligence (the ability to perceive and manipulate tone, melody, and rhythm), an interpersonal intelligence (the capacity for understanding the motivations of other people), an intrapersonal intelligence (conscious awareness of one's own talents and emotions), a spatial intelligence (the ability to visualize and manipulate forms and objects), and a bodily-kinesthetic intelligence (skill at using the body in energetic and creative ways). Later Gardner added an eighth distinct intelligence—naturalist intelligence (an intuitive understanding of living plants and animals). When he was minding his manners, Gardner characterized the concept of general intelligence as the theory of "the intelligence establishment." When he was in a less charitable mood, he railed against what he called "the intelligence Mafia"—psychologists who believed there was a general dimension of intelligence, that it could be measured, and that it stemmed, in part, from one's heredity.[2]

---

1   Howard Gardner, *Frames of Mind: The Theory of Multiple Intelligences* (New York: Basic Books, 1983) 16 and *passim.*; Linda Gottfredson, "Intelligence," *New Scientist*, 2 July 2011.

2   Howard Gardner, *Intelligence Reframed* (New York: Basic Books, 1999) 18;

Each of the intelligences was of great value, but Gardner noted that different societies had privileged different blends of aptitude. Five hundred years ago most western societies had "emphasized linguistic memory because printed books weren't readily available. Five hundred years from now, when computers are carrying out all reasoning, there may be no need for logical-mathematical thinking and again the list of desirable intelligences would shift." In modern Japan, Gardner continued, "interpersonal intelligence—the ability to work well in groups and to arrive at joint decisions," helped in achieving a cohesion and efficiency that bolstered industrial productivity. Hunting societies, on the other hand, considered it "more important to have extremely good control of your body and know your way around..." And in the islands of Micronesia, sailors navigated "among hundreds of islands, using only the stars in the sky and their bodily feelings as they go over the waves. To that society, this ability is much more important than solving a quadratic equation or writing a sonnet." If Micronesians had developed IQ tests, they would have come up with "an entirely different set of testing methods and a wholly distinct list of intelligences."[3]

In developing his theory of multiple intelligences, Gardner was influenced by his sense of what was fair, by scientific research, and by personal experience. He considered it unfair if a society emphasized the aptitudes for language and logic. In America and many other countries, young people were thought of as inherently smart or dull, in their own minds as well as by others. "We are wasting a lot of human potential by focusing on only linguistic and logical intelligence," Gardner said. "If an individual doesn't happen to be good in these, he or she often gets thrown on society's scrap heap." If a youngster

---

Gardner, *To Open Minds* (New York: Basic Books, 1989) 111; *Boston Globe* (5 November 1995); *The Straits Times* (Singapore) (8 June 2003).

[3] Howard Gardner, "The Seven Frames of Mind," *Psychology Today* (June 1984) 21-26; Gardner, "Human Intelligence Isn't What We Think It Is," *U.S. News & World Report* (19 March 1984) 75-78.

did poorly on an IQ test he would be "labeled as not very smart," and many schools and teachers would treat him accordingly.[4]

Gardner thought IQ tests had "destructive social effects" because they instilled feelings of superiority in some people but undermined the confidence of others. Teachers gave special encouragement to students who did well on the tests. With their confidence thus buoyed, these students then did well in school, were admitted to prestigious colleges, and eventually were welcomed into good jobs and professions. Conversely, IQ tests undermined the self-esteem of youngsters who did not have much aptitude for logic or language. When schools did not adjust their instructions to make learning easier for those with different intelligences, the schools gave the impression that other talents were not valued. Many "differently-abled" youngsters then started acting as if they were, in fact, mentally sluggish. "If for 20 years of your life school is the only show in town and you're labeled as dumb, it's going to have a huge effect on you," Gardner said. In school these pupils were regarded as, at best, not academically inclined, and many of them developed lifelong feelings of personal failure and inadequacy. "To my mind, this is the most unfair thing in the world. It puts one kind of intelligence on a pedestal and ignores every other kind even though 90 percent of the world doesn't happen to have the language-logic intelligence."[5]

Gardner also considered traditional views of intelligence "wrong in scientific terms." Medical research had shown that mental abilities did not break down equally when a stroke or tumor damaged the brain or central nervous system. If the left hemisphere of the brain was damaged, the patient would lose language ability almost entirely but musical, spatial, and interpersonal skills would not be affected to the same extent. Conversely, people with damage to the right

---

4   Howard Gardner, "Human Intelligence Isn't What We Think It Is."

5   Ibid.; *Irish Times* (13 September 1994); *Irish Times* (24 January 1995).

hemisphere often discovered that their capacity for language was intact, but that their spatial, musical, and interpersonal skills were seriously compromised. These findings seemed inconsistent with the idea that intelligence was a single trait. If intelligence was unitary, all the mental abilities of people with brain damage should have been affected equally.[6]

For Gardner, every stroke amounted to an accident of nature that called into question the traditional concept of intelligence. The ravages of brain damage argued both for the existence of a multiplicity of distinct intelligences and against the idea that there was a general intelligence that could be measured by a single test. Thus Gardner's theory of multiple intelligences not only expanded the concept of intelligence but also challenged the belief—one that he said was "held by many psychologists and entrenched—that intelligence is a single faculty and that one is either 'smart' or 'stupid' across the board."[7]

In essence, Gardner aimed a slingshot at one of the citadels of professional psychology. Unlike the Biblical David, however, Gardner did not score a knockout victory. The Goliath of standardized testing remained on its feet. At the turn of the 21st century, indeed, an emphasis on testing, logic, and language seemed to gain strength from an increased use of standardized tests as the measure of school accountability. Nevertheless, thanks to Gardner's theory of multiple intelligences, some psychologists and many school teachers and administrators began to think in new ways and tried to accommodate a wider range of intellectual capacities than the traditional aptitudes for logic and language.[8]

---

6   Howard Gardner, "The Seven Frames of Mind," 21.

7   Howard Gardner, *Intelligence Reframed*, 34.

8   *Boston Globe* (5 November 1995).

In accounting for his theories, Gardner also mentioned personal experiences. His parents and about fifty of his relatives had fled Nazi Germany and made their way to America. Nearly all of them settled in the New York area or in Scranton, Pennsylvania, where Gardner was born in 1943. Yet Gardner did not feel at ease in America. "As a Jew and (as all in my family perpetually feared) a potential victim of persecution," he considered himself "different." In Scranton, young Gardner did not socialize much with other youths, whose lives often revolved around athletic activities for which Gardner had little aptitude. Instead, he spent most of his time playing the piano and socializing with his extended family, "hearing the same stories and jokes and political views bandied about." Initially, Gardner thought he would become a professional musician. His skill with the piano, when combined with a lack of athletic prowess, may have contributed to Gardner's sense of separation from most of his American age-mates. As an adult, Gardner still recalled "with vividness" the "various activities I did not do or could not do." As a youth, he considered himself "a marginal person."[9]

Gardner also perceived a tension between the values of his family and the precepts of the larger American society. When he was living with his parents, Gardner had been "a devoted young Jew, attending Sunday school and Hebrew school regularly and being both 'bar mitzvah-ed' and confirmed." He was "obedient to authority" and understood that "it was more important to be loyal to the tradition than to strike out on one's own. Solace and happiness came from adhering to these norms, and from spending time in the company of people with similar points of view—family and others of the same religious and ethnic background." Yet there were "conflicting messages in the American atmosphere." In the streets Gardner also learned "that innovation is good . . . ; that examples drawn from the past are rarely useful and often pernicious; that it is more important to explore something on its own and come to know it directly than

---

9   Howard Gardner, *To Open Minds*, 20-28 and *passim*.

to honor received wisdom or practices that have been handed down uncritically from one generation to another."[10]

Although Gardner emphasized the importance of his ethnic background, he did not regard his later criticism of established psychologists (or a related critique of traditional teaching methods) as examples of an unassimilated Jew finding fault with the Gentile world. Instead, Gardner thought challenges to authority were quintessentially American. He had first learned this lesson in Scranton when he was a sixth grade student. His teacher, a Miss Clark, the sister of an important local politician, had "seized a paddle and whacked [Gardner] on the hands" after Gardner had corrected her on a question about which Gardner was "more knowledgeable . . . than was she." When the school principal learned of this, he forced Miss Clark to apologize, and Gardner "learned a valuable lesson about authority, American style." At home, he had been taught to "do what a figure in authority asks, and be respectful, even if the authority figure does not particularly merit respect." But in America "such obeisance to authority was not automatic."[11]

Unfortunately, most of Scranton's teachers had not learned this lesson. Gardner had little good to say about the public schools there. "The teachers were well meaning and virtuous but limited. We students sat at our desks, which were bolted to the floor; memorized lists of words, facts, arithmetical tables; and encountered little if anything in the way of . . . open inquiry of any sort." As a young teenager, Gardner attended Scranton Central High, where he learned "remarkably little from the well-meaning but largely ignorant faculty." Then he transferred to a small prep school, Wyoming Seminary, where he felt "somewhat less marginal." At Wyoming Seminary, he also encountered teachers who had attended first-rate universities

---

10 Ibid., 27, 30, 31.

11 Ibid., 31-32.

and who, while not themselves productive scholars, cared about intellectual pursuits. "These teachers lavished attention on Gardner and, perhaps best of all, allowed him to work on his own, without hav[ing] to buckle under to those in authority."[12]

After graduating from Wyoming Seminary, Gardner enrolled at Harvard College, which he entered as a freshman in 1961. At one time Harvard had been a bastion of the White Anglo establishment. By the 1960s, however, no one group seemed to be dominant on campus, and Gardner was especially impressed when he learned of a class that had elected four marshals—"one protestant, one Catholic, one Jewish, and one black." Gardner sensed that minority groups and dissenting individuals would be out of harm's way at a place where there was no majority.[13]

While at Harvard, Gardner gravitated toward the social sciences and eventually became a disciple of two well-known psychologists. As an undergraduate he worked with Erik Erikson, "an indisputably great man, at the height of his intellectual and personal magnetism, sharing with us his most recent thoughts on . . . issues that mattered." Then, as a graduate student, Gardner worked with Jerome Bruner, who was designing a new curriculum to teach social studies to middle-school students. Bruner's curriculum, called MACOS for "Man: A Course of Study," de-emphasized the transmission of basic information and focused instead on fundamental questions such as "What makes human beings human?" and "How could they be made more so?" These questions were approached in the exploratory, nondirective fashion associated with the open schools movement that was in fashion at the time. "This was progressive education, 1960s style," Gardner wrote, and he became "a strong convert." Given Gardner's predisposition from his youth in Scranton and at the Wyoming Seminary, "convert" was

---

12 *Ibid.*, 25, 33, 34, 33, 35.

13 *Ibid.*, 37.

not precisely the right word. Even in the 1950s, Gardner had already developed many of the dispositions that characterized progressives.[14]

After earning a Ph.D. at Harvard, Gardner became a postdoctoral fellow at the Boston Veterans Administration Medical Center. There he did research on the brain and central nervous system and became familiar with "the strange array of syndromes that follow brain damage." In time this led to the theory of multiple intelligences that he set forth in *Frames of Mind*. Some critics found fault with the theory, saying that Gardner had arbitrarily relabeled as "intelligence" a variety of "talents" which he found personally appealing. To qualify for Gardner's list of intelligences, however, there had to be a specific section of the brain where a particular aptitude was located.[15]

Gardner's early publications were intended for neuropsychologists who wanted to know more about the workings of the brain. But the theory of multiple intelligences soon achieved extraordinary popularity in the world of education. Perhaps this was because Gardner provided a Harvard imprimatur for something many teachers already sensed: that children have different qualities, that they learn in different ways and that it is a mistake to reward only the narrow range of verbal and mathematical talents that are related to traditional schoolwork. In the past, many teachers had intuitively tried to adapt their teaching to the different learning styles of their students, but *Frames of Mind* gave them a new rationale for doing so.

Nevertheless, Gardner was surprised by the extent of interest in his theory. *Frames of Mind* contained only two chapters discussing the educational implications of the theory of multiple intelligences, and these had been added to the book as something of an afterthought. Gardner had not expected them to spark a reform movement. But

---

14 Ibid., 47, 50, 52.

15 Ibid., 90.

that is what happened. In 1986, three years after the publication of *Frames of Mind*, an article in the *New York Times* reported that Gardner's theory was "having a major influence on the thinking of ... educators everywhere." A decade later the *Boston Globe* confirmed the point, saying there was "no question that MI had become a hot-ticket among reform-minded educators."[16]

One skeptical journalist opined that multiple intelligence theory achieved popularity because it encouraged "the egalitarian delusion that we are all utterly brilliant in equally important ways." More sympathetic observers attributed the popularity to a commonsensical understanding that people who did not do well in traditional schools or on standardized tests were often smart in different ways. Some were adept on the sports field but dull in examination rooms. Others had a talent for music but no head for dates or numbers. As one Chinese editor noted, Gardner held that people have a broad range of intelligences: "While some are word smart, others are number smart, picture smart, body smart, music smart, people smart, self smart, and nature smart." Because of this diversity, it was a mistake for schools to "focus most of their attention on students with good language and mathematical skills but not those who are talented dancers, musicians, and painters." Most children were excellent at something, and the teacher's job was to make the best of the situation.[17]

Thus, Gardner did more than identify a variety of intelligences; he also encouraged societies to appreciate diversity and encourage excellence in many forms. And he maintained that nations wasted a

---

16 Howard Gardner, *Multiple Intelligences* (New York: Basic Books, 2006), 53; *New York Times* (9 November 1986); *Boston Globe* (5 November 1995).

17 Robert Holland in the *Richmond Times Dispatch*, quoted by Mary Eberstadt, "The Schools They Deserve," *Policy Review* 97 (October/November 1999) 3-17; C. K. Lau, "Selection Process Scores Low Marks," *South China Morning Post* (26 August 2006).

lot of talent if their educational systems placed excessive emphasis on language and logic. As one Canadian newspaper noted, Gardner maintained "that North American culture, and by extension its school systems, reinforce and reward primarily two kinds of intelligence—linguistic and mathematical—when in fact there exist at least six other kinds of intelligence."[18]

As Gardner saw it, many youngsters were not doing well in school because their teachers were not using appropriate methods. "We showed that all kids have some areas where they are quite strong and some areas where they are quite weak," Gardner said. If teachers would recognize this and adjust to the diversity of aptitudes, many more students would become successful learners. Some students admittedly learned from the traditional reading, explanation, and testing. But others would respond only to different approaches. "Some of us learn mainly through actions or movement and are described as kinesthetic learners, others learn best through listening to sounds (auditory learners), while those ... who learn best through pictures or any other visual stimuli are known as visual learners." There was "no such thing as a good school, only a good school for this particular child at this particular time."[19]

Gardner called for the individualization of education. "Once you adopt the theory of multiple intelligences," he told one group of teachers, "you realize that the uniform school which teaches and tests all students on the same thing in the same way is . . . unfair." "When we can educate in a more personalized way, the children will learn better." If a student did not respond to traditional methods of education, MI called for the teacher to identify that student's particular strength and to orient the instruction accordingly. "If you're

---

18 *The Globe and Mail* (8 August 2001).

19 *New York Times* (9 April 1989); *Milwaukee Journal Sentinel* (7 June 2001); *The Scotsman* (27 October 2005).

not learning algebra in the usual textbook way, that's a challenge to the teacher . . . to ask, 'Is there another way to learn algebra?'" Gardner encouraged teachers to use what he called "multiple entry points." Students with linguistic intelligence would do better if algebra teachers introduced new concepts with a narrative. Students with artistic and musical intelligences would do better if topics were approached through drama, dance and song. "Kids with kinesthetic intelligence will respond to hands-on activities. People who have strong personal intelligences will like to debate and role-play. Those with inter-personal aptitude would do well if teachers asked them to work cooperatively with other students.[20]

When it came to criticizing traditional teachers, Gardner did not pull his punches. "When a child does not learn," he said, "it is premature to blame the child, because more often than not, the failure lies with the educator. When we educate better and when we can educate in a more personalized way, then children will learn better."[21]

Some of Gardner's disciples were even more outspoken. "Our schools are largely to blame for the failure and boredom that millions of children face as they trudge off unwillingly to their six-hour fate every weekday," said Thomas Armstrong, a former teacher and disabilities specialist. Writing under the headline, "Don't Blame the Child, Blame the School System," Dr. Michael Corry, a psychiatrist, attributed teenagers' increasing use of anti-depressants and amphetamines to traditional education—saying that many youngsters turned to drugs because their schools persisted with teaching methods irrelevant to their learning styles.[22]

---

20 *Education Digest* 65 (February 2000), 4-6.

21 *Phi Delta Kappan* 75 (March 1994), 563-566.

22 *Washington Post* (1 September 1987); *Irish Times* (1 March 2005).

Seymour Sarason, an educational psychologist at Yale, carried the critique a step further, saying that traditional education was responsible for the academic shortcomings of Black students. As Sarason saw it, "the high dropout rate in city schools" was a response "to classroom contexts that lack personal significance or stimulation." Sarason hoped that "as Blacks gained political influence and control in our cities" they would push for "a true paradigm shift . . . in our traditional conceptions of . . . education." In particular, he recommended a shift away from teacher-dominated whole class instruction. Instead, Sarason favored "cooperative learning," which he considered better tailored to the interpersonal intelligence of African-American youngsters.[23]

For some time federal law had required schools and teachers to create individualized education plans (IEPs) for students who had been diagnosed with special learning problems. But Gardner urged schools to expand this policy and develop IEPs to accommodate the diverse needs and learning styles of mainstream students. To that end, he called for the creation of two new groups of school administrators: "assessment specialists," who would try to understand the learning strengths and styles of each child, and "curriculum brokers," who would help match students' profiles, goals and interests to particular curricula and styles of learning. When this policy was implemented in some New York schools, journalists Melinda Beck and Pat Wingert reported that "specially trained teachers spen[t] months assessing every kindergartner one-on-one for strengths in all seven of Gardner's intelligences."[24]

Gardner's disciples took his message to heart. Instead of focusing primarily on books and note-taking, MI teachers approached

---

23 Seymour B. Sarason, "Some Reactions to What We Have Learned," *Phi Delta Kappan* 77 (September 1955) 84-85; Sarason, "The Public Schools: America's Achilles Heel," *American Journal of Community Psychology* 25 (December 1995) 771-786.

24 Howard Gardner, *To Open Minds*, 294; *Newsweek* (28 June 1993) 52.

subjects from many perspectives, using music, art, role-playing, cooperative learning, field trips, inner reflection, and much more. "You can't sit behind your desk in a beautiful suit and high heels and teach effectively," said Patricia Way, a teacher in East St. Louis. It's going to have to be interactive. "The modal of ... reading or being lectured to doesn't work," agreed Tami Carabello, a teacher in Seattle. Francesca Moen, another teacher in Seattle, explained why she had her third-grade students playing math games, from bingo to dice, that involved counting and numbers: "Not all kids learn in the same way, so I can't teach in only one way."[25]

Advocates of MI expressed special concern for "kinesthetic learners" who found it difficult to sit still while teachers did most of the talking. Some said that learners with this style were concentrated disproportionately, although not exclusively, in working-class families. Many of them dropped out of school, said Tony Mooney, a teacher at England's Rutlish School for Boys, because traditional approaches to education "failed to tap [their] talents." Plebian youths understood, if only subconsciously, that the established educational methods were not right for them but had been designed to foster docility among prospective workers while also insuring "the smooth rise of an educational elite into our universities." Mooney quoted a "working-class 13-year-old London girl" as complaining, "We have different teachers for different subjects, but the style is just the same. The teachers do most of the talking and the only time we get to do something for ourselves is when we do a few experiments or they ask us to write."[26]

Others doubted the connection between learning style and social class but nevertheless insisted that traditional education unfairly rewarded students who possessed what the Germans called *Sitzfleisch*: the discipline and stamina to sit quietly and concentrate. "Think about

---

25 *Seattle Times* (4 May 2005); *St. Louis Post Dispatch* (16 July 1998).

26 *London Independent* (10 February 1991).

what it takes to succeed in a typical American classroom," said Albert Shanker of the American Federation of Teachers. "Students who do well in school are those who can sit still for long periods of time, learn by listening to someone talk, think abstractly, and not talk to anyone around them. It's a style that may come naturally to fifteen percent of the population."[27]

Gardner's disciples provided many examples of how teachers could tailor their lessons to suit the aptitudes of diverse students. One enthusiast explained that students with "a highly developed . . . spatial-visual intelligence . . . might have terrible difficulty sitting through a lecture with an instructor who does nothing but talk." Such students would leave the classroom "being self-critical of their struggle to focus." Yet they would learn more and feel "like a success," if they had been taught to take "highly graphic notes that offer visual reinforcement for the words being spoken." Meanwhile, students with an interpersonal intelligence might be "hopeless at learning by just simply reading." A possible solution for them might involve the assignment of tasks that involved cooperative projects, role-playing, creating works of art, or singing songs that pertained to the topic. One teacher in Pennsylvania summed up a principal purpose of MI when she said the theory called upon teachers to find "new ways to teach the same old stuff."[28]

Yet the goal of MI schools went beyond accommodating children who found it hard to learn in traditional ways. Gardner conceded that in the early grades, for students from about age 7 to age 13, schools should teach "the three Rs." "You cannot even begin to study subjects like history or science unless you know how to read, write, and compute." But even here Gardner "disagree[d] totally with

---

27 Edward B. Fiske, *Smart Schools, Smart Kids* (New York: Simon & Schuster, 1991) 64-65.

28 *Education* 27 (Fall 2006) 83; *The Scotsman* (27 October 2005).

those who feel that these subjects must be taught in a dry, skill-and-drill manner." "Kids can learn the three Rs," he insisted, "by studying fascinating topics and asking important questions."[29]

Gardner's main emphasis, however, was on the use of MI in high schools and colleges, and his biggest concern was "that even our better students in our better schools are just going through the motions of education." He said that even physics students at Johns Hopkins and MIT (a group that surely would have clustered at the top of traditional IQ rankings) often remained "fundamentally unschooled . . . despite years of schooling." They did well on "classroom exercises and end-of-term tests" but stumbled outside the class when they were asked to synthesize information or to deal with new problems. This was the result, Gardner said, of an educational system that placed more emphasis on imparting knowledge than on cultivating understanding. "As long as we feel committed to cover all the material," he said, "most students will not understand." "One of the deepest critiques I have of the education system . . . is that we mistake factual knowledge, which parrots could learn, for understanding." Gardner encouraged teachers to aim for something higher—a level where students understood underlying concepts and grasped the connections among the materials with which they had been working.[30]

"Dating back to the time of the [ancient] Greeks," Gardner wrote, there had been "two contrasting approaches to educational issues." The "mimetic" method regarded teachers and textbooks as the main sources of knowledge; and students in mimetic schools were "expected to memorize information and then, on subsequent occasions, feed back

---

29 *Education Digest* 65 (February 2000) 4-6; *Washington Post* (29 August 1993); *Pittsburgh Post-Gazette* (2 July 2002).

30 *Phi Delta Kappan* 7 (March 1994) 563-66; Howard Gardner, *The Disciplined Mind* (New York: Simon & Schuster, 1999) 120; *Irish Times* Supplement (13 September 1994); *High School Magazine* 5 (January/February 1998), 50-53.

the information that had been presented to or modeled for them." The other approach Gardner labeled "transformative." In it, the teacher was "more of a coach" who encouraged students to become "creative," to engage in "critical thinking" and to develop a "deep understanding" of the general principles and concepts that underlay various subjects. "Transformational," "creative," and "critical" were three of the favorite words in the vocabulary of neo-progressive educators.[31]

For Gardner, "the ability to regurgitate information" indicated that students had good memories, not that they understood what they had learned. To foster better understanding, Gardner suggested that textbooks should be scrapped, because many of these books were unduly concerned with breadth of coverage. Gardner dismissed an emphasis on general knowledge, saying that this amounted to little more than superficial acquaintance with factual information "from Plato to NATO." He described one of his books as "a sustained dialectic—read 'disagreement'" with E. D. Hirsch, who emphasized the importance of "core knowledge." Gardner had little use for what he called "the rote drill-and-kill, scattershot processes which have dominated education." "Why do we need to teach kids so much information when they can access all they need to know on . . . a palm pilot?" "If we want to have understanding rather than good performance on [quiz shows like] *Wheel of Fortune*, we really need to do major surgery on the way we think about education."[32]

Many educators agreed. Thus, Deborah Stipek, Dean of the School of Education at Stanford University, was not impressed when a teacher told her daughter to learn the names of the rivers in South America. "That's silly," Stipek told the girl. "Tell your teacher that if

---

31 Howard Gardner, *To Open Minds*, 6.

32 *Ibid.*, Howard Gardner, *The Disciplined Mind*, 24; *Irish Times* Supplement (24 January 1995); *Irish Times* (29 April 2005); *Policy Review* 99 (February/March, 2000); *High School Magazine* 5 (January/February 1998) 50-53.

you need to know anything besides the Amazon, you can look it up on Google." Other educators felt similarly about traditional school assignments such as learning state capitals or the periodic table of the elements. Rather than cram students' heads with a succession of forgettable details, Stipek and most other progressive educators wanted schools to focus on key concepts and a few subjects that would be covered in depth.[33]

Gardner also believed that deep understanding could best be achieved in heterogeneous classrooms that combined different approaches. Using art, music, and cooperative projects would do more than make learning easier for students with different aptitudes and learning styles. It would also heighten the comprehension of traditionally-strong students by exposing them to different sorts of intelligence and stirring emotional connections. Gardner also fostered interdisciplinary learning, saying "we need minds that can synthesize massive amounts of information"—something that could be accomplished by breaking down the barriers that separated geography from language and art from science. Instead of organizing classes around traditional academic disciplines such as history or science, MI classes were often organized around themes such as oceans, the environment, technology, or "the self." By the 1990s, Gardner's preference for "critical thinking" and "transformational education" had become enshrined in the hearts of many teachers.[34]

The distinction between factual knowledge and deep understanding was also responsible, in part, for Gardner's opposition to grouping students by ability. At first glance, such opposition appeared inconsistent with a belief in multiple intelligences. Establishing homogeneous learning groups seemed to make sense if

---

33 *Time*, (18 December 2006) 54.

34 *Irish Times* (29 April 2005); *St. Petersburg Times* (2 December 1988).

people differed in aptitude and learning styles. It meant that teachers would no longer face the problem of using an approach that worked with some students even if other students found the approach boring or confusing. Thus Gardner's theory often was mentioned in discussions of ability grouping. It was an "injustice," one proponent said, to deprive "faster learners of curricula that allow them to make the most of their abilities." "By throwing all [students] together," said another, "you will obviously have to slow down the pace of instruction." On one occasion, Gardner himself uncharacteristically conceded that it was "malpractice for kids who are brilliant to have to sit around" and wait until their classmates were ready to move on to another lesson.[35]

Beginning in the 1960s, however, most liberals took exception to ability grouping. Some said that gifted students could do well on their own, without any extra help, while others thought that extra resources should be concentrated on programs to improve the performance of low-achieving students. Because of disparities in the average performance of racial and ethnic groups, some people also maintained that ability grouping was at odds with the movement for integration. In addition, Gardner acknowledged that he was "not particularly worried about students whose strengths lie in the logical-mathematical or linguistic areas. These students will do well in school [and] will feel good about themselves. . . ." He was "concerned rather about the students . . . who possess definite intellectual strengths but not in those areas traditionally valued in a school." Gardner therefore opposed the policy of separating the brightest students, saying that it alienated students from each other, overvalued the talents of some, and undervalued those of others. "It is malpractice to cordon off a group of kids as a matter of policy," he declared.[36]

---

35 Joseph Renzulli, quoted in *Boston Globe* (30 September 1991); Linda Gottfredson, "Schools and the *g* factor," *Wilson Quarterly* (Summer 2004) 35-45; *Houston Chronicle* (5 November 1993).

36 *Boston Globe* (30 September 1991); Howard Gardner, *To Open Minds*, 296.

Yet Gardner insisted that his opposition to ability grouping was not simply an attempt to accommodate the prevailing opinion of liberals. It stemmed, rather, from his conviction that multiple representation (and exposure to differing intelligences) fostered deeper understanding. Some observers nevertheless suspected Gardner was trimming his sails, and the suspicion increased when, in apparent deference to the teachers unions and to secular progressives, he also opposed charter public schools and vouchers for students who attended private schools. The charters and vouchers increased educational diversity, but Gardner warned, "I think we're going to ruin our public school system with thousands of different charters and vouchers."[37]

Instead of vouchers and charters, Gardner emphasized the importance of what was called "constructivism". This was the belief that if students were to achieve and retain an understanding that went beyond rote, memorized knowledge, they would have to use their particular ways of learning and participate actively in their own education. Constructivism held that students acquired a deeper understanding, and retained that understanding longer, when they worked through problems on their own.

To illustrate this point, Gardner mentioned an incident that occurred in a Chinese hotel when his son, Benjamin, was only a toddler. Benjamin enjoyed playing with the room key, trying to open the door, but because of his tender age and lack of manual dexterity he often failed to insert the key in the slot. Gardner and his wife were perfectly happy to allow Benjamin to fumble, since they usually were not in a hurry and Benjamin was enjoying himself. But the Gardners soon noticed that a Chinese attendant nearby, observing Benjamin's difficulty with the key, "would hold onto his hand and gently but firmly guide it directly toward the slot." "Alas

---

37 *The Oregonian* (7 November 2000); Howard Gardner, *The Disciplined Mind*, 227-229.

for the sake of Chinese-American amity," Gardner and his wife said nothing, although they did not appreciate the intervention. They wanted Benjamin to solve the problem on his own—because they wished to foster self-reliance and also because they thought that knowledge obtained on one's own was deeper and more abiding. Gardner wanted Benjamin "to view life . . . as a series of situations in which one has to learn to think for oneself, to solve problems on one's own and even to discover new problems for which creative solutions are wanted."[38]

Gardner wished the same for all students: an education that provided "encouragement, to be sure, but . . . relatively little direct supervision." He understood that many teachers wanted to explain matters in order to "cut short the discovery process and save students time." But Gardner believed that if students did not learn on their own they would fail to understand the underlying principles and would not be able to make use of knowledge after they left school. He recognized that there was "much more to learn than there is time for learning," but that only made it all the more essential for students to discover "how to learn."[39]

In addition to "constructivism," Gardner stressed the importance of "thematic learning" which involved taking several courses with different approaches to the same topic. For Gardner, the serious study of a limited number of topics gave students "a taste of and an inkling of truly profound ideas." One could begin with an introduction (a "pathway course," in the language of MI), but to achieve genuine insight students should probe deeper. To do this they would have to sacrifice breadth of knowledge, but that was a small price, since the goal of education should not be to acquaint students with a wide

---

38 Howard Gardner, *To Open Minds*, 3-5.

39 *Ibid.*, 282, 294; Howard Gardner, *The Unschooled Mind* (New York: Basic Books, 1991), 187.

range of factual information but rather to instill a deep understanding of a few "essential questions."[40]

Gardner recognized that educators differed when it came to identifying the essential questions. Therefore, "a system of multiple pathways ought to be administered with some flexibility." Traditionalists might focus on the classics of Western civilization. Multiculturalists could "study their own cultures and compare them with other groups, particularly those that have hitherto received unfair treatment at the hands of America's majority population." Technocrats could concentrate on technology and the latest strategies and tactics of the corporate-financial world. For his part, Gardner recommended a curriculum that focused on three essential qualities: truth, beauty, and evil, as exemplified by Charles Darwin's theory of evolution, the music of Mozart, and the treatment of Jews in Nazi Germany.[41]

Each of Gardner's topics afforded the possibility of fostering deep understanding through sustained consideration from several perspectives. In addition to reading about the Holocaust, for example, students could interview survivors, stage plays like *The Diary of Anne Frank*, and make posters and other artwork to commemorate heroes of the Resistance.

Each topic also revealed something about Gardner personally. His family had fled Hitler's Germany. He had devoted much of his youth to studying and practicing music. And by the time he matriculated at Harvard, an expurgated version of Darwinism had become *de rigueur* at most universities. When it came to discussing the multiple approaches that could be taken toward evolution,

---

40 Howard Gardner, *The Disciplined Mind*, 214ff; Gardner, *Intelligence Reframed*, 165ff.

41 Howard Gardner, *The Disciplined Mind*, 227, 225; Gardner, *Intelligence Reframed*, 167.

Gardner did not mention Charles Darwin's racialism or the extolling of competition and "survival of the fittest" by Social Darwinists like William Graham Sumner. Nor did he acknowledge that Darwinism could be reconciled with traditional religion by positing that a higher intelligence had worked His will through the process of evolution. Gardner insisted that the driving force behind the variety of species was wholly material and entirely random. He regretted the persistence, despite years of secularist tutelage, of "the mistaken belief that evolution is a teleological process."[42]

If Gardner were a benevolent dictator, he would have required all children to have the sort of education he favored. He considered it "the best education for now and for the foreseeable future." But he was willing to settle for less. He wanted his own children "to have the education of my choice," but he would give other parents the same freedom. In this one respect, at least, Gardner broke ranks with one of the founders of progressive education, John Dewey, who once maintained, "what the best and wisest parent wants for his own child, that must the community want for all its children." Gardner was "realistic enough to recognize that the rest of the world will not necessarily endorse my preferences or the reasons for them."[43]

Gardner also recognized that testing would be crucial to fostering the sort of reform he had in mind. He understood that as long as students were expected to perform well on standardized tests of general knowledge, the traditional approaches to education would remain in vogue. To promote MI, therefore, Gardner recommended a new method of assessment, the portfolio method, which called for students to submit, and for a committee of teachers to evaluate, projects that pertained to topics the students had chosen to emphasize. Such

---

42　Howard Gardner, *The Disciplined Mind*, 122.

43　Ibid., 223-224; John Dewey, *The School and Society* (Chicago: University of Chicago Press, 1990 [reprint of the original edition of 1900]), 7.

a portfolio might contain works of art and music, or videotapes of performances or interviews, as well as more conventional term papers, scientific reports, and mathematical proofs. In the language of MI, the evaluation of portfolios was called "authentic assessment," because it focused on work that individual students had actually done.[44]

Gardner also favored the authentic assessment of teachers. As things stood, most states demanded that prospective teachers take a number of education courses and make a satisfactory score on a test of general knowledge, the National Teachers Examination. But Gardner thought that this approach gave little indication of what someone could actually do in a classroom. He therefore recommended that candidates for teaching positions should also be required to present portfolios in which they documented their accomplishments and explained how they would assess the learning of their students.[45]

Many observers remained skeptical about MI. Indeed, in one of his books Gardner acknowledged that he had collected "a sheaf of hostile reviews." He recognized that some university professors, in particular, were critical of his theories. On one occasion Gardner speculated that this was because the professors' children tended, on average, to possess above-average aptitudes for logic and language. "In every jurisdiction some people like what I do," Gardner said. However, "most academics don't like my ideas—but as soon as they have a child with learning difficulties they become interested."[46]

---

44 Howard Gardner, *The Unschooled Mind*, 253-54.

45 Ibid., 259-60.

46 Howard Gardner, *To Open Minds*, 111; *Irish Times* (22 May 2001).

Some critics said that Gardner's reforms were impractical. Thus, University of Virginia professor E. D. Hirsch conceded that individualized education sounded good in theory but noted that, when one student was being tutored individually, the other members of the class would be left on their own—with the group as a whole usually learning less than it had previously and sometimes descending into an excess of disorder. Developing an individualized education plan for each student also placed a heavy burden on teachers, requiring sheaves of paperwork and hours of after-school meetings to determine what students needed. But Gardner rejected the argument that his reforms would drive good teachers from the profession, saying that if teachers did not have time to deal with their students individually they had "already stopped teaching."[47]

Others complained about the extra expenses at MI schools, especially the cost of hiring the two new groups of school personnel, assessment specialists and curriculum brokers. Yet Gardner dismissed the argument that resources did not exist to create new positions. He insisted that the problem was not due to an inadequacy in resources but to an insufficiency of will in the community. "So long as one wants to think of all students as alike, and to put on a pedestal a common curriculum and a single 'linguistic-logical' way of knowing, then there is little chance for individualized schooling. If, however, a community chooses to embrace the alternative goal—an education optimally devised for each child—I am convinced that it can be achieved."[48]

Another objection involved the practicality of submitting portfolios when students were applying for admission to colleges or to graduate schools. Gardner thought this approach was the best way to

---

47 E. D. Hirsch, "Why Traditional Education is More Progressive," *American Enterprise* 8 (March/April, 1997) 42; *Phi Delta Kappan* 75 (March 1994), 563-66.

48 *Guardian* (11 October 1993); Howard Gardner, *To Open Minds*, 296-97.

assess the qualifications of applicants. Many parents, however, wanted schools to emphasize the sort of traditional courses that boosted performance on standardized admission tests. After asking twenty colleges about their policies for evaluating portfolios, one parent reported, "not one would accept them in lieu of traditional grade point averages, in large part because they did not have the time to evaluate their quality." An admissions officer at Auburn University told this parent, "Ma'am, you are being grossly misled regarding portfolios. You need grades."[49]

Other critics focused on theoretical points. Yale University psychologist Robert Sternberg dismissed MI as "a theory of talents, not one of intelligences," while Sandra Scarr of the University of Virginia described MI as "faulty optimism that leads to dead-ends in both theory and practice." In general, journalist James Traub noted in *The New Republic*, "Gardner failed to persuade his peers." For his part, Gardner conceded, "a few psychologists liked [my] theory; a somewhat larger number did not like it; most ignored it."[50]

Some of the most trenchant criticism came from scholars and writers who adhered to the idea that IQ tests measured general intelligence (*g*). Because most academic work was "inherently analytical," wrote Linda Gottfredson, an educational sociologist at the University of Delaware, it was inevitable that youngsters with special aptitudes for language or logic would do well in school. Conversely, according to Charles Murray, co-author of *The Bell Curve* (1994), "our ability to improve the academic accomplishment of students in the lower half of the [IQ] distribution . . . is severely limited." Just as it

---

49 Douglas Frantz and Catherine Collins, *Celebration, U.S.A.* (New York: Henry Holt and Company, 1999), 254.

50 *Sunday Oregonian* (11 October 1992); James Traub, "Multiple Intelligence Disorder," *The New Republic* (26 October 1998) 20-21; Mary Eberstadt, "The Schools They Deserve," *Policy Review* 9 (October/November 1999) 3-17.

was beyond Murray's power to understand "a proof in *The American Journal of Mathematics*," so others, depending on their aptitudes, found it impossible to master arithmetic, or algebra, or calculus. Those with limited linguistic skills similarly found it impossible to understand complex written texts. This was "not to say that American public schools cannot be improved," Murray hastened to add. Some educational reforms had boosted the academic performance of low-achieving students. Nevertheless, even the best schools could not "repeal the limits on achievement set by limits on intelligence."[51]

Despite the criticism, Gardner and his theory of multiple intelligences enjoyed enormous influence at many levels of American education. Writing in *The New Republic* in 1998, James Traub noted that Gardner had become "a genuine academic superstar." By then Gardner had "won a MacArthur 'genius' grant; his books ha[d] been translated into 20 languages," and "his ideas ha[d] achieved extraordinary currency in even the most rarified reaches of the educational world." Writing in *Policy Review* in 1999, Mary Eberstadt reported that Gardner had received "12 honorary degrees and many honors. . . . [His] ubiquity both inside the world of education and out almost challenges description. He is a leader in more projects and studies than can be listed here." During the 1990s "MI schools" and "Gardner schools" blossomed all over the United States and in Europe and Asia as well. James O. Freedman, president of Dartmouth College, noted that Gardner was "the buzz in very important circles."[52]

---

51 Linda Gottfredson, "Schools and the *g* Factor," 35-45; James Traub, "Multiple Intelligences Disorder," *The New Republic* (26 October 1998) 20-21; Charles Murray, "Intelligence in the Classroom," *Wall Street Journal* (16 January 2007); Murray, "What's Wrong With Vocational School?" *Wall Street Journal* (17 January 2007).

52 James Traub, "Multiple Intelligence Disorder," *The New Republic* (26 October 1998) 20-23; Mary Eberstadt, "The Schools They Deserve," 3-17; *Boston Globe* (1 July 1999).

The Long Crusade

Gardner's influence was apparent at the University of Delaware, where this writer has been a member of the faculty since 1965. When I arrived at the campus all students in the College of Arts and Sciences were required to take a year-long course that surveyed the development of Western Civilization. Then, around 1970, when Gardner was still in graduate school, that requirement was replaced by a "distribution" plan that fostered familiarity with different modes of thought by requiring students to take at least a few courses of their choice in such different fields as history, science and literature. Then again, as Gardner and MI came into vogue in the 1980s and 1990s, there were demands that the distribution requirement give way to a new plan that would require students to take an introductory "pathway" course that would pursue "thematic learning" toward a "capstone" seminar in the senior year. Along the way, the faculty was told, students would benefit from "non-directive teaching" and "authentic assessment." We were assured that "hands-on" experimentation and "problem-based learning" were superior to the traditional textbooks and lectures. We were told that the new approach would foster "creative" and "critical" thinking. The experience would be "transformational." At that time I was not familiar with Gardner's theory and the accompanying vocabulary, and I recall telling one of the proponents, a colleague whom I admired professionally and liked personally, that I did not understand what she was saying.

To date, the general education requirements at Delaware have not been "Gardnerized." In large part, this is because the faculty in established departments feared that their enrollments would decline if this sort of revision were implemented. At the level of individual courses, however, Gardner's influence is apparent. Lectures are so out of fashion that the largest auditorium on campus is not used for classes, and the recently-constructed and largest classroom building contains no lecture hall. Meanwhile, some professors proclaim a commitment to non-directive methods that once would have been considered "not teaching." The new emphasis is also evident in the choice of required readings. In the School of Education, one of the textbooks assigned to future teachers asserts, "even the best IQ tests used today measure only a very specific type of intelligence." This textbook goes on to say there are many ways of "being equally intelligent as individuals who score high in IQ tests—but intelligent in a different way."[53]

Some people, of course, have turned away from neo-progressive education. Many parents did so when they enrolled their children in parochial schools or in charter schools such as the Core Knowledge schools, KIPP academies, and the Success for All programs that will be described in later chapters of this book. A growing number have also done so by educating their children at home. Some observers consequently have concluded that educational progressivism has been losing ground in recent decades.[54]

Nevertheless, progressive theories have remained fashionable at most well-regarded universities, especially in the schools of education. And Gardner's influence has been especially evident in the world of elite private schools. Indeed, Gardner first recognized that he had a following when he gave a speech to private-school administrators and observed the headmasters jostling one another to get a seat in the hall:

> Some months after the publication of [*Frames of Mind*], I was invited to address the annual meeting of the National Association of Independent [i.e., private] Schools. . . . I expected the typical audience of fifty to seventy-five persons, a customary talk of fifty minutes, followed by a small number of easily anticipated questions. Instead . . . I encountered a new experience: a much larger hall, entirely filled with people, and humming with excitement. It was almost as if I had walked by mistake into a talk given by someone who was famous. But the audience had in fact come to hear me: it listened attentively, and grew steadily in size until it spilled into the hallways on both sides of the room. . . . [A]fter the session had concluded,

---

53 Linda Gottfredson, "Schools and the *g* Factor," 41.

54 Mary Eberstadt, "The Schools They Deserve."

I was ringed by interested headmasters, teachers, trustees and journalists who wanted to hear more and were reluctant to allow me to slip back into anonymity.[55]

Gardner continues to enjoy enormous influence with the leaders of private schools. When the directorship of one of New York's most prestigious private schools came open in 1998, journalist and education writer James Traub reported, "almost every candidate for the job mentioned Gardner in his or her one-page educational philosophy statement." During the fifteen years after the publication of *Frames of Mind*, MI had progressed through stages. At first it was a disputed theory; then it became a rallying cry for school reformers; and by the 1990s it had become a cultural commonplace—at least in the rarified world of elite private education.[56]

After observing Gardner's great influence in elite circles, one skeptical journalist, Mary Eberstadt, asserted that his reforms were suitable only for advantaged children who automatically picked up the necessary general knowledge "from their reading and conversation outside the classroom." Because of their conversations with "high-functioning parents and peers," many upper-class students already understood allusions to history and literature. Even if their schools did not teach them the fundamentals of geography, they would find the major capital cities "from the airport when they get there." If they were not taught French or Italian, they would pick up the languages while traveling abroad.[57]

At one time Gardner had conceded an element of truth in this assessment. In *The Unschooled Mind* (1991), Gardner noted that "progressive education works best with children who come from richly endowed homes, whose parents are deeply interested in their children's education and who arrive at schools with motivation and curiosity."

---

55 Howard Gardner, quoted by Mary Eberstadt, "The Schools They Deserve."

56 James Traub, "Multiple Intelligences Disorder," 20-21.

57 Mary Eberstadt, "The Schools They Deserve."

He acknowledged that students who were "not independent-minded" and "lack self-discipline" would do better in more traditional schools. When it came to the best method of education, Gardner suggested, it was largely a matter of social class. In schools with lower-class children, it would be better to provide the "modeling and/or scaffolding that has often been seen as antithetical to the unstructured atmosphere of progressive education."[58]

Yet Eberstadt's critique was so strong that Gardner backed away from his earlier statements. Eberstadt accused Gardner of sacrificing "the very disadvantaged students that he claims to care about"—and of being unduly concerned about "privileged students who will acquire basics no matter what they study." But Gardner insisted that Eberstadt was "dead wrong" about this. He did not favor an education "designed just for an elite," but one that would be good "for all human beings."[59]

As national leaders began to emphasize the importance of reducing the racial and ethnic achievement gaps, Gardner and an associate, David Feldman of Tufts University, became especially interested in using MI to help African-American children. By 1989, the *New York Times* reported, Gardner and Feldman were "immersed in an ambitious program to apply their findings to children of economically deprived families, devising a curriculum they hoped could change the way these children are taught and encourage them not only to learn but to enjoy learning as well."[60]

Gardner recognized that this was a high-risk group of students, but he said that was all the more reason for aligning the education system with different sorts of intelligence. Although Gardner was wary about saying that different ethnic or racial groups had

---

58 Howard Gardner, *The Unschooled Mind*, 95.

59 Howard Gardner, "Howard Gardner, Unfiltered," *Policy Review* 99 (February/March 2000).

60 *New York Times* (9 April 1989).

different learning styles, some of his disciples believed that African-American children were especially endowed with "bodily-kinesthetic intelligence " and therefore found it difficult to learn while sitting quietly in traditional classrooms. From this it seemed to follow that Black students would benefit if their teachers refashioned lesson plans to allow for more activity. In history, for example, debates and plays could be staged, with students acting out the parts of different historical characters. When teaching basic arithmetic, teachers could depart from drills and memorization and instead allow for activities like stringing beads, manipulating differently-shaped blocks, clapping, hopping, and skipping. That 3 x 4 = 12 might be taught, for example, by performing four jumps, rest, four jumps, rest, four jumps, and then asking "How many jumps in all?"[61]

Some educators went so far as to say that the different races should be taught differently. In East St. Louis one panel of Black teachers and school administrators "strongly advocate[d] that the mostly black school districts should use Harvard University professor Howard Gardner's theory of multiple intelligences." And an article in the *New York Times* described the work of "education experts" who were creating "a stir by urging teachers and schools to recognize that students of various races and ethnic groups have such profound cultural differences that as a whole they learn in distinct, often incompatible ways."[62]

Janice Hale-Benson, a Black education professor at Cleveland State University, was one of the most prominent of these experts. At the outset of her book, *Black Children: Their Roots, Cultures, and*

---

61 Ibid; National Council of Teachers of Mathematics, *Curriculum and Evaluation Standards for School Mathematics* (1989) 26; Jody Kenny Willis and Aostre N. Johnson, "Multiply with MI," *Teaching Children Mathematics* (January 2001) 260-69.

62 *St. Louis Post Dispatch* (16 July 1998); *New York Times* (4 November 1990).

Learning Styles (1986), Hale-Benson praised Gardner's effort "to knock language and logic off their pedestal," saying that Gardner's theory would be "particularly useful in facilitating the development and achievement of black children." According to Hale-Benson, teachers should understand that students from different racial groups had different learning styles. White children took to symbols and abstractions, Asian children absorbed data easily, and Black children related better to people than to numbers.

Hale-Benson insisted that she was motivated by a desire to improve the academic achievement of non-Asian minority students, but her learning-style theories led to charges of racial stereotyping. Some critics said that any differences were rooted in class rather than race, and one Black journalist, William Raspberry, disputed the contention "that the differences are ethnically based: that there is some peculiarly European or African or Asian way of processing information, and schools have an obligation to reacquaint students with their cultural styles."[63]

Nevertheless, Hale-Benson stood her ground, insisting that if schools wished to reach Black students they would have to adapt their instructional methods to accommodate differences in both nature and culture. She cited research to the effect that Black children acquired motor skills sooner than White children, that they were more energetic and moved around more than other students, that they had "more verve than white children." Nevertheless, instead of tailoring lessons to accommodate this kinesthetic learning style, "Eurocentric" schools often punished Black youngsters for being rambunctious. Hale-Benson also persisted in maintaining that Black students had a "relational" learning style that featured "approximation" (a tendency to approximate space, number and time, instead of aiming for complete

---

63 Janice Hale-Benson, *Black Children: Their Roots, Culture, and Learning Styles* (Baltimore: Johns Hopkins University Press, 1986) xii; *New York Times* (4 November 1990); *Washington Post* (7 September 1990).

accuracy) and a focus on people (in contrast to a European style that was analytic, emphasized precision, and focused on things). Hale-Benson said the learning style of Black Americans had its roots in West African patterns of culture, which had given rise to "distinctive modes of child-rearing among African-American people."[64]

Some White educators adopted a similar approach, with one state in Australia assigning different intellectual abilities and fashioning different curricula for Caucasians, Asians, and Pacific Islanders. Yet this instance of racialism was too much for Howard Gardner. He "hit the ceiling" when he saw "a list of the various ethnic and racial groups that live in Australia arrayed in terms of intelligences that they had, and those they lacked." "The more I learned about this program, the less comfortable I was." "It was a mishmash of practices—left brain contrasts, sensory learning styles ... all mixed with dazzling promiscuity. They put together a mélange of faddish ideas...."[65]

Some critics believed this was true of MI in general. Gardner, however, insisted that such a description applied only to the excesses of a few disciples, and he continued to press for new approaches to learning. "At this point," one of Gardner's assistants explained, "I don't think that people should worry that traditional education [of low-achieving students] might be undermined. It's already undermined. It's really a decision about what you should do instead."[66]

Whatever the merits of MI theory, many people wondered, "Does it work?" Do students who attend MI schools really do better than comparable pupils at traditional schools? The answer is not clear.

---

64 *St. Petersburg Times* (2 October 1990); *New York Times* (4 November 1990); *Washington Post* (7 September 1990); Janice Hale-Benson, *Black Children*, 5. Also see Janice E. Hale, *Learning While Black: Creating Educational Excellence for African-American Children* (Baltimore: Johns Hopkins University Press, 2001).

65 *The Australian* (9 July 2005).

66 Mihaly Csikszentmihalyi, quoted in *New York Times* (9 April 1989).

MI appeared to work in some places but not in others. The success and failure were illustrated at the Key Schools in Indianapolis, Indiana and at the Celebration School near Orlando, Florida. It was no accident that the success occurred in a small public charter school that served only students who chose to attend school there. Nor was it coincidental that the failure happened at a much larger public school that tried to accommodate all the students in a city.

The Key Elementary School opened in 1987 with 150 students chosen from among 500 applicants in a lottery. An effort was made to match the demographics of the school with those of the city, and as a result most of the students were from poor African-American families. Yet students at the Key School differed from their counterparts elsewhere in one important respect: they were not assigned to the school but were volunteers from families that were required to work out transportation for their children and to attend regular parent-teacher conferences. The school also offered a distinctive curriculum—one based on the ideas of Howard Gardner as understood and implemented by eight local teachers who fought their way through the bureaucratic red tape of the school system and the teachers' union to establish their dream of an MI school. Gardner praised Key as "the first school in the world to declare itself an MI school," and in time Key and a sister school, the Key Renaissance Middle School, founded in 1993, were nationally recognized models of the MI approach.[67]

"Most schools focus on language arts and math, but we believe that children's capabilities are much broader," said Patricia J. Bolanos, the principal of Key Elementary. "We think they have a right to discover where they are particularly strong and develop these talents." Classroom posters kept the different aptitudes in the foreground of consciousness, and students spoke matter-of-factly about their strengths and weaknesses, "I'm really strong in art, I'm strong in math, I'm not so strong in music," said a fifth grade student

---

67 *Boston Globe* (5 November 1995).

who also cultivated his kinesthetic intelligence by learning to juggle. Another fifth grade pupil spent most of her time on the three Rs but also worked on an architectural drawing, played the trumpet, and did improvisational dancing. Each week teachers designed activities that helped kids develop different aptitudes. "Art class is usually classified as a frill," said one teacher. "But why shouldn't someone who is good at art be told that this is a wonderful strength?" "At the Key School arts are not an add-on but an essential part of the curriculum," one article in the *Washington Post* noted.[68]

In addition to emphasizing MI, the Key schools embraced many of the standard precepts of progressive education. They promoted self-esteem by teaching students that there were "certain intelligences you're good at, certain intelligences you're not good at, and everybody's good at something." They deemphasized the importance of memorizing facts and algorithms. When it came to reading, they warned of the dangers of boredom and frustration if students were required to practice phonic drills. It was better to teach reading by exposing students to engrossing stories and great literature, teachers said, since research supposedly showed that children did better if they discussed ideas. Instructors at the Key schools also engaged in a great deal of interdisciplinary team teaching, and students spent much of their time working on group projects.[69]

Most of all, the Key teachers proposed to "teach thinking" rather than "a bunch of isolated facts." The goal of education, Principal Bolanos affirmed, was not high test scores but "guiding students to deeper understanding." "Maybe I'm just foolish," Bolanos said, "but I don't like playing the numbers game, and that's what standardized tests really become." Instead of administering standardized exams,

---

68 *New York Times* (24 May 1988); *Boston Globe* (5 November 1995); *Washington Post* (3 May 1994).

69 *Washington Post* (3 May 1994).

Key teachers preferred to assess the sort of exhibitions and portfolios Howard Gardner recommended. The teachers compiled a video cassette of each student's schoolwork, a copy of which was given to the student upon graduation.[70]

Fortunately for the reputation of the Key schools, the average scores of their students on traditional examinations came in above the national average, even though a disproportionate number of the students came from poor minority families. The Key teachers (like godfather Gardner) strongly believed that standardized tests were not authentic assessments. But given that traditional opinions enjoyed much currency outside the realm of progressive education, and that a more traditional group of administrators would come to the fore in Indianapolis in the 1990s, it was the students' performance on standardized tests that enabled the Key schools to survive. These MI schools endured because even traditionalists conceded that their programs "worked."[71]

Yet similar programs foundered at the Celebration School near Orlando, and to understand the failure one must know something about the origins and nature of Celebration, the city. Celebration was a model town built by the Walt Disney Corporation for 20,000 people on undeveloped land near Disney World in Central Florida. The company came up with the idea in 1989, after research indicated that many Americans wanted to live in traditional towns that provided a sense of community. According to some polls, these people looked with nostalgia on a situation that had prevailed earlier in the twentieth century, when many urban Americans had lived within walking distance of schools, offices, and stores. But then the automobile, the post-World War II housing boom, and increasing crime rates gave rise to suburbs and isolated subdivisions. As one urban geographer

---

70 Ibid.; *Boston Globe* (5 November 1995).

71 *Portland Oregonian* (3 September 1990).

observed, "The trend in America has been to have specialized communities aimed at income groups, [with] balkanization . . . in the socioeconomic landscapes." At Celebration, Disney proposed to combat this trend, to turn back the suburban sprawl that some people blamed for alienating Americans from one another.[72]

To revive the earlier pattern, Disney did more than provide front porches, sidewalks, planned parks, swimming pools, and fitness centers. It also modified the practice of single-use zoning, which designated some areas for commerce, others for multiple dwelling apartment buildings, and still others for single-family homes. Instead, the company would create an integrated city, where the full spectrum of ethno-socio-economic groups would interact and where people could walk to stores and restaurants. Celebration was intended to be the sort of place where, as one Disney worker put it, "Someone gets home from work and, gosh, they don't have any milk. So they send their kid on their bike to the grocery store." As it happened, however, the properties were priced between $125,000 and $500,000 in the early 1990s, and Disney did not do subsidized housing. As a result, the buyers turned out to be predominantly middle class and overwhelmingly White. One local journalist noted. "As much as [Disney] likes to say that [Celebration] will be representative of a typical American town . . . it is of the middle class, white variety."[73]

The middle-class aspect of Celebration was evident in a film that was featured at the city's Visitor's Center. In it, several residents commended Celebration for its "traditional values." These values were not defined, but observers could infer that they included neatly

---

72   *Boston Globe* (18 February 1996).

73   *Boston Globe* (18 February 1996); *London Independent* (3 December 1995); Andrew Ross, *The Celebration Chronicles* (New York: Ballantine Books, 1999); Douglas Frantz and Catherine Collins, *Celebration U.S.A.* (New York: Henry Holt and Company, 1999).

laundered clothes and lawns, polished cars and painted white fences. "You can't help noticing that most of the residents are as white as the fences," one visitor said. "I'm sure Disney doesn't select for ethnicity, which would be illegal. . . . It's just that if you build the set for *It's a Wonderful Life,* you're going to attract people who think they'll fit."[74]

Many of the new residents regarded Celebration as a Norman Rockwell painting come to life. They found the new city attractive because housing was limited to six traditional styles of architecture and because additional restrictions prohibited practices such as abstract landscaping, repairing cars in driveways, and installing satellite dishes on front lawns. Company brochures also described the prospective Celebration School as "a model for education," with a curriculum custom-designed by a leading Harvard expert, Professor Howard Gardner. When the town opened, most of the families that moved to Celebration had school-age children, and the school was a major selling point. One company official acknowledged, "Frankly, the major reason for the school, and one that we as a company have been very up-front about from the beginning, is that not only would we attract families by having a school, but by having a school here first it sold homes."[75]

Disney's chief executive officer, Michael Eisner, supported Gardner's approach to education. So did Eisner's wife Jane. They believed their three sons had received "an exceptional elementary school education" at a similar school in Los Angeles, the Center for Early Education. At that school, Eisner wrote, the curriculum "was superb" and the "excitement about learning in the open classrooms was palpable."[76]

---

74   *Boston Globe* (27 February 1997).

75   *London Independent* (3 December 1995); *Globe and Mail* (Canada) (20 February 1999); Douglas Frantz and Catherine Collins, *Celebration, U.S.A.,* 135.

76   Michael D. Eisner, *Work in Progress* (New York: Random House, 1998) 408.

Yet most residents of Celebration had no idea what Professor Gardner and C.E.O. Eisner had in store for their children. According to two journalists who lived in Celebration and wrote a book about the city, "the old-fashioned architecture and marketing rhetoric about old-fashioned values lulled [many parents] into believing their kids would be going to a school just like the one they had attended."[77]

This was hardly the case. The $20 million-school (to accommodate an enrollment of about 1000 students in grades one through twelve) was a model of innovation in education. According to Andrew Ross, a professor at New York University and an educational progressive who spent a sabbatical year living in Celebration, "just about every method and principle from the last twenty years of educational reform was front-loaded into the curriculum." The school emphasized cooperation rather than competition, group projects, and deep knowledge of a few topics. Teachers sat down with each student and his or her parents and devised a personal learning plan (PLP) based on the strengths and weaknesses of the student's multiple intelligences. To facilitate interactive learning and multi-age group projects, several classrooms accommodated 100 students and five teachers. "A central 'hearth area,' evocative of the family living room . . . [was] furnished with couches, often facing each other like a hotel lobby." While some students were reclining or reading on the sofas, others discussed projects with teachers or classmates. As an alternative to standardized tests, students were assessed on the basis of exhibitions and portfolios. One math teacher expressed a popular opinion when he said, "We've got better things to do than preparing students for tests."[78]

---

[77] Douglas Frantz and Catherine Collins, *Celebration, U.S.A.*, 135.

[78] *The Globe and Mail* (Canada) (20 February 1999); Douglas Frantz and Catherine Collins, *Celebration, U.S.A.*, 128; Andrew Ross, *The Celebration Chronicles*, 123-25.

Progressives hailed the Celebration School. It was implementing the sort of program they had been recommending for some time. The school gave students more opportunities to learn from one another. It shifted the emphasis from acquiring knowledge to solving problems and mastering concepts. It downgraded advanced placement classes that had been taught by authoritative teachers who required students to take tests that covered quantities of information that had been presented in lectures and textbooks. Meanwhile, school leaders assured parents that research supported the new approaches and that researchers had also established that it was better to abolish ability groups and letter grades.

Many parents were taken aback. Far from welcoming the new policies, they regarded the innovations as a recipe for disaster. Andrew Ross, who personally favored progressive education, observed, "virtually everyone in town felt he or she had some bone to pick with the school's innovative learning design. But it was clear that the teachers' opposition to grading and test preparation—cramming and drilling in the 'basics'—was the chief source of parental discomfort." "Why aren't you teaching my son the basics?" exasperated parents asked. "How is he going to know your basic history, your basic geography?"[79]

Disgruntled parents also challenged some of the principles on which the Celebration School had been founded: that students thirsted for knowledge, that they could be trusted to take charge of their own education, that they would help one another do their schoolwork. These assumptions were reflected in the terminology at the Celebration School, where teachers were called "learning leaders"—because they were expected to act more as advisors than as instructors. The underlying assumption was that even young children were capable of self-discipline and able to help their classmates.[80]

---

79 Andrew Ross, *The Celebration Chronicles*, 125, 150.

80 Douglas Frantz and Catherine Collins, *Celebration, U.S.A.*, 129.

Many parents disagreed. One couple insisted that children needed "firm guidance and a clear sense of what is expected of them." Others complained that their children were not being challenged because of the lack of competitive incentives, were not motivated enough to choose or determine their own education, or were simply not learning as much as they were at their last school." Several families withdrew their children from the Celebration School in 1996-97, and others partially withdrew their children, "home-schooling them in academics, and sending them to the school for arts classes and wellness activities."[81]

One of those who gave up on the school was Rich Adams, a retired fire chief who had moved to Celebration from Bethlehem, Pennsylvania. Adams and his family had been featured as happy buyers in some of the city's promotional literature, but after just a few months they sold their house and returned to Pennsylvania. "We came here as a family with a dream, and all we received was an educational nightmare," Adams said. "My children not only did not progress in this school—they regressed." Roger Burton and his wife also sold their house and moved their children back to Illinois because they were disenchanted with the school. Michael and Luba Bilentchuk felt the same way. So did Frank Stone, a town doctor, and his wife Janette. At the end of their first year in Florida, they withdrew one of their daughters from the Celebration School and sent her to a Catholic school half an hour away. Later they followed suit with another child. "My gosh, we live on Campus Street," said Dr. Stone, "We expected to be able to watch our kids walk to the school down the street. But it was not working at all. Our fourth-grader did nothing the last nine weeks of school, and no one took responsibility."[82]

---

81 *Ibid.*, 146; Andrew Ross, *The Celebration Chronicles*, 146, 150-51, 163.

82 *Wall Street Journal* (3 June 1997); Douglas Frantz and Catherine Collins, *Celebration, U.S.A.*, 135-137.

It did not help when school administrators acknowledged that Celebration's curriculum was "not for everyone." This explanation was especially exasperating since most taxpayers believed that public schools should accommodate everyone, and there were few alternatives for families that had depleted their finances to borrow money for the purchase of homes in Celebration. They had not expected to pay still more for private school tuition.[83]

Others joined the disgruntled parents in criticizing the Celebration School. After a popular science teacher, Troy Braley, was fired for criticizing non-traditional education, another science instructor expressed his reservations anonymously and with irony, saying, "I'm not qualified to teach at a school like this. I just know chemistry." Meanwhile, the local chapter of MENSA, an organization for people with exceptionally high IQs, weighed in with more criticism of progressive education. The group scoffed when Mike Robinson, an education professor, reported that after reviewing some 400 studies he had concluded that students learned as much in multi-age groupings as when they were organized in single-age grades. "I seriously question the validity of the research," said MENSA member Joseph Palacios, a Stanford graduate who lived in Celebration. One observer opined that Palacios and other MENSA members believed they "were 'better educated' than the... educators who had designed the curriculum."[84]

As the controversy in Celebration simmered, a public interest group in New York released a report that pointed to a seismic fault line between the conventional wisdom that prevailed among education professionals and the thought of many parents. According to this report (conducted by Public Agenda), professional educators

---

83 Andrew Ross, *The Celebration Chronicles*, 151.

84 Ibid., 155, 164, 181; Douglas Frantz and Catherine Collins, *Celebration, U.S.A.*, 129.

were especially concerned with the process of learning. They wanted schools to promote collaborative learning in order to facilitate societal integration. They also believed that acquiring information and getting the right answers were less important than becoming accustomed to cooperative learning. Most parents, on the other hand, wanted schools to be safe and orderly, and to provide their children with basic skills, information, and work habits.[85]

With progressive education under siege, the Celebration School modified its course. In the late-1990s the sofas were removed from the hearth areas, and many classes returned to the traditional 50-minute schedule. At the same time, an Honors Track was established, textbooks were bought and issued, and more emphasis was placed on basic core subjects. Meanwhile, numerical grades (4, 3, 2 and 1) were substituted for previous, softer designations ("extending," "proficient," "developing" and "not yet"). To no one's surprise, progressives opposed these changes. They complained that "the schedule, and not the learner, was now driving the day." They said the new policies "made interdisciplinary teaching impossible." But that was the point: to placate disgruntled parents, the Celebration School turned to a more traditional form of education.[86]

Andrew Ross, the New York University professor who spent a sabbatical year in Celebration, offered one explanation of the counteraction. "This was surely a sign of the times. . . . All across the country, affluent, suburban parents of high-achieving children have strenuously resisted school reforms like detracking, noncompetitive learning, and alternative assessment. From their perspective, reform is unnecessary. The SAT testing system, after all, has evolved into a highly efficient delivery mechanism for propelling their children into elite colleges while relegating the less fortunate to less distinguished

---

85 Andrew Ross, *The Celebration Chronicles*, 154-55.

86 Ibid., 160-62.

points of the compass. Why would such parents support changes in a system that successfully awards their children labels of distinction at the expense of others?" Implicitly, Ross suggested a point of view that some other progressives stated explicitly: that parents of successful students would be profoundly upset if their children, who had enjoyed success in traditional classrooms, were joined by others who, thanks to school reform, overcame their previous problems and also succeeded in school.[87]

Parents of successful students generally rejected the assertion that their children had done well at the expense of others. They would not agree that traditional curricula damaged all but those who excelled in logic and language. Many educators on the left, however, agreed with Professor Ross's supposition. They thought traditional programs were indeed responsible for the failure of many students. And they accused well-to-do professional parents of being narrowly concerned with their own children, and of opposing changes that were needed to promote diversity and uplift students from underachieving minority groups. They noted with dismay that upscale residents in Ithaca, New York, like their counterparts in Celebration, strongly opposed a proposal (developed by a Black school superintendent who grew up in the segregated South) to merge students who had been taking honors and regular classes in science. They challenged statements such as those of Cornell University chemistry professor John McMurray, who warned that if classes for the gifted were eliminated, "They won't be prepared to take chemistry at Cornell . . . It's a shameful way to treat bright students." They were disappointed to learn that in May 1995, "more than 5000 voters—twice as many as in any recent school election [in Ithaca]—turned out to vote for three open seats [on the school board], and two of the three incumbents who favored abolishing honors classes were defeated."[88]

---

87 Ibid., 180.

88 *New York Times* (4 June 1995).

Such scenes were not limited to a few cities. Throughout the United States, "privileged parents" were undermining "school reform." This, at least was the opinion of the progressive education writer Alfie Kohn. According to Kohn, most parents of the professional class were "not concerned that all children learn; they are concerned that *their* children learn." As Kohn saw it, the events that transpired in Celebration and Ithaca were similar to what happened in Amherst, Massachusetts, "where highly educated white parents have fought to preserve a tracking system that keeps virtually every child of color out of advanced classes." Something akin also occurred in Palo Alto, California, "where a similarly elite constituency demands a return to a 'skill and drill' math curriculum and fiercely opposes ... [a] more conceptual [approach to] learning." Meanwhile, in an affluent suburb of Buffalo, New York, the "parents of honors students quashed an attempt to replace letter grades with standards-based progress reports."[89]

Kohn acknowledged that "educational conservatives" were not always conservative. "They may be pro-choice [on abortion] and avid recyclers with nothing good to say about the likes of Pat Robertson and Rush Limbaugh." Some allowed their schools to stress "higher-order thinking" and "a literature-based approach to teaching reading." Some even favored "the use of cooperative learning." But they supported these innovations only "within homogeneous groups." They liked the fact that their children attended desegregated schools, "but the fact that the white kids are in the top classes and the black kids are in the bottom is someone else's problem." As an especially egregious example, Kohn mentioned one liberal columnist for *The New Republic*. This columnist admitted that his daughter's public school operated what amounted to "a school within a school" for White students—since the honors classes were "dominated by whites," while the enrollment in regular classes was disproportionately Black. But the columnist also announced that

---

89 Alfie Kohn, "Only for My Kid: How Privileged Parents Undermine School Reform," *Phi Delta Kappan* (April 1998), 569-70.

if this sort of grouping were eliminated, he would withdraw his daughter from the school "in a nanosecond."[90]

Kohn conceded that some parents feared their children's education would be "dumbed down" in integrated, progressive schools. He acknowledged that these parents were "genuinely worried about the extent to which their children are learning, or would be learning, in a heterogeneous classroom." "Bringing those lower-achieving students into the classroom is going to water down things for my children," they said. "[Non-Asian minority students] are not going to be able to keep up, and the teachers are going to have to slow things down."[91]

Nevertheless, Kohn had more scorn than sympathy for such parents. As he saw it, these parents were pressuring schools "to maintain separate and unequal classes for their children." They were retrograde if not racist. They demanded that their children have access to instruction that would not be available to other students. To maintain harmony, school officials in Celebration (and also in Ithaca, Palo Alto and elsewhere) eventually accommodated such parents. Nevertheless, Kohn wrote, "in the final analysis there are some principles that have to be affirmed and some practices that cannot be tolerated." Public schools should not bow to the demands of upscale parents. "There are things that we must not do," he wrote. "That's a moral and professional issue."[92]

Upscale parents were not alone in favoring traditional education. Many successful students felt the same way. Certainly this was the case at Whitney High School in Cerritos, California. Although a public institution, Whitney was an academic magnet school open only to those who passed a stiff entrance examination. On statewide standardized achievement tests in the 1990s, Whitney was the top

---

90 *Ibid.*, 570, 571.

91 *Ibid.*, 574, 575.

92 *Ibid.*, 572, 576.

ranked school in California. Its students' performance on the national Advanced Placement tests was also impressive. The school was housed in a run down building in a lower-middle class area, and 75 percent of the students were of Asian (largely Korean) extraction.[93]

Whitney's successful students sometimes complained about excessive competition. But many of them were outspoken in opposing the introduction of progressive teaching methods at their school. When one teacher used progressive methods for teaching physics, the students said, "tell us what chapter to read, give us the lecture and we'll ace the test." They said, "We're doing great with the status quo. Why change things?"[94]

The opposition to progressive teaching methods was especially evident in 2001-2002, when Neil Bush, brother of President George W. Bush, visited Whitney High. Because of difficulties he had experienced as a student, Neil Bush harbored a strong distaste for traditional schooling. This dislike developed into a passion for school reform when Neil Bush observed his own son foundering. "My son is talented," Bush said, "but making him sit in a traditional classroom all day went against every grain of the way he thinks and works." Searching for an educational approach that would help his son, Bush eventually embraced Howard Gardner's theory of multiple intelligences. Like Gardner, Neil Bush believed that if a child was inattentive and unwilling to do schoolwork, either the teacher or the school curriculum was probably to blame.[95]

With this in mind, Bush established a company—Ignite! Inc.—that produced interactive software for students. The idea was to keep

---

[93] Edward Humes, *School of Dreams* (New York: Harcourt, Inc., 2003), 4, 113, 354.

[94] Ibid., 95.

[95] Ibid., 276, 277.

students' attention from wavering by appealing to their penchant for computer games. Instead of reading textbooks and listening to teachers, students could work individually—using computers for interactive lessons that were tailored to individual learning styles.[96] The students at Whitney High admitted that Bush's program "might have some utility for failing students who can't or won't respond to traditional classes." But it was far from what they wanted for themselves. When Bush pitched his program, some students disrespectfully mentioned Bush's previous mismanagement of the Silverado Savings and Loan Association. When Bush said schoolwork should be "interesting" and "fun," one student expressed concern "that learning might just slip away by making pleasure more important in school." Another said, "Active learning programs are great, they're fun, but there are limitations. Take an AP Biology course. There is a massive amount of information you must assimilate in order to pass the test. . . . You can't do that with active learning." When Bush described calculus as something most students considered "useless and obscure," another pupil answered, "I like calculus. It instills critical thinking. . . . It's definitely a challenge, but it forces you to think in creative ways. Some students may think school should be a cakewalk, that it shouldn't be hard, that you should play all day. But that's not the way to excellence."[97]

Bush was flummoxed, saying, "That's an interesting defense of what I consider to be a broken system." Perhaps Howard Gardner could have responded more effectively. Yet Gardner's theory (like Bush's interactive software) appealed primarily to reformers and to parents whose children were not doing well in school. Since many families had a child who was a problem student, Gardner's reputation remained high, and Bush successfully marketed his interactive software in many schools. But he did not do so at Whitney High or at many other schools where traditional academic education was working well for most students.

---

96 Ibid., 81-82, 284.

97 Ibid., 285, 81, 279, 280, 281.

3

Theodore R. Sizer and the Coalition of Essential Schools

Like Howard Gardner, Theodore Sizer was a man of ideas, many of which were put forward in an influential trilogy of books about a fictional teacher, Horace Smith. Writing in the *New York Times*, James Traub called the first of these books, *Horace's Compromise* (1984), "the most discussed school reform book of its time." With the publication of the sequels, *Horace's School* (1992) and *Horace's Hope* (1996), other observers chimed in. Writing in the *Boston Globe*, Paul Hemp described Sizer as "the most prominent school reformer in America." In *Teacher Magazine*, David Ruenzel called Sizer "the nation's most famous school reformer." Nathan Glazer, writing in *The New Republic*, described Sizer as "the most powerful advocate for [a neo-progressive] school of thought."[1]

In addition to writing about education, Sizer was a practitioner who at various times was a teacher, the dean of Harvard's graduate school of education, the headmaster of an elite prep school, a key advisor to foundation-grant programs, a professor of education at Brown University, and the principal of a public charter school. In

---

1 *New York Times* Educational Supplement (2 August 1998); *Boston Globe* (20 November 1994); *Teacher Magazine* (4 September 1996); *New Republic* (10 August 1998) 10; Theodore Sizer, *Horace's Compromise* (Boston: Houghton Miflin, 1984); Sizer, *Horace's School* (Boston: Houghton Miflin, 1992); Sizer, *Horace's Hope* (Boston: Houghton Miflin, 1996).

1992 he collaborated with Gardner and James Comer of Yale in crafting a proposal that received a multi-million dollar grant from the New American Schools Development Corporation, an organization that grew out of President George H. W. Bush's program to establish model schools that would inspire change in the broader educational system. In 1994, with support from the Annenberg Foundation, Sizer expanded a coalition of schools that tried to improve education by establishing common principles that other schools could adapt or emulate. Sizer's work also found favor with the Gates Foundation and other charitable organizations.

Sizer was born in 1932, the youngest of six children. His father was a professor of art history at Yale, but his mother was in charge of the family during much of Sizer's youth, especially after his father was called to military service in World War II and then spent years recovering from a stroke suffered in 1944. In his early school years Sizer was a mediocre student who suffered from dyslexia. "There were two clubs in our family, the smart club and the dumb club," he recalled. "I was in the dumb club." He did better at a private prep school, the Pomfret School, and then went on to study English literature at Yale. After graduating from Yale in 1953, he served for two years as an artillery officer in the U.S. Army.[2]

Sizer's army service influenced his thought about education. Some of the recruits in his unit were school dropouts, but they performed their duties well. "Nobody said, 'Well, some of [the soldiers] don't test well.' . . . There wasn't an assumption that some can't learn." According to Sizer, the Army assumed that "Whatever troops you got had to deliver. If one person didn't do it, he put everybody's life at stake. That made a deep impression. There was no tracking in the army, just the belief that somehow these young men had to be trained and had to be reliable and that all soldiers

---

2   *Boston Globe* (20 November 1994).

can learn." The result was that "semiliterate dropouts" took off "like rockets" and became "superb people."³

After the Army, Sizer spent one year teaching algebra and English at the Roxbury Latin School in Boston and another year at Harvard, where he received a master's degree in teaching. Then he spent two years as an instructor at an all-boys Church of England school in Melbourne, Australia.

Along the way, Sizer developed a number of likes and dislikes that influenced his thoughts about education. He liked much about the prep school he had attended as a youth. The Pomfret School was a progressive academy that had been established by Yale professors who wanted students to learn from informal activities such as English country dancing and raising frogs. However, the school also employed one teacher, Joseph Barrell, who used an old-fashioned approach to teaching Latin. Instead of approaching the ancient language as Sizer would have preferred, as an entry point for teaching about the history of Rome and "the constancy of humanity in its passions and terrors," Barrell drilled students on vocabulary, points of grammar, and the rules that governed the formation of phrases and sentences. Barrell also used a red pencil to record grades and highlight any mistakes that students made. Many teachers have used these methods, and some students have enjoyed the challenge of correctly applying a complicated system of rules and precedents. Pupils with a logical bent have found special delight in discerning the underlying structure of a foreign language. But Sizer considered Barrell's approach so off-putting that he later identified the

---

3   Mark F. Goldberg, "A Portrait of Ted Sizer," *Educational Leadership* 51 (September 1993) 53-56; Goldberg, "Here for the Long Haul," *Phi Delta Kappan* 77 (June 1996) 685; Tamar Henry, "Rebel Describes 'Hope' for Schools," *USA Today* (4 September 1996). The American armed forces of the 1950s were not as egalitarian as Sizer implied. After the Korean War, the Army accepted only those who scored above a threshold point on a standardized intelligence exam. The threshold was set at a level that disqualified about one-third of the White population and two-thirds of the Black.

teacher as an archetype of much he thought was wrong with education. His dislike of Barrell was such that in 2004, when he was 72-years-old, he gave his autobiography the ironic title, *The Red Pencil*—testimony to his enduring aversion to some of the standard practices of traditional teachers. When he had been a student, Sizer had expressed his distaste by calling the teacher "Joe" behind his back. To his face, it was "Sir" or "Mister Barrell," titles that Sizer considered too formal but that teachers expected to hear in 1946.[4]

Sizer also drew mixed messages from his experience in Roxbury, where he taught for a year in an impoverished, largely-Black section of Boston. Because the school needed a math teacher, the authorities disregarded Sizer's self-confessed "phobia about mathematics." Instead, they put him to work teaching algebra as well as English to more than 200 eighth- and ninth-grade students. Sizer got through the year by sticking to the textbooks, "controlling the class so kids never asked questions." This was the best that could be done in the circumstances, but it was far from ideal, and the experience left Sizer with an abiding dislike of textbooks. Yet he also developed empathy for African-American youths—an empathy that came to the fore in his subsequent careers as a dean, headmaster, principal, and education writer.[5]

Sizer also had a mixed experience in Australia. The school there was too proper for his taste, "more British than the British." The faculty wore black gowns and both teachers and senior students were allowed to administer corporal punishment. "But they also had constructive ideas," Sizer recalled, "such as using the older students as

---

4   USA Today (4 September 1996); Theodore R. Sizer, *The Red Pencil: Convictions from Experience in Education* (New Haven: Yale University Press, 2004) xix, xviii.

5   New York Times Educational Supplement (9 November 1986); *St. Louis Post-Dispatch* (15 July 1990).

coaches," and the headmaster, Sir Brian Hone, was an extraordinary leader and mentor who advised Sizer on books to read. "That Australian headmaster continues to influence me," Sizer said in 1993. Most of all, Hone was "a great advocate of small units." He insisted that schools should not enroll more than 500 students, and "nobody should be the principal of a school that has more than 25 teachers." These convictions would remain with Sizer.[6]

After two years in Australia, Sizer returned to Harvard and received a doctorate in 1961 with a dissertation on American high schools at the turn of the twentieth century. He remained at Harvard to head the Master of Arts in Teaching Program under Dean Francis Keppel. When Keppel was named U.S. Commissioner of Education, Sizer became a member of a small group that helped Harvard's President Nathan Pusey run the education school. Then, in January 1964, Pusey asked Sizer, who was only 31 years old at the time, to become the Dean of Harvard's Graduate School of Education. "The timing was extraordinary," Sizer said, "in that the rush of [President Lyndon B.] Johnson's education initiatives came at once." The budget of the Graduate School "went from $2 million to $10 million in just two years."[7]

The new money funded a great deal of research, including some important studies that dealt with race and class. With leadership from Professors Daniel Patrick Moynihan and Frederick Mosteller, some 80 professors from Harvard and elsewhere undertook an extensive, interdisciplinary reexamination that confirmed a principal finding of James S. Coleman's report of 1966, *Equality of Educational Opportunity*: that the academic performance of students corresponded more closely to the students' family background than to the quality of the schools they attended. This led to what Sizer called "a lot of pessimism."

---

6   Mark F. Goldberg, "A Portrait of Ted Sizer."

7   Ibid.; *New York Times* Educational Supplement (9 November 1986).

The Coleman report and its offspring [seemed to say], 'schools don't make a difference—tell me your income and I'll tell you your SAT scores,' that kind of thing." Sizer took particular note of "Coleman's troubling finding that the older the student—that is, the longer he or she had been in school—the wider the achievement gap between rich and poor became. There were few school-to-school variations. What mattered was social class. 'The sources of education [inequality] appear to lie first in the home itself and the cultural influences immediately surrounding the home,' Coleman wrote. 'Then they lie in the schools' ineffectiveness to free achievement from the impact of the home....'[8]

As Dean of the Graduate School of Education, Sizer went along with his colleagues in accepting Coleman's conclusion. Yet he found much of the scholarship "bewildering." Since Sizer's education had been in English and history, and his previous employment had been in the military and school teaching, he was "befogged and frequently cowed by the ferocious arguments ... about what struck me as dazzling but sometimes picayune statistical acrobatics, about the weight of different sorts of evidence, and about just what the humming new IBM computers at Harvard could and could not do with the thousands of Coleman's punched cards."[9]

Sizer's reservations became more pronounced after he moved from Harvard to become the headmaster of the prestigious Phillips Academy in Andover, Massachusetts. In some ways the move was surprising, for Sizer was not pressured to leave Harvard. Nevertheless, there were difficult problems at most colleges in the late-1960s, a time of student upheaval and revolts. For Sizer, 1969 and 1970 had been especially trying years of increasing crisis management. In addition, Sizer and his wife, Nancy, a teacher, had dreamed of working together in a high school. They had four children by 1970 and had discussed

---

8   *Washington Post* (9 August 1987); Theodore R. Sizer, *The Red Pencil*, 11-12.

9   Theodore R. Sizer, *The Red Pencil*, 11.

the possibility of teaching together at the high school their children attended. As it happened, the headmaster at Phillips Andover, the high school where their oldest children were enrolled, died in 1970, and Sizer was offered the job. It was too good an opportunity to pass up, and he took the position in 1972.[10]

Sizer headed Phillips Andover for nine years, during which many of his educational theories congealed. He became more pronounced in his preference for the sort of progressive education he had received in many classes at the Pomfret School (and equally confirmed in his distaste for the methods of Pomfret's renegade traditionalist, the Latin teacher). Because Andover was a wealthy school that could accept students irrespective of their ability to pay, Sizer was able to inaugurate a program that recruited poor African-American students. Many of these recruits went on to graduate and in the process confirmed the opinion that Sizer had formed in the Army—that many disadvantaged students could learn if taught properly. At Andover, Sizer also began to reconsider the import of the Coleman report. "While Coleman and others were saying schools didn't make a difference," Sizer "was looking at Andover, with its large endowment supports and many scholarship students, and it was making a difference." He became "more and more interested in why some of these kids coming from wretched schooling, poor kids, many of them minority kids, could change their futures very dramatically. There were things that worked—and they worked powerfully."[11]

In the 1970s Sizer started having regular meetings with other school administrators. "We'd sit there and puzzle over public education. Why was everything going bad out there? What was happening?" He decided to investigate on his own. With money

---

10   Mark F. Goldberg, "A Portrait of Ted Sizer."

11   *Washington Post* (9 August 1987); Mark F. Goldberg, "A Portrait of Ted Sizer."

from the Commonwealth and Carnegie foundations, and with joint sponsorship from the National Association of Secondary School Principals and the National Association of Independent [Private] Schools, Sizer assembled a staff and began a five-year project known as *A Study of High Schools*. Eventually the project took him to more than 100 high schools and led to the publication of three important books: *The Last Little Citadel* (1986), by Robert L. Hampel; *The Shopping Mall High School* (1985), by Arthur G. Powell, Eleanor Farrar, and David K. Cohen; and Sizer's own book, *Horace's Compromise* (1984). After that, there were two more offshoots about the fictional teacher, Horace Smith: *Horace's School* (1992) and *Horace's Hope* (1996). All of these books emphasized the shortcomings of American high schools and the challenges of teaching in less-than-ideal circumstances.

The metaphors of Sizer's fellow authors pointed toward one of their principle themes: that during the course of the 20th century, American high schools had been transformed from *citadels* to *shopping malls*—from outposts of taste and intellect to centers that offered intellectual merchandise tailored to a wide variety of different abilities, preferences, and levels of discernment. Sizer's colleagues conceded that there had never been a golden age for high schools. There were problems even at the turn of the twentieth century, when only 10 percent of the nation's teenagers had attended secondary schools. But the quality of high school education became more problematic as enrollments increased, to about 70 percent of the age cohort by 1960 and almost 90 percent by the end of the twentieth century.[12]

In 1900, most of the secondary school students were White youths from families that were financially comfortable. As a result of child labor laws and compulsory attendance policies, however, the

---

12 Arthur G. Powell, Eleanor Farrar and David K. Cohen, *The Shopping Mall High School* (Boston: Houghton Miflin Company, 1985) 238.

high schools began to enroll youngsters who previously had gone to work or roamed the streets. During the early years of the twentieth century, the high schools were filling up with immigrant and working-class youths who differed from the pupils that secondary teachers had taught previously. As a result, teachers were asked to provide more than book learning. Some of the new students had lice and, although the formal curriculum said nothing about bathing, teachers found themselves responsible for seeing to it that students took baths in school if not at home. "Not only baths, but a vast variety of other activities that could not be found in any syllabus began to appear. Manners, cleanliness, dress, the simple business of getting along together in a classroom—these things had to be taught more insistently and self-consciously than ever." "The whole battle with the slum [was] fought out in and around the public school," one observer wrote in 1902. The schools increasingly took responsibility for promoting the sort of socialization that previously had taken place in the family, in the neighborhood, or on the job.[13]

To attract a wider range of students, high schools also offered a greater variety of courses and extracurricular activities such as band, dances, and Friday night football. "Secondary education once had been reserved for the few," one educational historian has written. "But reformers wanted to bring the high school to all of America. They wanted to build a curriculum that would appeal to all comers." It was assumed that many of the new students "didn't have what it took to be serious about the great issues of human life, and . . . even if they had the wit, they had neither the will nor the futures that would support heavy-duty study."[14]

---

13 James B. Conant, *The Revolutionary Transformation of the American High School* (Cambridge: Harvard University Press, 1959) 6; Lawrence A. Cremin, *The Transformation of the School* (New York: Alfred A. Knopf, 1961); Jacob A. Riis, *The Battle with the Slum* (New York: The Macmillan Company, 1902) 404.

14 Arthur G. Powell et al., *The Shopping Mall High School*, 256, 245.

The shift was Copernican. Before 1900, all high school students (regardless of whether they planned to attend college) studied English, mathematics, history, and science. Afterward, elementary schools still provided a standard curriculum that stressed reading, writing, and arithmetic, but high school students were streamed in different directions. Some students continued to prepare for college, but others undertook vocational studies; and all students took courses that dealt with basic areas of human activity: health, dating, sex, driving, citizenship—subjects that were included in the category, "life adjustment education." Some of the weaker students took more life adjustment courses than academic studies.[15]

This gave rise to one of the great debates in the history of American education. In 1893 a Committee of Ten, headed by Harvard's president, Charles W. Eliot, had rejected the idea that high school students should be free to study vocational subjects and instead recommended that all secondary pupils should study English, foreign languages, mathematics, history, and science. According to Eliot, "the training of youth from fourteen to eighteen should be one and the same, whether he is going on to college or . . . going to earn his living."[16]

Eliot's emphasis on what amounted to a national high school curriculum did not sit well with President Theodore Roosevelt, who in 1907 declared America's school system "gravely defective in so far as it puts a premium upon mere literary training. . . . Nothing is more needed than the best type of industrial school, the school for mechanical industries in the city, the school for practically teaching agriculture in the country." Some influential academics agreed, among

---

15 Lawrence A. Cremin, *The Transformation of the School*, 104; William J. Reese, *America's Public Schools: From the Common School to "No Child Left Behind"* (Baltimore: Johns Hopkins University Press, 2005) 224 and *passim*.

16 Charles W. Eliot, Comment on G. Stanley Hall, "How Far is the Present High School . . . Adapted to the Nature and Needs of Adolescents?" *The School Review* 9 (December 1901) 671.

them Clark University professor G. Stanley Hall, who recommended that secondary schools adapt their courses of study to "the great majority who begin high school [and] do not finish, instead of focusing our energies on the few who get to college." Roosevelt's and Hall's point of view eventually found favor with the National Education Association, which in 1918 released a report (*Cardinal Principles of Secondary Education*) that held that it was anti-democratic and elitist to require all students to study subjects that were necessary only for those who planned to attend college.[17]

By early in the twentieth century the trend was unmistakably toward differentiation. As high school enrollments soared, the word went out from several centers of education. Instead of trying to familiarize all children with the culture and ideas of the ages, American schools should prepare students for their future lives in the United States. This was the message that Dean James E. Russell set forth from his perch at Columbia Teachers College; that Professor Elwood P. Cubberly propounded at Stanford; and that Professor John Dewey publicized at the University of Chicago. The trend was so strong that eventually even Harvard's President Eliot changed sides, abandoned his long-time defense of a common academic curriculum and conceded that some youths should "go into industrial schools, others into ordinary high schools, and others again into the mechanic arts high schools."[18]

The trend toward differentiation was reinforced in the 1950s and 1960s, when many communities followed the advice of another Harvard president, James B. Conant, closed their smaller schools,

---

17 Annual Message of the President, 3 December 1907, quoted in Diane Ravitch, *Left Back* (New York: Simon & Schuster, 2000) 79; statement of G. Stanley Hall, quoted in Arthur G. Powell *et al.*, *The Shopping Mall High School*, 242.

18 Charles W. Eliot, quoted in Edward A. Krug, *Charles W. Eliot and Popular Education* (New York: Teachers' College, 1961) 19-20.

and built larger "comprehensive" institutions. The purpose of the comprehensive schools was to accommodate the interests and aptitudes of quite different groups of students on the same campus. In addition to general courses that prepared all students for citizenship and life in the United States, there were vocational, commercial, and work-study programs for youths who were not bound for college, and advanced courses in mathematics, science, and foreign languages for students who were academically oriented.

Some dissenters opposed this development. Theodore Sizer and the authors of the companion volumes in Sizer's *Study of High Schools* were part of this opposition. Advocates of comprehensive schools had said it was elitist and even cruel to require all high school students to study Euclid's proofs and Shakespeare's sonnets. It was more democratic, they said, to allow students to choose courses of study that they or their parents considered appropriate. Sizer and his associates, on the other hand, believed such freedom amounted to classifying children by their home environment. They reached this conclusion because the children of workers and ethnic minorities were more likely to enroll in general and vocational courses while the offspring of well-to-do parents prepared for professions. As a result, working-class youngsters, African-Americans, and some ethnic minorities disproportionately gravitated toward low-skilled, low-paying jobs. According to the critics, all students, even those who did not plan to attend college, would have been better off if their high school studies had focused on traditional subjects like mathematics, history, literature, and foreign languages.[19]

Sizer's colleagues, the authors of *The Shopping Mall High School*, at times acknowledged that some students were "less able or less willing" than others. In one passage, they even expressed concern

---

19   Arthur G. Powell *et al.*, *The Shopping Mall High School*, *passim*. For similar views, see Diane Ravitch, *Left Back*, 91, 44; and William J. Reese, *America's Public Schools*, 151.

that enrollment of mediocre students would discourage top students from doing serious academic work. The situation would have been less problematic, they wrote, "if schools could be organized on the model of nuclear submarines, with watertight bulkheads sealing off some sections from others." But the structure of the comprehensive school was "more porous than that of a submarine—there are no bulkheads." Because of peer pressure, the anti-intellectual disposition of middling students infected the entire comprehensive school. Schools "could not be academically demanding unless they were demanding for all," *Shopping Mall* concluded. And if most youngsters were limited in their intellectual abilities and ambitions, it followed that comprehensive schools could not maintain high standards—not even for pupils enrolled in advanced classes.[20]

But there were only occasional lapses into this sort of realism. The *Shopping Mall* authors took pains to distance themselves from comments that might be considered elitist, and they included so many genuflections to political correctness that their book seemed schizoid. While occasionally admitting that many students had modest abilities and nonacademic ambitions, *Shopping Mall* also decried teachers who expressed pessimism about the intellectual capacity of these students. *Shopping Mall* railed against those who said that many students "didn't have what it took to be serious about the great issues of human life." Most students were capable of dealing with intellectual "meat," *Shopping Mall* said. It was not necessary to give them "pabulum." It was "naïve" to think "that occupations had a natural hierarchy of mental ability requirements, and that workers sorted themselves out accordingly."[21]

Shopping Mall also criticized comprehensive high schools for giving students too much choice. To accommodate the diversity of

---

20 Arthur G. Powell et al., *The Shopping Mall High School*, 245, 299, 299-300.

21 *Ibid.*, 245, 251, 249.

their students, the comprehensive schools provided a smorgasbord of courses and extracurricular activities, but the teachers did not push students "to choose wisely or engage deeply." Instead, the teachers established "a neutral environment where a do-your-own thing attitude prevails." According to *Shopping Mall*, this amounted to "an abdication of responsibility toward those students and families who, for whatever reasons, do not make the wise choice." The schools and teachers placed "too much of a burden on their teenagers to be already self-directed, already proficient in decision-making." Although comprehensive schools provided "wide curricular variety" and allowed "unfettered student choice," they took "few clear stands on whether some products or services are better than others."[22]

"If you want to learn here you can learn good," one student was quoted as saying, "but if you don't want to, no one will push you." According to *Shopping Mall*, this was a serious problem. The book had little to say about some of the usual villains of American education: disorder in the classrooms, disrespectful students, bullies in the hallways, and instructors who did not know much about the subjects they were teaching. Instead, *Shopping Mall* criticized teachers for not pushing students to be more serious about school, for negotiating "treaties" that allowed students to get by without difficult reading, writing, or homework, if the students agreed to behave in ways that were reasonably orderly and compliant.[23]

Shopping Mall said that American high schools were especially bad when it came to meeting the needs of average students. The book's subtitle proclaimed that there were "winners and losers in the educational marketplace," and the biggest "losers" were middling youngsters who suffered from an excess of freedom. These pupils could have thrived intellectually if their teachers had provided proper

---

22 Ibid., 3, 65, 5.

23 Ibid., 70, 199, 65.

direction, *Shopping Mall* maintained. But many students withered for lack of proper nurturing and encouragement. "Everything's here," the mother of one student said, but "the burden of choice falls on the students." Without advice and support, many adolescents were left without a sound education, "adrift on a sea . . . clutching at bits of flotsam and jetsam."[24]

The atmosphere at comprehensive schools was such that even the students in the advanced academic courses did not fare well. *Shopping Mall* conceded that many of these students made high scores on standardized tests and went on to attend selective colleges. But *Shopping Mall* distinguished between this sort of success and the development of intellectual intensity. Even in advanced classes, it was rare for students to become deeply engaged. There was little intellectual passion. And once again, *Shopping Mall* blamed schools and teachers for not providing active adult push and for failing to develop classes that were "lively" and "exciting."[25]

In his own writings, Sizer expanded on these themes. Like the authors of *Shopping Mall*, Sizer thought the United States had made a mistake when it developed comprehensive high schools. He blamed James B. Conant for pushing the nation in this direction. He criticized teachers for asking little of students who agreed to behave, an understanding that Sizer called a "conspiracy for the least." He found fault with schools whose students made good scores on standardized tests but did not develop "habits of serious thought, respectful skepticism and curiosity about much of what lies beyond their immediate lives." Most suburban schools were "happy places," Sizer reported, with "nice kids, nice teachers [and] people caring about one another." But beneath the surface, the intellectual life was

---

24 Ibid., 3, 178; Wayne Mollenberg, "Review of *The Shopping Mall High School*," *Educational Forum* 51 (Summer 1987) 410.

25 Ibid., 197, 105, 255-77.

"pretty shallow." Students were allowed to "wander through . . . taking undemanding courses," and hardly any learned much about "reasoning or applying ideas." Even the best students were "intellectually docile. . . . They could regurgitate material but not use it creatively. They could answer set questions but not come up with their own."[26]

Sizer was especially critical of traditional teachers. These teachers used textbooks and lectures to present information, and then gave multiple choice tests to see how much the students had learned. After that, traditional teachers gave essay exams to see if the students could identify and apply the portion of information that was relevant to particular questions. Finally, they asked students to prepare essays, term papers, science reports, or other projects. Along the way they graded and sifted students. They gave marks—"A," "B," or "C"—and in the process they either encouraged or discouraged students from pursuing work of a particular sort. Traditional teachers considered it their responsibility, part of their job, to sort and measure students.

As Sizer saw it, much of this was mistaken. High school should not be "about sorting people out, the presumed abler from the less able; it is about educating *all* children, generously and without qualification." It would be better if teachers refused to compare students with one another. It would be better still if teachers provided less information and gave fewer tests. Most teachers spent too much time talking and judging, and most students spent too much time listening and taking examinations."[27]

Many traditional teachers felt passionately about their subjects and tried to transmit what they knew in engaging ways. Yet Sizer

---

26 Theodore R. Sizer, *Horace's Compromise*, 210; James Traub, "Sizer's Hope," *New York Times* (2 August 1998); Sizer, *Horace's School*, 1; John Grapper, review of *Horace's School*, *London Financial Times* (16 April 1992); *Boston Globe* (15 December 1991); Mark F. Goldberg, "A Portrait of Ted Sizer."

27 Theodore R. Sizer, *Horace's School*, 143.

called for "a fundamental rethinking of the way teachers have taught and the way they should teach." "Sermons do not work well in engaging us," Sizer said. To show that lectures and books were "demonstrably inefficient" methods of teaching, Sizer proposed an experiment: "give students a test they took twelve to fifteen months earlier, and see how they perform." Sizer took special exception to advanced placement courses that were "fact-stuffed" with information. As he saw it, these courses "distort teaching and learning" because they "reward the mere display of knowledge." They required students to "regurgitate a set body of information."[28]

If students were to reach a higher level of learning, if they were to "reason independently," if they were to develop "habits of perspective, analysis, imagination [and] empathy," schooling would have to become "a dialectical process." Teachers should move away from lectures, textbooks, and grades, and engage students in conversation and collaboration. Instead of conveying information "from the front of the classroom," teachers should engage in Socratic questioning. Rather than answer questions, they should encourage students to "find the right (or at least defensible) answers themselves." "We're selling our children short," Sizer wrote, if we require only that they learn from books and lectures. Instead of emphasizing the passive accumulation of information, students should be encouraged to "grapple" by themselves. In the process, Sizer said, youngsters would progress from the mere acquisition of knowledge to serious thinking and an enlarged understanding of ideas and values.[29]

---

28 Theodore Sizer, quoted in *Chronicle of Higher Education* (7 November 1990); Sizer, *Horace's School*, 85, 86, 8, 104; Sizer, "The Trivial . . . Thing We Call High School," *New York Times* (31 October 1987); *Time* (20 February 1984) 81.

29 Theodore Sizer, *Horace's Compromise*, 82, 99, 119, 131-32; Sizer, *Horace's School*,89, 91, 97; Sizer, *The Red Pencil*, 67ff; *Washington Post* (25 March 1984); Sizer, "Grappling," *Phi Delta Kappan* 81 (November 1999) 184-90.

To provide the proper sort of non-directive education, Sizer stressed the need for a new kind of teacher. Things would not improve if instructors continued to regard teaching as telling and learning as remembering. Instead of giving lectures, teachers should induce students to learn by asking questions and making suggestions. Sizer wanted students to become "critical thinkers"—people who regarded the ideas of others with both respect and skepticism.

Perhaps because of unhappy memories of his own years as a schoolboy, Sizer harbored a fondness for teachers who either had not enjoyed their own schooling or had not been successful at it. Such people were more likely to depart from traditional practices. Yet most of those who entered teaching had admired their own teachers when they were students and continued to use similar methods after they became teachers. As Sizer saw it, these traditionalists posed one of the biggest obstacles to school reform. They perpetuated entrenched habits and routines. Instead of embracing new approaches, their classes continued to be "taken up with teachers talking and students listening, not the one-on-one engagement that good learning requires." Old-fashioned teachers continued "to feed students knowledge rather than expect them to forage on their own."[30]

In stressing the importance of learning on one's own, Sizer embraced the "constructivism" that Howard Gardner had touted—the idea that students achieved a deeper understanding if they became actively engaged in their own education. And that was not the only point that Sizer and Gardner agreed upon. Sizer also accepted the concept of multiple intelligences. "In the past, if a youngster did not 'get it,' he was identified as more or less incompetent. . . . The new assumption . . . is that if a kid does not get it in the usual way, the school should try to help him to get it in another way." "If a child does

---

30 *U.S. News and World Report* (26 February 1990) 50-55; *New York Times* (9 November 1986; 28 June 1983).

not learn, we must blame his school, not him." "We learn in different ways, and we must therefore be taught in different ways."[31]

To draw out individual students and discourage the use of traditional methods of instruction, Sizer made a number of recommendations. The load of the average high school teacher should be reduced from about 150 students to 80. Teachers should collaborate in teaching many courses. To allow teachers time to work with the whole class, with small groups, or with individuals as needed, the usual 45-50 minute class periods should be scrapped and replaced with periods of 90 minutes of more. Teachers should be given two hours of free time during the day—time that could be devoted to planning and conferring with other instructors. And the high school curriculum should be consolidated into just four areas: math and science, history and philosophy, literature and arts, and speech and writing.

Sizer called for in-depth study of fewer subjects. One of his slogans proclaimed, "Less is more." In what he called his "fantasy school," teachers would teach fewer subjects in greater depth. They would "cover a lot less, but . . . do it thoroughly." Students were more likely to become deep thinkers if, instead of rushing through topics, they focused on key events or concepts. Students of American history, for example, would learn more about immigration if they were allowed to dwell on the subject for more than the usual day or two. Students could also learn more about the history of business or labor if they were given time to prepare for mock trials of the industrialist Andrew Carnegie or the anarchist Emma Goldman. They could learn about the Constitution by doing research so that they could play the roles of lawyers who were arguing cases before the Supreme Court.[32]

---

31 Theodore Sizer, *Horace's Hope*, 35, 120.

32 *Chronicle of Higher Education* (7 November 1990); Theodore Sizer, *Horace's Hope*, 87; *New York Times* (2 August 1998).

At Sizer's ideal school, these projects would culminate in presenting what Sizer called an "exhibition of mastery." Before moving from one level to another, students would have to prepare an exhibit or portfolio that demonstrated what they had learned. The presentation might involve a work of art, a videotaped documentary, or a scientific experiment. Topics could range from racism to radioactivity, from the Vietnam War to architecture in New York City. After the fashion of doctoral students defending their dissertations, the presentations would be open to the public and would be judged by a committee that included some fellow students as well as at least two teachers.[33]

Sizer, however, did not recommend a substantial increase in school funding. He maintained, rather, that his program could be implemented with only a 10 percent increase in the expenditure per student. He admitted that it would cost more to reduce the number of students per teacher and allow teachers more time to meet with students individually and with one another to plan for collaborative activities. But he also pointed to offsetting economies. He said that some funds could be reallocated for use in the classroom rather than in administration. In addition, by narrowing the curriculum to four interdisciplinary courses for all students, there would be no need for expensive vocational programs, for counselors or coaches, or for teachers of subjects like health, driving, and home economics. Sizer said that schools could also reap "great financial savings" by increased use of interactive technology. While teachers were conferring with one another or with students, other pupils could use computers to exchange information and to consult with on-line tutors.[34]

---

33 *New York Times* (24 June 1998).

34 *Boston Globe* (10 January 1992); *Christian Science Monitor* (19 March 1984); Theodore Sizer, *Horace's School*, 42, 199-2000; *Boston Globe* (29 December 1996).

Sizer also plumped for smaller schools. He regarded comprehensive schools as elephantine legacies of an earlier age when bigness had been considered cost effective. In modern America, however, educators had come to recognize that many students in large schools suffered from feelings of anonymity. That was one of the principal reasons for disciplinary problems. Many people seemed to behave at their worst when they were not known in a community, and Sizer was not alone in thinking that the anonymity of large schools was partly responsible for vandalism and other antisocial behavior. "Give me a small school . . . and I'll show you a school that doesn't need a metal detector," he said. "I'll show you a school without a high dropout rate. I'll show you a school where children are doing well."[35]

Sizer thought behavior and school work would both improve at "human scale places" where most teachers and students knew one another. He therefore recommended the construction of smaller units with no more than 400 students. If students were already enrolled at mammoth institutions, he recommended the formation of smaller, separate "schools within schools," each with its own faculty, administration and programs. He welcomed the news that New York City had subdivided some of its larger institutions into smaller units with names like the Leadership Secondary School of the Future.[36]

Unlike James B. Conant, who favored large schools that made it easier to group pupils by achievement, Sizer was opposed to ability grouping. Since students varied individually, Sizer said there should be "as many tracks as kids." "Every child" should be "on his or her own track," and students should be expected to learn from one another.

---

35 *New York Times* (1 September 1987).

36 Theodore Sizer, *Horace's Hope*, 91; *New York Times* (19 June 1993; 15 April 1993; 24 June 1998).

Sizer's opposition to ability grouping was related to a belief that the practice damaged the self-esteem of students who were placed in the lower and middle groups. He said tracking drew lines "by race, class, and sometimes gender." It fostered rigidities and was unfair to late bloomers. "The waste" to individual students "and to society at large" was "prodigious." Beyond this, Sizer recognized that grouping allowed teachers to fashion lessons for entire classes. If a class contained students with widely different levels of preparation, teachers would have no alternative but to deal with students individually, as coaches or tutors rather than as authoritative instructors. As noted by Albert Shanker of the American Federation of Teachers, teachers of truly diverse classes "almost never lectured." They "knew that there wasn't much they could say simultaneously to a roomful of kids of different ages and stages of learning. So [they] moved from one group of two or three students to another." Like Sizer, Shanker thought this was "a superior way of getting [students] to learn"—because it "avoid[ed] teacher talk and [made students work] on their own or in small groups.[37]

In addition to calling for "detracking," smaller classes, and smaller schools, Sizer wanted each school to develop a distinctive ethos. As he saw it, many public schools were too large for the faculty to develop within itself a sense of community. Teachers at large schools tended to be independent operators who had been hired on the basis of credentials and expertise in a particular subject, rather than because they shared a particular religion, philosophy, or view of education. Thus it was not surprising that instructors at large schools rarely collaborated with one another. Team-teaching was far more likely at smaller schools where teachers could be "chosen to work . . . on the basis of a commitment to the philosophy of that school."[38]

---

37 Theodore Sizer, *Horace's Hope*, 98; Sizer, *Horace's School*, 36-44; Edward B. Fiske, *Smart Schools, Smart Kids* (New York: Simon & Schuster, 1991) 90.

38 Theodore Sizer, *Horace's Hope*, 23, 92.

These, then, were Sizer's core principles: (1) He wanted to reduce anonymity by personalizing education. (2) He wanted to educate every student, not just the stars. (3) He wanted teachers to place less emphasis on dispensing information and evaluating students. (4) He wanted students to take responsibility for learning and to become more skeptical in their thinking. (5) He wanted schools to place less emphasis on covering a range of subjects and more emphasis on in-depth study of fewer topics. (6) He wanted courses to conclude with an exhibition of the students' work instead of with a test. (7) He said it was time to get students more involved in their own learning and to discourage teachers from giving lectures.

Sizer also favored "reform from the bottom up." Because students differed from one another, and communities also had distinctive requirements, Sizer thought individual schools should be allowed to adapt their programs accordingly. He wanted to give the power to improve the schools to principals and teachers rather than to national or state organizations. He understood that the aim of national testing was to ensure that all students learned basic skills. But he sensed that much testing stemmed from a conviction that "locals don't have the smarts . . . to pull off what is needed." He thought that reliance on standardized tests grew out of "a deep suspicion of democracy," a belief that local teachers and principals could not run schools effectively. As if to confirm Sizer's suspicions, Chester E. Finn, a leading proponent of standardized testing, candidly asserted: "The education industry, left to its own devices, is doing a mediocre job. We are therefore as a society seeking to make it accountable in achieving specific results."[39]

Sizer took special exception to tests that rewarded breadth of coverage rather than depth of knowledge. He considered it "alarming" and "scary" that many government officials and some school reformers

---

39 *Boston Globe* (20 November 1994); Chester E. Finn, quoted in *New York Times* (26 December 1989).

had embraced national testing. Imposing standards "from the top down" was at odds with Sizer's desire to reform education by empowering students, teachers, and principals at the local level.[40]

Sizer believed, in addition, that assembling a good corps of teachers was a key to educational reform; and he said it took more than a fair wage and good working conditions to attract and hold the best teachers. Truly gifted teachers would not take jobs that failed to give them authority. They would not continue as teachers if distant bureaucrats were empowered to decide what their children should know. "After listening to many teachers," Sizer concluded that "the frustration of the best of them about being distrusted is corrosive." The more that government officials "decide how teachers should teach," the more they repelled "the kinds of people that ... I want our kids to be taught by."[41]

When he criticized standardized tests, Sizer was swimming against a strong current. He was swept into conflict not only with those who favored a more national approach to school reform, but also with people who recognized the importance of allowing schools to differ from one another. Many of these people were wary of government-run schools but nevertheless believed that, if taxpayers were paying for the education, government agencies would have to give tests to evaluate the quality of the education that was being provided. The editors of the *Boston Herald* expressed this view, saying it was "disappointing to see respected educators like Theodore Sizer" take exception to the use of standardized tests as a measure of school quality. According to the *Herald*, "sad experience" had shown that many educators, if "left to themselves," would take public money but fail to impart even basic skills. Richard Riley, U.S. Secretary of Education during

---

40 Theodore Sizer, "Silences," *Daedalus* (Fall 1995) 77-83.

41 Theodore Sizer, "A Better Way," *Daedalus* (Summer 2002) 26-29; *Christian Science Monitor* (11 September 1996).

the administration of President Bill Clinton, allowed that control of American schools should remain local, but Riley also insisted, "Reading is reading. Math is math. For these basics, let us not cloud our children's future with silly arguments about federal intrusion."[42]

Some of this criticism misunderstood Sizer. Sizer was adamant in opposing tests that required high-school students to acquire a wide range of information rather than to develop their critical faculties by grappling with a few topics. The idea of using a national exam to measure the quality of high school education impressed Sizer as "an absolutely terrible idea." Sizer was willing, however, to use tests to measure the mastery of basic reading, writing, and arithmetic. At his ideal schools, students would be required to take "a limited number of ... tests in (and only in) what may be called the critical enabling areas: reading, writing and basic mathematics."[43]

Indeed, Sizer said, if secondary education was to be effective, high schools should be open only to students who could demonstrate basic competence in literacy and arithmetic. If teenagers had not mastered the basics, they should be assigned for intensive remedial work. If "one-on-one tutoring" was needed to teach students to read, the public should "invest heavily" in such programs. Sizer resented suggestions that he was "driving illiterate kids out of [high] school." He wanted to see "teachers working intensively with these kids"—but in special schools. The group that some people "think I am pushing out of the schools is the very group which I am emphatically saying the state must hang with, well beyond the age of 16 or 18 in many cases."[44]

---

42   Nathan Glazer, "Back to Schools," *New Republic* (10 August 1998) 10-11; Diane Ravitch, "First, Save the Schools," *New York Times* (27 June 1994); *Boston Herald* (11 November 1999); *New York Times* (19 February 1997).

43   Theodore Sizer, *Horace's School*, 161.

44   *Boston Globe* (2 February 1992); *Washington Post* (9 August 1987; 15 February 1984); *Christian Science Monitor* (19 March 1984).

Because he insisted on what amounted to prerequisites for admission to high school, some observers considered Sizer an elitist. This impression was reinforced when Sizer acknowledged, "Most of my theories and ideas about education came to me in the '70s when I was headmaster at Andover." Yet Sizer said he was just trying to give public school students the same education that prep school students received. His experience at Andover had convinced Sizer that inner-city youths could benefit from this sort of training.[45]

Nevertheless, some observers regarded Sizer as "impractical to the point of romanticism." One wrote that, because Sizer approached school reform from the lofty heights of Yale, Harvard, and Andover, he seemed to have "both feet planted firmly in the air." While conceding the importance of stimulating students to think and reason, other critics noted that Sizer said very little about the content of the curriculum. Indeed, Chester E. Finn wrote, Sizer came "very close to arguing that the choice of content does not really much matter, that any book or fact or problem or event is as suitable as any other." Students could graduate from one of Sizer's schools without acquiring much of what E. D. Hirsch called "cultural literacy." Writing in the *New York Times*, Sara Mosle noted that, in essence, Sizer's approach to education was the opposite of the core knowledge program that Hirsch developed. Mosle then concluded with a stinging assessment of two books, one written by Sizer and the other by Hirsch. "To judge by [Sizer's] own criteria—that is, as an 'exhibition' of higher thinking—*Horace's Hope* is disappointing. Mr. Hirsch's [book] is far more substantial."[46]

---

45 *Christian Science Monitor* (11 September 1996; 19 March 1984); *Commentary* (May 1984) 64-70; *New York Times* (17 December 1995; 29 September 1996).

46 Sara Mosle, "Doing Our Homework" *New York Times Book Review* (29 September 1996).

Other critics took exception to Sizer's disparaging assessment of America's high schools. "At times I find Sizer, the old Andover headmaster, unduly condescending and overly pessimistic," wrote Dan Morgan in the *Washington Post*. "Descending into the steamy plain of U.S. secondary education was, one senses, a distressing and intensely personal experience ... for Ted Sizer."[47]

Many teachers also took exception. They doubtless agreed with Sizer's contentions that there were too many students in most classes. But they also recognized that Sizer presented a scathing indictment of most teachers. Traditional teachers, in particular, were averse to the sort of re-training that Sizer had in mind and, as *U.S. News* noted, "a resistant faculty can throw a wrench into the most well-meaning reform." The magazine described teachers as "the enemy within," saying that they, "the very people who should be advocating reform, have posed one of the biggest obstacles. Far from embracing new ideas, teachers often feel threatened by them." The greatest resistance came from instructors Sizer had marked for extinction: coaches, counselors, and teachers of driving, health, home economics, and vocational education.[48]

Many students and parents also expressed reservations about Sizer's proposals. Opinion polls reported that, at least in most suburbs and smaller cities, most people were satisfied with their schools. "The students are happy taking subjects," Sizer admitted. "The parents are happy because that's what they did in high school." Larry Cuban, an education professor at Stanford, believed that Sizer had hit bulls-eyes on the shallowness of most schools, but Cuban also recognized that, "unfortunately," since most people liked their schools, "there is likely to be little fundamental change."[49]

---

47 *Washington Post* (25 March 1984).

48 *U.S. News & World Report* (26 February 1990) 50-55.

49 *Phi Delta Kappan* (October 1984); *Washington Post* (6 October 1985).

Despite the criticism, for a few years Sizer's plan for reforming high schools enjoyed an extraordinary vogue of popularity. After the publication of *Horace's Compromise* in 1984, Sizer organized a group called the Coalition of Essential Schools. The initial idea was to work with five or ten schools that would embrace Sizer's principles and become models for other educators who wanted students to become deeper, self-directed critical thinkers. By 1994, about 500 schools were affiliated with the coalition, and a reporter for the *Wall Street Journal* concluded, "Not since John Dewey . . . has one person's philosophy taken hold in so many classrooms." By the end of the 1990s, when more than 1000 schools were included in the network, the *Boston Globe* reported that Sizer loomed "as a giant on the American educational landscape." The editors of the *Providence Journal-Bulletin* opined that insofar as the field of education could be said to produce celebrities, "Mr. Sizer is most assuredly near the top of the list."[50]

Sizer's celebrity was due, in part, to his ability to engender admiration and devotion from a large number of fellow educators. His personality was frequently described as "inspirational" and "charismatic." With craggy good looks and a preference for tweed jackets, Sizer seemed the very personification of a benevolent Yankee schoolmaster. His Brahminesque elocution and ability to enliven conversations with vivid anecdotes doubtless added to his appeal. "Ted had a vision," one educator said. And he could "promote that vision as well as anybody I've ever seen." Another educator, a Jewish principal in New York City, said she had "great suspicion of New England WASPS from Harvard." But she nonetheless considered Sizer "one of the small number of people I've met in my life whom I can completely trust and respect."[51]

---

50 *Wall Street Journal* (28 December 1994); *Boston Globe* (19 September 1999); *Providence Journal-Bulletin* (1 January 1995).

51 Deborah Meier and Grant Wiggins, quoted in *Wall Street Journal* (28

Sizer also had a knack for raising money. During the decade after the publication of *Horace's Compromise* (1984), Sizer received about $100 million from education foundations and donors such as AT&T, Exxon, and Citicorp. Then, in 1994, the publisher Walter Annenberg gave $500 million to promote the reform of America's public schools. Fifty million went to Sizer's Coalition of Essential Schools, and the rest was earmarked for projects Sizer deemed worthy. Annenberg's gift was one of the largest in the history of educational philanthropy. It seemed to indicate that Annenberg considered the condition of U.S. schools dire but not hopeless. "This is an only-in-America story," wrote columnist David Broder. "The Annenberg fortune had its origins with his father, who used very tough tactics to make the Daily Racing Form the 'bible' for bettors at bookie joints and race tracks. The coins those gamblers placed in Annenberg's hands while looking for the usually mythical big payoff now come back to help rescue the institution with the best payoff record in American history—the public school system."[52]

With the money, Sizer established the Annenberg National Institute for School Reform at Brown University. Then he began to confer with educational organizations around the country. "I will be glad to give advice when asked," Sizer said. With a smile he noted that "long-lost professional acquaintances were calling, insisting that they had intended to call for months—and then hinting broadly that perhaps a portion of the Coalition's new fortune might tumble in their directions."[53]

Some people wondered if Sizer's model really was more effective than the traditional pattern of instruction, but there was

---

December 1994).

52 *New Orleans Times-Picayune* (22 December 1993).

53 *Boston Globe* (28 July 1998; 12 January 1994).

no doubt about the sort of schools that would share the largess. The Annenberg grant seemed to validate both the new-progressive version of educational reform and the "bottom up" approach that measured improvement on a small scale, school by school, rather than the "top down" method that held schools accountable for the performance of their students on nationally standardized exams. This point was important. According to Andrew Porter, the head of the Wisconsin Center for Education Research, "The big thing about the Annenberg grant is that it appears very much to be running to the opposite direction from . . . the U.S. Department of Education."[54]

Beginning in 1999, the Bill and Melinda Gates Foundation chipped in with additional grants that, by 2006, amounted to some $1.5 billion. Although the Gates grants did not go directly to Sizer or his Coalition, Gates consulted with Sizer and most of his grants were tailored to promote Sizer's principles. Like Sizer, Gates wanted to create "small learning communities" and "schools within schools." In particular, Gates created or converted some 1500 high schools into academies that enrolled about 400 students. The idea was that by cultivating a sense of community, educators could foster academic achievement and discourage students from dropping out of school. Tom Vander Ark, the executive director of the Gates Foundation, noted that 30 percent of the nation's high school freshmen were not graduating from secondary school, and among African-Americans the dropout rate was about 50 percent. If the U.S. was to continue to lead the world economically, Vander Ark told a Congressional committee, high schools had to be redesigned "to prepare *all* students for the 21st century."[55]

Bill Gates expanded on these points in a 2005 speech to the National Governors Association. Gates acknowledged that the best-educated young people in the United States were educated as well

---

54 *Boston Globe* (12 July 1998; 2 January 1994).

55 Statement of Tom Vander Ark, *Congressional Quarterly* (9 June 2005).

as any youths in the world, but he said that millions of American students were falling behind, not because of their race, poverty, or cultural values, but because their schools were old-fashioned. "Our high schools were designed 50 years ago to meet the needs of another age," Gates told the governors. By the year 2000, America's high schools had become "obsolete." "Until we design them to meet the needs of this century we will keep limiting, even ruining, the lives of millions of Americans every year." "In district after district," Gates said, "wealthy white kids are taught algebra . . . while low-income kids are taught how to balance a checkbook."[56]

Some observers believed that traditional schools were based on ideas that were "classist" if not racist. Thus Sandy Weil and John Ferrandino, the chairman and president, respectively, of the National Academy Foundation, maintained that American schools were "accomplishing exactly what they were designed to do." Earlier in the twentieth century, high schools had been planned with the expectation that many students would not graduate but would drop out and go into "the many unskilled and semi-skilled jobs of that time." Times had changed, however, and by the year 2000 the American economy was said to need larger numbers of workers who were broadly educated. A system that allowed so many of its teenagers to drop out of high school may have been sufficient for the Industrial Age. But no more, said Robert T. Jones, president and CEO of the National Business Alliance: "In today's labor market, we need 100%." "If we don't fix American education," Bill Gates declared, "I will not be able to hire [American] kids."[57]

Summarizing the ideas that supported the move toward smaller schools, the *Milwaukee Journal Sentinel* explained,

---

56 *Washington Post* (27 February 2005); *New York Times* (27 February 2005).

57 *London Financial Times* (1 June 2005); *Business Week* (21-28 August 2000) 190; *New York Times* (30 April 2005).

> [S]maller schools of 100 to 400 students give teachers and staff a chance to know every student and to develop ties that bind them together in a common learning community.... In the end, it's the culture of the classroom that counts the most. Schools... must ignite a passion for learning in their students. When fired with that passion all children have a better chance of academic success.

The *Portland Oregonian*, on the other hand, regarded such comments with skepticism:

> Two generations ago, the ideal high school was a factory. One generation ago, it was a shopping mall. Today the ideal is whatever the rich people will give us. Since about 2000, Microsoft founder Bill Gates has given us small. A billion dollars' worth of small.... His foundation seized on small high schools with the single-mindedness of a computer programmer, the relentlessness of an anti-trust lawyer, the fervor of an evangelist, and the checkbook of the richest man in the world. Educators stood in their pews and said, 'Amen, brother. Let's get small.'[58]

In the case of Manual High School in Denver, the *Oregonian*'s skepticism was warranted. Before the Gates Foundation intervened, Manual had enrolled 1100 students, 90 percent of whom were either Black or Hispanic. The dropout rate was about 50 percent, and scores on standardized tests were among the worst in Colorado. Then, with a million dollars from the Gates Foundation, reformers split the school into three smaller schools and instituted Sizer-style changes: interdisciplinary classes, exhibitions instead of examinations, and the expectation that students would take responsibility for their education. Electives such as choir, debate, and athletics were curtailed and advanced placement courses cut back. Many athletes, musicians, and college-bound students responded by transferring to other schools. After six years, Manual's enrollment declined to 580 students, and

---

58 *Milwaukee Journal Sentinel* (15 June 2006); *Portland Oregonian* (4 December 2005).

authorities decided to end the experiment and close the school. By then, one teacher said, "The only kids left were the hardest to educate."[59]

Skeptics were criticized for calling attention to the situation at Manual High. Gates deserved "an A for making the effort," one editor wrote, adding that there were other examples of "bona fide Gates successes." This was undoubtedly true. Between 2000 and 2006, the Gates Foundation gave more than $100 million to help create some 1500 small schools that enrolled more than 50,000 students. Some of the new schools in New York City reported that 70 percent of the students who began ninth grade four years earlier managed to graduate—a rate well above the city's overall graduation rate of 54 percent. These success stories received ample coverage in the nation's press, with one study reporting that there were 13 positive stories about educational reform for every critical assessment.[60]

Nevertheless, when the Gates Foundation hired outside groups to compare Gates-funded small schools with others in the same districts, the overall results were mixed. The Gates schools tended to be less violent and have higher attendance and graduation rates. But test scores were only slightly better in English and reading, with 35 percent of the small schools' students doing satisfactory work, compared with 33 percent at large high schools. The scores in mathematics were especially problematic: "only 16% of students at Gates schools made the grade . . . vs. 27% at traditional schools."[61]

Chastened by this experience, Gates acknowledged, "many of the small schools that we invested in did not improve students'

---

59 *Business Week* (26 June 2006) 64; Diane Ravitch, "Bill Gates: The Nation's Superintendent of Schools," *Los Angeles Times* (30 July 2006).

60 *Business Week* (10 July 2006) 92; Frederick Hess, "Inside the Gift Horse's Mouth," *Phi Delta Kappan* 87 (October 2005) 131-137.

61 Jay Greene and William C. Symonds, "Bill Gates Gets Schooled" *Business Week* (26 June 2006) 64.

achievement in any significant way." The Foundation then adjusted and, as historian Diane Ravitch noted, "apparently . . . recognized that curriculum (what students are taught) and instruction (the quality of teachers) may be no less important than school size." Some observers suggested that the poor math scores resulted from a lack of direct instruction and from an excess of group work. Jay Greene and William C. Symonds, for example, maintained, "the small-school goal of engaging students in projects that combined math with other subjects produced poor results because rigorous math instruction often got short shrift." Executives at the Gates Foundation conceded that it had been naïve to expect progress just because schools had been made smaller. "Today we are much more explicit about the curriculum," the director of the Foundation said in 2006.[62]

Eventually, the Gates Foundation shifted its emphasis to stress technology as well as to promote smallness. Thus the Gateses invested $17 million in an innovative charter school in San Diego, High Tech High. Technology was "infused throughout the curriculum," as most students worked on networked laptops and maintained digital portfolios. Some wrote poetry and novels, while others made documentary films. Following the advice of Ted Sizer, 50-minute classes were scrapped in favor of fewer classes that lasted far longer. Some students spent half the day in a class that blended English, social studies, and work on the environment. Most teachers were recruited from nontraditional backgrounds and, instead of using standard textbooks, encouraged students to work on projects that combined subjects like math, science, and history. Twelve seniors were sent to Baja California for eight weeks of work on various projects.[63]

---

62 *Ibid.*; Bill Gates, annual letter, 2009, GatesfFoundation.org; Diane Ravitch, "Bill Gates."

63 *Business Week* (26 June 2006) 64, (28 August 2000) 190; *Philadelphia Inquirer* (8 January 2006).

Meanwhile, after three years of planning, in 2006 the Gates Foundation opened another "school of the future." The gleaming white, modern facility looked out of place amid row houses in a working-class area of Philadelphia. Unlike its counterpart in San Diego (where 70 percent of the students were White or Asian), the students in Philadelphia were nearly all Hispanic or African-American and mainly low-income. Both schools were stocked with computers and interactive "smart boards" and were infused with management techniques that had been used at Microsoft.[64]

Optimists predicted success ahead, but others looked on with eyes grown weary from observing the failure of other expensive efforts to reform education. "The Gateses believe they have seen ... a return on the $17 million their foundation has sunk into San Diego's High Tech High," a story in *Business Week* noted. But "the experience there also underscores how difficult it is to duplicate success on a broad scale."[65]

Would "school reform" work? That was the question many observers posed with respect to the Gates grants and a number of institutions associated with Theodore Sizer's Coalition of Essential Schools. These schools were united by their adherence to Sizer's principles—small size, emphasis on depth of knowledge over breadth, and use of teachers as mentors and coaches rather than as knowledgeable authorities. As has been noted, the Coalition grew from only 12 schools in 1984 to more than 1000 by the end of the 1990s.

There remained what one New England newspaper called "the matter of the bottom line." Apart from attracting publicity and money, just how well did Sizer's Coalition succeed in the real world? According to a lengthy news story in the *Wall Street Journal*, the answer was "not very well." The *Journal* reported that five research studies—based

---

64 Ibid.

65 Ibid.

on visits, interviews, and questionnaires at more than two dozen coalition schools—found a state of disarray, with the previous order dismantled and nothing substantial in its place. "What you were left with, after our five years of studying, were a few teachers who were still continuing to try to do things in their individual classroom or in small teams, but very little schoolwide had changed," said Donna Muncey, an anthropologist who examined eight Coalitions schools. Samuel Stringfield, a Johns Hopkins University researcher who studied five schools in a different evaluation, also reached a negative conclusion: "For anyone to say that this is a reform that has been proven to work is simply not true." Some other assessments were more upbeat. Edward Ahnert, the director of the Exxon Education Foundation, reported that Coalition schools had created "a better learning climate, a more civil or humane environment, [and] better adult-student relations." Nevertheless, the *Providence Journal-Bulletin* grumbled, "We don't need multimillion dollar projects that, at best, make teachers and students feel better about being in school. What we really need are reforms that produce measurable improvements in academic performance. In this regard, there seems to be little evidence that, during its first ten years, the Coalition of Essential Schools project has helped much."[66]

Nevertheless, under the right circumstances, Sizer's approach did work. Two examples that Sizer frequently mentioned were Thayer High School in Winchester, New Hampshire, which was the first school to become an official member of Sizer's Coalition, and the Central Park East elementary and secondary schools in East Harlem, New York, which received a great deal of publicity in the New York press.

---

66 *Providence Journal-Bulletin* (1 January 1995); *Wall Street Journal* (28 December 1994). For a summary and commentary on the research studies of the Coalition schools, see Margaret M. MacMullan, "The Coalition of Essential Schools: A National Research Context," in Theodore Sizer, *Horace's Hope*, Appendix B, 160-176.

Before Dennis Littky became its principal in 1981, Thayer High had been a troubled school in an economically depressed area. Winchester had once been a bustling mill town, but plant closings in the 1960s and 1970s left many residents without jobs and the town with the highest welfare load in the region. The 330-student high school had a mixed reputation. The dropout rate was about 20 percent, high for a small school in a small town, and the proportion of graduates who went on to college was relatively low. But many of Winchester's 4000 residents did not wish to live anywhere else. "It's a poor town, but it's a good town," said the police chief. People walked to church. They were personally acquainted with the librarian, the postman, and the grocery store owner. The Pisgah Diner and Don's Barber Shop were comfortable centers for local gossip. And the support for Thayer High's basketball team was such that local fans flocked to the games like Texans to high school football. "There's a very strong sense of community in this town," one of the locals explained.[67]

Given this satisfaction, it was surprising that local authorities chose Dennis Littky as the principal of Thayer High. Winchester was a small town in a rural region, but Littky had grown up in Detroit before receiving a bachelor's degree and eventually a doctorate in education from the University of Michigan. His previous jobs had been in urban and suburban areas—as director of a reading program in New York City's controversial community-controlled schools of Ocean Hill-Brownsville and as the principal of a middle school on Long Island. In these venues, Littky had independently arrived at a philosophy of education similar to that of Theodore Sizer. As Sizer noted with approval, Littky abolished ability grouping at Thayer High and "assumed that everyone was college bound." The curriculum was narrowed and students were funneled into academic courses that

---

67 *New York Times* (27 April 1986); *Boston Globe* (26 January 1990; 13 December 1992); Susan Kammeraad-Campbell, *Doc: The Story of Dennis Littky and His Fight for a Better School* (Chicago: Contemporary Books, 1989) 7.

"emphasized problem solving over rote learning." The teachers taught in "grade level teams," and the students engaged in "individual and collective work."[68]

Littky arrived at Thayer three years before Sizer published *Horace's Compromise* and, like Sizer, wanted to break away from 50-minute classes and allow much longer periods for team teaching and interdisciplinary projects. He also insisted on a great degree of autonomy in hiring, so that he could fashion a teaching staff that was "pretty much together" on the direction the school should go. Believing students learned most when involved and excited about what they were doing, Littky wanted each pupil to follow a course of study that was tailored to his or her individual interests. "SAT scores mean nothing if individual students are not actively engaged in their own education, making decisions, taking responsibility," Littky said. "Thayer will never send the most kids to college or get the best test scores," but it was more important to teach youngsters to "learn to think and become decent human beings."[69]

At first, most things went well. The number of dropouts declined and a larger portion of the graduates went on to college. One sympathetic journalist wrote that Littky had transformed "a small, poor rural school from an educational basket case into a place where students and teachers seemed excited about what they were doing." Sizer was so impressed that he chose Thayer High in 1985 as the first school in the country to join the Coalition of Essential Schools. Noting that Littky brought students with him when he attended meetings, Sizer praised Littky especially for his "deep respect for youngsters."[70]

---

68 Susan Kammeraad-Campbell, *Doc, passim*; Theodore Sizer, *Horace's Hope*, 19-20.

69 Susan Kammeraad-Campbell, *Doc, passim*; *Christian Science Monitor*, (3 January 1985); *Boston Globe* (26 January 1990); *Newsweek* (25 May 1987) 76.

70 *Boston Globe* (26 January 1990); Susan Kammeraad-Campbell, *Doc*, 246.

Yet this rapport eventually became a problem. It was not just that Littky believed that building trust was facilitated by an informality that troubled some citizens of Winchester—and some did wonder about the practice of allowing students to call their principal "Doc" or "Dennis." Littky also sought to foster sympathetic relations by encouraging teachers and students to "share feelings." To this end, he permitted class discussions of homosexuality and birth control, and students in English were required to keep journals, with assurance that teachers would be non-judgmental and would not divulge the contents to anyone. Some students proceeded to record their innermost feelings about parents and siblings, while others discussed sexual matters, drinking alcohol, and smoking marijuana. One of the English teachers defended the practice, saying, "This is the one time when they can write without fear of somebody standing over them with a red pencil. I like them to explore, to clear their minds ... [and] sort out feelings."[71]

Some parents did not see it that way. Instead, they circulated a statement that demanded an end to such assignments and asserted that parents should make sure "that their children's beliefs and moral values are not undermined by the schools." One mother was appalled to find vomit and child murder among the topics discussed in her daughter's writing class. Another mother observed, "If a kid writes [in his or her journal], 'My mother's so mean. I hate my mother,' ... That's an invasion of family privacy, that's all there is to it." To make matters worse, this mother said, the teachers at Thayer High did not

---

> According to Littky, the dropout rate at Thayer High was "between 16 and 20 percent" in the years before he became principal, 1980-81. "The next year, 1981-82, we cut the rate in half, to about 8 percent, actually bringing back students that had dropped out in previous years." The rate stayed at about 8 percent in subsequent years. However, the *Keene Sentinal* noted that at 8.19 percent Thayer's dropout rate remained among the highest in New Hampshire. Susan Kammeraad-Campbell, *Doc*, 338.

71 Susan Kammeraad-Campbell, *Doc*, 310, 264.

care about what the students did to the English language. "It can be loaded with misspellings, bad grammar and punctuation, and the student can still receive a high mark."[72]

While Sizer and his Coalition supported Dennis Littky and his teachers, the protesting parents received encouragement from other outside groups, especially the Heritage Foundation and the Eagle Forum. According to Eagle founder Phyllis Schlafly, journal writing had "nothing whatever to do with developing the ability to read and write the English language." It entailed, rather, an unwarranted intrusion into "personal problems—family fights, divorces, deaths, drugs and alcohol, peer conflicts and love affairs...." Schlafly thought these topics should be off limits: "Most parents didn't authorize the school to pry into private family problems and affairs. Those are none of the school's business."[73]

The dispute over journal writing was just one aspect of a culture war that occurred in Winchester. There was, in addition, Littky's unconventional appearance. He was a small man whose graying beard and fringe of curly hair made him look like an aging hippie. "He's the highest-paid individual in town and, instead of setting a dignified example, he acts like a tramp," complained Elmer Johnson, a member of the state legislature. Littky's unconventional personal life led to still more complaints. As a young man, Littky had been married for three years, but thereafter he said he had "no time or desire for a family." Instead, in the words of an admiring biography, "he would have many more intense relationships with women, all of which would end after a few years when [Littky's] attention flagged...."[74]

---

72 *Ibid.*, 264; *Newsweek*, (25 May 1987) 76.

73 Susan Kammeraad-Campbell, *Doc*, 263, 338-39.

74 *Newsweek* (25 May 1987) 76; *Boston Globe* (26 January 1990); Susan Kammeraad-Campbell, *Doc*, 29.

Local residents complained that the principal was not setting a good moral example for students. In addition to living arrangements that some considered scandalous, Littky and other teachers were accused of allowing obscene musical lyrics to be blasted about the school's parking lot and of tolerating public petting and vulgar dancing at parties they chaperoned. There were additional complaints that students in one class had been required to view a film about a gay San Francisco activist, Harvey Milk, while students in another class had to write a story based on a Dear Abby letter concerning a girl who had endured years of incest with her father. In another course entitled "Life after Thayer," a course required of all seniors, students addressed questions such as whether gay males and females were equally prone to engage in "cruising" and whether homosexual men and women have more interest in sex than do heterosexuals.[75]

Most of all, some local people took exception to Littky's educational philosophy. Littky's style was "reminiscent of the experimentalism of the '70s—and that is what has exercized many townspeople," *Newsweek* observed. In London, the *Sunday Telegraph* similarly opined: "Littky's whole approach smacked of vintage Sixties drool—the sort of thing utopians on both sides of the Atlantic had been dreaming up for decades only to find that it was an infallible recipe for classroom anarchy."[76]

The National Broadcasting Company (NBC) eventually made a TV movie about Littky's sojourn in Winchester. Under the title "A Town Torn Apart," the film depicted a conflict that led the school board, by a vote of 3-1, to fire Littky in 1986. Believing that the situation in the public schools had deteriorated, board member Bobby Secord, who had been the 1967 prom king at Thayer High,

---

75   Susan Kammeraad-Campbell, *Doc*, 322, 353-54.

76   *New York Times* (27 April 1986); *Newsweek* (25 May 1987) 76; *Sunday Telegraph* (3 April 2005).

sent his own children to a Christian school. Board member Susan Winter said she wanted Thayer to "go back to the basics of reading, writing, and arithmetic." And Allen Barton, the third board member who voted against Littky, said the issue was "the philosophy of the modern education system." "I have no personal vendetta against [Littky]," Barton said. The problem was that Littky, "a modern educationist," would not provide a curriculum that was "structured enough" to satisfy Barton, an engineer.[77]

Littky and his supporters fought the firing. Their initial point was that the school board had violated his rights by firing him without a hearing. After reviewing the evidence, Judge George Manias ordered that a hearing be held and that Littky be allowed to keep his job until then. After such a hearing the board had the right to remove him, as long as it provided a reason that was not arbitrary or capricious. Deciding that Littky was "too progressive" probably would have sufficed, but before the hearing was held there was another school board election, which turned out to be too close to call even after two recounts. Finally, in yet another election, Littky's supporters got the upper hand, rescinded the firing, and he remained principal of Thayer High for eight more years. In the meantime, Winchester had been split apart as cousin turned against cousin.[78]

As many newspapers told the story, the turmoil in Winchester was a familiar tale of provincials resisting change. Readers were given to understand that Littky's reforms had improved Thayer High School and that objections were either frivolous, the result of a dogged determination to stand athwart history, or perhaps a product of repressed sexuality. Thus, after noting that the dropout rate at Thayer had declined while more graduates went on to college,

---

77 *Boston Globe* (13 December 1992); *Newsweek* (25 May 1987) 76; Susan Kammeraad-Campbell, *Doc*, 306, 318-20.

78 Susan Kameraad-Campbell, *Doc*, chapters 23 and 24.

Newsweek asked, "So why is the school board trying to fire Dennis Littky?" Answering its own question, *Newsweek* opined that the battle in Winchester was "mostly . . . a clash between old and new values." The magazine quoted one of Littky's critics, a man who lived "in the same farmhouse he was born in 67 years ago," as saying, "Us old-timers resent liberal newcomers coming in and telling us how backwards we are." *The Boston Globe* similarly declared, "old-timers in Winchester see their town changing. And they don't like what they see. . . . They are used to doing things the way they have always been done." For his part, Littky was less charitable. When asked why he "got fired, after completely turning the school around and making it a wonderful place," Littky said: "[It was] because real education is a subversive act. It empowers the child."[79]

Whatever the interpretation, the controversy was good for Littky's career. After learning about the situation in Winchester, other school administrators made telephone calls asking for advice, and Littky regularly received job offers for much more than his salary in New Hampshire. Nevertheless, Littky remained at Thayer High until 1994, when he headed for Asia with nothing in mind. After a hiatus of several months, he returned to work on school reform as the first resident fellow at the Annenberg Institute that Theodore Sizer had established on the campus of Brown University. From there, Littky was recruited to establish a nontraditional public vocational school in Providence, Rhode Island.[80]

Because of the changing job market, Rhode Island's educational commissioner, Peter McWalters, thought there was no longer a need for traditional vocational schools. So in 1997, he invited Littky to develop a different kind of program. Littky then fashioned a curriculum for

---

79 *Newsweek* (25 May 1987) 76; *Boston Globe* (24 June 1990); *Sunday Oregonian* (29 November 1992).

80 *Boston Globe* (13 December 1992; 26 January 1990; 20 February 2000).

what was called the Met School. It called for students to spend two days a week working as interns at local enterprises and for schoolwork to be individually tailored and to revolve around projects that pertained to student interests. Instead of formal lessons, students would discuss current issues and affairs. "There would be no classrooms, no formal lessons, no bells, no grades, no uniforms, no detentions—and no teachers, at least not in the accepted sense of the word." Most of all, there would be no textbooks. "I think textbooks are the most boring things in the world," Littky said. "I would much rather my students read a historical novel than some dreary list of facts and figures. Or better still, went out and discovered things for themselves."[81]

Littky's Met School was popular with students in Providence. Within a year, more than 580 people were enrolled. About 70 percent were either Black or Hispanic, and more than 80 percent came from low-income families and qualified for federal meal subsidies. Upon enrolling, these students, on average, trailed three years below the norm in literacy skills. But they rarely skipped school, and after four years more than three-quarters of them decided to give college a try.[82]

Some skeptics believed the Met students became "engaged" because they were not required to do any academic work. But by 2005, with funding from the Gates Foundation, some two-dozen schools around the country had been modeled on the Met, and more were in the works. The cloning was organized by a Gates-funded corporation, the Big Picture Company, where Littky was employed as an executive. Littky also explained the venture in a book, *The Big Picture: Education Is Everyone's Business* (2004).[83]

---

81   *London Sunday Telegraph* (3 April 2005).

82   Ibid.; *Washington Post* (28 September 2004).

83   *Newsweek* (16 May 2005) 58; Dennis Littky, *The Big Picture: Education is Everyone's Business* (Alexandria: Association for Supervision and Curriculum Development, 2004).

Meanwhile, back at Thayer High School, there was still more change. After Littky left, the school returned to a more traditional curriculum. But that lasted for only a few years. In 2005 Thayer High was closed, and its 350 students were bused some 20 miles to a comprehensive high school in Keene, New Hampshire. Many longtime residents of Winchester opposed the change, believing that community spirit would decline if there were no basketball games in the winter and no prom in the spring. Others, however, said the move would save taxpayers money, and some predicted that students would benefit from the greater variety of courses, especially advanced placement courses, that would be available at a school whose enrollment was five times greater than that at old Thayer High.[84]

Theodore Sizer's approach to education was also implemented in New York City, in East Harlem, where Deborah Meier established the Central Park East Schools. Like Sizer, Meier was educated at elite private schools. In her case it was the Fieldston School in the Riverdale section of the Bronx, followed by undergraduate studies at Antioch College and graduate work at the University of Chicago. And like many women who were born in the 1930s, Meier married when she was young, at the age of 20, and before long she was the mother of three children. She then found part-time work as a kindergarten teacher in Chicago—not because she wanted a career in education but to pay for housekeeping and to allow enough time for activities connected with the civil rights movement. "I had absolutely no intention of becoming a teacher," Meier recalled, "but then I became fascinated, hooked for good." After returning to New York in 1966, Meier began to work full time in elementary schools that were testing what came to be known

---

84 Telephone interview with Carol Howe (1 May 2007).

as "open education." She was known as an innovative educator who developed a personalized approach to teaching.[85]

Meier eventually came to the attention of Anthony Alvarado, the superintendent of public schools in District Four, which encompassed Harlem. Alvarado was eager to try different approaches to deal with a difficult situation. In the early 1970s, only 16 percent of the children in the district were reading at or above grade level. On an average day, only 44 percent of the enrolled students attended classes at Benjamin Franklin High School. And less than 10 percent of the students who enrolled in ninth grade were graduating from the high school four years later. Alvarado asked Meier to start an alternative school that might serve as a model for better education.[86]

Meier then established the Central Park East Elementary School. Beginning with just 32 students in the fall of 1974, the school was originally housed in a wing of a larger school building. The enrollment increased quickly, and within a few years there were three Central Park East Elementary Schools, each with an enrollment of about 400 students. By the mid-1990s about 50 schools in metropolitan New York were based on the principles of Central Park East.[87]

Like Dennis Littky and Theodore Sizer, Meir believed enrollments should remain small to allow for the personalization and interaction that she considered necessary for effective education. In addition, Meier never forgot that she began her career teaching kindergarten, and she retained a deep commitment to using informal methods of instruction. When she was asked to establish an

---

85 *Current Biography* (May 2006) 67-75; *New York Times* (16 June 1987); *Washington Post* (7 September 1994).

86 Seymour Fliegel, *Miracle in East Harlem* (New York: Times Books, 1993) 31.

87 Ibid., 36; *New York Times* (27 June 1995).

elementary school, she recalled, "we decided to build it around the simple proposition that children between the ages of 5 and 12 could best be educated in a school that sought to prolong kindergarten for six more years." Later, when Meier established the Central Park East Secondary School, a school that enrolled students in grades 7 through 12, the purpose was "to hold on to our kindergarten philosophy for another six years."[88]

"If we could keep the kindergarten mentality going all the way through [high] school," Meier said, it would be more likely that students would "feel confident that nothing, or very little anyway, was beyond their capacities." Thus the Central Park East schools focused on making school interesting and on "keeping students . . . more involved in decision making." Instead of comparing students with one another or with national norms, there were no grades and as few standardized exams as higher authorities would allow. There were no textbooks, except in math; classes were scheduled for two-hour time blocks, and students worked cooperatively on various projects— studying snails in science, the history and architecture of New York City in social studies. The curriculum was designed to instill "a good deal of self-confidence in [the students'] basic capacities as learners." In addition, as at other progressive schools, "children at CPE [Central Park East] were not simply presented with a set of facts to learn." Meier's concern was with "how students become critical thinkers and problem solvers."[89]

Meier recognized that graduates of her schools "might not be quite as well prepared" for high school or college as students who had received a more traditional education. Nevertheless, she insisted, "if we had stayed with the traditional curriculum, many [students] would

---

88 Deborah Meier, "Supposing That ..." *Phi Delta Kappan* (December 1996) 271-276.

89 Ibid., 273, 272; Seymour Fliegel, *Miracle in East Harlem* 41.

never have gotten a shot at being in a college. . . . They would have dropped out along the way." As proof of the success of her approach, Meier frequently mentioned the numbers "ninety and ninety." Ninety percent of the freshmen who matriculated at CPE's secondary school graduated from high school four years later. And ninety percent of the graduates went on to attend a college. For Meier, attending college was of key importance because "most of the good technical jobs require students who also could get into college." This was not because most jobs required mastery of any particular skills or bodies of knowledge, Meier implied. It was because employers were screening potential employees on the basis of whether they had attended (or graduated from) college.[90]

When it came to graduating from high school and continuing on to college, the record at CPE was extraordinary—especially when one considered that, as Meier observed, the enrollment in her schools was "about 40% Hispanic, 45% African-American, and 15% other (Asian and white)." More than two-thirds of the students were "poor enough to be eligible for free or reduced-price lunches, and at least 20% [were] labeled as 'special ed' or 'handicapped.'" When it came to keeping students in school, and moving them on toward college, few New York schools with similar demographics could match the record of CPE.[91]

Because of this success, Meier was widely regarded as a leading school reformer. According to Jerome Murphy, the Dean of Harvard's School of Education, Meier became "a legend because when everybody was saying it was impossible for urban schools to make much progress, she was doing it." Her status was confirmed in 1987

---

90 Ibid, 273-274; Deborah Meier, "How Our Schools Could Be," *Phi Delta Kappan* (January 1995)

371-372; "Interview with Deborah Meier," *Techniques* 72 (February 1997) 30-35; Deborah Meier, "Supposing That . . ." 273-74.

91 Deborah Meier, "How Our Schools Could Be," 372.

when the MacArthur Foundation recognized Meier with one of its "genius" grants, the first one ever conferred on a teacher. Writing in the *Washington Post*, education writer Jay Mathews hailed Meier as "one of the best-known and most celebrated educators in the country." She was a "teacher who threw away the book" and "tore down the walls standing in the way of learning." In the *New York Times*, another education writer, Sara Mosle, also praised Meier for designing a "school experiment that actually works" in a city whose schools were widely regarded as a collection of cracked-window disasters. Meier's reputation was burnished still more between 1990 and 1995 when the Annenberg Foundation, acting on the recommendation of Theodore Sizer, gave New York City some $50 million to create more schools like Meier's.[92]

Although Meier became one of the saints of school reform, she had her share of detractors. Seymour Fliegel, an administrator in the school board hierarchy has written that some Hispanic and African-American parents expressed misgivings "about having their children's education controlled by 'a white Jewish lady.'" Some others were concerned about Meier's philosophy of education. They may not have known what Meier was getting at when she said she did not share E. D. Hirsch's "notion about what it means to be educated." But they understood that students at CPE did not spend time learning the sort of information that was conveyed in many other schools. Some parents were also dismayed when Meier said it was a mistake to "spend years teaching paper-and-pencil arithmetic" when calculators were readily available. Nor did they accept Meier's explanation: that "we don't keep a horse and carriage in our garage just in case our car breaks down." Seymour Fliegel went to the parents and told them "in the nicest possible way that even though some of their complaints were true, they were far outweighed by the fact that [CPE] was a

---

92 *New York Times* (13 January 1999; 28 May 1995); *Washington Post* (7 September 1994).

really good place for kids." Nevertheless, when Fliegel offered critics the option of transferring their children to another school of their choice, fifteen families left CPE.[93]

Sometimes it was hard to disentangle the motives of Meier's critics. According to Seymour Fliegel, much of the opposition stemmed from the fact that Meier was "white, female, and Jewish." But critics seldom expressed this objection openly. Instead, "they attacked Meier's methods . . . they claimed not to understand open education. They objected to a hands-on, 'search and discovery' approach to learning, which they called 'play.' Basically, they favored a return to a more conventional classroom situation, where the teacher stood at the front of the class and lectured the students."[94]

Additional criticism came from educators who thought it was not enough for Meier to cite statistics on dropouts and college attendance. Writing in *The Journal of Negro Education*, Herbert Walberg noted that there was "no hard evidence" as to what the students at CPE had actually learned. According to Walberg, this was the inevitable result of using portfolios and exhibitions (whose assessments were inevitably subjective, all the more so because the assessments were conducted by the students' own teachers and peers). It would have been better, Walberg implied, to give standardized tests that compared Meier's students with those who attended other schools. Abigail Thernstrom similarly took exception to Meier's contention that outsiders should trust her and other teachers to determine whether the schools were succeeding. As it happened, Thernstrom noted, Meier's students performed below the statewide

---

[93] Seymour Fliegel, *Miracle in East Harlem*, 33-40; Deborah Meier, *The Power of Their Ideas* (Boston: Beacon Press, 1995) 81, 166; Marge Scherer, "On Schools Where Students Want to Be: A Conversation with Deborah Meier," *Educational Leadership* (September 1994) 4-8.

[94] Seymour Fliegel, *Miracle in East Harlem*, 139.

average on one of the few standardized tests that were administered. However, a comparison with other schools that enrolled students with similar demographics probably would have shown that CPE was doing well.[95]

Other critics challenged one of Meier's basic assumptions. Writing in the *Wall Street Journal,* Charles Murray said it was utopian to assume that, as Meier once put it, "every citizen is capable of the kind of intellectual competence previously attained by only a small minority." After all, Murray noted, "half of all children are below average in intelligence." Some could not understand "an exposition written beyond a limited level of complexity," and only a few had what it took to understand the arguments in scientific journals. Fortunately, however, youngsters who attended traditional vocational schools could make a good living. While conceding that some employers used attendance at college as "a screening device," Murray pointed to a tremendous increase in the demand for craftsmen. "Finding a good carpenter, painter, electrician, plumber, glazier, mason—the list goes on and on—is difficult, and it is a seller's market. Journeymen craftsmen routinely make incomes in the top half of the income distribution while master craftsmen can make six figures." Murray's implication was clear. He thought Meier would have served many students better if she had encouraged them to train for a skilled vocation rather than to pursue a liberal arts education.[96]

Meier did not refute the criticisms, but her schools survived. It helped that, as one article in the *New York Times* noted, "Meier and company ... stayed away from hot-topic debates." Unlike Dennis Littky in New Hampshire, Meier and her colleagues at CPE did not

---

[95] *Journal of Negro Education* 65 (Winter 1996) 93-95; Deborah Meier, *Will Standards Save Public Education* (Boston: Beacon Press, 2000) 35-39.

[96] Deborah Meier, *The Power of Their Ideas*, 4; *Wall Street Journal* (16, 17, 21 January 2007).

get involved in what the *Times* called "culture wars." Although Meier frequently wrote for left-wing magazines and journals like *The Nation* and *Dissent*, she understood that it was "not only the Right that's queasy about early sexual activity, or even early explicit talk about it." "There are progressives like me who are not in favor of sex for the young, even *with* condoms. There are liberals who feel as passionately as conservatives when schools insensitively expose children to threatening issues."[97]

School choice was another key to Meier's success. She knew that in the 1950s some segregationists had favored choice as a way to escape desegregation. She understood that in more recent decades many people worried that choice, even if occasionally beneficial, would become a method for creating elite public schools that would increase the distance between the haves and have-nots and that might ultimately undermine public education. But Meier also recognized that by the 1970s it was only the poor who lacked choice in most urban areas, since people with money already could afford to move to the suburbs or to send their children to private schools. Most of all, Meier recognized that choice was a necessary prerequisite for schools like CPE. She knew that students (or parents) who did not like her approach to education could transfer to other New York schools. In Harlem, many of these schools remained quite traditional, with one adopting the "core knowledge" program of E. D. Hirsch. Others focused on subjects like science or music. Thus, from the outset, CPE was able to enroll only students who chose to be there. In the words of union leader Albert Shanker, "Debbie screens applicants. Students must come with their parents for an interview, and they must agree to do the work."[98]

---

97   *New York Times* (28 May 1995); Deborah Meier, *The Power of their Ideas*, 82.

98   Deborah Meier, *The Power of Their Ideas*, 97, 93; *Boston Globe* (2 January 1994).

Because CPE eschewed the culture war, and because New York City allowed for choice in schools, Meier avoided the sort of controversy that engulfed Dennis Littky in New Hampshire. Nevertheless, choice was a double-edged sword. Because Meier screened the students (and also because her schools avoided standardized tests whenever possible), observers generally believed that Central Park East was not a model for reforming all of education. Even if the demographics of CPE students were matched with those at a regular public school, the comparison broke down because no students attended CPE simply because they had been assigned to the school.

For 20 years, from the inception of CPE in 1974 into the early 1990s, city-wide school administrators touted smaller schools as crucial to improving education throughout New York City, especially the high schools, where less than half of all students graduated in four years. By offering an antidote to the alienation and anonymity that allegedly beset large comprehensive schools, supporters said, smaller schools pointed the way to better schools for all. Yet by the 1990s the success of a few thousand carefully selected CPE students seemed inconsequential in a school system that had enrolled literally millions of students over the same period. The success of CPE was also tarnished when critics noted that, thanks to grants from the Annenberg Foundation and other philanthropies, CPE was funded more generously than other schools in New York. The future of Meier's schools was also jeopardized when it was learned that Meier had overspent her budgets, if only slightly, and when CPE's most influential supporter in the central school administration, Anthony Alvarado, was found guilty of serious financial improprieties.[99]

Finally, in the mid-1990s, Chancellor Rudy Crew, the top education administrator in New York City, deemphasized the

---

99 For discussion of these financial matters, see Seymour Fliegel, *Miracle in East Harlem*, chapters 10 and 11.

importance of small, alternative schools. Crew's critics said he wanted to centralize things. Crew, however, insisted that the advantages of small schools had been exaggerated, and he expressed concern about the extent to which CPE relied on foundation grants and on the leadership of an extraordinary individual. According to Crew, one problem was that CPE was "so totally dependent upon . . . external resources," the likes of which were not available throughout the school system. Another problem stemmed from over-reliance on charismatic leaders, "maybe a principal . . . or a teacher." For one reason or another, Crew thought it unlikely that CPE (or other small schools) could be "brought to scale." That was a bureaucratic way of saying that, however much Deborah Meier might succeed with a few individual schools, Crew did not regard CPE as a model that could be expanded to improve education throughout New York City.[100]

To achieve the larger goal, Crew turned to standardized testing. While Meier had been developing small schools during the 1970s and 1980s, spending for public education increased throughout the United States. Unfortunately, academic achievement (as measured by performance on standardized tests) did not change much, and there were especially problematical gaps in the achievement of different demographic groups. In response, by the 1990s a new trend emerged among educational reformers. Increasingly, there were demands that schools and teachers should be held accountable for the performance of their students. A new wave of reformers believed there was (or should be) a consensus about what students should know and that educators should be rewarded or punished according to how students performed on standardized tests.

Meier rejected the idea that standardized tests could determine if students had been well educated. She continued to insist that certain

---

100 Frank J. Macchiarola, "Giuliani Is Half Right on Schools," *New York Times* (17 August 1995); Sol Stern, "Rudy, We Hardly Knew Ye," *New York Daily News* (5 December 1999); *New York Times* (13 October 1997).

habits of mind ("caring and compassion," "empathy and skepticism") were just as important as skill in reading and math. But in the 1990s she understood that "given the current climate of standardized testing" her approach was cutting "against the grain." In 1997, at the age of 66, Meier left New York for Boston, where she established another small school, the Mission Hill School, which was located in a Black neighborhood and enrolled 180 students from kindergarten through eighth grade. Meier said she was for "high standards" but "not for standardization." "I'm not in favor of more multiple-choice tests, or important decisions being made using only one instrument—while ignoring the input of the teachers who know these kids.... There is no evidence that standardization produces more equality. This is a lazy and cheap way of trying to provide equity."[101]

Like Deborah Meier, Theodore Sizer was pro-choice. In an article published in 1968, he proposed that government agencies "give money *directly* to poor children (through their parents) to assist in paying for their education." At that time, most liberals considered "voucher " a vile word. Some even regarded the concept as "a tactic for capturing public education for the private/religious and for-profit sectors." Sizer, however, believed the idea deserved better. He noted that in the 1950s the G.I. Bill had allowed him to attend a private university, Harvard. "If this governmental device worked for me," he wrote, why not for poor students? After the G.I. program ended, wealthier parents could still educate their children wherever they chose. They had the wherewithal to buy houses in whatever

---

101 Mitchell Bogen, "An Interview with Deborah Meier," *Reclaiming Children and Youth* 10 (Spring 2001) 50; *Newsweek* (12 June 2000) 79; *Current Biography Yearbook 2006*, 371-374.

neighborhood they selected, often on the basis of the reputation of the local public schools. And if they were not satisfied with the public schools, they could afford to patronize private schools. "If this works well for wealthier folks," Sizer asked, "why not for everybody?" In addition, Sizer recognized that children differed. He believed that many would benefit from his approach, but he also knew that some others would do better in more structured, traditional schools.[102]

Eventually, Sizer received the opportunity to practice what he had been preaching. The opportunity arose in 1996, when a group of parents persuaded Sizer and his wife to become co-principals of the Francis W. Parker Charter School in Ayer, Massachusetts. When the Sizers gave up the reins three years later (when Theodore Sizer reached age 67), the school enrolled 360 students whose scores on the Massachusetts Comprehensive Assessment System tests were among the highest in the state. Despite this good showing, Sizer expressed reservations, saying the test did not measure "a lot of things we care about." He also complained that the school had been disrupted for the three weeks it took to administer the exams. "You wonder what you could have done with the time," Sizer said.[103]

As was to be expected, the Parker school corresponded to the popular conception of progressive education, Sizer-style. The school did not have a football team, there was no cafeteria, and Spanish was the only foreign language. There were no formal classes, but students worked on projects while teachers held counseling sessions. The faculty did not give letter grades, and students were not assigned to traditional classes. Instead, they were grouped in one of three divisions, through which they progressed after demonstrating mastery in a public exhibition.[104]

---

[102] Theodore Sizer and Phillip Whitten, "A Proposal for a Poor Children's Bill of Rights," *Psychology Today* (August 1968) 59-63; Sizer, *The Red Pencil*, 80-84.

[103] *Worcester Telegram & Gazette* (6 July 1999); *Boston Globe* (10 January 1999).

[104] James Traub, "Sizer's Hope," *New York Times* (2 August 1998).

Sizer readily acknowledged that his school was not right for every student. "That's why Parker is a school of choice," he said, "not a comprehensive school." Some students thrived at Parker, but others missed their former schoolmates and felt uncomfortable with new, progressive routines. "There are four children in my carpool," said one mother, Janet Bumpus. "Two of them, who did not like their previous schools, are delighted with [Parker], the other two, who enjoyed their former schools, are not quite as sure." As it happened, Bumpus's son, Brad, dropped out of Parker after one year. "The traditional education system is what he is comfortable with," his mother explained with regret. "He has been accustomed to a . . . structured setting."[105]

While recognizing that students varied individually, Sizer did not believe that educational approaches should vary according to ethnicity or social class. Many critics, however, said that Sizer's methods of schooling for understanding and depth worked well only with youngsters whose family travels and dinner table conversations had exposed them to a broader education at home. For other students, the critics said, structured schools were better. The critics would come to the fore during the first decade of the 21st century, as more people came to recognize that the racial and ethnic achievement gaps were as large as ever. As elected officials placed more emphasis on educating disadvantaged youths, Sizer's theories began to seem out-of-date. Some critics even blamed progressive education for the fact that non-Asian minority groups were, on average, doing poorly in school. These critics said that progressives were so concerned with creativity and critical thinking that they failed to teach the basics of reading, writing, and arithmetic.[106]

Thus Sizer's influence waned as policymakers emphasized student testing and the schools' and the teachers' responsibility for test scores. In 1997 more than 1,000 schools were affiliated with Sizer's

---

105 *Boston Globe* (8 October 1995; 16 June 1996).

106 For an example, see Nathan Glazer, "Back to Schools," *New Republic* (10 August 1998) 11.

Coalition of Essential Schools, but by 2010 only 150 remained as dues-paying members of the Coalition. Sizer acknowledged that he was "disappointed that we haven't gotten more traction," and it came as no surprise when he opposed the No Child Left Behind law of 2001, saying that it relied too heavily on test scores. When Sizer died in 2009, Lewis Cohen, the director of the Coalition of Essential Schools, conceded that Sizer's ideas "were not compatible with the current vernacular of standardization and testing."[107]

By the end of his life, Sizer had become passé. Nevertheless, he had once been a great visionary. From about 1970 to 2000, Theodore Sizer was, as Howard Gardner has put it, "the most articulate, most forceful, and most convincing voice for American progressive education."[108]

---

107 Theodore Sizer and Lewis Cohen, quoted by Debra Viader, "Sizer's Legacy," *Education Week* (23 October 2009; updated 8 May 2010).

108 Howard Gardner, quoted by Bryan Marquard, "Theodore Sizer: Leader in Effort to Overhaul Education," *Boston Globe* (25 October 2009).

Part II

Back To Basics

4

Chris Whittle and the Edison Schools

With his Edison Schools, Chris Whittle offered an approach to education that was at once innovative and old-fashioned. The Edison Schools were privately managed, operated for profit, and up to speed with the latest technology. But they also emphasized a back-to-basics curriculum.

Whittle was born in 1947 and reared in a small town, Etowah, Tennessee. Together with some fellow students at the University of Tennessee, in 1968 Whittle began publishing *Knoxville in a Nutshell*, a guide to the college town. The section on dining recommended 30 restaurants—all advertisers—and other sections gave information about prices and advice about clothing, entertainment, and other services. Impressed by the amount of paid advertising, an economics professor provided $100,000 to bankroll the publication of similar *Nutshells* for other universities. The first spinoff was at the University of Kansas in Lawrence (*Lawrence in a Nutshell*), and soon there were still more *Nutshells* that were stocked with a combination of information, advertising, and advice. After that there were additional guides for students interested in travel, music, cameras, careers, and other matters—all published by "13-30," a publishing corporation that took its name from the age of the intended audience. By 1977, the annual sales amounted to more than $5 million, and Whittle and two partners became millionaires when they sold a one-half interest in 13-30 to the Bonnier Group of Stockholm, Sweden, for $3.2 million.[1]

Whittle did not rest with $1 million. With his college pal and 13-30 partner, Philip Moffitt, Whittle bought a venerable but financially-troubled New York magazine, *Esquire*. In the 1930s and 1940s *Esquire* had been linked with urbane sophistication, but circulation declined during the 1970s and advertisers found other places to spend their money. By 1979 the owners of the magazine were ready to sell, and Whittle and Moffitt, flush with money from the Bonnier deal, were convinced that they had what it took to save *Esquire*. With support from their new Swedish partner, Whittle and Moffit bought the magazine for $3.5 million and an agreement to assume the magazine's debts of about $7 million. The sale came as a surprise to *Esquire*'s editor, Clay Felker. "I didn't even know negotiations were going on," Felker told reporters, "and all of a sudden I hear I'm going to lose my magazine to two guys who arrive out of the blue from Knoxville." *Esquire*'s national editor, Richard Reeves, blurted out, "I've never heard of these people. They could have landed from Mars."[2]

Despite their youth and limited experience, Whittle and Moffitt turned *Esquire* around. By the early 1980s the magazine was making a profit, and in 1986 Whittle sold his interest in the venture to Moffitt for $10 million. Seven years later, after selling *Esquire* to Hearst Publications for $80 million, Moffitt bought a beautiful house on the California coast and set off on a new career as a writer and photographer.[3]

---

1   Vance H. Trimble, *An Empire Undone: The Wild Rise and Hard Fall of Chris Whittle* (New York: Carol Publishing Group, 1995) *passim*; N. R. Klinefield, "In Search of the Next Medium," *New York Times* (19 March 1989).

2   Vance Trimble, *An Empire Undone*, 145, 146, 152.

3   Ibid., 200.

In the meantime Whittle returned to Knoxville and to 13-30, where he employed several hundred people who annually produced about $75 million worth of niche magazines for airlines and doctors' waiting rooms. In what some critics considered an ostentatious celebration of his wealth, in 1988 Whittle began to build "Historic Whittlesburg," a monumental two square block headquarters for 13-30, which was renamed Whittle Communications. The architecture was Georgian, and the buildings, which cost somewhere between $50 million and $70 million, resembled a college campus. Yet the expense was not a problem, for Whittle had sold half interest in his company to Time Warner for $185 million, $40 million of which went to Whittle personally.[4]

Along the way, Whittle acquired a taste for lavish living. He became an art collector with "a level of taste that stamped him more as a connoisseur, a modern-day Medici, than as a vulgar consumer." To refurbish his 10-room apartment in New York (and later a 12-room town house there), Whittle employed Peter Marino, a decorator who specialized in providing opulent settings for exceptionally wealthy people. Whittle also bought a 16-acre estate on Long Island, and he leased not one but two company jets, an annual expense of several million dollars.[5]

To support this lifestyle, Whittle developed additional niche magazines and a major new venture called Channel One. After hearing teachers say that most students "don't pay attention to the news" and "don't know what is going on," Whittle produced a news show for high school students in their morning homerooms. To make the news more appealing to this audience, Whittle featured teenage reporters and familiar television stars. To make a profit, he included two minutes of commercials with each ten minutes of current events programming.

---

4   Ibid., *passim*.

5   James B. Stewart, "Grand Illusion," *New Yorker* (31 October 1994) 66, 72.

As it happened, advertisers were willing to pay network-level rates to reach teenage consumers who could not change the channel.[6]

Channel One was controversial when it began in 1989, as debate raged over the propriety of allowing advertising in America's classrooms. But Whittle promoted Channel One by giving schools free television sets and other audiovisual equipment. At a time when satellite dishes were still quite large, Channel One placed them on 12,000 school buildings, installed 300,000 TVs in classrooms, and laid thousands of miles of cable within school buildings. Within three years, 40 percent of all American middle schools and high schools had signed on to the program, and 8 million teenagers were watching Channel One every day. Advertising went from zero to $80 million a year, about $30 million of which was profit. Some of the money was used to cover the cost of the initial investment in electronic equipment, but the net profit was such that in 1994 Whittle was able to sell Channel One to Primedia for $250 million. The sale was another coup for Whittle, although it turned out to be disappointing for the new owners. The size of Channel One's audience remained about the same for the next decade, and advertising revenues declined in the wake of complaints about subjecting a captive audience of teenagers to advertisements for junk food and expensive sneakers.[7]

In the course of developing Channel One, Whittle had met with many school boards and had attended numerous conferences on education. Then, while he was basking in the success of his sale of

---

6   Vance Trimble, *An Empire Undone*, 207 and *passim*.

7   Chris Whittle, *Crash Course* (New York: Riverhead Books, 2005), 64-66; Russ Baker, "Conservatives Clash Over Advertising in Schools," *The New Republic* (22 October 1999) 22 [noting that while much of the criticism came from liberal critics of commercialism, some conservatives also had complaints—about advertisements for violent movies and reports that seemed to promote the legalization of drugs]; Claire Atkinson, "Channel One Hits Bump," *Advertising Age* 76 (4 March 2005) 3.

Channel One, the Business Roundtable of Tennessee asked Whittle to speak, not about Channel One but about education in general. Specifically, the Roundtable asked Whittle what he would do to improve America's schools. "I'd start over," Whittle replied. "I'd make it a business." "When [Thomas] Edison invented electric illumination, he didn't tinker with candles to make them burn better. Instead he created something entirely new: the light bulb. In the same fashion American education needs a fundamental breakthrough, a new dynamic that will light the way to a transformed educational system."[8]

As Whittle saw it, education was "America's last great cottage industry." Most local enterprises had been nationalized over the course of the twentieth century, as grocery stores affiliated with national chains, while national retailers came to dominate the malls and local hardware stores struggled to compete against Home Depot and Lowe's. Almost everywhere except education, the efficiencies associated with big business and professional management had compelled fragmented local enterprises to consolidate. Whittle said the time had come for education to follow suit. He said "the power of scale" would enable reorganized schools to benefit from research and development. He estimated that most successful corporations spent between 2 and 6 percent of their total revenue on "R&D," but school districts either "don't have R&D budgets, or in those few cases where they do, the budgets are microscopically small in the scheme of serious R&D." School districts did not have anything equivalent to the test tracks of the leading automobile companies. They had nothing comparable to the research parks that pharmaceutical companies established to develop new drugs or to the Bell Labs that stimulated innovation in telecommunications.[9]

---

8 *New York Times* (19 January 1994); Vance Trimble, *An Empire Undone*, 262-63.

9 Chris Whittle, *Crash Course*, 28, 31, 29, 3.

Believing that Whittle had what it took to reform and reorganize education, many people urged the young entrepreneur to take over at least some of the nation's public schools. Four state governors were especially supportive in this respect: Lamar Alexander of Tennessee, George W. Bush of Texas, Tom Ridge of Pennsylvania, and William Weld of Massachusetts. Venture capitalists and investors also became enchanted with the prospect, "lured by presentations from Merrill Lynch, an early Whittle-backer, that spoke of an inefficient secondary-education industry that spent $1 billion a day, only half—half!—of which was spent directly on education."[10]

The idea that public schools were operating inefficiently found support in the research of economists and social scientists who reported that the average expenditure per public school student had doubled since the 1960s, but the average scores on several tests had actually declined. Some observers noted that much of the expenditure went for the special education of handicapped and otherwise disadvantaged students. But others observed that some of the expenditures went for frills that could be eliminated by cost-conscious business people. By the 1990s, competition and cost-cutting were seen as keys to educational improvement. There was renewed support for a concept that the Nobel laureate Milton Friedman had broached in 1955: the idea that private enterprise would do more than anything else to improve the quality of American education.[11]

---

10 Brian O'Reilly, "Why Edison Doesn't Work," *Fortune* (9 December 2002), 148ff.

11 Milton Friedman, "The Role of Government in Education," in R. A. Solo, ed., *Economics and the Public Interest* (New Brunswick: Rutgers University Press, 1955). As will be noted below, average scores declined between 1970 and 2010. But this was largely because non-Asian minorities came to constitute a larger portion of the student population. If scores were "disaggregated"— that is, if the test scores of discrete ethnic groups were compared from one generation to the next—there was improvement between 1970 and 2010.

Whittle agreed. He knew that most of the increased spending on public education had gone to finance smaller classes and what he called a "deserved increase in teacher compensation." But he insisted that the quality of education would not improve unless schools engaged in modern research and development and made use of "the inexorable advantages of scale."[12]

Entrepreneur that he was, Whittle doubtless regarded the reorganization of education as another way to increase his wealth. But Whittle's concern for education went beyond mere opportunism. While still in his 30s, Whittle had already earned a fortune. Thereafter he appeared to be propelled by an idealistic belief that business could succeed where government and earlier generations of school reformers had failed. If schools were organized properly, Whittle said, the educational achievement of American youths would improve. "It is not our children who are failing," he wrote, "but we who are failing millions of them." In some schools, less than 10 percent of the students had achieved minimal levels of proficiency in reading and mathematics, and throughout the nation "roughly 30 percent" of the children were "languish[ing] in functional illiteracy." Whittle recognized that "everyone cannot be at the top of the class. Not all will go to Harvard, not all will even go to college." Yet "virtually all can be literate," he insisted. Whittle said it was "racist" to think otherwise.[13]

To improve education, Whittle launched what he called the Edison Project—a plan to make public schools better by privatizing them. When he announced the project in 1991, Whittle spoke of raising $1.2 billion to build 1,000 private schools by the year 2,000—schools that would outperform the established public schools and thus revolutionize American education. He scored yet another sales coup when Phillips Electronics (from which Whittle had previously

---

12   Chris Whittle, *Crash Course*, 96.

13   *Ibid.*, 4, 11, 16, 20.

purchased some 300,000 television sets for Channel One) paid $175 million for a one-quarter stake in the Edison Project. Time Warner and Associated Newspapers, a British enterprise, chipped in with additional capital. And in what many people considered an even bigger triumph, Whittle persuaded Benno Schmidt, the president of Yale University, to become Edison's chief executive officer.

With Schmidt as its CEO, the Edison Project had a trophy hire if ever there was one. As one report in the *New York Times* noted, Whittle "gained instant credibility . . . when he landed" Schmidt. Many observers thought Whittle had to be on to something big if Schmidt, the president of one of the world's great universities, was prepared to give up lifetime tenure, prestige, and security. Schmidt himself acknowledged that, at first, "the notion that I would leave the presidency of a 300-year-old institution for something so new and risky was outlandish, like leaping into the abyss."[14]

A lucrative offer was partly responsible for Schmidt's move, as Whittle agreed to pay Schmidt more than four times the $187,000 a year that Schmidt had been earning at Yale. But Schmidt was also impressed by Whittle's public purposes. "I was impressed by [Whittle's] vision and intelligence, and the degree to which he was committed to the public good," Schmidt said. "As important as Yale is," Whittle told Schmidt, "taking on this project would make a much more important contribution to the country." Whittle reminded Schmidt of the "immense problem . . . in our country that needed solving: the difficulties within our K-12 schools," and Schmidt recognized that if Edison succeeded, "there's nothing . . . that would be more constructive for our society." If the venture worked, Edison would enroll several hundred thousand students, and its schools would be "models . . . that public schools

---

14 *New York Times* (27 May 1992; 26 May 1992); Chris Whittle, *Crash Course*, 70.

can... emulate if they wish." Schmidt regarded Edison as "a private project with a public mission."[15]

Whittle and Schmidt both thought that research and development would be crucial for the success of their Edison Schools. With that in mind, Edison allocated some $60 million for R&D on a few key questions: what it took to be an effective school principal, what teachers should do to increase the academic achievement of students, and how educational technology could be used more effectively. To design the research, Whittle assembled a team of well-regarded educators. John Chubb had been a scholar at the Brookings Institution and at two prestigious universities, Princeton and Stanford. Chester Finn was a professor at Vanderbilt and a former undersecretary of education. Nancy Hechinger came from Apple Inc. with the idea that schools should provide students with free computers.[16]

There was little surprise when Edison's research touted "accountability," and the use of bonuses, policies that had long been in place at many business corporations but had not been the standard operating procedure at most schools. The base pay of principals should be increased by about 50 percent, Whittle said, and there should be annual bonuses of $25,000 to $35,000 for principals who met their budgets and whose students posted impressive gains on standardized achievement tests. The pay of teachers should also be increased substantially. "If we want a certain level of talent in our classrooms, we must pay for it," Whittle wrote, and Americans should understand "that a 5 percent increase is not going to get the job done." Since the average teacher earned about $46,000, Whittle wrote in 2005, "a $1,000 bonus potential... will not materially alter behavior. But imagine the power

---

15 James B. Stewart, "Grand Illusion" 74; *New York Times* (26 May 1992); Vance Trimble, *An Empire Undone*, 9, 14, 16; Benno Schmidt, "Educational Innovation for Profit," *Wall Street Journal* (5 June 1992).

16 Chris Whittle, *Crash Course*, 73-74.

of a $15,000 bonus potential on a $46,000 base. That has the ability to attract a teacher's attention and drive results."[17]

Edison's "system design" called for a longer school day (from about 8 a.m. until 5 p.m.) and a longer school year (200 days instead of the usual 180). As a result, Edison's students would spend about 50 percent more time in school than the average for public school students. Some observers applauded this approach, saying that it would be especially beneficial for Black and Hispanic students who would not do well in school unless they spent more time away from their home environments. "These are kids who need to learn to stand apart from their family, the culture of their neighborhood and their peers on the street," wrote political scientist, Abigail Thernstrom. Other scholars, however, took exception to the notion that Black and Hispanic students had to separate themselves from their communities and families in order to achieve academically. Ronald Ferguson, a lecturer on public policy at Harvard, insisted that Thernstrom had "simplifie[d] the identity trip that kids have to go through," and Thernstrom herself later conceded that her language may have been ill-advised.[18]

Edison also established a strict (some said "regimented") curriculum that included 90 minutes of daily instruction in reading and one hour of math. Neo-progressive educators lamented that the curriculum was too "disciplined," "rule-bound," and "test-driven." After observing classes at one Edison school in Missouri, education writer Peter Campbell complained that there was "no project-based learning or hands-on activities." Instead, "most of the teachers 'taught at' the students." From the first day of classes in September, the curriculum revolved around preparation for a state-mandated test that was

---

17 *New York Times* (26 May 1992); Chris Whittle, *Crash Course*, 124, 127.

18 Abigail Thernstrom and Ronald Ferguson, quoted by Ronald Roach, "In the Academic Think Tank World, Pondering Achievement-Gap Remedies Takes Center Stage," *Blacks in Higher Education* 18 (2001) 26.

administered in April. Each month, students were given practice tests, and then the teachers adjusted their approaches with an emphasis on uplifting students who were just below the passing line. As a result of this approach, instructional time was reduced for subjects other than reading and math—and for students who were either well-above or well-below passing. According to Campbell, most of the instruction was at a "superficial level," but teachers who managed to get enough kids over the threshold were rewarded with bonus money.[19]

In addition to saying that Edison's curriculum was designed primarily to improve test scores, Campbell complained that Edison's teachers placed too much emphasis on discipline. In one school where all the students were Black, "the conceptual model" was that the children were "wild and needed to be tamed." "The teachers constantly berated the children for the slightest infraction." They made the students walk to lunch in orderly lines, with their hands folded, and in one instance "the boys' line could not go forward because one of the boys was wiggling . . . The teacher commanded him to become absolutely still before she would let the boys go to lunch."[20]

In defense of Edison's strict discipline, the board member who escorted Campbell on his visit, said, "Sure, the structure of the Edison schools is a bit tough. Yes, we make the kids walk in lines wherever they go. But it works. You don't have to waste six minutes at the beginning of class telling Johnny to sit down and be quiet. And you don't waste 15 minutes in the middle of every class trying to get students to be quiet and stay on task. Even the very brightest kids can't learn in an environment like that. No one can." The board member might have noted also that, as part of the overall design, the curriculum at Edison included a sizeable infusion of social studies

---

19 Peter Campbell, "Edison is the Symptom, NCLB Is the Disease," *Phi Delta Kappan* 88 (February 2007) 438-43.

20 Ibid.

that pertained to African-Americans and other minority groups. And no students attended Edison's schools except by choice, for Edison insisted that "all students attend our schools voluntarily—either by affirmative choice or by rejecting the choice of opting out (in cases where our school replaces the neighborhood school)."[21]

Yet Edison was on a collision course with many teachers and their unions. Many teachers had chosen their profession because they liked education and enjoyed working with young people, even though they knew that teaching would entail some financial loss. Now it seemed that they were being insulted for their sacrifice, for a tacit implication of Edison's message was that America's schools were failing because the pay in education was insufficient to attract good professional people. On occasion, this point was made explicitly. In 2011 *New York Times* columnist Nicholas Kristof wrote that "until a few decades ago, employment discrimination perversely strengthened our teaching force. Brilliant women became elementary school teachers, because better jobs weren't open to them." In modern America, however, "brilliant women become surgeons and investment bankers—and 47 percent of America's kindergarten through 12th grade teachers come from the bottom one-third of their college classes."[22]

Teachers also complained that Edison disregarded the progressive precepts that they had been taught in their schools of education. And Edison also made light of the problems of poverty and single-parent families. All would be better, Edison implied, if better people were attracted to the field of education, if schools were more orderly, and if the curriculum focused on basic academic subjects.[23]

---

21 *Ibid.*; John E. Chubb, "Lessons in School Reform from the Edison Project," in Diane Ravitch and Joseph P. Viteritti, eds., *New Schools for a New Century* (New Haven: Yale University Press, 1997) 91-92, 100, 116.

22 Nicholas D. Kristof, "Pay Teachers More," *New York Times* (12 May 2011).

23 Benno Schmidt did make passing reference to some of the "many reasons

Teachers mentioned additional problems. They said their work was as much art as science, and they insisted that the quality of teaching involved more than students' scores on tests of reading and mathematics. They said Whittle's bonus plan would give short shrift to art and music and would disregard the importance of teachers who had a special gift for inspiring pupils or boosting the self-confidence of troubled youths. They rejected Whittle's premise that teachers could be fairly judged on the basis of the students' performance, saying that would penalize teachers who were working with youngsters who were mentally slow, who did not try to do well in school, or who came from environments that were not conducive to learning. They mentioned the danger of favoritism when evaluating something as elusive as the quality of teaching. They also noted that many students had no interest in traditional academic subjects but remained in school for the social and athletic activities. If the emphasis shifted toward test preparation, they predicted, non-academic students were more likely to drop out.

Whittle, however, rejected the argument "that we do not have the methods to administer [a bonus] system fairly." "Teachers," he insisted, "should be rewarded for utilizing clear best practices instead of 'freelancing' with favorite protocols that have not been shown by research to work." Whittle also called for more mundane adjustments to a changing world. He said the nine-month school calendar was "developed in agrarian times" and "the common 6-hour-and-30-minute school day" was "wildly inconvenient for working parents." In the modern world, Whittle insisted, it made good sense to extend the school year to 11 months and the school day to at least 8 hours.[24]

---

progress has been thwarted: the changing nature of America's families, deep economic and social divisions, [and] urban disintegration." But Schmidt insisted that "the problem" lay primarily in "the system itself." Benno Schmidt, "Educational Innovation for Profit."

24 Chris Whittle, *Crash Course*, 127, 31; David Gardner and Chris Hill, The Motley Fool Interview With Edison Schools Founder and CEO Chris Whittle, *TheMotleyFool.com* (28 September 2000) transcript available at:

Yet a question inevitably arose. How did Whittle propose to pay for the Edison schools? Whittle recognized that there probably would not be any extra money. Because inflation-adjusted spending for public education had doubled in the preceding generation, without any marked increase in the academic achievement of students, it was not likely that taxpayers would provide still more money. "Billions of dollars [have already been] spent on funding initiatives that have not generated results," Whittle admitted. Consequently, "one of the design requirements of schools in the future should be that the cost per pupil does not increase by more than 10 percent in real-dollar terms." Yet Whittle was so confident that Edison could provide superior schools for no more than the average cost of conventional public schools that he also had a "'Plan B,' which says that the cost must be *equal* to current spending." For about $5,500 (1992) dollars per student, Whittle envisioned a nationwide network of schools that would provide each pupil with a computer and would be open for 11 months a year and at least eight hours a day. And he also promised to make a profit from the venture.[25]

To show a profit, Edison would have to keep its expenses down, and to this end Whittle proposed a number of cost-saving programs. He would pay teachers more than they had been earning, Whittle said, and the *Wall Street Journal* mentioned that Edison hoped to establish a base salary of $85,000. But Whittle said Edison would employ "far fewer" teachers.[26]

For decades the mantra of educators had been to increase the number of teachers and pay them more. But Whittle thought this was

---

www.fool.com/foolaudio/transcripts/2000/stocktalk000928.htm.

25 Chris Whittle, *Crash Course*, 37, 97-98; also see Benno Schmidt, "Educational Innovation for Profit."

26 James K. Glassman, "An Entrepreneur Goes to School," *Wall Street Journal* (7 September 2005); Chris Whittle, *Crash Course*, 128.

only "half-right—the pay part." Instead of spending almost all day in classes with teachers, Edison's students would spend a good deal of time at individual, computer-equipped carrels, where they would be engaged with interactive computer programs and curricula. And the cubicles would not be patrolled by highly-paid teachers but by top students who would be assigned the chore of three hours of tutoring each week. To those who questioned the qualifications of this "student tech force," Whittle posed a rhetorical question: "At home when your computer has a glitch, whom do you turn to for help, your twelve-year-old or your spouse? Answer: the twelve-year-old. Why? Because twelve-year-olds know more about a computer than most adults will ever learn."[27]

Edison's chief development officer, John Chubb, acknowledged that in the past progress in education had been "slow and unimpressive." Nevertheless, Chubb insisted that there was "reason for optimism—and the reason is technology." He explained that "given [the] instructional technology that exists today," it was "quite feasible" to send grade school students to computer labs for an hour a day—and thus reduce the number of certified elementary teachers by about one-sixth." "At the middle school level, two hours a day with computers would reduce staff requirements by a third." And "high schools, with three hours of usage, could reduce staff by up to half." To achieve further savings, Chubb recommended that computers be used to connect the remaining teachers with tutors in India, who would work "for a fraction of the wages of teachers in the United States and Europe." Chubb also noted that the after-school tutoring market was "growing 15 percent annually in the United States, with Indian firms leading the way, either alone or in partnership with U.S. firms needing low-cost, high-quality tutors."[28]

---

27 Chris Whittle, *Crash Course*, 128, 149, 115.

28 Terry M. Moe and John E. Chubb, *Liberating Learning* (San Francisco: Jossey-Bass, 2009), ix, 80, 68, 69.

Yet Chubb did not recommend technology simply as a way to cut costs. He noted that the financial savings could be plowed back "into teacher compensation to attract and retain stronger teaching staffs." Higher pay "would help attract and retain better talent," and better talent was "the most important ingredient of better schools." Chubb said that research had shown "that a highly effective teacher . . . can raise a student from the lowest quartile of the national achievement to the highest quartile, up to 50 percentiles, in just three years."[29]

To illustrate his points, Chubb mentioned two schools in Dayton, Ohio, where, thanks to technology, "a *single* classroom teacher" was able to handle "double-size classes of about sixty students." Most of the students in these schools came from "families in great economic and academic need," but, over the course of seven years, from 1999 to 2006, the achievement of the students on standardized exams "clearly improved." Chubb said that much of the improvement was due to the fact that the schools had used their savings "to raise the compensation of teachers and administrators, which in turn has enabled the schools to attract and retain stronger teaching staffs."[30]

Yet the quality of the teachers was not the only factor at work. Chubb also noted that as the Dayton students made progress, "their achievement levels became increasingly heterogeneous, requiring teachers to work with kids who sometimes varied as much as six grade levels in achievement by third grade." The standard approach to this level of variation was to regroup students for reading and to provide individualized tutoring. But "although these measures helped, they were not satisfactory." The Dayton schools "therefore embraced a radical new-approach. They invested heavily in technology to allow them to differentiate instruction on a very large scale." Students were then "assigned the right programs to meet their individual needs." And the positive results were "unmistakable."[31]

---

29 Ibid., 82, 80, 79.

30 Ibid., 3, 80, 81, 82.

31 Ibid., 82, 83.

As Chubb described it, the Dayton students entered their technology rooms enthusiastically, sat down at their assigned pods, and consulted an assignment "individually determined by their teacher based on prior diagnostics." It was "striking," Chubb reported, to see "how easily students have adapted to the call to work independently." Part of this was due to "the almost inherently engaging nature of technology—kids are experiencing in school the same bright, interactive multimedia presentations they know so well from computers outside of school." Students were also engaged "because the work they are doing precisely meets their needs." They were not frustrated "by work above their level or bored by work below their level." This was often the case in traditional classrooms, and, according to Chubb, it was the reason that many students had "behavioral issues and discipline problems." By way of contrast, the customizing of interactive technology promoted engagement, "which in turn promotes learning." For Chubb, the path of the future was clear: "more technology and fewer teachers."[32]

Chris Whittle and the Edison Schools proposed to save yet more money by paring the expensive bureaucracies that were familiar in public schools—the guidance counselors, librarians, psychologists, coaches, transportation directors, and other administrators. About half of all money spent in public schools was not spent directly in classrooms but on support services, Whittle noted. Most of all, Whittle pointed to what he called the "advantages of scale"—the extra efficiencies that would go along with the development of a national school system, just as additional efficiency had accompanied the development of national systems in the business world.[33]

Some observers were skeptical. Theodore Sizer doubted that Whittle's cost-saving ideas would save enough money to offset the investments in new technology and other services. When Harry

---

32 Ibid., 83-84, 85, 86.

33 *New York Times* (26 May 1992; 27 May 1992); Chris Whittle, *Crash Course*, 267.

Levin, an education professor at Stanford, was asked if Edison could recoup its investment, Levin replied: "I'd say flat out, 'No.'" There was no way that Edison, for the per-pupil expense of an average public school, could make a profit while also lengthening the school day and school year and providing each student with a personal computer.[34]

Others were more optimistic. Michael Moe of Lehman Brothers noted that the education market was "huge," and consequently "companies with innovative solutions represent significant investment opportunities." "When you look at the amount of money that is spent on public education," Moe said, "the possibility of bringing some rationalization to the services provided and still enhancing the quality of the services is very, very real." When Edison issued $172 million worth of stock in 1999, the value of the shares doubled in less than a year—from an Initial Public Offer (IPO) of $18 to $36. Investors were betting that Edison would become a profitable corporation. Unlike some other programs to improve education—some of which are discussed in this book—Edison did not rely on financial grants from private foundations or government agencies. It raised its money from investors who purchased Edison's stock.[35]

Yet the Edison Project was hardly underway when adjustments were made. It turned out that in most areas people were satisfied with their local schools and saw no need for drastic changes. There was nothing resembling a crisis in the middle-class suburbs. The problems were concentrated in schools where most of the students were either Blacks or non-White Hispanics, and soon Whittle received inquiries from urban superintendents and school boards saying, "Would you be interested in running a public school of ours, using the Edison system? You wouldn't have to put up buildings because we already

---

34 *New York Times* (27 May 1993; 17 March 1995).

35 *Ibid.* (17 March 1995); David Moberg, "How Edison Survived," *The Nation* 278 (15 March 2004) 22.

have them. We would contract with you to in effect run a ... school for the public system."[36]

Whittle agreed, and Edison moved away from the original plan to build 1,000 for-profit, technologically advanced schools and settled for contracting to run a number of especially troubled public schools. Whittle put an optimistic spin on the transition, saying it allowed Edison to "achieve what we really set out to do in the first place, which is to bring quality education to ordinary kids." Nevertheless, Edison's eventual customers turned out to be quite different from the students Whittle initially had in mind. Instead of teaching students who were representative of the nation at large, Edison took over "desperately troubled inner-city schools with rock-bottom test scores ... 'They were the ones most willing to take the chance, who felt they had nothing to lose.'"[37]

Judging from the reaction of the stock market, many investors doubted that Edison would succeed where so many others had failed. This was understandable. In the past a flood of money and a succession of teaching fads had failed to eliminate the racial and ethnic achievement gaps. The value of Edison's stock, which had doubled in 1999, plummeted from a high of $36 to less than $1 in 2002, before rebounding to about $1.75 in 2003.

Some investors may have thought that the academic problems of Black and Hispanic students and schools were insoluble. But there were additional problems. For one, the teachers' unions were adamant in their opposition to for-profit schooling. Much of this opposition was philosophical. Some business groups and free market ideologues were reflexively in favor of privatizing public education. They were convinced that private enterprises could "provide quality education

---

36 Vance Trimble, *An Empire Undone*, 300.

37 *Ibid.*, 300; Brian O'Reilly, "Why Edison Doesn't Work."

and still make a profit from the same tax dollars and with the same children that public schools have often failed." The teachers' unions, on the other hand, believed the public schools had a good record of educating students while also providing fair working conditions. The unions therefore looked askance at market-based nostrums. They were also taken aback when most of the teachers at profit-seeking Edison schools turned out to be inexperienced novices who, despite the longer hours and lack of tenure that Edison generally demanded, were employed at less than half the $85,000 "base pay" that the *Wall Street Journal* once mentioned.[38]

Opposition from the teachers' unions turned out to be only one of Edison's obstacles. Politics was another. Many Republicans hailed Edison as the nation's most prominent EMO (Educational Management Organization), the exemplar of privatization. But Democrats were more skeptical. So were many school boards. During its first decade, Edison was so eager to acquire public school partners that it signed many contracts that allowed local boards to terminate agreements after three to five years—and some contracts that allowed cancellation at any time and for any reason. Newly elected boards often had their own ideas about educational policy, and as one board succeeded another there was a tendency to adopt different programs. In some cases, this caused Edison to lose its startup costs before there was sufficient time to demonstrate the value of its programs. In Sherman, Texas, where Edison won its first school contract in 1995, a new school board canceled the deal five years later, although most teachers and parents considered the program a success. In Chula Vista, California, the teachers at one elementary school eventually chose not to renew Edison as their manager, saying that after 10 years of working with the company, they had absorbed all that Edison had

---

38 Peter Schrag, "Edison's Red Ink Schoolhouse," *The Nation* (25 June 2001) 20; Kenneth J. Saltman, *The Edison Schools* (New York: Routledge, 2005) *passim*; James K. Glassman, "An Entrepreneur Goes to School."

to offer and no longer needed to pay some $1 million annually for management and advice.[39]

Altogether, about one-fourth of Edison's contracts were not renewed, among them contracts in Boston, Chester (PA), Dallas, San Francisco, and Wichita. The most consequential of the cancellations occurred in Philadelphia. The stakes were especially great in this "City of Brotherly Love," where Edison, in 2002, won an $11.8 million contract to run 20 of the city's worst-performing schools. The contract had been secured with the assistance of two Republican governors who enthusiastically supported privatization as a reform strategy and praised Edison for having gone further than any other firm in showing what could be done for inner-city students. As it happened, Edison's students in Philadelphia recorded substantial gains on achievement tests. But the gains were not enough to offset the opposition of the local teachers' union, which continued to oppose private companies running public schools. There was additional opposition from some parent groups and one well-publicized "walkout" by students. Finally, after six years of skirmishing and during the administration of a Democratic governor, public authorities in Philadelphia voted to take back control of four of Edison's schools, while warning that the others had one year to show more progress or they, too, would revert to public control.[40]

If educational performance had been the only yardstick, Edison's schools would have passed muster in Philadelphia. Edison "did a

---

39 David Evans, "Trouble Looms for Edison Schools," *New York Times* (26 June 1996); Chris Moran, "Charter school Severs Most Ties with N. Y. Firm," *San Diego Union-Tribune* (10 September 2007).

40 Jay Mathews, "The Philadelphia Experiment," *Education Next* (Winter 2003); Alissa Quart, "Classroom Consciousness," *TheNation.com* (10 June 2002); Keith B. Richburg, "Setback for Philadelphia Schools Plan," *Washington Post* (29 June 2008); Kristen A. Graham, "Study Shows Math Advances in Phila. For-Profit Schools," *Philadelphia Inquirer* (11 February 2009).

number of things right," said James Nevels, the chairman of a state-appointed Philadelphia School Reform Commission. "They've done a superb job with the most difficult schools." Nevertheless, although test scores had gone up during the years of Edison's management, scores had also improved at other schools that had remained under public control, and the difference in improvement was not enough to assuage the teachers' unions and other groups who continued to resent the very idea that a private company might make a profit operating public schools. As journalist Brian O'Reilly noted, "for-profit schools have to be orders of magnitude better than their public school rivals in order to overcome the political opposition that confronts them."[41]

However unwarranted, the termination of Edison's contract in Philadelphia, coming as it did on the heels of other terminations, dealt a heavy blow to the reputation of the company and to the cause of privatization. And there were yet more problems. In addition to underestimating the suspicion and opposition that Edison would arouse among teachers and parents, it turned out that the economies of scale were much smaller than Chris Whittle had predicted. Edison was also overloaded with executives making six-figure salaries, and the company was set back further in 2002 when the Securities and Exchange Commission reported that Edison had inflated its revenues. During its first decade, Edison Schools lost about $354 million, and it did not show even a small profit until the second quarter of 2003. As it happened, that would turn out to be the company's only profitable quarter. "This isn't a stock for everybody," one analyst said. "If you follow your stocks every day, Edison could give you a heart attack."[42]

---

41 Mary Beth McCauley, "A City's Schools Test a New Way," *Christian Science Monitor* (30 November 2004); Jay Mathews, "The Philadelphia Experiment"; Brian O'Reilly and Julia Boorstin, "Why Edison Doesn't Work," *Fortune* 146 (9 December 2002) 148-154.

42 David Moberg, "How Edison Survived"; Nelson D. Schwartz, "The Nine Lives of Chris Whittle," *Fortune* 148 (27 October 2003) 103; David Evans, "Trouble Looms for Edison Schools."

Nevertheless, Edison survived. To keep the project afloat, in 1995 Whittle sold some of his houses, one of which was put on the market for $45 million, and invested the proceeds in Edison stock. With the company continuing to hemorrhage money, Whittle took Edison private in 2003, purchasing stock at a deflated price just a few months before he announced that Edison had finally turned a profit. The company's principal benefactor was an unlikely savior, the Florida Retirement System (FRS)—a pension fund for public employees, about half of whom were teachers whose union strenuously opposed Edison and the idea of for-profit schools. Yet neither the union nor the teachers had a voice in the matter, since the purchase was made by Liberty Partners, an investment company that managed a portion of the FRS pension fund.[43]

There were complaints, of course. "The assets of public employees are at serious risk," one union leader declared. In addition, this leader said, "there's nothing you can point to to believe [Edison] will turn around and be profitable." "With all the possible investments that you could make in our economy where the likelihood of making a significant profit is so much more evident, why would [Liberty Partners] pick [Edison]?" "One of the big problems we have is that the people with the most at stake, whose retirement security is vested in this fund, have absolutely no voice in governing the fund."[44]

Edison's stock never recovered, and eventually Liberty's investment did become a problem for Florida's retired teachers. The stock did not recover because test scores never lived up to Edison's original expectations. In the early years, CEO Benno Schmidt had described the pursuit of educational equality as "the civil rights struggle of today," and education officer John Chubb had said, "Our experience is that racial and ethnic gaps can be solved." From the

---

43 Brian O'Reilly, "Why Edison Doesn't Work"; David Moberg, "How Edison Survived"; Leigh Allen, "Schooled on Edison Evolution," *Dayton Daily News* (26 May 2005).

44 David Moberg, "How Edison Survived."

outset, Chris Whittle had recognized that Edison's success would ultimately depend on test scores. As it happened, however, "modest progress" was the most that Edison could substantiate.[45]

The analysis of test scores is a complex undertaking. Edison coached its students for standardized tests, and there were allegations that the company did not admit a proportional share of disabled students. But Edison also managed mostly low-performing schools, while comparison schools often enrolled a wider range of students. Then again, most students at Edison began at such low levels that they were likely to make larger gains than students at other schools. Edison's clientele also differed from the norm in impoverished areas because the parents tended to be especially concerned about their children and the students either chose Edison or were given the option of attending a different school.[46]

Given the complexities, test scores were susceptible to differing interpretations. "We're knocking the cover off the ball," Chris Whittle declared after reviewing one set of scores. The American Federation of Teachers, on the other hand, reported that "averaged across all states, the typical Edison school performed below average." Taking a middling position, researchers at the University of Western Michigan concluded, "While our findings do not suggest that Edison did less, they do not suggest that the company did more ... in terms of gains on standardized tests."[47]

---

45 Benno Schmidt and John Chubb, quoted by Ronald Roach, "In the Academic and Think Tank World, Pondering Achievement Gap Remedies Takes Center Stage."

46 "Edison Schools to Serve More than 250,000," *Public Relations Newswire* (20 September 2004); Dana Goldstein, "Business Schools," *American Prospect* (5 August 2008) web only (Prospect.org/cs/articles); Jacques Steinberg and Diana B. Henriques, "Complex Calculations on Academics," *New York Times* (16 July 2002).

47 Chris Whittle, quoted by Alison Gendar, Paul H. B. Shin and William

In an extensive analysis of Edison's test scores, the Rand Corporation reported in 2005 that schools that Edison had operated for at least four years equaled or outperformed public schools with similar student populations. This Rand report ran to 290 pages and, since Rand was one of the nation's premier independent research organizations, the report was widely credited. Yet the Rand scholars offered only measured praise, especially in comparison with Edison's John Chubb, who said that his company's "track record in helping raise student achievement and closing the achievement gap is the best in the industry"; that "data shows that African-American and economically disadvantaged students are making clear, and sometimes spectacular, academic progress in their Edison partnership schools." In 2007, another Rand report on Edison's schools in Philadelphia was more cautious, finding "no evidence of differential academic benefits that would support additional expenditures on private managers." In 2009, yet another study, conducted by scholars at Harvard University, reached yet another conclusion: that Philadelphia students who "attended a school under for-profit . . . management . . . learned substantially more in reading and math."[48]

It is hard to know what to make of such divergent studies. This writer believes that Edison generally did a good job with its students, but the progress was only incremental. This was disappointing, and even surprising, since Edison emphasized testing and its students spent almost 50 percent more time in school each year. Taking everything into account, Edison's gains failed to live up to the company's promises.

Sherman, "Saving Schools a Risky Business," *New York Daily News* (11 February 2001); AFT Reports by the American Federation of Teachers and the Western Michigan Evaluation Center, quoted by Kenneth J. Saltman, *The Edison Schools*, 72, 70.

48 *Public Relations Newswire* (17 June 2004; 1 April 2004); EdisonSchools. com (25 November 2005); Dana Goldstein, "Business Schools," *American Prospect* (5 August 2008); Kristen A. Graham, "Study Shows Math Advances in Phila. For-Profit Schools."

As the test results came in, more cities canceled contracts that had authorized Edison to manage their public schools. And as enrollment in its schools declined (from a peak of about 90,000 in 2005 to some 50,000 three years later), the company continued to lose money. Equally important, Edison lost its cachet. In 2005, *Wall Street Journal* columnist James K. Glassman wrote that Edison, "instead of owning 1,000 private schools [as Chris Whittle had once envisioned,] ...merely manages 157 public ones. Quite a comedown."[49] Eventually, the company faded from public view. Recalling the publicity that Edison had once received, journalist Caroline Grannan opined in 2008, "It's surprising that more people aren't wondering whatever happened to that miracle that was supposed to be bringing private sector efficiencies to public education."[50]

After spending 16 years and some $500 million trying to make a profit managing public schools, Edison turned instead to providing supplemental services. The No Child Left Behind Act of 2001 provided federal funds for companies that tutored students who failed to make what was called "adequate yearly progress" on standardized tests. This provision, in turn, kindled the growth of tutoring companies that rushed in to tap the available money. Edison took advantage of this opportunity and also branched into selling technology products to regular public schools. To make clear that Edison was changing its direction, in 2008 the company changed its name from Edison Schools to EdisonLearning. And in 2007, Chris Whittle stepped down as CEO.[51]

---

49 Thomas Toch, "Chris Whittle Launches Chain of Private Schools," *New York Magazine* (20 July 2008); Dana Goldstein, "Business Schools," *American Prospect* (5 August 2008).

50 James K. Glassman, "An Entrepreneur Goes to School"; Caroline Grannan, "The Light Goes Out for Once-hailed Edison Schools," *San Francisco Examiner* (22 July 2008).

51 See information at EdisonLearning.com and Elissa Gootman, "Report on

Whittle's resignation did not bespeak a complete departure from the field of education. Instead, Whittle joined again with Benno Schmidt to launch an international chain of for-profit elite private schools. The chain was to be called "Nations Academies," and the new schools were designed to appeal especially to people who wanted the best education that money could buy. In particular, the schools would cater to the children of diplomats and corporate executives, and a year's tuition would approach $40,000, the level of an Ivy League university. Whittle and Schmidt planned to begin in 2011, with schools in New York and Washington, each enrolling around 1,700 students from preschool through high school. Their larger goal was to have 60 campuses worldwide by 2021. They predicted that these schools would make a profit by operating efficiently, by finding economies of scale, by making greater use of technology, and by reducing the number of teachers, counselors, and other staff that were typically employed at elite private schools.[52]

Time will tell. In the meantime, Edison's pioneering use of educational technology became popular with many families that chose to homeschool their children. Many of the charter schools that will be discussed in Part Three of this book also embraced the innovative technology that Edison had pioneered. Some online charter schools came to be known as "virtual schools." "By 2012," historian Diane Ravitch has written, "there were more than 200,000 full-time students enrolled in virtual charter schools in the United States." According to Ravitch, publicly funded charter schools made "handsome profits" despite receiving "less funding per student than bricks-and-mortar schools."[53]

Tutoring Firms Cites Problems," *New York Times* (8 March 2006).

52 Thomas Toch, "Chris Whittle Launches Chain of Private Schools," *New York Magazine* (20 July 2008); Dana Goldstein, "Business Schools," *American Prospect* (5 August 2008).

53 Diane Ravitch, *Reign of Error* (New York: Alfred A. Knopf, 2013), 182.

5

Robert Slavin and Success for All

In the 1990s, when Chris Whittle's influence on American education was still rising, the Edison Schools placed a great deal of emphasis on reading. "We believe reading is the most important subject." Whittle said. "If you can't read, you're not going to pass science, and we spend more time and more money on reading than on any other subject." In its schools Edison used the Success for All reading program that had been developed by another educational reformer, Robert Slavin of Johns Hopkins University.[1]

In many ways Robert Slavin was far from a back-to-basics conservative. He grew up in Washington, D.C., and he chose to attend Reed College in Oregon because of Reed's reputation as a haven for liberal and radical students. While at Reed, Slavin met his future wife and Success for All partner, Nancy Madden, who herself had chosen the school for its liberal reputation as well as for its academic strength. After completing his formal education with a Ph.D. (1975) from Johns Hopkins University, Slavin became a professor of psychology at Hopkins, and his early studies hewed to the standard lines of progressive education. He opposed grouping students by ability, and he favored two approaches that most progressive educators favored: cooperative learning and inquiry-oriented activities.[2]

---

1   Gardner and Hill, "Interview with Chris Whittle."

2   *Reed Magazine* (February 2001).

Yet when it came to the best method for teaching reading, Slavin rejected the conventional wisdom of progressive education. For decades educators had debated whether it was better to present information and teach skills directly, or to allow children to discover them on their own. Most progressives preferred nondirective, student-centered teaching methods that allowed children to learn at their own pace, with teachers acting as facilitators, as guides rather than as authoritative instructors. Progressives stressed the importance of exposing students to good literature and interesting stories, saying that if the students' interests were engaged they would become enthusiastic about school and would automatically learn how to read. Traditionalists, on the other hand, emphasized the importance of phonics and the need for students to sound out words by memorizing the sounds of letters and combinations of letters. Progressives opposed memorization and drill, which they sometimes disparaged as mind-numbing "parrot learning." They said that drills would stifle the students' budding interest and cause them to lose interest in school. Traditionalists, in return, accused the progressives of having a romantic view of learning, one that was imbued with love and hope but, sadly, would leave many children uncomprehending, without the ability to read.

Progressives could point to international studies. They mentioned that Finnish students came out on top in a 1991 worldwide study of the reading ability of 9-year-old children. One reason was that Finland produced few television programs of its own, and Finnish children consequently learned to read from cartoon subtitles that flashed so quickly that word recognition, not sounding out, was the only way to read. Progressives also noted that the Chinese and Japanese languages had no letters to sound out—and that children in these countries learned to read by recognizing the import of characters.[3]

---

3   Richard Rothstein, "There's More to Reading than Phonics," *New York Times* (14 March 2001).

Robert Slavin

Initially, Slavin was disposed toward the progressive approach. Progressivism, after all, was consistent with a liberal political tendency to seek freedom from authority and tradition. Slavin also knew that the faculties at schools of education tended to believe that most learning was accomplished in student-centered, non-directive classrooms.[4]

In 1986, however, Baltimore's superintendent of schools asked Slavin to design a program for disadvantaged elementary school students. Slavin then reviewed the literature on reading and discovered that a gulf separated the conventional wisdom of many reading teachers from that of researchers. "Whole language was the craze [among teachers of reading,]" Slavin said, "and it would have been a lot easier for us to have just gone along with that. But we ... did a review of the literature ... and the literature was crystal clear that phonics was more effective. Study after study found that children who struggled in reading had to be taught a phonetic, systematic strategy for unlocking the reading code." Some children admittedly learned to read without phonics, but Slavin concluded that no group of children had been harmed by phonics while "a large group of children" was "harmed by the lack of phonics."[5]

---

4   For more on this point, see Jeanne S. Chall, *The Academic Achievement Challenge* (New York: Guilford Press, 2000) 34 and *passim*.

5   Robert Slavin, interview with Hedrick Smith, (PBS: Hedrick Smith Productions, September 2005). In *The Academic Achievement Challenge* 80-83, Jeanne S. Chall has written: "Neville Bennett's (1976) comparison of open schools with more traditional schools found that formal teaching produced higher achievement." "Kennedy of the U.S. Office of Education (1978) concluded that the less effective education programs for disadvantaged children were those where the children were the planners and the teachers acted as facilitators of their learning." "In 1996 Adams and Engleman came to essentially the same conclusions." "In 1978 Gage published his first synthesis of quantitative studies done in the elementary grades and found that, in general, students in those schools that were more open (student-centered) had lower academic achievement than those in traditional (teacher-centered) schools." "Good and Brophy's synthesis of quantitative studies in 1987 generally confirmed Gage's 1978 synthesis."

Especially in the early years of elementary school, Slavin explained, "you have a fairly well-defined task. The kids have got to be able to decode." With that in mind, Slavin's Success for All program (SFA) taught phonic awareness (the ability to discriminate and hear sounds within words) to kindergarten and prekindergarten children. Systematic instruction in phonics then began in the first grade. Slavin's critics complained that this led to excessive drills and to the use of simplistic texts that bored even elementary students. Yet Slavin insisted, "research supports 'teaching kids to unlock the code, as well as using decodable text with a high proportion of words that kids can decode.'"[6]

Slavin further insisted that all children could learn to read, if they were taught properly. Slavin admitted that the title of his program, Success for All (SFA), was "kind of corny," but he chose the name to convey the idea "that the school must relentlessly stick with every child until that child is [reading]." Slavin conceded that most teachers had good intentions. Yet, because many teachers were using the wrong methods, Slavin said, they were "murdering these children." "You see these little kids coming into school; these are wonderful children. They are just so full of creativity and enthusiasm." And yet after a few years of formal schooling, "many of these same children will have lost the spark they all started with." "That has to change." "Children deserve better than that." "Schools can be far more effective than they have been for children from disadvantaged homes."[7]

Beginning in first grade, SFA students started their school days with a 90-minute session of intensive reading instruction. This was longer than elementary schools typically spent on reading, and the

---

6   Robert Slavin, Interview with Hedrick Smith; *New York Teacher* (4 June 2003) at NYSUT.org, http://www.pbs.org/makingschoolswork/sbs/sfa/slavin.html (accessed 1 August 2014).

7   Robert Slavin, interview with Hedrick Smith; Robert E. Slavin and Nancy A. Madden, *One Million Children* (Thousand Oaks, CA: Corwin Press, 2001) 5; Robert E. Slavin and Nancy A. Madden, eds., *Success for All* (Lawrence Erlbaum Associates, 2001) 3.

sessions were definitely teacher-centered. "For the first twenty minutes, the teacher stands in front of the class and reads to the children," one observer noted. After that, sessions were divided into precisely-timed lessons on skills and sub-skills. In one class, the teacher gave a phonics lesson on the sound made by the letter, "P." For inspiration, she had put out a plastic potato, a pepper, and a pear, and the SFA curriculum specified the use of a call-and-response format. "What sound does it make?" the teacher asked, "Puh, puh, puh, puh," the children responded. Another teacher used rhymes and chants to teach the sounds of a combination of letters. "Tick tock, tick tock, said the clock."[8]

Progressives took exception to what they called "joyless chants" and "vapid literature." They were further dismayed when they discovered that SFA required teachers to use a minute-by-minute script. Novice teachers were reproached for engaging in friendly banter with students. If teachers strayed from the script, their SFA mentors said, there would not be enough time for vocabulary drills or other parts of the pre-packaged lesson plan.

Success for All specified exactly what a teacher should do between, say, 8 and 8:43 a.m. and then, after a break of only two minutes (!), between 8:45 and 9:28. A headline in the *New York Times* characterized SFA as "Teaching by the Book" with "No Asides Allowed." Another article appeared in the *Wall Street Journal* under the headline, "Now Johnny Can Read if Teacher Just Keeps Doing What He's Told." It described a SFA school where teachers and students spent "precisely three minutes on the choral litany, two minutes on words they can't sound out, three working with a partner composing sentences using the words—and more, for 90 minutes. No variations allowed."[9]

---

8   James Traub, "Success for Some," *New York Times* (10 November 2002); Anemona Hartocollis, "Citing Success Among Worst City Schools," *New York Times* (13 November 1997).

9   *New York Times* (23 May 2001); *Wall Street Journal* (19 July 1999).

Many progressives were appalled. "Highly scripted lessons don't just handcuff teachers," complained education writer Alfie Kohn. "They cheat students—especially poor and minority students—by substituting a diet of isolated skills for the thoughtful exploration of ideas." "Creativity . . . is being stifled," declared Bob Nathanson, a professor of education at Long Island University. Critics said that SFA focused too narrowly on the basics, and teachers were being turned into robots. "A trained monkey could do this program," said Janice Auld, the president of the North Sacramento Education Association.[10]

To illustrate the point, the *New York Times* published a feature story on one novice teacher who was "brimming with idealism and determined to put a unique stamp on her classroom." In her SFA school, however, this teacher encountered a highly structured environment that dictated how she should spend every minute. The *Wall Street Journal* told of another teacher who retired because SFA was "killing creative teaching." "It's Stepford teaching," the teacher said, referring to a movie about robotic wives. "They tell you what posters to have in your room and they tell you where to put them."[11]

Many school administrators nevertheless defended the system. "Some critics out there will say, 'Oh my God, you're lobotomizing teachers,'" said Paul Vallas, who at different times headed the public school systems in Chicago, Philadelphia, and New Orleans. "No. What we're saying is, 'What every successful corporation is doing, what the military is doing, is giving teachers a model of quality instruction and curriculum.'" "Instead of everyone trying to figure out their own way in the classroom, which is the way schools used to work," explained Judith Rizzo, the deputy chancellor for instruction in New York City, "new teachers in particular need a very clearly defined program. . . . It's

---

10 *New York Times* (29 May 2001); Sarah Colt, "Scripted Lessons," appendix to Robert Slavin, interview with Hedrick Smith.

11 *New York Times* (23 May 2001); *Wall Street Journal* (19 July 1999).

like learning to cook. You learn the basics first." Yet another observer, journalist Nicholas Lemann, compared the SFA curriculum with the protocols for airline safety. All pilots were required to follow the same safety checks. All aircraft had to be equipped with radar and oxygen masks. Admitting that SFA was an "affront to the progressive sensibility in education," Lemann nevertheless noted, "almost every school that uses [SFA] previously had a greater degree of teacher autonomy and was failing to teach students well." Autonomy was hard to defend when students did not learn to read.[12]

Progressives also criticized SFA for embracing ability grouping. This came as a surprise, for Robert Slavin had once insisted that grouping students by ability was misguided. After reviewing the literature in 1989, he had concluded that the main result of grouping was to depress the self-esteem of weak students. "As far as achievement is concerned, the effect for both high- and low-achieving students is neutral," he had written. In the 1980s, Slavin had also been a national leader in the movement to improve race relations by grouping students heterogeneously. He had touted cooperative learning as the best way to improve race relations. He had said that "activities that put students together in cooperative contact to achieve common goals [are] more powerful than studying other groups, special programs on race relations or other obvious efforts to improve intergroup relations." "There's nothing as strong as personal cooperative contact," he had said.[13]

SFA students continued to work in teams, and time was allotted for students to quiz and to read to one another. But to boost

---

12 *New York Times* (26 November 1999; 23 May 2001); Nicholas Lemann, "Ready, Read" *The Atlantic* (November 1998).

13 *New York Times* (3 January 1990; 16 July 1991); Robert E. Slavin, *Cooperative Learning* (New York: Longman, 1983); Slavin, "Cooperative learning," *Review of Educational Research* 50 (Summer 1980) 315-42.

achievement scores on standardized tests, SFA also grouped students according to their skill in reading. Slavin said he "wouldn't call it ability grouping, we'd call it performance grouping." One difference, he said, was that SFA students were tested every eight weeks, and the groups were reshuffled according to test scores. "It gives the kids a chance not to get stuck," Slavin said. Knowing that "grouping" was a dirty word in progressive circles, Slavin continued to insist that he opposed rigid grouping and tracking. Yet, since the purpose of the eight week-shuffle was to maintain homogeneity in "learning communities," some critics concluded that Slavin was making a distinction without a difference.[14]

Progressives were mollified somewhat because SFA relied on tutors and social workers to complement the work of classroom teachers. Each SFA school employed social workers whose job was to persuade parents to read to their children and to take an interest in any attendance or behavior problems. Social workers were also charged with responsibility for reporting problems that students might have with health, eyesight, inadequate nutrition, or abuse at home. In one instance, a social worker discovered a pupil who was not eating because his mother had died and his father could not cook. Another involved a student who was sleeping in class because he had no bed at home, and a third dealt with a child who was missing school because he had no winter coat. Slavin stressed the importance of "intensive services from infancy to age 8," including "high quality infant care [and] preschool . . . services."[15]

By dispatching social workers to the surrounding community, SFA gained a reputation for truly caring about its students. "What

---

14 Robert Slavin interview with Hedrick Smith; Alicia Woodard Green, "Performance Grouping" (appendix to Slavin, interview with Hedrick Smith).

15 *New York Times* (23 May 1998); Meg Bozzone, "An Interview with Robert Slavin," *Instructor* (1990) 104; Robert E. Slain, "Can Education Reduce Social Inequality?" *Educational Leadership* 55 (December 1967) 6.

has happened is that the community is no longer thinking of the schools as a place where a bunch of white teachers who don't really care are just collecting a paycheck," said Alberto Reinoso, the principal of the Thurgood Marshall Elementary School in Asbury Park, New Jersey. "And all of this has happened because Success for All really believes in parental involvement." A parent in the state of Washington said that SFA "definitely made school more family-oriented because it does entail the parents getting involved.... It's kind of learning for the parents as well."[16]

SFA also emphasized the need for frequent testing and for intervention as soon as problems were observed. "We ... monitor children's progress very closely," Slavin said. "We ... identify the point at which children start to fall behind and provide intensive remedial support or whatever is necessary for the child." Slavin was committed to "the idea that every single child [is] going to be successful no matter what." If a child fell behind in reading, he or she would receive extra one-on-one tutoring each day. If there were problems at home, extra social services would be provided.[17]

Some of this resembled what could be called "Title I reforms." Since the mid-1960s the federal government had spent billions of dollars for programs to assist students who were impoverished and having problems with schoolwork. Much of this money had gone to Head Start, but other funds were appropriated for teachers' aides and special tutors, for breakfasts and for healthcare. Slavin supported these special services but also recognized that the best research called into question their effectiveness, at least insofar as having a lasting effect on academic achievement. Indeed, the National Assessment of Educational Progress (NAEP) reported that after the late-1980s

---

16 *New York Times* (23 May 1998); Carrie Dunshee, quoted in *Seattle Times* (16 June 2004).

17 Robert Slavin, interview with Hedrick Smith.

the achievement gap between Black and White students was actually increasing. Some observers wondered if Title I programs were not partly to blame, because they frequently took disadvantaged students away from regular schoolwork for counseling, field trips, and other special services.[18]

Slavin thought it was time to try a new approach. In the recent past, he said, there had been "a kind of 'let a thousand flowers bloom' quality" to school reform. In the 1980s, many communities had embraced Theodore Sizer's emphasis on choice and on allowing individual schools to have considerable independence and autonomy. "Site-based management" had been the vogue, and "each principal and group of teachers was supposed to help to create their own destiny and to determine what they thought was best for their children." The idea was that public education would improve if teachers and students could choose a particular sort of school. But, according to Slavin, "that . . . ran into all the problems of trying to coordinate many different things." In Memphis, he said, "there was a wonderful superintendent who was very much behind the site-based management idea, but by the time she left she had nineteen different reform models . . . And it just couldn't be managed."[19]

Because school choice and site-based experiments were difficult to administer, and because Title I programs had often pulled students out of their regular classes, the time seemed right for SFA. "The education of disadvantaged students is at a crossroads," Slavin wrote in 1998. He said that Title I funds should be used for "school-wide change." It was time to establish programs that would reform the curriculum of elementary schools. To that end, SFA supplemented its

---

18 Slavin made special mention of one critical assessment of Title I spending: Michael J. Puma et al., *Prospects: Final Report on Student Outcomes* (Cambridge, Mass: ABT Associates, 1997).

19 Robert Slavin, interview with Hedrick Smith.

phonics-based reading program with Roots and Wings, a program for teaching elementary school mathematics, social studies, and science.[20]

Thus SFA involved what was called "whole school reform." Unlike previous programs that Title I had funded, programs that provided special services like tutoring, counseling, breakfasts, and field trips to expand the horizons of disadvantaged children, SFA provided a new, scripted curriculum and mentors to make sure that teachers followed the scripts. Instead of minor surgery, Slavin said, "We do a heart-lung transplant." Because SFA involved such wide-ranging change, and such a sacrifice of the teachers' autonomy and independence, Slavin insisted that at least 80 percent of the teachers must vote to adopt SFA before he would bring the program to a particular school. In most instances this meant that SFA was used only in schools where past test scores had been so low that there was no question about the need for change. Even most of these schools adopted only the reading and language arts portions of the SFA curriculum, and continued with traditional approaches to mathematics, social science, and science. This may have been because Roots and Wings, the non-reading portion of SFA, used constructivist and inquiry methods of instruction that were drawn from the playbook of progressive education.[21]

Thus SFA, as actually implemented, usually dealt only with reading and language arts. And as students moved beyond first grade, some progressive methods were used, although attention was still given to decoding. "In the second grade," Slavin said, "we begin a process that's then played out in many ways all the way through eighth grade." Students were organized "in cooperative teams to help each other develop skills for comprehension." "Treasure hunts" would be held, with the students searching for treasures such as

---

20 Olatokunbo Fashola and Robert E. Slavin, "Schoolwide Reform Models," *Phi Delta Kappan* 79 (January 1998) 370

21 Eric Clearinghouse on Educational Management (ED427388, 1998-12-00)

"the main idea of the book or story they were reading." Instead of having children plod through textbooks or read out loud, SFA urged teachers to illuminate key points, "but at advancing levels of difficulty in sophistication as the children move along." As with the approach to decoding in the early years, the teachers were given precisely-scripted "strategies for comprehension." "The difference [was] that in second grade you're applying these things to *Charlotte's Web*. In the sixth grade you're applying them to . . . much more complicated texts."[22]

For all its sweep and innovation, SFA was not an especially expensive program. The tutors, social workers, healthcare, and free breakfasts were already covered by Title I, and Slavin said the scripted lessons added an additional annual expense of only about $150 per student in 2005, when the average expenditure per public school student was about $8,000 a year. First year start-up costs were in the vicinity of $75,000 per school, with another $10,000 required each year for a school to keep up with curriculum materials and technology. According to Slavin, these expenses were "typically well within the Title I resources available to high-poverty school[s]."[23]

Slavin insisted that test results justified the expense. He reported that "research comparing SFA with control schools in many parts of the United States has consistently shown that SFA has substantial positive effects on student reading achievement throughout the elementary grades." In Texas, for example, the scores of 55,000 students who were enrolled in 111 SFA schools rose significantly more than those of comparable students in other schools. And so it went in other places. At one school of the Quinault Indian Nation, the average score of sixth graders on a test of basic skills rose from the 37th percentile to the 58th. In Meridian, Mississippi, the percentage of students who achieved proficiency in reading increased from 34 to

---

22 Robert Slavin, interview with Hedrick Smith.

23 Ibid; *Seattle Times* (16 June 2004).

60. And in Devils Lake, North Dakota, the percentage of students reading at grade level increased spectacularly, from 23 percent to 79. The results for African-American students were especially gratifying because SFA reportedly narrowed the gap between the scores of Black and White students substantially. It did so, Slavin said, "not by taking away from the middle class but by building a high floor under the achievement level of all children."[24]

Throughout the 1990s Slavin and his associates at Johns Hopkins University published research that purported to show that SFA had been especially successful in raising the test scores of disadvantaged students in urban school districts. SFA schools were matched with other schools with a similar history of test scores and a similar proportion of impoverished students (as measured by the percentage who were eligible for free or reduced-price lunch programs). Time after time, the SFA schools did better. The studies were published in leading professional journals and seemed compelling. Even Richard Rothstein, a *New York Times* education writer who generally looked askance at back-to-basics approaches, acknowledged in 1998 that Success for All was "probably the most effective reading program available today for disadvantaged youngsters."[25]

The evidence was such that in New Jersey, where the state Supreme Court established a judicial tribunal to see to it that the

---

24 Robert E. Slavin, "Built to Last: Long-term Maintenance of Success for All," *Remedial and Special Education* 25 (January/February 2004) 61; Eric A. Hurley, Anne Chamberlain, Robert E. Slavin, and Nancy A. Madden, "Effects of Success for All on TAAS Reading Scores," *Phi Delta Kappan* 82 (June 2001) 750; Robert E. Slavin, "At Odds—Mounting Evidence Supports the Achievement Effects of Success for All," *Phi Delta Kappan* 83 (February 2002) 469; Robert E. Slavin, "Can Education Reduce Social Inequality?" *Educational Leadership* 55 (December 1997) 6; SFA website postings for Quinault, Meridian, and Devils Lake.

25 Richard Rothstein et al., "Charter Conundrum," *The American Prospect* 39 (July/August 1998) 46.

state spent as much on public education in the poorest cities as in the wealthiest suburbs, the judges virtually ordered 277 impoverished schools to implement Success for All. The state's Education Commissioner, Leo F. Klagholz, recommended specifically that all urban elementary schools adopt the SFA reading program. The "research" led him to this recommendation, Klagholz said. Professor Slavin's program had produced "demonstrable success" in high-poverty schools, not just in New Jersey but also in "several hundred schools around the nation." Tom Jannarone, an urban schools consultant, acknowledged that some teachers opposed the use of precisely-scripted lesson plans. But, Jannarone said, "When you get the state pushing to choose this model, Success for All becomes not just an educational model, but the state's model."[26]

Eventually, SFA was widely implemented not only in New Jersey and Texas but also in many other states. By 2005 more than 1500 schools were using the program. At first Slavin and his wife, Nancy Madden, worked out of Johns Hopkins University. But by 1998, their program was so large that they split off and established a separate non-profit foundation called the Success for All Foundation. Slavin retained his professorship but Madden moved on to become the full-time chief executive of the foundation, which by 2005 was employing more than 300 people at its headquarters in Towson, Maryland. By then the foundation was also receiving millions of dollars annually in research grants and funding.

When it came to funding programs to improve inner-city schools, public officials and private foundations had to choose among many ambitious applicants. Thus Success for All inevitably came in for criticism from rivals who were less successful in their appeals for funds. In this regard, it helped that the Success for All Foundation

---

26   Abbott v. Burke, 119 N.M. 287 (5 June 1990); New York Times (23 December 1997; 30 April 2000).

was non-profit. "It would have been ... easy to have done this as a for-profit," Slavin said. "Investors are a whole lot easier than grants—and we had investors beating down our door." Yet Slavin also sensed that he would have an advantage if he could tell critics and rivals, "we're not-for profit." "That makes a big difference."[27]

Yet even non-profit organizations could earn a great deal of money in educational consulting. A professor's fee for speaking could amount to thousands of dollars, and "consultation" is a vague term that accommodates almost any advice that the imagination or ambition of consultants may desire. Thus SFA came in for criticism, some of it from rivals who, as one article in *Forbes* phrased it, wanted "to lap up some of the thick gravy the government pours on reform efforts."[28]

Some of the criticism challenged the integrity of the SFA research. According to Stanley Pogrow, a professor of education at the University of Arizona, "there never was any valid supporting research." "What had happened," Pogrow wrote, "was that the developers of Success for All, Robert Slavin and Nancy Madden, were also directors of a research center at Johns Hopkins University." From this perch "they were able to secure tens of millions of dollars to conduct research on their own program." Thus, when the U.S. Department of Education commissioned an assessment of programs that dealt with at-risk students, the contract went to Slavin and Madden's center at John Hopkins. "When Congress asked for a national study to determine the best approach for helping Title I students," the same group was commissioned to make the study.[29]

---

27 *The Gazette Online: The Newspaper of Johns Hopkins University* (9 November 1998).

28 Seth Lubove, "Success for Whom?" *Forbes* (13 November 2000) 210.

29 Stanley Pogrow, "Success for All Never Had a Research Base and Never Worked," Teachers.net Gazette (Boston University Online) May 2001.

According to Pogrow, Slavin and Madden then "flooded publications and professional research meetings with tons of articles, speeches, and sophisticated tables showing how successful [SFA] was." They "convinced everyone of the success of their program through the sheer volume of technical reports, to the extent that . . . no one looked into whether the research was actually valid."[30]

This eventually changed. In 1991 an independent evaluation of the SFA program in Baltimore noted that some SFA studies did not report on whether students were performing at grade level but reported instead that SFA students were doing better than comparable students in control schools. This represented some progress, if the control schools were truly comparable. But it fell short of SFA's announced goal of having all children reading at or near grade level by the end of third grade. The original goal had not been mere relative success in comparison to other inner-city schools that were not using any special programs. The original goal "was never simply to be better than other low-income schools," researcher S. J. Ruffini observed. Ruffini also said there were problems with the methods SFA used for comparing its schools with the control schools.[31]

Richard L. Venezky, a professor at the University of Delaware, expanded on these points. Venezky acknowledged that it was problematical to compare SFA students with national norms, "because few schools in major urban areas that serve predominantly minorities score at or above the national average." Nevertheless, Venezky refused to consider SFA a success simply because its students reportedly did

---

30 Ibid.

31 S. J. Ruffini et al., *Evaluation of Success for All* (Unpublished Report, Department of Research and Evaluation, Baltimore City Public Schools, 1991); Richard L. Venezky "An Alternative Perspective on Success for All," *Advances in Educational Policy* 4 (1998) 148.

better, on average, than "the abysmal performance normally obtained in reading with inner-city students."[32]

Venezky also questioned the quality of some of the research that was cited in support of SFA. In one instance, he said, SFA dropped the bottom 29 percent of its first-grade students from a comparison with other students, and in another SFA reported the scores of less than half the fifth grade students who had been tested for comparison with control students. Another critic accused SFA of "remov[ing] lots of high risk students from the samples . . . and in at least one case special ed students just disappeared." In addition, SFA was accused of "stack[ing] the deck by not reporting if students in the control group [were] spending as much time reading." Venezky also noted that "almost all of the claims for success of [SFA] derive from the project itself and few from disinterested outsiders."[33]

Moving beyond concerns about the methodology of evaluation, Venezky reported that the gains associated with SFA seemed to occur only in the first grade. After that, Venezky said, "SFA students begin to fall behind the average students nationally and by the end of fifth grade are almost 2.4 years behind." Even when compared with other inner-city control schools, Venezky reported, the advantage of SFA was concentrated in "the early primary grades." Venezky recommended that SFA "reevaluate how it instructs reading after first grade and how it assesses outcomes at the higher elementary levels."[34]

According to Venezky, SFA placed so much emphasis on phonics and the ability to decode simple stories that it gave short

---

32 Richard L. Venezky, "An Alternative Perspective," 155, 163.

33 Ibid., 151, 163; Stanley Pogrow, "Success for All Does Not Produce Success for Students," Phi Delta Kappan (September 2000) 71; Pogrow, "Success for All Never Had a Research Base," Teachers.net Gazette (May 2010).

34 Richard L. Venezky, "An Alternative Perspective," 161-162.

shrift to "higher-level reading and thinking skills, particularly those required for content-area reading." Thus, Venezky said, it was no surprise that SFA students fell further behind the national norms after the early grades. "The SFA approach to reading instruction is particularly good for what is assessed in the initial stages of reading," Venezky wrote, "but is not as well designed for the later stages where vocabulary and comprehension become more important than basic word attack skills."[35]

SFA came in for additional criticism from Herbert J. Walberg, a research professor at the University of Illinois, Chicago. Walberg acknowledged that SFA was a non-profit corporation but nevertheless insisted that with "huge amounts of money at stake program developers, administrators, and evaluators have strong financial interests in showing progress." Since 1965, Walberg wrote, the federal government had spent "more than $100 billion on the Chapter 1/Title I program to raise the achievement of poor children." Therefore, Walberg said, it was not surprising that "the Success for All developers and independent reviewers differ hugely in their estimates of its effectiveness." Disinterested research was hard to come by when so much money was at issue.[36]

Walberg further insisted that the problem was not just with those who received grants to fund their programs. The government

---

35 Ibid., 163, 160.

36 Herbert J. Walberg and Rebecca C. Greenberg, "The Diogenes Factor," *Phi Delta Kappan* (October 1999) 18. There was yet more criticism from Elizabeth M. Jones, Gary D. Gottfredson, and Denise C. Gottfredson, who reported that the effects of SFA were positive, though small, for grades 1 through 3; but "the positive effects were not found in the later grades." In some instances "control groups outscored Success for All students" and overall the average effect was "near zero—that is, Success for All students scored at about the 50th percentile or the same as matched control groups." Jones, Gottfredson, and Gottfredson, "Success for Some," *Evaluation Review* 21, 643-670, 659.

agencies that provided the funds also wanted to show that they had not wasted money, and they therefore "allow[ed] program developers to evaluate the programs." In these circumstances, Walberg concluded, skepticism was in order. Walberg urged readers to consider the sources of the research, quoting both the Romans who asked, "*Cui bono?*" (Who benefits?) and fellow Chicagoans who warned, "Don't ask your barber whether you need a haircut."[37]

Robert Slavin predictably took exception to the criticisms, and especially to allegations that his research was self-serving and that he had used data selectively. As one journalist noted, politics could be "tame compared with an academic whose integrity is questioned." When Richard Venezky noted that "almost all the claims for the success of [SFA] derive from the project itself and few from disinterested outsiders," Slavin's supporters accused Venezky of not being objective. They noted, for example, that Venezky had been associated with the International Reading Association, one of the premier organizations that promoted progressive approaches to teaching reading. And when Walberg complained that "the federal government has long supported failed programs financially and cannot seem to sort the good from the bad," Slavin's defenders accused Walberg of coming "close to slander" for suggesting that SFA was prompted by "financial concerns . . . rather than the drive to solve our literacy problem."[38]

Slavin was especially incensed with the criticism of University of Arizona professor Stanley A. Pogrow. According to Pogrow, SFA was "another in a long line of programs that have failed to accelerate

---

37 Herbert J. Walberg and Rebecca C. Greenberg, "The Diogenes Factor," 127-128; Walberg and Greenberg, "Educators Should Require Evidence," *Phi Delta Kappan* (October 1999) 132.

38 *Forbes* (13 November 2000) 210; Richard L. Venezky, "An Alternative Perspective," 163; Herbert J. Walberg and Rebecca C. Greenberg, "Educators Should Require Evidence," 135; Bruce R. Joyce, "The Great Literacy Problem and Success for All," *Phi Delta Kappan* (October 1999) 130.

student learning after the third grade. In terms of results, it is the same old, same old—with lots of bucks and political influence behind it." "The research behind SFA never used valid methodology or appropriate reporting of results." "All the advocacy by Slavin . . . is simply that—advocacy, not science. The work is not that of researchers but of marketers with a lot at stake."[39]

Yet Pogrow himself was not a disinterested critic, for he had developed a rival program called Higher Order Thinking Skills (HOTS). And even Pogrow acknowledged that SFA was effective in the early years of elementary school. Up to grade three, Pogrow wrote, there was a place for "drill, rote learning, and direct instruction." Yet even in the early grades, Pogrow considered it a mistake to have "at-risk students doing these things all the time." "Skill development" and "test prep" were important, but teachers should also strive "to develop a sense of understanding." "To build the thinking skills of educationally disadvantaged students," Pogrow recommended at least 35 minutes of unstructured discussion in the early grades and longer discussion periods for grades 4 through 7.[40]

Unfortunately, Pogrow wrote, programs such as HOTS were being crowded out because government agencies had accepted the validity of bogus SFA research. According to Pogrow, "a small group of researchers had convinced educators and legislators that . . . Success for All was uniquely and dramatically successful in raising the performance of disadvantaged students in urban districts." Then

---

39 Stanley Pogrow, "Success for All Does Not Produce Success for Students," 78-79.

40 Stanley Pogrow, "Challenging At-Risk Students," *Phi Delta Kappan* (January 1990; on-line, paragraph 5 of the section, "Implications of the Findings."); Pogrow, "Accelerating the Literacy of Educationally Disadvantaged Students after the Third Grade," *California English Teacher* (April 2002); Pogrow, "HOTS: Helping Low Achievers in Grades 4-7" *Principal* 76 (November 1996) 34-35.

states such as New Jersey, when ordered by courts to spend more for the education of impoverished students, virtually demanded that the upgraded schools implement the SFA program. "As SFA and its approach are increasingly favored, the choices that schools and teachers are allowed to consider to serve educationally disadvantaged students are increasingly restricted."[41]

The result would be tragic, Pogrow predicted. He maintained that the academic problems of inner-city students did not stem solely from their difficulty with basic reading. A larger problem set in when inner-city students were about 10 years old. Beginning around the fourth grade, they fell further behind as schoolwork began to require generalization and abstraction. This was not because a disproportionate number of the youngsters inherently lacked the capacity for sophisticated thought. "At-risk students have tremendous levels of intellectual and academic potential," Pogrow insisted. "Disadvantaged students are as capable of abstract thought as anyone." But they suffered because "the adults in their lives simply do not model thinking processes for them."[42]

Pogrow emphasized the importance of additional educational "gaps," especially an "understanding gap" that allegedly stemmed from a "conversation gap." He said there was a major difference in the child-rearing styles of parents in "caring professional households" and parents in "caring welfare households." The former supposedly spent far more time discussing issues with their children and explaining the reasons for various rules. The latter eschewed such discussions in favor of short commands, "the majority being of a negative admonishing nature."

---

41 Stanley Pogrow, "Rescuing Abbott," *Times of Trenton* (8 June 2003); Pogrow, "Success for All Does Not Produce Success for Students," 67.

42 Stanley Pogrow, "Challenging At-Risk Students," *Phi Delta Kappan* (January 1990; point 3 in "findings from HOTS"); Stanley Pogrow, "The Missing Element in Reducing the Learning Gap," *Teachers College Record* (3 October 2004).

According to Pogrow, "students from low-income households arrive in school with . . . millions fewer language interaction opportunities in the home. The interactions they do have largely involve listening to literal commands: 'do this' and 'do that.'" And "most of the adult talk is negative in nature, admonishing and criticizing." By the age of 4, Pogrow wrote, professional-class children had been exposed to five times as many words as children from welfare families.[43]

To compensate for the dearth of conversation at home, Pogrow advised schools to provide an "intensive conversation environment." Even in the early grades, teachers should do more than drill students on the basics. They should also set aside time for Socratic conversation and developing thinking skills "via ongoing conversations about ideas." To foster this sort of instruction, teachers should be "trained to maintain proper levels of ambiguity in discussions so that students would have to resolve ambiguity and construct meaning." If this were done, even disadvantaged students would develop higher order thinking skills and would no longer find their progress stunted after age 10. "Instead of lots of teacher talk," Pogrow and HOTS would provide "the dinner table conversations that [disadvantaged] students did not have in the home."[44]

Without such conversation, Pogrow opined, the progress of most disadvantaged students would slow down after fourth grade. Students who had not been exposed to the give and take of conversation would become frustrated and resentful when middle and high school teachers asked more complex questions. Students with limited vocabularies would become bored and resentful because their teachers would be

---

43 Stanley Pogrow, "Reducing the Gap . . . A Thinking Development Approach," *New Horizons for Learning* (Fall 2004); Pogrow, "The Missing Element."

44 Stanley Pogrow, "The Missing Element"; Pogrow, "Accelerating the Literacy of Educationally Disadvantaged Children"; Pogrow, "Reducing the Gap," HOTS.org.

speaking "in a strange foreign language." Such students did not need more drill and test preparation. They were already drilled too much. If they were to move beyond the plateau of elementary school, they needed to develop higher order thinking skills.[45]

Pogrow also mentioned research studies that allegedly had established the effectiveness of the HOTS program. He said the program was being used successfully in many schools where students "generally made twice the gain in overall reading as compared to comparison groups, and about three times the growth in reading comprehension." The success, moreover, was not limited to the early grades but continued into middle school and beyond. Unfortunately, Pogrow lamented, HOTS itself might not survive in the twenty-first century. It was at risk because Success for All had become the overwhelming choice among schools that wanted to tap into the money that private philanthropies and the federal, state, and local governments were spending on the reform of elementary education.[46]

After visiting ten SFA schools, education writer Jonathan Kozol also weighed in with a litany of criticisms. Like others before him, Kozol complained that SFA teachers had "little chance to draw upon their own inventiveness." Instead, they were required "to stick closely to the script." There was no time for "even the most pleasant and old-fashioned class activities," such as parties with the children at Halloween or an exchange of cards on Valentine's Day. Everything was directed toward improving the scores on standardized tests. Even recess was "truncated or abolished in the desperation to carve out a bit more time for drilling children for exams."[47]

---

45 Ibid.

46 Stanley Pogrow, "Reducing the Gap."

47 Jonathan Kozol, *The Shame of the Nation*, 71, 72, 79-80, 120.

To make matters worse, children who did poorly on the tests—those who were "re-shuffled" downward at the end of each eight week period—faced the "ever-present danger of humiliation when their reading levels ... were announced." When Kozol asked one girl about her classmates, the girl told Kozol that "Reginald is a Level One" and "Melissa and Shaneek are Level Threes." When Kozol asked the girl how she was doing, the girl "wrinkled her nose and looked at me unhappily. 'I'm just a Level Two.'"[48]

Many teachers were also unhappy with SFA. Some resented the loss of autonomy and understood that the emphasis on standardized tests stemmed, at least in part, from a loss of confidence in the teachers' ability to assess their students. "What stultified the atmosphere of education more than anything," one teacher said, "was "not the scripted reading method" but the implication that it was necessary to rely almost solely on external measurements. School administrators said that, because there was a high incidence of teacher turnover at inner-city schools, prepackaged lessons were needed to ensure that all teachers—even novices and substitute teachers—would be competent. But Kozol, while conceding that SFA had been imposed "in part, to compensate for staffing needs of schools that had a hard time in recruiting teachers," concluded that SFA ironically ended up by driving out well-qualified teachers who could not abide the loss of autonomy.[49]

Kozol took special exception to methods SFA used for maintaining order. "Silent lunches had been instituted in the cafeteria and, on days when children misbehaved, silent recess had been introduced as well." SFA also trained the school's teachers to use a number of terse commands: "Active listening!" "Every eye on me!" "Zero noise!" Yet this last command was rarely required, for SFA had an extraordinary system of hand signals. The "silence salute" was

---

48   Ibid., 73-74.

49   Ibid., 305, 85.

supposed to be given with the elbow bent, but Kozol reported that it was delivered with "Stiff arm. Hand up. Flat palm." As described by Kozol, the signal was akin to "Heil Hitler!"[50]

As Kozol described it, SFA also reeked of racism. Although Robert Slavin spoke in broad language that seemed applicable to all students, his program was used primarily at inner-city schools that had long histories of failure and frequent turnover of teachers. In New York City, only 1 percent of the students in Success for All schools were White. "If we were not a segregated school," one teacher said, "if there were middle-class white children here, the parents would rebel at this curriculum and they would stop it cold." According to Kozol, SFA amounted to "an educational apartheid system with one method of instruction for poor kids and another for middle-class kids." Instead of encouraging students to think independently, SFA was preparing students for service in subordinate economic roles—as nursing aids and health assistants and workers in restaurant kitchens. Because inner-city children were "not perceived as having the potential of most other citizens," their schools operated on the premise that schools for disadvantaged children should have "a different set of goals than schools that serve the children of the middle class."[51]

Some writers on the right seemed to confirm this assessment. In 1969 the prominent Berkeley psychologist Arthur Jensen had maintained that memorization, drill, and direct instruction were especially appropriate for students with low IQs. And in 1993 Charles Murray, the co-author of *The Bell Curve*, advised ghetto schools to "start thinking about what preparation students really need to become productive workers." According to Murray, it was especially important that children from "disorganized homes" learn "to come to the same place every day, stay there for a prescribed number of hours

---

50 Ibid., 65, 66-67, 345-346.

51 Ibid., 64, 81, 75, 87, 105, 98; *New York Times* (19 January 2003).

and follow the teacher's (boss's) instructions, even if they didn't feel like it." Nor were Jensen and Murray alone in offering such advice. As journalist Abby Goodnough reported in the New York Times, many other experts also maintained that both poor children, "whose lives outside school may be highly unstable," and their teachers, "who are often new and have little training," needed "as much structure and top-down direction as possible."[52]

Robert Slavin understandably took exception to Kozol's strictures. Slavin insisted that it was false to say that SFA was "intended only for schools that serve large numbers of disadvantaged students." SFA admittedly hoped "to help disadvantaged students," but there was "nothing in the program that would not be appropriate in middle-class communities." In fact, Slavin asserted, "about 100 SFA schools across the country could be described as middle class."[53]

Slavin further maintained that Kozol told only part of the SFA story, the part that "confirm[ed] his preexisting biases." "[Kozol] chose not to inform his readers" that students in SFA schools were making substantial gains. In fact, at P.S. 65 in the Bronx, the SFA school where Kozol spent the most time, "the percentage of students passing the New York reading test rose from 17 percent in 1999 to 46% in 2003." By way of contrast, at P.S. 30, which Kozol offered as an example of what a good urban school should be, the percentage passing declined from 30.5 to 27.8. Nor were these two schools atypical, Slavin insisted. The success of SFA had been shown "in dozens of rigorous experimental/control comparisons done by many researchers."[54]

---

[52] Arthur R. Jensen, "How Much Can We Boost IQ and Scholastic Achievement?" *Harvard Educational Review* 39 (1969) 1-123; Charles Murray, "Bad Lessons," *New York Times* (8 January 1993); Abby Goodnough, "Fearing a Class System in the Classroom," *New York Times* (19 January 2003).

[53] Robert E. Slavin, "Shame Indeed," *Phi Delta Kappan* 87 (April 2006) 621.

[54] Ibid.

Like most liberal educators, Slavin opposed the policy of assigning minority students to racially imbalanced schools, if the disproportion was predominantly Black. He deplored the fact that some of these "segregated" schools were "underfunded for the job they are asked to do." But he considered it deplorable, even "shameful," for Kozol to ignore the importance of using the best, research-tested ways for teaching basic subjects. Slavin insisted that it would be calamitous "to deny these children effective instructional methods." "By failing to tell the whole story of what happened at [SFA schools]," Slavin concluded, "Kozol only aid[ed] those who believe that improving inner-city schools is hopeless."[55]

Progressive educators generally sided with Slavin's critics while traditionalists rallied in support of Success for All. The debate, however, involved more than theories of education. As has been noted, from its founding onward Success for All outpaced its rivals in the contest for grants from private philanthropies and government agencies. This trend was confirmed in 2010 when the Department of Education chose just four groups from among 1,600 applicants in the competition for "scale up" awards worth $50 million each. Success for All was one of the four. Two of the others—Teach for America and the KIPP Foundation—will be described below, in Chapters 7 and 8.[56]

---

55 *Ibid.*

56 Michele McNeil, "49 Applicants Win 3 Grants," *Education Week* (4 August 2010). The fourth winning application for "scale up' funds came from Ohio State University, which proposed to train 3,750 additional first grade teachers in a tutoring program called Reading Recovery.

6

E. D. Hirsch and Core Knowledge

In 2010, some 1,184 schools used all or part of what is called the Core Knowledge Curriculum. This made Core Knowledge one of the largest school curricula in the United States. The curriculum focused on the elementary grades and emphasized the importance of giving students the basic knowledge that would serve as a foundation for more advanced learning. Core Knowledge drew its inspiration from E. D. Hirsch, Jr.

Hirsch was born in 1928, the son of a rabbi in Memphis, Tennessee. He was educated at Cornell, where he received a B.A. degree in 1950, and at Yale, where he received a Ph.D. in English literature in 1957. In 1960, he published a book on the Romantic poets and literary theorists William Wordsworth and Friedrich Schiller. Other books followed, and by the 1970s Hirsch was well established as a literary theorist whose ideas were often discussed at academic conferences. Hirsch eventually received an endowed professorship at the University of Virginia and became the chairman of the university's Department of English.[1]

---

1   E. D. Hirsch, quoted by Alan Wolfe, "In Defense of a Common Culture," *Christianity Today* (4 February 2010); Mark Bauerlein, "The Remarkable Turn of E. D. Hirsch," *Chronicle of Higher Education* (2 August 2008).

Hirsch had what he called "a 'Eureka!' moment" in 1978, when he and some colleagues were testing the reading comprehension of students at the J. Sargent Reynolds Community College in Richmond. Hirsch discovered that as long as the students were asked to read passages about familiar topics like roommates or automobiles, the students from the community college did almost as well as those from the University of Virginia. But the community college students faltered when they encountered passages that required unfamiliar background information. Hirsch was especially surprised to discover that many community college students, even though they were from Richmond, had difficulty understanding a passage on Robert E. Lee's surrender to Ulysses S. Grant at Appomattox Court House. They had problems, Hirsch observed, "because they had no idea who Lee was, who Grant was, what the context was." By contrast, students from the University of Virginia read and understood the passage with ease, because they had heard of Lee and Grant, knew about the Civil War, and were not seeing the name Appomattox for the first time. The university students did not face comparable difficulty until they were asked to read a passage about Hegel's metaphysics.[2]

This experience "changed my life," Hirsch said. It led him to shift his focus away from literary studies and toward education. After observing the community college students closely, Hirsch concluded that "their basic intelligence was sound." But they had been cheated. "They hadn't acquired important general knowledge in their homes and communities, and their schools hadn't compensated for that.... They simply did not have the knowledge they needed to make sense of many texts." For the rest of his professional career, Hirsch would maintain that successful reading required more than an ability to decode or sound out words. It

---

2   E. D. Hirsch, "Many Americans Can Read But Can't Comprehend," *USA Today* (24 February 2004); Mark F. Goldberg, "Doing What Works," *Phi Delta Kappan* 78 (September 1997) 83; Christopher Hitchens, "Why We Don't Know What We Don't Know," *New York Times* (13 May 1990).

also required background knowledge without which students would not understand what they were reading.³

Hirsch recognized that elementary schools had recently done a better job teaching the fundamentals of reading. Thanks to researchers such as Jeanne Chall of Harvard, fewer teachers subscribed to the belief that reading was a natural process. The tide had turned against the progressive notion that just as children learned to speak without formal instruction, so they would also learn to read naturally if they were exposed to good literature and had reached a level of developmental readiness. Instead, reading teachers were coming to understand that persistent instruction, a little at a time, was the best way to teach reading. After surveying the research on reading, Hirsch, like Robert Slavin, concluded that the evidence in favor of phonics-based, direct instruction was "strong and ... voluminous."⁴

After they had learned to decode words fluently and accurately, many children understood what they were reading. But comprehension was more likely if children had been exposed at home to a wide range of enabling information. Comprehension was also more likely if the children's experience at home had made them familiar with large vocabularies and with complex modes of syntax and grammar. Hirsch noted with approval the work of University of Kansas researchers Betty Hart and Todd Risley, who had "demonstrated that toddlers in low-income homes tend to hear fewer words and less complex sentences than higher-income children. Low-income children therefore enter kindergarten or preschool with smaller verbal repertoires than high-income children."⁵

---

3   E. D. Hirsch, quoted by Sol Stern, "E. D. Hirsch's Curriculum for Democracy," *City Journal* (Autumn 2009).

4   E. D. Hirsch, *The Knowledge Deficit: Closing the Shocking Education Gap for American Children* (Boston: Houghton Miflin Company, 2006) 23-24.

5   E. D. Hirsch, *The Making of Americans* (New Haven: Yale University Press, 2009), 138.

It turned out that for many youngsters becoming a skilled decoder was not the same as becoming a skilled reader. Although children from disadvantaged backgrounds could sound out words, they often did not understand what they were reading—apparently because they had grown up in information-barren circumstances and were not exposed to the articulate use of language. According to Hirsch, the academic achievement gap originated "outside school, in the language that toddlers hear." By the age of two, there existed "large differences in children's familiarity with unusual words, standard pronunciation, and complex syntax." "The typical disadvantaged child enters kindergarten knowing only half as many words as the typical advantaged child."[6]

This led Hirsch to discuss a phenomenon that is sometimes called the "Matthew Effect." The term derives from a Biblical preacher who, in the Gospel of Matthew, spoke of faith growing stronger among true believers while declining among the less faithful. ("For whosoever hath, to him shall be given, and he shall have more abundance; but whosoever hath not, from him shall be taken away even that he hath.") In terms of vocabulary and reading, the rich became richer and the poor became poorer because prior knowledge of key words and information enabled advantaged children to learn still more, whereas children who knew little were hindered in learning.[7]

Hirsch asked his readers to "picture a classroom where the more fortunate students know at least 90 percent of the words being used by a teacher or in a textbook. That enables them to gain knowledge about the other 10 percent of words that they did not already know. But the students who did not already know 90 percent of the words,

---

6   *Ibid.*, 2; E. D. Hirsch, "Overcoming the Language Gap," *Education Week* (2 May 2001); Hirsch, "Reading Comprehension Requires Knowledge," *American Educator* (Spring 2003) 21.

7   Matthew 13:12.

and were therefore mystified by what the teacher or book said, would make little progress in learning new words and so would fall still further behind. They start off behind and then fall further behind. They also feel left out and discouraged and are likely to tune out and create discipline problems. For such students the verbal gap tends to grow ever larger as they go through school. The rich get richer and the poor get relatively poorer with exposure to the same discourse. That is the Matthew Effect."[8]

Hirsch nevertheless maintained that disadvantaged youngsters could catch up, if their schools taught students the vocabulary, syntax, and basic information that most educated Americans held in common. He especially stressed the importance of breadth of knowledge. Reading was not just a mechanical skill, Hirsch reiterated. To understand most written works, one had to know something about the subject. Because they knew nothing of the Civil War, the students at the Richmond community college had difficulty with the passage that described the surrender at Appomattox Court House. Similarly, a literate English person who was not familiar with American baseball, would know all the words but would not understand a newspaper story that said, "Jones sacrificed and knocked in a run." Most Americans, for their part, would be "baffled by a sentence about the sport of cricket."[9]

To underscore the importance of background knowledge, Hirsch mentioned a 1988 study where researchers divided seventh- and eighth-grade students into two groups—strong and weak readers as measured by standardized reading tests. The students in each group were then subdivided according to their knowledge of baseball. After that, all the students were given a reading test with passages about baseball,

---

8   E. D. Hirsch, *The Making of Americans*, 139.

9   *Ibid.*, 58-67; E. D. Hirsch, "The Latest Dismal NAEP Scores," *Education Week* (2 May 2001); Hirsch, *The Knowledge Deficit*, 68

and "low-level readers with high baseball knowledge significantly outperformed strong readers with little background knowledge."[10]

For Hirsch, this study made an important point: "that knowing something of the topic you're reading about is the most important variable in comprehension." And there was a corollary: many disadvantaged youths knew about baseball but were less familiar with common knowledge about geography, history, science, and literature. Thus, when it came to passages on these topics, disadvantaged children could sound out the words but still did not understand. It turned out that "a reading test is inherently a knowledge test" because new information was almost always "embedded in a mountain of taken-for-granted knowledge."[11]

Hirsch believed that "adequate progress in knowledge" was "the sure road to adequate progress in reading." Therefore, he urged teachers and schools to deal with deficits in vocabulary and background information. They should acknowledge that when the proportion of unfamiliar words exceeded 10 percent of a passage, readers had difficulty inferring the meaning from context and were left uncomprehending. Equally important, they should recognize the importance of background knowledge. "Knowledge builds on knowledge," Hirsch often said, explaining that, after children had mastered the rudiments of reading, their progress depended on acquiring knowledge that would enable them to make connections between new and previously learned content. Since children who already knew something about the Civil War (or any other subject) found it easier to understand passages on the topic, it followed that schools should impart the information that students needed to become good readers.

---

10 E. D. Hirsch, "Reading Test Dummies," *New York Times* (12 March 2009).

11 E. D. Hirsch, "The Knowledge Connection," *Washington Post* (16 February 2008); Hirsch, "The Truth about Learning to Read Well," *Yale Alumni Magazine* (September/October 2009).

Fortunately, the two tasks went hand-in-hand. For decades, experts had debated whether children would gain a large vocabulary naturally, if they were exposed to a range of information, or whether they would learn more if their teachers devoted a significant portion of class time to the explicit study of word meanings. In a reversal of the situation with respect to decoding, the weight of evidence indicated that the natural method (as opposed to direct instruction) worked better for vocabulary enhancement. For Hirsch, this meant that schools could simultaneously provide background knowledge and build vocabulary. While emphasizing phonics-based decoding in the early years of elementary school, teachers should also expose students systematically to a body of widely-shared knowledge, metaphors, and allusions. In this way, students would be able to make sense of texts that could not be understood without prior knowledge.

Although Hirsch had written technical papers on reading and comprehension as far back as 1960, he did not receive wide attention until the publication in 1987 of his best-selling book, *Cultural Literacy*. In it Hirsch observed that teaching "the ways of one's own community has always been and still remains the essence of the education of our children." He noted that "the weight of human tradition across many cultures supports the view that basic acculturation should be completed by age thirteen. At that age Catholics are confirmed, Jews bar or bat mitzvahed, and tribal boys and girls undergo the rites of passage into the tribe." The job of elementary and junior high schools, as Hirsch saw it, was to transmit the basic information needed to thrive in a society, which in practice meant "the transmission to children of the specific information shared by the adults." Like it or not, Hirsch said, America had a body of cultural information and allusions that most successful people shared.[12]

---

12 E. D. Hirsch, *Cultural Literacy: What Every American Needs to Know* (Boston: Houghton Miflin Company, 1987) 18, 30, xiii, xvi.

Hirsch's espousal of cultural literacy did not stem from an elite notion of culture and tradition. Politically, Hirsch was a liberal Democrat who thought wealth should be distributed more evenly. "I've never voted Republican. I've always voted Democrat," Hirsch said in 2006. "I've always thought of myself . . . as a quasi-socialist, and a sense of social justice is my chief animating emotion. I don't like great inequalities . . . I'm egalitarian." [13]

But Hirsch was an analytical egalitarian who had observed that the higher one ascended in professional worlds, the more cultural literacy was needed. It was not a formal requirement, but familiarity with a range of references was taken for granted in the upper spheres. Those who did not have these familiarities did not seem to belong. That was the way things were, and instead of lamenting the situation, Hirsch wanted to make sure that students from disadvantaged backgrounds had the opportunity to learn what was needed to get ahead.[14]

Cultural Literacy provided an appendix that listed some 5,000 names, dates, aphorisms, and metaphors that were familiar to literate Americans. Without this fund of information and references, it was difficult to get ahead, or even to grasp the implications of many newspaper articles. This was so, Hirsch explained, because writers inevitably took some things for granted. To communicate effectively, writers had to sense what could be left unexplained, on the assumption that readers already shared this information. And since most professions (or texts) assumed that members (or readers) shared a certain amount of background information, this common knowledge was a prerequisite for both social mobility and reading comprehension. According to Hirsch, "any reader who doesn't possess

---

13   E. D. Hirsch, interview with Andrew J. Rotherham, "Core Convictions," EducationSector.org (22 September 2006).

14   Mark Bauerlein, "The Remarkable Turn of E. D. Hirsch," *Chronicle of Higher Education* (2 August 2008).

the knowledge assumed in a piece he or she reads will in fact be illiterate with respect to that particular piece of writing."[15]

Perhaps because Americans love lists, and also because Hirsch's list could be regarded as a test of cultural intelligence, *Cultural Literacy* enjoyed tremendous sales success. To the surprise of the publisher, who had initially hoped to sell about 5,000 copies, the book spent months on the *New York Times*' list of non-fiction best sellers. Eventually, several hundred thousand copies of the book were sold, and Hirsch dedicated the royalties to what became the non-profit Core Knowledge Foundation. The foundation then published primers that spelled out in detail what every child should learn in elementary school. Eventually, there was a book for each grade—*What Your 1st Grader Needs to Know, What Your 2nd Grader Needs to Know*—and a packaged plan that specified how teachers and students should spend about 50 percent of their time at schools that purchased the Core Knowledge curriculum. Underlying the venture was Hirsch's conviction that literacy depended on "the breadth of one's acquaintance with a national culture."[16]

As the United States became more diverse and multicultural after the 1960s, and as a larger proportion of high school graduates enrolled in colleges, average scores plummeted on some tests. This was especially evident on national assessments of reading and on the verbal part of the Scholastic Aptitude Test (SAT). Between 1972 and 1991, for example, the percentage of students scoring over 600 on the SAT Verbal test declined from more than 11 percent of the test takers to less than 7 percent. Some observers thought this was the inevitable result of changes in the pool of test takers. This opinion was so widespread that one well-informed writer declared in 2010 that "everybody (or nearly everybody)" knew but was "fearful of expressing

---

15 *Ibid.*, 13.

16 *New York Times* (26 September 1993); *Time* (17 August 1987) 56.

in public" that "America's educational woes just reflect our current demographic mix of students. Today's schools are filled with millions of youngsters, many of whom are Hispanic immigrants struggling with English plus millions of others of mediocre intellectual ability disdaining academic achievement."[17]

Hirsch, however, did not accept this view. He thought test scores had plummeted because the nation's elementary schools no longer provided the breadth of knowledge that was needed to understand written works. As Hirsch saw it, the primary schools did not provide this information because, beginning around the turn of the 20th century with John Dewey and his disciples at the University of Chicago and at Columbia Teachers College, the nation's colleges of education had developed a new approach to elementary education. Progressive educators scuttled the traditional academic curriculum, which had imparted basic information, and instead allowed students to work on projects that the students themselves found interesting. The progressives conceded that graduates of their schools might not acquire as much standard information about history, geography, and science, but they said that progressive education would encourage the development of self-confidence and inquiring minds. As a result, the progressives said, their students would have an edge when it came to critical thinking and problem solving.[18]

Hirsch regarded the progressives' theory as unfounded romanticism. He thought specific knowledge about a broad range of topics was the key to understanding written material, and that the failure to provide enabling knowledge was the chief cause of the decline in reading comprehension. As Hirsch saw it, the racial, ethnic,

---

17 E. D. Hirsch, *Cultural Literacy*, 4; Richard J. Hernstein and Charles Murray, *The Bell Curve*, 428; Robert Weissberg, *Bad Students, Not Bad Schools* (New Brunswick: Transaction Publishers, 2010) vii.

18 E. D. Hirsch, *The Making of Americans*, passim.

and socio-economic achievement gaps in the United States were "not chiefly caused by diversity of ethnic and family background but by diversity of academic preparation." "The chief cause of the ... equality gaps" was the progressive "anti-curriculum movement" that had germinated for decades and reached full flowering in the 1960s and 1970s. Instead of preparing students for what progressive educators called "higher-order thinking," the new approach had deprived pupils of the knowledge that was needed to understand most books, newspapers, and magazines.[19]

Hirsch repeatedly stressed that an emphasis on core knowledge was especially beneficial to children from underprivileged homes. Unlike children who had been exposed at home to some of the taken-for-granted background knowledge, most disadvantaged children came to school knowing less of what society deemed important. But this did not mean that well-to-do students did not suffer from what Hirsch called "the new anti-curriculum theories [that] dominated teaching at Teachers College, and thence came to dominate dozens of education schools across the nation." The reading scores of the best American students had also declined as the influence of progressivism expanded.

"In 1972, 17,560 college-bound seniors scored 700 or higher on the SAT Verbal. In 1993, only 10,407 scored 700 or higher on the Verbal—a drop of 41 percent in the raw number of students scoring 700 and over, despite the larger number of students taking the test in 1993 compared to 1972." Some observers attributed this decline to egalitarianism and blamed the civil rights movement for shifting the emphasis in public education away from grouping students by ability and toward uplifting the disadvantaged. But Hirsch insisted that every group would benefit if the nation's elementary schools imparted a rich foundation of general knowledge.[20]

---

19 Ibid., 116-17, 40-41, 115.

20 Ibid., 39; Richard J. Herrnstein and Charles Murray, *The Bell Curve*, 428;

Hirsch described himself as "a political liberal" but "an educational conservative." He wanted to reduce racial and ethnic achievement gaps and achieve a more equal distribution of academic skills. But to do this, the elementary schools had to make sure that students were acquainted with essential common knowledge. Progressives, on the other hand, were opposed to the specific, grade-by-grade subject-matter curriculum that Hirsch favored. They pointed to research that supposedly showed that knowledge was truly mastered only as it was acquired personally in real situations. They understood what Howard Gardner was getting at when he reprimanded observers who tried to show his toddler son how to insert a key in a locked door. Gardner wanted the lad to figure it out by himself. Because of the fundamentally internal nature of deep learning, progressives insisted, teachers should not present rules and information. Nothing should be fixed in advance. Instead, teachers should encourage children to discover on their own and to *construct* their own understandings. Progressives emphasized the importance of "non-directive teaching" and "personally-constructed learning." Eventually, modern progressives came to be known as "constructivists."[21]

It was a "tragic paradox," Hirsch wrote, that "the *Brown* decision which desegregated our schools" was handed down in 1954, shortly before a combination of educational trends "finally succeeded in abolishing the emphasis on traditional academic content in the early grades." As Hirsch saw it, during the 1960s, 1970s and 1980s children were being integrated into schools where "the traditional lore necessary to communication and full participation in our society was very inconsistently taught." "In the wake of the *Brown* decision, at the very moment of our highest hopes for social justice, the victory of progressivism over academic content had already foreclosed the

---

Robert Weissberg, *Bad Students, Not Bad Schools*.

21 E. D. Hirsch, "Why Core Knowledge Promotes Social Justice," *Common Knowledge* 12 (1999); Hirsch, *The Making of Americans*, 37, 44-45.

chance that school integration would equalize achievement and enhance social justice."[22]

Hirsch thought that political liberals "ought to oppose progressive educational ideas because they have led to practical failure and greater social inequity. The only practical way to achieve liberalism's aim of greater social justice is to pursue conservative educational policies." But most liberals did not see it that way. When liberals controlled school boards, Hirsch observed, schools tended to oppose the explicit teaching of phonics and to disparage the importance of traditional, knowledge-based education. Instead, most liberals favored the informal method of teaching reading and criticized the direct teaching of subject matter. Liberals complained that traditional instruction imposed "the same content on every student, without taking into account the child's individual strengths, weaknesses and interests." Instead of teaching a pre-determined body of information to an entire class, liberals and progressives said it would be better for students to have individual tutorials and special projects. They advised teachers to become "guides" or "coaches" rather than authoritative instructors.[23]

Hirsch acknowledged that individualized tutorials were "the most effective mode of teaching." Nevertheless, he maintained that most students learned "more and better in schools where greater emphasis is placed on whole-class instruction." The answer to this paradox lay in simple arithmetic. "It is impossible to provide effective one-on-one tutoring to 25 students at a time," Hirsch explained. "When one student is being coached individually, 24 others are being left to their own

---

22 E. D. Hirsch, "Why Core Knowledge Promotes Social Justice."

23 E. D. Hirsch, interview with Andrew J. Rotherham, *EducationSector.org* (26 September 2006); Hirsch, "Why Traditional Education is More Progressive," *American Enterprise* 8 (March/April 1997) 42; Hirsch, "Finding the Answers in Drills and Rigor," *New York Times* (11 September 1999).

devices... When, on the other hand, knowledge is effectively given to the entire group simultaneously, more students are learning much more of the time." In addition, Hirsch said that an emphasis on individual projects led teachers to skip over many topics and left elementary students without much of the basic common knowledge.[24]

Hirsch insisted that people who lacked "effective mastery of English, including mastery of the shared background knowledge that enables its nuanced use," were likely to remain poor. Minority leaders could not challenge the vested interests without mastering the rhetoric and content of the traditional culture; and without the knowledge that schools could provide, disadvantaged youths would not obtain the jobs that would enable them to improve their condition. Therefore, Hirsch urged Americans to reach an agreement on the content and sequence of what was taught in the elementary grades, just as they had come to agree on the standard spelling of words like *Mississippi*. The content, moreover, should be determined by asking a question: "Is this information taken for granted in writing that is addressed to the general, informed readers of this nation?" If such readers were not expected to know about the Black African cultures of Nubia and Kush, then that information could be omitted. If generally educated readers were expected to be familiar with the achievements of African-American leaders, then students should be told about W. E. B. Du Bois and Martin Luther King. Since the standard background knowledge was always changing, the elementary curriculum had to be modified from time to time. Hirsch included a good deal of African-American history as core knowledge—enough to receive endorsements from the noted black scholars Orlando Patterson and Henry Louis Gates.[25]

But Hirsch was concerned that "under the pressure of the multicultural movement" students might know of Rosa Parks "but

---

24 E. D. Hirsch, "Why Traditional Education is More Progressive."

25 *Ibid.*

not Eleanor Roosevelt." Therefore, he insisted that schools should continue to inform students about traditional cultural allusions and references like the *Mayflower*. Schools should also come to an agreement about the sequence of the agreed-upon topics. Otherwise, some students would never hear about the *Mayflower* and others—especially those who transferred from one school to another –might hear about the *Mayflower* in one grade after another.[26]

Some observers were bothered by Hirsch's insistence on the *Mayflower* (and other matters that pertained to White America). They accused Hirsch of trying "to impose his narrow values on the diversity of a many-splendored nation." In *The New Republic*, Louis Menand complained that stories like that of George Washington and the cherry tree "reinforce a myth about the superhumanity of the Founding Fathers." After acknowledging that Americans would benefit from a "sense of national unity, which a shared understanding of certain basic information provides," Robert Stevens declared in the *New York Times* that it was "highly unlikely" that such information "could be provided in a way not in some sense geared to the values and assumptions of a rather narrow elite." Stevens noted that "the concerns of the Chicano community in Southern California" were "not the same as those of the Cuban community in Miami, let alone those of a predominantly WASP community in New England or the Midwest."[27]

Stevens's comment pointed toward a new emphasis that was emerging among professors of literature and history. As Gabrielle M. Spiegel explained in a presidential address to the American Historical Association, historians were increasingly concerned with "questions of diaspora ... and the rapidly developing field of transnational history."

---

26 E. D. Hirsch, "Americanization and the Schools," *The Clearing House* 72 (January/February 1999) 136.

27 *Nation* 244 (30 May 1987) 714; *New Republic* 196 (22 June 1987) 42; *New York Times* (26 April 1987).

Instead of regarding themselves as essentially "Americans," a growing number of citizens of the United States—especially Blacks, Asians, and Hispanics—were emulating the traditional approach of some Jewish sojourners. They were developing "de-territorialized identities." They no longer identified with their "hostlands" but instead regarded themselves as part of dispersed ethnic "communities"—diasporas of Africans, Mexicans, Chinese, or Jews. Because they celebrated this redefinition of home, community, allegiance, and identity, many scholars rejected E. D. Hirsch's emphasis on core knowledge.[28]

These criticisms were especially popular in university circles, as Hirsch learned during a conversation with a young professor from the academic Left (a category Hirsch previously had used for himself). The young professor upbraided Hirsch "for wanting to perpetuate the language and culture of the elite . . . instead of working to change American culture." In response, Hirsch said that "during the long period it would take before professors managed to change the linguistic competence required to get a job at IBM or to understand a serious newspaper, the withholding of 'elite' culture from disadvantaged students would simply prevent them from earning a good living." Hirsch was left speechless when the young professor then said, "That's a sacrifice I'm willing to make." Hirsch treasured the memory as an "epitomizing moment." For the sake of a theory, "the cultural left" was willing "to risk condemning a generation to ignorance and therefore to poverty."[29]

As it happened, the young professor's comment was only one instance in what became an avalanche of criticism. In 1987,

---

28 Gabrielle M. Spiegel, "The Task of the Historian," *American Historical Review* 114 (February 2009) 1-15.

29 E. D. Hirsch, "Americanization and the Schools," 136; Christopher Hitchens, "Why We Don't Know What We Don't Know," *New York Times* (13 May 1990).

sociologist Lewis A. Coser criticized Hirsch for not recognizing that "mainstream culture" reflected the "strong class bias" of the elite. In 1991, the English faculty at Syracuse University produced a document that found fault with Hirsch for "privileging a particular body of culturally sanctioned texts." At his own University of Virginia, Hirsch recalled, the faculty of the School of Education said that core knowledge was "traditional, Eurocentric, rote memorizing, racist, and developmentally inappropriate."[30]

As a professor, Hirsch had a reputation for outstanding scholarship on the English romantic poets. He also enjoyed a high reputation as a teacher at the University of Virginia, where for years his large-lecture courses on English literature had received top ratings. Then, after he began to write about education, Hirsch arranged with the dean of Virginia's college of education to teach a course "on the causes and cure of the achievement gap between, on one hand, blacks and Hispanics, and, on the other, whites and Asians." Since this was "a hot topic," Hirsch expected "to attract a lot of curious students and expose them to heterodox views." He was surprised when his new course attracted only ten students. "The next year the story was the same, as it was the year after that. In the third year, one of my students mentioned to me privately that I should be proud of the courage shown by my students; that they were all in my class despite having been explicitly warned by members of the education faculty not to take the course."[31]

Hirsch was "astonished" at the time and still "stunned" years later when he thought about how students were "shielded from heterodox ideas in education schools, which are less like university departments

---

30 Lewis A. Coser, "Cultural Literacy," *Science* 236 (22 May 1987) 973; Ann Hulbert, "Revise, Revise," *The New Republic* 204 (28 January 1991) 42; E. D. Hirsch, "Heroes of Education Reform," *Common Knowledge* 11 (1998).

31 E. D. Hirsch, *The Making of Americans*, 49.

than theological institutes where heresy is viewed as an evil that its members have a civic duty to suppress." According to Hirsch, "anti-curriculum" progressives regarded "pro-curriculum" educators as despots who wanted "to impose soul-deadening burdens on children and discourage lively, child-friendly teaching." Those who stressed the importance of subject matter were regarded as "authoritarian, undemocratic, and right wing." It was "the duty of the education professor to protect prospective teachers from exposure to their ideas. Their writings must not be assigned."[32]

One after another, progressive professors of education piled on with criticism of Hirsch's approach. One notable example was *The Manufactured Crisis* (1995), by David C. Berliner, a professor at Arizona State University, and Bruce J. Biddle, a professor at the University of Missouri. Berliner and Biddle deprecated core knowledge for its "drill and practice," its "rote learning of facts," and its teacher-dominated classrooms, where adults poured information and ideas "into passive students." Instead, Berliner and Biddle said that "higher order thinking" should be "a central goal." Like Howard Gardner and Theodore Sizer, Berliner and Biddle advised against attempts "to cover the curriculum." They wanted "sustained involvement with a small number of topics, rather than superficial coverage of many topics," and they recommended "greater stress" on "student-initiated projects." For Berliner and Biddle, "meaningful knowledge is never really transmitted from an authority to a passive learner; instead, knowledge is created anew by learners as they … construct their own interpretations of ideas." Adding insult to their critique, Berliner and Biddle accused many teachers of opposing progressive approaches for fear of surrendering their "power and authority" and because they recognized that traditional approaches had been "designed, in part" to provide "unfair advantages … for affluent children" and to disadvantage "impoverished and minority students."[33]

---

32 Ibid., 49-50.

33 David C. Berliner and Bruce J. Biddle, *The Manufactured Crisis* (Addison-

E. D. Hirsch

Hirsch continued to regard himself as a political liberal, and he lamented that progressive professors were using the peer review process to deny funding for research projects that might support basic education. He said that progressives did not want to know "about practical results that show that explicit, coherent subject matter counts for more than anything else in early education and produces results that far exceed anything done under the anti-curriculum creed." Rather than study core knowledge schools where disadvantaged students made good scores on standardized tests, progressives cast aspersions. They said that traditionalists favored "rote memorization and parroting back facts." They said that core knowledge was "antipathetic to independent-mindedness, love of learning, and critical thinking." They said that progressive teachers, unlike traditionalists, "inculcate[d] general skills, independent thought, love of learning, and critical thinking." According to Hirsch, these "polarizing slogans" were part of "a propaganda effort . . . to preserve the anti-curriculum doctrine in the face of failure and decline. Ever since the 1930s, the identification of a set academic curriculum with an anti-liberal, reactionary, authoritarian, elitist, right-wing point of view has continued to be the most successful and persistent rhetorical maneuver of the anti-curriculum movement. It has won over many liberals and has influenced major philanthropies to oppose an elementary core curriculum."[34]

In 1999, the *Harvard Educational Review* published an especially spirited progressive critique of Hirsch's contention that disadvantaged students would benefit from a core curriculum. According to Kristin L. Buras, core knowledge inevitably focused "on dominant groups while according the experience of women, labor, and other such

---

Wesley Publishing Company, 1995) 301, 304, 305, 309, 307, 328, 323 and *passim*. Berliner and Biddle also endorsed the main lines of Jonathan Kozol's economic analysis of American education: *Ibid.*, 216-25, 267 and *passim*.

34 E. D. Hirsch, *The Making of Americans* 129, 177, 53.

groups marginal status." Buras said it was not enough to insert "cultural and historical information about oppressed groups into the already dominant organization of school knowledge." Disadvantaged children would become alienated from schools that emphasized the common knowledge of elite White people. If textbooks celebrated the achievements of white men, minority youths and female students would conclude that they were inferior and should be content with an underprivileged status. They would wonder about their place in society. They would become ill at ease and less secure in their identities. If the experiences of their groups were "deemed insignificant," they would "resist schooling" and turn to "nihilism."[35]

To guard against this, Buras recommended a "socially just curriculum" that would be centered on "the knowledge of the least advantaged." "Gender arrangements" should be taught "from the standpoint of women," race relations from the perspective of disadvantaged minorities, and "questions of sexuality from the standpoint of gay people." Instead of "advantaging the knowledge of the elite and powerful," schools should "promote a more just society" by nurturing "cultural struggle" and by legitimizing and celebrating "the cultural and historical experiences of oppressed groups."[36]

Education writer Herbert Kohl echoed these criticisms. According to Kohl, Core Knowledge was "an overreaction of whites to keep people of color in their place" by "pushing the dominant Western culture and belittling the culture of minority students." In his book *I Won't Learn From You* (1991), Kohl maintained that when students sensed that they were being taught racist or sexist material, or material that somehow dishonored their culture, they would shut down and refuse to learn. As Kohl saw it, Hirsch's notions were "stupid

---

35 Kristen L. Buras, "Questioning Core Assumptions," *Harvard Educational Review* 69 (Spring 1999): 75, 73, 82, 83, 84 and *passim*.

36 Ibid., 87.

and dangerous," the product of "cultural and class biases" that tried to "channel young people's thinking" so that they would not see the need for "fundamental economic or social changes." Instead of sanctioning the core knowledge of the elite, Kohl wanted schools to "promote democratic thinking and give children tools and understandings that will help them confront inequity."[37]

Other writers weighed in with additional criticism. Writing in *The Atlantic*, Neil Postman said Hirsch was mistaken to believe "that teachers were no longer concerned with academic content but are instead obsessed with the process of skills of learning." Classroom observations established that, despite the theories of progressive professors at the nation's colleges of education, most teachers continued to use textbooks and to cover conventional information. Since this was the case, Postman wrote, it followed that more disadvantaged children had failed in traditional schools than in progressive classrooms.[38]

Hirsch was not dissuaded by this criticism. He acknowledged that many teachers, when faced with the practicalities of managing their classes, moved away from progressive theories. Most teachers did impart information. They continued to give examinations. But Hirsch said it was a mistake to conclude that progressivism had not failed because it had never been tried in the schools. As Hirsch saw it, the "'never tried' hypothesis" was a pathetic defense of those who were not willing to face reality. Even those teachers who were imparting

---

37 Kathleen Vail, "Core Comes to Crooksville," *American School Board Journal* (March 1997); Herbert Kohl, "What Your 1st Grader Needs to Know," *The Nation* 254 (6 April 1992) 457; Kohl, *I Won't Learn From You* (Minneapolis: Milkwood Edition, 191).

38 Neil Postman, "Cultural Literacy," *The Atlantic* 264 (December 1989) 119. Also see Larry Cuban, *How Teachers Taught: Constancy and Change in American Classrooms* (New York: Teachers College Press, 1993); and David F. Larabee, *The Trouble with Ed Schools* (New Haven: Yale University Press, 2004).

information were doing so on an *ad hoc* basis. One teacher (or school system) might teach world geography while another taught about space exploration. There was no coherent curriculum that specified what was to be learned in each grade.[39]

Additional criticisms of core knowledge pointed to race, ethnicity and poverty, not progressive education, as the causes of low academic achievement. According to these lines of thought, the problem was that the United States, unlike some other countries, was challenged with demographic and economic problems. Robert Weissberg, a professor at the University of Illinois, noted that an increasing number of students hailed from groups that were either sub-par in academic aptitude or burdened with cultures that did not take schoolwork seriously. Other authorities, such as Richard Rothstein, an educational columnist for the *New York Times*, placed the onus on poverty. Rothstein thought it was a mistake to blame schools for the achievement gap. That only diverted attention from the need to reduce the economic disparities that thwarted poor children long before school started.[40]

Other critics raised additional points. For decades many liberals had touted integration—the balanced mixing of students from different races and economic classes—as the key to improving the academic work of low-scoring students. But "White flight" militated against this sort of mixing, as did a series of Supreme Court opinions that were handed down between 1991 and 2007. Some liberals predictably took exception when Hirsch, by emphasizing the importance of the curriculum and saying almost nothing about the importance of balanced mixing, did not rail against racially imbalanced school enrollments. Hirsch was "so insistent on the centrality of a common *curriculum*," wrote Richard D. Kahlenberg, "that he actually

---

39 E. D. Hirsch, *The Making of Americans*, 126-27.

40 Robert Weissberg, *Bad Students, Not Bad Schools*; Richard Rothstein, *Class and Schools* (New York: Teachers College Press, 2004; and Washington: Economic Policy Institute, 2004).

dismisses the importance of schools that bring together children from all walks of life. [Instead,] he points to the success of high-poverty Core Knowledge schools...."[41]

Hirsch dismissed much of the criticism. He said that those who pointed to changes in the nation's ethnic demography had uttered "an implicit slur on the innate academic abilities of certain groups of low-income students." "Ethnicity" did not suffice as an explanation, Hirsch said, because "the gap in the reading tests of whites versus blacks and Hispanics is far greater than the gap in their IQ scores.""Poverty" was also an inadequate explanation, for it did not take account of the success that many schools had achieved with poor minority students. This was true not only of Core Knowledge schools, Hirsch noted, but of other schools that were also organized around a coherent, content-based curriculum.[42]

Most conservatives agreed with Hirsch's basic proposition."One applauds when [Hirsch] posits that countries are bound together not only by common languages and customs but also by shared bodies of knowledge," Daniel Seligman wrote in Fortune. "When [Hirsch] bemoans the disappearance from American curriculums of 'the traditional, history, myth, and literature,' one bemoans with him." Seligman nevertheless thought it was a mistake to believe that "bad schooling" was "the root cause of cultural illiteracy." It was simplistic to think the solution to the achievement gap "begins and ends with curriculum reform." Seligman criticized Hirsch for ignoring the importance of basic intelligence and for not acknowledging that IQ, as measured by standardized tests of intelligence, was "the best predictor" of a student's success in school.[43]

---

41 Richard D. Kahlenberg, "The Common Good," *The American Scholar*(Autumn 2009).

42 E. D. Hirsch, *The Making of Americans*, 127-28.

43 Daniel Seligman, "Cultural Literacy," *Fortune* 116 (14 September 1987) 133; Seligman, "Dictionary of Cultural Literacy," *Fortune* 128 (18 October 1993), 169.

Seligman was not alone in complaining that "IQ" were missing letters in Hirsch's discussion of the achievement gap. Many of those familiar with the research on genetics and human biodiversity also believed that racial differences were not only real but intractable. Whatever the cause of racial disparities in academic achievement, wrote Charles Murray, the co-author of *The Bell Curve*, new educational policies were not likely to make much difference. Columnist Steve Sailer, who specialized in writing about education and human biodiversity, was especially caustic in criticizing academic writers (like Hirsch) for ignoring "the IQ elephant" in the schoolroom. Sailer thought Hirsch had succumbed to "euphemisms" when he blamed textbooks and curriculums for the shortcomings of America's schools. "Almost everybody" knew that "bad schools" meant "bad students"— but professors were afraid to say so for fear that they would become pariahs on campus. Rank-and-file Whites, however, were less constrained by the canons of political correctness. They were, in fact, "swept up in a bidding war, competing furiously with one another for their most important possession: a house in a decent school district." In a desperate effort to keep their children away from students who were thought to be disproportionately dim or dangerous, many White families were "literally spending themselves into bankruptcy." Studies of urban affairs reported that "school quality was the single most important determinant of neighborhood prices." In the suburbs of Washington, D.C. the White fear of Blacks was so great that Whites were willing to pay much more to live in White areas—with houses in predominantly White Fairfax County selling for about 45 percent more than comparable homes in integrated Prince George's County. After observing that "this phenomenon of overpriced or out-of-reach whiteness pervades real estate markets throughout the country," Sheryll Cashin, a Black professor at Georgetown University, reported that the "white premium" amounted to about 13 percent nationwide.[44]

---

44 Charles Murray, "The Inequality Taboo," *Commentary* (September 2005) 14; Steve Sailer, "You Have to Tell the Truth," Vdare.com (28 September 2003); Sailer, "Bad Schools ... and the Great Middle-Class Massacre," Vdare.com

Some writers on the right pointed to the cultures of disadvantaged groups as the root cause of the achievement gap. In his best-selling book, *The End of Racism* (1995), Dinesh D'Souza maintained that genetics accounted for nothing and instead argued that Black students suffered from a dysfunctional set of attitudes and values. Yet D'Souza sent some Blacks into a frothing rage when he described "black culture" in vivid detail. Scott Phelps, a Caltech graduate who taught science at a mostly-Black John Muir High School in Pasadena, elicited a similar reaction after he spoke candidly on a radio talk show. Phelps said he did not believe in genetic explanations for poor Black performance but pointed, rather, to cultural causes. "Different cultures have different behaviors," Phelps said, adding that after a dozen years of teaching he had concluded that African-American students did not take school work as seriously as Asian and Caucasian students. Phelps's intent had been "to get the district to stop blaming teachers or holding them solely responsible for performance," but he was suspended from his job nevertheless. School administrators said Phelps's comments had created a hostile environment at his high school. "We must be tolerant and understanding," said Superintendent Percy Clark. "Diversity should be our asset."[45]

Rather than answer most of his detractors, Hirsch proceeded with an unsparing critique of progressive education. "The reason" for "the large reading gap between demographic groups," Hirsch wrote, was that "an army of American educators and reading experts are fundamentally wrong in their ideas about education and especially

---

(28 September 2003); Sheryll Cashin, The Failures of Integration (New York: Public Affairs, 2004) 7, 10, 13, 123, 130-31, 185-193.

[45] Dinesh D'Souza, *The End of Racism* (New York: Free Press, 1995); Steve Sailer, "The Case of the Truth-Telling (But Racially Incorrect) Teacher," Vdare.com (27 October 2002); Sailer, "Diversity v. Freedom," Vdare.com (3 November 2002). Phelps was later reinstated, and some school officials "while of course not apologizing to Phelps, admitted that some of what he had said was correct and that they needed to look into the problem."

about reading comprehension. Their well-intentioned yet mistaken views are the significant reason (more than other constantly blamed factors, even poverty) that many of our children are not attaining reading proficiency...."[46]

Hirsch persisted in tracing America's educational problems to the theories of John Dewey, especially as those theories were modified and popularized by William Heard Kilpatrick, who taught some 35,000 students during a long career as a professor at Columbia Teachers College. Rather than emphasize the importance of basic common knowledge, Kilpatrick and other progressive educators urged prospective teachers to promote "critical thinking" by having students work on special projects. They disparaged the acquisition of broad knowledge as "rote learning" of "mere facts." They deprecated whole class instruction and instead stressed the value of cooperative group activities. They said that much of what children learned came through interaction with one another; and they insisted that students were far more likely to retain knowledge that they learned on their own. They said that children learned naturally, if adults did not stifle their innate creativity. They opposed drill, repetition, and memorization of facts. They said that full understanding occurred only when students learned on their own, without direct instruction from teachers. Instead of providing students with a coherent sequence of content, progressive and constructivist educators stressed the importance of personalized learning and higher-order thinking.

By the 1980s, Hirsch said, these views had become "a theology" that education professors "drilled into prospective teachers like a catechism." "For five decades ... American schools had accepted the primacy of process over content, arguing that specific knowledge is almost irrelevant, whereas thinking skills are of paramount importance." During this time, the progressives gained control of

---

46   E. D. Hirsch, *The Knowledge Deficit*, 3.

the colleges of education, the state educational bureaucracies, and the largest teachers union, the National Education Association. And as the progressives "came to dominate our public schools . . . [they] precipitated a social misfortune."[47]

Given the dominance of progressives in the nation's colleges of education, it was not likely that Hirsch's ideas would ever come to the fore in most American schools. "Millions of teachers" had already become "a captive audience for [progressive] indoctrination," Hirsch declared. Nevertheless, Hirsch continued to publish articles and books that developed his basic themes. He emphasized that without basic knowledge it was not possible to think critically about any subject. Without knowing about the era of the Great Depression, one could not assess (or even comprehend serious writing about) the presidency of Franklin D. Roosevelt. This was true also of global warming, conservation, and other topics. Prior knowledge facilitated basic comprehension and enabled readers to make connections, draw inferences, and ponder implications. "To teach content is to teach higher-order skills," Hirsch wrote. "To teach higher skills explicitly is to pursue a phantom." Real critical thinking was impossible without the knowledge that progressive educators slighted.[48]

Critics on the left and right, for their part, continued to ascribe the nation's educational problems not to deficiencies in the school curriculums but to other factors. After noting that wealth was distributed more unevenly in the United States than in some other countries, writers on the left maintained that greater economic equality was an essential prerequisite for narrowing the

---

47 Jennifer Roback Mores, "The Schools We Need," *Forbes* (16 November 1998) 72; E. D. Hirsch, *The Knowledge Deficit*, 21; Wilfred M. McClay, "The Schools We Need," 70; Hirsch, "Americanization and the Schools," *The Clearing House* 72 (January/February, 1999) 136; Hirsch, "Why Core Knowledge Promotes Social Justice," *Common Knowledge* 12 (Fall 1999).

48 E. D. Hirsch, "Not So Grand a Strategy," *Education Next* (Spring 2003) 68.

racial and ethnic achievement gaps. Until the society ended poverty, they said, it was not fair to expect the schools to equalize academic achievement. Meanwhile, writers on the right said it was unfair to compare American students with students from countries that were homogeneously White or East Asian.[49]

Hirsch nevertheless continued to focus on his basic theme: the problem was not with the students, their families, or the diversity of the larger society. Educational problems could be solved and the achievement gaps narrowed if American schools would "begin to follow alternative ideas that stress the importance of a gradual acquisition of broad, enabling knowledge." Hirsch noted that about one-fourth of the students in Paris and Marseilles were "non-naturalized, non-French students," mostly from Africa. But in France "the initial gap between advantaged and disadvantaged students, instead of widening steadily as in the United States, decrease[d] with each school grade." Rather than make excuses, the French had narrowed their achievement gap by establishing "a school system that has explicit requirements for each grade." The same had happened in Germany where, thanks to another national curriculum, "the highly disadvantaged offspring of Turkish 'guest workers'" were brought up to grade level, "despite the enormous educational handicaps of Turkish children in Germany." After observing these results, the British Parliament disregarded the opposition of educational professionals and voted in 1987 to introduce a national curriculum in England. Like Hirsch, the French, German, and British leaders believed that their nations would suffer not from demographic diversity but from a diversity of academic preparation.[50]

---

49   E. D. Hirsch, "Not So Grand a Strategy," 68, 15; Richard Rothstein, *Class and Schools* (New York: Teachers College Press, 2004); Hirsch, *The Schools We Need*, 92.

50   E. D. Hirsch, *The Knowledge Deficit*, 17; Hirsch, *The Schools We Need*, 81, 42, 96; Hirsch, "Class Size," *Common Knowledge* 11 (Summer 1998).

E. D. Hirsch

In time, Hirsch came to regard core knowledge and national standards as "the new frontier of the civil rights movement"—saying that "the continual widening of the learning gap" could not be halted "unless schools make a systematic effort to build up the specific background knowledge that disadvantaged children need." This was especially true because Americans, more than most peoples, were constantly changing schools, and the percentage of minority and economically disadvantaged students who moved from one school to another was "appallingly high." Hirsch thought that much of the achievement gap was mistakenly attributed to race, ethnicity, or poverty when it was actually a consequence of mobility. Impoverished children found schoolwork particularly difficult, Hirsch said, because so many of them had to deal with different textbooks and curriculums as they moved from one school to another.[51]

Hirsch's support for a national curriculum put him at odds with the many conservatives who wanted local citizens rather than either the state or national governments to decide what should be taught. These conservatives feared that liberals would use their influence to shape a national curriculum that presented a hyper-critical view of American history and promoted *avant-garde* policies like gay marriage (by requiring students to read books like *Heather Has Two Mommies*). Hirsch, however, said this danger could be avoided if the public schools agreed not to take sides in still-disputed areas. Since school attendance was compulsory, students should "not be compelled to attend a school that inculcates ideas that their parents and caregivers find repugnant."[52]

Conservatives sensed that this was problematical. Because progressives were dominant in the world of education, liberals were not likely to desist from pushing their views on controversial questions.

---

51 E. D. Hirsch, "Fairness and Core Knowledge," http://www.coreknowledge.org/articles-and-speeches, 1991; Hirsch, *The Knowledge Deficit*, 109-119.

52 E. D. Hirsch, *The Knowledge Deficit*, 113.

Given the disposition of most professional educators, wrote Wilfred M. McClay, a professor at the University of Tennessee, "an about-face in the direction of 'conservative educational policies' is as likely to happen as Edward M. Kennedy's enlisting in the Christian Coalition." If the near monopoly of progressive education was to be broken—as Hirsch acknowledges it must be before anything could change, it would not suffice to expect the schools to desist from promoting a liberal agenda. Jerome J. Hanus of American University similarly stated that "the existing intellectual monopoly will be broken only if . . . an end-run is made around the 'directorate.' While we may grant that there is no silver bullet of reform, surely a tax-funded school-voucher system that included all schools, religious and secular, would offer at least some buckshot."[53]

Hirsch agreed—but only partially. He wanted parents to have the freedom to use tax-funded vouchers at schools of their choice. He supported the charter schools movement. "How could I not?" he asked in 1998, when "nineteen percent of the charter schools in the nation are Core Knowledge schools." Hirsch favored "pluralism, competition and choice." He noted that "families and communities have different tastes and priorities," and he insisted, "In a free society people must have the power to shape the decisions that affect their lives and the lives of their children."[54]

Yet Hirsch did not regard choice as a panacea. He said that unlike the situation with respect to most consumer goods, where customers know what they want, most parents do not have a clear conception of what they want schools to be doing to educate their

---

53 Wilfred M. McClay, "The Schools We Need"; Jerome J. Hanus "The Schools We Need," *Public Interest* 126 (Winter, 1997) 124.

54 E. D. Hirsch, "Heroes of Education Reform," *Common Knowledge* 11 (4 November 1998); E. D. Hirsch et al., "A Nation Still at Risk," *Policy Review* 90 (July/August 1998) 23.

children. Informed choice was especially difficult because most schools espoused the same general philosophy of education, "the same concern for 'the individual child and his or her needs,' for 'critical thinking,' 'self-esteem,' 'joy in learning,' 'respect for others'; and the same pledge by the school staff to use the latest research-based pedagogical methods, such as 'site-based decision making,' 'cooperative learning,' 'child-centered pedagogy.'" Bemused by such jargon, most parents decided to send their children to the closest school.[55]

To improve American education, Hirsch stressed the importance of standards and assessments. He thought it would be a great step forward if the United States would implement a national system of testing students on agreed-upon information. This was what Japan, Germany, and France had done, and their students performed well. Hirsch, like many political liberals, looked to the national government for a solution to problems. He favored a "nationalized, bureaucratic, non-market education system." Unlike most conservatives, he thought problems would ensue if more competition were introduced into American schooling. "The market is a fickle beast," Hirsch wrote. "You can't assume that if people are free to choose, the system will automatically improve, and that an invisible hand will cause our children to be well educated. I call this 'free-market romanticism.'"[56]

Because he believed so strongly in the value of testing students on the content of a national curriculum, Hirsch was taken aback when, in one instance after another, the standards movement in the United States fell under the sway of people who opposed the sort of content that Hirsch favored. When New York revised its social studies curriculum in the late 1980s, for example, a committee of educators

---

55 E. D. Hirsch, "Heroes of Education Reform"; Hirsch, *The Schools We Need*, 60-62.

56 E. D. Hirsch, "Not So Grand a Strategy," 68; Hirsch, "The Tests We Need," *Common Knowledge* 13 (Winter 2000).

proceeded with changes that inflated the importance of ethnic groups at the expense of White Europeans and Americans.

So it went also when a group of historians at UCLA prepared a set of National History Standards for the National Endowment for the Humanities. Even before these standards were published, they came under attack from observers who accused the professors of too much liberal bias and of a hyper-critical assessment of the American experience. The criticism was so searing that eventually the United States Senate, by a vote of 99-1, passed a resolution that disavowed the UCLA standards. Meanwhile, a set of National English Standards also came under fire for its disregard of traditional grammar, punctuation, and composition.[57]

Nor was this all. "One had expected that ideological biases might well show up in standards for history and literature," Hirsch wrote. But he was surprised and dismayed to discover that the standards in math and science, approved by the National Council of Teachers of Mathematics and the National Science Foundation, were also "ill-thought-out [and] needlessly infected with ideology." In one academic subject after another, the standards movement had been "hijacked" by politically correct ideologues of the left. Nevertheless, Hirsch continued to maintain that curriculum-based tests, especially if administered state-wide or nationally, were "the most promising educational development in half a century," "the fairest and most effective means of achieving the aims of democratic schooling," "the most promising way for schools to overcome inequities created by class and caste."[58]

---

57 The literature on the history and English standards is voluminous. For discussion of the vote in the U.S. Senate, see Gary B. Nash et al., *History on Trial* (New York: Alfred A. Knopf, 1997) 235 and *passim*.

58 E. D. Hirsch, "What's at Stake in the K-12 Standards Wars," *Academic Questions* 13 (Fall 2000) 87-90; Hirsch, "The Tests We Need," *Common Knowledge* 13 (Winter 2000); Hirsch, "The SAT," Hoover Institute essay (28 May 2001).

When making his case, Hirsch continued to maintain that "overcoming educational injustice" was "the new frontier in the struggle for civil rights," albeit a battlefield that was more "subtle and confusing than the one involving sit-ins and freedom rides." Hirsch acknowledged that most of the reforms he advocated "happen to be on the so-called conservative side of the ledger," but he insisted that he was really a liberal "because the most urgent aim of the Core Knowledge movement has been and remains social justice, the aim of giving all children an equal chance in life regardless of who their parents are." Because Hirsch's rhetoric was spiked with concern for uplifting disadvantaged students, even his most severe critics conceded that Hirsch's position was articulated with "a certain benevolence, an air of good will, a concern that democratic ideals be upheld."[59]

Given his oft-repeated views, it was no surprise that Hirsch welcomed the passage of the No Child Left Behind Act (NCLB) of 2001. This law aimed to improve American education by focusing on the lowest achieving students. It required every public school that received federal funds (as nearly all of them did) to test third- through eighth-grade students annually in reading and math. It also required the schools to disaggregate the test scores by race, ethnicity, disability, and low-income status, and if any of the subgroups failed to make "adequate yearly progress" the school would face sanctions that would become more punitive with each passing year.[60]

Hirsch hailed NCLB as "the most hopeful and important federal education legislation that has been enacted in recent years." He said that "tests of academic progress are the only practical way to

---

59 E. D. Hirsch, "Heroes of Education Reform"; Hirsch, "Ideas, Convictions, and Courage," *Common Knowledge* 14 (2 November 2001); Hirsch, "Fairness and Core Knowledge"; Mark F. Goldberg, "Doing What Works," *Phi Delta Kappan* 78 (September 1997) 83; Kristen L. Buras, "Questioning Core Assumptions," 81.

60 Diane Ravitch, "Question and Answer: The Truth about America's Schools," *The American* (July/August 2007).

hold schools accountable for educating all children. . . ." He thought that testing would force elementary schools to focus on the basics of reading and math—and to move away from the progressive emphasis on critical thinking and teaching students how to learn.[61]

Yet Hirsch's support for NCLB was short-lived. After NCLB was implemented, the youngest students recorded gains. But those gains eventually washed out. "The eighth-grade students of 2008 had recorded gains in fourth grade, but these have not led to improvements in later grades," Hirsch noted. In addition, "the large reading gap between advantaged and disadvantaged children—'the achievement gap'—has stayed where it was." "Facts must be faced," Hirsch wrote in 2010. "We are making no progress at all in teaching children to read in the United States. Our massive and well-intentioned effort to focus the work of our schools on improving reading instruction has failed."[62] In fact, Hirsch came to think, NCLB had inadvertently made things worse. In a classic instance of unintended consequences, NCLB had placed so much emphasis on test scores that it undermined the quality of education. Because NCLB imposed stiff penalties if elementary students did not make adequate yearly progress on year-end tests, many schools focused on "how-to strategies and test-taking skills." Much of this time was spent taking practice exams. That led to higher test scores—up until about age 9. After that, however, the scores stagnated.[63]

Hirsch thought he knew why. It was because elementary teachers were teaching to the test. They were devoting so much time to phonics and test strategies that they had to curtail the essential

---

61 E. D. Hirsch, *The Knowledge Deficit*, 19, 91.

62 E. D. Hirsch, "The Knowledge Connection," *Washington Post* (16 February 2008); Hirsch (guest columnist), "The Answer Sheet," *WashingtonPost.com* (6 April 2010).

63 E. D. Hirsch, "Primer on Success," blog.Core Knowledge.org (26 September 2012).

E. D. Hirsch

common knowledge of history, literature, and science. Moreover, they neglected core knowledge because of a *mésalliance* between NCLB and progressive education. "Theories are 'more powerful than is commonly understood,'" Hirsch wrote, and "the dominant ed-school idea" opposed teaching all students a sequenced curriculum that focused on knowledge that everyone was expected to know. Instead, progressives continued to oppose a preset, "one size fits all" curriculum that ensured a coherent, grade-by-grade buildup of knowledge.[64]

"Why do so many schools fail to meet the goals established by the No Child Left Behind Act?" the Core Knowledge Foundation asked in one of its press releases. "Our children are not learning how to read," the Foundation answered, "because they are subjected to a ... curriculum that fails to build the background knowledge essential to reading comprehension. Many schools excel at teaching the mechanics of reading, at giving kids the decoding skills they need to make out individual words. However, by fourth grade, students' deficit in background knowledge trips them up." Because NCLB led to so much preparation for tests but said nothing about the importance of a common curriculum, students were starved for facts about history, geography, science, literature, mathematics, music, and art. And because of this knowledge deficit, many students could not understand the texts they were asked to read in fourth grade and beyond.[65]

Hirsch made few converts in the educational establishment. When *Cultural Literacy* was published in 1987, Hirsch recalled, he received "a lot of enthusiastic response from teachers and from the general public.... But then I started getting [academic] reviews, and ... everything that came from the education world was hostile." As a

---

64 E. D. Hirsch, "How Schools Fail Democracy," *Chronicle of Higher Education* (28 September 2009).

65 Core Knowledge press release, quoted at *Instructivist.blogspot.com* (6 September 2005).

favorable reviewer noted in the *Washington Post*, "Hirsch's work [had been] distorted and his views vilified." When a reporter from *Phi Delta Kappan*, a mainstream education journal, asked for an interview in 1997, Hirsch was "so convinced . . . that the general education community [wished] to shun him that he expressed doubt that the piece would actually be published." The reporter inferred that Hirsch was "more than a little frustrated by all the criticism he has received from professional educators." Yet, although Hirsch's influence at education schools was minimal, he soldiered on, saying that his father had taught him to "follow a conviction even if it's not what the crowd believes."[66]

Outside the academy, Hirsch's ideas found a more receptive audience. With royalties from the sale of *Cultural Literacy*, Hirsch established the CORE Knowledge Foundation, and eventually there were additional funds from the Exxon Education Foundation, the National Endowment for the Humanities, the Walton Family Foundation, the Olin Foundation, and the Brown Foundation of Houston. With this money, Hirsch and a small staff published a series of textbooks, organized annual conferences, and offered advice on establishing and operating core knowledge schools. The first such school, the Three Oaks School in Fort Myers, Florida, was established in 1991, and by 2010 more than 1,000 core knowledge schools were up-and-running.[67]

Most Core Knowledge students made superior scores on standardized tests. In Delaware, the Core Knowledge charter school in Newark regularly led all elementary schools on the state's annual assessment tests. Most of the students at the Delaware school were from the middle and upper-middle classes, but Core Knowledge achieved dramatic gains with other students as well. At the Mohegan School in

---

66 E. D. Hirsch, interview with Andrew J. Rotherham, *EducationSector. org* (22 September 2006); Jay Mathews, "I Pledge Allegiance to Core Knowledge,"*Washington Post* (30 August 2009); Mark F. Goldberg, "Doing What Works."

67 E. D. Hirsch, "Ideas, Convictions and Courage."

the Bronx, where most of the students were either Latinos or African-Americans, test scores went up more than twice as much as the scores at schools in a matched control group. At the Morse School, which served a blue-collar neighborhood in Cambridge, Massachusetts, test scores also increased significantly. At the Paul H. Cale Elementary School in Albemarle County, Virginia, scores not only improved but there was clear evidence of narrowing the performance gap between students of low socio-economic status and others. After studying the situation in Maryland, Johns Hopkins University researcher Samuel Stringfield reported that gains at the Core Knowledge schools "clearly exceeded those of the state and of the demographically and geographically matched schools." In another study of twelve Core Knowledge schools, Stringfield found that the more the Core Knowledge curriculum was implemented, the more test scores improved.[68]

These results were not definitive. Although social scientists tried to compare the Core Knowledge students with others who had virtually identical characteristics, it was not possible to have exact comparisons with regular public schools. Even if the pairings were nearly exact in terms of socio-economic characteristics, the Core Knowledge students were not assigned and required to attend certain schools. They were volunteers from families that chose to have a subject-centered curriculum. Nevertheless, the Core Knowledge experience suggested that test scores were not entirely determined by either IQ or poverty. The experience suggested that, even with poor minority students, better results could be achieved if schools provided an orderly environment, a structured curriculum, and explicit instruction including drill and practice.[69]

---

68 See U.S. Department of Education, "Lessons Learned from FIPSE Projects" (May 2000); "An Overview of Research on Core Knowledge," Core Knowledge Foundation, available at CoreKnowledge.org (January 2004); Johns Hopkins Magazine (June 1999); Mary Summers, Defining Literacy Upward," *Forbes* 164 (26 July 1999) 70.

69 E. D. Hirsch, "The Latest Dismal NAEP Scores," *Education Week* 20 (2 May 2001); Hirsch, "Good Genes, Bad Schools," *New York Times* (29 October

Perhaps the best example of the effectiveness of Hirsch's approach occurred in the state of Massachusetts, where the Education Reform Act of 1993 prescribed that the year-end tests would be linked to knowledge-based standards that covered specific information that was taught in each grade. The superiority of this approach seemed to be established when Massachusetts students surged upward on the biennial National Assessment of Educational Progress (NAEP). In 2005 the state ranked first in the nation in fourth- and eighth-grade reading and fourth- and eighth-grade math, and it then repeated this feat in 2007. On another test, the Trends in International Math and Science Studies (TIMSS), fourth-graders in Massachusetts ranked second globally in science and third in math, while the eighth-graders tied for first in science and placed sixth in math. The United States as a whole finished tenth.[70]

One should not place too much emphasis on test scores. As will be noted below, and especially in chapters 10 and 12, there are many ways in which test scores can be manipulated. Nevertheless, the results in Massachusetts were for a state-wide system, as opposed to individual schools of choice. And the results in Massachusetts did suggest that students in other states would have done better if their schools had also adopted a content-rich, grade-by-grade curriculum. According to education writer Sol Stern, the "Massachusetts miracle" showed that "Hirsch's theories, long merely persuasive, now have solid empirical backing."[71]

Yet Massachusetts was an exception. In most states, teachers continued to proceed without a standard curriculum and with a variety of instructional approaches. In addition, as will be noted in

---

1994).

70 Sol Stern, "E. D. Hirsch's Curriculum for Democracy," *City Journal* (Autumn 2009).

71 Ibid.

Part Three of this book, when a "new guard" of educational reformers came to the fore in the 1990s, they shifted the emphasis away from the importance of curriculum and focused instead on the quality of individual teachers, as measured by their students' scores on whatever tests happened to be used. E. D. Hirsch may have been, as Sol Stern has written, "America's most important education reformer of the last century." But in the 1990s and the first decade of the 21st century, the new guard of school reformers rejected Hirsch's approach as surely as Hirsch rejected the theories of progressive education professors. Unlike Hirsch, whose basic idea was that background knowledge was essential for academic achievement, the new guard emphasized the importance of "teacher quality." The concept of core knowledge never took hold. In the early years of the 21st century, school reformers increasingly would blame the nation's education problems not on progressive education but on "bad teachers."[72]

---

72   Ibid; Robert Pondiscio, "Nineteen Points and One Very Bad Idea," *blog. CoreKnowledge.org* (24 July 2009).

Part III

Teach For America and *its Progeny*

7

Wendy Kopp and Teach for America

In 1988, Wendy Kopp was "in a funk for the first time in my life." A senior at Princeton University, Kopp was "searching for a place to direct my energy," but she "could not figure out what I wanted to spend my life doing." She had applied for jobs with consulting firms and an investment bank, but not because she was deeply interested in business or finance. She "just couldn't think of anything else to do." She also sensed that many of her classmates felt the same way. They wanted to do "something meaningful." But what?[1]

Kopp was the last student in her department to settle upon a topic for a senior thesis. Then, finally, she had a moment of inspiration. Why, she asked herself, shouldn't the United States "have a national teacher corps of recent college graduates who would commit two years to teach in urban and rural public schools?" This became the topic of Kopp's senior thesis—and eventually the focus of her life's work. In the thesis, Kopp proposed to create a national teacher corps that would be patterned after the Peace Corps and called Teach for America (TFA). TFA would "use the Peace Corps model—lots of publicity, a selective application process, [and] active recruitment—to

---

1 Wendy Kopp, *One Day, All Children* (New York: Public Affairs, 2001), 3, 10, 8, 4, 5; Kopp, as quoted by Adam Bryant, "Charisma: To Her It's Overrated," *New York Times* (5 July 2009); Kopp, quoted by Donna Foote, *Relentless Pursuit* (New York: Alfred A. Knopf, 2008), 30.

attract top recent graduates, train them, and place them as teachers in inner cities and rural areas which suffer from persistent teacher shortages." "So many of my peers were completely undecided about what to do after college," Kopp has written. "They seemed ready to be recruited by something like what I had in mind."[2]

Kopp thought that graduates of America's leading colleges would spend two years teaching in the nation's most needy schools—but only if such assignments could be structured so as to radiate "an aura of status and selectivity." As Kopp saw it, most Ivy League students never considered teaching "because of its downwardly mobile image." To turn things around, talented students would have to be recruited as aggressively as they were being recruited to work on Wall Street. Kopp wanted to establish TFA as the Harvard of national service. She wanted people to talk about TFA "the way they talk about the Rhodes scholarship." To persuade the best and the brightest to work in inner-city schools, status would have to be attached to teaching disadvantaged students. And to obtain the necessary status, Kopp calculated that TFA should accept no more than 20 percent of its applicants. The goal for the first year was to "place 500 recent college graduates in five or six urban and rural areas across the country." To generate the necessary number of candidates, TFA would need about $2.5 million for its first year of advertising and recruitment.[3]

In some ways, Kopp was an unlikely candidate to lead an effort to improve the education of disadvantaged students. She had grown up in a well-to-do neighborhood in Dallas, Texas, where she graduated as the valedictorian of the Highland Park High School. Instead of

---

[2] Wendy Kopp, *One Day, All Children*, 6, 31; Fred Hechinger, "Education," *New York Times* (6 December 1989).

[3] Wendy Kopp, *One Day, All Children*, 7, 10; Avi Zenilman, "Now, That's Classy," *Washington Monthly* (September 2006); Kopp, quoted by Rachel Shteir, "Teaching Teachers," *New York Times* (7 January 1996).

tutoring needy children, as many of the eventual TFA recruits would do, Kopp had been the editor of the high school newspaper, president of the debate team, and a lead actress in her school's production of Neil Simon's *California Suite*. At Princeton she was involved with a student group that organized conferences and published its own magazine, *Business Today*. Her interest in the problems of America's inner-city schools began during the fall of her senior year, when she heard one of the conference speakers say that there was "always a shortage of qualified teachers in very low income areas"—and that "individuals who haven't majored in education" were being hired "to meet the need in underprivileged areas."[4]

When Kopp mentioned that she would need a great deal of money to do the sort of advertising and recruiting she considered crucial, her thesis adviser was skeptical. "Do you know how hard it is to raise twenty-five *hundred* dollars?" Professor Marvin Bressler asked. Nevertheless, Bressler approved the thesis, and Kopp turned it into a thirty-page proposal that she sent to the CEOs of companies such as Mobil Oil, Delta Airlines, and Coca-Cola. Union Carbide was the first to offer assistance—free office space in Manhattan. Mobil followed with a seed grant of $26,000, and others soon chipped in. Within a year, philanthropists had promised the $2.5 million that Kopp had envisioned. The largest of the initial contributions came from Dallas billionaire Ross Perot, who gave a challenge grant of $500,000.[5]

With this support, TFA chose 500 candidates from a pool of 2,500 applicants. After eight weeks of training during the summer of 1990, 489 "corps members" were dispatched for two-year stints in some of the nation's most needy schools. The *New York Times* deemed

---

4   Sam Dillon, "Two School Entrepreneurs Lead the Way," *New York Times* (19 June 2008); Kopp, *One Day, All Students*, 9; Donna Foote, *Relentless Pursuit*, 28.

5   Kopp, One Day, All Children, 11, 14-16, 42-46; *New York Times* (31 May 1990).

this achievement worthy of coverage on its front page and saluted Kopp for "infusing public education's understaffed and overburdened teaching ranks with bright and devoted college graduates who might not have otherwise turned to teaching." In little more than one year, Kopp had turned her brainstorm into a senior thesis and had raised $2.5 million. She had recruited hundreds of prospective teachers and had persuaded schools to give them the same regular starting salary as full-fledged teachers.[6]

It was hard to quarrel with TFA's basic idea, which was to place bright, energetic recent college graduates in school districts that were in dire need of teachers. Initially, the focus was on six such districts. Some were in inner cities—South Los Angeles, the South Bronx, and New Orleans. Others were in impoverished parts of rural Georgia, North Carolina, and the Mississippi Delta. Because of bad student behavior and difficult working conditions, these areas had a problem retaining teachers. At Locke High School in the Watts area of Los Angeles, for example, about fifty teachers quit in the course of each school year, leaving many students with a succession of uncertified temporary substitute teachers. In these circumstances, an article in UCLA's *Daily Bruin* noted, TFA would fill "a gaping hole." The TFA corps members would "do no worse than the untrained teachers that are already in these schools. In fact ... they may be even better." An article in the *New York Times* noted that in these school districts the alternative was "less likely to be a certified teacher with a degree in education than someone recruited at the local Wal-Mart."[7]

---

[6] Michel Marriott, "For Fledgling Teachers," *New York Times* (5 December 1990); Susan Chira, "Princeton Student's Brainstorm," *New York Times* (20 June 1990).

[7] Jodi Wilgoren, "Wendy Kopp," *New York Times* (12 November 2000); *Daily Bruin* (11 January 2007); Donna Foote, *Relentless Pursuit*, 24.

Kopp envisioned TFA as doing much more than providing a higher caliber of substitute teachers. She also thought of TFA as a movement to uplift the disadvantaged by transforming education. Like many other observers, Kopp believed that disadvantaged students were doing poorly in school because they suffered from poverty, poor nutrition, inadequate healthcare, and lack of preschool education. She also believed that these students would do much better if their teachers compensated for the disadvantages by having faith in the students and by working relentlessly to instill an understanding of the importance of education.

Yet Kopp's emphasis differed from the constructivist views of neo-progressive educators and also from the views of most traditional teachers. Traditionalists tended to think that some students were "smart," others were "hard workers," and still others were neither. Traditionalists also thought that some families exceeded others in their support for education. Believing as they did, traditionalists assigned responsibility for doing well in school to the students and their families. Intellectual ability was regarded like other abilities, from sports to music. Teachers were expected to maintain order and present information clearly, but traditionalists assumed that the performance of students was largely a function of their aptitude and exertion. "If children failed, it was thought to be due either to their inability or their lack of effort; if they excelled, it was due to their talents and their industry. The one qualifier in this construction held that, regardless of ability, children could, through hard work, 'overachieve,' or, if they failed to work, 'underachieve.'"[8]

Some traditionalists also believed that groups differed in their cultural patterns. Even in antiquity, for example, Cicero had warned his fellow Romans not to buy slaves from Brittania, for he

---

8   Tommy M. Tomlinson, "The Troubled Years: An Interpretive Analysis of Public Schooling since 1950," *Phi Delta Kappan*, 62 (January 1981) 373ff.

found their attitudes toward education and technology lacking. As if to prove Cicero's point, when the Romans pulled out of Britain in the fifth century, the British economy and political structure both collapsed. One thousand years later the British rose to lead the world industrially—but this only underscored how abiding and influential cultural attitudes could be. It took a millennium for the inhabitants to absorb the cultural advances brought by their Roman conquerors.[9]

In modern times, many researchers and scholars continued to believe that racial and ethnic achievement gaps were due to the persisting influence of culture, while some others said that a significant portion of the disparities in academic achievement was genetic in origin. Yet after the civil rights revolution and with the rise of multiculturalism, "cultural realism" increasingly came to be regarded as "blaming the victim" and "race realism" as "racism." On many campuses it was considered a moral outrage to attribute achievement gaps to either culture or race. If either influence was acknowledged, some people seemed to fear, then efforts to close the gaps would be discontinued and some groups of students would be considered too backward or too dim to be worth the effort.[10]

By the 1970s, new views had come to the fore, especially on the campuses of the nation's elite universities. At Harvard in 1971, one prominent psychologist, Richard Herrnstein, received death threats and had to cancel lectures after he published an article that emphasized the importance of heredity. Students also disrupted the lectures of Harvard's Professor E. O. Wilson after Wilson's seminal book, *Sociobiology* (1975), argued that evolutionary biology had influenced many aspects of human behavior. On one occasion, when

---

9   Thomas Sowell, *Race and Culture* (New York: Basic Books, 1994) 156-57.

10 *Ibid.*; Sowell, *Race, Culture, and Equality* (Stanford: The Hoover Institution, 1998) 13; Mark Snyderman and Stanley Rothman, *The IQ Controversy*(New Brunswick: Transaction Publishers) 285 and *passim*.

Wilson tried to speak at a meeting of the American Association for the Advancement of Science, a young critic poured a pitcher of water over Wilson while demonstrators chanted, "Wilson, you're all wet." Since Wilson was a tenured professor, he was not fired; but he recalled that he "received little support from my colleagues on the Harvard faculty," and he "withdrew from department meetings for a year to avoid embarrassment." Wilson recognized that he was out of step with the prevailing ethos at Harvard because, like Herrnstein, he had stressed the abiding influence of biology (and thus implied that there were limits to what social reform could accomplish).[11]

Intolerance for biological explanations of human behavior continued for decades and reached something of a climax in 2006 when Lawrence Summers was forced out of the presidency of Harvard. Over the years, critics had taken exception to several of Summers' statements and policies. But the incident that finally forced Summers from the presidency involved his suggestion that discrimination was not the only reason that men outnumbered women as professors of science, engineering, and mathematics. It was possible, Summers suggested, that men might have more intrinsic aptitude for these fields. Although men and women had about the same average scores on most aptitude tests, Summers mentioned that there was greater variability in the range of scores. Far more men were concentrated at both the very low end and the very high end of the distribution. "I would like nothing better than to be proved wrong," Summers said. He hoped an equal gender balance could be achieved by eliminating social barriers. But he added, "My guess is that there are some very deep forces that are going to be with us for a long time."[12]

---

11 "The Education of Stephanie Grace," AmRen.com (4 May 2010); Edward O. Wilson, "Science and Ideology" *Academic Questions* 8 (June 1995); Wilson, *Naturalist* (Washington: Island Press, 1994) 349.

12 Lawrence Summers, quoted by John Tierney, "Daring to Discuss Women in Science," *New York Times* (8 June 2010).

The treatment of Herrnstein, Wilson, and Summers was only the tip of an iceberg. On elite campuses the prevailing popular wisdom led students to understand that any mention of heredity or culture was in poor taste. Conversely, perceptive students sensed that they could ease their way to the top of the status heap by embracing egalitarian views and by manifesting special concern for uplifting underrepresented minority groups.[13]

This lesson was underlined in the aftermath of a 2009 dinner conversation among three students at the Harvard Law School. The topic of discussion had been affirmative action, and one of the students was Stephanie Grace, who had graduated from Princeton with honors after writing a senior thesis on race relations. During the conversation, Grace had questioned the view that racial differences in IQ had a genetic basis.

Afterwards, however, Grace had second thoughts. "I just hate leaving things where I feel I misstated my position," she wrote in an e-mail to her friends. "I absolutely do not rule out the possibility that African-Americans are, on average, genetically predisposed to be less intelligent.... I think it is at least possible that African-Americans are less intelligent on a genetic level, and I didn't mean to shy away from that opinion at dinner."[14]

A few months later Grace had a falling out with one of the friends, and the previously private e-mail was sent to the Black Law Students Association at Harvard and thirteen other schools. By that time Grace had become an editor of the *Harvard Law Review* and had been hired as a clerk for a federal judge. The BLSAs then demanded

---

[13] For more on this point, see Steve Sailer, "Americans First," *The American Conservative* (13 February 2006); and Sailer, "The 'Whiteness Studies' Game," Vdare.com (8 September 2002).

[14] Full text of Stephanie Grace's e-mail, at boston.com/news/local/Massachusetts/articles/2010/04/30/042010.

that Grace be fired, on the grounds that she would be in a position to oppress Blacks if she was employed by a federal court.[15]

Grace then learned what lay in store for people who questioned the idea that all groups have equal potential. The dean of the Harvard Law School, Martha Minow, denounced Grace for expressing skeptical open-mindedness on the forbidden topic of race and IQ. "I am writing," Dean Minow stated in an open letter, "to address an email message in which one of our students suggested that black people are genetically inferior to white people." Dean Minow insisted that Grace's comments did "not reflect the views of the school or the overwhelming majority of the members of this community.... Here at Harvard Law School, we are committed to preventing degradation of any individual or group, including race-based insensitivity or hostility."[16]

Rather than stand by her skepticism, Grace apologized. "I am deeply sorry for the pain caused by my email. I never intended to cause any harm, and I am heartbroken and devastated by the harm that has ensued. I would give anything to take it back. I emphatically do not believe that African-Americans are genetically inferior in any way. I understand why my words expressing even a doubt in that regard were and are offensive."[17]

The Grace incident, like the previous incidents involving Herrnstein, Wilson, and Summers, was an indication of the climate of opinion on the campuses where Wendy Kopp proposed to recruit for Teach for America. From the outset, Kopp recognized that she must tailor her message to suit a climate where the dogma of zero

---

15 Kashmir Hill, "Racist E-Mail Goes National," at AboveTheLaw.com/2010/04.

16 Steve Sailer, "Arizona, Britain, and Harvard Law," Vdare.com (2 May 2010); "Full Text of Stephanie Grace's E-mail."

17 "Full Text of Stephanie Grace's E-mail."

group differences—what journalist John Derbyshire has called "the DZGD"—reigned supreme. One way to do this was by marketing TFA as a program to close the racial and ethnic gaps in academic achievement. If I had one thing going for me," Kopp has said, "it was that I understood the mindset of the people we were trying to attract."[18]

When recruiting corps members for TFA, Kopp described the achievement gaps as "this generation's issue." TFA could solve the problem, she insisted. Genes and culture did not doom kids who lived "in rural and urban areas." These children would excel if they were given better teachers. "We have the potential to end educational inequity," Kopp said. "I truly believe that." If she had only two minutes to deliver a commencement address, her message would be that graduates of elite colleges should "take on the world's inequities ... They are solvable."[19]

Abolishing racial and ethnic gaps in academic achievement thus became TFA's central goal. When TFA began, Kopp noted, the "conventional wisdom" held "that there is only so much schools can do." "Most Americans view[ed] educational inequity as an intractable problem." Ever since sociologist James S. Coleman published his massive study, *Equality of Educational Opportunity* (1966), most social scientists believed that "socioeconomic circumstances determined educational outcomes." They "assumed that fixing education would require fixing poverty first." Other social scientists followed the lead of psychologist Arthur Jensen and concluded that IQ influenced academic achievement—and that heredity was at least partially responsible for the fact that the IQ of African-Americans, on average, trailed that of White Americans by about 15 points.

---

18 John Derbyshire, *We Are Doomed* (New York: Crown Forum, 2009); Wendy Kopp, quoted in "Biography Resource Center," at *GaleNet.com*. Kopp was speaking in the context of accounting for her success in convincing corporations that she could persuade students to volunteer for two years of service with TFA.

19 Wendy Kopp, quoted in *Money.cnn.com* (27 November 2006); *CNN.com* (20 June 2007); and *New York Times* (19 June 2008; 5 July 2009; 16 July 2009).

But most of the young people associated with TFA did not know this. They were not *au courant* with social science. "Teach for America is ... a story about the power of inexperience," Kopp wrote. TFAers had endless energy to combat "a problem that many have long since given up on."[20]

Thus Kopp and TFAers talked at length about the importance of education and increasing the academic achievement of non-Asian minority students. TFA's website proclaimed: "We believe we must change the prevailing ideology around educational inequity. We need to move from a world where most people believe this is an intractable problem to one where it is commonly understood that we can solve this problem if we make the right social choices." Dustin Oldham, the executive director of TFA's operations in St. Louis, summed up the prevailing view: "We know that the achievement gap can be closed and that it is a solvable problem, and we are building the movement so that this fact is recognized and proven, time and again, in school districts across the nation." At Emory University, the student newspaper, *The Emory Wheel*, published an account of TFA's recruiting under the headline, "Teach for America Strives to Close the Achievement Gap."[21]

There were several parts to TFA's program. Despite disparaging the importance of heredity and culture, TFA proceeded on the assumption that disadvantaged students would benefit if their teachers were high-IQ college graduates who would disseminate the customs and values that prevailed at elite universities. When

---

20 Wendy Kopp, commencement speech at Mt. Holyoke College, 2007, available at EdReform.blogspot.com (July 2007); Kopp, *A Chance to Make History* (New York: Public Affairs, 2011) 5, 177-78

21 Tamar Levin, "Top Graduates to Teach the Poor," *New York Times* (2 October 2005); Elena Schulman, "Teach for America Strives to Close Achievement Gap," *Emory Wheel* (12 November 2007); formerly on TFA website, quoted at apps.tfanet.org/mission/theory_of_change.htm; Dustin Oldham, quoted by Jim Nicholson, "Teach for America," at stlcommercemagazine.com/archives/february 2007.

Kopp noted that the average SAT score for corps members was "over 1,250," she conveyed the impression that she believed great teachers were born rather than shaped by several years of education courses. Like Kopp, who also said that "certification" of teachers was "a weak predictor of effectiveness," most TFAers discounted the importance of giving teachers years of training before they began teaching. TFAers believed that disadvantaged students would achieve if their teachers were especially intelligent, if the teachers set the bar high, and if the teachers invested their students with the proper attitudes and skills.[22]

TFA was circumspect in expressing this view, but some of TFA's supporters showed less restraint. One article in *Education Next*, a journal published by the Hoover Institution at Stanford University, noted that TFA's "underlying idea" was "that many smart, accomplished college graduates would make significant contributions to public education—if it weren't for the fact that they must have majored in education or be willing to spend one to two more years (and significantly more in tuition) earning a master's in education in order to get certified." In the course of praising TFA for recruiting teachers from selective colleges, one editorial in the *New York Times* described traditional teacher training programs as "little more than diploma mills." It was hardly surprising, then, that some professors of education, such as David C. Berliner of Arizona State University, complained that TFAers thought they could "solve the problems of urban education because we're smarter than everybody else." "There's some arrogance there," Professor Berliner said.[23]

---

22 Wendy Kopp, *One Day, All Children* 149; Kopp, "Building the Movement to End Educational Inequity," *Phi Delta Kappan*, 89 (June 2008) 743; Susan Chira, "Idealism Vies with Failures," *New York Times* (6 July 1992).

23 "Teach for America" *New York Times* (16 May 2008); Margaret Raymond and Stephen Fletcher, "Teach for America," *Education Next* (Spring 2002); "Praise for Teach for America," *U.S. News* (20 June 2008); David Berliner, quoted by Sam Dillon, "Two School Entrepreneurs," 16.

To ease tensions with the schools of education, TFA encouraged its members to take evening and summer courses that would eventually lead to their receiving official certification as teachers. Many members, however, expressed distaste for the education courses. Rachelle Snyder, a corps member who taught in Los Angeles, considered her four-to-nine evening credentialing classes "a waste of time." And when Mike Feinberg, who taught for TFA in Houston, discovered that the information for a required summer workshop could be mastered by reading the textbook, Feinberg signed in each morning but then headed for the golf course, sneaking back each afternoon to sign out.[24]

TFA also stressed the power of positive thinking. Kopp believed that too many teachers had the wrong mind-set. They thought, "it's not possible to succeed" with disadvantaged students. If there was one thing that TFA recruits needed, Kopp said, it was "the instinct to remain optimistic in the face of a challenge." A good teacher did much more than impart knowledge, Kopp insisted. In addition to presenting information clearly, good teachers "inspire their students to assume responsibility for meeting ambitious academic goals," and then committed themselves "to doing whatever it takes to ensure their students succeed." To close the achievement gap, Kopp wrote, TFA would "*redefine the role of the teacher* to mean more than providing access to learning experiences."[25]

TFA's approach appealed to many observers, among them New York City's school chancellor, Joel Klein, who tersely explained why he eventually became one of TFA's biggest employers: "TFA teachers are much less excuse-bound." TFAers prided themselves for taking full responsibility for student achievement, refusing to blame outside

---

24 Donna Foote, *Relentless Pursuit*, 181; Jay Mathews, "Maverick Teachers," *Washington Post* (18 June 2007).

25 Donna Foote, *Relentless Pursuit* 168, 328; Wendy Kopp, *A Chance to Make History* 30 (italics in original).

factors, such as poverty or truancy or lack of parental support, for underperformance.[26]

Instead of placing blame on laggard students, unsupportive families, or problematic socioeconomic conditions, TFA placed the blame on societal racism and veteran teachers. Thus Sara Mosle, a member of TFA's first class, wrote that "the biggest problem" at her school in the Bronx "had nothing to do with violence or drugs. It had to do with expectations. Because the kids ... came from an impoverished background, expectations for them were low." Another corps member also made a point of not blaming students or their parents. "It is society's lack of expectations for these children that are to blame," Priya Roy insisted. Among TFA's recruits, the prevailing belief was that "all students will rise to meet the challenge" if teachers would only "set a rigorous academic course." When the Gallup organization asked the public, "Why do we have low educational outcomes in low-income communities," the public's top three responses were, "lack of student motivation," "lack of parental involvement," and "home life issues." By way of contrast, TFA teachers pointed to "teacher quality," "principal quality," and "expectations."[27]

When she learned of this poll, Wendy Kopp was so pleased that she commented at some length. "Those responses strike me as capturing accurately the views of most Americans—even most thoughtful and civic-minded Americans." They attributed the achievement gaps to "lack of student motivation" and "home life issues" such as "lack of

---

26 Wendy Kopp, quoted by Adam Bryant, "Charisma,"; Joel Klein, quoted by Patricia Sellers, "Schooling Corporate Giants on Recruiting," *Fortune* (27 November 2006); Sara Mosle, "Teach for America Grows Up," posted at Slate.com (19 May 2008).

27 Sara Mosle, "Scenes from the Class Struggle," *The New Republic* 208 (16 December 1991) 24; Joshua Kaplowitz, "How I Joined Teach for America and Got Sued for $20 Million," *City Journal* (Winter 2003); Lincoln Caplan, "Great Expectations," Slate.com (19 October 2007); Priya Roy, quoted by Elana Schulman, "Teach for America Strives to Close Achievement Gap."

parental involvement." By way of contrast, TFA's corps members had blamed "teacher quality" and "school leadership." "There is such hope in this," Kopp said. "Our corps members are telling us that this problem is within our control." The *Washington Post* chimed in with an editorial praising TFAers for "overwhelmingly believ[ing] that schools underrate children, fail to challenge them and resist imposing higher standards because they simply don't believe the students will meet them." Instead of blaming "the deeper causes of low student achievement," the *Post* editorial said, educators should recognize that "higher expectations ... can actually lead to higher test scores."[28]

In addition to recruiting teachers who were especially smart and confident about their ability to close the achievement gaps, TFA also sought to develop a cadre of civic leaders who would be committed to larger social reforms that would improve education and reduce poverty. From the outset, Wendy Kopp envisioned TFA's alumni as a crucial part of her program. Kopp did not expect or even want corps members to make a career of teaching. Rather, she hoped that, after a few years in the classroom, TFAers would move on and become leaders in law, politics, and business. Once corps members were ensconced in government bureaucracies and in executive suites, Kopp predicted, they could build on their experience of having taught in low-income areas. The presidential advisor and public intellectual David Gergen summed up this aspect of TFA when he wrote that "the most serious contribution of the corps members" would come "after they finish their two-year TFA commitment," when the TFAers would emerge "from their two years of service as the vanguard of a new generation of social entrepreneurs committed to education equity and social justice."[29]

---

28 Wendy Kopp, quoted in *Schools Matter* (19 June 2006), available at SchoolsMatter.blogspot.com; *Washington Post* (13 November 2005).

29 David Gergen, "Teaching for a Better America," *Boston Globe* (22 October 2005).

This was the most far-reaching part of Kopp's vision. She hoped "not just to place teachers in schools for a few years but to incubate a national corps of educational leaders" who "might then be in a position to create genuine, systematic reform." Kopp visualized TFA as "a pipeline of leaders" whose "initial teaching experience" would be "foundational to their lifelong commitment to effecting the systemic changes necessary to ensure educational opportunity for all." In a letter to a TFA alumnus, Kopp explained that her goal was not "to get our people to stay [in teaching] longer than two years, but rather to build a force of leaders who will work for fundamental change from within education and from positions of influence in every other sector. . . . We think it's critical that many of our corps members do enter other sectors, taking with them the commitment and insight that comes from their Teach for America experience so that they can work for the kind of changes in policy and public opinion that are necessary for ed[ucation] reform to take hold."[30]

Given this theory of change, Kopp recognized that "numbers are everything." If the organization did not grow beyond the 500 placements of 1990, it would be disparaged as, in the words of Stanford education professor Larry Cuban, "a relatively minor force" that could hope to kindle only "incremental change." To close the achievement gaps, TFA would have to expand its influence. The only way to do that would be to grow in size.[31]

Kopp therefore devoted much of her time to raising the money that would allow TFA to expand. From the outset, she sensed that

---

30 Sara Mosle, "Teach for America Grows Up"; Wendy Koss to Whitney Tilson, at EdReform.blogspot.com (March 2007); Kopp, quoted by Robert Pondiscio "Wendy Kopp Responds," posted at *blog.CoreKnowledge.org* (27 May 2008).

31 Wendy Kopp, quoted by Justin Pope, "Teach for America Surging in Popularity," *Washington Post* (17 June 2006); Larry Cuban, quoted by Sam Dillon, "Two School Entrepreneurs"; Donna Foote, *Relentless Pursuit*, 192.

there was "an incredible amount of money in the world and people who are looking for good things to support," and she was relentless in pursuing grants and donations. "If you can just get in the door," Kopp said, "you can have a good chance." To make time for telephone calls and meetings with potential donors, Kopp limited the amount of time she spent observing how TFA teachers were faring in their classrooms. In her meetings with potential donors, Kopp reiterated that the achievement gaps could be closed—that corps members were deeply committed "to realizing dramatic gains in students' academic achievement," that they knew their disadvantaged students "had the *potential* to achieve at the same level as students anywhere," that "given [this] potential to achieve at the same level" corps members "refused to settle for anything else."[32]

Kopp also recognized that most philanthropists and corporate executives were results driven. In the course of accumulating their fortunes, they had focused on making a profit, and Kopp similarly focused on an educational bottom line. Although Kopp acknowledged that there was "a danger in relying on low-level standardized tests as the ultimate bar," TFA emphasized the importance of what Kopp called "measurable results." Beginning in the mid-1990s, TFA identified a single, overriding goal: "significantly boosting achievement (defined as a one-and-a-half to two-year jump in grade level)," as measured by standardized tests. TFA then became a pioneer in using students' test scores as a way of comparing and measuring the effectiveness of teachers. Eventually, TFA developed a data-driven system that linked student achievement scores with seven teacher traits that TFA measured during the application process.[33]

---

32 Wendy Kopp, quoted by Susan Chira, "Princeton Student's Brainstorm"; Kopp, *One Day, All Children*, 161, 163.

33 Wendy Kopp, *One Day, All Children*, 177, 161; Sara Mosle, "Teach for America Grows Up"; Donna Foote, *Relentless Pursuit*, 37, 293; Foote, "Lessons from Locke," 47.

In addition to emphasizing the importance of test scores, Kopp urged schools to emulate the methods of successful business leaders. She said these leaders set goals. They inspired workers to meet the goals. And they measured progress toward achieving the goals. So it should also be with teachers. Their goal should be to have their students achieve at grade level. They should motivate their students to achieve this goal. And they should monitor their students' progress. As Kopp saw it, the key to great teaching was not mastery of subject matter but a knack for "figuring out what motivates people" combined with a willingness to do whatever was needed to meet concrete goals.[34]

Adding a touch that must have appealed to well-to-do philanthropists, Kopp also urged school principals to emulate the practices of business magnates. Just as teachers should keep track of the progress of their students, so principals and superintendents should track and manage their teachers. "If you want to create an exceptional school," Kopp wrote, "You have to . . . manage your team members." As Kopp saw it, school leaders should "act on all the principles of effective management." Their "number-one priority" should be "to know which of their employees are most effective" and "to keep [only] those people." To do this, school managers would have to assemble "basic reliable data on performance . . . to know who is most and least effective based on fair and objective metrics." Kopp pointed with special approval to one principal who said, "If you don't see children progressing or the teacher progressing, then it is not a good fit and the adult needs to go somewhere else." "Leadership," Kopp insisted, was "at the core of the solution to educational inequity."[35]

---

34 Wendy Kopp, interview with Charlie Rose, *CharlieRose.com* (1 July 2008); Kopp, *One Day All Children*, 161; Adam Bryant, "Charisma? To Her, It's Overrated"; Erin Donahue, "Wendy Kopp's Teach for America and Its Critics," student paper, University of Delaware (18 February 2010).

35 Wendy Kopp, *A Chance to Make History*, 66-67, 151, 154, 69, 11.

Kopp's approach paid off. After raising $2.5 million in 1990, TFA's fundraising increased exponentially. By the year 2000 grants to TFA covered an annual expense of $10.5 million, and by 2007 TFA's budget had grown to $120 million. At one fund-raiser at New York's Waldorf Astoria Hotel, tables went for as much as $100,000, and the overall collection amounted to $5.5 million. The *New York Times* reported that for this event, "stretch limousines jammed Park Avenue for blocks."[36]

Meanwhile, Kopp's salary increased from $25,000 in 1990 to $250,736 in 2005, and TFA's staff of recruiters, officers, and administrators grew to 835. With each year, TFA recruited ever more aggressively—"insanely aggressively," Kopp conceded. In 2005, 12 percent of the senior class at Yale applied for positions with TFA, as did 11 percent of the graduating classes at Dartmouth and Amherst, and 8 percent at Princeton and Harvard.

By then, the TFA recruits were averaging 1,310 on the SAT exam, and only one-third of the Ivy Leaguers (and 12 percent of all applicants) were accepted into the corps. One article in the *New York Times* reported that TFA had become "the post college do-good program with buzz." Another article, in the *Yale Daily News*, praised TFA for "making the classroom a prestigious destination for college grads, many of whom would have never otherwise considered the teaching profession."[37]

---

36 Wendy Kopp, quoted by Susan Chira, "Princeton Sudent's Brainstorm"; Kopp, *One Day All Children*, 184; Lincoln Caplan, "Great Expectations"; "The Media-Muddled Story of Teach for America," *Undernews* (13 January 2009) at ProRev.com/2009/01/media-muddled-story-of-teach-for.html; Sam Dillon, "Two School Entrepreneurs"; Negar Azimi, "Why Teach for America," *New York Times* (30 September 2007).

37 "The Media Muddled Story of Teach for America"; Donna Foote, *Relentless Pursuit*, 27; Tamar Lewin, "Options Open," *New York Times* (2 October 2005); *Yale Daily News* (19 September 2008).

After 2008, with the overall economy mired in a recession, applications to TFA soared, reaching a total 46,359 in 2010. At Harvard the number of applicants increased from 100 in 2007 to 293 in 2010 (18 percent of the senior class, a proportion that exactly matched the record at Yale). Even when choosing at Harvard and Yale, however, TFA selected only a minority of the candidates. This led one wry observer to write that the solution to America's educational problem was at hand: "Evidently, all we have to do is to fire all the schoolteachers and replace them with the best Harvard graduates—but *not* run of the mill Harvard grads. Just the *best* Harvard graduates."[38]

By 2010 TFA was spending about $22,000 to select and train each new corps member and its recruiting operation had become so effective that many corporations were eager to cooperate. "We think Teach for America is the best college recruiting organization in the U.S.," said one executive at Wachovia Bank. An executive at Goldman Sachs acknowledged that teaching for TFA was "one of the few jobs that people pass up Goldman Sachs for." At J. P. Morgan, yet another executive insisted that his financial group was like TFA, because "We [also] want employees who are committed to serving the community as well as to serving shareholders."[39]

Some major corporations were so taken with Kopp's program that they allowed recent college graduates to defer job offers to spend two years with TFA. J. P. Morgan even gave TFA's recruits signing bonuses before their two years of teaching and also offered well-paid summer internships to keep the corps members involved with the company while they were teaching. Google and General Electric

---

38 Steve Sailer, "All We Have To Do," iSteve.blogspot.com (14 July 2010).

39 Shannon McFayden, Edie Hunt, and David Puth, quoted by Patricia Sellers, "Schooling Corporate Giants," *Money.cnn.com* (27 November 2006); Donna Foote, *Relentless Pursuit*, 27.

did likewise, with one of GE's vice presidents explaining, "We [GE and TFA] look for the same types of people." Meanwhile, some one hundred graduate schools offered deferred admission and scholarships to applicants who wished to join TFA. For its part, TFA made clear its expectation that many of its recruits would move on to other work after completing their teaching stints. "I told them right up front that I was going to go to med school," said Dartmouth graduate Kristen Wong. "They liked that even better. They pick people who become leaders in the community." Boston College graduate Kilian Betlach served three terms with TFA—a total of six years, but he "never was encouraged to stay on as a teacher. It's almost as if the program perpetuates the idea that if you went to Harvard, a teaching career is below you. As soon as you join TFA, the focus is on being an amazing teacher. Then, all of a sudden, it stops. And you start getting e-mails from Goldman Sachs."[40]

By the late 1990s, TFA was generally recognized as a tremendous success, one that was celebrated by both Democrats and Republicans. In 2000, Wendy Kopp dined with President Bill Clinton, who "nodded vigorously" when Kopp said, "the only way to truly ensure that all children have the opportunity to achieve is to inspire more determined, talented leaders to turn their attention to our nation's poorest regions." Two years later, Kopp was seated in a box with First Lady Laura Bush when President George W. Bush declared, "I am proud to stand up and talk about the best of America and Wendy Kopp. I hope young Americans all across the country will think about joining Teach for America." Bush's aides then approached

---

40 Patricia Sellers, "Schooling Corporate Giants"; Bob Corcoran, quoted by Lindsey Gerdes and Sophia Asare, "Teach for America Taps Titans," *Business Week* (13 September 2007); Wendy Kopp to Whitney Tilson, EdReform. blogspot.com (4 March 2007); University of Chicago Law School, "Teach for America Partnership," at www.law.uchicago.edu/prospective/teach-for-america.html; Kristin Wong, quoted in Justin Pope, "Teach for America Surging in Popularity"; Kilian Betlach, quoted by Negar Azimi, "Why Teach for America."

Kopp and encouraged her to quadruple the size of her corps. In 2009, *Time* magazine named Kopp as one of the nation's 100 most influential people. In 2010, Kopp reported that 12 percent of all Ivy League seniors applied to work for TFA, and she and her government affairs team were working with members of Congress to build support for a $50 million federal appropriation for Teach for America. In 2011, Teach for America received a total of $100 million from philanthropists Laura and John Arnold, Eli and Edythe Broad, Steve and Sue Mandel, and Julian Robertson. Also 2011, the U.S. Department of Education announced that Teach for America was one of four groups (among a field of 1,600 applicants) chosen for a $50 million "scale-up" award that would enable TFA to double the size of its teaching corps by 2016. Another $50 million went to a TFA spin-off, the Knowledge Is Power Program (KIPP), which will be discussed in Chapter 8. Yet another $50 million went to the a Success for All (SFA) program described in Chapter 5. In announcing the awards, Secretary of Education Arne Duncan said that his Department was rewarding "creative thinkers who test good ideas and take proven approaches to scale so that more children can benefit."[41]

Along its road to success, TFA did experience some hard times. From the outset, there were critics within the corps, and professors at the nation's schools of education also found faults with

---

41   Wendy Kopp, *One Day, All Children*, 144-45; Joe Klein, "Who Killed Teach for America," *Time* (17 August 2003); *Time* (30 April 2009); Wendy Kopp to Friends, posted at EdReform.blogspot.com (25 March 2010); Michele McNeil, "49 Applicants Win 3 Grants," *Education Week* (4 August 2010); Arne Duncan, quoted in Department of Education Press Release (5 August 2010) at press@ed.gov; "Teach for America Attracts $100 Million," *Philanthropy.com* (27 January 2011).

the organization. One of the earliest criticisms came from Jonathan Schorr, a member of the first corps of teachers that TFA dispatched in 1990. Schorr acknowledged that before he was assigned to teach at a public high school in Southern California, he "could have counted on my fingers the number of times I had been inside a public school." Nevertheless, Schorr thought he was ready for the job. After all, Schorr wrote, he "had had the best education money can buy"—nine years at the prestigious Sidwell Friends School in Washington, followed by four years at Yale. He harbored dreams of liberating disadvantaged students "from public school mediocrity and offering them as good an education as I had received."[42]

It turned out that Schorr was "not ready" for a ninth-grade class that was "filled with 'social promotions'—students who had not passed the eighth grade but were simply moved along...." In addition to the social promotions, there were learning disabled students who were reading at third-grade level and other students with "severe behavior problems, students who spoke little English, petty (and not-so-petty) criminals, and so on." Many of the students dropped out during the course of the school year, which led Schorr to conclude, "I was not a successful teacher." "Just eight weeks of training may be long enough to train neighborhood clean-up workers or even police auxiliaries, but [it is not] enough for teachers." Indeed, Schorr wrote, "a quick course and a year in the classroom without the support to make that year successful is a waste of the enormous potential of a young, energetic teaching force."[43]

None of this would have come as a surprise to veteran teachers who have taught in urban public schools, and eventually TFA revised its training program. By 1994, TFA was employing 40 veteran teachers to support corps members and, although the summer program was

---

42 Jonathan Schorr, "Class Action," *Phi Delta Kappan* (December 1993), 315-18.

43 Ibid.

reduced to five weeks, TFAers were required to enroll in education courses and to meet periodically to discuss common problems. Yet this was not what Schorr had in mind. After spending two years taking education courses in pursuit of a California teaching credential, he reported, "virtually nothing of what I know came from those classes." In fact, "spending three or four hours at this after a day of teaching ... nearly drove me mad." Schorr recommended that novices spend a year or two as an apprentice with "a master [teacher] by their side."[44]

Critics continued to wonder if the TFA teachers were prepared for the challenges they would face. At Locke High School in Los Angeles, a major employer of TFA teachers, only 11 percent of the school's students could read at grade level, and some students could not read at all. "I don't mean they were stumbling over words or couldn't pronounce—they could not read!" wrote journalist Donna Foote, who spent a year observing TFA teachers at the school. In one class, the TFA teacher was "actually going through phonetic sounds ... trying to get [students] to understand words like 'cat.'" Foote also described the students' behavior as "rude, crude, and disrespectful"—a generalization that Foote supported with many specific examples.[45] And the problems were not limited to high schools. Stanford graduate Katherine Onorato reported that the annual staff turnover at her school in Oakland was 50 percent. "One teacher would go in, quit, and be out—over and over again. . . . My kids bragged about how many teachers they had run off."[46]

---

44 Ibid; Jay Mathews, "Assessing Teach for America," *Washington Post* (6 November 1994); Wendy Kopp, "TFA Revisions Under Way," *Phi Delta Kappan* (May 1994), 734-35.

45 Donna Foote, quoted by Lucia Graves, "What Is Teach for America Really Like?" *U.S. News* (February 4, 2009); Foote, *Relentless Pursuit*, 4, 26 and *passim*.

46 Katherine Onorato, quoted in Molly Ness, *Lessons to Learn* (New York: Routledge, 2004), 56. For a satirical take on the harsh realities faced by TFA recruits, see "Teach for America Chews Up, Spits Out Another Ethnic Studies Major," *The Onion* (16 February 2005).

Yale graduate Joshua Kaplowitz had an especially vivid experience at the Emery Elementary School in Washington. He learned there that TFA's philosophy—"the idea that if you set a rigorous academic course, all students will rise to meet the challenge"—left him "completely ill equipped when I stepped into my own fifth-grade classroom." Most of Kaplowitz's fifth-graders wanted to learn, "but all it took to subvert the whole enterprise were a few cutups." As it happened, there were more than a few. There was Kanisha, who would scream like an air-raid siren. There was Lamond, who would get up, walk across the room, and try to slap Kanisha. There were others whose parents were "mistrustful and tended to question or even disbelieve outright what I told them about their children."[47]

After one semester with the fifth grade, Kaplowitz was reassigned to teach second grade students, but, "unbelievable as it sounds, my second-graders were even wilder than my fifth-graders. Just as before, a majority of kids genuinely wanted to learn, but the antics of a few spun my entire class into chaos. This time, though, my troublemakers were even more immature and disruptive, ranging from a boy who roamed around the room punching his classmates . . . to a borderline-mentally retarded student, who would throw crumpled wads of paper all day."[48]

Kaplowitz sent disruptive students to the principal, but "nearly every student I sent to the office returned within minutes," and the lack of punishment "encouraged a level of violence I never could have imagined. . . . Fights broke out daily—not just during recess or bathroom breaks but also in the middle of lessons. And this wasn't just playful shoving: we're talking fists flying, hair yanked, heads slammed against lockers." On one occasion, Kaplowitz asked other teachers to help him stop a fight, but they refused because they said the District

---

47 Joshua Kaplowitz, "How I Joined Teach for America—and Got Sued for $20 Million," *City Journal* (Winter 2003).

48 Ibid.

of Columbia forbade teachers from laying hands on students "for any reason, even to protect other children."[49]

Experience would prove the other teachers right. One day an exasperated Kaplowitz placed his hand on the back of a disruptive student, nudged the student toward the hall, and closed the door. The student told his mother than he had been "violently shoved," and the mother filed a $20 million lawsuit against the school district. The D.C. police also charged Kaplowitz with a misdemeanor count of assault against the student.

Eventually, Kaplowitz was acquitted—but only after a criminal trial that spanned six days in 2002. For its part, the school system settled the mother's claim for $75,000—"chump change compared with the cost of defending the litigation." "It wasn't $20 million, but it was still more money than . . . this woman had seen in her life."[50]

There were additional problems that had little to do with students. Yale graduate Sarah Sentilles described her first- and second grade students in Compton, California, as "bright, energetic, hopeful, and really smart." Sentilles also had a favorable impression of the students' parents. But after teaching in Compton, Sentilles wrote a book that was so critical of her school's Black administrators that for five years the school district refused to accept any more TFA teachers. According to Sentilles, the administrators were an inept lot who failed to replace broken windows or repair loose electrical wiring; they forgot to order textbooks, and they did not provide a security guard or an intercom system, despite the high incidence of shootings near the school. On her way to school one morning, Sentilles passed a body on the side of a street, and on

---

49 Ibid.

50 Ibid.

other occasions she saw a drive-by shooting and heard gunshots while watching her students play at recess. Two men were killed in gunfire that erupted one afternoon as Sentilles drove her car out of the school's parking lot.[51]

Despite the problems, most TFAers thought well of the program. When University of Illinois graduate Ravina Daphtary began teaching in the Mississippi Delta, her first few months were characterized by daily battles with "65 adolescent students who didn't know me, didn't trust me, didn't look like me, didn't like me, and, for the most part, wouldn't work for me." Nevertheless, after two years, Daphtary had "fallen in love with my classes." As the TFA script had predicted would happen, Daphtary "discovered that students and new teachers alike can rise to meet unreasonably high expectations, as long as those expectations are set for them in earnest." After interviewing 154 TFAers, Johns Hopkins graduate and TFA alumna Molly Ness reported that Daphtary's experience was by no means atypical. Many interviewees, and Ness herself, remained "incredibly hopeful" for their students.[52]

Nevertheless, interviewees also reported that they were "by no means, adequately prepared for the classroom." Ness was "disappointed by the lack of guidance and mentoring that Teach for America provided." Abby Fee, a corps member from Harvard, seconded this view. "You have all these grandiose ideas. And then you get there and you're like, holy shit, my kids won't even sit in their desks.... It makes the high minded goals of Teach for America seem

---

51 Matthew Burke, "Teacher Saw Hope Amid L.A. Violence," *Boston Globe* (2 October 2005); Sarah Sentilles, *Taught By America* (Boston: Beacon Press, 2005) *passim*; Seema Mehta, "Controversial Reunion: Teach for America Has Returned to the Compton District after Five Years," *Los Angeles Times* (27 January 2009).

52 Ravina Daphtary, "Teach for America's Benefits," *The Daily Illini* (27 January 2009); Molly Ness, *Lessons to Learn*, 227.

really far away and kind of impossible." "It's not enough that I want it for [the students]," added Nick Pyati, a graduate of Columbia University. "It's not enough that I work hard."[53]

The problems came as no surprise to critics of TFA, who said it was naïve to think that bright, enthusiastic, 22-year olds who had no teaching experience would be ready to handle the challenges that TFA's corps members would face. In August 1990, even before the first TFA recruits were dispatched to their new schools, Deborah Appleman, a professor of education at Carleton College, "bridle[d] at the notion that anyone, regardless of how bright or how selective his school, would be ready to teach after a summer's worth of 'intensive' training." It was "insidious," Appleman wrote, to assume "that anyone who knows a subject and is willing to be with kids can teach." Sixteen years later, Appleman wrote another essay in which she took exception to "the notion that underprepared teachers can teach effectively in the nation's most challenging schools." Expressing similar dismay, Susan Mintz, an education professor at the University of Virginia, maintained that "research reveals that it takes a novice teacher three to five years to develop the skills necessary for working with any child." According to Mintz, research also showed that disadvantaged children were especially in need of "highly trained teachers who are familiar with child development, principles of effective instruction, and strategies for addressing the unique academic and social needs associated with this student population."[54]

---

53 Molly Ness, *Lessons to Learn*, xiii; Abby Fee and Nick Pyati, quoted by Gillian Gillers, "The Inside Scoop on Teach for America," *Current Magazine* (10 April 2006).

54 Deborah Appleman, "Teach for America," *Christian Science Monitor* (8 August 1990); Appleman, "A Poor Pairing: Underserved Students and Underprepared Teachers," downloadable at ReconsideringTFA.wordpress.com/commentary (17 February 2006); Susan Mintz, "America Needs Teachers, Not Teach for America," *Cavalier Daily* (23 October 2001).

The criticism eventually became an orthodoxy in the nation's teachers' colleges, where professors and officials instinctively recoiled from what they called "the bright person myth " of teaching—the idea that smart young people could do as well as veteran teachers, even if the young people had no extensive training in education. After all, if TFA corps members could succeed in the nation's toughest classrooms, with just a few weeks of preparation, what was the point of education schools?[55]

It was hardly a surprise, then, when education professors and administrators criticized TFA. Patricia Wasley, the dean of the Bank Street College of Education, found fault with TFA's "implicit assumption that you don't need to be prepared." David Immig, the CEO of the American Association of Colleges of Teacher Education, said it was "just impossible ... to turn people in [a few] weeks into highly skilled practitioners." Arthur E. Wise, the president of the National Council for Accreditation of Teacher Education, said it was "simplistic" to ignore the importance of courses on classroom management, teaching methods, and learning theory. John Palmer, the dean of education at the University of Wisconsin, said that TFA projected an attitude that was contemptuous of dedicated, career teachers. According to Palmer, "We would never say because there's a shortage of doctors or engineers, 'Take a bright person, give them a few weeks of preparation, and let them build bridges or perform surgery.'"[56]

---

55 Gail Russell Chaddock, "Teach for America Turns Ten," *Christian Science Monitor* (26 October 1999); Wendy Kopp, *A Chance to Make History*, 11.

56 Patricia Wasley, quoted by Stephaan Harris, "Volunteer Teachers," *USA Today* (13 October 1999); David Immig, quoted by Tamara Henry, "Intense Training," *USA Today* (16 July 2001); Arthur Wise, quoted by Jay Mathews, "Education Effort Meets Resistance," *Washington Post* (10 June 2003); John Palmer, quoted by Marcus Mabry, "The New Teacher Corps," *Newsweek* (16 July 1990), 62.

Many rank-and-file teachers also took exception to TFA. Lori Harte, a 20-year teacher in New York City, was so annoyed that she established a website called Debunk TFA. Scores of teachers then posted comments on the mismatch of inexperienced teachers and high-risk children. At another anti-TFA website, one veteran teacher decried "the time when Ms. Wendy Kopp first started TFA and decided, from her Princeton perch and without a day in the classroom, that inexperienced teachers were inherently better than experienced ones." Another veteran lambasted Kopp for waging a "class war" against "teachers who serve our nation's toughest schools." Others found fault with TFA corps members for being "cliquish," for exhibiting "a total disdain for veteran teachers," for "insinuate[ing] that these 'bleeding hearts' can be lauded as the best teachers in the school." At Vanderbilt University, a prospective teacher, Stacy Clark, penned an especially trenchant critique. "Why bother majoring in [education]," Clark asked, "if a little over a month is enough to teach you everything you need to know?" As Clark saw it, TFA was "demeaning the very profession it says it is trying to improve." TFA did not regard teaching as "a respected career" but as "something savvy people do on their way to bigger and better things."[57]

TFAers incurred special resentment when they suggested that the achievement gaps could be closed if only teachers worked harder. One example occurred when Wendy Kopp gave a speech at Washington University in 2006. To illustrate TFA's philosophy, Kopp mentioned the experience of a TFA corps member named Aurora, who had been teaching in a 4th grade classroom in Houston. As Kopp told the story, Aurora "discovered that the students were nowhere near the 4th grade proficiency benchmarks. So she got the

---

57 *DebunkTFA.wordpress.com* (now defunct); "The Little Reform that Doesn't," *The Daily Howler* (9 December 2008; 20, 24, 26 August 2008; and 22 December 2008); Stacy Clark, "Teach for America: Let's Play Teacher," *The Vanderbilt Torch* (October 2007); Donna Foote, quoted in Lucia Graves, "What Is Teach for America Really Like," *U.S. News* (5 March 2008).

key to the school from the janitor and came in early and stayed late every day. She asked the parents to let the students stay late each day. She also had her students come in on Saturdays. [As a result,] at the end of the year, the students all passed the 4th grade test." If only more teachers were like Aurora, Kopp seemed to say, the achievement gaps would be closed.[58]

Critics, however, said that most teachers could not devote this much time to their jobs. "This is not because they are lazy or deficient," education writer Peter Campbell noted. "It's because they want to have lives that include something other than work." Kopp was asking more of teachers than was asked of most other professionals. Without saying so explicitly, Kopp was urging teachers to forego children and lives outside the classroom, and for this reason her plan was "predicated on a workload that virtually ensures that it cannot scale." To make matters worse, Kopp had mentioned with pride that Aurora "was now a student at Harvard's National Institute for Urban School Leaders" and was "on track to become the youngest graduate of the Institute ever." For Campbell, this was no cause for celebration. "[I]f Aurora emerged from her own TFA experience convinced that all we need to do is have teachers work longer and harder and better, and all students need to do is work longer and harder and better, then she will be in a very powerful position to convince others that this is all we need to do."[59]

The resentment of veteran teachers was such that TFA teachers often stepped into a minefield of anger. One example of this occurred at Locke High School in Los Angeles, where some activist teachers, with support from TFA newcomers, proposed to boost test scores by adding an extra period of instruction to each school day. The

---

58 Wendy Kopp, quoted by Peter Campbell, "Teach for America's Popularity Grows," *TransformEducation.blogspot.com* (26 May 2006).

59 *Ibid.*; Jay Mathews, "Dangerous Minds," *Washington Post* (15 June 2008).

proposal touched off an outburst of indignation. "I don't think you need to bring up how hard you work and how much you care," said one veteran teacher just before the plan was rejected by a faculty vote of 72-36. "Most of you aren't gonna be here."[60]

TFA's critics also expressed concern about the high turnover among corps members. Only 70 percent of TFA's initial class of 1990 fulfilled their two-year commitment—342 of 489. In later years some 85 percent of the recruits put in two years, but only 28 percent continued for a third year. "You lose them just when they are becoming effective," said one professor of education. "It took me years to get 'good,'" one veteran teacher wrote—"more than two years." "My worry [is that] just as Teach for America people ... approach proficiency..., they are done. What a shame!" Critics jibed that TFA should stand for "Teach for Awhile." "There is something wrong with a system that floods poorly performing schools with inexperienced teachers who leave just as they are becoming experienced teachers."[61]

TFA could write off ed school professors and veteran teachers as defenders of the status quo. But some of the criticism involved more general, theoretical considerations. To be sure, hardly any critics ever mentioned the possibility that low-scoring students had inherent problems. This writer knows of no instance in which a TFA corps member mentioned low IQs as a possible reason for academic problems. Discussing the abiding influence of anti-academic cultures

---

60 Jay Mathews, "Dangerous Minds."

61 Molly Ness, *Lessons To Learn*, 11; "Teach for America," NationMaster.com/ encyclopedia; Avi Zinilman, reporting on the findings of the Teacher Policy Research Project, "Now, That's Classy," *Washington Monthly* (September 2006); Linda Darling Hammond, quoted by Sam Dillon, "Two School Entrepreneurs"; anonymous blogger, "Teaching is not something anyone can do," DebunkTFA.wordpress.com (24 September 2008; available through the Internet archive at *Archive.org*); Stacy Clark, "Let's Play Teacher"; Anna, "Why I Hate Teach for America," at Feministe.us/ blog/archives/2008/08/23.

was almost as taboo. Nevertheless, some critics recognized that, as one commentator put it, "the problems ... go beyond the teachers."[62]

In looking "beyond the teachers," a few observers expressed views that might be labeled "realistic." The problems had "little to do with the quality, quantity, or funding of teachers," one wrote. "You CANNOT teach a group of kids that consists of even 10% that simply do not care, are not interested, have NO incentive, and are bent on constant disruption and MUCH worse. The ACTUAL number is probably well OVER 50% of the 'students' that fall into that category in the schools that TFA is involved in." "Maybe we can at least admit what the source of the problem is."[63]

Expanding on this point, another observer wrote, "The problem isn't the teachers, but rather the sub-cultures they're teaching in. . . . A lot of parents like to say they value education and they 'get involved' but really their idea of getting involved is just bitching at teachers for stuff that isn't the teacher's fault." Taking a more academic stance, a teacher from Baltimore referred to the research of University of Kansas child psychologists, Betty Hart and Todd R. Risley. Hart and Risley had reported that the three-year-old children whose parents were professionals had vocabularies that were twice as large as three-year-olds whose parents were on welfare. According to the Baltimore teacher, no amount of "polite talk" could make a "critical fact go away." In terms of academic preparation, some groups of children were, on average, well behind others even before they entered school.[64]

---

62 Comment by debunktfa on "True Grit" *DebunkTFA.wordpress.com* (17 September 2008; available through the Internet archive at *Archive.org*).

63 Comment of "Bob" (27 November 2008) on entry "The disturbing hype of Teach for America" (4 October 2005) *Brendan-nyham.com/blog*.

64 "David Spade Says" (24 August 2008) at Feministe.us/blog/archives; "The Biggest Problem with Wendy Kopp," *The Daily Howler* (16 July 2008).

Some comments took aim at TFA "from the left." In saying that poverty was "no excuse" for failure, TFA was suggesting that urban schools could be fixed on tBhe cheap, with low-paid young teachers. This message was at odds with the argument that more money should be spent at low-scoring schools. Some liberals also accused TFA of ignoring social conditions and, "by overlooking these factors, enabling them." Others suggested that TFA was pursuing its organizational self-interest by crafting a theory that appealed to well-to-do philanthropists and business people who opposed higher taxes for social spending. According to Peter Campbell, "the implicit message of TFA is, 'All we need to do is hire great teachers and all our problems will be solved.' This lets these conservative, right-wingers off the hook." Bill Strom, a TFA alumnus, acknowledged, "if, in fact, the harmful effects of poverty are mere excuses, then there is no special incentive to work against or eradicate poverty."[65]

Advocates of progressive teaching methods weighed in with additional criticisms. Some said it was a mistake for TFA to "narrow their focus on the so-called achievement gap," since this led teachers to teach to the test by identifying " . . . the discrete skills and tasks that were going to be tested... and then [making] sure that students were proficient in these areas." Dave Prugh, who taught for TFA in Texas, was "appalled" when he was told to stop reading novels with his students and instead pay more attention to preparing them for tests. "My biggest frustration as a teacher," Prugh said, "has been watching test scores improve yet feeling as if the students weren't learning more. The critical thinking was being lost." Sylvia Corona, who taught for TFA in California, also chafed at restrictions on using the progressive instructional methods she had studied at Columbia University. In Los Angeles,

---

65 Comment of James, posted at *TheStoppedClock.blogspot.com* (18 December 2008); comment of Peter Campbell (26 May 2006) at *TransformEducation.blogspot.com*; comment of Bill Strom (15 December 2008) available at JoesSchool.blogs.com.

the students' scores "started to climb" after corps member Taylor Rifkin "began to teach to the tests." But instead of making Rifkin happy the results worried her. "Are they really learning?" Rifkin wondered. "Do they understand the concepts?" One art teacher in New York City expressed sympathy for the TFA teachers at his school, saying, "Math, history, physics are all really cool things too, but [TFA teachers] have so much BS and red tape they have to go through. It cannot be fun teaching for the regents [exams]. I sometimes feel guilty about this sweet deal I get where we just hang out, eat, make art, and interact with young people."[66]

Most of all, left-wing critics complained that TFA absolved the well-to-do while blaming their victims. According to Bil Johnson, an education professor at Brown University, TFA allowed the ruling class to say, "'Look, something's being done,' when in fact no significant change is occurring." Even worse, some radicals said, TFA allowed the dominant powers to tell inner-city youths, "now, if you fail, well, it's your own fault. We gave you a chance, but you didn't take advantage of it." This was an especially "cruel lie," radicals said, because the real problem lay with the changing nature of the American economy. These critics noted that academic skills were of little importance for most jobs in the inner cities, where "50% of the new jobs being created are in the minimum wage service sector."[67]

---

66 Online, comment (25 August 2008) on "Why I Hate Teach for America" EdNotesOnline.blogspot.com/2008/08 (24 August 2008); Peter Campbell, quoted by "Terry," (15 December 2008) available at *JoesSchool.blogs.com*; Dave Prugh and Sylvia Coroa, quoted by Seth Kugel and Ting Yu, "A Class All Their Own," *One Day: Teach for America Alumni Magazine*(Summer 2008); Donna Foote, *Relentless Pursuit*, 111; "Billy Says," 26 August 2008) at Feministe.us/blog/archives.

67 Bil Johnson, quoted in "Teach for America: Another, More Radical Perspective," *Brown Policy Review* (November 3, 2007); Reggie Dylan, "Restructuring Inner-City Schools for the Global Marketplace" (24 September 2008) at *4LAKids.blogspot.com*.

The many strands of criticism came together most influentially in a 1994 essay that Linda Darling-Hammond published in the *Phi Delta Kappan*, the bi-monthly journal of a professional association that had several hundred chapters in the United States. When she published her essay in the *Kappan*, Darling-Hammond was a professor of education at Teachers College, Columbia University. Before that, she had been a professor of education at the Bank Street College of Education, and later she would become a professor of education at Stanford.

Darling-Hammond was an unapologetic advocate of the progressive approaches that most colleges of education promoted. An extended discussion of her educational theories would be a digression at this point. Suffice to say that Darling-Hammond embraced most of the ideas put forward by the reformers who were discussed in the first three chapters of this book.

Like Jonathan Kozol, Darling-Hammond made light of evidence that most inner-city schools received funding that was at or above the average for their state. Like Kozol, she downplayed the significance of instances where inner-city students lagged despite per-pupil expenditures that far exceeded the state-wide average. Like Kozol, she emphasized that some suburban school districts spent more than their inner-city counterparts. Like Kozol, she disregarded the research of scholars who found no correlation between the money schools spent and the test scores of students. Darling-Hammond insisted that "money matters," and she wanted much more to be spent for the education of low-income children.[68]

Like Theodore Sizer, Darling-Hammond's ideal teacher was a "guide on the side" rather than a "sage on the stage." She wanted teachers to lecture less and to use fewer textbooks. She said that

---

68 Linda Darling-Hammond, *The Flat World and Education* (New York: Teachers College Press, 2010) 20 and *passim*; Darling-Hammond, *The Right to Learn* (New York: Jossey-Bass Publishers, 1997) 278-79 and *passim*.

standardized tests "impede student learning." She wanted teachers to aim for the deeper understanding that could be achieved if they abandoned direct instruction and recognized the students' need for conversation and coaching.[69]

Like Howard Gardner, Darling-Hammond thought schools should be restructured so that students would focus on a few subjects. Like Gardner, she lamented that many well-educated college students did not truly understand "concepts they have supposedly learned." To promote "higher order thinking," she encouraged teachers to abandon the "coverage culture" and to emphasize only a few of the many topics that were covered in a typical textbook.[70]

Lest there be any doubt about her advocacy of progressive education, Darling-Hammond also repudiated the importance of core knowledge. She said that E. D. Hirsch had "caricatured" progressive education and that it was a mistake to maintain, as Hirsch had, "that direct whole-group instruction emphasizing drill-and-practice is the path to developing disciplined understanding." Darling-Hammond characterized Hirsch as a "fundamentalist" who thought, "If schools would just go back to the basics, all would be well." Darling-Hammond believed that Black and Hispanic students were lagging because their curricula and teachers mistakenly stressed the importance of accumulating knowledge at the expense of "deep understanding."[71]

Given her background in teachers' colleges and in progressive education, Darling-Hammond's criticism of Teach for America was hardly a surprise. TFA, after all, encouraged bright young people to bypass the schools of education on their way to becoming teachers. And because TFA aimed to close the achievement gaps, TFA also emphasized

---

69 Linda Darling-Hammond, *The Right to Learn* 65, 8, 15, 115.

70 Ibid., 32, 57, 54, 55, 114.

71 Ibid., 8-9, 22.

the importance of the basic information that is covered on standardized tests. Most TFAers therefore emphasized direct instruction rather than the development of higher-order thinking skills.[72]

Although Darling-Hammond's criticism was predictable, her essay for the *Kappan* was an especially scathing shot across the bow. Its intent was to make TFA's benefactors recognize that, despite praiseworthy statements of purpose and expert public relations, TFA missed its mark. Darling-Hammond wanted to expose the discrepancy between what TFA promised and what it achieved. She felt like the disgruntled father of one TFA recruit, who complained about the contrast "between the façade of [TFA's] press releases and staged media tours and the grim realities of what the young recruits really experienced."[73]

Darling-Hammond began by decrying the fact that many TFA recruits were "placed in elementary and middle schools but have had no training in child development, learning theory, or such essential skills as how to teach reading." Although TFAers were highly intelligent and idealistic, they were not familiar with the teaching strategies that teachers needed to be successful. Instead, TFA seemed to assume that because of the corps members' superior intelligence, they did not need—and need not bother with—extensive preparation for teaching. According to Darling-Hammond, TFA believed that, "beyond subject-matter knowledge and general intelligence, no serious preparation is needed to teach effectively." But here, Darling-Hammond insisted, "the evidence is extremely clear. Beyond a threshold level, subject-matter knowledge makes less difference to teachers' effectiveness than does

---

72 Linda Darling-Hammond, "Who Will Speak for the Children? How 'Teach for America' Hurts Urban Schools and Students," *Phi Delta Kappan* 76 (September 1994), 21-34.

73 Lawrence Beymer, letter to the editor, *Phi Delta Kappan* 76 (December 1994) 340.

their preparation in child development, learning theory, curriculum development, and teaching methods."[74]

Darling-Hammond also noted that some TFA teachers quit and others "had to be let go." She maintained that this was the case because TFA's young recruits had little knowledge "of how children learn [and] how to create a learning environment." Yet before they departed, Darling-Hammond alleged, many of these teachers "undermined the education of the children they were assigned to teach." For Darling-Hammond, this was the nub of the problem. TFA was bad for the very students it proposed to uplift.[75]

Darling-Hammond further maintained that TFA was deeply resented "in minority communities, where good intentions that fail to produce good teaching for African-American and Latino children look like a thin veil for arrogance [and] condescension." TFA was "a frankly missionary program." Its corps members hoped to "save the cities and their poor students," but rank-and-file Blacks and Latinos recognized that TFAers were short-term sojourners who never "really identified with the community and the culture of the students." Beyond that, 68 percent of TFA's recruits were Whites or Asians who were being placed in schools where most of the teachers had been Black or Hispanic.[76]

In addition, Darling-Hammond said the very brilliance of the TFAers undermined their effectiveness in inner-city schools. "Underprepared TFA recruits may be the least likely to succeed with students whose experiences they cannot easily understand . . . People who learn effortlessly . . . often find themselves at a loss as teachers. They can't remember how they learned, and so they cannot construct

---

74 Linda Darling Hammond, "Who Will Speak for the Children?"

75 Ibid.

76 Ibid.

a process for teaching others." According to Darling-Hammond, it would have been better if TFA sent its recruits "to privileged suburbs and private schools, where their chances of success will be greater, and their failures will do less harm. In turn, these privileged schools could lend highly qualified teachers to urban schools, where their expertise would be of more use." As will be noted in Chapter 9, a modified version of this idea would come to the fore fifteen years later when the administration of President Barack Obama developed its Race to the Top Program.[77]

As Darling-Hammond saw it, TFA demonstrated that "quick fixes" don't work in education. The preferable alternative was to make sure that all teachers were prepared at one of the "many very good teacher education programs that are structured to ensure the kind of high-quality coursework and clinical experiences that fly-by-night operations like TFA cannot provide." In an article published in *The Nation*, Darling-Hammond urged the federal government to establish a "Marshall Plan for Teaching." "For an annual cost of $3 billion," the nation could "underwrite" the preparation of 40,000 teachers at "top-quality urban teacher-education programs."[78]

Professional educators applauded Darling-Hammond's critique. Lydia A. H. Smith, a professor of education at Simmons College, reflected the views of many ed school professors. "It is not right to waste children's lives with poor teaching; nor is it right to persuade idealistic people with all the best intentions . . . that they can teach when they are poorly prepared and therefore helpless in the actual classroom setting." Arthur E. Wise, the president of the National Council for Accreditation of Teacher Education, penned an especially forceful critique of TFA. Like Darling-Hammond, Wise

---

77 Ibid.

78 Ibid.; Linda Darling-Hammond, "Evaluating 'No Child Left Behind," *The Nation* (2 May 2007).

professed concern for "the unfortunate school-children who are the guinea pigs for this quick-fix approach that assumes that teaching is a craft to be picked up on the job." According to Wise, "over 100 studies have documented that fully prepared teachers are more effective . . . than those who come from the 'quick-fix' approaches." Nevertheless, because of the influence of misguided groups like TFA, Wise feared that the nation would move away from "devot[ing] more resources to teacher preparation" and would instead regard teaching as "an amateur activity" that smart people could learn "through practice alone."[79]

Wendy Kopp immediately recognized that she would have to respond to Darling-Hammond's criticisms. While she was still on vacation in 1994, Kopp penned a letter to the editor of the *Kappan*. In it, Kopp noted that TFA had recently polled the principals of the schools where its recruits were teaching. Of the 233 principals who replied, more than 95 percent reported that TFAers were "at least average in relation to other beginning teachers," 67 percent said that corps members were better than their other new teachers, and "more than 60 percent rated them as better than their *overall teaching faculty*." Another survey of 40 school superintendents, found that 97 percent believed TFAers were as competent as or better than the overall faculty.[80]

These surveys assuaged some critics. Colman McCarthy, a progressive columnist at the *Washington Post*, conceded, "Well away from the high professorial perches of Columbia [University] . . . those in the trenches every day with TFA teachers—school superintendents and principals—have other views." Writing in the *New York Times*, Rachel Shteir mentioned yet another TFA report that seemed to rebut

---

79 Lydia A. H. Smith and Arthur E. Wise, letters to the editor, *Phi Delta Kappan*, 76 (December 1994) 342, 338.

80 Wendy Kopp, letter to the editor, *Phi Delta Kappan* 76 (November 1994) 262; Kopp, *One Day, All Children*, 99.

Darling-Hammond. Contrary to Darling-Hammond's implications, over the years TFA had recruited a far greater proportion of minorities than the education profession overall. In the nation at large in 1996, 86.5 percent of all teachers were White, 7 percent African-American, 4 percent Hispanic, and 1 percent Asian. But 40 percent of TFAs corps members were minorities (24 percent African-American, 8 percent Hispanic, and 8 percent Asian). In 2011, 40 percent of Harvard's graduating Black seniors applied for work with TFA.[81]

It was harder to discredit some other allegations. After learning that TFA had accepted forty-four of one hundred applicants from Yale but only four of the nearly one hundred Fordham students who applied, one Fordham professor said TFA was a program "for those already privileged." Corps members occasionally reinforced the impression of elitism. One wrote, "97 percent of the teachers at schools like the one I was in need to be replaced. Seriously. Of the 100+ teachers at my school, excluding the TFA teachers, there were no more than three where you or I would tolerate having one of our children in the classroom."[82] Another key question concerned whether TFA was succeeding in closing, or even narrowing, the racial and ethnic achievement gaps. Here the evidence was not conclusive. Frederick M. Hess, a resident scholar at the American Enterprise Institute, was as familiar as anyone with the relevant research. And Hess concluded that the research was "entirely ambiguous."[83]

---

81 Colman McCarthy, "Teachers for America Get an 'A,'" *Washington Post* (29 April 1995); Rachel Schteir, "Teaching Teachers," *New York Times* (7 January 1996); Kyle Olson, "NYC Teachers Union Plays Race Card against Progressive Teachers Group," *New York Times* (22 April 2011).

82 Mark Naison, "Why TFA Is Not Welcome in My Classroom," HNN.us/node/140713 (17 June 2011); comment posted at EdReform.blogspot (July 2011).

83 Frederick Hess, quoted by Jay Mathews, "A New Focus for Teachers in Training," *Washington Post* (17 May 2005).

In 2002, a Stanford-based research group called CREDO (Center for Research on Education Outcomes) evaluated the performance of TFA teachers relative to both new teachers and all teachers in the Houston Independent School District. According to CREDO, "all the [evidence] show[ed] the average TFA teacher improving her students' performance by more than new teachers and at least as much as all teachers in Houston."[84]

At almost the same time, however, Linda Darling-Hammond and another team of Stanford researchers reached an opposite conclusion. Based on their study of some 271,000 students who had attended fourth and fifth grade in Houston between 1992 and 2002, Darling-Hammond et al. reported, "certified teachers consistently produce significantly stronger student achievement gains than do uncertified teachers." TFA recruits were "less effective than certified teachers" but performed "about as well as other uncertified teachers." Although most TFA recruits left teaching within three years, those who continued and became certified did "about as well as other certified teachers."[85]

Other studies were more favorable to TFA. One, by the Urban Institute in Washington, reported that TFA teachers who worked in North Carolina between 2000 and 2006 did better than traditional teachers, as measured by student performance on end-of-course tests. Another study, conducted by Mathematica Policy Research at an expense of $2 million, concluded that TFA's corps members outperformed even the veteran and certified teachers in Houston and five other school districts.[86]

---

84 Margaret Raymond and Stephen Fletcher, "Teach for America," *Education Next* (Spring, 2002).

85 Linda Darling-Hammond, Deborah J. Holtzman, Su Jin Gatlin, and Julian Vasquez Heilig, "Does Teacher Preparation Matter?" available at Education Policy Analysis Archives *EPAA.asu.edu*; Jill Tucker, "Study: Teaching Credential Matters," *Oakland Tribune* (16 April 2005).

86 "Teach for America," *New York Times* (16 May 2008); Mathematica Policy

The Mathematica study concluded that TFA's advantage was "statistically significant." But some observers cautioned that there was little to cheer about. Jay Mathews, an education writer for the *Washington Post*, explained that the problem was that "although TFA teachers outperformed the non-TFA teachers in the control group, they did not bring their students anywhere near to where they ought to be." The math scores in TFA classes increased by three percentile points. But this was like a baseball player who improved his batting average from an anemic .100 to a barely-better .125. At the outset of the school year, TFA's math students had scored on average at the 14th percentile, and at the end they had risen to the 17th percentile. "This was better than the control group students, who were at the 15th percentile in the fall and still there in the spring." In reading, the numbers were "similarly depressing." Overall, Mathews concluded, "TFA teachers look better than other poorly trained hires but none of them actually improve student achievement to any great degree."[87]

Wendy Kopp recognized that progress was slow in closing the achievement gaps. When she was asked about this after a 2009 speech to the Commonwealth Club of California, Kopp conceded that nationally the gaps were as large as they had been in 1990, when TFA sent its first corps of teachers into some of America's poorest schools. In 2011, Kopp acknowledged, "If you look at the data on the aggregate level, the achievement gap has not closed at all in the last twenty years."[88]

Research, "The Effects of Teach for America on Students," (9 June 2004).

87 Jay Mathews, "Class Struggle: When Good Isn't Good Enough," *Washington Post* (13 July 2004).

88 Wendy Kopp, quoted by Eric Tipler, "Why Is Wendy Kopp Hopeful?" (15 May 2009) available at *EricTipler.com*; Kopp, quoted by Dana Goldstein, "Does Teach for America Work?" *TheDailyBeast.com* (25 January 2011); Wendy Kopp, *A Chance to Make History*, 6.

Nevertheless, Kopp was not discouraged because, she said, "every major city in America now has at least one high-performing inner-city school—some have more—something that was not true 10 or 15 years ago. If you think about it, this is a big deal. Not only are these schools proving that the achievement gap can be narrowed, they also have the potential to be seeds, catalysts for larger-scale change." As Kopp saw it, before TFA "we simply did not know how to teach children handicapped by poverty and its accompaniments—family disintegration and destructive community cultures." But now, thanks to the success that many individual schools had enjoyed, Kopp concluded that demography did not have to be destiny. Effective teaching could overcome student indifference, parental disengagement, and poverty.[89]

Critics versed in the social sciences made light of the individual success stories—saying that the disadvantaged minority students who attended these schools were not a representative sample of the students in their communities. Nevertheless, the interests that funded school reform, the big foundations, state legislators, and Governors, were swept away by Kopp's optimism. When TFA began in 1990, recalled hedge fund manager (and former TFA teacher) Whitney Tilson, there was a question as to whether "unmotivated students with uninvolved parents" could be transformed "into hard-working, high-achieving college bound students." But by 2011, Tilson said, he had "visited over 100 schools that are generating extraordinary academic success with the most disadvantaged children." Tilson recognized that many people believed that a combination of "lousy students, parents and communities" had made it impossible for public education to thrive in the inner cities. But, like most of those associated with TFA, Tilson rejected this "'blame

---

89 Wendy Kopp, quoted by Eric Tipler, "Why Is Wendy Kopp Hopeful?"; Kopp, paraphrased by George F. Will, "Teach for America Transforms Education," *PressDemocrat.com* (27 February 2011); Kopp, *A Chance to Make History*, 2, 8; Kopp, "In Defense of Optimism in Education" *Huffington Post* (13 March 2012).

the victim' mentality" and insisted: "children are not failing our schools; rather, our schools are failing far too many children."[90]

Many philanthropists eventually agreed. In the aftermath of Linda Darling-Hammond's critical assessment, TFA had staggered in the mid-1990s. At that time, Kopp recalled, "Funders called for reassurances and answers to the questions that Darling-Hammond had raised." Some backers reduced their contributions, forcing Kopp to fire sixty members of her staff and to reduce TFA's bi-monthly payroll by 40 percent. In November 1994, the *Washington Post* reported that TFA was "financially troubled," and for a while, Kopp even "contemplated the possibility that Teach for America would not make it."[91] Nevertheless, several donors eventually stepped up and saved TFA. At one especially dark moment, the Carnegie Corporation chipped in with $300,000. At another, the Ahmanson Foundation provided $350,000. In the year 2000, Don and Doris Fisher, the founders of The Gap clothing chain, offered TFA its largest private-sector grant—$8.3 million, which TFA managed to match on a one-to-one basis. With that, Kopp noted, "[We were] on our way." In 2011, Eli Broad and three other donors established a $100 million endowment for TFA. And by then the nation's richest man, Bill Gates, had also embraced TFA and school reform in general because, Gates explained, a growing number of schools had "smash[ed] old prejudices about what low-income and minority students can achieve." These schools showed that "you can have a good school in a poor neighborhood," Gates said. "So let's end the myth that we have to solve poverty before we improve education. I say it's more the other way around: Improving education is the best way to solve poverty."[92]

---

[90] Eric Tipler, "Why Is Wendy Kopp Hopeful?"; Whitney Tilson, "Correlation vs. Causation," EdReform.blogspot.com (August 2011); Tilson, "Does School Matter," EdReform.blogspot.com (September 2011).

[91] Wendy Kopp, *One Day, All Children* 110, 111, 119; Jay Mathews, "Assessing Teach for America," *Washington Post* (6 November 1994).

[92] Wendy Kopp, *One Day All Children* 42, 90, 181, 184; *Los Angeles Times* (27 January 2011); Bill Gates, quoted by Steven Brill, *Class Warfare* (New

Wendy Kopp

With support from these and other philanthropists, TFA reshaped the common understanding of school reform. In earlier years when the influence of Jonathan Kozol had loomed large, reformers had stressed the need for smaller classes and more money. After that, there was an era when reformers had emphasized the importance of the curriculum—be it the constructivism of Howard Gardner and Theodore Sizer or the core knowledge of E. D. Hirsch. Most TFAers, however, regarded Kozol as a cranky purveyor of nostrums that had not worked, while they thought of Gardner, Sizer, and Hirsch as "old guard education warriors... from a different era."[93]

By 2010, when Marquette University chose Wendy Kopp as its commencement speaker, Kopp could say that she had "personally seen hundreds of [TFA] teachers who are proving... that when our nation's most economically disadvantaged children are given the opportunities they deserve, they excel on an absolute scale." As an example, Kopp mentioned Kalyn Gigot, who had graduated from Marquette in 2009. When Gigot began teaching sixth and seventh grade in Milwaukee, most of her students were several years below grade level. But Gigot turned things around, Kopp said, by recognizing that "success is about all the fundamentals of leadership." Gigot set an ambitious goal (getting students to achieve at grade level). "She went about investing her students in this goal." "She reached out to the students' families to enlist their support." And she "work[ed] incredibly hard." She held extra office hours at McDonald's every Saturday morning, and she kept students after school for extra help until about 7 p.m. on Tuesdays, Thursdays, and Fridays.[94]

York: Simon Schuster, 2011) 348; Gates, quoted in *Wilmington News Journal* (29 July 2011).

93 Comment of Whitney Tilson, EdReform.blogspot.com (December 2009).

94 Wendy Kopp, "Commencement Address at Marquette University 2010," posted at Marquette.edu.

Of course Gigot was only one teacher, but Kopp insisted that TFA had "hundreds of such 'proof points'"—and that this evidence was changing the nation's thought about what was possible. "In the most elite of journalistic and policy circles," Kopp said, people no longer believed that "socioeconomic circumstances are determinative of educational outcomes." They were beginning to think that by replicating TFA's program it would be "possible to put children growing up in poverty on a level playing field." Kopp predicted that, as that belief took hold, the course of school reform would be transformed.[95]

In the course of the transformation, an important change would occur. When discussing the importance of teachers, Kopp accentuated the positive. She emphasized that underachieving minority students did better if they had outstanding teachers. There was, however, a tacit implication that if some groups of students did not do well, it was because their teachers were deficient. As will be noted in the next chapter, during the first decade of the 21st century, the emphasis in school reform shifted. Instead of praising special teachers, reformers increasingly attributed the achievement gaps to schools that were bad because bad teachers' unions made it difficult for schools to fire bad teachers. By 2010, the bad unions, bad teachers, bad schools idea (what pundit Steve Sailer called the Three Bads Theory) had become the conventional wisdom of school reform.[96]

---

95 *Ibid.*

96 Steve Sailer, "Guggenheim's Waiting for 'Superman' Is Shoddy Filmmaking at Best," *Takimag.com* (27 September 2010).

8

Kopp's Kids: KIPP, DFER, and Michelle

In 1998, Wendy Kopp married Richard Barth, who had been one of Kopp's closest aides during the early years of Teach for America. Kopp and Barth eventually became the parents of three sons. In addition to these biological children, and in keeping with TFA's overall design, Kopp also pointed to a great many TFA "alumni children" who, after completing their tours in classrooms, moved on to other occupations but continued to push for educational and public policies to uplift disadvantaged students. She took special pride in the work of Mike Feinberg and Dave Levin, who established a celebrated group of charter schools, the KIPP academies; in Whitney Tilson, who organized an influential pressure group within the Democratic Party, DFER (Democrats for Education Reform); and in Michelle Rhee, who moved on to become the schools chancellor in Washington, D. C. Kopp expressed the common sentiment of these and most other TFA alumni when she insisted, "disparities don't need to exist. We can ensure that children in the poorest communities in America have the same average achievement rates as more privileged children."[1]

---

1 Wendy Kopp, *One Day All Children*, 174.

KIPP

After graduating in 1992 from Pennsylvania and Yale, respectively, Mike Feinberg and Dave Levin joined Teach for America and shared an apartment while teaching in Houston, Texas. They eventually developed a special rapport with their students, but at the outset it was far from smooth sailing. One student in Levin's sixth grade class was "often angry and mean. He teased, taunted, and slapped other children. He ignored teachers who told him to stop." Another student "walked across the room during class, zipped down his fly, pulled out his penis, and asked a girl for oral sex." Levin sent him to the principal, but the student "was sent back in thirty minutes." Feinberg had an easier time. His students "saved that kind of activity for lunch or recess." In general, there was chaos in their schools. "Children raced up and down the halls. Few of them did their homework. Noise was a constant problem."[2]

There was an exception to the general pattern, however. Across the hall from Levin's classroom at Bastian Elementary School was the room of a veteran African-American teacher, Harriet Ball. Ball's fourth-grade students behaved well and made good scores on standardized tests. One day Levin approached her. "Ms. Ball?" he said. "I'm Dave Levin. I have the class across the hall. I've been noticing your class. . . . Do you mind if I sit in your room during my breaks and just watch what you do?" What Levin observed was "lots of choreographed movement, rhymes, [and] songs." Ball had devised one chant after another to get across the essential rules of grammar and arithmetic—a technique that, Ball said, built "long-term memory and boost[ed] the ability to easily transfer to higher level thinking." Eventually Ball would establish a corporation, Harriett Ball Enterprises Inc., and market her chants and activities throughout

---

2   Jay Mathews, *Work Hard, Be Nice* (Chapel Hill: Algonquin Books, 2009) 25, 23.

the United States. Her company's web site discussed "multi-sensory teaching" and cited the work of Harvard educational psychologist Howard Gardner, especially his views about the importance of tactile-kinesthetic intelligence.[3]

Back at their apartment after school, Levin told Feinberg about what Ball was doing. Feinberg then took time off to observe personally as Ball drilled her students on verb conjugations, multiplication tables, and place names. But it was not all chants. There was also a good deal of reading, silent and aloud, followed by questions, comments, and conversation. *Washington Post* education writer Jay Mathews has written that for Levin and Feinberg, "it was the beginning of the Ball tutorial, one master teacher and two rookies meeting for the next two years. They watched her in class. They asked her questions over drinks at King Leo's and other Houston clubs she favored. They invited themselves to her home on weekends for more instruction."[4]

During the course of this training, Ball convinced Feinberg and Levin that "learning could only occur in a well-run classroom, and that no classroom ran smoothly unless the teacher was firm." Feinberg and Levin thus came to believe that they had "to be strict with their students or the behavioral distractions would overwhelm the class." Ball also insisted that *all* children could learn. She disagreed with teachers who said that little could be accomplished if students and parents had no interest in school. Like Wendy Kopp and Teach for America, Ball believed that teachers should do whatever it took to see to it that students learned their lessons—even if it meant staying late after school or visiting the parents at home.[5]

---

3   Ibid., 32, 35, 288-89.

4   Ibid., 33.

5   Ibid., 53, 37.

Dave Levin absorbed this lesson so thoroughly that it led to his reassignment away from Bastian Elementary in 1994. Texas required students to take an exam, the Texas Assessment of Academic Skills (TAAS), and the policy was that a school would be rated unsatisfactory if fewer than 75 percent of its students passed the test. There was a loophole, however, that allowed students with a learning disability or those who did not speak English to be exempted from taking the test, if their parents would request an exemption. Several teachers at Levin's school asked parents to sign form letters requesting such exemptions, and the principal urged Levin to do the same for 11 of his students. Levin refused, however. He was "not going to give in to the popular but dispiriting notion that low-income children could not make much progress." As it happened, all but one of Levin's students passed the math section of the test, all but two passed the reading, and the school did not suffer in the TAAS ratings. Nevertheless, because Levin had refused to go along with the school's policy, he was given a letter of reprimand and told that his services would no longer be required at Bastian.[6]

After teaching elementary school students in Houston for two years, Feinberg and Levin were inspired by their pupils' potential but troubled by the bureaucracy and frustrated "at what was happening with our kids when they left our classrooms and went off to the local middle schools." The children had done well "in our . . . classrooms," Feinberg recalled, "but when they left . . . there was no long-term impact that was noticeable. Our kids would go off to the middle schools and by Christmas time, unfortunately, even though they [had been] in our classrooms well behaved, intelligent, enthusiastic students, they quickly would start skipping just as many classes, start smoking just as much dope, start joining just as many gangs, and start becoming just as many parents as all the other kids in those middle schools and high school[s]. And that was extremely frustrating."[7]

---

6 Ibid.

7 Mike Feinberg, interview with Hedrick Smith, *Making Schools Work* (Hedrick Smith Productions, 2005).

Kopp's Kids

Rather than concede defeat, in 1994 Feinberg and Levin persuaded the authorities in Houston to let them start their own middle school for grades 5 through 8. Eventually known as the KIPP Academy, the new school took its name from one of Harriett Ball's chants: "Knowledge is power, Power is money, and We want it."[8]

Houston's school authorities had several reasons for sanctioning KIPP. As has been mentioned, by the mid-1990s Texas schools were being rated according to how their students did on the annual Texas Assessment of Academic Skills. It helped that Feinberg and Levin were willing to do whatever was needed to ensure that their students did well on this test. KIPP had a nine-and-a-half-hour school day, from 7:30 a.m. to 5 p.m., with half-day classes on Saturdays, several weeks of summer school, and extra time for homework. Feinberg and Levin also studied older versions of the TAAS and discussed similar questions in their classes. This was a controversial practice called "teaching to the test," but Feinberg and Levin said the practice "was simply review of skills and concepts that state test makers—most of them teachers—had decided were important for students to learn." This approach increased the likelihood that KIPP's students would do well, and this in fact was the case. The end-of-year test scores in 1995 showed that "almost every KIPP student had moved up two grade levels in just one year." "Based on the test scores," Jay Mathews has written, KIPP was "an unqualified success." "Only about half [of these] students had passed the state tests when they were fourth graders. After a year of Feinberg and Levin, more than 90 percent of them had passed both the math and reading tests."[9]

Despite the academic success, it was not always easy to persuade students to enroll at KIPP. In most areas, students were routinely assigned to schools in their neighborhoods. Because Feinberg and Levin were operating a specialty school, however, they had to recruit

---

8   Jay Mathews, *Work Hard, Be Nice*, 74.

9   Ibid., 74, 112, 141.

their pupils, and many prospects lost interest when they heard about the longer school days and year. "Who'd want to do that?" said one boy who was wearing a baseball cap sideways. Some critics called KIPP the "Kids in Prison Program."[10]

To persuade pupils to enroll, Feinberg and Levin promised "all kinds of fun." In addition to the joy of learning, there would be Saturday lunches at McDonald's and school trips to nearby places like AstroWorld. For students who followed KIPP's rules, there would be additional trips to distant locations like Disney World in Florida and the nation's capital, Washington, D.C. This would cost money, of course, but Feingold and Levin thought they could cover the expense with contributions.

As it happened, one of KIPP's first benefactors was Jim McIngvale, better known in Houston as Mattress Mack. McIngvale owned Gallery Furniture, and over the years he had become something of a celebrity by starring in his own television commercials. "Come to Gallery Furniture, where we *really* will save you money," McIngvale would shout from the TV screen, while throwing a fistful of dollars at the camera. Since Feinberg and Levin had enjoyed the commercials, they decided to drive over to the furniture store and ask Mattress Mack if he would support KIPP.

> 'Hi, Mr. Mack,' Feinberg said. 'We're two teachers from . . . down the road. . . . We're starting a program called KIPP. . . . We believe there are no shortcuts . . . 'You know what?" [Mack said]. 'That is *absolutely right*. There are no shortcuts. It's all about hard work, right? So . . . what are you here for, boys?' Feinberg talked fast. 'Well, we're starting this program and having the kids come from seven thirty to five and having summer school for everybody...' McIngvale smiled broadly. 'This is *great*!' he said. 'This is exactly what public education needs. So what can I do to help?'[11]

---

10 Ibid., 216, 210.

11 Ibid., 94-97.

Kopp's Kids

Before the day was over, McIngvale had agreed to underwrite some of KIPP's extra expenses. "From then on," Jay Mathews has written, "no one in Houston was a bigger supporter of Levin, Feinberg, and KIPP than Mattress Mack, who enjoyed throwing money at them as much as he liked tossing it at television cameras."[12]

Beyond the need to give disadvantaged students extra time to learn the basics, there were other reasons for KIPP's extended school day and year. It allowed time for enrichment in music and art without taking away from the basics. And Feinberg and Levin also wanted to reduce the influence of peers from their students' neighborhoods.

Altogether, KIPP students spent about 67 percent more time in class than their counterparts at regular public schools. As a consequence, the KIPPsters (as KIPP students came to be called) did not have time to "hang out" in their neighborhoods. Because he spent so much time at school, explained Adaobi Kanu, an eighth grade student, "I don't have time to play. I don't get home until around 7, and I get straight to my homework. After three years of doing it, it's fun."[13]

With such a schedule, admission to KIPP necessarily was limited to volunteers. And having students spend more time in class and away from the influence of peers in their neighborhoods was only one of KIPP's distinguishing features. There was also a strong emphasis on parental involvement. Feinberg and Levin visited the homes of prospective students to explain that parents were required to sign a contract, the KIPP Commitment to Excellence. It specified that parents must check their children's nightly homework and visit the school any time a problem arose. One officer of the National Education Association later mentioned this feature as a key to KIPP's success. "Parents have to be active enough to put their kids in those

---

12   *Ibid.*, 97.

13   *New York Times* (20 October 1999).

schools. So by the very nature they're going to be pretty active in their child's education."[14] As news about KIPP spread, more students volunteered (with a lottery in those years when there was not enough space to accommodate all who wished to enroll). In 1996 Levin moved to New York to start a second KIPP, while Feinberg hired extra teachers to accommodate a growing enrollment in Houston. Before long there were four KIPP academies, and the number continued to grow. Soon KIPP had to hire more new teachers—many of whom had previously worked for TFA.

Like TFA, KIPP expected much of its teachers. To begin, there were the longer school days and year. In New York, for example, KIPP teachers were required to be at school for a minimum of 47 and one-half hours each week, while middle school teachers elsewhere in the city were required to be in their buildings for only 31 hours a week. KIPP teachers were also expected to carry cellular telephones and to respond each evening to calls from students who had questions about homework or projects. In KIPP schools, moreover, the teachers were not tenured and, if their performance was considered unsatisfactory, they could be fired without complying with the usual bureaucratic procedures. To compensate for this and for the extra time, KIPP paid its teachers about 20 percent more than the going rate in their district.

KIPP also expected much of its students. Feinberg and Levin developed a system of classroom behavior called SLANT, which required students to Sit up, Listen, Ask questions, and Nod and Track the teacher with their eyes. Visitors often commented on how keenly KIPP's students appeared to be paying attention, and on occasion Feinberg and Levin would ask students to demonstrate the opposite of SLANTing. "Give us the normal school look," they would say, and the students would start slouching and staring into space. After visiting one KIPP class, journalist Paul Tough conceded, "To anyone

---

14 Denise Cardinal, quoted in *Houston Chronicle* (12 August 2005).

raised in the principles of progressive education, the uniformity . . . in KIPP classrooms can be off-putting." Nevertheless, Tough added, "the kids I spoke to said they use the SLANT method not because they fear they will be punished otherwise but because it works: it helps them to learn."[15]

Some KIPP schools also developed distinctive sets of punishments. If students misbehaved, failed to do their homework, or even delayed in calling for help with an assignment, they would be sent to "the bench," where they would still attend class but where they would have to wear their shirts inside out and would not be allowed to speak with other students. During lunch period, these students would be sent to a special "porch," where they would not be allowed to talk to their friends. Since many peccadilloes were counted as infractions, most KIPP classes usually had two or three pupils on the bench at a time. Nevertheless, according to journalist Ira Carnahan, "compared with the barely controlled chaos in some middle schools (inner city and suburban), [KIPP] students sit quietly and focus when the teacher lectures."[16]

Feinberg was candid in explaining KIPP's approach to discipline. "We don't believe in suspending children," he said. "We do not want to punish children by taking away their education . . . When we suspend children they go home for a week on suspension . . . and they'll come back worse than ever." So, in place of suspension, KIPP came up "with the idea of the bench in terms of not being on the team. And on the bench what we've taken away is the social aspect which the kids at middle school level so crave. So they're still

---

15 Paul Tough, "What It Takes to Make a Student," *The New York Times Magazine* (26 November 2006).

16 Angela Pascopella, "Judging the KIPP Academy," *Curriculum Administrator* 37 (January 2001) 45; Ira Carnahan, "No Shortcuts," *Forbes* 172 (10 November 2003), 114.

in the classroom, they're still learning; but they have to sit apart from their teammates, and the only one they can talk to in that classroom is the teacher. They can't talk to their friends and their friends can't talk to them. So it applies not just to the classroom but the entire school day so when they go eat lunch, they have to sit at a separate table . . . They can't eat with their friends. They have to eat either in silence or they can work on their homework and reading when they're at the table."[17]

Ruminating on why discipline was a big part of KIPP's student life, Feinberg explained: "Anyone who's been successful in this world [knows] that part of their success was owed to . . . [the] discipline that they either created themselves or they received from someone else to help them along."[18] There were rewards as well. At some schools "KIPPsters" could earn up to 20 KIPP dollars a week, which could be used to buy supplies at the school. Scrip was distributed for turning in homework, for participating in class, and for going above and beyond what was expected. The students were given a piece of paper that looked like a regular bank check, one that had to be countersigned by parents before the children could deposit it to their school checking account. If a parent saw that a weekly check was for only $4 or $5, the parent would know that the child was having problems.[19]

In addition, there were more substantial incentives. At one KIPP Academy, fifth grade students who earned enough dollars over the year received a trip to Disney World. Elsewhere, there were class trips to other far-flung spots. KIPP's teachers displayed their college diplomas and organized trips to visit college campuses, and one KIPP academy also displayed the pennants of every college its alumni had attended,

---

17 Mike Feinberg, interview with Hedrick Smith.

18 *Ibid.*

19 Kelly Patricia O'Meara, "Education Reform," *Insight on the News* (18 September 2000), 16.

with plaques listing the names of the graduates as a continual reminder to present students. To go on field trips, or even to participate in extra-curricular activities such as the school orchestra, students were required to have a pre-determined amount of money—"Scholar Dollars"—in their KIPP checking accounts. These KIPP schools were avowedly trying to instill in students an understanding that privileges had to be earned.[20]

Another goal was to stimulate the ambitions of students who might not otherwise think about going to college. One visiting scholar noted that KIPP blended the social with the academic. "KIPP is creating a social world that thinks that academic effort is cool," said Lauren Resnick. The rewards were part of an effort to give students "a social world to live in that's consonant with the academic world that they're trying to build." Writing in the *New York Times*, columnist David Brooks noted that "students who lack cultural and social capital because they did not come from intact, organized families" generally fell "further and further behind—unless they come into contact with some great mentor who can not only teach, but also change values and behavior." Brooks intended the word "mentor" in a broad sense that included entire schools, because, as TFA alumnus Whitney Tilson noted, "every successful school I've seen serving low-income minority communities (which, it goes without saying, usually lack the cultural and social capital Brooks is talking about) somehow instills this capital (certainly KIPP does)."[21]

Although KIPP's system of rewards and punishments was innovative, the courses were quite traditional. "There's nothing flashy about the curriculum," Feinberg said. With its stress on basic

---

20 *Forbes* 172 (10 November 2003) 114; *New York Times* (20 October 1999); Lauren Ferrillo, "KIPP," undergraduate student paper, University of Delaware, December 2005.

21 Lauren Resnick, quoted by Courtney Singer, "KIPP," appendix to Mike Feinberg, interview with Hedrick Smith; David Brooks, "Questions of Culture," *New York Times* (19 February 2006); Whitney Tilson's comment at EdReform.blogspot.com (February 2006).

arithmetic skills, paving the way to algebra by eighth grade, and the general belief that facts were good, KIPP was clearly outside the mainstream of progressive education. The classes were teacher-centered, and students were required to memorize a great amount of information. As has been noted, KIPP was also known as a land of chants, where students recited the multiplication tables, the names of state capitals, and the standard rules of grammar and spelling. They would also bang on desks and stomp their feet as they chanted bigger thoughts: "Knowledge is Power. Power is freedom. And I want it." A reporter for the *New York Times* described the KIPP Academy in the Bronx as "perhaps the city's most regimented public middle school, with a highly structured approach to learning."[22]

The traditional methods were prompted by a sense of mission. KIPP's founders wanted to give students a chance to take advantage of opportunities. Feinberg and Levin were determined "to provide kids with the academic, intellectual, and character skills they need to succeed in high school, college, and the competitive world beyond." In America's post-industrial economy, they said, there was a connection between the gaps in academic achievement and a growing disparity in the distribution of income. Their goal was to bridge the gaps by preparing youngsters from poor communities to get better-paying jobs in the new economy.[23]

Unfortunately, Feinberg said, too many people made excuses for the academic shortcomings of inner-city students. Because of poverty, family instability, and the anti-academic values of the peer

---

22 Mike Feinberg, quoted by Kelly Patricia O'Meara, "Education Reform"; Abigail Thernstrom and Stephan Thernstrom, *No Excuses*, 63; Amy Goodnough, "Structure and Basics Bring South Bronx School Acclaim," *New York Times* (20 October 1999).

23 Mike Feinberg, interview with Hedrick Smith.

group, some observers thought inner-city children had so many cards stacked against them that they could not do well in school. Others placed the blame on the persistence of societal racism, the abiding influence of anti-academic sub-cultures, or inherent shortcomings in intelligence. According to Feinberg, many people "either say or believe, without stating it quite directly and openly, that a lot of these kids of color who come from poor homes, across the track so to speak, can't learn, they can't be reached, it can't be done." Many people still had the "mindset that because of a zip code you're born in or the color of your skin or something like that, that there's limitations to what one can achieve in this world." Many people "don't . . . truly believe an achievement gap is possible to get rid of."[24]

Some observers believed that KIPP was proving that this thinking was mistaken. With more than 75 percent of its students qualifying for federal lunch subsidies, KIPP's students were clearly "disadvantaged." Yet on standardized tests of reading and mathematics, KIPP's students scored far above students who attended other schools for disadvantaged children. For seven straight years, the KIPP Academy in the Bronx outperformed all other public middle schools in the borough in math and reading, a result that so impressed the borough president that he pushed all the districts to start similar programs. According to Feinberg, "on average our kids come in one or two grade levels behind where they should be by fifth grade. But by sixth grade, after only one year at KIPP, these students are up to grade," and by seventh and eighth grade they were scoring well above the average "as measured by the Stanford 10, a nationally administered normative test."[25]

---

24 Ibid.; Cynthia Howell, "Educator Speaks Up," *Arkansas Democrat-Gazette* (23 March 2005).

25 Jay Mathews, "Expert Takes a New Look at KIPP Schools," *Washington Post* (12 May 2005); *New York Times* (20 October 1999); Mike Feinberg, interview with Hedrick Smith; "KIPP 3D Academy," appendix to *Ibid.*

This success impressed many observers. An editorial in *USA Today* identified KIPP as "probably the most successful charter schools in the U.S." Writing in the *Arkansas Democrat-Gazette*, journalist Cynthia Howell described KIPP as "the nation's premier organization of charter schools." Jay Mathews of the *Washington Post* concluded that KIPP's success made "a good case . . . for introducing . . . longer school days and . . . stronger motivational techniques ... into all low-performing schools." In the *New York Times*, Amy Goodnough noted that KIPP had received praise "from left and right"—from liberal reporters and from George W. Bush, who featured a group of KIPP students chanting, "Read, baby, read," at a Republican national convention.[26]

KIPP also received much praise from the Harvard historian Stephan Thernstrom and his wife and co-author, Abigail Thernstrom. In their book of 2003, *No Excuses: Closing the Racial Gap in Learning*, the Thernstroms touted the KIPP academies as examples of what schools could accomplish. If more schools would emulate KIPP's combination of long hours, dedicated teachers, and innovative discipline and rewards, the Thernstroms said, Black and Hispanic students would do much better. For the Thernstroms, KIPP was good news. It showed that educational innovation could reduce, and perhaps even eliminate, the achievement gaps. KIPP had developed a blueprint for addressing what the Thernstroms called "the most important civil rights issue of our times." The Thernstroms even took the title of their book from KIPP. For years "No Excuses" had been a favorite slogan of KIPP's founders.[27]

There were various explanations for KIPP's success. One retired teacher in San Francisco gave the credit to KIPP's formula for

---

26 *USA Today* (4 January 2005); *Arkansas Democrat-Gazette* (23 March 2005); *Washington Post* (12 May 2005); *New York Times* (20 October 1999).

27 Abigail Thernstrom and Stephan Thernstrom, *No Excuses*, 274 and *passim*.

getting teachers, parents, and students to work together—saying that any school would stagnate if any one part of this "secular trinity" were absent. The Thernstroms, for their part, emphasized the importance of developing an academic culture. In their view, the average academic achievement of Blacks and Hispanics lagged because their community cultures did not value education as much as the cultures of Whites and Asians. As a result, Black and Hispanic students did not work diligently in school, and the schools consequently came to expect little of these students. At the KIPP academies, however, the teachers' expectations were higher, the discipline was tougher, and the curriculum focused on the basics.[28]

Extra money, however, was not part of the equation. Because they wished to establish additional KIPP academies, Feinberg and Levin insisted that KIPP should operate on "the same amount of money that it takes to run a public school in whatever community those public schools are operating." Feinberg acknowledged, "Money is, certainly, an important factor." But he also recognized that money was "not the ultimate answer." "Money is not going to guarantee success." There were "too many school districts out there that are spending twice as much as they get here in Houston, that are just failing the children miserably."[29]

Besides, if KIPP received extra funds, Feinberg said, many people would say, "Well they [succeeded] because of the money." Consequently, KIPP "figured out how to run all these extra hours on the same nickel." Feinberg and Levin dunned donors for contributions to defray the expense of school trips. They bragged about "being very lean on the administrative side." And although KIPP's teachers were paid more than their counterparts in a given area, the total expenditure for salaries

---

28 Richard L. Heidelberg to *New York Times* (17 August 2000); Abigail Thernstrom and Stephan Thernstrom, *No Excuses, passim.*

29 Mike Feinberg, interview with Hedrick Smith.

was reduced because KIPP's teachers were younger (and thus at lower steps on the salary scale) than their counterparts at most other schools. In addition, because of KIPP's emphasis on order, the KIPP schools did not have to rely upon small classroom size to maintain control. As the Thernstroms noted, KIPP's "disciplined atmosphere allow[ed] large classes, reducing the number of teachers on the payroll."[30]

As the nation continued to grapple with the question of how to improve the academic achievement of poor and minority children, many observers were intrigued by the prospect of spawning KIPP academies throughout the United States. "I don't know how easy it would be to repeat KIPP's . . . success on a massive scale," wrote *New York Times* columnist Bob Herbert. "But schools that thrive in the inner city and in poor rural areas deserve . . . some very close attention."[31]

With this in mind, in 2002 Donald and Doris Fisher gave $15 million (later increased to $25 million) in seed money to establish a KIPP Foundation that fostered KIPP clones. And the Fishers, who had made their fortune as founders of The Gap clothing chain, knew something about building a franchise. To promote more KIPPs, they instructed educators in the nuts and bolts of operating charter schools. The first group of "fellows" received $45,000 stipends plus free room and board during an eight week "residency" at an already-established KIPP school and at a six week seminar held at the University of California, Berkeley. Then they would become eligible for a $1 million loan for school buildings. "It was literally an opportunity," said Caleb Dolan, a sixth grade teacher from Gaston, North Carolina. "It's always been my pipe dream . . . It's been my late-night conversation for about three years now: If we ran the school, if we ran the school."[32]

---

30 Ibid.; Abigail Thernstrom and Stephan Thernstrom, *No Excuses*, 57.

31 Bob Herbert, "A Chance to Learn," *New York Times* (16 December 2002).

32 Jodi Wilgoren, "Seeking to Clone Schools of Success for Poor," *New York Times* (16 August 2000).

Thanks to the KIPP Foundation, the dream would become a reality, not just for Dolan but for others as well. In 2007 KIPP raised an additional $65 million to finance an ambitious plan to create 42 schools in Houston. Houston philanthropists Laura and John Arnold contributed $30 million, and much of the rest came from the leaders of three of America's best-known corporations: Microsoft, Wal-Mart, and The Gap. The Bill and Melinda Gates Foundation (which had previously given $8 million to create up to eight KIPP high schools) pledged $10 million, the Walton Family Foundation, $8.7 million, and Doris and Don Fisher, another $5.3 million.[33]

Eventually, the United States Department of Education joined in. In 2010, it opened a new competition to foster the development of more schools like KIPP. Funded with $650 million from the American Recovery and Reinvestment Act (the so-called "stimulus package"), the new program provided assistance for educators who wished to replicate or expand "high-quality charter schools with demonstrated records of success." KIPP emerged as one of the big winners—one of only four organizations that received the maximum grants of $50 million.[34]

By 2013 fifty thousand students were enrolled in 141 KIPP schools. By then, Feinberg and Levin had also persuaded Richard Barth, a TFA alumnus who had been working for Edison Schools, to take over administrative direction of the KIPP Foundation. Barth's appointment cemented the close relationship between KIPP and TFA, for Barth was the husband of TFA founder Wendy Kopp.[35]

---

33 Jay Mathews, "Charter School Effort Gets $65 Million Lift," *Washington Post* (20 March 2007).

34 www2.ed.gov/programs/charter/index.html; Michele McNeil, "49 Applicants win i3 Grants," *Education Week* (4 August 2010). The other "victorious" organizations were Teach for America, the Success for All Foundation, and Ohio State University.

35 Jay Mathews, "KIPP Founders... To Focus on Bigger Picture," *Washington*

Some observers regarded KIPP as a key to closing the achievement gap. *USA Today* celebrated KIPP's schools as "probably the most successful charter schools in the U.S. . . . Three of every four KIPP graduates go on to college, compared with fewer than half the students in the neighborhood schools they left." In their book *No Excuses*, Abigail Thernstrom and Stephan Thernstrom reported that at the KIPP Academy New York "66 percent of the students in math and 55 percent in reading had scores above grade level by New York State Standards," while elsewhere in the community from which KIPP drew its students "only 9 percent in math and 16 percent in reading were above grade level."[36]

If KIPP's students were truly representative of students in their neighborhoods, the KIPP model could be seen as a panacea. Nevertheless, some observers were skeptical. After noting that the achievement gap had persisted in most places despite the numerous, expensive reforms of the past—"everything from Progressive child-centered education, the self-esteem movement, court-ordered busing, [and] Afro-centric education (among countless others)," Robert Weissberg, a professor at the University of Illinois, scoffed that the Thernstroms were offering "the faintest glimmer of hope to those craving betterment against all odds."[37]

Post (13 July 2011); Tamar Levin, "Charter Group Will Enroll More Pupils in Houston" *New York Times* (21 March 2007); Mathews, *Work Hard, Be Nice*, 312; Mike Feinberg and Dave Levin, "What 'Yes, We Can' Should Mean for Our Schools," *Washington Post* (9 January 2009), posted at EdReform.blogspot.com (January 2009); posting at Diane Ravitch's blog, 5 February 2014.

36 "Charters: Success or Failure?" *USA Today* (4 January 2005); Martin Carnoy, Rebecca Jacobsen, Lawrence Mishel, and Richard Rothstein, *The Charter School Dust-Up* (Washington: Economic Policy Institute, 2005) 51; EdReform.blogspot.com (August 2009).

37 Robert Weissberg, "Review of No Excuses," *Society* (September/October 2004) 80-85.

Other critics noted that, in important ways, KIPP's students differed from the rank and file of public school students in disadvantaged communities. Richard Rothstein, who had reported on education for the *New York Times* before becoming a research associate at the Economic Policy Institute and a lecturer at Columbia Teachers College, noted that KIPP's students could hardly be considered typical when they volunteered to be attend school from 7:30 until 5, and on Saturdays and during the summer as well. And KIPP's teachers, with an average of only 3 to 6 years of experience in the classroom, were considerably younger and arguably more energetic and idealistic than their counterparts in other public schools. There was also some evidence that the KIPP families were a little better off financially than the average in their neighborhoods and that KIPP's students all along had slightly better test scores than the average in their communities.[38]

Rothstein scrutinized KIPP's statistics. He noted, for example, that KIPP's students were disproportionately girls, and girls usually did better than boys on the tests that were given in elementary and middle schools. Rothstein also noted that many teachers in regular public schools made a point of recommending KIPP only to their better students. And he noted that KIPP insisted that the KIPPsters' parents must sign a letter of commitment in which they agreed to "check our child's homework every night," to "make arrangement for our child to come to KIPP on appropriate Saturdays," and to "make sure that our child follows the KIPP dress code."[39]

Some observers emphasized the importance of involving the parents—and just how atypical this was in low-income districts. Rothstein quoted one teacher as observing, "Parental involvement is the main ingredient and that is what they [KIPP leaders] want.

---

38 Martin Carnoy et al., *The Charter School Dust-Up*, 51-65.

39 Martin Conroy et al., *The Charter School Dust-Up*, 51-65; Jay Mathews, *Work Hard, Be Nice*, 89-90.

It is the crucial factor in their success." Another teacher said she "didn't want to be skimming the best kids." But when this teacher talked to the parents of weaker students—"the kids I thought most needed it"—the parents said "stuff like 'sounds too serious' and 'he needs another year to grow up.' . . . I couldn't get many of these parents to apply. . . . Who ended up going to KIPP were kids with better-than-average test scores and parents who cared, motivated parents." Yet another teacher said, "Parental support is extremely important. This is the common denominator that all of the students I nominated have."[40]

Two Internet journalists, Caroline Grannan and Peter Campbell, called attention to yet another aspect. In California, a remarkable number of students were dropping out of KIPP's schools. "In the 2005-6 school year, six of the nine KIPP schools . . . saw decreases in entering fifth-grade cohorts from 20 to 59 percent. The worst case was KIPP Bridge College Preparatory in Oakland, whose original fifth grade of 87 students was down to just 36 students by the time they reached eighth grade." The withdrawals made KIPP's results look better. "The students who left were most likely low-performing students. KIPP's average eighth grade scores at those schools looked terrific compared to their average fifth grade scores, but that might be because the lowest-scoring fifth graders had transferred to other schools, leaving only the higher scorers."[41]

KIPP Bridge in Oakland was atypical. The loss of more than fifty of eighty-seven certainly was extreme. But thirty-two of the "lost" students moved out of the area, and there was nothing KIPP could do about that. As for the others, nine left because the student or parents did not like the extended school day and year; and the remainder were not happy because KIPP was insisting that the students must repeat

---

40 Martin Conroy et al., *The Charter School Dust-Up*, 58, 60, 59.

41 Jay Mathews, *Work Hard, Be Nice*, 274-75.

a grade. Some parents said their children were already good students who would be stars back at their regular schools. KIPP's success was not an illusion, but the "dropouts" showed that KIPP did not work for every student.[42]

KIPP and its boosters had stepped on thin ice when they suggested that KIPP was THE solution to the problems that beset inner-city schools. There was no one solution. Nevertheless, KIPP's achievements were outstanding, and even Richard Rothstein, after scrutinizing the statistics and noting the unrepresentative nature of KIPP's students and parents, acknowledged that it was "likely" that KIPP was "in fact unusually effective." "We do not intend to suggest that [KIPP's] effectiveness is not real," Rothstein wrote. "KIPP's supporters claim, and we have no evidence that disputes this, that KIPP provides children with the motivation and opportunity to excel that they might not have in their regular public schools. Our evidence is also not inconsistent with the notion that regular public schools might have a great deal to learn from KIPP's philosophy and strategy."[43]

Some progressives refused to concede this much. William Crain, a psychology professor at the City University of New York, complained that it was a "limited definition" to equate "success" with test scores. After all, Professor Crain wrote, tests "primarily assess students' ability to memorize facts and formulas that they half understand . . . [and] say nothing about children's creativity, empathy, sensitivity to nature, love of learning, or ability to think for themselves." Harvey Daniels, another progressive professor, took exception to the "widespread belief that the most effective school for city kids is a kind of authoritarian, knuckle-knocking, skill-and-drill, back-to-basics approach [with] a focus on tight discipline." Education writer Alfie Kohn complained that KIPP students were "subjected to

---

42 "KIPP and Retention," EdReform.blogspot.com (April 2007).

43 Martin Conroy et al, *The Charter School Dust-Up*, 58, 60, 59.

a level of control that is downright militaristic." As Kohn saw it, the KIPPsters, were being "turned into trained seals who have to bark out correct answers on command."[44]

Most observers, however, were more upbeat. After attending a gala dinner in New York City, at which more than 1,000 people celebrated KIPP's 15th anniversary in 2009, hedge fund manager Whitney Tilson expressed the prevailing opinion. "Looking around the room, I got goose bumps. The only thing that rivals what KIPP has done is TFA." KIPP had shown "that if you give [disadvantaged] kids great teachers, set high expectations, and ask (no, demand) that they work hard and be be nice, THEY ACHIEVE AT VIRTUALLY THE SAME LEVEL AS OTHER KIDS !!!!"[45]

Some critics noted, however, that KIPP's success was limited to young (pre-high school) students. Others doubted whether KIPP, despite its success with highly-motivated volunteers, could also succeed as a system for all disadvantaged students in a given area. This skepticism was reinforced by the experience in New Orleans. After Hurricane Katrina, all the public schools in New Orleans were converted into privately run charter schools. Yet the students' scores on standardized tests barely budged. In 2014, after eight years of experimenting with charter schools, the test results, as reported by the Louisiana Department of Education, showed that students in New Orleans ranked in the 17th percentile among all Louisiana public school students; that is, the average score for students in New Orleans's reorganized schools, was below the average score in 83 percent of the state's school districts —just about where they were before publicly-funded charter schools replaced regular public schools.[46]

---

44 William Crain to *New York Times* (17 August 2000); Angela Pascopella, "Judging the KIPP Academy."

45 EdReform.blogspot.com (August 2009; January 2007).

46 Michael Deshotel, "The Success of the Louisiana Recovery District is a Great Big Fraud," *Louisiana Teacher*, 3 June 2014; Diane Ravitch, "New Orleans:

DFER

Despite the occasional criticism, most observers regarded KIPP favorably, and this esteem burnished the reputation of Teach for America. By 2007, some 60 percent of KIPP schools had been founded by TFA alumni, and some 285 former corps members had become school principals. Many other "graduates" had moved on to better-paid careers but continued to campaign for what they called "educational equity and social justice." Writing in the New York Sun, journalist Elizabeth Green called attention to one group who wanted "to shift the political debate by getting the Democratic Party to back innovations such as merit pay for teachers, a longer school day, and charter schools."[47]

Green was referring to DFER—Democrats for Education Reform—a group that was launched at a series of cocktail parties hosted in the Trump Plaza penthouse of New York money manager Ravenal Boykin Curry IV. DFER's eight-member Board of Directors included four men who worked at various capital funds. Five of the eight members of DFER's Board of Advisors were also connected with capital funds. The group's Executive Director was Joe Williams, who had previously worked as an education journalist for the New York Daily News and the Milwaukee Journal. One of DFER's moving spirits was Whitney Tilson, a Harvard graduate who had been a member of TFA's first class in 1990. After completing his stint with TFA, Tilson managed a hedge fund in New York, Tilson Funds. Tilson also served on the board of several KIPP schools in New York, and he maintained an Internet school reform blog that provided information about the philosophy and activities of DFER.

Appalling Academic Performance," DianeRavitch'sBlog, wordpres.com, 6 June 2014,

47 Elizabeth Green, "How New Generation of Reformers Targets Democrats on Education," New York Sun (31 May 2007).

As DFER saw it, millions of African-American and Hispanic children were "trapped in persistently failing schools." Their academic achievement trailed far behind that of Caucasian and Asian students not because of any inherent deficiencies in their scholastic intelligence or because of intractable, anti-academic cultural values. According to DFER, non-Asian minority students lagged because society had allowed their public schools to become "captive to powerful, entrenched interests that too often put the demands of adults before the educational needs of children." Republicans and Democrats were both responsible for the problems with public education in Black and Hispanic areas, but DFER insisted that it was "the Democratic Party— our party—which must question how we allowed ourselves to drift so far from our mission." DFER's goal was "to create a counterweight to the forces of the status quo in the Democratic Party."[48]

Executive director Joe Williams explained DFER's approach in his book, *Cheating Our Kids* (2005). "The truth is that our once-heralded system of education . . . has been captured by groups . . . whose interests . . . are protected and advanced through competent and powerful organizations, including unions." Public education had become "so consumed with meeting the frequent demands of employees and other adult constituencies that the needs of the customers—parents and children—often are an afterthought." Inner-city schools had become "primarily sources of employment for adults rather than educational enterprises [for] children."[49]

Since politics involves conflicts over the distribution of public resources, Williams thought it inevitable that employee unions, vendors, and other groups would struggle for their piece of the pie. There was no way to get around that. Williams believed, however, that the right

---

48 Ibid; EdReform.blogspot.com (October 2007; April 2008).

49 Joe Williams, *Cheating Our Kids* (New York: Palgrave MacMillan, 2005) 3, 14, 15.

kind of politics would pay more heed to the interests of disadvantaged students and their parents. Unfortunately, there was a "disconnect between Democratic candidates and party constituents." Although many Democratic voters wanted their children to have better schools, the Democratic party was "closely linked to the teachers unions"— and those unions were not fighting for students but for the teachers who paid union dues. "The unions don't exist to help kids or improve education, despite what marketing-savvy union leaders may claim.... The union's responsibility is to protect employees, not children."[50]

Williams wrote carefully, as one would expect of an author whose book was intended for a general audience. For a more outspoken version of DFER's critique, one could turn to the comments posted at Whitney Tilson's School Reform Blog. Here there was a full-throated condemnation of public school teachers and their two principal unions, the National Education Association (NEA) and the American Federation of Teachers (AFT). These unions gave substantial contributions to the Democratic Party and also constituted the largest single bloc of delegates to the Democrats' quadrennial national conventions. Equally important, the teachers' unions supplied the personnel for mailings, telephone calls, and get-out-the-vote drives. As a result, the unions had come to exercise a great deal of influence in the Democratic Party. But DFER insisted that this influence came at the expense of inner-city students.

When it came to casting aspersions at inner-city teachers, Tilson's blog rivaled Jonathan Kozol's book of 1967, *Death at an Early Age*. Kozol had criticized one of his White colleagues, an art teacher, for contemptuously dismissing a Black student's drawings as "garbage" and "junk." Forty-two years later, one of the postings at Tilson's blogspot similarly reported that another art teacher was spending "almost every minute of every day screaming at the top of her lungs in the faces of

---

50   *Ibid.*, 103, 108, 81.

5-8 year olds who had done horrible things like coloring outside the lines." The posting conceded that "not everyone in the school was a racist," but said "the leadership of the school and a number of the most senior teachers [were] either utterly disdainful of the students they taught, or [have] completely given up on the educability of the kids." "The saddest thing about the whole damn mess was that our K-3 kids still REALLY WANTED TO LEARN. Every day they came eager for knowledge. And every day this cabal of cynicism, racism, and laziness did everything within their powers to drain it out of them. . . . In many classrooms, the main lesson learned was that school became something to dread, many adults thought you were capable of very little, and some adults couldn't be bothered to lift a finger."[51]

DFER wanted to make these stories known, but the group had more than publicity in mind. DFER stood for *Democrats for Education Reform*, and the organization was intent on reducing the influence of teachers' unions within the Democratic Party. The unions demanded that their members receive seniority benefits and tenure after a probationary period. Without seniority and job security, the unions said, the salaries at most schools would not be enough to persuade able people to pursue careers in teaching. DFER, on the other hand, regarded tenure and seniority as major reasons for the sorry state of inner-city schools. Tenure made it difficult for principals to fire ineffective teachers; and seniority allowed good teachers to transfer away from inner-city schools to easier assignments in predominantly White areas.

Tilson considered it "madness" to structure layoffs according to the tradition of "last hired, first fired." That only ensured that schools would "push out some of their highest performing teachers while keeping their least effective ones." Nor did it make sense to allow "the best and most experienced teachers . . . to choose where they teach." This made it easier for good teachers to move away from schools "with

---

51   EdReform.blogspot.com (July 2009).

a high population of needy children" and to "congregate in schools with the easiest workloads." In Illinois, Tilson wrote, teachers were divided into four quartiles, according to their scores on standardized tests, and "in majority-white schools, bad teachers are rare: just 11 percent of the teachers are in the lowest quartile. But in schools with practically no white students, 88 percent of the teachers are in the worst quartile. The same disturbing pattern holds true in terms of poverty. At schools where more than 90 percent of the students are poor—where excellent teachers are needed the most—just 1 percent of teachers are in the highest quartile."[52]

In raising this issue, DFER touched on a point that sociologist James S. Coleman had mentioned in his landmark report of 1966, *Equality of Educational Opportunity*. Coleman had noted that there was substantial equality when it came to the formal training of teachers in majority-Black and majority-White schools. But Coleman's research also indicated that both Black and White children did slightly better on tests if their teachers had done well on a standard test of vocabulary. This was problematical because Black teachers generally had lower vocabulary scores than their White counterparts. Coleman thus recognized that students might do better if there were fewer Black teachers, but this possibility was so heterodox that Coleman's report did not pursue the matter. During the modern era of school reform, however, some observers made the connection: "Better teachers means whiter teachers."[53]

Without explicitly mentioning the racial implications, Tilson and DFER stressed the importance of teacher scores. "Teacher training and preparation" were "only a small part of the effort to raise teacher quality." It was more important to recruit "higher caliber people into the profession." And Tilson's blog left little doubt about the meaning

---

52 EdReform.blogspot.com (March 2010; January 2009; March 2007; November 2006).

53 James S. Coleman, "Sins of Sensitivity," *National Review* 43 (18 March 1991) 28ff; Steve Sailer, iSteve.blogspot.com (15 April 2009).

of "higher caliber." "The most effective teachers are those with high SAT or ACT scores and grade point averages." "Teacher quality trumps everything else when it comes to student achievement." Tilson attributed the success of Finland and Singapore, whose students led the world on standardized tests, to the fact that these nations "only take teachers from the top 10 percent of college graduates." And he mistakenly alleged that in America "only the lowest caliber college students become teachers." When called on this misstatement, Tilson retreated, but only slightly, saying, still mistakenly, "new teachers are mostly drawn from the bottom tier of college graduates."[54]

While lauding the quality of teachers in some foreign nations, Tilson emphasized the shortcomings of teachers in the United States. If a KIPP school was required to hire rank-and-file American teachers, he wrote, the KIPP school "would struggle to achieve even half the gains it currently achieves with its students." He reiterated that in America "new teachers are mostly drawn from the bottom of college graduates."[55]

Tilson's allegations were exaggerated, but some scholars also reported that the quality of America's teachers had declined since the 1950s. Before then, sex discrimination had the effect of steering high-IQ American women toward teaching. But as more opportunities opened for women, the test scores of new teachers declined. After investigating the matter, economist Eric Hanushek, of the Hoover Institution at Stanford, reported that "recent birth cohorts who score near the top of IQ . . . tests are much less likely to want to be teachers than those in earlier birth cohorts." The decline was also reflected in teachers' salaries, which kept up with the rate of inflation but fell

---

54 "Train, Pay Our Teachers Better," *Atlanta Journal-Constitution* (26 December 2007) posted at EdReform.blogspot.com (January 2008); Whitney Tilson, "Rebutting Seven Myths about Teach for America," *Huffington Post* (21 February 2011).

55 *Ibid.*; Whitney Tilson, "Israel Trip," EdReform.blogspot.com (November 2010); Tilson, "Correction from Previous Post, EdReform.blogspot.com (November 2010).

behind the pay levels in other professions. In 1950, teachers were paid about the same as other people with college degrees, but by the year 2000 their average salaries were 30 percent lower. The change was especially dramatic for women. According to Harvard professor Paul E. Peterson, "In 1950 the salaries of women teachers under the age of thirty were right at the median of all college-educated women in that age category. But fifty years later, two-thirds of all young college-educated women were earning more than a teacher of that age." It was hardly a surprise, then, that "the percentage of students with high SAT scores saying they plan to become teachers dropped precipitously from the 1960s to the 1990s. So did the percentage of teachers coming from selective colleges and universities." Frederick Hess, of the American Enterprise Institute, reported, "the likelihood that a new teacher was a woman who ranked in the top 10 percent of her high school cohort fell by 50 percent between 1964 and 2000."[56]

While this research indicated that fewer high achievers were becoming teachers, other scholars developed methods for measuring the effect teachers had on the academic achievement of students. This was hardly a new question. After controlling for IQ and socioeconomic background, James Coleman's research team had reported in 1966 that there was only a very slight correlation between the average achievement of students, as measured by scores on standardized tests, and the teachers, facilities, and programs that schools provided. Almost all the variation in academic achievement corresponded to differences in the students' socioeconomic and family backgrounds. Later, after a sophisticated computer-driven reassessment of Coleman's work, a team of researchers at Harvard University confirmed Coleman's findings. This led many observers to conclude that "family" mattered "more than schooling." It led

---

56 Eric A. Hanushek and Finis Welch, "Teacher Quality," chapter 18 of *Handbook of the Economics of Education*, Volume 2 (Elsevier, 2006); Paul E. Peterson, *Saving Schools* (Cambridge: Harvard University Press, 2010) 136, 153-54; Frederick Hess, "How to Get the Teachers We Want," *Education Next* (Summer 2009).

Coleman to say that inner-city schools could not prepare students to compete in the modern world unless these students were somehow freed "from the impact of the home."[57]

Coleman's research and conclusions did not sit well with Tilson, DFER, and school reformers in general. One posting explained why. "I don't think we can fix parents," but "we can fix—or at least substantially improve schools." Tilson conceded, "If I could fix either all of the parents . . . or all the schools in America, I'd choose the former in a heartbeat." But while it was impossible to fix the parents, recent research showed that "it's possible to fix the schools."[58]

Rather than focus on the academic performance of students from different races and classes, as Coleman had done, researchers in the 1990s began to focus on individual students who either did or did not experience marked improvement over the course of a school year. In doing so, the new research followed a path blazed by William Sanders, an agricultural statistician at the University of Tennessee. Sanders had previously developed measures for separating farm practices (like using different amounts of fertilizer) from the influence of environmental features (like the quality of the soil or the amount of sunshine or rain). After that, Sanders proceeded to develop a "value added" method that separated the influence of teachers on student achievement from that of the children's family circumstances, health, and aptitude. By comparing the test scores of specific students from year to year, Sanders was able to identify the youngsters who made the biggest gains and, since the family background and IQ of these youths had

---

57 James S. Coleman et al., *Equality of Educational Opportunity*; Frederick Mosteller and Daniel P. Moynihan, *On Equality of Educational Opportunity*; Richard D. Kahlenberg, "Learning from James Coleman," *Public Interest* 144 (Summer 2001) 54-72; James S. Coleman, "Equality of Educational Opportunity, Reexamined," *Socio-Economic Planning Sciences* 2 (1969) 347-54.

58 Whitney Tilson, "Do Schools Matter," *Huffington Post* (18 September 2011).

not changed, he was also able to rank teachers by their ability to produce large gains in their students.[59]

Other researchers then followed up with additional studies which confirmed that, after controlling for IQ and family background, the students of some teachers obtained high test scores while students with other teachers experienced low learning growth. Two of the most influential of these researchers were Eric Hanushek and Steven G. Rivken of the Hoover Institution at Stanford University. These Hoover scholars reported that year after year students in some classrooms made exceptional gains, while others in the same building languished. According to Hanushek and Rivken, teachers were "the key... to improving student performance." Hanushek and Rivken also reported that teachers whose students did well one year were effective the next year, too, while those whose students performed badly one year continued to perform badly. Indeed, they said, "If a student had a good teacher as opposed to an average teacher for 4-5 years in a row, the increased learning would be sufficient to close entirely the average gap between a typical low income student and one who is not on free or reduced lunch."[60]

---

59 Robert Gorden, Thomas J. Kane and Douglas O. Staiger, *Identifying Effective Teachers Using Performance on the Job* (Washington: The Brookings Institution, 2006); S. Paul Wright, Sandra P. Horn, and William L. Sanders, "Teacher and Classroom Context Effects on Student Achievement: Implications for Teacher Evaluation," *Journal of Personnel Evaluation in Education* 11 (April 1997) 57-67; Sanders, "Value-added Assessment from Student Achievement Data," *Journal of Personnel Evaluation in Education* 14 (December 2000) 319-339; EdReform.blogspot.com (October 2007); Richard Rothstein, *Class and Schools* (New York: Teachers College Press, 2004) 63-71; Diane Ravitch, *The Death and Life of the Great American School System* (New York: Basic Books, 2010) 179-182.

60 Eric A Hanushek, "Teacher Deselection," chapter 8 of Dan Golhaber and Jane Hannaway, eds., *Creating a New Teaching Profession* (Washington: Urban Institute Press, 2009); Eric A. Hanushek and Steven G. Rivkin, "How to Improve the Supply of High Quality Teachers," in Diane Ravitch, ed., *Brookings Papers on Education Policy* (Washington: Brookings Institution Press, 2004), 7-25.

The Brookings Institution weighed in with another influential report that also emphasized the existence of huge differences in teacher effectiveness, if efficacy was measured by the test scores of students. The Brookings report was entitled, "Identifying Effective Teachers Using Performance on the Job." Its authors were Robert Gordon of the Center for American Progress, Thomas J. Kane of Harvard, and Douglas O. Staiger of Dartmouth.[61]

Gordon, Kane and Staiger noted that "traditionally, policymakers have attempted to raise the quality of the teaching force by raising the hurdles for those seeking to enter the profession." Thus teachers were required to have not only a college degree but also a special license that was awarded only after taking several courses on education. The Brookings report maintained, however, that this "credential-centered regime" was based on a questionable premise. According to Gordon, Kane, and Staiger, there was no evidence that the effectiveness of teachers, as measured by students' scores on standardized tests, was related to the teachers' degrees, their grades, their completion of a specific set of courses, or anything else the researchers measured. This led philanthropist Bill Gates to exclaim, "I remember being really impressed with their data about the differences between good teachers and bad teachers. But I was also dumfounded that they had nothing in there about what makes a teacher good. Nothing."[62]

Because paper qualifications were not very useful in identifying effective teachers, the Brookings report recommended that requirements for entering the teaching profession be removed and

---

61 Gorden, Kane and Staiger, *Identifying Effective Teachers*.

62 *Ibid.*, 5-6; Bill Gates, quoted by Steven Brill, *Class Warfare*, 179; Hanushek and Rivkin, "How to Improve the Supply of High Quality Teachers"; Hanushek, "The Trade-off Between Child Care Quantity and Quality," *Journal of Political Economy* 100 (February 1992) 84-117; Hanushek, "Measuring Investment in Education," *Journal of Economic Perspectives* 19 (Autumn 1996), 9-30.

that teachers be rewarded or punished according to the "value" they added to their students. Instead of raising the salaries of teachers as they gained seniority or earned advanced degrees—the existing policy in most school districts—the Brookings scholars proposed a two-step program. First they would create "data systems . . . that can track the teachers." Then they would dismiss teachers whose students scored in the bottom 25 percent on standardized tests. They would keep only those teachers who could "demonstrate success on the job" by increasing the scores their students made on standardized tests. In time, this approach came to be known as the value-added model (VAM) for assessing teachers.[63]

Some reformers recommended that several thousand teachers should be fired each year and replaced with "novice" teachers who would have a trial period of two or three years to show that their students made higher test scores. To those who questioned whether this approach was practical, the Brookings scholars said that "recent experience has shown that there is a reserve army of Americans" who are interested in teaching—if only they were not required "to take . . . years of education school classes." The Brookings report further maintained that "the economic value" of their policy would be "enormous." They calculated that the increase in achievement test scores "would be worth about $72,000 to $169,000 per high school graduate. When multiplied by 3 million public high school graduates per year, such an increase would be worth $216 billion to $507 billion per year, if the policy were applied nationwide."[64]

Since many states and school districts would have trouble finding funds to build the requisite data infrastructure, the Brookings report recommended an expansion of federal grants. In addition to funding the development of "longitudinal data systems linking teachers and

---

63 Gorden, Kane and Staiger, "Identifying Effective Teachers," 12, 5-6, 2, 13.

64 Ibid., 13, 10, 11, 15.

students," the report also urged the federal government to help local governments pay annual bonuses of at least $20,000 to teachers who were VAM-rated as "effective" and who were "willing to teach in high-poverty schools." The Brookings scholars calculated the additional cost for data systems and salary bonuses would come to "slightly more than $3 billion per year"—a mere fraction of the prospective benefits but an amount that, as it happened, was exactly the sum that, as noted in Chapter 7, Linda Darling-Hammond had urged the federal government to spend as part of her quite different "Marshall Plan" to improve teacher training in the existing colleges of education.[65]

There were skeptics, of course. Some questioned the availability of a reserve army of effective teachers. They recalled that student test scores had not improved after California, at a cost of $1.5 billion per year, had mandated in 1996 that class size in the elementary grades be reduced from what had been an average of 28 students to a maximum of 20. The conventional explanation attributed this stability in test scores to the fact that, in its efforts to staff the additional classes, the state had been forced to hire many uncertified teachers.[66]

Other skeptics said the value-added measure of teacher effectiveness was highly unstable. Historian Diane Ravitch reported that in North Carolina, 11 percent of teachers who were in the lowest quintile in their early years of teaching reading eventually moved up to the highest quintile. And only 44 percent of reading teachers and 42 percent of math teachers who started out in the top quintile were still there later in their careers. This meant that if a principal assigned low performing students to a teacher who was once ranked in the top quintile, there was a good chance that the teacher would no longer be in the top quintile. "Most teachers who ranked in the top quintile one year were not the 'best' teachers the

---

65   Ibid., 5, 17, 23, 25.

66   "Class Size Reduction in California," at classsize.org/Summary/98-99.

next year, and most teachers who ranked in the lowest quintile one year got better results the next year."[67]

Ravitch also noted that VAM was highly speculative. "Nowhere was there a real-life demonstration in which a [school] district had identified the top quintile of teachers, assigned low-performing students to their classes, and improved the test scores of low-performing students so dramatically ... that the black-white test score gap closed." The prediction that achievement gaps would be closed if low-scoring students spent several years with high quintile teachers was not based on actual observation of any large number of students but, rather, on extrapolating from the progress that some individual students made over the course of an academic year. If high quintile teachers enabled some students to make a great deal of progress in a single year, supporters of VAM reasoned, achievement gaps could be eliminated if such teachers were paired with low-achieving students for several successive years.[68]

Another critic of VAM, Judge Richard Posner, of the Seventh Circuit Court of Appeals, predicted that the value added method would "induce all sorts of wasteful strategizing." In addition to giving teachers and students an incentive to cheat on standardized tests, the VAM method would encourage teachers to engage in office politics—"what organizational economists call 'influence activities.'" In VAM schools, Posner speculated, a teacher would be tempted to truckle, in hopes that principals and counselors would then assign the best students to his classes, thereby increasing the likelihood of the teacher's obtaining a good quality rating.[69]

---

67 Diane Ravitch, *The Death and Life of the Great American School System*, 185-86; Dan Goldhaber and Michael Hansen, *Assessing the Potential of Using Value-added Estimates of Teacher Job Performance for Making Tenure Decisions* (Washington: CALDER, Urban Institute, 2008).

68 Diane Ravitch, *The Death and Life of the Great American School System*, 188.

69 Richard Posner, "Rating Teaches," *Becker-Posner-blog.com* (9 December 2012).

Yet another skeptic, Steve Sailer, noted that the value-added theory did not take account of one of the most famous concepts in economics: the law of diminishing marginal returns. To illustrate this point, Sailer said that he played golf only a few times a year and his average score was 108—about 40 strokes per round worse than the superstars of the game. Sailer speculated that if he somehow convinced the superstars' coaches to drop their famous clients and instead work with him for a year, it might be possible to cut 10 strokes off his average score, from 108 to 98. But it did not follow that Sailer would then be on track, over the course of four years, "to cut 40 strokes, all the way down to 68, and thus challenge my teachers' former pupils." It did not follow that if Sailer received a fifth year of world-class golf instruction, he would be winning every pro tournament with an average score of 58 strokes per round.[70]

Continuing with another analogy to sports, Sailer later wrote that he knew "a lot about the history of the evolution of baseball statistics over the last 150 years, a lot more than I know about the development of teacher rating statistics." Nevertheless, Sailer thought the teacher rating statistics were "about where baseball stats were in the late 1800s." He was especially critical because most reformers, for fear of seeming politically incorrect, refused to factor IQ into their VAM formulae.[71]

Despite the problems, important elements of the mainstream media embraced the value-added approach. In one editorial, the *Wall Street Journal*, praised the Hoover and Brookings scholars for proposing to "get rid of bad teachers and reward good ones," for saying

---

70 Steve Sailer, "Diane Ravitch, 'No Child Left Behind,' and the Racial Achievement Gap's Kryptonite Cause," Vdare.com (28 March 2010).

71 Steve Sailer, "Judge Richard Posner on IQ by Race and How to Rate Teachers," iSteve.blogspot.com (14 October 2012); Sailer, "You Have to Tell the Truth," Vdare.com (28 September 2003).

"the current practice of demanding certification based on teacher-training courses has outlived its usefulness, that routinely granting teachers lifetime tenure after two or three years is stupid, and that student test scores and other systematic ways to evaluate teachers are good enough to act on."[72]

Other newspapers agreed. The *Los Angeles Times* invested $50,000 in a project that linked student performance to individual teachers and said there were large disparities among teachers, with some teachers regularly propelling students from below grade level to above, while the students of other teachers just as consistently made sub-par scores. In 2010 and 2011 the *Times* published the value-added ratings of some 11,500 third- through fifth-grade teachers, despite complaints that publication of personal information amounted to an unprecedented invasion of the privacy of individual teachers. In 2010, New York's three daily newspapers decided to emulate Los Angeles and asked for records that linked teachers to student performance in their city.[73]

In 2010, the Gates Foundation also endorsed the value-added approach. It did so by giving sizeable grants to school districts that allowed for linking student and teacher data. "Defining teacher effectiveness is the key first step," the Foundation declared, and teacher effectiveness was to be measured by "value-added scores based on student assessment scores." The first four winners were the Hillsborough

---

72 *Wall Street Journal* (6 April 2006).

73 Steven Brill, *Class Warfare*, 363-69. Jason Song, Jason Felch, and Julie Marquis were the principal journalists for the "value added" articles in the Los Angeles Times. The articles, and extensive discussion of the articles, are available at *LATimes.com*. In New York City, the United Federation of Teachers sued to block the release of VAM ratings on privacy grounds. It was not until 2012 that the courts cleared the City to release performance reports for some 12,500 teachers. See Lisa Fisher, "Court Declines to Hear Appeal on Teacher Data," *Wall Street Journal* (14 February 2012).

County School District in and near Tampa, which received a grant for $100 million; the Memphis school district, which received $90 million; the Pittsburgh school system ($40 million), and the College Ready coalition of five charter networks in Los Angeles ($60 million).[74]

Bill Gates and his wife, Melinda, explained the rationale. "It's amazing how big a difference a great teacher makes versus an ineffective one," Bill Gates said. "If you want your child to get the best education possible, it is actually more important to get him assigned to a great teacher than to a great school." Melinda Gates concurred: "The key to helping students learn is making sure that every child has an effective teacher every single year. Teachers are at the center of our strategy at the Gates Foundation. . . . The schools across the country that have implemented the Knowledge Is Power Program [KIPP] invariably get excellent results from the very same low-income students who tend to struggle at traditional high schools."[75]

Two influential pundits chimed in. Writing in the *New York Times*, columnist Nicholas D. Kristof declared that "good teachers matter more than anything; they are astonishingly important. It turns out that having a great teacher is far more important than being in a small class or going to a good school with a mediocre teacher." At the *New Yorker*, best-selling author Malcolm Gladwell similarly maintained that great teachers could be identified by the test scores of their students.[76]

---

74 Bill and Melinda Gates Foundation, "Empowering Effective Teachers" (pamphlet: February, 2010) 6, 9; Steven Brill, *Class Warfare*, 201-05, 229-35.

75 Bill Gates, quoted by Steve Sailer, "Diane Ravtich, No Child Left Behind, and the Racial Achievement Gap's Kryptonite Cause"; Melinda French Gates, "Education Reform, One Classroom at a Time," *Washington Post* (18 February 2008); Jonathan Alter, "Bill Gates Goes to School," *Newsweek* 152 (December 15, 2008) 42.

76 Nicholas D. Kristof, "Our Greatest National Shame," *New York Times* (15 February 2009); Malcolm Gladwell, "Most Likely to Succeed," *New Yorker*

Kopp's Kids

There were some differences among the value-added researchers. William Sanders calculated that low-scoring students who were assigned to top-quintile teachers would gain so much that racial and ethnic achievement gaps could be closed in three years. The Brookings scholars—Robert Gordon, Thomas Kane, and Douglas Staiger—estimated that it would take four years to close the Black-White gap. And the Hoover researchers—Eric Hanushek and Steven Rivken—calculated that "having five years of good teachers in a row" (that is, teachers in the 85th percentile) "could overcome the average seventh-grade mathematics achievement gap..."[77]

Whatever the time frame—three years, four years, or five—a new conventional wisdom emerged—one that regarded teachers as the key to closing the racial and ethnic achievement gaps. The new view held that, if students succeeded, the teacher deserved the credit. If students got low scores, the teachers were to blame. Teachers were responsible for both good performance and bad performance. Therefore, to close the achievement gap, schools should hire good teachers and fire bad ones.[78]

As time passed, there was a subtle shift in emphasis. When Wendy Kopp established Teach for America in 1990 the emphasis had been on what committed teachers could achieve. The KIPP academies continued to emphasize what outstanding teachers could accomplish. However, the leaders of the value-added movement increasingly argued that low-performing students were lagging because they had been assigned to

---

(15 December 2008); Donna Foote, "Lessons from Locke," *Newsweek* (11 August 2008).

77 Gordon, Kane and Staiger, "Identifying Effective Teachers,"; Eric A. Hanushek and Steven G. Rivkin, "How to Improve the Supply of High-Quality Teachers," Diane Ravitch ed., *Brookings Papers on Educational Policy* (Washington: Brookings Institution Press, 2004).

78 Diane Ravitch, *The Death and Life of the Great American School System*, 182.

a string of mediocre or bad teachers. In 2008, for example, the focus in one of Eric Hanushek's papers was on "the impact of low quality, or ineffective, teachers." Hanushek lamented "the aggregated impact of the bottom teachers." He stressed the importance of "identify[ing] the most ineffective teachers and . . . mov[ing] them out of the classroom." The best way to improve education, Hanushek maintained, was to "systematically remov[e] the worst teachers." Education reformers should emulate the example of corporate leaders who fired inefficient workers "on an on-going basis."[79]

Several education writers seconded this view. Writing in the *Durham Herald-Sun*, John Hood opined, "If North Carolina policymakers want to boost economic growth and job creation, they should fire some teachers." Hood speculated that if "the worst 7 percent of American teachers" were fired and replaced by "those whose skills were simply equal to today's average teacher," this seemingly small change "would have revolutionary results, by raising the average student performance of America to that of Finland, the highest-scoring country in international tests." Hood proceed to quote "Stanford University economist Eric Hanushek," who had written that improving academic scores this way would have "astounding benefits, increasing the annual growth rate of the United States by 1 percent of GDP." And this improvement, "accumulated over the lifetime of somebody born today . . . would amount to nothing less than an increase in total U.S. economic output of $112 trillion in present value."[80]

As has been noted, DFER's founders were investors and managers of capital funds. As such, they had been trained to regard exuberant predictions skeptically. Those who posted comments at

---

79 Eric A. Hanushek, "Teacher Deselection."

80 John Hood, "A Case for Firing Teachers," *Durham Herald-Sun* (11 December 2011).

Whitney Tilson's blog recognized that the value-added research was problematical. "There are plenty of nits to be picked," Tilson himself acknowledged. Nevertheless, Tilson insisted, "every study shows that teacher quality matters far more than anything else when it comes to student learning and achievement." "The dirty little secret" of public education was that able teachers were allowed to congregate in "'better' schools" while the "high-needs schools (and low-income minority kids—the ones who most need the BEST teachers) are instead endlessly screwed by a system that provides them, every year, with the worst teachers." "If you give a group of the most privileged kids an ineffective teacher, they don't learn very much. Conversely, if you give even the most disadvantaged kids a great teacher, they will learn and achieve at levels that would amaze you."[81]

According to Tilson, the best way to improve education in the inner cities was to "fire bad teachers." "Every sensible person knows that there are WAY too many lousy teachers," Tilson wrote. "Schools with a high proportion of low-income and minority students are far more likely to have teachers who are inexperienced, did not major or minor in the subject they're teaching, who failed the basic skills test on the first attempt, who went to a noncompetitive college, and who had very low grades and test scores in high school and college." According to Tilson, 30 to 40 percent of the inner-city teachers should be discharged. "Millions of students nationwide" were suffering "in classes headed by ineffective, incompetent, barely literate, and/or burned out teachers." As Tilson saw it, "the key factor" responsible for the racial and ethnic achievements gaps was "that most poor kids are forced to attend mediocre to catastrophically bad schools and are taught by way too many mediocre to catastrophically bad teachers. That's the main problem we face as a nation." "The problem is not too many bad kids, it's too many bad schools."[82]

---

81 EdReform.blogspot.com (November 2007; January 2007; April 2007).

82 *Ibid.* (March 2010; September 2007; April 2008; December 2006;

Tilson recognized that many people viewed education "as a noble profession, involving great sacrifice." As a consequence, some would interpret what he had written as "anti-teacher." But Tilson insisted that his major targets were the unions that protected not just the "crappy teachers" but also the "principals, administrators, bus drivers, cafeteria workers, [and] janitors." "These entrenched interests, unlike low-income, minority students and their parents, [were] well funded, well organized . . .—and will fight to the death to protect their interests." According to Tilson's DFER colleague Joe Williams, the unions were "the elephant in the room," and "the future of the Democratic Party" depended on "what it decides to do about the high-profile role the teachers unions play."[83]

To counter the influence of the teachers' unions within the Democratic Party, DFER's wealthy leaders dug into their own pockets. "In May 2011, when the New York State agency that monitors lobbying issued its annual report, DFER was found to have outspent the United Federation of Teachers and New York State United Teachers combined, spending $6.6 million for its 2010 media blitz and an army of Albany lobbyists, compared with $6.2 million dispensed by the unions." Between 2008 and 2010, DFER spent more than $17 million on political advocacy.[84]

Most of all, DFER challenged the prerogatives that the teachers' unions had gained for their members. As has been noted, DFER criticized seniority provisions that allowed experienced teachers to move away from inner-city schools. DFER took exception to the policy of "last-in, first out" (LIFO)—on the ground that this policy compelled schools to begin layoffs with the most recently hired

---

November 2007; January 2008).

83 *Ibid.* (January 2006; November 2006; November 2007); Joe Williams, *Cheating Our Kids*, 76, 97.

84 Steven Brill, *Class Warfare*, 416-17, 379.

teachers, even if those teachers had been especially effective. And DFER criticized union contracts that based teachers' salaries on how many years a teacher had been teaching, and on what graduate degrees the teacher held, rather than on the performance that the teachers' students made on standardized tests. DFER said that if school superintendents and principals were not bound by union contracts and rules, they could dismiss ineffective teachers and hire newcomers who would prove, in time, that effective teaching could overcome poverty and other obstacles. Then, DFER maintained, America would learn that, as New York schools chancellor Joel Klein liked to say, "Demography does not have to be destiny." Then, the nation would learn that New York principal Kayrol Burgess-Harper was on the right track when she said, "Give me the ability to hire and fire the [teachers] I want and give me a school day from eight to five . . . and I'd have hundreds of little Einsteins running around here."[85]

DFER also raised questions about the nation's traditional colleges of education. Seventy percent of them "can't be fixed and should be shut down," Tilson wrote. "They are worse than useless: not only do they add no value (every study I'm aware of shows that ed school grads do no better at educating students than other teachers), but they actually do harm" by encouraging prospective teachers "to pity their low-income students." "Lest you think I exaggerate," Tilson cited similar comments by Arthur Levine, a former President of Columbia Teachers College, and Bob Compton, the executive producer of a documentary film on education, *Two Million Minutes*.[86]

These matters came to the fore during the Presidential campaign of 2008. On balance, the leading Republican candidates were closer to DFER's position than the leading Democrats.

---

85 Joel Klein, paraphrased by Steven Brill, *Class Warfare*, 303; Kayrol Burgess-Harper, quoted by Brill, *Ibid.*, 18.

86 EdReform.blogspot.com (November 2007; March 2010).

Republican Mitt Romney, for instance, criticized seniority, proposed to give superintendents and principals more authority to "deploy resources ... and remove nonperformers," and supported extra pay for teachers who accepted "the most challenging assignments." The Republicans' eventual nominee for President, John McCain, hit what Tilson called "all the right buttons" when it came to "what he said about education." And the nominally Republican Mayor of New York City, Michael Bloomberg, and his schools chancellor, Joel Klein, pushed to deny tenure to probationary teachers who failed to raise their students' test scores and to prevent senior teachers from congregating in middle-class schools. After hearing Bloomberg deliver an "absolutely brilliant and spot on" speech at the annual conference of the National Urban League, Tilson "long[ed] for the day" when a Democratic leader would have "the guts—and the wisdom—to give a speech on education like this one!"[87]

As Democrats in 2008, DFER had to choose between Hillary Clinton and Barack Obama, and in this comparison Clinton came in second—largely because at the beginning of the year she was the prohibitive favorite and therefore did not need to take any risks. "Unless something significant changes," Tilson wrote, "she can put it on cruise control, coast to the nomination and *then* run to the center. Thus, if I were her political advisor, I'd have told her to give the exact speech to the NEA that she did—pander like crazy and only stick a toe in the water on reform." As a longshot candidate, on the other hand, Obama could present himself as a New Democrat who was less beholden to the unions. If Obama did so, Tilson wrote, Obama could model his approach after that of Hillary Clinton's husband, Bill, who in 1992 "was an obscure former governor of Arkansas running 5th in the polls" until he "position[ed] himself as a New Democrat in part by embracing welfare reform." By thus "stealing" one of the Republicans'

---

87 Mitt Romney, "Reforming Education," EdReform.blogspot.com (April 2008); EdReform.blogspot.com (October 2008; March 2007; July 2007).

best ideas, Bill Clinton had done "both the right thing . . . *and* the politically smart thing."[88]

Tilson was elated when Obama took advantage of the opportunity and endorsed DFER's approach to school reform. Speaking in Flint, Michigan, Obama proposed to "start by investing $10 billion to guarantee access to quality, affordable, early childhood education for every child in America." But that was not all. Obama also said the nation needed "to recruit an army of new teachers" who would be "deploy[ed] to under-staffed school districts" and promoted and rewarded only if they produced "better results."[89]

Tilson believed that Obama's comments on education were more than part of a clever campaign strategy. In his autobiography, *Dreams from My Father*, first published in 1995, long before Obama became a candidate for president, Obama had written that "school reform was the only possible solution for the plight of the young [Black] men I saw on the street." Obama had noted that people "rarely talked about ... the biggest source of resistance" to school reform—"namely, the uncomfortable fact that [in Black communities] every one of our churches was filled with teachers, principals and district superintendents. Few of these educators sent their own children to public schools; they knew too much for that. But they would defend the status quo." Rather than reform the schools, middle-class Blacks mistakenly regarded reform as "part of a white effort to wrest back control."[90]

During his campaign for the presidential nomination, Obama followed up on these thoughts. Speaking in New Hampshire, Obama reiterated DFER's emphasis on the importance of teachers. "We know

---

88 EdReform.blogspot.com (July 2007).

89 Ibid. (June 2006).

90 Barack Obama, *Dreams from My Father* (New York: Three Rivers Press, 1995) 256-57.

that from the moment our children step into a classroom, the single most important factor in determining their achievement is not the color of their skin or where they come from; it's not who their parents are or how much money they have. It's who their teacher is." It was vitally important, Obama said, to get better teachers, especially in the hard-to-staff schools. To do this, it would be necessary to "evaluate the outcomes so that we know which ones are doing the best job." And if "we find that there are teachers who are . . . underperforming . . . we should find a quick and fair way to put another teacher in that classroom."[91]

After Obama secured the presidential nomination, he continued to talk about the need for school reform. As Tilson noted, "Normally at this point, the presidential nominee owes the world to the NEA for all the work it did to get him to the general election, except, uh, Obama doesn't owe nuthin this time around." So Obama declined to speak at the NEA's annual conference in Washington but instead had his speech beamed in via satellite. In the speech, Obama caused a stir, including some loud booing, when he said, "Under my plan, [school] districts will . . . be able to reward those who teach underserved areas ... or if they consistently excel in the classroom, that work can be valued and rewarded as well." When he learned of the booing, Tilson was elated. "I LOVE IT!" he wrote. "Three cheers for Obama for having the guts to say something he knew wouldn't be popular with the most powerful Democratic interest group." Obama himself acknowledged, "I know this wasn't necessarily the most popular part of my speech, but . . . I'm saying it . . . because it is what I believe."[92]

For many years, teachers and their unions had harbored reservations about the combination of "merit pay" and "empowered principals." In the 1970s, when psychologist Kenneth Clark

---

91 Barack Obama, quoted at EdReform.blogspot.com (December 2007).

92 Whitney Tilson, statement at EdReform.blogspot.com (July 2008).

developed such a plan for Washington, D.C., many teachers had mentioned how difficult it was to evaluate something as elusive as the quality of teaching. They said the danger was especially great because many school principals and administrators were former teachers who had gravitated toward management after discovering that they either did not like teaching or were not good at it. The leader of the teachers union also said it was unfair to equate good teaching and good test scores. After all, William Simons had noted, students attended school for only a few hours, after which they returned to their neighborhoods and homes. "What do you do," Simons asked, "about the teacher who happens to have a group of students who do not get proper food at home or come from an environment that is not conducive to learning?"[93]

Union leaders repeated these points and added some new ones in the age of Obama. Thus UFT President Randi Weingarten raised questions about the extent of what she called "3-D Reform"—data-driven decision making. Weingarten conceded that there was a place for testing, but she detected more than a whiff of condescension in DFER's approach. Rather than work with teachers, the reformers regarded teachers as "interchangeable cogs" on an educational assembly line. The reformers insisted on "cook book curricula" and "step-by-step instructional practices" for "standardized multiple choice tests." Weingarten said that gifted teachers tried to teach "civility, aesthetic appreciation, and moral values in addition to skills and facts." But the reformers did not understand that. They did not recognize that "not everything that counts can be counted, and not everything that can be counted counts." "Sadly," Weingarten wrote, "too often, testing has replaced instruction; data has replaced professional judgment; [and] ... leadership has replaced teacher professionalism."[94]

---

93 Raymond Wolters, *The Burden of Brown* (Knoxville: University of Tennessee Press, 1984) 50-51.

94 Randi Weingarten, postings at *Eduwonk.com* (20, 23, 24 August 2007). In

Tilson tacitly conceded some of Weingarten's points. Like Wendy Kopp, who sent her sons to a progressive private school, Tilson sent his daughters to private schools that took a constructivist approach to learning. But Tilson said that this approach would not work "with inner-city kids." The schools that succeeded in closing the achievement gap—like the KIPP schools where Tilson served as a member of the board of directors—used testing "extensively, first to measure where students are when we get them (on average, two years below grade level coming into 5th grade), and then to track them every step of the way." Thanks to "regular (roughly monthly) internal testing," KIPP's teachers were able to "make appropriate adjustments" if their students were not learning the material. KIPP also used tests as "one way ... to evaluate our teachers and principals. Given how far behind our kids are when we get them, average or even good teachers won't cut it for us—we need superstars, who can teach and inspire kids to DOUBLE their rate of learning ... while they're with us."[95]

Tilson believed that direct instruction, an emphasis on the basics, and preparation for tests were especially appropriate for inner-city schools. Since those schools "get the bottom of the barrel when it comes to teachers," it made sense to insist upon a structured curriculum that followed a step-by-step approach. This method might limit the teachers' creativity, but it would also reduce mistakes. Some people complained about a "McDonald's approach to education," but others said, "That's nothing to be ashamed about. McDonald's isn't creative French cooking ... [but] they don't leave anything to chance. The food is always OK no matter where the store is." Tilson acknowledged that he did not like "the idea of mostly low-income minority kids not having art, etc." Nevertheless, "when 60% of African-American 4th graders in this country (ALL of them, not just low-income ones) can't read a simple children's book, we have a national crisis on our hands.

---

her "not everything" statement, Weingarten was quoting Albert Einstein.

95 Wendy Kopp, *A Chance To Make History*, 48; EdReform.blogspot.com(October 2006; April 2006; February 2007).

Desperate times require desperate measures, and nothing is more important that being able to read and do basic math."[96]

When Tilson emphasized testing and structured instruction, he (probably unconsciously) seconded an assessment that the Berkeley psychologist Arthur R. Jensen had broached in a controversial article of 1969. Jensen is best known for work that concluded that at least half of the racial gap in average IQ is genetic in origin. But Jensen also sought to discover how education could be fashioned to serve the needs of low-achieving students. In his 1969 article, Jensen maintained that "compensatory education programs" had uniformly failed to close the racial achievement gap "wherever they have been tried." But Jensen also insisted, "All the basic scholastic skills can be learned by children with normal learning ability." He further speculated that non-Asian minority children were lagging because their schools were using "cognitive" approaches that stressed the importance of "understanding" and "conceptual learning." Jensen said that a disproportionate number of Black students were not advancing because their teachers were using methods that were at odds with the "genetic and cultural heritage" of African-Americans. Children with low IQs and children who were disadvantaged in terms of cultural background or socioeconomic circumstances had "different ... modes of learning." "If diversity of mental abilities, as of most other human characteristics, is a basic fact of nature ... it seems a reasonable conclusion that schools and society must provide a range and diversity of educational methods ... The ideal of equality of educational opportunity should not be interpreted as uniformity of ... instructional techniques ... Diversity rather than uniformity of approaches ... would seem to be the key to making education rewarding for children of different patterns of ability."[97]

---

96 EdReform.blogspot.com (March 2007; March 2006); Raymond Wolters, *The Burden of Brown*, 60.

97 Arthur R. Jensen, "How Much Can We Boost IQ and Scholastic Achievement?" 3, 116-117; Thomas Sowell, *Race and Culture*, 169-170.

Whatever the reasons for the low scores in inner-city schools, DFER wanted to empower principals. This was reflected in several of the comments posted at Tilson's blog. "[T]he biggest problem with the typical failing public school system is that principals don't have the power . . . to do what's necessary to build a team of badass teachers." Because of the teachers unions, public school principals faced "the almost total impossibility of firing *any* tenured teacher." "The main problem principals face is *not* figuring out who their best and worst teachers are, but rather finding a way to overcome union resistance." Top performers should be rewarded and, equally important, principals should be empowered to "get rid of teachers who were unwilling or unable to effectively impart knowledge to children."[98]

With these thoughts, and also because many members of DFER lived in New York City, DFER often commended New York's Mayor Michael Bloomberg and Schools Chancellor Joel Klein. DFER did so because Bloomberg and Klein overcame opposition from the city's teachers union and implemented several of DFER's favorite policies. Between 2002 and 2009, the Bloomberg administration increased teachers' salaries by some 43 percent, while overall spending for education went up by 57 percent. In return, Bloomberg and Klein persuaded the teachers union to extend the work week by more than two hours, to accept a shorter summer vacation, and to limit seniority transfers. The union also accepted a number of policies that, if not quite merit pay, were steps in that direction. In 2006, Bloomberg and Klein provided housing subsidies of up to $15,000 to entice new math, science, and special education teachers to work in the city's most challenging schools. In 2007, Bloomberg and Klein negotiated agreements with the teachers union to allow school-wide bonuses for teachers in about two hundred schools if their school's test scores went up, and individual signing bonuses of $15,000 for teachers of mathematics and science. Bloomberg and Klein also developed a plan to pay teachers an extra

---

98   EdReform.blogspot.com (December 2006; January 2008).

$10,000 to teach in low performing schools, and additional bonuses of up to $25,000 for principals who agreed to spend three years in troubled schools. Principals whose schools made the greatest gains on standardized tests were eligible for still another bonus of $25,000. There were additional cash rewards for students who had good attendance records and test scores. Acting independently but with the approval of Chancellor Klein, Whitney Tilson raised $1 million for a program called Rewarding Achievement (REACH), which paid low-income students up to $1,000 for each Advanced Placement exam they passed, with a matching grant for the student's school.[99]

In offering these bonuses and cash incentives, Bloomberg, Klein, and Tilson were speaking the language of the financiers who led DFER and who themselves were accustomed to much larger bonuses. But Bloomberg and Klein went beyond bonuses. They also developed a new system of testing and data collection that rated teachers according to the performance of their students—so that "top performing teachers can be identified and acknowledged (and underperformers can be improved or removed)." Tilson was especially pleased when Chancellor Klein announced in 2007 that the city school system would spend $80 million on a new battery of tests. Going well beyond the national No Child Left Behind program (which mandated testing in grades 3 through 8, and one more time in high school), Klein proposed to test pupils in grades 3 through 8 five times a year in both reading and math, while high school students would be tested four times a year in each subject.[100]

---

99 Diane Ravitch, *The Death and Life of the Great American School System*, 91, 85; Michael Bloomberg, speech to National Urban League, reprinted at EdReform.blogspot.com (July 2007); Helen Zelon, "The Education Business" *City Limits* (1 June 2009); Peter Meyer, "New York's Education Battles," *Education Next* (Spring 2008); EdReform.blogspot (April 2007; November 2007; March 2008).

100 EdReform.blogspot.com (July 2007; February 2007; June 2007).

Because Bloomberg and Klein wanted to be judged by their success in raising student test scores, they awarded large contracts to companies that specialized in preparing students for the tests that New York gave each year. According to historian Diane Ravitch, "Beginning in September each year, the elementary and middle schools dedicated large blocks of time to practice for the state tests."[101]

The policy seemed to pay off in reading and mathematics, which were the subjects that counted on standardized tests. Between 2006 and 2009 the number of New York City students scoring at level 1 (and therefore required to repeat a grade) declined from 70,090 to 14,305. In 2007 the city won the $500,000 Eli Broad Prize for Urban Education for raising student achievement, reducing the achievement gaps, and helping greater proportions of African-American and Hispanic students achieve at higher levels.[102]

Bloomberg and Klein often mentioned the improvement on standardized tests. It turned out, however, that the gains were largely an illusion. The number of students at level 1 had declined, but only because New York lowered the standard and made it easier for students to reach level 2. When testing sixth-grade readers in 2006, students had to earn 41 percent of the points to attain level 2; but in 2009, students in that grade needed only 17.9 percent. Moreover, when the results of the National Assessment of Educational Progress (NAEP) were released in 2007, it turned out that (except in fourth grade mathematics) students in New York City had made no significant progress during the first four years of the Bloomberg-Klein regime. Critics also accused the Bloomberg team of cooking the test-score books. According to Diane Ravitch, the single instance of improvement—in fourth grade math— was the result of providing "accommodations," extra time or assistance,

---

101 Diane Ravitch, *The Death and Life of the Great American School System*, 76.

102 *Ibid.*; Peter Meyer, "New York City's Education Battles," *Education Next* (Spring 2008).

to "an extraordinary 25 percent of the students in that grade ... a figure far higher than in any other city tested by NAEP and double the rate in New York City in 2003."[103]

Despite the overall lack of progress on the NAEP tests, the press celebrated "the Bloomberg miracle" with laudatory articles appearing in *Forbes*, *The Economist*, *Time*, *Newsweek*, and *USA Today*. This made it easier for Klein to proceed toward reforming the schools' policies on tenure and termination. But due to existing contractual promises, firing tenured teachers proved to be more difficult.

DFER and Whitney Tilson commended Bloomberg and Klein for paying teachers for performance, not just seniority. DFER and Tilson were pleased when Bloomberg said he was running the schools "the same way I ran my company [Bloomberg LP—a financial news and information service]." DFER and Tilson supported the mayor for developing incentives to encourage the retirement of senior faculty who could be replaced by junior teachers—at a savings of some $30,000 per replacement. They approved when Klein said he was "converting the role of the principal into a CEO role." They applauded when, to drive home the point, Klein hired Jack Welch to train New York's school principals. When Welch had been the chief executive at General Electric, Welch had famously developed a "20-70-10 plan." It called for "rigorous appraisal" and "meaningful differentiation" among employees. The top 20 percent would receive extra recognition and cash bonuses. The next 70 percent would receive cost-of-living adjustments. The bottom 10 percent would be marked for termination.[104]

---

103 Diane Ravitch, *The Death and Life of the Great American School System*, 79, 88; Ravitch, "Mayor Bloomberg's Report Card," *Education Next* (Summer 2008).

104 Michael Bloomberg, quoted by Helen Zelon, "The Education Business"; Michael Mulgrew, "How the Mayor Can Prevent Teacher Layoffs," *New York Daily News* (30 July 2010); Joel Klein, quoted by Jia Lynn Yang, "NY School Chancellor: Head of the Class" *Fortune* (15 February 2007); Geoff Colvin,

Tilson was so pleased that he failed to notice that Bloomberg and Klein implemented a curriculum that differed markedly from the program that KIPP used at its schools. After establishing central control of New York City's schools, Bloomberg and Klein proceeded, in the words of journalist Sol Stern, to give "the progressive-education movement near-total power and influence." Despite objections from several reading researchers, Bloomberg and Klein replaced phonics programs and insisted upon a "Balanced Literacy" curriculum ("whole language plus a dollop of phonics"). They imposed a "writing process" approach that, according to Stern, called for young students to write "without worrying (or being taught much) about formal grammar or spelling." And they opted for "Everyday Mathematics" and "Impact Mathematics"—two "fuzzy math" approaches that emphasized mathematical concepts and problem solving instead of the importance of calculating precisely.[105]

In essence, as historian Diane Ravitch has noted, Bloomberg and Klein "adopted a 'left-right' strategy. [They] selected instructional programs that pleased the pedagogical left, awarded large contracts to vendors of these programs, and created large numbers of jobs for consultants and coaches who were knowledgeable about progressive approaches. And [they] satisfied the business community by vigorously promoting choice, standardized testing, and accountability."[106]

Some parents complained about the progressive approaches to teaching. One mother was aghast when she learned that a teacher at her child's school had been reprimanded for teaching punctuation and for emphasizing the importance of correct spelling. Another parent took exception because administrators at her school considered it "serious

---

"The CEO Educator," *Money.cnn.com* (1 October 2009).

105 Sol Stern, "Bloomberg and Klein Rush In," *City Journal* (April 2003); Stern, "A Marshall Plan for Reading," *City Journal* (September 2008); Diane Ravitch, *The Death and Life of the Great American School System*, 72.

106 Diane Ravitch, *The Death and Life of the Great American School System*, 71.

offenses" if teachers asked children "to memorize multiplication tables [or] to find nations on a globe."[107]

With their commitment to "top-down reform," Bloomberg and Klein initially manifested what one parent called "disdain for any parent who asks questions." In designing their curricula, the Mayor and the Chancellor had consulted experts. And most of the experts in New York City were professors at Teachers College, Columbia University, which for several decades had been the mother church of progressive education. In keeping with this progressivism, Bloomberg and Klein's deputy chancellor, Diana Lam, insisted that there must be a "reading rug" in every classroom. Teachers were to spend less time teaching students how to sound out words, so that children could spend more time sitting on the rug—where they would either read independently or interact with one another amidst a joyful buzz.[108]

When the criticism persisted, Bloomberg and Klein modified their approach. Lam resigned in 2004, after facing a nepotism charge (putting her husband on the payroll), and in 2006 Bloomberg and Klein accepted decentralization and allowed principals a greater amount of autonomy. In Region 5, for example, a veteran administrator, Kathleen Cashin, was allowed to form a "Knowledge Network" that offered a curriculum based on E. D. Hirsch's Core Knowledge system. Hirsch then traveled to New York and explained how important it was for students to build upon a body of factual information, and for reading teachers to use phonics when they were showing students how to decode and sound out words.[109]

---

107 Betsy Combier comment at *ParentAdvocates.org* (13 April 2003); Robert Pondiscio comment at *blog.CoreKnowledge.org* (23 September 2009).

108 Diane Ravitch, *The Death and Life of the Great American School System*, 35; Sol Stern, "Bloomberg and Klein Rush In"; Stern "A Marshall Plan for Reading."

109 Peter Meyer, "New York City's Education Battles," *Education Next* (Spring 2008).

Tilson must have had some reservations about Bloomberg and Klein's progressivism. But he was so impressed with their management style, their support for merit pay and their opposition to tenure, that he urged President Obama to choose Klein as the nation's new Secretary of Education. Tilson recognized that, by the time of Obama's election in 2008, Klein had been "blackballed by the unions." But this only made Klein all the more attractive to Tilson. It showed that Klein was "a true reformer" who had "the strength, courage, passion and willingness to run through walls and suffer endless slings and arrows to always do what's right for kids." Tilson was "100% certain" of this. And there was "another important factor as well: politics." If Obama chose Klein, "the teacher union bosses will weep, gnash their teeth, and get their knickers in a twist." But "you owe them nothing," Tilson wrote to Obama. "In fact they did everything they could to squash your candidacy during the primaries." Now Obama had a chance not only to get even with the unions but to send "a powerful message that you're truly a New Democrat, focused on doing what is best for the country, even if it means angering entrenched interests in your own party."[110]

Michelle Rhee

As has been mentioned, when Barack Obama was choosing his cabinet in 2009, Whitney Tilson urged that Joel Klein be appointed as Secretary of Education. Others in DFER, however, acknowledged that there was another candidate whom the group also regarded as a splendid choice. As reported in the *New York Times*, "Joe Williams, executive director of [DFER]," said that his group "would be delighted to see [either] Mr. Klein or Ms. Rhee appointed." "Ms. Rhee" was Michelle Rhee, the superintendent of schools in Washington, D. C.[111]

---

110 EdReform.blogspot.com (December 2008).

111 *New York Times* (16 December 2008).

Kopp's Kids

In many ways Michelle Rhee was a representative member of the generation of school reformers who came of age after 1990. Rhee was reared in Toledo, Ohio, in a family of prosperous Korean-Americans. Rhee's father was a physician and her mother the owner of an upscale dress shop. Rhee was educated at the Maumee Valley Country Day School, an elite private school where there were only 55 students in the high school graduating class. She then attended an Ivy League university, Cornell, where she fell in with a group of students who urged her to reject bourgeois assumptions (which Rhee's older brother, Eric, characterized as the "expectation" that one should become a "doctor, lawyer, something like that"). While she was at Cornell, Rhee came to think that many Black kids in the inner cities were being sentenced to impoverished lives because their teachers assumed that these children could not learn.[112]

After graduating from Cornell in 1992, Rhee joined Teach for America and spent three years teaching at the Harlem Elementary School in Baltimore. Rhee then enrolled in a graduate program at Harvard's Kennedy School of Government. In 1997, when she received a master's degree from Harvard, Rhee also received a telephone call from Teach for America's founder, Wendy Kopp. Kopp explained that TFA had established a sister program called TEACH. The initial idea was for TEACH to provide training and support for TFA recruits. Before long, however, TEACH morphed into a program for training mid-career professionals who wished to become teachers without attending a school of education. Directing both TEACH and TFA was too much for Kopp, who persuaded Rhee to take charge of TEACH, which was then renamed the National Teacher Project (NTP). Over the course of the next decade, Rhee and NTP recruited some 28,000 teachers for more than 200 school systems.[113]

---

112 Sean J. Miller, "Is Michelle Rhee the New Face of Education Reform?" *Christian Science Monitor* (28 January 2009); Marc Fisher, "In Search of the Real Michelle Rhee," *Washington Post* (27 September 2009); Richard Whitmire, *The Bee Eater* (San Francisco: Jossey-Bass, 2011) 7-8.

113 Wendy Kopp, *One Day, All Children, passim*; V. Dion Haynes et al., "Fenty's

Rhee's earlier experience as an elementary school teacher in Baltimore was especially influential. When she was working for TFA, Rhee had been assigned to teach the third grade, but during her first year she was not able to control her class of 35 children. Due to stress, Rhee suffered from hives, and at one point she told her father that she was ready to give up on teaching. But she had second thoughts and stuck it out, insisting that she "was not going to let 8-year olds run me out of town." During her second and third years of teaching, Rhee took two classes that, she said, had been scoring "at almost rock bottom on standardized tests" to "absolutely the top." According to Rhee's resume, "Over a two-year period, [she] moved students scoring on average at the 13th percentile on national standardized tests to 90 percent of students scoring at the 90th percentile or higher."[114]

Some observers were skeptical. "Gaines like that would be more than dramatic," one writer noted. "Such score gains would be historic." The principal of the Harlem Elementary School confirmed Rhee's story about her students' improvement, as did two other teachers. But there were no documents to back up the claim. This was surprising since Rhee and TFA placed great emphasis on documented test scores.[115]

Whatever the skeptics thought, Rhee insisted that her students had improved markedly. And she thought she knew why. During her second and third years, Rhee held many conferences with the parents of her students and, after obtaining the consent of the parents, she gave her students two hours of nightly homework and made them

---

Agent of Change," *Washington Post* (2 July 2007).

114 Michelle Rhee, quoted by Evan Thomas et al, "An Unlikely Gambler," *Newsweek* 152 (1 September 2008) 54; Rhee's resume quoted at *DailyHowler.com* (2 July 2007); Lucia Graves, "The Evolution of Teach for America," *U.S. News* (17 October 2008); Richard Whitmire, *The Bee Eater*, 25-44.

115 *DailyHowler.com* (2 July 2007; 11 July 2007); V. Dion Haynes et al, "Fenty's Agent of Change."

attend school on Saturday. The key to success, Rhee said, was "sweat," on the part of the teacher and the students.[116]

Rhee also drew a larger lesson from her experience in Baltimore. It was easy for inner-city teachers to become resigned to poor results and to blame the environment rather than the schools or the teachers themselves. Rhee recognized that poverty, broken families, crime, and drugs all worked against academic achievement. But she also concluded that teachers could make a critical difference. "It drives me nuts when people say that two-thirds of a kid's academic achievement is based on their environment," she said. Pointing to her students whose scores allegedly had risen from worst to best, she continued: "Those kids, where they lived didn't change. Their parents didn't change. Their diets didn't change. The violence in the community didn't change. The only thing that changed for those 70 kids was the adults who were in front of them every single day teaching them."[117]

Rhee's emphasis on the importance of good teaching was reinforced when she observed that many of her students seemed to lose interest in school as they moved along. KIPP founders Mike Feinberg and Dave Levin had observed a similar pattern with their students in Houston. But Feinberg and Levin had attributed this to what some observers called "the lure of street life"—gangs, sex, drugs, and rock and roll. Rhee, on the other hand, placed the blame on other teachers. In a conversation with one reporter, Rhee said, "All of those kids would go on to other teachers and totally lose everything because those teachers were lousy." "Rhee used an earthier adjective," the reporter added. On another occasion, Rhee declared: "What was most disappointing was to watch these kids go off into the fourth grade and just lose everything because they were in classrooms with teachers who weren't engaging them."[118]

---

116 Michelle Rhee, quoted by Evan Thomas et al., "An Unlikely Gambler."

117 *Ibid.*

118 Jay Mathews, "Baptism by Fire," *Washington Post* (27 October 2008);

Given Rhee's criticism of her fellow teachers, it was hardly surprising that, as education writer Richard Whitmire has noted, "Other teachers at Harlem Park turned against her." So did many informed scholars, some of whom mentioned the importance of heredity and culture while others stressed the importance of environmental factors. Those on the left often attributed low academic scores to various sorts of oppression: poverty, racism, sexism. Those on the right pointed to social pathologies: illegitimacy, welfare dependency, and dysfunctional cultural values. In 2008, 150 scholars signed a statement to the effect that many changes would have to be made before non-Asian minority groups would achieve parity in academic achievement. Stanford's professor Larry Cuban expressed a widespread opinion when he said that Rhee's views reflected "a serious misreading of why urban students fail to reach proficiency levels."[119]

Nevertheless, Rhee downplayed the effects of IQ, poverty, violence, and family instability. She was convinced that bad teachers were the biggest problem with public education in the inner cities. "It's the adults," she said. "There's nothing wrong with the kids." "As a teacher," Rhee said, "you have to be willing to take personal responsibility for ensuring your children are successful despite obstacles. You can't say, 'My students didn't get any breakfast today,' or 'No one put them to bed last night,' or 'Their electricity got cut off in the house, so they couldn't do their homework.'"[120] In one sense, Rhee was complimenting teachers when she insisted on the importance of their work. But veteran teachers sensed that Rhee was also demanding that they work longer and harder and take responsibility for the test scores of their students. Some said that

---

Amanda Ripley, "Can She Save Our Schools," *Time* (8 December 2008) 39.

[119] Melissa Williams-Gurian, quoted by Richard Whitmire, *The Bee Eater*, 21; Statement released by the Economic Policy Institute, June 2008; Larry Cuban, "Michelle Rhee," *Washington Post* (23 November 2008).

[120] Michelle Rhee, quoted by Sean J. Miller, "Is Michelle Rhee the New Face of Education Reform?"

Rhee was asking for "superhuman efforts, consistently, for decades to come." Others took exception to an implicit assumption: that schools should recruit "waves of energetic young teachers, who would spend five or six years in the classroom before moving on, rather than career teachers, who might tire as they grow older." "Michelle does not view teaching as a career," union leader Randi Weingarten maintained. "She sees it as temporary, something a lot of newbies will work very hard at for a couple of years, and then if they leave, they leave, as opposed to professionals who get more seasoned." Critics said that Rhee did not treasure veterans who were rooted in their communities and developed a deep and abiding identification with their schools. Instead, Rhee relied on transient young missionaries, if their students scored well on standardized tests.[121]

Rhee did not say explicitly that she was trying to change the teaching profession. But she attributed her success in Baltimore to working like a demon, and she thought other teachers should do the same. As Evan Thomas noted in *Newsweek*, Rhee wanted to change the requirements of the job from 8 a.m. to 3 p.m. with summers off to "something that bears more resemblance to joining the Green Berets." Rhee wanted teachers to follow the example of KIPP's longer workdays and shorter vacations. Another like-minded reformer, Kati Haycock of the Education Trust, conceded that there were "some absolutely fabulous teachers who have taught in very tough settings for 20 years and have consistently produced stunning growth, and have somehow found the stamina to do it, while some energetic 24-year olds aren't up to it. But what we need to do is change the idea that education is … [a] career that needs to be done for life. There are a lot of smart people who change careers every six or seven years, while education ends up with a bunch of people on the low end of the pile who don't want to compete in the job market."[122]

---

121 Clay Risen, "The Lightning Rod," *The Atlantic* (November 2008) 85; Randi Weingarten, quoted by Sam Dillon, "A School Chief Takes on Tenure," *New York Times* (13 November 2008).

122 Evan Thomas et al., "An Unlikely Gambler."

While alienating veteran teachers, Rhee's emphases endeared her to those who sought to bypass traditional approaches. It was hardly a surprise, then, that Rhee and her National Teacher Project received acclaim from DFER and from Joel Klein. Like them, she insisted that low-income urban students could catch up with youngsters in the suburbs. For Rhee, as for DFER and Klein, there was a straight-forward way to improve America's inner-city schools: get the best teachers and principals to work in the worst schools. This could be done by firing bad teachers and hiring more recruits from Teach for America and from the New Teacher Project.

Yet Rhee did not remain with the New York-based NTP. As a result of an election in Washington, D.C. in 2006, she was propelled into national prominence. The election saw Adrian Fenty, a 35-year old African-American graduate of Oberlin College, chosen as the youngest-ever mayor of the nation's capital city. During his campaign, Fenty promised to upgrade Washington's public schools, which by many measures were among the worst in the country. Only 43 percent of the high school freshmen graduated within five years, and on standardized tests administered by the National Assessment of Educational Progress (NAEP), Washington ranked last among 11 urban school systems in math and second-to-last in reading. Fenty promised to make education his top priority and to turn things around by instituting "a new culture of accountability."[123]

Fenty asked Joel Klein for advice on choosing a new school chancellor, and Klein recommended Michelle Rhee. It was hardly surprising that Klein recommended Rhee. As Richard Whitmire has noted, Klein and Rhee shared a "mind lock." They thought the existing education system was "built on three pillars of mediocrity: lockstep pay [for teachers], life tenure, and seniority." They thought

---

123 Clay Risen, "The Lightning Rod," 80; Press Release at *DCWatch.com* (4 January 2007); Yolanda Woodlee, "Fenty Lauds School System Changes," *Washington Post* (15 March 2008).

there would be no progress until the system was reconstructed "on a foundation of performance [and] accountability." They emphasized the importance of giving educational administrators the authority to fire or to retain teachers on the basis of the students' performance on standardized tests.[124]

This emphasis on "firing your way to success" called attention to a difference between what many school reformers called "old guard education warriors" and a new breed of younger reformers. In the 1980s and early-1990s, the campaigns for better schools had revolved around established educational leaders. On the progressive left, there were liberals like Howard Gardner and Theodore Sizer, and on the educational right there were traditionalists like E. D. Hirsch. At the outset of the 21st century, however, the momentum shifted away from the old guard and passed to a closely connected group of younger people who had been associated with Teach for America. Most of these reformers had no fixed opinions about the curriculum or about teaching methods. They focused instead on issues of tenure, union strength, and merit pay. Most of all, they proposed to collect data that would allow computers to measure the effectiveness of teachers by calculating the amount that the teachers added to their students' scores on standardized tests. With a touch of sarcasm, journalist Ezra Klein noted that "the debate over education policy" had become "very strange." On one side were "'old' style" liberals" and on the other were "new style reformer[s] who have two! separate! Blackberries!"[125]

At first, Rhee said she was not interested in moving to Washington. But Mayor Fenty eventually persuaded her with his response to one of Rhee's questions. "What would you be willing to risk [for] the chance of being able to transform the schools?" Rhee

---

124 Richard Whitmire, *The Bee Eater*, 58-59.

125 EdReform.blogspot.com (December 2009); Ezra Klein archive, *The American Prospect* (9 December 2008).

had asked. "Everything," Fenty answered. Rhee warned Fenty that she might become a political liability, but Fenty insisted, "I don't want to look back on our time and say we were careful; we did the politically correct thing."[126]

Many people were taken by surprise when Fenty appointed Rhee as school chancellor in 2007, for Rhee, who was 37-years old at the time, had never been in charge of a school, let alone a district with 46,000 students. Rhee's appointment made her an instant celebrity. She was the first of her generation of new-guard school reformers to become the superintendent of a major school system, and she soon became a symbol of a new approach to helping inner city students—one that recruited energetic new teachers while challenging the power of the established teachers' unions.

Rhee proceeded to recruit hundreds of instructors from Teach for America and to choose two TFA alumnae as her deputy chancellor and as assistant to the deputy mayor for education. Before long, TFA alumni were also appointed as principals at more than 10 percent of Washington's 123 schools. Rhee acknowledged that there was "a core group of education reformers who are driving a disproportionate amount of the great things going on right now."[127]

After becoming chancellor, Rhee also settled in for a long battle with the Washington Teachers Union. Believing that the school system had a great many employees with "what I think are sort of [inflated] perceptions of their performance and of their work," Rhee closed 23 schools in 2007, fired 100 central office workers, and discharged 36 principals (one out of every four). None of these decisions abrogated tenure agreements with teachers, which were protected by a collective

---

126 Evan Thomas, "An Unlikely Gambler."

127 *Ibid.*; Jay Mathews, "Maverick Teachers Key D.C. Moment," *Washington Post* (18 June 2007); Lucia Graves, "The Evolution of Teach for America."

bargaining contract that the teachers union had negotiated with the school district. But from the outset it was clear that Rhee's reform strategy revolved around improving the quality of instruction by making radical changes in the way teachers were hired and fired. That could not be done without negotiating a new contract with the teachers' union.[128]

In the meantime, in 2008 and 2009, Rhee purged some 266 teachers she considered ineffective (including many tenured instructors). These teachers were dismissed on account of "financial necessity," which was one of the justifications that, under traditional academic contracts, allowed the abrogation of tenure without filing charges against individual teachers. Some observers believed that Rhee had overstated the extent of the district's financial crisis in order to justify terminations that she had in mind all along. This suspicion gained credence because, just a few months before the firings, Rhee had hired more than five hundred new teachers, some of whom were Asian immigrants who had entered the United States on H1-B visas. This reinforced a suspicion that "the Korean chancellor" was out of touch with the predominantly Black population of Washington. On the Internet, one blogger published several hundred words of commentary under a headline that offered this capsule summary of Rhee's approach: "To Improve Schools—Fire Black Teachers, Hire H1-B Asians."[129]

In her effort to persuade the teachers union to forsake tenure and seniority rights, Rhee dangled the carrot of money. With the

---

128 Richard Whitmire, *The Bee Eater*, 109.

129 Evan Thomas et al., "An Unlikely Gambler"; RiShawn Biddle, "Fenty Gets Schooled," *American Spectator* (30 June 2010); Barbara Hollingsworth, "Importing Teachers in the District of Columbia," *Washington Examiner* (10 November 2009); Tamar Lewin, "School Chief Dismisses 241 Teachers," *New York Times* (23 July 2010); Patrick Cleburne, posting at Vdare.com (10 November 2009).

aid of some $375 million contributed by the Broad Foundation, the Walton Family Foundation, and other philanthropies, Rhee proposed to make Washington's teachers the best paid in the country. If the teachers would give up seniority privileges and tenure, and if they could successfully show that the test scores of their students were improving, they could earn large salary increases that would bring them to as much as $130,000 a year. If they chose to keep their tenure, on the other hand, they would receive only modest raises for the next five years. In any case, Rhee wanted all new teachers to choose the first option. In August, 2008, one poll commissioned by the union indicated that teachers opposed Rhee's plan by three to one, and, taking no chances, the union declined to put the proposal to a vote.[130]

Nevertheless, Rhee pressed on, and in the spring of 2010 she succeeded in persuading the teachers union to accept a contract that ended most preferences for seniority and allowed for the use of student test scores in evaluating the performance of teachers. An article in *The Atlantic* described the agreement as a "revolutionary teachers' contract" that "essentially broke the union," and another article in the *New York Times* explained that the new contract made it possible for Rhee to fire any teacher if the teacher was evaluated as "ineffective" for one year or "minimally effective" for two years. "The criteria used to define 'ineffective' or 'minimally effective' are, according to another clause [in the contract], 'a nonnegotiable item' determined solely by Rhee and her staff." Rhee modestly said that she had "bargained with the teachers' union for 2½ years and won significant concessions."[131]

---

130 Evan Thomas, "An Unlikely Gambler"; Amanda Ripley, "Can She Save Our Schools?"; Sam Dillon, "A School Chief Takes on Tenure," *New York Times* (13 November 2008).

131 Natalie Hopkinson, "Why Michelle Rhee's Education 'Brand' Failed in DC," *The Atlantic* (15 September 2010); Steven Brill, "The Teachers' Unions' Last Stand," *The New York Times Magazine* (17 May 2010); Michelle Rhee and Adrian Fenty, "The Education Manifesto," *Wall Street Journal* (20 October 2010).

Questions naturally arose as to how Rhee persuaded the teachers' union to accept the terms of the 2010 contract. Part of the answer was that the new contract offered 20 percent raises plus large bonuses for "highly effective" teachers—with the rating determined largely by the scores students made on standardized tests. "Momentum" was another part of the answer. By 2010, a number of state legislatures had revamped their laws to link teachers' pay with students' scores. The Washington Teachers Union may have calculated that Rhee's terms were as good as could be obtained in this environment. Under the terms of the new contract, the "highly effective" teachers—who made up 16 percent of Washington's teachers in 2009—would be eligible for as much as $25,000 in one-time bonuses. Those rated as "highly effective" for two years in a row could see their base pay increase by as much as $26,000 a year.[132]

A few months after signing the new contract, Rhee fired 241 teachers, including 165 who received poor appraisals under an evaluation system that was linked to student scores. Although those dismissed for poor performance represented only 4 percent of the city's 4,000 teachers, 737 other teachers were rated "minimally effective" and were given one year to improve their performance or face dismissal. Rhee refused to speculate about how many more teachers eventually might be dismissed, but she predicted that by 2012 "a not insignificant number of folks will be moved out of the system for poor performance."[133]

Many observers were surprised by the large number of teachers who had been fired and the even larger number who had been warned of impending termination. As Richard Whitmire has noted, Rhee was "flushing out huge numbers of teachers" while "no schools superintendent anywhere [else] in the country was dismissing more

---

132 Richard Whitmire, *The Bee Eater*, 123-27; Tamar Lewin, "School Chief Dismisses 241 Teachers," *New York Times* (23 July 2010); *Washington Post* (12 September 2010).

133 RiShawn Biddle, "Fenty Gets Schooled"; Bill Turque, "Rhee Dismisses 241 D.C. Teachers," *Washington Post* (24 July 2010).

than a handful of teachers for ineffectiveness." Whitmire calculated that between 2007 and 2010 "roughly half of the ... teaching staff [in Washington's public schools] turned over (a combination of layoffs, resignations, and retirements)." Even that was not enough for Whitmire, who believed that "only a third" of the teachers in Washington were up to par. "The reality," Whitmire wrote, "is that [Rhee] fired too few teachers, not too many."[134]

Some academic researchers went further and estimated that to reform schools, nationwide, the United States would have to fire about 2.8 million of its corps of 3.5 million teachers. This was the conclusion of Ivy League professors Doug Staiger and Jonah Rockoff, who prepared a quantitative analysis of the relevant value-added statistics. In a paper presented at a conference at Columbia University, Staiger and Rockoff concluded that to maximize the performance of students, 80 percent of new teachers should be fired after two years' probation—and replaced by teachers who were just as effective at raising test scores as the top 0.7 million teachers currently are. Staiger and Rockoff said there were "enormous costs to having mediocre teachers burdening the school system, and once they get their union cards, we're stuck with them for decades." Conversely, "the benefit of keeping only the superstars is enormous."[135]

Some observers scoffed that an 80 percent dismissal rate was wildly impractical. Others simply looked askance at this exercise in simulation research. It was like calculating how good a baseball team would be if all its pitchers except Sandy Koufax were replaced by hurlers who were as good as Koufax, and all of its batsmen except Babe Ruth were replaced by hitters as good as Ruth. Steve Sailer said

---

134 Richard Whitmire, *The Bee Eater*, 117, 214, 217.

135 Ray Fisman, "Is Firing (A Lot Of) Teachers the Only Way to Improve Public Schools?" Slate.com (11 August 2010); iSteve.blogspot.com (11 August 2011).

it was preposterous to assume that millions of academic Koufaxes and Ruths would eventually come to the fore, if only mediocrities were not protected by tenure and unions.[136]

When Rhee's critics complained that she was foolishly trying to fire her way to success, defenders insisted that Rhee's approach had led to higher test scores. Before Rhee became the superintendent, Richard Whitmire wrote, low-income children in Washington scored much lower than students from similar backgrounds in Boston, Houston, and New York City. "Nothing but bad schools" could explain this, Whitmire maintained. And then, after Rhee took control, test scores in Washington improved by about 11 percent on locally-administered tests of reading and arithmetic. Rhee's defenders cited this as proof that she was on the right track. The results of the National Assessment of Educational Progress (NAEP), however, were not so encouraging. In 2011, NAEP reported that the test scores of White, Black and Hispanic children in the District had all improved slightly since 2003, but the achievement gaps among the various demographic groups had not narrowed significantly, and the average scores of Black and Hispanic students in Washington remained below the average scores for peers of the same race and class in other cities.[137]

Despite the modest progress, the mainstream media generally supported Rhee's approach. "No joy can be taken in knowing the hardship caused to individuals [the 241 teachers dismissed in 2010] who likely are nice people and good neighbors," the *Washington Post* noted. But the *Post* nevertheless commended Rhee "for taking the

---

136 Steve Sailer, "Slate: All We Have To Do is Fire 2.8 Million Out of 3.5 Million Teachers," iSteve.blogspot.com (11 August 2011).

137 Richard Whitmire, *The Bee Eater*, 70; June Kronholz, "D.C.'s Braveheart," Education Next (Winter 2010); Matthew Yglesias, "Is School choice Failing DC?" Slate.com (5 December 2011); Dana Goldstein, "In Post-Rhee DC, Achievement Gaps Remain Staggeringly Wide," *TheNation.com* (8 December 2011).

difficult but necessary steps to rid the system of ineffective teachers." The *Wall Street Journal* praised Rhee for fighting an entrenched bureaucracy that allegedly did more to protect adults than to educate children. And the *New York Times* commended the teachers' union for "wisely" accepting an agreement that gave Rhee "greater leeway to pay, promote or fire teachers based on performance." Out in middle-America, the editors of the *Oklahoman* chimed in, saying that it was "not often" that they could "look to the nation's capital for sensible ideas." But Rhee had provided "a rare opportunity" by confronting "a status quo system that puts the job protection of teachers above the needs of students."[138]

There was grumbling, however, and not just from teachers. In *The Death and Life of the Great American School System* (2010), historian Diane Ravitch showed how test scores could be manipulated by altering the number of right answers required for a pass or by increasing the number of students who were excused from taking the tests. And in the *Washington Post*, education writer Jay Mathews pointed to one specific way in which testing had been manipulated in the District of Columbia. Shortly before Rhee became chancellor, the schools had switched from one set of tests to another (from the Stanford-9 to the DC-CAS). As often was the case, scores plummeted when pupils faced unfamiliar questions, and then the scores rebounded as teachers (and their students) had a better idea of what to expect.[139]

Other reporters at the *Post* published accounts that differed markedly from what one of them called the "steadfast, protective and, at times, adoring" views of Rhee that prevailed on their own editorial

---

138 "The D.C. Teacher Firings," *Washington Post* (25 July 2010); "Who's Got Michelle Rhee's Back?" *Wall Street Journal* (14 December 2009); "Washington's Teachers Contract," *New York Times* (13 June 2010); "D. C. Superintendent Puts Teacher Tenure in Crosshairs," *Oklahoman* (2 August 2010).

139 Diane Ravitch, drawing on research by G. F. Brandenburg, *The Death and Life of the Great American School System, passim*; Jay Matthews, "Class Struggle," *WashintonPost.com* (3 August 2010).

page. Valerie Strauss noted that because Rhee was using test scores "to make important decisions about kids and teachers," many teachers had narrowed their focus and were "mindlessly drilling kids so they can do well on standardized tests." And Linda Perlstein, a reporter who spent five years writing about education for the *Post*, wrote an especially impressive book-length account of the new emphasis on test scores. To discover whether this approach was producing better education, Perlstein spent an entire year at an elementary school once considered a failure but later held up as an example of reform done right. As it happened, Perlstein's sojourn was at the Tyler Heights Elementary School, which was not in the District of Columbia but in nearby Annapolis, Maryland. But Perlstein's book, *Tested* (2007), provided a disturbing account of relentless drilling and test preparation. It called attention to "the unintended and undesirable consequences of our current testing obsession."[140]

When it came to the alleged testing gains, reporters from *USA Today* were especially skeptical. After analyzing documents and data secured under D.C.'s Freedom of Information Act, the newspaper reported that during Rhee's tenure as chancellor there had been "extraordinarily high numbers of erasures on standardized tests," and "the consistent pattern was that wrong answers were erased and changed to right ones." In some schools there were as many as 12.7 wrong-to-right erasures, as compared to a district-wide average of less than 1. In 2011 the District's Board of Education announced that it would investigate this matter but would "not release any information about its investigations unless wrongdoing is found."[141]

---

140 Valerie Strauss, "The Answer Sheet," *WashingtonPost.com* (29 June 2010); Linda Perlstein, *Tested* (New York: Henry Holt and Company, 2007); Edward Humes, as quoted on the back cover of the paperback edition of *Tested*.

141 Bill Turque, quoted by Robert Pondiscio at *CoreKnowledge.com* (28 January 2010); Jay Mathews, "Class Struggle," *WashingtonPost.com* (3 August 2010); *USA Today* (28 and 29 March 2011).

The scrutiny of test scores damaged the case for Rhee's program, for that case was based on her alleged success in improving the test scores of low-performing students. Critics said, "The scores did rise, but they didn't represent genuine learning." Critics said Rhee had "incentivized desperate behavior by principals and teachers trying to save their jobs . . . and comply with their boss' demands." Even some of Rhee's staunch supporters, such as Whitney Tilson of DFER, acknowledged, "If one introduces rewards for good performance and performance is evaluated . . . via tests, then there is strong incentive to cheat on these tests and, given the opportunity, many people will do so."[142]

Some wondered whether the cheating had been so widespread that it created a picture of progress that never occurred. Nobody knew for sure, but Rhee shrugged off the criticism, and also the strictures of those who said that Washington's schools were placing so much emphasis on test scores for reading and arithmetic that they were neglecting other important subjects—art, music, history, geography, and literature. When some teachers pointed out that test scores did not take account of creativity and the love of learning, Rhee replied, "You

---

[142] Diane Ravitch, "Shame on Michelle Rhee," *TheDailyBeast.com* (29 March 2011); Whitney Tilson, "Eager for Spotlight," *EdReform.blogspot.com* (August 2011). When it came to problems with cheating, Washington was far from alone. For the situation in some other cities, see Heather Vogell, John Perry and Aaron Judd, and M. B. Pell, "Cheating our Children: Suspicious School Test Scores Across the Nation," *Atlanta Constituton* (24, 25, 27 March 2012). Reformer Whitney Tilson was "not at all surprised to learn that there are pockets of cheating," but Tilson was "stunned at how widespread it appears to be. This means we reformers have to make this a TOP priority, or we risk undermining everything we're achieving." *EdReform.blogspot.com* (April 2012). The Black economist and syndicated columnist Walter Williams wrote that teachers in Philadelphia "have joined public school teahers in cities such as Atlanta, Detroit, Los Angeles, Columbus, New York and Washington in changing student scores on academic achievement tests. Teachers have held grade fixing parties, sometimes wearing rubber gloves to hide fingerprints." Walter Williams, "Solutions to Black Education," *CNS News*. 25 February 2014

know what? I don't give a crap." Then she said, "Don't get me wrong. Creativity is good and whatever. But if the children don't know how to read, I don't care how creative you are. You're not doing your job."[143]

Rhee's manner annoyed many people, including some who agreed with her ideas. Rhee attributed her directness to her ethnicity, saying, "Korean people are not the most tactful." She recalled that she had been uncomfortable with ambiguity and pleasantries for "as long as I can remember." She said it drove her "crazy when people beat around the bush instead of saying, 'Look, I need you to do this.'" Rhee's mother remembered that as a young girl Rhee had said whatever was on her mind, even if it stung. Finally, one day, Inza Rhee had more than she could take of her daughter's blunt manner. "What is wrong with you?" Inza asked Michelle. "You just don't care what people think of you."[144]

Concern about Rhee's lack of tact reached a peak when *Time* magazine published a cover story about Rhee in December 2008. The text of the article was informative and placed Rhee in a favorable light. But with Rhee's approval, the editors illustrated the story with a cover photograph that pictured a grim-faced Rhee, with her arms folded in front in a typical tough guy pose, holding a large broom to sweep away the many bad teachers that she blamed for the plight of Washington's students. Instead of depicting Rhee as strong but caring, surrounded by students and teachers who were working together, the photo conveyed a different impression—one that affirmed Rhee's standing as a national symbol of tough-minded, no excuses urban school reform.[145]

---

143 Amanda Ripley, "Can She Save Our Schools?", 40.

144 Marc Fisher, "In Search of the Real Michelle Rhee," *Washington Post* (27 September 2009).

145 Marc Fisher, "In Search of the Real Michelle Rhee"; Bill Turque, "Up Close: Rhee's Image Less Clear," *Washington Post* (8 December 2008).

Rhee nevertheless persisted with her approach, which one union official characterized as a "destructive cycle of hire, fire, repeat." Rhee was so enamored with firing bad teachers that on one occasion she invited a TV crew to accompany her. "I'm going to fire somebody in a little while," she said. "Do you want to see that?" The cameraman filmed the termination from behind, thus obscuring the identity of the victim, who happened to be a school principal. Even Rhee's backers conceded that this incident smacked of disrespect for employees. But there was an upside, in that the publicity helped to attract financial support from business executives who resented unions for limiting the authority to hire and fire at will.[146]

Many Washingtonians were dismayed. Teachers' union president George Parker described the cover photo as "just more teacher-bashing." It was "disrespectful and denigrating," said Cathy Reilly, the head of the Senior High Alliance of Parents, Principals and Educators. It was part of "a constant portrayal of the system as nothing but bad," said Margot Berkey, whose daughter attended Woodrow Wilson High School. Pointing to the cover, Vincent Gray, the chairman of the District of Columbia's City Council, asked, "What does it get you, to constantly bash those you're trying to get to help you?" Rhee acknowledged that it may have been a mistake for her to approve the cover. But she never lost her certitude. "If I go down because I didn't play the politics game right, that's OK with me. At least . . . you're making decisions that you believe are in the best interests of the kids."[147]

---

[146] Randi Weingarten, quoted in Richard Whitmire, *The Bee Eater*, 188; Whitmire, *Ibid.*, 222.

[147] Marc Fisher, "In Search of the Real Michelle Rhee"; Bill Turque, "Up Close, Rhee's Image Less Clear"; Robert Pondiscio, "One, Two, Three, All Eyes on Rhee," *blog.CoreKnowledge.org* (15 June 2009).

Council Chairman Gray was known for his support of education reform. He had approved Rhee's appointment when she was named as schools chancellor in 2007. Yet Gray was so disappointed with Rhee's performance in office, and with some of mayor Adrian Fenty's other policies, that Gray challenged Fenty when Fenty came up for re-election in 2010. Fenty said education was his "number one priority," and Gray listed education first among his three top priorities. Rhee considered the election a referendum on her policies. She campaigned with Fenty and indicated that she would not stay in her post if Fenty lost his bid for re-election.[148]

The hints about resigning only increased the ardor of Rhee's critics. Straw polls taken two months before the election indicated that Fenty was sinking, with 54 percent of parents disapproving of Rhee's performance and 62 percent of Black residents also expressing disapproval. By election eve, the results were even more skewed, with one poll reporting that Fenty had a lead of 42 percentage points among Whites, while Gray had a 38-point lead among Blacks. The polls also revealed a stark racial divide in favorability ratings. Sixty-three percent of the White voters in Washington viewed Fenty favorably, but only 33 percent of the Blacks. Seventy percent of the Blacks viewed Gray favorably, as compared with only 39 percent of the Whites.[149]

Fenty and Rhee stood by one another throughout the election of 2010, but Rhee always regarded test scores, not re-election, as the ultimate measure of her policies. Despite the allegations of cheating and the intractability of the achievement gaps, she continued to point to test scores as "signs of progress" but said that it would take five to eight years "to achieve dramatic results." Outside observers agreed. "It

---

148 Bill Turque and Nikita Stewart, "Rhee Hints Her Job as DC Schools Chief Hinges on Fenty's Re-Election," *Washington Post* (1 July 2010).

149 *Ibid.*; Deborah Simmons, "D.C. Mayor Race Defined by Race," *Washington Times* (7 September 2010).

will be years before anyone can evaluate" the effects of Rhee's policies, wrote historian Diane Ravitch.[150]

As it happened, Rhee did not have that much time. In a Democratic primary held on September 14, 2010, Council Chairman Gray defeated Mayor Fenty, 53 percent to 46 percent. Gray received 82 percent of the votes in the Black majority wards on the east side of the Anacostia River, while 76 percent of the voters in the city's two Whitest wards cast their ballots for Mayor Fenty. Many people, especially Black people, rejected Rhee's critique of Washington's predominantly Black teachers. Most rank-and-file voters could claim one or more teachers as a friend or neighbor. So, instead of regarding tenure and seniority as the causes of the achievement gap, Black voters rallied in support of veteran teachers who, they thought, had done as well as could be expected in difficult circumstances. The White side of the city saw Rhee as rescuing the school system; the Black side "saw heads of households—people they knew and couldn't imagine being bad teachers—losing their jobs."[151]

A few days after the election, Michelle Rhee resigned as the chancellor of Washington's public schools. Her departure brought to mind a comment that Stanford professor Larry Cuban had made at the outset of Rhee's stint in Washington. Cuban had advised that it was "better to be a marathoner" than a "sprinter." He had said, "Sprinter superintendents err in jumping on unions too early in their long-distance race for better achievement. They suffer from ideological myopia." They mistakenly believed that "low test-scores and achievement gaps between whites and minorities result in large part from knuckle-dragging union leaders defending seniority and tenure rights." But "once union

---

150 June Kronholz, "D.C.'s Braveheart," *Education Next* (Winter 2010); Diane Ravitch, *The Death and Life of the Great American School System*, 173.

151 Freeman Klopott, "Fenty Couldn't Overcome Racial Divide," *Washington Examiner* (15 September 2010); Richard Whitmire, *The Bee Eater*, 176.

leaders were convinced that they were fighting for their survival, they converted the battle into an 'us vs. them' struggle. When that happens, kiss reform goodbye."[152]

In a farewell message, Rhee and Fenty conceded that they had failed to persuade the public to support their "aggressive educational reform agenda." But they insisted that the problem was not with their program but with the packaging. "[W]e did not communicate with [the public] effectively. We did not explain why we were doing what we were doing. . . ."[153] When it came to explaining their defeat at the polls, some school reformers recognized that Rhee and Fenty had barely scratched the surface. Pointing to the deeper reason for the defeat, Whitney Tilson confessed that the school reform movement had "a HUGE area of weakness." It was "mostly a movement of rich white people in general (myself included)" who had "failed to build a broad and diverse base of support, especially among minorities and in minority communities." Another reformer observed that when reformers denigrated urban public schools, they were attacking one of the bulwarks of the Black middle class. When he was new to the movement, this reformer recalled, "A minister took me aside and said, 'look, I know you're right . . . but you have to understand—I can't support [you] publicly because all my Deacons and their wives are employed by the school system!'" This consideration was especially important during the deep economic recession of 2009-2010, when Rhee fired five percent of Washington's teachers and issued warnings to another 15 percent.[154]

---

152 Larry Cuban, "Better to Be a Marathoner," *Washington Post* (23 November 2008); Joseph Veteritti, quoted by Ian Urbina, "Washington Mayor Loses to City Council Chairman," *New York Times* (15 September 2010).

153 Michelle Rhee and Adrian Fenty, "The Education Manifesto," *Wall Street Journal* (30 October 2010).

154 Whitney Tilson, "Sample of Feedback," EdReform.blogspot.com (December 2011).

Even some of Rhee's supporters turned pessimistic. After the election, President Barack Obama said at a town hall meeting in Washington that testing was boring and should be cut back. And Richard Whitmire, the author of an admiring book about Rhee, sensed "that the school reform movement—roughly defined as those who believe that schools alone can make a dent in the seemingly intractable problems arising from the influence of race and poverty— is headed toward a major beat-down."[155]

Nevertheless, even as Fenty went down to defeat, Rhee became a personification of the latest trend in school reform. Her reputation was then enhanced when she was featured in a widely praised, anti-union documentary film, *Waiting for 'Superman'*. From Iowa to New Jersey, leading politicians said they thought Rhee would be a good choice to lead their states' departments of education. But as Rhee traveled the country promoting *Superman*, she "sounded more like the standard bearer for a national movement than an appointed official focused on a single public school system." Rhee had undermined Fenty's chances for re-election, but Fenty had made Rhee a star.[156]

After leaving Washington, Rhee launched a new organization, "Students First," that aimed to export her approach to schools throughout the nation. "I am going to start a revolution," Rhee told Oprah Winfrey during a guest appearance on Winfrey's TV show *Oprah*. Within 48 hours after that appearance, Rhee received 100,000 donations totaling more than $1 million. There were so many donations that they "blew out the computers serving the 'donate' section of the Students First website, which actually was a section of the DFER website, because DFER was

---

155 Barack Obama, quoted by Richard Whitmire, "Why the Education Reform Movement Is in Trouble," *DailyCaller.com* (9 April 2011); Whitmire, comment at *DailyCaller.com* (9 April 2011).

156 Bill Turque, "Most Popular Subject: Rhee's Next Position," *Washington Post* (9 October 2010); Ian Urbina, "Washington Mayor's Loss May Imperil School Reform," *New York Times* (16 September 2010).

... serving as the fund-raising conduit for Rhee's start-up organization." Rhee then set her sights on attracting one million supporters and $1 billion as an endowment for Students First. She got off to a good start with $100 million in donations or pledges from major philanthropists such as Eli Broad, Rupert Murdoch, and the Fisher family that had founded the Gap clothing chain (and that had been a major benefactor of KIPP and Teach for America). Although Rhee had been shunned by most voters in Washington, D.C., she seemed likely to remain a force in school reform.[157]

9

Recent Trends in School Reform

I: Barack Obama, Arne Duncan, and the Race to the Top

Had the circumstances been different, the defeat of Mayor Adrian Fenty and the departure of Chancellor Michelle Rhee might have set back their approach to school reform. By 2010, however, Fenty and Rhee were no longer the most prominent advocates of the theory that great teachers are the key to closing the racial and ethnic achievement gaps (and that, conversely, it is the teachers' fault if the gaps persist). By then, President Barack Obama and his Secretary of Education, Arne Duncan, were also espousing this theory.

When Obama was seeking the Democratic presidential nomination in 2008, he sometimes sounded as if he himself had served a stint with Teach for America. Obama said that school administrators should scrutinize test scores to see which teachers were doing the best jobs. In addition, he said that after the administrators had also identified teachers who were "underperforming," the administrators should find "a quick and fair way to put another teacher in that classroom." Obama talked about the need for recruiting "an army of new teachers," and he sided with reformers who said America's educational system would be better if school principals had greater freedom when it came to discharging teachers they considered unsatisfactory. Obama also recommended extra pay for teachers who volunteered to teach in inner-city schools as well as for teachers whose students made substantial gains on standardized tests.[1]

Much of this did not sit well with teachers and their unions. Most teachers attributed the achievement gaps to poverty, unmotivated students, and unsupportive parents. They also regarded tenure for teachers as a protection against politics and arbitrary firing. They said tenure did not guarantee lifetime employment but required only that teachers who had served a probationary term of three to five years could not be fired unless there was a hearing at which convincing evidence of incompetence, moral turpitude, or financial necessity was presented. They said that fewer able people would choose to become teachers, and fewer teachers would stick with their profession, if teachers were denied tenure and other rights that accompanied seniority.

Obama knew the teachers' unions had made substantial financial contributions to the Democratic Party and had provided many of the workers who distributed fliers, made phone calls, and encouraged voters to get to the polls. Therefore, he proceeded cautiously. Even as Obama spoke in favor of focusing on student scores on standardized tests, and of rewarding or punishing teachers accordingly, he also tried to appease the teachers unions by appointing Linda Darling-Hammond as an advisor during his presidential campaign. Then, after Obama won the presidential election, he appointed Darling-Hammond as the head of his education policy transition group.

As noted in Chapter 7, Darling-Hammond had come to public attention in 1994 when she published a critical assessment of Teach for America. In the years that followed, Darling-Hammond continued to expound a version of reform that differed from that put forward by Wendy Kopp and Michelle Rhee. Rather than bring eager but untrained young teachers into the classroom, and link teachers'

---

1 Barack Obama, quoted at EdReform.blogspot.com (December 2008; December 2007; July 2008).

pay to students' test scores, Darling-Hammond said the nation should provide better training for teachers through the established colleges of education. She derided drilling for multiple-choice tests and endorsed the progressive trinity of project work, discovery learning, and critical thinking. Most of all, Darling-Hammond emphasized the importance of investing more money in the training of teachers.[2]

Obama's appointment of Darling-Hammond alarmed many reformers. *New York Times* columnist David Brooks recalled that he received "a flurry of phone calls from reform leaders nervous that Obama was about to side against them." DFER's Whitney Tilson summed up the opinion of these callers when he declared that Darling-Hammond was "influential, clever, and (while she does her best to hide it) an enemy of genuine education reform." Tilson conceded that Darling- Hammond had good intentions. "She really cares about kids, closing the achievement gap, and doing what's right to improve schools." But this made Darling- Hammond especially dangerous. "All sensible people are rightly skeptical when union bosses call for more spending and smaller class size," Tilson wrote. "Gee, what a shocker that they favor more money to more teachers." But many people were misled when "well-credentialed, well- intentioned people like Prof. Darling-Hammond" recommended reforms that would "end up costing a lot of money and won't change anything." Darling-Hammond was "a thinly disguised shill for the teachers unions. . . . Her ideas, if adopted, would likely result in much higher spending and little or no improvement in our schools." She was "about as bad as it gets in terms of education reform."[3]

---

2   Linda Darling-Hammond, "Evaluating 'No Child Left Behind,'" *The Nation* (2 May 2007); Seyward Darby, "Old School," *The New Republic* (24 December 2008).

3   David Brooks, quoted by Gerald Bracey, "The Hatchet Job on Linda-Darling Hammond," *HuffingtonPost* (4 January 2009); Whitney Tilson, quoted by Sam Dillon, "Uncertainty on Obama Education Plans," *New York Times* (14 December 2008); EdReform.blogspot.com (December 2007).

Tilson's views were not unique. Beginning with Teach for America, a network of new-guard reformers had been growing in strength and numbers, and by the time of Obama's election as president this group was ensconced in key positions almost everywhere. They had established hundreds of charter schools. They were administrators in many regular public school districts. They were legislating in state capitals and serving on the staffs of mayors and governors. They were writing position papers for public policy think tanks, and they were dispensing grants from billion-dollar philanthropies like those bearing the names of Bill and Melinda Gates and Eli and Edythe Broad. They were doing what Wendy Kopp had envisioned when she wrote her senior thesis in 1990.[4]

After receiving telephone calls and e-mails from new-guard reformers, David Brooks wrote an essay that criticized Darling-Hammond for being against school reform. The editors of the *Los Angeles Times* and the *Washington Post* did likewise, and Obama soon recognized that, as Jonathan Alter wrote in *Newsweek*, "if he chooses [as Secretary of Education] a union-backed candidate such as Linda Darling-Hammond . . . he'll have a revolt on his hands from the swelling ranks of reformers." Supporters of Darling-Hammond were left sputtering that the mainstream media did a "hatchet job" by describing the debate as "pitting education reformers against those representing the educational establishment or the status quo." Professor Bruce Fuller, of the University of California, Berkeley, explained that the debate actually pitted "professionalization advocates such as Darling-Hammond," who believed the emphasis should be on raising student achievement by helping teachers improve their instruction, against "efficiency hawks like [Joel] Klein and [Michelle] Rhee," who emphasized standardized testing and purging bad teachers.[5]

---

4   Steven Brill, "The Teachers' Unions' Last Stand," *New York Times Magazine* (17 May 2010).

5   David Brooks, "Who Will He Choose," *New York Times* (5 December

Recent Trends in School Reform

With Klein, Rhee, and Darling-Hammond representing different approaches to how schools should be reformed, President-elect Obama picked Arne Duncan, the superintendent of the Chicago Public Schools, as his Secretary of Education. In making this choice, Obama settled upon a man who had implemented much of the new guard's approach in his school district without thoroughly alienating the teachers' unions. "Mr. Obama has opted not to pick a fight," the editors of *The Economist* wrote. Unlike Klein and Rhee, who "both have infuriated unions," Duncan was a "rare reformer unions can stomach."[6]

Duncan's success was influenced by his familiarity with Chicago. His father was a psychology professor at the University of Chicago, and Duncan grew up in Hyde Park, a racially mixed, middle-class area near the university. Duncan eventually attended Harvard University, but he took one year off to work at an after school center that his mother, a social worker, had established in one of Chicago's Black neighborhoods. While working at the center Duncan did the research for his senior thesis on the aspirations and opportunities of the urban underclass.

Duncan became even more familiar with Black Chicago because he eventually grew to a height of six feet, five inches, and developed a special talent for basketball. Basketball often took Duncan into gang territory in search of games for, as Duncan explained, "If you want to get better, you have to find the best people to play with. It was pretty simple for me." The combination of playing basketball and working at his mother's center introduced Duncan to life in the ghettos. Later he would talk about "a photo of our group," taken back in the 1970s,

---

2008); "Which Way on Education," *Los Angeles Times* (12 December 2008); "A Job for a Reformer," *Washington Post* (December 2008); Jonathan Alter, "Bill Gates On Education," *Newsweek* (15 December 2008); Gerald Bracey, "The Hatchet Job on Linda Darling-Hammond"; Bruce Fuller, quoted by Sam Dillon, "Uncertainty on Obama Education Plans."

6   *The Economist* (20 December 2008).

"and some of those guys are dead. Growing up down there and having friends from the program and from the streets die when I was twelve, thirteen—that scared me. . . . As much as the success stories have shaped me and given me hope, those deaths might be an even bigger motivator. The guys who got killed were the guys who didn't finish high school. It was literally the dividing line between you live or you die. Nobody who went to college died young."[7]

After graduating from Harvard in 1987, Duncan decided to pursue a career in education rather than attend graduate school or take a job on Wall Street. But first he tried his luck at basketball. He failed in a tryout with the Boston Celtics but then moved to Australia, where he played pro ball until 1991. Then Duncan returned to Chicago, where he worked for seven years doing mentoring and administrative work at the Shakespeare Elementary School. After that, Duncan joined the staff of school superintendent Paul Vallas, whom he eventually succeeded as the chief executive officer of Chicago's public schools. As the superintendent of Chicago's schools, Duncan promoted several of the policies that new-guard reformers favored. His signature policy was to shut down schools that had a record of poor performance on standardized tests, and then reopen the schools with an entirely new staff. Duncan also opened dozens of new charter schools, and he worked to extend the school day, to provide merit pay for teachers, and to tie the teachers' evaluations to the scores that students made on standardized tests.[8]

Duncan's policies did not sit well with many teachers and their unions, but Duncan nevertheless managed to retain his reputation as someone who could work with diverse groups. In December 2008,

---

[7] Amanda Paulson and Stacy Teicher Khadaroo, "Education Secretary Arne Duncan," *Christian Science Monitor* (30 August 2010); Carlo Rotella, "Class Warrior," *The New Yorker* (1 February 2010).

[8] Ibid.

Joe Williams, the executive director of DFER, acknowledged that his group would be delighted if either Joel Klein or Michelle Rhee was appointed as Secretary of Education. But Williams sent the Obama administration a memorandum recommending Duncan. "He is the kind of guy who can work with all sorts of people with different viewpoints." In a policy paper, DFER noted that Duncan had sought the assistance of the Chicago Teachers Union in developing a performance-pay plan, and consequently enjoyed "credibility with various factions in the education policy debate and would allow President Obama to avoid publicly choosing sides in that debate."[9]

It was an exaggeration to say, as one article in the *Washington Post* did, that Duncan was "embraced by the teachers unions . . . as well as reformers." Yet Duncan did avoid antagonizing the unions while pushing for policies that, by 2008, had become the standard fare of corporate-backed school reform: charter schools, merit pay, and data-driven decision making. At the same time, Duncan made a point of *not* blaming either students or their parents. During a hearing in 2008, Duncan said he had "worked in the inner-city community for some time and had seen that parents despite whatever lack of education they had, . . . were extraordinarily interested in their children's education and in wanting something better. So before we blame parents, I think we need to be really self-critical and look in the mirror first."[10]

Duncan was not thinking of himself when he talked about looking in the mirror. He thought that when it came to student achievement, teachers mattered more than any other factor. Therefore, no reform was more crucial for closing the nation's racial and ethnic achievement gaps than improving the quality of teachers in predominantly Black

---

9 *New York Times* (16 December 2008); *Washington Post* (16 December 2008).

10 *Washington Post* (16 December 2008); Angus Davis to Rhode Island Regents (15 December 2008) at EdReform.blogspot.com (December 2008).

and Hispanic schools. President Obama agreed, saying, "the single most important factor in determining [student] achievement is not the color of their skin or where they come from. It's not who their parents are or how much money they have. It's who their teacher is."[11] "We have to identify teachers who are doing well," Obama said. "And if some teachers aren't doing a good job, they've got to go."[12]

Shortly after he became Secretary of Education, Duncan started a contest that became the most important education initiative of the Obama administration. The Race to the Top (RTTT) contest used

---

11 This statement is at odds with the findings of a vast amount of research that has been accumulating since James S. Coleman published his landmark study, *Equality of Educational Opportunity* (Washington: Government Printing Office, 1966). This research indicates that, after controlling for the socioeconomic background of students, there is very little correlation between average achievement, as measured by scores on standardized tests, and the facilities and services that schools provide. Teachers are the most important influence on student test scores inside the school but their influence is dwarfed by non-school factors, especially the native intelligence of students, parental support for education, and family income.

12 Barack Obama, speech to NEA, at USLiberals.about.com (5 July 2007); Barack Obama, quoted by Joel Klein, "In Grading Teachers, Value-added Test is Indispensable," *Houston Chronicle* (20 February 2010); Obama, quoted by Sean Olson and Hailey Heinz, "Obama Arrives in N.M.; Bad Teachers 'Have Got To Go,' President Says," *Albuquerque Journal* (28 September 2010).

When speaking more carefully, Obama said, "I always have to remind people that the biggest ingredient in school performance is the teacher. That's the biggest ingredient within a school. But the single biggest ingredient is the parent." As Richard Rothstein has noted, "There is a world of difference between claiming . . . that the single biggest factor in student success is teacher quality and claiming . . . that the single biggest school factor is teacher quality. Decades of social science research have demonstrated that differences in the quality of schools can explain about one-third of the variation in student achievement. But the other two-thirds is attributable to non-school factors." Barack Obama, quoted by Rothstein, "Statement on How to Fix Our Schools," EPI.org/publication/ib286 (14 October 2010).

a relatively modest amount of federal money ($4.5 billion) to induce states to embrace the principal tenets of the latest trends in school reform. The RTTT money initially amounted to only 1 percent of all federal, state, and local spending for education. But the promise of federal funds in a time of strapped state budgets, combined with the prestige of winning a contest, proved to be seductive. Duncan's purpose was not to fund public schools but to encourage reform in exchange for dollars.[13]

For Duncan's strategy to work, the RTTT grants had to be limited, at least during the first round, to states that embraced reform. Otherwise, laggard states would have no incentive to change. Duncan therefore announced in the spring of 2010 that there were only two winners in the first round—little Delaware (which received $107 million) and Tennessee ($502 million). Each of these states had a data system that it promised to use for matching student scores with teacher evaluations, compensation, and tenure; each offered incentives to "effective" teachers who volunteered to teach in inner-city schools; each enlisted the support of its teachers' unions; each claimed to have made progress in raising achievement and closing gaps; and each made it relatively easy to establish independent charter schools.[14]

Other states got the message. In California, Governor Arnold Schwarzenegger declared that the Obama administration "won't allow any state to compete in the Race to the Top if we have laws that restrict linking performance with teachers." The *Los Angeles Times* then published a *Consumer Reports*-like guide to education

---

13 Ezra Klein, "Race to the Top," *WashingtonPost.com* (30 March 2010); David Brooks, "Race to Sanity," *New York Times* (3 June 2010).

14 Nick Anderson and Bill Turque, "Delaware, Tennessee Win Education Awards in First Race to the Top Competition," *Washington Post* (30 March 2010); AmRen.com (26 April 2012); Amanda Paulson, "Race to the Top Winners: How Did Delaware and Tennessee Succeed," MinnPost.com (30 March 2010).

that its reporters and an educational economist had compiled. After reviewing seven years of elementary school test scores, the economist made a "value added analysis to see how much the students' test scores had improved, from one year to the next, under each of some 6,000 third-through- fifth-grade teachers. The *Times* then reported that students had made great strides under some of the teachers; but under others there was little progress. The *Times* named a few of the top and bottom teachers and said that it planned to release the rankings, by name, for all teachers.[15]

Meanwhile in New York, the state legislature learned what lay in store for those who opposed new-guard reforms. When the Obama administration first announced the availability of the RTTT funds, Duncan made it clear that states that impeded the growth of charter schools or prohibited the use of students' test scores when evaluating teachers would not fare well in the contest. Most states responded by lifting caps that limited the number of charters and by scrapping laws that barred the use of student test scores in teacher assessments. At the behest of the teachers' unions, however, the New York legislature enacted provisions that limited the expansion of charter schools. To no one's surprise, New York then failed in its request for RTTT funds.[16]

In an effort to improve its chance for RTTT money in the future, the New York legislature re- convened at the behest of Democrats for Education Reform (DFER), which "ran $4 to $5 million worth of television ads blaming the teachers union for losing the chance to win

---

15 Arnold Schwarzenegger, quoted in Robert Cruickshank, "Arne Duncan and Arnold Schwarzenegger," *Calitics* (20 August 2009); *Los Angeles Times* (15 August 2010) (the first of a series of articles on value-added assessments of teachers); David Leonhardt, "Stand and Deliver," *New York Times* (5 September 2010).

16 Charles Upton Sahm, "New York Races to the Bottom," *City Journal* (22 January 2010).

$700 million in round one." After reconvening, the legislature made an about face. It lifted its cap on charter schools (from 200 to 460), and it rescinded statutes that made it difficult to use student test scores when evaluating teachers. As a result, when the second round of RTTT grants were announced later in 2010, New York (with $700 million) became one of nine states and the District of Columbia that received $3.4 billion. These states showed "what is possible when adults come together to do the right thing for children," Duncan said. They "showed a tremendous amount of ... commitment to education reform."[17]

During the recession of 2009-2010, Duncan's Department of Education also received about $100 billion in what was called an "economic stimulus package." This money was supposed to be parceled out to all fifty states in an effort to save jobs and balance budgets. There were some who believed, however, that at least a portion of the stimulus money was also used to "provide incentive to everyone, from teachers to state officials, to think in terms of reform."[18]

School reformers were ecstatic. In one of its press releases, DFER declared that RTTT had "effected more positive change in state and local education laws and policies than any other federal education program in history." According to DFER, "the boost that the Administration's Race to the Top initiative" gave to state and local education reform efforts was "the Administration's biggest domestic policy success." "If the Administration continues to keep the bar high

---

17 Jeffrey Medina, "New York State Votes to Expand Charter schools," *New York Times* (28 May 2010); Alexander Hefner, "Teaching to the Test Does a Disservice to Learning," *Newsday* (8 October 2010); "Nine States, District of Columbia Win Second Round Race to Top Grants," *US FED News* (25 August 2010); Statement of Arne Duncan, quoted by Peter Meyer, "Assessing New York's Commissioner of Education," *Education Next* (Summer 2011).

18 Arne Duncan, quoted in "Nine States, District of Columbia Win Second Round Race to Top Grants"; Alexandra R. Moses, "$100 Billion to Education in Obama's Stimulus Package," EdUtopia.org (13 February 2009).

for Race to the Top, and stays on the path of real change by making major investments only in those states and school districts that have shown the willingness to break out of the old ways of doing things, it will mark a major turning point in U.S education policy, the effects of which will reverberate for decades."[19]

It is still too early to know how the initiatives of the Obama administration will work out. However, there already has been a good deal of debate about Duncan's policies in Chicago. President Obama has said that during Duncan's seven years as superintendent of Chicago's schools, elementary school test scores went "from 38 percent of students meeting the standards to 67 percent"—a gain of 29 percentage points. But another report found that, after adjusting for changes in tests and procedures, the students' pass rates increased by only 8 percentage points. This led education blogger Alexander Russo, who specialized in writing about Chicago schools, to conclude that the city's school system "isn't nearly as improved as many have been led to believe."[20]

Other critics also weighed in. Kenneth Saltman, a professor at DePaul University, described Duncan as a "privatizer" who labeled regular public schools as failures in order to justify opening new charters that skimmed off the highest-achieving students, "thereby widening the gap between winners and losers." Another Chicago professor, Diane Whitmore Schanzenbach of the Harris School of Public Policy Studies, said there was only limited evidence that Duncan's policies were making things better. Diane Ravitch, a prominent historian of education, characterized Duncan's statements as "teacher-bashing 'baloney'" and said that Duncan's "dramatic school

---

19   DFER statements, posted by Whitney Tilson, EdReform.blogspot.com (July 2010, January 2010).

20   Barack Obama and Alexander Russo, quoted by Gregg Toppo, "Chicago Schools Report Contradicts Obama and Duncan," *USA Today* (12 July 2009).

closings and his enthusiasm for opening charters had resulted in 'no gains.'" Ravitch, whose critique of new guard education reform will be discussed in Chapter 10, found fault with RTTT for mandating that schools evaluate teachers by their students' test scores, even though, she said, such ratings were unreliable and inaccurate. She called RTTT a "Race to Nowhere." Other critics said the contest was a "Dash for the Cash" and a "Race to the Trough."[21]

Professor Bill Ayers wrote an especially interesting critique of Duncan's policies. As noted in Chapter 1, Ayers was a radical activist who once spent several years as a fugitive from justice. But at the time of Obama's presidency, Ayers was a professor of education at the University of Illinois at Chicago and, like Arne Duncan (and Barack Obama as well) a resident of the Hyde Park district. Ayers noted that "Duncan as well as the Obama children attended the University of Chicago Laboratory Schools (as did my three sons)." He also noted that the Lab Schools, which were established by John Dewey early in the 20th century, featured a progressive or constructivist curriculum that differed markedly from the test-driven approach that Duncan and Obama favored for regular public schools. "Oh, and, not incidentally," Ayers added, the Lab Schools also had "a respected and unionized teacher corps."[22]

If these features were "good enough for the Obamas and the Duncans," Ayers wrote, they ought "to be considered an aspiration . . . to work toward for the kids on the west side of Chicago, south Los Angeles, the nation's capital, and public schools everywhere." Instead of "the relentless pounding on teachers that we are treated

---

21 Kenneth Saltman, Diane Whitmore Schanzenbach, and Diane Ravitch, quoted in Carlo Rotella, "Class Warrior," *New Yorker* (1 February 2010) 10; "New Yorker Buries the Lede in Puff Piece on Secretary Duncan," LaughterHopeSockInTheEye.wordpress.com (31 January 2010); Diane Ravitch, "Teachers Furious at Duncan," *The Daily Beast* (10 May 2011).

22 Bill Ayres, "Response to 'Class Warrior,'" *Huffington Post* (12 October 2010).

to daily," Ayers urged school reformers to heed the advice of John Dewey. As Ayers paraphrased the advice, Dewey had said, "Whatever the wisest and most privileged parents want for their children must serve as the baseline for what the broader community deems essential for all of its children."[23]

Duncan also came in for criticism from educators who took exception to the Obama administration's approach to student discipline. In 2010, Duncan announced that his department would do more than look for evidence of intentional discrimination against minority students. It would also scrutinize disciplinary policies that had a disparate impact on minority students. If the proportion of suspensions or other punishments meted out to Black or Hispanic students exceeded their proportion of the overall student enrollment, Duncan said, his department would investigate to make sure that the punishments were warranted. Implying that he believed there were no racial differences in levels of misbehavior at school, Duncan said that he personally was "deeply troubled by rising discipline rates and disparities in discipline." In 2012, Attorney General Eric Holder authorized legal actions that aimed to foster proportionality in school discipline.[24]

Many observers complained. In their book, *No Excuses* (2003), Abigail Thernstrom and Stephan Thernstrom had reported, "African-Americans are two-and-a-half times as likely to be disciplined as white students." But the Thernstroms gave readers to understand that the disparity was not due to discrimination but, rather, to the misbehavior of Black students. In their view, "a wealth of evidence

---

23 Ibid.

24 "Duncan Plans to Prod Schools of Civil Rights Laws," AllBusiness.com (9 March 2010); Mary Ann Zeh, "Obama Administration Targets 'Disparate Impact' of Discipline," *Education Week* (7 October 2010); Zeh, "Obama Administration's 'Disparate Impact' Policy Draws Criticism," *Education Week* (15 February 2011); Joseph Kay, "Eric Holder and School Discipline," AmRen.com (1 May 2012).

indicates that African-American children—and especially black boys—are far more likely than others to break school rules, disrupting their own and their classmates' education."[25]

Thus the Obama administration encountered a good deal of skepticism when it challenged "disparate impact" in disciplinary punishments. At the U. S. Commission on Civil Rights, Commissioner Todd F. Gaziano explained that the new policy placed "an extremely heavy burden on the school to justify any disparity." Steve Sailer observed, "the big, unmentioned story in American education" concerned "how institutional . . . support for teachers in maintaining discipline in the classrooms has been undermined over the decades by disparate impact worries. The Obama Administration . . . has only *increased* the persecution of schools that try to maintain order."[26]

Other observers chimed in. When the Obama administration challenged disparities in Huntsville, Alabama, one member of the county and state Republican executive committees replied, "Blacks misbehave on average more frequently than whites do." Writing in *American Renaissance*, white rights activist Jared Taylor insisted that "racial differences in suspension rates" simply reflected "differences in offense rates." Taylor thought it "contemptible . . . to pretend that there are no race differences in student behavior—and to blame 'prejudiced' teachers for differences in suspension rates."[27]

---

25 Abigail Thernstrom and Stephan Thermstron, *No Excuses*, 138.

26 Todd F. Graziano, quoted by Mary Ann Zeh, "Obama Administration's 'Disparate Impact' Policy Draws Criticism"; Steve Sailer, "PISA Forever," iSteve.blogspot.com (29 December 2010).

27 James Fulford, "The Fulford File," Vdare.com (23 October 2007; 4 March 2011); Crystal Bonvillian, "Huntsville Public Schools Still Racially Inequitable, DOJ Says," *Huntsville Times* (21 February 2011); Jared Taylor, "School Suspensions: More Official Baloney," AmRen.com (26 April 2012); Joseph Key, "Eric Holder and School Discipline," AmRen.com (1 May 2012).

Still others endorsed an argument that the Black economist Thomas Sowell had made in the past: that when government officials made it more difficult "to crack down on classroom disrupters," the officials destroyed "all the other children's education." Intervening to coddle what Sowell called "a handful of hoodlums" offset any beneficial effects of school reform. According to Sowell, Secretary Duncan and Attorney General Holder were playing "the race card . . . at the expense of the education of black students. Make no mistake about it, the black students who go to school to get an education are the main victims of the classroom disrupters whom Duncan and Holder are trying to protect."[28]

II: Comparing Test Scores: NAEP, No Child Left Behind, and PISA

Twelve times since 1971, the Department of Education and its predecessors have given math and reading tests known as the National Assessment of Educational Progress (NAEP). The tests were given to sample groups of students, and the samples were constructed so carefully that the NAEP tests came to be known as "the nation's report card." For a while the ethnic and racial achievement gaps narrowed, but then the progress stopped and since 1990 there has been some retrogression. Harvard's Professor Paul E. Peterson has charted the trends in his book *Saving Schools* (2010). The improvement among Black and Hispanic students seems to have been due to the fact that their reading improved as more schools turned to direct instruction and phonics. The desegregated schools of the post-*Brown* era may also have been better than the schools that southern Blacks had attended

---

28 Thomas Sowell, "Judicial Havoc," TownHall.com (6 July 2005); Sowell, "The Big Hoax," TownHall.com (13 March 2012).

before 1954. The retrogression since 1990 was probably influenced by two trends: a steep increase in the proportion of Black children who were born to unwed mothers, and a growing disparity in the number of children who were born to women who had, or had not, graduated from high school.[29]

The results of the NAEP tests were far from bleak. The average reading and math scores of White students improved slightly over the course of 40 years, while those of Blacks and Hispanics were well above the level of 1970 (although below the level of the mid-to-late 1980s). Despite the post-1990 slippage among non-Asian minority students, the history of American education since 1950 would be considered a success if the goal had been to improve academic achievement rather than to close gaps.

However, ever since *Brown v. Board of Education* (1954), and especially since the No Child Left Behind Act of 2001, school reformers have aimed for equalization. Therefore, reformers bemoaned the "failure" of American education. One of the most influential laments came in 1983 when a commission established by the U.S. Department of Education published *A Nation at Risk*. This report emphasized that average SAT scores had declined since about 1970, while the average scores of U.S. students also lagged behind the average scores of students in many other nations.[30]

In truth, the declines in average scores were not evidence of deterioration. The first decline resulted from a substantial increase in the number of middling students who were going to college (and therefore taking the SAT exams). The second decline was due to

---

29 Paul E, Peterson, *Saving Schools* (Cambridge: Harvard University Press, 2010), 271.

30 National Commission on Excellence in Education, *A Nation at Risk* (Washington: The Commission, 1983).

another demographic shift that transformed the pool of American students so that there were far more lower-scoring minorities in relation to Whites. In 1971, 87 percent of the students who took the NAEP tests were White or Asian, while non-Asian minorities were 12 percent. Thereafter, the proportion of Whites declined steadily until, in 2008, Whites and Asians made up only 59 percent of the test takers while the proportion of Blacks and Hispanics had increased to 40 percent.[31]

By emphasizing the importance of average scores, school reformers conveyed the impression that America's schools were in decline. At regular intervals, reformers publicized the results of tests that compared modern college applicants with the applicants of earlier generations. Then they called attention to international studies that compared the scores of American students with the scores of students from other countries. Again and again, the results were similar. The average scores of modern collegians were not as high as the scores of earlier generations of college students. And on international comparisons, the average scores of American students were in the middle range—behind the scores registered in Northeast Asia and Western Europe but ahead of the scores in most of the rest of the world. In 2009, when the Programme for International Student Assessment (PISA) tested students in 34 countries, MSNBC reported that American students were "continuing to trail behind their peers in a pack of higher performing nations. . . . Out of 34 countries assessed, the U.S. ranked 14th in reading, 17th in science, 25th in math."[32]

School reformers then spread an alarm. Chester Finn characterized the release of the PISA scores in 2010 as another

---

31 Sam Dillon, "'No Child' Law is Not Closing a Racial Gap," *New York Times* (29 April 2009).

32 Christine Armario, "Wake-up Call: U.S. Students Trail Global Leaders," MSNBC.com (7 December 2010).

"Sputnik Moment." "Sixty-three years after Sputnik caused an earthquake in American education by giving us reason to believe that the Soviet Union had surpassed us," PISA showed that other nations were "bent on surpassing us ... in education." Arne Duncan agreed. "This is an absolute wake-up call for America," Duncan said. "The results are extraordinarily challenging to us, and we have to deal with the brutal truth. We have to get much more serious about investing in education." President Obama concurred. "Our generation's Sputnik moment is back," Obama said. Now that people all over the globe were "plugged into the world economy," the nations with the most educated workers would prevail and, "as it stands right now, America is in danger of falling behind." The PISA scores seemed to confirm a point Obama had made at the outset of his presidency when he had told the Hispanic Chamber of Commerce, "despite resources that are unmatched anywhere in the world, we've let our grades slip, our schools crumble, our teacher quality fall short, and other nations outpace us."[33]

    This conventional wisdom eventually came under attack from critics who "disaggregated" the test scores. The No Child Left Behind Act of 2001 had required schools to do more than report the average of the scores their students had attained on standardized tests. Schools were also required to report the average scores of different ethnic groups and different economic classes. Then, if any group failed to make what was called "adequate yearly progress" toward parity with higher scoring groups, their school would be targeted for sanctions.

---

33 Chester E. Finn, "A Sputnik Moment for U.S. Education," *Wall Street Journal* (8 December 2010); Arne Duncan, quoted in Christine Armario, "'Wake-up Call: U.S. Students Trail Global Leaders'"; Barack Obama, quoted by Sam Dillon, "Top Test Scores from Shanghai Stun Educators," *New York Times* (7 December 2010); Steve Sailer, "Education, the Sailer Scheme, and the Bush-Obama Era," Vdare.com (15 March 2009; with a link to the transcript of Obama's talk to the Hispanic Chamber of Commerce).

Eventually, the scores on international tests were also disaggregated. When that occurred, the results confounded school reformers. In 2010, when the PISA scores were broken down by race and ethnicity, and when American students were compared with students in the countries from which the Americans' ancestors came, it turned out that Asian-American students outperformed the students in all Asian nations; that White Americans did better than students from all 37 predominantly White nations (except Finland); that U.S. Hispanics scored higher than the students of all eight Latin American countries that participated in the PISA tests; and that Black Americans outperformed the only Black country that participated, Trinidad and Tobago, and probably would have outscored any sub-Saharan African country if any had participated in the PISA testing.[34]

The major media eventually published several stories on the disaggregated PISA scores, but this was not "news" to informed observers. Five years earlier, in 2005, economist Edwin S. Rubenstein had reported that the average scores of American-born Asians and Caucasians were the second highest among twenty high-income countries tested by the Educational Testing Service (ETS). And in 2006, *New York Times* reporter Sam Dillon had noted that all American ethnic groups had improved on a battery of NAEP reading and math tests, although Dillon's emphasis had been on the persistence (and recent increase) in racial and ethnic achievement gaps.[35]

---

34 Tino Sanandaji, "The Amazing Truth about PISA Scores," Super-Economy.blogspot.com (22 December 2010); Steve Sailer, "PISA Scores Show Demography is Destiny in Education," Vdare.com (19 December 2010); Patrick J. Buchanan, "Who Owns the Future," HumanEvents.com (28 December 2010).

35 Edwin S. Rubenstein, "National Data," Vdare.com (22 December 2005); Rubenstein, "National Data," Vdare.com (27 March 2007); Sam Dillon, "Schools Slow in Closing Gaps between Races," *New York Times* (20 November 2006).

The principal disaggregators differed in some respects. One of them, economist Tino Sanandaji, emphasized the importance of non-racial factors: "language, culture, home environment, income of parents ... and social problems in the neighborhood and peer group norms ..." Sanandaji said he operated on "the assumption that there are NO RACE DIFFERENCES IN IQ, and that differences in school outcome between countries and groups are entirely due to culture..." Steve Sailer, on the other hand, believed that "human bio-diversity [HBD]" was "destiny." Sailer believed that about half of the disparity in group averages was due to genetic inheritance and that "the bottom line" for "keeping the US. globally competitive" involved fixing "the demographic trends" rather than the "endlessly-discussed need to 'fix the schools.'"[36]

Despite these differences, Sanandaji and Sailer agreed on a key point. According to Sanandaji, "the biggest myth that the media reporting of PISA scores propagates is that the American public school system is horrible." Sanandaji said it was a mistake to "assume that the cause of the disappointing American mean is the school system." "A lot more ... goes into the human capital production function than just the school system," Sanandaji wrote. "By attempting to at least correct for one of those factors, demography, we find suggestive evidence that the American school system doesn't seem to be the problem." Sailer concurred, saying that the disaggregated PISA scores discredited reformers who were "always wailing and gnashing [their] teeth about how the U.S. is doomed by the failures of the U.S. educational system relative to the rest of the world." According to Sailer, the problem was not bad schools but an increasing number of weak students.[37]

---

36 Tino Sanandaji, "The Amazing Truth about PISA Scores" (22 December 2010; comment on 23 December 2010); Steve Sailer, "Alchemists Can't Turn Lead into Gold," Vdare.com (4 May 2008); Sailer "PISA Scores Show Demography is Destiny."

37 Tino Sanandaji, "The Amazing Truth about PISA Scores," and comment (28 February 2011); Steve Sailer, "PISA Scores Show Demography Is Destiny."

Many rank-and-file readers expressed frustration in blunt language. One described school reform as "a racket" whose principal beneficiaries were "educrats." After arguing that American education was in dire states, school reformers would dun taxpayers for extra funds for costly reforms. Another commenter declared, "Our school system is sound." "If you look at the test scores of Asian American and white American kids ALONE, they stand up well (better) than the kids of ANY OTHER MAJOR COUNTRY ... Our education system is NOT broken ... The problem is elsewhere. No one just wants to admit it."[38]

Such comments were not limited to ordinary readers. Disaggregation also led to a perceptible shift in informed opinion. In 2007, Patrick J. Buchanan had written that *A Nation at Risk* had "document[ed] the deterioration of American public education." But after the results of the 2009 PISA tests were disaggregated, Buchanan concluded, "America's public schools ... are not abject failures. They are educating immigrants and their descendants to outperform the kinfolk their parents or ancestors left behind when they came to America. America's schools are improving the academic performance of all Americans above what it would have been had they not come to America."[39]

Buchanan was a conservative writer, but his conclusion was echoed by Judge Richard Posner, one of the nation's most frequently cited liberal writers. After reading the disaggregated PISA scores, Posner acknowledged, "the white and Asian kids in American schools are already doing fine, for the most part." Non-Asian minority

---

38 Jeff Williams, comment at iSteve.blogspot.com (3 January 2009); Kipper, comment at *ibid.* (20 August 2010); Susan, comment Becker-Posner-Blog.com (7 January 2011).

39 Patrick J. Buchanan, "Dumbing Down of America," Vdare.com (5 March 2007); Buchanan, "Who Owns the Future?"

students were doing poorly, on the other hand, and Posner speculated that this was due to "genetic and cultural factors"—especially "IQ" and "economic inequality."[40]

Writing in the *Richmond Times-Dispatch*, columnist David Sirota expanded on the economic aspect. "To help impoverished kids overcome comparatively steep odds," Sirota wrote, "schools in destitute areas naturally require more resources than those in rich ones." Sirota complained that "billionaire-executives-turned-education-dilettantes" ignored this reality and instead pretended "that incessant union-busting, teacher-bashing, and standardized testing represented successful school 'reforms.'"[41]

In response, some reformers acknowledged that there was not much that schools could do about either IQ or economic inequality. But they said that even if America's disaggregated average scores were good, the percentage of American students who had reached a very high level of mathematical achievement was well below the proportion in several of the world's leading industrialized nations. Nor was this due to the large numbers of Black and Hispanic students in the American sample. According to Eric Hanushek, "the diversity excuse" would not suffice. "Twenty-four countries have a larger percentage of highly accomplished students than the 8 percent achieving at that level among the U.S. white population in the class of 2009." "Even our most-advantaged students are not all that competitive."[42]

---

40 Richard Posner, "The PISA Rankings and the Role of Schools in Student Performance on Standardized Tests," Becker-Posner-Blog.com/2011/01.

41 David Sirota, "What Real Reform Looks Like," *Richmond Times-Dispatch* (15 December 2011).

42 Eric A. Hanushek, Paul E. Peterson and Ludger Woessmann, "Teaching Math to the Talented," *Education Next* (Winter, 2011); Amanda Ripley, "Your Child Left Behind," *The Atlantic* (December 2010).

Hanushek's point seemed to be reinforced in January, 2011, when NAEP reported that two-thirds of U.S. fourth-grade students failed to satisfy NAEP's standard for proficiency in science, while 70 percent of eighth- graders and 79 percent of high school seniors also fell short of this mark. Critics, however, noted that statistics could be manipulated by shifting the definition of proficiency. NAEP used the word "proficient" to describe students who would be known in common parlance as "'A' Students." To be considered proficient, fourth graders were expected to explain the benefit of an adaptation for an organism; eighth graders were asked to relate oxygen levels to atmospheric conditions at higher elevations; and high school seniors were expected to solve a design problem related to the electrical force between objects.[43]

In accounting for the relatively small proportion of "highest" achieving White students in the United States, some school reformers pointed to a documentary film of 2008, *Two Million Minutes*. The film depicted the high school experiences of three pairs of strong students—a boy and a girl from the United States, a boy and a girl from China, and a boy and a girl from India. The title of the film referred to the amount of time American students spent in high school. As depicted in the film, the Chinese and Indian students spent almost twice as much time in school and study as their American counterparts. The Americans were good students. The girl was eventually accepted as a premed student at Indiana University, and the boy received a tuition scholarship to study computer graphics at Purdue. But unlike their Chinese and Indian counterparts, who had focused almost exclusively on academic studies while they were in high school, the Americans had participated in extracurricular activities such as football, student government, the school newspaper, and socializing with friends.

---

43 Nick Anderson, "National Science Test Scores Disappoint," *Washington Post* (25 January 2011); Diane Ravitch, *Reign of Error* (New York: Alfred A. Knopf, 2013), 47-51.

Bob Compton, the producer of *Two Million Minutes*, implied that the students in China and India were putting their time to good use by concentrating on science and mathematics. But not everyone agreed. Stanford education professor David F. Labaree noted that what might be called "the informal curriculum"—learning how to interact effectively with both peers and superiors—is an important part of education. And Gary Becker, a Nobel-prize-winning economist at the University of Chicago, noted that Japan and other Asian countries typically placed "greater emphasis on rote learning and memorization than does the United States." As Becker saw it, this might account for the Asian predominance at the highest end of math scores. But Becker also noted that America was "the world leader in game-changing creativity and innovations, far above these other countries." Becker speculated that America's lead might be "related in part to the emphasis that the American education system places on creative thinking rather than memorizing . . . " Lending credence to Becker's suspicion, in the 21st century an increasing number of Asian educators began to visit American schools in search of clues as to how to increase the creativity of their students. Meanwhile, school reformers in the United States continued to call for more test preparation—for gifted students as well as for those "at risk."[44]

III: A Turn to Early Childhood Education

Given the limited success of the efforts to close the racial and ethnic achievement gaps, some observers scoffed at the prospects for school reform. Thus correspondents at AlternativeRight.com, a website that emphasized the importance of race and human bio-

---

44 David F. Labaree, *Someone Has to Fail* (Cambridge: Harvard University Press, 2010) 211-21; Gary Becker, "Implications of International Comparisons of Student Performance," Becker-Posner-Blog.com/2011/01.

diversity (HBD), found fault with reformers for giving heredity short shrift and for assuming, as one writer put it, that the problem was "largely (mostly?) cultural" and could be "fixed with enough intervention from Busybodies."[45]

Most of the contributors at *Alternative Right* (and some other webzines and publications) believed that studies of twins had established that at least 50 percent and perhaps as much as 80 percent of the variation in intelligence was due to genetic inheritance. They pointed in particular to the Minnesota Study of Identical Twins Reared Apart, which reunited separated twins from around the world. Led by Professor Thomas Bouchard, researchers at the University of Minnesota studied 62 pairs of genetically identical twins and 43 pairs of fraternal twins, many of whom had not seen each other since infancy. Many of the twins had been reared in strikingly different circumstances. In one extreme case, one twin had been reared as a Nazi in the Sudetenland and the other as a Jew in Trinidad. Nevertheless, these twins shared a great many traits and eccentricities. The same was true of most other identical twins. In fact, identical twins reared apart from one another turned out to be much more similar than fraternal twins reared in the same family. The similarity was especially great in terms of measured IQ. And on many measures of personality and temperament, identical twins reared apart were almost as similar as identical twins reared together. To proponents of HBD, the explanation was obvious: the twins' genes had guided their development.[46]

Adoption studies also pointed to the importance of heredity. One especially well regarded project in Texas found "little similarity between

---

[45] Richard B. Spencer, "Did Richard Posner Discover HBD?" AlternativeRight. com (2 March 2011) comments by "Phaedon" and "fxem."

[46] T. J. Bouchard et al., "Sources of Human Psychological Differences: The Minnesota Study of Identical Twins Reared Apart," *Science* 250 (12 October 1990), 223-28.

adopted children and their siblings and greater similarity between adopted children and their biological parents." Together, the twins and adoption studies seemed to show that heredity was largely (although not completely) responsible for human differences. In their best-selling book *Freakonomics*, Steven Levitt and Stephen Dubner summed up the conventional wisdom of those familiar with the research: "Studies have shown that a child's academic abilities are far more influenced by the IQs of his biological parents than the IQs of his adoptive parents." In measured academic prose, psychologist Arthur Jensen explained that, when it came to accounting for the 15 point IQ gap in the racial averages for Whites and Blacks, "The preponderance of the evidence is ... less consistent with a strictly environmental hypothesis than with a genetic hypothesis, which, of course, does not exclude the influence of environment or its interaction with genetic factors."[47]

Yet the racial implications of genetic or "hereditarian" thinking placed HBD beyond the pale for most mainstream Americans. Most school reformers continued to say that all would be well if the curriculum was improved, if bad teachers were weeded out, and good teachers were rewarded with extra pay. When the achievement gaps persisted into the 21st century, however, some reformers shifted their approach, de-emphasized the reform of K-12 schools, and stressed the importance of early childhood education.

---

47 J. M. Horn et al., "Intellectual Resemblance among Adoptive and Biological Relatives: The Texas Adoption Project," *Behavior Genetics* 9 (1979) 177-207; Steven D. Levitt and Stephen J. Dubner, *Freakonomics* (New York: William Morrow, 2005) 171. Also see Sandra Scarr and Richard A. Weinberg, "IQ Test Performance of Black Children adopted by White Families," *American Psychologist* 31 (1976) 726-739; R. A. Weinberg, S. Scarr, and I. D. Waldman, "The Minnesota Transracial Adoption Study: A Follow-up of IQ Test Performance," *Intelligence* 16 (1992), 117-135; M Levin, "Comment on Minnesota Transracial Adoption Study," *Intelligence* 19 (1994) 13-20; Richard Lynn, "Some Reinterpretations of the Minnesota Transracial Adoption Study," *Intelligence* 19 (1994) 21-27; Arthur Jensen, quoted by Steve Sailer, "A King Among Men," Vdare.com (1 December 2002).

Judge Richard Posner was a case in point. After speculating that IQ had played "a significant role in America's mediocre showing on the PISA tests," Posner conceded that "improvements in secondary school education" were "unlikely to have dramatic effects." He thought that "black and Hispanic kids may not do much better until their early childhood environment is improved to the point at which black and Hispanic IQs are raised significantly." Other observers experienced a similar epiphany and, during the first decade of the 21st century, the pendulum of school reform began to swing away from emphasis on K-12 schools and toward concern for early childhood education. Some early childhood reformers focused on extending formal education downward to include the two years before kindergarten, when children are three- or four-years old. Others stressed the importance of the time from birth to age three.[48]

The emphasis on early childhood education received a special boost from James J. Heckman, a Nobel Prize-winning economist at the University of Chicago. One of Heckman's econometric models measured the benefits of early childhood education by comparing the life histories of youngsters who either did or did not receive such education. After comparing the recipients' rate of employment, welfare dependency, criminal behavior, and incarceration with that of a control group, Heckman concluded that the economic benefits of early education were substantial. "Rates of return are 15 % to 17 %. The benefit-cost ratio is eight to one."[49]

---

48 Richard Posner," Implications of International Comparisons of Student Performance," Becker-Posner Blog, Becker-Posner-Blog.com/2011/01; Arne Duncan, quoted *ibid*.

49 James J. Heckman, "Catch 'em Young," *Wall Street Journal* (10 January 2006). Much of Heckman's work was published in scholarly journals, but in 2003 he summarized his views in an accessible book co-authored with Alan. B Krueger, *Inequality in America* (Cambridge: The MIT Press, 2003).

Heckman based this conclusion on studies of a few exemplary programs that had targeted disadvantaged youths and continued to study them until they were adults. One of these programs was the Perry Preschool in Ypsilanti, Michigan. From 1962 to 1967, Perry provided three-year old disadvantaged Black children with two and a half hours of daily preschool. Perry also placed teachers with advanced degrees in the children's homes, where the teachers spent ninety minutes each week instructing the Perry parents with respect to child rearing. The Perry students were then compared with a control group at ages 14, 15, 19, 27, and 40. The Abecedarian Program in Chapel Hill, North Carolina, was another exemplary program. Abecedarian enrolled children at the age of three to four months and continued with substantial intervention up to age eight.[50]

After noting that the Perry and Abecedarian children did better than similar children who did not receive enriched early childhood education, Heckman concluded that academic problems and achievement gaps stemmed from "the lack of stimulation afforded young children." As Heckman saw it, families were "the major source of inequality in American social and economic life." Heckman recognized that "American society has been reluctant to intervene in family life, especially in the early years," but he thought "paternalistic interventions in the early life of children in certain dysfunctional families" were needed to close the achievement gaps. Such intervention had become especially urgent due to "the growth in single-parent families"—especially in Black America, where about 70 percent of the babies were born out of wedlock. Because "an increasing fraction of all U.S. children are growing up in adverse environments," Heckman wrote, "the best way to improve schools is to improve the students sent to them." And students could be improved by reforming the way parents reared their children.[51]

---

50 James Heckman, "Catch 'em Young"; James J. Heckman and Alan B. Krueger, *Inequality in America*, 24-30, 163-172.

51 James J. Heckman, "Catch 'em Young"; Heckman and Alan B. Krueger,

If reformers were to succeed in narrowing the racial and ethnic achievement gaps, Heckman said, the reformers should "catch 'em young." They should recognize that the traditional methods of school reform came too late to make much difference. Once students started school, Heckman wrote, "test scores across socioeconomic groups are stable, suggesting that later schooling has little effect in reducing or widening the gaps that appear before students enter school." At the age 5 and 6, when most students began kindergarten and first grade, the average Black student already scored below 85 percent of the Whites on tests of school readiness, and the proportion of African-Americans scoring below the White median hardly budged over the course of the next twelve years. Since "a major finding from the research literature" was that intractable gaps emerged even before students started school, Heckman concluded that "schools and school quality contribute little to the emergence of test-score gaps among children." Heckman did not say that all essential aptitudes were determined by age three. Yet because he was an economist, Heckman wanted to go where the return was highest, and he thought the payoff from "early interventions targeted toward disadvantaged children" was greater than the return from programs for older students.[52]

In addition to touting the benefits of early childhood education, Heckman disparaged the quality of parenting in Black and Hispanic America. "The simple fact is that [Black and Hispanic children] typically have not received the massive doses of cultural enrichment that children from middle-class and upper-class families have," he wrote. One of Heckman's articles included a picture that purported to show that the brain of a three-year-old child who suffered parental neglect was only half the size of an average three-year-old. Another

---

Inequality in America, 148, 163-165, 207.

52 James J. Heckman, "Invest in the Very Young" (Chicago: Ounce of Prevention Fund and University of Chicago Harris School of Public Policy Studies, 2000), 5; Heckman and Alan B. Krueger, *Inequality in America*, 337; Heckman, "Catch 'em Young."

article indicted Black parents for not emphasizing the importance of conscientiousness and empathy. According to Heckman, minority parents did not talk enough with their children; and when these parents did speak, they were more likely to admonish than to nurture. To compensate for these deficiencies, Heckman endorsed an array of expensive government policies and interventions "to improve the cognitive and socio-emotional skills of disadvantaged children."[53]

University of Michigan psychologist Richard E. Nisbett concurred. Like Heckman, Nisbett maintained that most "school-age interventions" had "only modest effects on student achievement." Nisbett also reported that the research on the Perry Preschool and the Abecedarian Program, as well as studies of a similar program in Milwaukee, showed that early childhood education could accomplish a great deal.[54] Nisbett's book of 2009, *Intelligence and How to Get It*, also challenged the view that "intelligence and academic talent are substantially under genetic control." Nisbett acknowledged that "many if not most experts on intelligence" were "hereditarians." He knew that a generation of studies of twins and adopted children had led many experts to conclude that between half and three-quarters of the ethnic differences in IQ and academic achievement were due to heredity. Nevertheless, Nisbett insisted that "the accumulated evidence of research, much of it quite recent, provides good reason for being far more optimistic about the possibilities of actually improving the intelligence of individuals [and] groups . . . than was thought by most experts even a few years ago."[55]

---

53 James J. Heckman, "Promoting Social Mobility," *Boston Review* (September/October 2012); Heckman, Lex Borghans, Angela Lee Duckworth and Bas ter Weel, "The Economics and Psychology of Personality Traits," Working Paper 13810, NBER.org/papers/w13810.

54 Richard E. Nisbett, *Intelligence and How to Get It* (New York: W. W. Norton, 2009), 136, 121-141.

55 Ibid., 1, 2 and *passim*.

In addition to mentioning the success of youngsters who had attended exemplary preschools, Nisbett also cited studies that indicated that the IQs of adopted children increased substantially if they were reared by upscale White parents. Nisbett knew that earlier studies of adopted children had led many scholars to conclude that intelligence was relatively immune to changes in environment. Nisbett, however, criticized, the earlier studies, on the ground that the environment of adopted children did not change much, since the children usually moved from one middle-class family to another. Instead, Nisbett placed great emphasis on eight recent studies that compared poor children who were adopted by well-to-do parents with similar poor children who were not adopted. According to Nisbett, the IQs of the adopted kids increased by an impressive 12 to 18 points. Nisbett made much of these studies because they supposedly demonstrated not just the importance of home environments but also suggested that preschool programs could boost the intelligence of disadvantaged children, if the programs simulated the practices of upscale adoptive families. Nisbett consequently went into detail about how differences in parenting styles could affect a child's intelligence.[56]

Along with these recent adoption studies, two books were especially influential in preparing the way for a new emphasis on early childhood education. One was *Meaningful Differences in the Everyday Experience of Young American Children* (1995), by University of Kansas psychologists Betty Hart and Todd Risley. This book maintained that by the time children were four years old, youngsters from disadvantaged families had been exposed to far fewer spoken words than children from professional families. According to Hart and Risley, IQ and academic achievement correlated with the amount and sort of language that young children heard. Hart and Risley also reported that hearing

---

56 Ibid., 21-38 and *passim*; David L. Kirp, "After the Bell Curve," *New York Times* (23 July 2006).

a relatively large number of criticisms had a negative effect on IQ, and that hearing more praise, conversation, and complex sentences had a positive effect. Hart and Risley said that children's experience with language mattered more than socio-economic status, more than race, more than anything else that they measured.[57]

Another influential study came from California, where anthropologist Annette Lareau found significant differences in the child rearing approaches of working- and middle-class parents. In the not-so-distant past, most parents in both groups had been at once authoritative and *laissez-faire*. They had told their children what to do rather than try to persuade them with reasoning, but they had also allowed for a great deal of freedom when it came to friends and social activities, proverbially telling their children to "go out and play, but be home for dinner." Beginning in the 1960s, however, middle-class childrearing was characterized by more "discussions between parents and children," and parents were more careful in choosing their children's playmates. Middle-class parents also engaged in a great deal of "concerted cultivation"—stocking their homes with books, planning family outings to concert halls and museums, and pushing their children toward extra-curricular activities that would enhance a college application. By way of contrast, Lareau reported that working-class parents continued to allow their children to develop "naturally." Working-class parents centered their social lives on interacting with relatives "who typically live close by"; and they gave their children "long stretches of leisure time," during which the youngsters were allowed to play with whatever children lived nearby. Lareau did not say that one approach was morally superior to the other, but she maintained that the "cultural logic" of the approach that prevailed among working-class and poor families was "out of synch" with what the children needed to do well in school. Like Hart and

---

57 Betty Hart and Todd Risley, *Meaningful Differences in the Everyday Experience of Young American Children* (Baltimore: P. H. Brookes, 1995).

Risley, and like Heckman and Nisbett, Lareau attributed the gaps in academic achievement to lack of stimulation at home.[58]

While rejecting the idea that the races of humanity differed inherently in reasoning power and imagination, Richard Nisbett embraced the theory that there was something wrong with the child rearing practices of African-Americans. He attributed some of the problem to socio- economic status (SES). "Compared with higher-SES parents, lower-SES parents are less likely to be warm and supportive of their children and are more likely to punish infractions harshly." "The lower-SES child is likely to have peers who are on average less intellectually stimulating than those available to higher-SES children." According to Nisbett, the environment in single-parent families was especially bleak."[59]

In addition to SES-related problems, Nisbett maintained that even middle-class Blacks reared their children "in ways that are less likely to encourage high IQ scores." Compared with Whites "of comparable social and economic circumstances," Blacks did not "interact verbally with their children." They were less likely to provide books or educational toys. They were "more likely to frown and scowl." They did not encourage children to make "problem-solving efforts." Nisbett reported that "the IQs of black and interracial children raised by white adoptive parents were 13 points higher than those of black and interracial children raised by black adoptive parents."[60]

Nisbett softened the criticism by insisting, "Genes account for none of the difference in IQ between blacks and whites." Environmental factors, especially dysfunctional child rearing

---

58 Annette Lareau, *Unequal Childhoods* (Berkeley: University of California Press, 2003) 1-3 and *passim*.

59 Richard E. Nisbett, *Intelligence and How to Get It*, 82, 83, 101.

60 *Ibid.*, 111-118.

practices, "plausibly account for all of it." "Aspects of black culture—at every social-class level—are less likely to promote cognitive performance compared with white culture." Despite his efforts to soften the criticism, Nisbett recognized that he was saying things that might "bring the wrath of people down on me. I'm saying that working-class parents need to do some stuff differently. I'm saying black parents need to do some stuff differently."[61]

Had Nisbett published his book in 1969 instead of 2009, he would have been raked with criticism. The conventional wisdom among reformers of the 1960s and 1970s held that underclass African-American students knew they belonged to a despised group and therefore quickly turned against people who manifested even a semblance of patronizing condescension. It was said that students in the inner cities would not cooperate with anyone who considered their values deviant or inferior. The conventional wisdom therefore posited that middle-class teachers were doomed to fail unless they recognized and built upon cultural strengths that already existed in the Black community. Writing in the *Harvard Educational Review* in 1970, psychologists Stephen S. Baratz and Joan C. Baratz maintained, "failure to recognize and utilize existing cultural forms of the lower-class Negro community . . . not only dooms intervention programs such as Head Start to failure, but also constitutes a form of institutional racism." Another psychologist, Frank Riessman, elaborated on this point in a widely-read book, *The Culturally Deprived Child* (1962). Education writer Herbert Kohl summed up this explanation in an influential essay, "I Won't Learn from You." According to Kohl, disadvantaged minority students would shut down and refuse to learn if they sensed that they were being taught in ways that somehow dishonored their culture.[62]

---

61 Ibid., Richard E. Nisbett, quoted in Carey Goldberg, "Get Smart," *Boston Globe* (9 March 2009).

62 Stephen S. Baratz and Joan C. Baratz, "Early Childhood Intervention: The

The Baratzes, Riessman, and Kohl criticized scholars who had seized upon a "social pathology model as a replacement for the genetic inferiority model." They scoffed at "the inadequate mother hypothesis" as surely as they disdained "inherently low IQ" as an explanation for the relatively low scores that Black children made on academic tests. They rejected the theory that Blacks were doing poorly in school because their mothers' vocabularies were limited, because lower-class Black mothers were sullen and authoritarian when dealing with their children, because these mothers did not provide their children with enough intellectual stimulation. The Baratzes, Riessman, and Kohl regarded the social pathology rationale as a way of blaming Black victims rather than White racism. They rejected proposals to "take the [inner-city Black] child completely out of the home . . . for the purpose of providing him with the experiences unavailable to him during his first three years of life."[63]

Richard Nisbett expected to be criticized for resurrecting the social pathology rationale in the twenty-first century. "I've said some things that I really thought would bring the wrath of people onto me," Nisbett told one reporter. Nisbett expected his fellow social scientists to take exception to a narrative that blamed Black families for the shortcomings of Black students. But such criticism did not surface—at least not in the mainstream media—when Nisbett's book was published in 2009. Instead, a number of influential activists, scholars, and education writers embraced Nisbett's approach. For many liberal reformers, it became a new orthodoxy. The *New York Times* published a précis of *Intelligence and How to Get It*, and *Times'*

Social Science Base for Institutional Racism," *Harvard Educational Review* 40 (Winter 1970) 29; Frank Riessman, *The Culturally Deprived Child* (New York: Harper and Row, 1968). Kohl's essay was later reprinted in his book, *I Won't Learn from You* (Minneapolis: Milkweed Editions, 1991); *The Nation* 254 (6 April 1992), 457.

63 Stephen S. Baratz and Joan C. Baratz, "Early Childhood Intervention," 32, 36, 44.

columnists Jim Holt and Nicholas Kristof weighed in with special applause. It was better to attribute the achievement gaps to bad child rearing practices than to inherent intelligence, Kristof explained: "If intelligence were deeply encoded in our genes, that would lead to the depressing conclusion that neither schooling nor antipoverty programs can accomplish much."[64]

Accounting for the scarcity of mainstream criticism necessarily involves some speculation. One possibility is that by 2009, when *Intelligence and How to Get It* was published, so many academics were turning toward genetic explanations of racial differences in average IQ that egalitarians were reluctant to criticize Nisbett, since Nisbett rejected the idea that genetic variation played a role in group differences in IQ scores. In 1988, when more than 600 experts in the field of psychological measurement had been surveyed, most of the experts had asserted that IQ tests measured the ability to reason abstractly. Most experts thought that heredity accounted for much of the variation within families and within racial groups. And most believed that the IQ gap between Blacks and Whites was due in part to genetic inheritance.[65]

During the first decade of the twenty-first century, new evidence from biology reinforced that from psychology. One story *New York Times* reported that "genetic information" was "slipping out of the laboratory and ... carrying with it the inescapable message that people of different races have different DNA." "There are clear differences between people of different continental ancestries," said Marcus W. Feldman, a professor of biological sciences at Stanford. The differences

---

64 Richard Nisbett, quoted by Carey Goldberg, "Get Smart"; Nisbett, "All Brains Are the Same Color," *New York Times* (9 September 2007); Jim Holt, "Get Smart," *New York Times* (29 March 2009); Nicholas D. Kristof, "How to Raise Our I.Q.," *New York Times* (16 April 2009).

65 Mark Snyderman and Stanley Rothman, *The IQ Controversy* (New Brunswick: Transaction Publishers, 1988).

apparently arose during the tens of thousands of years that human populations adapted to different climes on separate continents, after their ancestors had dispersed from humanity's birthplace in Africa. As they became aware of the different distributions of DNA, scientists increasingly questioned the egalitarian assumption that intelligence was distributed equally among groups that had evolved separately.[66]

Whatever the reason, most liberals of 2009 declined to criticize Nisbett's updated version of "the inadequate mother thesis." In Harlem, the noted Black educator, Geoffrey Canada, was so favorably impressed by Nisbett's approach that Canada supplemented a KIPP-style curriculum of preparing students for standardized tests with what one observer called "a ferocious commitment to middle-class values" and an array of health and psychological services. One of these services was a nine-week program that taught young people the latest lessons on child rearing. Funded by grants from several foundations, the Harlem Children's Zone encouraged parents to replace "physical punishment with a system of rules enforced by talk, negotiation, rewards, the withdrawal of privileges, and time outs." High school students and young parents were told that their children would suffer if they were exposed to "the typical experience of children in Harlem—few books, too much TV, insufficient language exposure."[67]

Writing in the *New York Times*, columnist David Brooks called the Harlem Children's Zone a "miracle." According to Brooks, this combination of KIPP and early childhood education was "the equivalent of curing cancer for these kids." It was "amazing." "It eliminated the black-white achievement gap." In another article for the *Times*, journalist James Traub conceded that in most places

---

66 Amy Harmon, "In DNA Era, New Worries about Prejudice," *New York Times* (11 November 2007).

67 David Brooks, "The Harlem Miracle," *New York Times* (8 May 2009); Paul Tough, *Whatever It Takes* (Boston: Houghton Miflin, 2008), 80, 79.

the "accomplishments of [school] reform" had been "modest." But, according to Traub, that was because of bad parenting practices. Black children grew up "in a world without books or even stimulating games." This was true even of middle-class children, for there was a significant "difference in child-rearing habits and peer culture between the black and white middle classes." As Traub saw it, schools could not solve the problem. The only hope was "a kind of . . . paternalism in which mothers are expected to yield up their children to wise professionals."[68]

Other influential scholars also stressed the need for more early childhood education. In 2011, Ronald Ferguson, a Black professor at Harvard, reported that "black parents on average are not as academically oriented in raising their children as whites." In one wealthy suburb that Ferguson surveyed, "40 percent of blacks owned 100 or more books, compared with 80 percent of whites. In first grade, the percentage of black and white parents reading to their children daily was about the same; but by fifth grade, 60 to 70 percent of whites still read daily to their children [!], compared with 30 percent to 40 percent of blacks."[69]

Thomas J. Espenshade, a White professor at Princeton, summed up an emerging consensus in an essay he published in the *New York Times* in 2012. Racial and ethnic achievement gaps had persisted "despite the No Child Left Behind law, the Race to the Top initiative and endless debate over K-12 school reforms," Espenshade noted; and this led Espenshade to conclude that there was all the more reason for "an expansion of early-childhood education" and for increased university research on "the impact of factors like diet and nutrition [and] the amount of time parents talk and read with

---

68 David Brooks, "The Harlem Miracle"; James Traub, "What No School Can Do," *New York Times* (16 January 2000).

69 Ronald Ferguson quoted by Michael Winerip, "Closing the Achievement Gap without Widening a Racial One," *New York Times* (14 February 2011).

their kids." Bruce Perry, a child psychiatrist at the Baylor College of Medicine, concurred, saying, "We need to change our child rearing practices. We need to change the malignant and destructive view that children are the property of their biological parents. Human beings evolved not as individuals, but as communities.... Children *belong* to the community."[70]

Traub, Ferguson, Espenshade, and Perry were liberals, but some conservatives expressed similar opinions. "To compensate for conversational, educational, and cognitive shortfalls at home," Chester E. Finn wrote, "boys and girls from acutely deprived environments need more intensive instruction . . . Their parents . . . need help." According to Finn, preschool education could give "needy kids a boost up the ladder of educational (and later-life) success by narrowing or eradicating the achievement gaps that now trap far too many of them on the lower rungs." To do this, preschool programs should be "intensive, tightly targeted . . . [and] means tested." They should start "early in a child's life, perhaps even before birth," and the yearly expenditure per pupil should be at least $35,000.[71]

There were some skeptics. Robert Weissberg, a professor at the University of Illinois, opined that those who attributed the racial and ethnic achievement gaps to the influence of faulty childrearing had succumbed to "a public policy version of the gambler's fallacy." Weissberg noted that after repeatedly losing on wagers, some gamblers mistakenly believed that they were due for a success that would wipe

---

70 Thomas J. Espenshade, "Moving Beyond Affirmative Action," *New York Times* (4 October 2012); Bruce Perry, quoted by John T. Bruer, *The Myth of the First Three Years* (New York: The Free Press, 1999) 15.

71 Chester E. Finn, Jr., *Reroute the Preschool Juggernaut* (Stanford: Hoover Institution Press, 2009) 86-88, 90, 7. $35,000 is my estimate, based on splitting the difference between the annual expenses of two widely-lauded preschool programs, the Perry Preschool in Ypsilante, Michigan, and the Abecedarian Program in Chapel Hill, as calculated by Bruce Fuller, *Standardized Childhood* (Stanford: Stanford University Press, 2007), 192, 195.

out all previous losses. So it was also with desperate gap closers. Despite the failure of previous school reforms, they refused to concede the futility of their enterprise and instead came to think that poor Black children were victims of dysfunctional family environments. They believed that racial and ethnic achievement gaps could be closed, if only reformers could monitor the ways that Black and Hispanic parents interacted with their two-, three- and four-year olds. The key to successful school reform was teaching non-Asian minority parents how to talk to their children, how to enforce discipline, and how to think and develop a sense of autonomy.[72]

Steve Sailer seconded Weissberg's view. After noting that "the racial gap is measurable *two years before children enter kindergarten,*" Sailer asked, "how [could] schooling, important as it is, ever be a cure-all for inequality." Sailer attributed the reformers' "susceptibility to the latest cult craze" to "the dogma of racial equality." "Since only evil people suspect that nature as well as nurture plays a role in the black-white gap," Sailer wrote with a touch of sarcasm, it followed that Black children must be "victims of their family environments, and thus should be . . . kept away from their families and raised by whites and middle-class blacks." Sailer said "out loud" what he surmised the early-childhood reformers were thinking: that school reformers should spend "a lot of government money taking poor black children away from their crack-addict mothers and their moms' knucklehead ex-con boyfriends and have them raised by nice white ladies for as much of each 24 hour cycle as possible."[73]

---

72 Robert Weissberg, "Why Biology is the Friend of Liberty," Vdare.com (27 January 2011).

73 Steve Sailer, "Bill Gates Admits He's Blown $2 Billion on Ayers Brothers Small Schools Boondoggle," iSteve.blogspot.com (5 February 2009); Sailer, "The Michigan Mess," Vdare.com (29 June 2003); Steve Sailer, "Bill Gates Admits He's Blown $2 Billion on Ayers Brothers Small Schools Boondoggle"; Sailer, "Obama's Universal Preschool Push," iSteve.blogspot.com (11 May 2009); Sailer, "The Test Score Gap," Vdare.com (7 October 2012).

In his book *Maximizing Intelligence* (2003), George Mason University professor David J. Armor eschewed inflammatory rhetoric but similarly maintained that disadvantaged Black and Hispanic infants and young children would benefit if their mothers gave them up for several hours of daily child care. Armor, however, recognized that most mothers did not wish to be separated "from their infant and toddler children for substantial periods of time." He doubted that it would be possible to convince these parents that they should let others become substitute parents.[74]

Indeed, many parents were uneasy about proposals that would place very young children in child care for long periods of time. This was evident in 2006 when voters in California rejected an initiative proposal to expand the public schools downward to provide prekindergarten for three- and four-year-old children. Elsewhere, however, the campaign for prekindergarten education gained momentum. Between 2004 and 2009, the nationwide enrollment of four year olds in state-funded prekindergartens increased by 40 percent. And during his 2008 campaign for the presidency, Barack Obama called for increased spending for both early childhood education for infants and toddlers and pre-K programs for three- and four-year olds. The editors of *Education Week* calculated that Obama's proposals would add about $30 billion per year in additional spending for education. The Democratic Party platform of 2008 promised to "make quality, affordable early childhood care and education available to every American child from the day he or she is born."[75]

---

74 David J. Armor, *Maximizing Intelligence* (New Brunswick: Transaction Publishers, 2003), 192, 171.

75 Lawrence J. Schweinart, "Creating the Best Kindergartens," in Editors of Education Week, *The Obama Education Plan* (San Francisco: Jossey-Bass, 2009) 21; Editors of Education Week, *The Obama Education Plan*, vii; Democratic Platform, quoted by Chester E. Finn, *Reroute the Preschool Juggernaut*, 1.

"If we close the achievement gap," Obama said, "then a big chunk of economic inequality in this society is diminished." With that in mind, candidate Obama promised to spend an additional $10 billion for early childhood education, an amount that would be the largest new federal initiative for young children since Head Start began in 1965. He also promised to establish "Promise Neighborhood Grants" that would encourage low-income communities to establish parenting programs. After he became president in 2009, Obama directed an additional $4 billion in Recovery Act funds for Head Start and Early Head Start, and he promised that the federal budget for 2010 would provide another "significant increase in these programs." "We know what a difference early childhood programs make in the lives of our kids," Obama said.[76]

Obama's support for early childhood and prekindergarten programs derived, at least in part, from his friendship with Irving B. Harris, a Chicago philanthropist who had helped finance Obama's campaigns for the Illinois State Senate. Harris has been called "the godfather of early childhood education in Chicago." In Chicago, Harris and his foundation, the Ounce of Prevention Fund, have played a leading role in pushing for early childhood education.[77]

Throughout the country, as in Chicago, earnest foundations, government officials, and university professors have led the campaigns for early childhood and pre-K programs. One of the most influential of the elite advocacy groups was "Pre-K Now," an organization funded by the Pew Charitable Trusts. Its theme was "prekindergarten for *all.*" While Pew spread this message nationwide, "Preschool California,"

---

76 Barack Obama, quoted by Cynthia Gordy, *Essence* (17 August 2009), available at AmRen.com (18 August 2009); Sam Dillon, "Obama Pledge Stirs Hope in Early Education," *New York Times* (17 December 2008); Obama, speech in Manchester, New Hampshire (20 November 2007) in Editors of Education Week, *The Obama Education Plan*, 3.

77 David L. Kirp, *The Sandbox Investment* (Cambridge: Harvard University Press, 2007), 58.

funded by the Packard Foundation, focused on that state, and the Gates Foundation supported a like-minded campaign, "Thrive by Five," in Washington state. The oil and banking entrepreneur George Kaiser pushed for a similar program in Oklahoma, and investor Warren Buffet's daughter, Susan, directed the Buffet Early Childhood Fund. Taken together, these organizations committed many millions of dollars to support early childhood and pre-K education.[78]

Elite reformers found some grass roots support, especially from teachers' unions, which recognized that their membership would swell if two more grades were added to the elementary school curriculum. Feminism also played a role in fostering the early childhood movement. When large numbers of middle-class mothers joined the workforce, there was an increased demand for childcare centers and early childhood education. Welfare reform also forced many mothers out of the home and into the workplace.

Nevertheless, "universal pre-K " proved to be controversial. In recent years, programs have been enacted in states where elite foundations and the teachers' unions have great influence, but the policy was rejected when an initiative proposal was submitted to California voters in 2006. In explaining this defeat, proponents of early childhood and pre-K education stressed that well-to-do people feared they would be "taxed into oblivion"—and therefore mounted a campaign of disinformation. According to David L. Kirp, a professor of public policy at the University of California, Berkeley, wealthy entrepreneurs "went on TV, reinforcing people's cynicism about any government program." Critics also said the California proposal would amount to "a giveaway to well-off parents who could easily afford to pay the preschool tuition." According to Michael Boskin, an economist at the Hoover Institution, the plan would "hand out subsidies to middle-income and rich people to pay for services they

---

78 Ibid., passim.

are already getting." These subsidies would be financed by "huge tax increases on small businesses and successful entrepreneurs."[79]

There were additional concerns. For some Blacks and Hispanics, the phrase *"universal* pre-K " raised the specter of *requiring* families to send their children to schools where teachers from the White/Anglo middle class would be in charge. This concern was sparked by provisions such as one, later approved by the House of Representatives, to authorize $8 billion for an Early Learning Challenge Program. The funds would go to local programs that were deemed "excellent"—with excellence measured by the proportion of teachers who had received college degrees in early childhood education. When asked why many parents preferred day care in their neighborhoods to pre-K centers situated in an elementary school, one Hispanic activist in California explained that the people who were already providing day care in Hispanic neighborhoods were "98 percent . . . Latina" and "really conscious of the children's culture."[80]

Although Berkeley's professor Kirp emphasized the fears and resentments of taxpayers as key to the defeat of universal pre-K in California, another Berkeley professor, sociologist Bruce Fuller, noted

---

79 Ben Qustin, quoted by David Kirp, *The Sandbox Investment*, 214; Kirp, *The Sandbox Investment*, 216; Michael Boskin, "Off and Running: Quit Taxing the Rich to Fund Your Pet Projects," *Los Angeles Times* (28 May 2006).

80 *Wilmington News Journal* (28 September 2009); Bruce Fuller, *Standardized Childhood*, 186-187. In the spring of 2011, the Obama administration appropriated $500 million for an early-childhood counterpart to its Race to the Top Competition. Taking its cue from RTT, the Early Learning Challenge program (ELC) would award funds to states with the best plans to improve children's readiness for school. The ELC established a Quality Rating and Improvement System (QRIS), and one of the standards by which competing states would be judged was whether the states required pre-school teachers to have degrees in early childhood education. See Sara Mead, "Obama's Education Legacy for America's Youngest Kids," *The New Republic* (3 December 2011).

that many African-Americans and Hispanics feared that universal pre-K would undermine their sense of ethnic identity, ethnic community, and ethnic pride. According to Fuller, these African-Americans and Hispanics wanted their young children to be cared for close to home, either by relatives or by friends in their neighborhood. When offered a choice, African-American and Hispanic parents often preferred home-based providers and smaller organizations. They did not want what one of them called "a straight middle-class system." Rather than emulate the child rearing style of upper- middle-class Caucasian families, they wanted their offspring to be reared "with an eye toward their own cultural and linguistic community."[81]

African-American and Hispanic parents understood that in the modern world, examinations were regularly given to K-12 students. But many of them resisted demands to extend the emphasis on cognitive development downward into the prekindergarten years. Ronald Ferguson, a Black professor at Harvard, expressed the opinion of many parents when he said, "Black folks don't want white folks coming into their communities and saying, 'You ought to be more like us.'"[82]

At one time, progressive reformers themselves had favored a sort of informal, community- based socialization that many African-Americans and Hispanics preferred. Progressives had once embraced the theories of French psychologist Jean Piaget, who had maintained that very young children should be allowed to develop at their own pace. As Piaget saw it, preschool children should not be required to sit passively while being instructed by adults. They should engage in playful activities. Skilled adults might informally channel this play toward school readiness, but the emphasis should not be on formal teaching or on preparation for standardized tests.

---

81 Bruce Fuller, *Standardized Childhood*, 141, 33 and *passim*.

82 Ronald Ferguson, quoted by Abigail Thernstrom and Stephen Thernstrom, *No Excuses*, 137.

In the first decade of the 21st century, however, as the new-guard school reform movement focused on test scores and achievement gaps, direct instruction seeped down into the preschools. The emphasis shifted toward what Professor Fuller called the "academic *skilling*" of very young children. Many parents were taken aback when they were told, as one group of Hispanic parents was, that "As parents of preschool children who will be coming to kindergarten next school year, you need to know what we expect of them. The standards are very high these days; you will be surprised, compared to when you were in school. Back then, you only had to worry about playing. Nowadays, children are expected to write sentences, to know all their letters and sounds."[83]

Many parents found the new emphasis off-putting, and their misgivings merged with the vested interests of those who were already providing day care in the neighborhoods. In 2007 there were some 113,000 child care enterprises in the United States. Many of these centers did not provide the sort of upper-middle-class socialization that early childhood reformers recommended, but they existed nevertheless. Some of them could afford to hire only high school graduates who supervised play but offered few learning activities.

The existence of low-budget child care centers was reinforced by the federal welfare reform legislation of 1996, which gave eligible parents vouchers that could be used by any child care provider, whether licensed or not. In 2008, the federal Child Care Development Fund provided about $10 billion in vouchers for 1.75 million preschool kids. One scholar at the Brookings Institution joked that welfare reform had turned out to be "a money machine for child care."[84]

---

83 Bruce Fuller, *Standardized Childhood*, 33, 62, 79, and *passim*.

84 Chester E. Finn, Jr, *Reroute the Preschool Juggernaut*, 27; Ron Haskins, quoted by David L. Kirp, *The Sandbox Investment*, 147.

Another consideration should also be mentioned. Professor Fuller has calculated the yearly expense at the Perry Preschool at $15,166 per student (in 2000 dollars), about twice what Head Start spent per pupil. For the more interventionist Abecedarian Program, the estimated annual expense was $34,476. And proponents of early childhood education insisted that nothing less would suffice. According to Professor Kirp, "well-designed programs have been shown to benefit kids," but "low-quality preschools don't."[85]

Some observers were skeptical. Columnist Mona Charen described the early childhood "nostrums" as "hackneyed and stale"—a reprise of policies that had failed during President Lyndon B. Johnson's War on Poverty. Another columnist, Heather Mac Donald, characterized them as "wishful thinking." Some comments on the Internet were even more critical: "like putting money in a bottomless pit"; "just one more liberal program that'll . . . blow millions of dollars . . . [and] go nowhere."[86]

Much depended on whether one believed the research, such as that of James Heckman and Richard Nisbett, which claimed that money spent on early childhood programs eventually saved the taxpayers money. This research involved complicated calculations and assumptions that correlated the money spent with later income from taxes and with later spending on welfare and prisons. As has been noted, Heckman calculated the benefit to cost ratio at Perry and Abecedarian at eight to one. But other scholars have put the ratio at about 2:1, and even that may be too high. Robert Weissberg has written, "this is advocacy research" and "biases are everywhere." "Faulty

---

[85] Bruce Fuller, *Standardized Childhood*, 192, 195; David L. Kirp, *The Sandbox Investment*, 52, 7, 18.

[86] Mona Charen, comment posted at *National Review Online* (25 February 2009); Heather Mac Donald, "Losing Ground," *National Review Online* (29 October 2009); comments posted at AmRen.com (18 August 2009).

assumptions are just piled one on top of another." Richard Nisbett has conceded, "a huge amount of research needs to be done to establish whether something like the Perry or ... Abecedarian program would be effective and feasible if scaled up to national proportions."[87]

Certainly, there are questions about the small number of students who participated in the Perry and Abecedarian programs. Between 1972 and 1977 there were a combined total of 111 mostly African-American children in Abecedarian's full- time program and in the control group. If even a few of these children had undergone atypical experiences, the overall results would have been thrown out of kilter. And although interventions were intensive, with one adult for every three infants and toddlers and one adult for every six of the three- and four-year-olds, the results were not spectacular. In her book *It Takes a Village* (1996), Hillary Rodham Clinton reported that the average IQ of the Abecedarian three-year-olds was 17 points higher than that of the control group. Clinton did not mention that by age eight the advantage had faded to three points.[88]

The interventions at the Perry Preschool were less intensive, but the results were similar. Altogether, there were only 123 students in the Perry study—58 Perry students and 65 in the control group. And although the differences were statistically significant, they were not enormous. Forty-three percent of the Perry graduates were employed at age 40, compared with 35 percent of the control group. Twenty-one percent of the Perry graduates had been arrested more than five times, compared with 31 percent of the control group. According to Professor Fuller, "exposure to Perry explains less than 3 percent of all

---

87 Robert Weissberg, *Bad Students, Not Bad Schools*, 256.; Richard Nisbett, quoted by Steve Sailer, "Selling Out and How To Do It—The Case of Richard E. Nisbett," Vdare.com (14 June 2009).

88 David Armor, *Maximizing Intelligence*, 155; Hillary Rodham Clinton, *It Takes a Village* (New York: Simon and Schuster, 1996), 60-61; John T. Bruer, *The Myth of the First Three Years*, 163.

the variation in earnings ... and about 4 percent of the variability in school attainment levels."[89]

These results did not satisfy one blogger. According to "education realist," the Perry experiment was nothing to celebrate. At this "gold standard" of preschool programs, the racial achievement gap was reduced by "barely a nudge." And "the jail gap isn't quite as spectacularly awful." What it boiled down to was this: "If we take really incredibly at-risk kids and spend billions on them in preschool and manage to replicate the very best outcomes we've ever managed, only one in three of them will be arrested five times by their 40th birthday, instead of one in two!"[90]

Skepticism about early childhood education has been countered to some extent by the popularity of the nation's most celebrated pre-K program, Head Start. This program taught playground etiquette, provided nutritious meals and medical checkups, familiarized children with letters and numbers, and generally gave three- and four-year-old children some good times and care they would not have received otherwise. Some researchers have also reported that Head Start children are less likely to repeat a grade and more likely to graduate from high school.[91]

Other researchers, however, concluded that the academic benefits of Head Start fade with time. On academic tests, Head Start

---

89   Bruce Fuller, *Standardized Childhoods*, 193.

90   EducationRealist.wordpress.com (5 April 2013).

91   See Consortium for Longitudinal Studies, *As the Twig is Bent: Lasting Effects of Preschool Programs* (Hillsdale, N.J.: Lawrence Erlbaum Associates, 1983), 461-463 and *passim*; "Everybody Likes Head Start," *Time* (20 February 1989), 49-50. Edward Zigler, the author of several important scholarly books on early childhood education, has also edited a useful anthology of the arguments for and against Head Start, *The Head Start Debates* (Baltimore: P. H. Brooks Publisher, 2004).

children do better than control groups in the early years of elementary school, but the advantage fades to almost nothing by the time the youngsters are in middle school. In 2010, the Department of Health and Human Services published a carefully constructed *Head Start Impact Study* which concluded, "children's attendance in Head Start has no demonstrable impact for their academic, socio-emotional, or health status."[92]

One liberal journalist, Joe Klein of *Time* magazine, conceded that the HHS study had provided "indisputable evidence" that "the positive effects" of Head Start were "minimal and vanished by the end of first grade." Most liberals, however, were loath to criticize early childhood education. They said that, even if Head Start did not have a lasting effect on academic achievement, there was evidence that it fostered the development of important non- cognitive attitudes like self-control, self-confidence, determination, persistence, and the ability to work with other people. They said that people with these personality traits were more likely to succeed.[93]

For its part, the major media give the impression that the distribution of academic achievement could be equalized if Hispanic and African-American parents embraced the family style and parenting practices of most Asian families and of most White professionals from the upper- and upper-middle classes. Racial and ethnic achievement gaps could be closed (or, at the least, substantially reduced) if Black and Hispanic parents allowed others to become, in effect, substitute parents who provided the right sort of child care.

---

92 Grover J. Whitehurst, "Is Head Start Working for American Students?" The Brookings Institute, www.brookings.edu/blogs/up-front/posts/2010/01/21-head-start-whitehurst.

93 Joe Klein, "Time To Ax Public Programs that Don't Yield Results," *Time* (7 July 2011). Paul Tough has expanded on this point in his book, *How Children Succeed* (Boston: Houghton Mifflin Harcourt, 2012).

A best-selling nonfiction book and hit movie provided an example of celebrating good child rearing. *The Blind Side* told the story of Michael Oher, an African-American boy from the slums of Memphis, Tennessee. After a wealthy white family adopted the teenaged Oher, and provided him with a personal tutor and other advantages, Oher's IQ rose from 80 to 96. He eventually attended the University of Mississippi, where he became a Dean's list scholar as well as a football star. After that, Oher moved on to a lucrative career in the National Football League. John Lee Hancock, the director of the movie, regarded Oher's story as "a test case" for determining the relative importance of nature and nurture. "And nurture wins in a big way. You've got a kid who's cast on the junk heap of life, socially and from an educational standpoint, and it's amazing what a roof, a bed, meals, and an emphasis on schools can do, when everybody had written him off."94

The *New York Times* has published several articles that developed this theme. One, "The Inner City Prep School Experience," expressed concern that, despite an annual expenditure of $35,000 per pupil, a public boarding school in Washington, D. C. could not afford to keep its students on campus during weekends and summers—when the students might be ruined by exposure to the slum culture of their home neighborhoods. The *Washington Post* chimed in with similar articles and essays, such as one entitled, "Making the Grade Isn't About Race. It's About Parents." This essay maintained that student achievement was "deeply affected by issues of family," that "the reason [Black] students were lagging academically had nothing to do with race," that it was "because their parents just weren't there for them—at least not in the same way that parents of kids who were doing well tended to be."95

---

94 John Lee Hancock, quoted by Michael Granberry, "The Texan Behind 'The Blind Side,'" *Dallas Morning News* (15 November 2009); Michael Lewis, *The Blind Side* (New York: W. W. Norton, 2006).

95 Maggie Lee Jones, "The Inner-City Prep School Experience," *The New York*

Many people nevertheless remained skeptical. Commenting on the *Post*'s article, one reader acknowledged, "it would help . . . if black men would . . . stay with their offspring." Nevertheless, this reader added, "genetics would still be a factor." Other readers conceded that the reformers were correct "to a degree." "Cultural differences should not be underestimated." But these readers also insisted, "A dullard is still a dullard." One noted that blacks also made low scores in Africa, where they had "a whole village raising the kids." C. Van Carter, of the blogspot *Across Difficult Country*, added a droll comment: "Many blacks are [already] provided income and housing by the government. Supplying a staff of white servants to maintain the home and raise the children is the next logical step." These skeptics may not have been aware of the already-mentioned 1988 survey of more than 600 psychologists. But, like most of these psychologists, many ordinary people thought the racial and ethnic gaps in academic achievement were due, in part, to genetic inheritance.[96]

One more point deserves mention. If early childhood education is expanded, and if very young children actually benefit from spending more time away from their homes and parents, the racial achievement gap is likely to increase. To understand this ironic point, one should recognize that most children from well-to-do families already attend private preschools. And thanks to Head Start, which is means tested—that is, restricted to children from families that are near or below the poverty line—the proportion of preschoolers from disadvantaged families is larger than the proportion from working- and lower-middle-class families. Thus, if preschool became universal and publicly financed, and if youngsters actually benefit

---

Times Magazine (25 September 2009); Patrick Welsh, "Making the Grade Isn't About Race. It's About Parents," *Washington Post* (18 October 2009).

96 Comments posted at AmRen.com (18 October 2009); C. Van Carter, quoted by Steve Sailer, "The Next Liberal Fad: A 'Stolen Generation' of Black Children?" Vdare.com (22 November 2009).

from early childhood and pre-K education, the advantages would go disproportionately to children who previously had not been attending preschools. As it happens, these children are not from the most disadvantaged families but from the working-and lower- middle classes. A great many of them are White.

This brings us back to "the Matthew Effect" that was mentioned in Chapter 6. As noted there, the term derived from a passage in the Gospel according to Matthew, which told of faith growing stronger among true believers while declining among the less faithful. The phrase "the rich get richer" is an economic version of the same point. Something similar occurs in schools. When *all* children are offered advantages, the greatest benefits accrue to children with high IQs and supportive families. If extra books are added to the library, these children are more likely to take advantage than those who are truly disadvantaged. Similarly, able students are more inclined to take advantage of computers and Internet connections. *Sesame Street* provides yet another example. This television show was designed to narrow group differences. But working- and lower-middle-class children viewed the show more frequently and gained more from the experience than children from truly disadvantaged backgrounds.[97]

Nor are these examples atypical. Far from effacing achievement gaps, effective reforms increase disparities. When public schools provided only a few years of elementary education, group disparities were slight. But what if these schools were given better textbooks, computers, a library, capable teachers, science labs and all the rest? The outcome, Robert Weissberg has answered, "would *necessarily* be wider gaps, as brighter more motivated students better utilized newly available resources." This result could be prevented only by denying access to advantaged students. By this logic," Berkeley's Professor

---

97 Herbert J. Walberg and Shiow-Ling Tsai, "Matthew Effects in Education," *American Education Research Journal* 20 (Fall 1983), 359-373.

Kirp has observed, "the only way to help poor children [by which Kirp means, the only way to close racial and ethnic achievement gaps] would be to deny opportunities to the middle class." With its income barrier to access, Head Start was an exception to the rule.

Political considerations generally require that government programs must be available for all. And then, as Berkeley's Professor Fuller has noted, "the gain experienced by low-income kids may not ever be enough to catch up with the gain by middle-class kids."[98]

---

98 Robert Weissberg, *Bad Students, Not Bad Schools*, 105; David L. Kirp, *The Sandbox Investment*, 216; Bruce Fuller, quoted by Carrie Sturrock, "Preschool Study Finds Bright Side, Dark Side," *San Francisco Chronicle* (1 November 2005); Stephen J. Ceci and Paul B. Papierno, "The Rhetoric and Reality of Gap Closing: When the 'Have-Nots' Gain but the 'Haves' Gain Even More," *American Psychologist* 60 (February/March 2005), 149-60.

Part IV

Contrarian Views of School Reform

10

Diane Ravitch

Born in 1938, Diane Ravitch was and educated in the racially segregated public schools of Houston, Texas. After graduating from San Jacinto High School, Ravitch attended a desegregated, elite college (Wellesley in Massachusetts) and did graduate work in history at Columbia University, where she wrote a doctoral dissertation under the direction of Professor Lawrence Cremin. At one time Cremin was widely regarded as the dean of America's historians of education, but Ravitch eventually supplanted her mentor. Over the course of four decades, she wrote several scholarly books and edited many more. *Time* and the *Christian Science Monitor* have described Ravitch as "prominent" and "renowned," and others have been equally lavish in their praise. In 2010, *New York Times* writer Richard Bernstein called Ravitch "probably America's leading historian of education." In the *Los Angeles Times*, Peter Schrag described Ravitch as "this nation's most respected historian of education." In the *Washington Post*, Jay Mathews wrote that Ravitch was not just "our best living historian of education" but "in my view ... the best ever." In *The New York Review of Books*, E. D. Hirsch declared that Ravitch was "without rival as a historian of modern American schooling."[1]

---

1   Gilbert Cruz, "The Skimmer," *Time* (24 July 2008); Bob Blaisdell, "The Death and Life of the Great American School System," *CSMonitor* (16 March 2010); Richard Bernstein, "A Change of Heart on Education," *New York Times* (5 May 2010); Peter Schrag, "The Death and Life of the Great American School System," *Los Angeles Times* (28 February 2010); Jay Mathews, "Class Struggle," *WashingtonPost.com* (26 March 2010); E. D. Hirsch, "How to Save the

The Long Crusade

In the course of her career, Ravitch has been a professor at Columbia Teachers College and at New York University, a senior fellow at the Brookings Institution, a national policy expert, and a best-selling author. One of her early books, *The Revisionists Revised* (1978), was a spirited rebuttal of radical scholars who tried to discredit the belief that America's public schools fostered social mobility. On the contrary, the radicals maintained, the schools actually shored up an unjust, exploitative social order. In another book, *Left Back* (2000), Ravitch criticized progressive education, and in other writings she expressed skepticism about multiculturalism and support for a core curriculum that some people considered Eurocentric.

Since Ravitch established her intellectual reputation with works that criticized left-wing and liberal approaches to education, she became especially popular with conservative readers and policy makers. Nevertheless, Ravitch had been reared and educated in predominantly liberal circles and she remained on good terms with many Democrats. She served as an Assistant Secretary of Education in the Republican administration of President George H. W. Bush, but she also served on the board that oversaw national testing during the administration of Bush's Democratic successor, Bill Clinton. After Clinton, another Republican President, George W. Bush, invited Ravitch to the White House to hear the announcement of the younger Bush's program for No Child Left Behind. Meanwhile, Ravitch also served on advisory boards at two prominent foundations that promoted school reform, the Hoover Institution and the Thomas B. Fordham Institute. All things considered, Ravitch has had a remarkable career, "part star scholar and part national policy wonk."[2]

Prior to the Bush and Clinton administrations, most school

Schools," *New York Review of Books* (13 May 2010).

2   Richard Greenwald, "A New Lesson Plan," www.BrooklynRail.org/2010/06/express/a-new-lesson-plan (3 June 2010).

reformers had emphasized the importance of racially-balanced integration. But, as noted at the outset of this book, this sort of mixing had never been popular with most Americans and between 1991 and 2007 the Supreme Court changed its interpretations so as to require desegregation but not busing for racial balance. In doing so, the Court adjusted its jurisprudence to take account of the flight of many Whites, the opposition of many Blacks, and the persistence of racial and ethnic achievement gaps in those areas where courts had required racially-balanced enrollments.[3]

After the demise of court-ordered busing, two new approaches to school reform came to the fore: choice and accountability. Choice was manifest in proposals for vouchers, tax credits, magnet schools, and charter schools. Accountability was manifest in the establishment of state educational standards, in the testing associated with the No Child Left Behind program, and in demands that teachers be rated by the value-added method. Ravitch was only one of many reformers who, in her words, "jumped aboard a bandwagon." In the 1990s and early 2000s, she regarded testing as a way to "shine a spotlight on low-performing schools" and school choice as a method that would "enable poor children to escape failing schools." From her perches in Washington and at New York University and the Hoover and Fordham institutes, Ravitch sought to shape school choice and accountability to "close the achievement gap between rich and poor, black and white."[4]

Yet by 2007 Ravitch had become "increasingly skeptical about these reforms, reforms that I had supported enthusiastically." "Where once I had been hopeful, even enthusiastic about the potential benefits of testing, accountability, choice, and markets, I now found myself

---

3 Raymond Wolters, *Race and Education, 1954-2007*, passim.

4 Diane Ravitch, *The Death and Life of the Great American School System* (New York: Basic Books, 2010) 3-4.

experiencing profound doubts..." Although Ravitch had enjoyed the camaraderie and intellectual stimulation at Hoover and Fordham, she eventually resigned from her positions at both institutes. She was "increasingly disaffected from both the choice movement and the accountability movement." She was "beginning to see the downside of both and to understand that they were not solutions to our educational dilemmas."[5]

Even before Ravitch's turnabout, some critics had predicted that testing would be problematical. One of the early critics, Peter Sacks, complained that "Dr. Ravitch" should have seen trouble ahead because she "had access to the same evidence that the rest of us had, but chose to ignore it." Yet this judgment seems harsh, since Sacks' purpose had been to convince people like Ravitch. His main points were that test-based accountability encouraged teachers to focus on math and reading, the only subjects tested, to the neglect of other important subjects; and that preparing for tests led to incessant drills that subverted authentic interest in math and reading.[6]

There was also the possibility that emphasis on boosting scores eventually would corrupt education. In the 1970s, sociologist Donald T. Campbell had formulated a theory that came to be known as "Campbell's Law." It held that the quality of any service would be compromised if the service were assessed by a single basic test rather than by careful, complex evaluations. In every field, organizations and individuals would change their behavior to do well on the test. If heart surgeons were rated by the number of patients who survived their operations, some surgeons would refuse to operate on the sickest patients who most needed surgery. If job placement numbers

---

5   Ibid., 1, 2, 12.

6   Peter Sacks to *New York Times*, quoted by Richard Rothstein, "Moment of Clarity," *The New Republic* (15 March 2010); Sacks, *Standardized Minds* (Cambridge: Perseus Books, 2000).

were used to measure the effectiveness of employment agencies, some agencies would focus on the most easily filled jobs. If college "selectivity" was measured by the number of students rejected, some schools would send applications to unqualified high school students they planned to reject.[7]

In *The Death and Life of the Great American School System* (2010), Ravitch explained how Campbell's Law applied to school accountability. In doing so, she once again manifested the skill she had shown in her early debates with radical and progressive educators. *Death and Life* explained that accountability led teachers to drill their students on basic skills but to pay less attention to other subjects. Ravitch said that, in response to increased emphasis on test scores in math and reading, many schools had diverted "hundreds of instructional hours each year from history, social studies, science, the arts and physical education, and redirect[ed] those hours to test preparation."[8]

That was only the beginning of Ravitch's critique. Since Ravitch lived in New York City, she was familiar with some of the methods that had been used to inflate the scores of students there. Ravitch reported that during the first decade of the 21st century, when Michael Bloomberg was Mayor and Joel Klein the Schools Chancellor, New York's schools had fudged the numbers by excusing weak students from taking standardized tests. They had also lowered the scores required to pass. And to boost graduation rates, they had introduced "a dubious practice called 'credit recovery' that allowed students who failed a course or never even showed up for it [to] get credit by turning in an independent project, whose preparation was

---

7   Donald T. Campbell, "Assessing the Impact of Planned Social Change," in G. M. Lyons, ed, *Social Research and Public Policies* (Hanover: Public Affairs Center, Dartmouth College, 1975); Richard Rothstein, "Moment of Clarity."

8   Diane Ravitch, *The Death and Life of the Great American School System*, 73, 76 and *passim*; Ravitch, quoted by Fred Bortz, "The Death and Life of the Great American School System," *Seattle Times* (17 April 2010).

unmonitored, or by attending a few extra sessions." For Ravitch, it was no surprise that in 2007, when the city's students were tested by the National Assessment of Educational Progress(NAEP) as well as the familiar New York state tests, NAEP reported that New York's students had made no significant gains since the NAEP test was last given in 2003. According to Ravitch, New York's students had done no better on the NAEP tests because these tests were more conceptual and because federal officials took care to attain comparable samples of the students that were tested from year to year. Ravitch reported that on New York's state tests, on the other hand, there had been "a lot of cheating ... a lot of gaming the system." This was true elsewhere as well. "Instead of raising standards," the emphasis on test scores had "actually lowered standards because many states have ... changed the scoring of their tests to say that more kids are passing than actually are." High-stakes testing had "encouraged teachers to teach to the test and states to cheat the federal government."[9]

Ravitch took special aim at the value-added method for assessing effective teachers. As has been noted, the turn of the 21st century saw the emergence of "data-driven reformers" who assessed teacher quality by measuring the scores that students made on standardized tests. Many of these reformers believed, as *New York Times* education writer Michael Winerip wrote with irony, that the science of value-added assessment had progressed to the point where school administrators could "calculate a teacher's worth to the third decimal point." "For the first time, human bias was removed from student assessment and replaced with scientific accountability.... No longer did teachers' subjective opinions of children distort things."

---

9   Diane Ravitch, *The Death and Life of the Great American School System*, 89; Ravitch, quoted in *Daytona Beach News-Journal* (8 March 2010); Ravitch, quoted by Eric Dunn, "Ravitch Critiques Education Reform," *Stanford Daily* (15 April 2010); Ravitch, "Pass or Fail," NewRepublic.com (15 March 2010).

"Scores on standardized tests" had become "the gold standard."[10]

Winerip was exaggerating to make a point. Most reformers acknowledged that, as Whitney Tilson once put it, "test-scores and value-added systems shouldn't be the SOLE mechanism for evaluating teachers." But Tilson insisted that test scores should count for "40-60%" of teachers' evaluations in New York. Meanwhile in Colorado, state Senator Mike Johnston, a former Teach for America teacher, was the driving force behind a new law that provided that 51 percent of every teacher's professional valuation score must be based on student achievement data. The 51 percent figure then became a rallying cry, as an increasing number of reformers insisted that at least 51 percent of a teacher's annual evaluation should be tied to student test scores. Meanwhile several states—Florida, Louisiana, New Jersey, and New York among others—revised their teacher evaluation systems to incorporate student achievement data.[11]

Ravitch conceded that test scores were useful as one of many indicators of overall quality. But she warned about the danger of using students' test scores to determine teacher pay. Ravitch said the value-added reformers failed to recognize that teachers who did well with one group of students often did not do well with another group the next year. "The scores depend to a large degree on which students are in a teacher's class, and a teacher may have a highly motivated group of students one year that gets wonderful scores, but an unmotivated group the next year that gets average or poor scores. What's more ... test scores are highly correlated with income and social status. Just as teachers can't control which students they have in class each year, they can't control where those students come from." "A teacher who produces big score gains one year may produce none the next year,

---

10 Michael Winerip, "In Public School Efforts," *New York Times* (18 April 2011).

11 Whitey Tilson, posting at EdReform.blogspot.com (9 May 2011); Dana Goldstein, "The Test Generation," *American Prospect* (11 April 2011).

depending on which students happen to be in his or her class."¹²

To support her comments on the instability of test scores, Ravitch mentioned an analysis by University of California, Berkeley, economist Jesse Rothstein, which said that value-added calculations often "misidentifie[d] which teachers are more effective and often [are] not much better than a coin toss." A teacher who was rated high or low by the value-added had only a one-third chance of getting a similar score the following year.¹³

Nevertheless, many school reformers continued to regard "value added" as the key to assembling a faculty of high quality. They defined "a great teacher as an 'effective' teacher, and an 'effective' teacher [as] one whose students get higher test scores." Then, taking their cue from Jack Welch, the CEO at General Electric, the reformers said the best way to assemble an outstanding faculty was to fire teachers whose students did not make good scores. As Ravitch explained, the value-added reformers believed "we should fire the bottom 10 percent every year, and over time we will have a staff of 'great' teachers because all the bums will be gone."¹⁴

Yet implementing this policy would not be easy. If test scores

---

12 Diane Ravitch, "Pass or Fail," *The New Republic* (15 March 2010); Ravitch to Deborah Meier at blogs.EdWeek.org/edweek/Bridging-Differences (cited hereafter as *Bridging Differences*; 6 April 2010).

13 Diane Ravitch, "Pass or Fail"; Dana Goldstein, "The Test Generation"; Diane Ravitch to Deborah Meier, quoted by Valerie Strauss, "The Answer Sheet," *WashingtonPost.com* (18 January 2011). For a defense of value-added calculations, while also acknowledging that the calculations are complicated, see Steven Glazerman et al., "Value-added: It's Not Perfect, But It Makes Sense," *Education Week* (15 December 2010) available at ed.Stanford.edu/news/value-added-it039s-not-perfect-it-makes-sense.

14 Diane Ravitch and Mike Rose, "Taking Back School Reform," EdWeek.org/tm/articles/2010/05/12/roseravitchschoolreform.html?tkn=XZTFMK0b%2FtQf7lLAo502mURXR%2Ftrg84KPJJz&cmp=clp-edweek (12 May 2010); Ravitch to Deborah Meier, *Bridging Differences* (10 February 2009).

became the basis for evaluating teachers, teachers would be given a probationary term of three-to-five years. At the end of that period, the students' test scores would be assessed and the teachers who did not produce gains would be fired and replaced by new teachers who had no track record. "Every year a new group of teachers who had not produced gains would be fired, and another untested group of teachers would take their place."[15]

In recommending this approach, school reformers apparently believed that recruiting great teachers would not be a problem, since they assumed that recent graduates of leading colleges would replace the departing teachers. When Ravitch asked reformers how they proposed to improve the schools, she was given to understand that the reformers would "change 'the quality' of teachers by recruiting Ivy League graduates and Teach for America folk." They were "going to push out all those experienced fogies." Ravitch, however, had a problem "trying to understand the math." By 2010, Teach for America was recruiting 5,000 teachers a year, but there were more than 3 million teachers in the United States. Consequently, Ravitch concluded, "Harvard, Yale, Princeton, Brown, and Berkeley" would never "supply enough teachers to fill the need for new teachers."[16]

Ravitch also regarded the reformers as "clueless about what a good education is and how to make it happen." She noted that most of the reformers had "never taught; have never been in a classroom since they were students; know nothing of the history of education and nothing about research; but [they think] they know how to fix the nation's schools." Ravitch considered it "a certain kind of madness" to "override the judgments of those who work in schools and are in daily contact with teachers and children" and to rely instead on philanthropists and social scientists "who never set foot in a classroom [to] create a statistical

---

15 Diane Ravitch to Deborah Meier, *Bridging Differences* (3 November 2009).

16 Diane Ravitch to Deborah Meier, *Bridging Differences* (10 February 2009; 25 November 2008).

measure to tell us how best to educate children." She found it "amazing that so much genius about how to run a terrific education system has been sequestered in child-free, student-free offices..."[17]

As Ravitch saw it, there were two main problems with the reformers' theory. It did not take account of teaching to the test. And it was based on the mistaken assumption that the data should be taken at face value. Ravitch acknowledged that some reformers honestly believed "that school data are as meaningful as profit-and-loss statement[s] or price-to-earning ratio[s]." They did not recognize that they were "living . . . in an age when test scores are so easily manipulated and so often fraudulent." Therefore, Ravitch made a point of explaining the methods that were used to manipulate the scoring of the tests. In *Death and Life* she showed how schools and states had reported higher scores, "by hook or by crook." Some played "statistical games (like dropping the cut point, or creating conversion tables to change low scores into high scores)." Others "dumb[ed] down their tests." Some "scrub[bed] their scores to remove low-scoring students." Ultimately, this led to a situation "wherein scores go up, but actual educational improvement does not occur."[18]

Beyond that, Ravitch said the value-added approach led to an hostility toward teachers that "poisoned the atmosphere" and left many teachers "feel[ing] fearful, beleaguered, and disrespected." No matter the cause of a student's low performance, value-added reformers held the schools and teachers accountable. If the teachers said their students made low scores because of poverty or family

---

17 Ibid.; Diane Ravitch to Deborah Meier, *Bridging Differences* (4 June 2008); Ravitch to Meier, in Valerie Strauss, "The Pitfalls of Putting Economists in Charge of Education," *WashingtonPost.com* (18 January 2011).

18 Diane Ravitch to Deborah Meier, *Bridging Differences* (1 December 2009; 16 March 2010).

problems, the value-added reformers accused the teachers of making excuses. The reformers insisted that good teachers could transform the lives of their students, if only the teachers worked harder, set higher standards, and had higher expectations.[19]

Ravitch admitted that at one time she herself had been "encouraged by the 'no excuses' rhetoric," but eventually she came to think it was "either naïve or duplicitous" to discount the "devastating effects of poverty on a child's life in school." Schools would not improve, Ravitch wrote, "if we use them as society's all-purpose punching bag, blaming them for the ills of the economy, the burdens imposed on children by poverty, the dysfunctions of families." "Something is fundamentally wrong," Ravitch wrote, "with an accountability system that disregards the many factors that influence students' performance on an annual test . . . except for what teachers do in the classroom for forty-five minutes or an hour a day." What is more, Ravitch insisted, "we won't attract better teachers by demonizing and scapegoating them whenever students fail to get higher scores."[20]

Ravitch took particular exception to a cover story that journalists Evan Thomas and Pat Wingert wrote for *Newsweek*. The story was entitled, "The Key to Saving American Education." To illustrate its central point, the cover of the magazine showed a classroom blackboard on which students had written a phrase, repeated again and again, "We must fire bad teachers." According to Thomas and Wingert, "in recent years researchers have discovered something that may seem obvious, but for many reasons was overlooked or denied. What really makes a difference . . . is the quality of the teacher."

---

19   Diane Ravitch to Andrew Rotherham, NewRepublic.com (21 March 2010).

20   Diane Ravitch, "Pass or Fail"; Ravitch and Mike Rose, "Taking Back School Reform"; Ravitch, *The Death and Life of the Great American School System*, 197; Ravitch, quoted by Steve Wood, "Educators' News" (9 March 2010) at MathDittos2.com/ednews/features/f100309.

Thomas and Wingert also said research had established that "much of the ability to teach is innate" and that little was to be gained by attending "graduate schools of education . . . with [their] insipid or marginally relevant theorizing and pedagogy." And since researchers had looked at different variables—such as certification and level of education—and had concluded that nothing was predictive when it came to anticipating which prospective teachers would succeed in the classroom—it seemed to make sense to open the profession to anyone. The recruits could then be given a limited term to show whether they could produce better test scores from their students.[21]

Ravitch was aghast. "Since credentials do not predict who will consistently produce higher scores," she wrote to one friend, "there is no reason to pay attention to certification, master's degrees, even National Board certification. So, anyone should be able to enter teaching, without any of the usual professional training. I find myself wondering why schools should even require future teachers to be college graduates, since there is no research demonstrating the necessity of an undergraduate degree in the test-score production function. Perhaps high school seniors (or juniors?) could master the trick as well as someone with lots of credentials."[22]

Ravitch had still more to say about Thomas and Wingert's article for *Newsweek*. In a letter to another friend, Ravitch called the article "a parody of right-wing rant." "It seems that the nation's classrooms are overrun with 'bad teachers,' ... 'weak' teachers, ineffective teachers, dumb teachers, and others who remain in the classroom only because they have 'lifetime tenure.' Evil teachers' unions protect these people who are harming our nation's children.

---

21 Evan Thomas and Pat Wingert, "Why We Must Fire Bad Teachers," *Newsweek* (March 6, 2010); Sara Mosle, "Facing Up To Our Ignorance" (11 March 2010) Slate.com.

22 Diane Ravitch and Mike Rose, "Taking Back School Reform."

Researchers now know, [Thomas and Wingert] say, that if we could fire all these malingerers, the notorious achievement gap between the races would soon close and America would once again lead the world in education."[23]

Ravitch was especially alarmed about legislation that would strip teachers of tenure and prohibit school districts from paying teachers according to the teachers' years of experience, their advanced degrees, and their varied experiences. Instead, such proposals would base the teachers' compensation in large part on student scores on standardized tests. Ravitch characterized this approach as "an onslaught against [the] professionalism of teachers." In a letter to the members of the Florida legislature, Ravitch predicted that the legislation would harm education and also "cause many of your best teachers to leave the profession."[24]

In the past, Ravitch's work had appealed primarily to scholars and serious readers. She had done "what I can with my pen but generally stay[ed] at arms-length from political action." But Ravitch felt too strongly about the problems with value-added reform to remain cloistered in her study. The value-added reformers had riled her, and although she was 70 years old in 2008 she still felt "ready to go into the ring and take on all comers for 15 rounds." She was further buoyed when *The Death and Life of the Great American School System* enjoyed major sales success. In less than a month Basic Books sold out several printings, and before long Ravitch's book was on the *New York Times* list of best-selling books. Ravitch then embarked on a cross-country tour to promote the book. Over the course of the next two years, she gave scores of lectures and also spoke to union members, to school board members, to many members of Congress,

---

23 Diane Ravitch to Deborah Meier, "The Shame of Newsweek," *Bridging Differences* (16 March 2010).

24 *Ibid.*

and to high-level members of President Barack Obama's staff. Ravitch became, in the words of *Washington Post* reporter Nick Anderson, "an unlikely national spokeswoman," warning that "a cult of testing and accountability has hijacked school reform." "My personal journey," Ravitch explained, "has been to rally the grassroots" of parents and teachers. Speaking to a large crowd at the Cobo Center in Detroit, Ravitch insisted: "The teaching profession is under attack by those who blame teachers for conditions beyond their control. They want to take away your professionalism and turn you into testing technicians. . . . You must not let them do that."[25]

As Ravitch saw it, "Sec. Duncan . . . the Gates Foundation . . . the Broad Foundation . . . all of these very wealthy and powerful people are taking us on the wrong track because they're focused . . . on 'how do we fire the bad teachers.'" "I don't think America is overrun by bad teachers. I think America is overrun by too much poverty . . . among children. . . . We should be talking about how do we make sure that our children have adequate healthcare, and that we have pre-K education, birth to 5-year-old education, because there's a gap when kids start school . . . because they don't have access to healthcare or vocabulary." Ravitch questioned whether school reformers truly wanted to improve education. What they're really doing, she said, "is tearing education apart and demonizing teachers."[26]

Wherever Ravitch spoke, teachers rallied in support, saying "virtually the same thing: They have never been more demoralized in their professional lives. They feel that they are scapegoats for everything

---

25 Diane Ravitch to Deborah Meier, *Bridging Differences* (2 July 2008; 2 March 2007); Nick Anderson, "Business Principles Won't Work for School Reform," *Washington Post* (26 February 2010); Ravitch, quoted by David Denby, "Public Defender," *The New Yorker* (19 November 2012) 74, 66.

26 Whitney Tilson, "Diane Ravitch was on The Daily Show," EdReform. blogspot.com (8 March 2011); Ravitch, remarks to Michigan Education Association, EdReform.blogspot.com (7 March 2011).

that is wrong in American education." When Ravitch spoke at Stanford University, the student newspaper reported that she had to pause several times "to receive overwhelming applause." The first question after her talk came from a teacher in Salinas who taught the children of migrant farm workers. This teacher "burst into tears" as she said that, because the students had not made good scores on standardized tests, school reformers were "about to close her school where the teachers are working hard to instruct a transient and high-needs enrollment." A few hours later, Ravitch spoke at Berkeley, where the response was much the same. She attributed this "wonderful reception" primarily "to the fact that what I am saying resonates with teachers." After all, Ravitch explained, "teachers feel, with justification, that they are being...blamed whenever test scores don't go up." Increasingly, when teachers went on strike, the disputes were not over traditional bread and butter issues of pay and benefits. Instead, many disputes centered on the criteria that were to be used in evaluating teachers. This was the case, for example, for Chicago's public school teachers, who in 2012 staged their first strike in 25 years. Their eventual "victory" involved reducing the weight of "value added" evaluations to 25 percent in the first two years of a new contract, 30 percent in the third year, and 40 percent in year four, instead of the 40 percent weight that the city had wanted in the first year.[27]

Each day Ravitch received "on average, about 100 emails... from readers of my book, mainly teachers, who either say 'thank you' or 'help.'" Meanwhile, the teachers' largest union, the National Education Association, gave Ravitch its "2010 Friend of Education Award." In accepting the award, Ravitch said that in the course of her tour she had met thousands of teachers—"possibly 20,000," and she "did not meet a single one who likes what is happening.... Not one who was unaware of the rising tide of hostility towards teachers."

27 Diane Ravitch to Deborah Meier, *Bridging Differences* (20 April 2010; 9 March 2010); Gary Becker, ""Rating Teachers," *Becker-Posner-Blog.com*(23 September 2012); Diane Ravitch, "Two Visions for Chicago's Schools," NYBooks.com/blogs/nyrblog/2012.sep/12.

Again and again, teachers asked Ravitch, "What can we do? How can we stop the attacks on teachers and the teaching profession? Why is the media demonizing unions? . . . Who will stand up for public schools and their teachers? Again and again, teachers came up to me and said: Be our voice. Speak up for us."[28]

Ravitch "spoke up," and in the process she took exception not only to testing and accountability but also, and more questionably, to school choice. This was surprising since in the 1990s Ravitch had written powerful defenses of educational freedom. As she watched ghetto schools become engulfed in disorder and anti-academic attitudes, Ravitch had recommended that public policy be fashioned so that inner-city families would be able to send their children to better schools. She found it unacceptable that motivated students from low-income families had no alternative but to attend a nearby public school that was serving them badly.[29]

Yet a decade's experience with value-added "testism" made Ravitch so distrustful of school reformers that she eventually turned against school choice as well as accountability. Whereas before she had thought it preferable for some inner-city youths to have a better chance for a good education than for all of them to remain in underperforming schools, during the first years of the 21st century Ravitch criticized school choice and said that publicly-funded students should attend regular schools in their neighborhoods. She seemed not to recognize that the major problem with neighborhood schools was the neighborhood. She did not mention that, even after controlling for socio-economic circumstances, a disproportionate

---

28 Eric Dunne, "Ravitch Critiques Education Reform"; Diane Ravitch to Deborah Meier, *Bridging Differences* (6 April 2010); Ravitch, speech to the NEA, available at EdReform.blogspot.com (July 2010).

29 For an example, see Diane Ravitch and Joseph P. Viteritti, *New Schools for a New Century: The Redesign of Urban Education* (New Haven: Yale University Press, 1997).

number of Black students misbehaved, and that this misbehavior detracted from the education of all the other students. Nor did she seem to recognize that, due to massive demographic changes, many families in the same neighborhood no longer spoke the same language. Thanks to racial integration, multiculturalism, and a rising tide of secularism, many families no longer shared the same values. It was no longer possible for many communities to provide anything like the neighborhood schools that Ravitch had attended in Houston during the 1940s and 1950s. Ravitch, however, ignored the downside of diversity and insisted, "Our schools cannot improve if charter schools siphon away the most motivated students and their families in the poorest communities from the regular public schools."[30]

In some respects, Ravitch's argument against school choice was similar to one that Jonathan Kozol had previously made. Ravitch noted that most poor families did not encourage their children to take advantage of after-school tutoring, even when the tutoring was free of charge. She noted that most poor families continued to patronize neighborhood schools, even when educational standards at the schools were low and even when there was the possibility of attending a better charter school. She noted that charter schools appealed to "the most motivated students in poor communities, those whose parents push them to do better." But the departure of motivated students had the side effect of causing enrollment in nearby public schools to consist even more disproportionately of less motivated students, "including some who just want to get by and some who are not interested in school work." Ravitch considered this "an ominous development for public education and for our nation." She believed that school choice was leading to "a two-tier system of widening inequality." She warned, "As charter schools increase in number and able students enroll in them,

---

30 Diane Ravitch, *The Death and Life of the Great American School System*, 227; Steve Sailer, "Diane Ravitch, 'No Child Left Behind', and the Racial Achievement Gap's Kryptonite Cause," Vdare.com (28 March 2010).

the regular public schools will be locked into a downward trajectory."[31]

At one time, Ravitch had favored school choice. In 1997 she had written, memorably: "I do not advocate full choice solely on grounds that competition is good, although I do think that competition is good. No, what I argue is that it is unjust to compel poor children to attend bad schools." Nevertheless, a decade later Ravitch maintained that it was wrong to allow inner-city students to choose their schools if the choices increased "the burden on the regular public schools" by "skim[ming] the most motivated students." She complained that "under the rubric of choice" a great many children were "sorting themselves (and being sorted)," and she said that ambitious public school students should be required to attend the regular public schools in their neighborhoods, even if those schools were overwhelmed by the challenges of dealing with troublesome and unmotivated students. To gloss over this harsh policy, Ravitch said that "the future of the next generation" depended on "improving the system, not on tinkering around the edges." For that reason, Ravitch told a friend, it made better sense "to uplift and transform the vast majority" of inner-city schools than to develop charter schools as alternatives for the motivated minority.[32]

In the earlier years when she had supported choice, Ravitch had not expected charter schools to become as popular as they became in many inner cities. In the suburbs and smaller towns, most people were satisfied with the existing public schools. Consequently in the nation as a whole, only 4 percent of students patronized charter schools in

---

31 Diane Ravitch, *The Death and Life of the Great American School System*, 144-45.

32 Diane Ravitch and Joseph P. Viteritti, *New Schools for a New Century*; Ravitch, quoted by James Traub, "What Can Public Schools Learn?" *New York Times* (9 November 1997); Ravitch to Deborah Meier, *Bridging Differences* (19 November 2009; 19 February 2008); Ravitch to Andrew Rotherham, "Is Education on the Wrong Track?" NewRepublic.com (21 March 2010).

2009, while the proportion of students enrolled in private schools remained steady at slightly more than 10 percent (with a sharp decline in Catholic school enrollments offset by increased patronage for other private schools). But in several major cities, a much larger proportion of people were not satisfied with the regular public schools. In 2012 about half the students in Washington, D.C., were enrolled in charter schools, while at least 30 percent were enrolled in charter schools in at least six other cities, and at least 20 percent in 18 others. Ravitch feared that continuing on this path would undermine public education in most of America's major cities. To prevent this, Ravitch would deny motivated students the freedom to attend a better school.[33]

If she had her way, Ravitch would require motivated inner-city students to attend bad neighborhood schools. Perhaps to justify this harsh policy, Ravitch reviewed a number of studies that compared the test scores of students at charter schools with those at regular public schools and noted that a NAEP study of 2003—a study that seemed to contradict the argument about "skimming"—reported that matched samples of charter and public school students made similar scores in reading but regular public school students performed slightly better in mathematics. Yet this was only the beginning of what sometimes were called "the data wars." In 2004, a Harvard economist, Caroline M. Hoxby, "analyzed the performance of every charter elementary school student in the nation and found that they were more likely to be proficient in both reading and math..." Then in 2009, Margaret Raymond, the director of the Center for Research on Educational Outcomes at Stanford's Hoover Institution, reported that only 17 percent of charter schools had better results than regular public schools. One year later, however, Raymond presented a more positive assessment of charter schools in New York City. Other studies followed, comparing the educational performance in private

---

33 Diane Ravitch to Deborah Meier, *Bridging Diffferences* (19 November 2009);Ravitch, *Reign of Error*, 159.

schools and public schools, and charter schools and regular public schools. According to Ravitch, "The only surprise was how small and usually insignificant were the gains recorded by any sector." There were exceptions, to be sure. Ravitch acknowledged that the KIPP schools had obtained "impressive results." But overall, she reported, the test scores at charter schools were not spectacular.[34]

Ravitch said little about one of the major reasons for the general equivalency in test scores: the fact that many people favored school choice not to boost scores but to maximize freedom. When it came to college, most observers recognized that many students eschewed the academically-elite schools, preferring instead to enroll at institutions that were less distinguished academically but charged lower tuition or had reputations for social life (or comfortable surroundings to acquire future spouses, or opportunities for networking in one's home region). So it was also when it came to elementary and secondary education. Many families had priorities other than the highest possible test scores. Some stressed the importance of moral training or religious orthodoxy. Others sought social prestige, or distinction in athletics or music or art. Nevertheless, Ravitch scoffed when, in response to reports that test scores in the charter schools generally were not higher than those in the regular public schools, "some conservative commentators declared that choice was not supposed to raise test scores. It was just supposed to provide choice, which was a good thing in itself." Ravitch must have nodded with approval when one such commentator, Charles Murray, wrote that standardized test scores were "a terrible way to decide whether one school is better than another." But Ravitch took exception because Murray also maintained that charter schools were desirable simply because they gave parents the opportunity to send their children to the sort of school they preferred.[35]

---

34 Diane Ravitch to Deborah Meier, *Bridging Differences* (19 November 2009).

35 Diane Ravitch to Deborah Meier, *Bridging Differences* (11 May 2010); Charles Murray to *New York Times* (4 May 2010).

Whatever the reasons for the similarity in test results, Ravitch was severely critical of well-to-do philanthropists whom she considered the main force behind the campaign to promote accountability, school choice, and value-added assessments of teachers. Ravitch only rarely complained about inner-city students who chose to attend charter schools, and about suburban youngsters whose families preferred an alternative to the regular public schools. Most of Ravitch's animus was directed at wealthy philanthropists who championed the value-added method for assessing teachers. In *The Death and Life of the Great American School System*, Ravitch called them the "billionaire boys," and she showed that some of these billionaires had previously acquired quite a record of failure as school reformers. Ravitch noted, for example, that in the 1960s the Ford Foundation had promoted an ill-fated effort to establish "community control" of the public schools of New York City. Thirty years later the Annenberg Foundation had squandered $500 million in a dubious attempt to improve public education by funding a network of small progressive schools. Then the Bill and Melinda Gates Foundation wasted another $2 billion promoting small schools, while the Walton Family Foundation and the Eli and Edythe Broad Foundation joined Gates in committing substantial sums to advocacy for school choice and value-added accountability.[36]

As Ravitch saw it, these foundations were setting the policy agenda, and she lamented, "To date [2010], not a single book has been published that has questioned their education strategies." Ravitch explained the absence of searching criticism on the grounds that "academics carefully avoid expressing any views that might alienate the big foundations" or jeopardize "future contributions to their projects." "Never before," Ravitch wrote of the Gates Foundation, "was there a foundation that gave grants to almost every major think tank or advocacy group in the field of education, leaving almost no one

---

36 Diane Ravitch to Deborah Meier, *Bridging Differences* (19 November 2009); Ravitch, *The Death and Life of the Great American School System*, 195-222.

willing to criticize its vast power and unchecked influence." Ravitch said there was "something fundamentally antidemocratic about relinquishing control of the public education policy agenda to private foundations run by society's wealthiest people." It was ironic as well. While insisting that teachers be held accountable for their students' test scores, the foundations themselves were never held accountable. They gave billions of tax-exempt dollars to promote reforms, but the Internal Revenue Service did not ask for evidence that the reforms actually improved education.[37]

Ravitch focused especially on the Gates Foundation, which she said was doing more than any other entity to promote "de-professionalization and high-stakes testing as fixes for American public schools." She complained in particular about Gates' "dazzling PR blitz." She said the Gates Foundation had spent $373 million on education in 2009, with $78 million devoted to "advocacy." Some of this went to like-minded researchers. Some went to media organizations. Some went to young public school teachers who criticized the practice of granting tenure to veteran teachers. Some went to new advocacy groups that interpreted education issues for journalists. Eventually, *Newsweek* reported, Bill Gates came to regard Ravitch as his "biggest adversary." The news pleased Ravitch. "Now that's really funny," she wrote to her friend Deborah Meier. "[Gates], with all those billions and a huge staff. Me, with a computer . . . and a voice. In the end, what wins: ideas or money? We'll see."[38]

---

37 Diane Ravitch, *The Death and Life of the Great American School System*, 200-201; Robert Weissberg, *Bad Students, Not Bad Schools*, 176.

38 Diane Ravitch to Deborah Meier, *Bridging Differences* (11 September 2007; 30 September 2008; 18 May 2010; 4 May 2010; 30 November 2010; 28 June 2011); Ravitch, "Bill Gates: Selling Bad Advice," *TheDailyBeast.com* (23 May 2011); Sam Dillon, "Behind Grass-Roots School Advocacy, Bill Gates" *New York Times* (21 May 2011).

This statement was made in jest. In fact, Ravitch had much more than a computer. She could count on support from thousands of teachers who agreed with her criticism of corporate-style school reform—and from an even larger number of parents who were pleased with the schools in their communities and skeptical about endless rounds of standardized testing. Many of these parents would allow for school choice to accommodate individual students who, for whatever reasons, wished to transfer to another school. But in most communities the great majority of parents and students were satisfied with their schools and looked askance at efforts to drastically change the overall school system.

For a while, Ravitch was a lonely critic of corporate-style school reform. But as she traveled the country, she noticed that the crowds attending her talks were growing. On occasion, she was speaking to groups of a thousand or more. Ravitch's speaking style was that of a no-nonsense scholar who avoided flights of rhetoric and adhered to the philosophy of *Dragnet*'s Joe Friday, the TV detective who was interested in "just the facts, ma'am." Despite this dry speaking style, Ravitch became as close to a rock star as any professor in the United States. She received standing ovations in one auditorium after another.

It is still too early to know who will win this "school war." In the short term, the billionaires were ascendant, as one state after another embraced the corporate approach to school reform. But reformers were worried. Whitney Tilson, for example, conceded that because of Ravitch's "sterling resume and the fact that she was once a reformer, her views are quite influential and thus she is one of the greatest obstacles to the reform our schools so desperately need." "Ravitch often kicks our butts," Tilson acknowledged in an e-mail to one of his friends. The friend agreed, saying it was humiliating to "get our butts kicked by a 73-year old woman."[39].

---

39 Whitney Tilson, comment at *RebuttingRavitch.com* (March 2011)' comment

Ravitch was elated by the "pushback" she observed in one community after another. Most teachers had friends in their communities, and many local people thought it was unfair for social scientists and billionaire philanthropists to blame teachers—their friends—for the problems of failing students. Critics of corporate-style school reform also connected with people who considered the federal and state governments' insistence on frequent rounds of standardized testing to be at odds with America's tradition of local control of education. Critics also connected with people on both the left and right—with liberals who favored more "progressive" approaches to education, and with conservative traditionalists who thought standardized testing had been taken to an extreme. In New York, many parents complained that it was not right for the State to require 8-13 year old students to take math and reading tests that lasted for more than 7 hours—at a time when the SAT was scheduled for 3 hours and 45 minutes and the MCAT for medical schools was scheduled for 4 hours and 5 minutes. In New Jersey, parents and students complained that over the course of ten years, 2004-2014, the State had increased the number of required high school tests from 6 in 2004 to 34 (30 for seniors) in 2014.[40]

Critics of corporate-style school reform dominated the social media, where thousands of activists exchanged information, sent out tweets, and generally gave the Gates, Broad, Koch, and Walton foundations a hard time. As Ravitch saw it, the billionaire boys had "bought off the U. S. Department of Education." They had given millions of dollars to "every 'think tank' and advocacy group in D.C." But they "didn't buy everyone." Because they had ignored teachers and parents, the corporate reformers were "on the defensive."[41]

---

at EdReform.blogspot.com)12 March 2012).

40 "How Many Hours shoulc ait take to Test Children in Grades 3-8?" Diane Ravitch's Blog, April 16, 2014; "How Many Tests Must a High School Teacher in New Jersey Give,?" *ibid.*

41 Diane Ravitch, "Bill Gates is Running Scared," Diane Ravitch's Blog,

Ravitch said that she had one regret. "I only wish I might be alive and vigorous enough 20 years from now to write this story. I know it won't be me, but I see the outlines already. It will make a fascinating read. There will be heroes, villains, naïve collaborators, rigid ideologues intent on imposing their failed philosophy . . . and those who were just following orders or unthinkingly carried away by the latest idea. Of one thing I feel sure. History will not be kind to those who gleefully attacked teachers, sought to fire them based on inaccurate measures, and worked zealously to reduce their status and compensation."[42]

According to Ravitch, Gates and other billionaire philanthropists were worse than mistaken. They were acting with ulterior motives. She noted that in 2008 and 2009 hardly a week passed without news of a financial scam, but the foundation-funded think tanks and universities rarely exposed the way school reformers manipulated the statistics about education. "Something about this scenario is troubling," Ravitch wrote. "I guess it is the fundamental unfairness in which one side has an all-star list of billionaires . . . and the other side has parents and teachers whose resources are meager." Ravitch believed "the so-called 'consensus'" in favor of value-added school reform was "purely a fiction manufactured by elite opinion makers."[43]

As she criticized the "billionaire boys," Ravitch reversed the trajectory of her own ideology. Ravitch had once been regarded as a liberal-turned-conservative, but now she returned to espousing the views of her youth—views that were generally liberal and sometimes left-wing. After graduating from college in 1960, Ravitch had worked at the *New Leader* magazine, "a wonderful publication where I learned about democratic socialist politics." "At that time and for most of my

---

18 March 2014; G. F. Brandenburg, "At the First National Conference," gfbrandenburg.com (3 March 2014)

42 Diane Ravitch to Deborah Meier, *Bridging Differences* (28 June 2011).

43 *Ibid.* (11 September 2007; 30 September 2008; 18 May 2010; 4 May 2010).

life," Ravitch noted, "I was a registered Democrat." It was not until the 1990s that she registered as an Independent.[44]

As she began to write "from the left" once again, Ravitch complained that America had fallen "effortlessly into the control of Know Nothings from the world of business, law, and politics." One such was philanthropist Eli Broad. After conferring with Broad for an hour "in his gorgeous penthouse in NYC, overlooking Central Park," Ravitch reported that this real-estate-magnate-turned-school-reformer knew little about education but believed that "what was needed to fix the schools was not all that complicated: a tough manager, surrounded by smart graduates of business and law schools." Ravitch apparently took Broad's measure, for Broad himself has said, "I didn't know anything about curricula and had no idea how to teach. So we decided to focus on governance and management of school systems."[45]

Other magnates emulated Broad. In New York, for example, Michael Bloomberg, a media-mogul-turned-mayor, was "a big believer in the notion that winners could win on any field." According to journalist Steven Brill, Bloomberg's company "had been famous in media circles for being the ultimate sink-or-swim shark tank. Not even the top executives had contracts. They could be at their desks one day and gone the next." It all depended on "effectiveness" and "results."[46]

Insistence on the prerogatives of management inevitably led to a clash with the teachers' unions, but Ravitch was surprised by the breadth and depth of anti-union sentiment. She noted that Steve Jobs, the CEO at Apple Computers, had given a speech, saying, "the biggest problem in American education was the teachers' union." Jobs

---

44 "Introducing Diane Ravich," *Bridging Differences* (26 February 2007).

45 Diane Ravitch to Deborah Meier, *Bridging Differences* (5 January 2008; 11 September 2007; 19 March 2007; 3 February 2009; 28 February 2007).

46 Steven Brill, *Class Warfare*, 88, 90

then explained that because of union work rules the nation's principals were not allowed to judge the merit of teachers and to hire and fire accordingly. "Until the teachers' unions were broken," Jobs said, "there is almost no hope for education reform."[47]

Ravitch believed that Jobs's remarks reflected the prevailing opinion in his social circle, where many others also said "the obstacle to educating all children well is the union because the principal cannot hire and fire and assign teachers as he or she wants." Ravitch, on the other hand, believed that teachers needed unions more than ever because the billionaires of the 21st century wanted "to hire and fire at will."[48]

As Ravitch saw it, the value-added billionaires and the data-driven decision makers had already made a mess of the American economy. In their search for maximum profits, they had exported jobs and manufacturing overseas, and Jack Welch, the chief executive officer at General Electric, was one of the major culprits. While annually purging the bottom 10 percent of General Electric's workers, Welch also transformed "what was once a household brand known by every American [into] a financial services business, with profit as the only goal and the only value. . . . GE was a 'leader' in exporting jobs and manufacturing overseas and destroying a large sector of the consumer products industry in this nation." Instead of advancing the interests of their country and their fellow Americans, Welch and other CEOs were bent on maximizing profits. The United States was "losing jobs to India and China" for one reason: "because employers can get well-educated workers there for far less

---

47 Diane Ravitch to Deborah Meier, *Bridging Differences* (5 January 2008; 11 September 2007; 19 March 2007; 3 February 2009; 28 February 2007); Steve Jobs, quoted and paraphrased by Whiney Tilson, EdReform.blogspot.com (October 2011).

48 Diane Ravitch to Deborah Meier, *Bridging Differences* (5 January 2008; 11 September 2007; 19 March 2007; 3 February 2009; 28 February 2007).

than they must pay here."⁴⁹

In 2008 this strategy—a combination of "outsourcing" manufacturing jobs while "growing" financial services—making deals instead of making things—led to a major economic recession, but the billionaires still had enough money left over to bring their mindset to schooling. "Conveniently overlooking the fact that business practices and the ruthless pursuit of a competitive edge nearly destroyed our national economy," Ravitch wrote, "our business leaders" now said, "the schools must be redesigned to function like business . . . " "Schools with low scores must be closed, and states must open the flood gates to unlimited numbers of . . . charter schools. Schools must compete for students. Teachers must compete with one another for higher test scores. Everyone must be evaluated by those scores. Everything else is an 'insignificant' idea."⁵⁰

Some school reformers have jocularly referred to the controversies over education reform as "class warfare." Steven Brill's important book on the subject was published under that title, *Class Warfare* (2011). Yet Ravitch thought there was nothing funny about what amounted to an upper-class war on the middle class. As Ravitch saw it, the billionaire boys had already off-shored much of American manufacturing. And now they were waging war against another pillar of the middle class, America's teachers. They were using the shortcomings of Hispanic and African-American students as excuses for blaming teachers, for breaking unions, and for increasing the prerogatives of management.

Some observers doubtless considered this theory far-fetched. But the "billionaire boys" had shifted responsibility away from students and families, whom most people had traditionally blamed (or

---

49   Diane Ravitch to Deborah Meier, *ibid.* (21 October 2008; 16 April 2007).

50   *Ibid.*, Diane Ravitch to Deborah Meier (1 December 2009).

credited) for academic achievement. Instead, they blamed the teachers and their unions. Joel Klein, the schools chancellor in New York City, expressed a view that prevailed among value-added reformers when he complained that there were "many teachers who work by the clock. They show up a minute before 8:30 and leave a minute after 3, and when in school they do the barest minimum. They get dreadful results with students and... it's painfully obvious that they belong in another line of work." But they could not be fired because of union rules. Klein went on to complain that union contracts provided senior teachers with a salary of $80,000 a year when a beginning teacher could do just as well for $40,000. This made no sense, Klein wrote. "Why pay someone more for simply working another year?"[51]

Other reformers agreed. Whitney Tilson wrote that at his hedge fund "and in virtually any business in the country" employers could fire whomever they liked for whatever reason (except for legally proscribed discrimination). Because of the teachers unions, however, this could not be done in most public schools. To make matters worse, wrote another reformer, Steven Greenhut, thanks to their unions teachers had become the new "idle rich"—people who could retire while still in their 50s and then "spend 30 or more years receiving pensions that are the equivalent of millions of dollars in savings." In a scholarly paper sponsored by the Heritage Foundation and the American Enterprise Institute, Jason Richwine and Andrew G. Biggs also reported that teachers were overpaid. Richwine and Biggs conceded, "public school teachers earn less in wages on average than non-teachers with the same level of education." But after comparing teachers and non-teachers "on an objective measure of cognitive ability," IQ and SAT scores, one supposes, and after taking account of job security and retirement benefits, Richwine and Biggs concluded that "total compensation" for teachers was "52 percent greater than

---

51 Joel Klein, "What the School Reform Debate Misses About Teachers," *Washington Post* (13 March 2011); Klein "The Failure of American Schools," *The Atlantic* (June 2011).

fair market levels."⁵²

This argument resonated with many business magnates, who proposed to "reform" education by eliminating tenure and seniority. In the late 19th and early-20th centuries, civil service reform had been a leading progressive cause, and teachers had been given these protections as a defense against partisan reprisals. Similar protections had also been given to judges, professors, and many civil servants. As Judge Richard Posner has noted, "I happen to have a job as a federal court of appeals judge, in which everyone is securely tenured and paid the same salary, even though the judges vary in ability, experience, and effort." Posner further observed that there were "many jobs of that sort ... and it would be a mistake to think that all such jobs would be performed better if they were restructured along the Darwinian lines that prevail in business."⁵³

Such restructuring, however, was exactly what many business magnates considered the *sine qua non* for improving the academic achievement of Black and Hispanic students. Steve Jobs was far from a solitary voice when he said America's schools were "crippled by union work rules." Bill Gates also insisted that teachers' compensation should not be based on advanced degrees or years of service but, instead, should be based on how well students performed on standardized tests. Writing in the *Wall Street Journal*, New York schools chancellor Joel Klein said his goal was "a full-scale transition from a government-run monopoly to a competitive marketplace."⁵⁴

---

52 Whitney Tilson, "Teacher Evals," EdReform.blogspot.com (August 2011); Steven Greenhut, "Union Force Opposes Real Education," oaoa.com/article_a9cbedbf-dc32-575e-836d-f92723d040db.html (6 January 2011); Jason Richwine and Andrew G. Biggs, "Assessing the Compensation of Public-School Teachers," AEI.org/papers/education/k-12/assessing-the-compensation-of-public-school-teachers (1 November 2011).

53 Comment of Richard Posner, Becker-Posner-blog.com (9 September 2012).

54 Steve Jobs, quoted and paraphrased by Whitney Tilson, EdReform.blogspot.com (October 2011); Bill Gates; Joel Klein, "What the School Reform

Some rank-and-file bloggers concurred. One complained about public employees who received pensions while still in their 50s and then allowed taxpayers to pay them "to sit in front of the one-armed bandit or whatever for the next forty years." Another said the Democratic Party in California had become the party of retired government employees, many of whom spend 30 or more years receiving pensions that are the equivalent of millions of dollars in savings"—paid for by taxpayers, "the poor, the downtrodden, and the working class."[55]

Ravitch was astonished. She sensed that the nation was "hurtling back a century or more, to the age of the Robber Barons," when power was concentrated in the hands of corporate magnates who were not checked and balanced by the force of union workers. The billionaires were fielding an army of lobbyists. They were financing think tanks that put the billionaires' spin on policy issues. By offshoring manufacturing jobs, the billionaires had already destroyed the countervailing power of industrial unions. And now, in the early years of the 21st century, they were trying to get rid of public sector unions a well.[56]

The billionaires' approach to school reform eventually led Ravitch back toward the socialist opinions that had prevailed at the *New Leader* magazine when she had been a member of the staff there. In one letter of 2009, Ravitch affirmed, "I believe that the most important challenge to our society today is poverty." She also signed

---

Debate Misses about Teachers," *Washington Post* (13 March 2011); Klein, "The Failure of American Schools"; Klein, "When I Was Chancellor," *Wall Street Journal* (10 May 2011).

55 Mary Morrison, "Back to School in Los Angeles," *American Renaissance*, AmRen.com (5 October 2012) and comment of mutt 3033); Steven Greenhut, "Union Force Opposes Real Education."

56 Diane Ravitch, quoted by Whitney Tilson, "Ravitch: A Moment of National Insanity," EdReform.blogpot.com (March 2011); Paul Krugman, "Wisconsin Power Play," *New York Times* (21 February 2011).

a manifesto ("A Broader, Bolder Approach to Education") that said that schools alone could not eliminate the achievement gaps; that in addition to improving schools, the government should invest more in early-childhood programs, in health services, and in out-of-school enrichment programs.[57]

This was a point that writers on the left had been making for years, and one of these writers, Richard Rothstein of the Economic Policy Institute, applauded Ravitch for saying that "disadvantage children need . . . preschool and medical care. They need small classes . . . and . . . extra learning time. Their families need . . . coordinated social services that help them acquire necessary social and job skills . . ." Education could not be improved "if we ignore the disadvantages associated with poverty." Families needed "jobs and housing," and schools were only one important "part of a web of public and private agencies that buttress families."[58]

As Ravitch returned to her roots on the Left, as she stressed that "schools alone are insufficient to overcome the burdens imposed by poverty and that poor kids need preschool, health services, and other supports," Ravitch increasingly took aim at what she called "the underlying narrative" of the corporate approach to school reform. She said "the Gates Fund, the Broad Fund . . . all these very wealthy and powerful people" were taking reform on the wrong track because they focused on firing teachers and breaking unions. They said, "we can safely ignore growing income inequality and poverty and concentrate instead only on specific school reform policies." They assumed that "teachers are to blame if scores are low; that if

---

57 Diane Ravitch to Deborah Meier, *Bridging Differences* (2 June 2009); "A Broader, Bolder Approach to Education," at BoldApproach.org.

58 "A Broader, Bolder Approach to Education"; Richard Rothstein, "Moment of Clarity," NewRepublic.com (15 March 2010); Ravitch, *The Death and Life of the Great American School System*, 229.

we fire principals and teachers ... and have more testing, scores and graduation rates will rise, more students will go to college, and our society will prosper."⁵⁹

In 2011, Ravitch said that she did not think that Gates-style school reform was part of a conscious plot, although she recognized that the foundation-favored narrative was made to order for well-to-do people who wished to reduce their own taxes, for politicians who wished to slash the budget for public education, and for conservatives who wished to bust unions that had been supporting liberal causes. As time passed, Ravitch became even more critical of the billionaires. In one blog posting, Ravitch asked, "What do they want?" "To make money," was the answer. Education was a multi-billion dollar industry. There were "$$$$$ everywhere" and the billionaires were eager to see "how much money can be made off of this!" That was why they had launched "a massively well-financed campaign ... that seeks to replace our current system of public education—which for all its flaws is probably the most democratic institution we have...—with a market-based, non-unionized, privately managed system."⁶⁰

When it came to explaining the relatively poor performance of Black and Hispanic students, Ravitch did not blame bad teachers. Instead, she stressed a different story line, one that emphasized that America was "overrun by too much poverty, too much poverty among children." Instead of focusing "solely on 'how do we fire the bad teachers,'" she said, "we should be talking about how to make sure that our children have adequate health care, and that we have pre-K education, birth to 5-year old education."⁶¹

---

59   Diane Ravitch, comments on "The Daily Show" quoted by Whitney Tilson, EdReform.blogspot.com (March 2011).

60   Diane Ravitch, "Deborah Meier: Follow the Money," Diane Ravitch's blog, 9 February 2014; Ravitch, "Walton Family Foundation," DianeRavitch's Blog, 2 April 2014.

61   *Ibid.*; Diane Ravitch to Deborah Meier, *Bridging Differences* (12 May 2009; 21 September 2010; 7 June 2011).

In her book of 2013, *Reign of Error*, Ravitch argued that the nation's educational problems stemmed from a toxic mix of poverty and segregation. To combat poverty she called for an expanded version of Lyndon B. Johnson's War on Poverty. Going beyond 1960s-style social services such as food stamps, rent subsidies, and welfare payments to single mothers, Ravitch recommended a bevy of what she called "wraparound services": pre-natal care, high-quality early childhood education, and after-school and summer enrichment programs for children from poor families. She argued that every school should have a nurse, a psychologist, a guidance counselor, and smaller classes.

And this was not all. According to Ravitch, poverty was "not the only factor that affects academic achievement. Racial segregation also contributes to low academic achievement." To deal with the "problem" of differing patterns of ethnic concentration, Ravitch favored a return to the court-ordered busing policies of the 1970s. She did not accept the definition of *desegregation* that the Supreme Court established in *Brown v. Topeka Board of Education* (1954) and that Congress specified in the Civil Rights Act of 1964 : "'Desegregation' means the assignment of students to public schools and within such schools without regard to their race, color, religion, or national origin, but 'desegregation' shall not mean the assignment of students to public schools in order to overcome racial imbalance." Instead, Ravitch equated "segregation" with "racial imbalance" and implicitly called for a return to the sort of busing that the Supreme Court had authorized in the 1970s but repudiated in the 1990s and 2000s.

Some observers dismissed Ravitch's critique of the corporate approach to school reform. *New York Times* columnist David Brooks conceded that Ravitch had once been "one of the leading intellects behind the education reform movement." Nevertheless, in 2011 Brooks dismissively characterized Ravitch as "the nation's most vocal educational historian." At DFER, Whitney Tilson declared it "blindingly obviously that Diane Ravitch is nothing but a shill for the unions." Although Ravitch was widely regarded as a prominent historian, Tilson insisted, "The empress has no clothes." Ravitch was no longer "an objective researcher, fairly and accurately presenting both sides of an argument." She had become, rather, a defender of a status quo that served school employees rather than students. To make matters worse, she was maligning charter schools that had succeeded in uplifting youngsters in many inner cities.[62]

Another school reformer, Kevin Carey of the Education Sector, a Washington think tank, attacked Ravitch *ad hominem*. Writing in *The New Republic*, Carey said that Ravitch's turnabout on school reform was not based on new facts and evidence, as Ravitch claimed. It stemmed, rather, from personal pique over Joel Klein's decision not to appoint Ravitch's friend Mary Butz as head of a program that trained school principals, although Butz had headed just such a program in the past. Carey insinuated that Ravitch took this rebuff personally, since after a divorce from her husband in 1986 Ravitch and Butz had been "longtime partner[s]."[63]

Ravitch said her friend "did not seek a job from [Klein]." "I did not change my views about education because of anything Klein did or did not do nearly a decade earlier. That's ridiculous." Carey's story was based on interviews with unidentified sources and partook of a personal smear. It showed how far some school reformers were

---

62 David Brooks, "Smells Like School Spirit," *New York Times* (30 June 2011); EdReform.blogspot.com (29 April 2009).

63 Kevin Carey, "The Dissenter," *The New Republic* (23 November 2011). Eventually, Ravitch and Butz were married in a civil ceremony.

willing to go when it came to discrediting their critics. Carey did not mention that between 2006 and 2011 the Gates Foundation gave Carey's organization, EdSector, three grants for a total of $3,800,000. For a small organization, that was a lot of money.[64]

One of Ravitch's former colleagues, Michael J. Petrilli of the Thomas B. Fordham Institute, presented a more balanced critique. Petrilli acknowledged that Ravitch had hit the mark with many of her criticisms of corporate school reform. Because Ravitch was once "one of us," Perilli wrote, "she knows the weaknesses in our arguments"—"chief of [which] is the move to create prescriptive, top-down, statewide teacher-evaluation systems based largely on classroom-level test score gains." But Petrilli thought Ravitch's reform program—the combination of another war on poverty with a return to busing for racial balance—was naïve and romantic. Petrilli also found fault with Ravitch for "saying not a word about . . . family-structure woes," and for ignoring the influence of "a culture that shrugs at 14- or 16- or 18-year olds' getting pregnant (often not for the first time)." Petrilli might have added (although he did not do so) that Ravitch had little to say about disruptive students who undermined the education of their peers. According to Petrilli, "The skeptical, hard-nosed . . . Ravitch of the first half of her book [*Reign of Error*] turns into a pie-in-the-sky dreamer in the second half."[65]

Steve Sailer presented an even more telling critique of Ravitch. Sailer concurred with many of Ravitch's "newfound doubts about the current conventional wisdom on K-12 education reform." He agreed that it was "arrogant" for "the billionaire boys" to think they knew how to "reinvent schools from the ground up." He was especially skeptical about what he called "the educational fad of the 2010's: Blame

---

64 Diane Ravitch to author (18, 19, 24 February 2012); Ken Libby to author (24 February 2012).

65 Michael J. Petrilli, "Rain of Errors," *National Review Online*, 17 October, 2003.

Teachers." He considered it "self-evidently silly" to judge the quality of schools by measuring their students' test scores. Sailer, however, differed from Ravitch when it came to explaining why this was silly. According to Sailer, test scores were "IQ-dominated," and therefore indicated "how smart the students were before they even enrolled." In both *Death and Life* and *Reign of Error*, however, Ravitch ignored the importance of native intelligence.[66]

Sailer implied that Ravitch ignored intelligence because she wished to maintain her standing and influence in an egalitarian society. Yet a perusal of some of Ravitch's correspondence suggests that the omission was due to more than prudent calculation. Ravitch did not understand the arguments that IQ researchers had been making for years. Writing to her friend Deborah Meier, Ravitch recalled that when Richard Herrnstein and Charles Murray published *The Bell Curve* (1994), "I was not persuaded by their claims." "I still am not persuaded," Ravitch wrote, and by way of explanation Ravitch mentioned her own family. "I am one of eight children. We all had exactly the same parents and the same grandparents. Yet our school smarts and coping skills varied widely.... Based on what I knew from my own life, I was not willing to concede that heredity and genetics predetermined one's intelligence.... If Murray and Herrnstein's arguments were wrong in my family, I was willing to bet they were wrong in lots of other families as well."[67]

Actually, Ravitch's family experience was an argument *for*, not *against*, the importance of heredity. Psychologists have established that siblings differ a lot in IQ—on average by 12 points, compared with 17 for random strangers. But since parents provide similar environments for rearing their children, it seems unlikely that such

---

66 Steve Sailer, "Diane Ravitch, 'No Child Left Behind, and the Racial Achievement Gap's Kryptonite Cause"; Diane Ravitch, *Reign of Error* (New York: Alfred A. Knopf, 2013)

67 Diane Ravitch to Deborah Meier, *Bridging Differences* (30 May 2008).

great variation within families would be due to environmental differences. Most parents and most psychologists understand that the variation among siblings results from differences that inhere in the individual children.[68]

Nevertheless, Ravitch ignored the importance of intelligence. Neither *Death and Life* nor *Reign of Error* discussed the work of Arthur Jensen or other leading authorities on IQ. Nor was there any discussion of E. O. Wilson's evolutionary approach to sociobiology or to Henry Harpending's evolutionary approach to anthropology. These matters—IQ and evolutionary studies—will be discussed in Chapter 11 of this book. But Ravitch paid no attention to research that suggested that Mother Nature was partially responsible for the racial achievement gap.

As Steve Sailer had suggested, Ravitch probably sensed that IQ and evolution (and dysfunctional cultural values as well) had become taboo subjects that, if discussed, would banish her from the mainstream of American discourse. Instead, Ravitch emphasized that test results showed a correlation between family income and test scores—with the children of more well-to-do families scoring higher, on average, than children from poorer families. She did not mention that testing also showed a correlation between race and test scores, with the achievement gap between matched groups of well-to-do Blacks and Whites even larger than the gaps between middle- and lower-income Blacks and Whites. Nor did Ravitch mention that the mean SAT score for Whites from families with an annual income of less than $20,000 was as high as the mean score of Blacks from families with an annual income of more than $200,000.[69]

Critics have also said that Ravitch did a better job of criticizing

---

68 Linda S. Gottfredson, "The General Intelligence Factor," *Scientific American* (Winter 1998).

69 "Why Family Income Differences Don't Explain the Racial Gap in Sat Scores," *Journal of Blacks in Higher Education*, 62 (2008): 10-12; Steve Sailer, "2008 SAAT Scores by Race and Income," Vdare.com (15 March 2014).

school reformers than of proposing a program to improve American education. Whitney Tilson, for example, posed a challenging question: "even if some of [Ravitch's] critiques of reformers have some validity what is she offering as an alternative to the status quo that even she admits is unacceptable?" Tilson said he had "read her book carefully (and read/ follow her closely) and I've never heard ANYTHING." When Ravitch said the abolition of poverty was the *sine qua non* for school reform, Tilson insisted that she was "say[ing] nothing of any practical use."[70]

In point of fact, however, Ravitch has proposed more than a re-run of Lyndon B. Johnson's war on poverty. "We need better teachers," she has acknowledged. But she also maintained that the best way to achieve this goal is to require that teachers must have a college degree in the subject they are teaching. She conceded that teachers should be "assessed" and "evaluated," but maintained that this should be done by "peer review teams." In addition, since alternative job opportunities for American women have improved in recent decades, Ravitch said that, to attract more good teachers, schools must now provide "higher salaries, better support and mentoring systems, and better working conditions."[71]

In addition, over the course of four decades, Ravitch emphasized the importance of a core curriculum, based on the Western cultural canon. Through many twistings and turnings, Ravitch remained a trustee of E. D. Hirsch's Core Knowledge Foundation. "I do worry about the risk of Balkanization," Ravitch confided to her friend Deborah Meier. Ravitch feared that the United States could not have "a common democratic culture without some shared knowledge, shared discussions, shared poems, and shared history." For Ravitch,

---

70 Whitney Tilson, "Email Discussion with Gary Rubenstein,' EdReform. blogspot.com (July 2011).

71 Diane Ravitch to Andrew Rotherham, "Is Education on the Wrong Track," *The New Republic* (21 March 2010); Ravitch, "The Myth of Charter Schools," *New York Review of Books* (11 November 2010).

the key to better schooling is a rich curriculum, not high-stakes testing and data-based merit pay.[72]

By the turn of the twenty-first century, however, America had become too diverse to agree on any core that went beyond elementary reading and arithmetic. Many people still treasured American history and Western Civilization, but others celebrated varieties of multiculturalism. Many people favored directive schools where teachers told students what was important. Others said that students should construct their own understandings.[73]

Ravitch nevertheless clung to the idea of a liberal arts curriculum. She recognized that an attempt to establish National History Standards had failed in the 1990s. But Ravitch thought this was because the scholars in charge, a group of historians at UCLA, had larded their standards with too much political bias—"pretty strong partisan language" was the way Ravitch described the UCLA standards in one letter. Surely, Ravitch wrote, it should be possible "to reach a consensus" in other fields, such as mathematics. As it happened, however, the standards developed by the National Council of Teachers of Mathematics (NCTM) were almost as controversial as the UCLA history standards. In the name of "constructivism," the NCTM standards emphasized "conceptualizing" while scanting the importance of precise calculation. The NCTM standards were no sooner promulgated than many mathematicians, scientists, and engineers decried them as "fuzzy" and "intellectually vacuous." Eventually, the NCTM standards were abandoned—but only after it turned out that adopting those standards had led to a decline in test scores.[74]

---

72 Diane Ravitch to Deborah Meier, *Bridging Differences* (27 March 2007; 25 September 2007; 27 June 2007); Sherman Dorn, "The Death and Life of Market-Based Reform," *Educational Review* 13 (22 April 2010).

73 Diane Ravitch to Deborah Meier, *Bridging Differences* (23 October 2007).

74 Diane Ravitch to Deborah Meier, *Bridging Differences* (27 June 2007;

The demise of the UCLA history standards and the NCTM math standards cast doubt on Ravitch's assumption that professional educators could be trusted to manage America's schools. Ravitch acknowledged that the UCLA and NCTM standards were problematic, but she seemed not to recognize that the problems stemmed from the very nature of the educational establishment. The UCLA standards were politically biased, but similar biases were pervasive among professional historians and high school teachers throughout the United States. The NCTM standards went off the deep end of progressive constructivism, but the NCTM reflected views that were widespread among education professors all over the nation. As mathematician David Klein has noted, "Ravitch's solution" was "to return control to 'professional educators.'" But it was the shortcomings of the professional educators—their failure to insist that students learn the basic facts of history and mathematics—that had paved the way for business-based reformers to move into education. America's schools had been caught in a giant pincer movement between the intellectual trendiness and liberal politics of professors and teachers, on the one hand, and the coercion and ideology of the billionaire boys on the other.[75]

---

7 October 2008; 11 December 2007); Ravitch, *The Death and Life of the Great American School System*, 17; David Klein, "A Quarter Century of U.S. 'Math Wars' and Political Partisanship," *British Society for the History of Mathematics* 22 (2007) 22-33; Suzanne Wilson, *California Dreaming: Reforming Mathematics Education* (New Haven: Yale University Press, 2003).

75 David Klein, "The Death and Life of the Great American School System," *Educational Horizons* 88 (Summer 2010), 194-199.

II

The Race Realists

As has been noted, Diane Ravitch criticized many of the recent trends in school reform. But Ravitch paid no attention to IQ studies that suggested that the racial achievement gap stemmed from the fact that White and Asian students, on average, are smarter than African-Americans and Mestizo Hispanics. When she ignored the research on IQ, Ravitch followed the example of most other education scholars and writers. She apparently recognized that most societies have pervasive orthodoxies that are maintained by a tacit agreement not to discuss certain matters. She probably sensed as well that many people would regard any such discussion of race and IQ as bad manners.[1]

Other scholars and writers, however, believed that the racial gap in achievement was based on a racial gap in average IQ, which was derived, in part, from genetic inheritance. Many of these scholars believed that the influence of genes was so great that racial and ethnic achievement gaps could not be eradicated or even reduced substantially. Those who emphasized the importance of inherent differences often were called "hereditarians." In recent years, many hereditarians have called themselves "race realists."

---

1   For an astute discussion of this point, see George Orwell, "Freedom of the Press," a proposed preface to *Animal Farm*, *Times Literary Supplement*, 15 September 1972.

The mainstream media gave the impression that only a few maverick racists subscribed to hereditarianism and that the great majority of well-informed observers were egalitarians who believe that group differences are purely the result of cultural influences. Egalitarians maintain, for example, that the effects of slavery, segregation, and discrimination account for the fact that the average IQ of Black Americans trails that of Whites by about one standard deviation.

Yet egalitarianism is not the prevailing opinion among experts in the field of psychological measurement. When Mark Snyderman and Stanley Rothman surveyed more than 600 such experts in 1988, most of these experts agreed with the assertion that IQ tests accurately measured the ability to solve problems and to reason abstractly; and most also agreed with the statement that the IQ gap between Blacks and Whites was due in part to racial inheritance. Among these experts, the prevailing opinion was that "nurture" counted but that "nature" was responsible for at least half of the racial disparity in average IQs.[2]

Snyderman and Rothman did "survey research" that allowed respondents to answer anonymously. The answers might have been different if the experts had been identified. In modern America, after all, the penalty for linking intelligence with heredity and race can be severe. This point was illustrated in the reaction to *The Bell Curve* (1994), in which Richard J. Herrnstein and Charles Murray made the case for the importance of IQ (and also suggested that, in accounting for racial disparities, "the data . . . tip toward a mixture of genetic and environmental influences"). The 845-page book enjoyed phenomenal sales success—with more than 500,000 copies sold in the first six months. But *The Bell Curve* also sparked tremendous controversy. Herrnstein died shortly before publication, but the surviving author, Murray, was widely denounced for broaching topics that had been considered unmentionable—that the races differed in intelligence and

---

2   Mark Snyderman and Stanley Rothman, *The IQ Controversy*.

that the differences probably were based, at least in part, on genetic inheritance. Murray found himself ostracized by many academics even as others signed a statement affirming that the principal conclusions of *The Bell Curve* were "mainstream science on intelligence."[3]

The *Bell Curve* controversy reinforced the inclination to shy away from research on and writing about IQ. Education scholars and writers recognized that almost every society has taboo topics that members are expected to avoid. But the United States also has a tradition of free speech and unfettered scientific investigation. Although most people who wrote about education respected the prevailing prohibition with respect to IQ, research on genetics and DNA continued and seemed to reinforce the argument of *The Bell Curve*. Yet this did not make hereditarianism any less controversial.

The experience of biologist James D. Watson illustrated this point. There was hardly a more distinguished scientist than Watson, who had received a Nobel Prize in 1961 for his work as co-discoverer of the double helix structure of DNA. For several years, this renown allowed Watson to speak with uncommon candor. Thus, in a conversation with Harvard's president Derrick Bok, Watson estimated that by the year 2020 "the key genes affecting differences in human intelligence would be found." In his autobiography, published in 2007, Watson went on to say that "many persons of goodwill" saw "only harm in our looking too closely at individual genetic essences." They did not wish to "face up to facts that will likely change the way we look at ourselves." But Watson predicted that science would continue its march, and the truth would emerge. Eventually, American society

---

[3] Richard J. Herrnstein and Charles Murray, *The Bell Curve*, 311 and *passim*; Linda Gottfredson et al., "Statement on Intelligence," *Wall Street Journal* (13 December 1994). For one collection of the criticisms, see Rusell Jacoby and Naomi Glauberman, eds., *The Bell Curve Debate* (New York: Random House, 1995).

would recognize that there was "no firm reason to anticipate that the intellectual capacities of peoples geographically separated in their evolution should prove to have evolved identically. Our wanting to reserve equal power of reason to some universal heritage of humanity will not be enough to make it so."[4]

Watson's candor eventually precipitated a backlash. It did so in 2007 when Watson told an English reporter that he was "inherently gloomy about the prospect of Africa because all our social policies are based on the fact that their intelligence is the same as ours—whereas all the testing says not really." Upon reading this statement in the press, the Science Museum in London immediately canceled one of Watson's lectures, with a spokesman for the museum explaining, "We feel that Dr. Watson has gone beyond the point of acceptable debate and we are, as a result, canceling his talk." Shortly thereafter, Watson was suspended from his positions at the Cold Spring Harbor Laboratory in New York, which he had led for 39 years, first as director, then as president, and then as chancellor. An article in the *New York Times* told readers that Watson "hadn't a scientific leg to stand on" when he implied "that black Africans are less intelligent than whites." But others said that Watson had been denounced for "saying aloud what most well-informed people more or less assume is true."[5]

Watson capitulated. He apologized for his statements. Though Watson had received the highest of praise and respect for 50 years, the firestorm that resulted from his comments was apparently unbearable. In an attempt to placate critics, Watson released a statement saying,

---

4   James D. Watson, *Avoid Boring People: Lessons from a Life in Science* (New York: Alfred A. Knopf, 2007) 326-27.

5   James D. Watson and museum spokesperson, quoted by Steve Sailer, "James D. Watson—A Modern Galileo," Vdare.com (21 October 2007); George Johnson, "Bright Scientists: Dim Notions," *New York Times* (28 October 2007); William Saletan, "Created Equal," Slate.com (18 November 2007).

To those who have drawn from my words the inference that Africa, as a continent, is somehow genetically inferior, I can only apologize unreservedly. That is not what I meant. More importantly, from my point of view, there is no scientific basis for such a belief.[6]

In some quarters, Watson's apology was greeted with dismay. Pat Buchanan asked, "Why, with all his honors, prestige, and security, did Dr. Watson feel the necessity to apologize for what he wrote, said, and believes?" Buchanan then made an unflattering comparison of Watson with Christian martyrs who had sacrificed their lives rather than renounce their beliefs. Watson, however, said that the controversy over his remarks led him to think "ever more intensely on the values passed on to me by my father . . . and by my mother . . ." who had stressed the importance of "social justice, especially the need for those on top to care for the less fortunate."[7]

Nevertheless, even as Watson apologized, other scholars disregarded the possibility of reprisals and continued to express hereditarian views. Their research was driven in large part by a belief that lack of knowledge would harm sick people. President Bill Clinton mentioned this "immense new power to heal" in 2000. "Genomic science will have a real impact on all our lives," Clinton said. "It will revolutionize the diagnosis, prevention, and treatment of most, if not all, human diseases."[8]

---

6   Statements of James D. Watson, *The Independent* (19 October 2007) and *New York Times* (25 October 2007).

7   Patrick J. Buchanan, "The Recantation of Dr. Watson"; Statement of James D. Watson, *New York Times* (25 October 2007).

8   Bill Clinton, quoted by Nicholas Wade, *Life Script: How the Human Genome Discoveries Will Transform Medicine and Enhance Your Health* (New York: Simon & Schuster, 2001) 14-15.

Genetic research has not yet revolutionized medicine, but there have been important advances. Thanks to this research, doctors have learned that enalapril, a standard treatment for chronic heart failure, is less helpful to Blacks than to Whites. They have learned that Blacks should be given lower doses of Prozac because they metabolize antidepressants more slowly than Caucasians and Asians; that Whites respond better than Blacks to the standard treatment for active hepatitis C; that Blacks and Whites tend to respond differently to treatments for high blood pressure.[9]

In addition to improving medical treatment, these discoveries challenged the premises of people who maintained either that race did not exist or that racial differences were insignificant. And as genomic research proceeded, the balance of scientific opinion shifted more and more toward the importance of heredity. One article in the *New York Times* noted that in the age of DNA genetic information was "slipping out of the laboratory" and pointing toward "appreciable differences between races in the genes that influence socially important traits." Richard A. Schweder, a professor at the University of Chicago and the president of the Society for Psychological Anthropology, observed that in the debate over the relative importance of nature and nurture, "the pendulum" had swung "from nature in the first decades of the [twentieth] century, to nurture in the 1930s, 40s, 50s, and 60s, to nature once again in the 70s, 80s, and 90s."[10]

The extent and significance of inherent racial differences is not yet a settled question, but there is little doubt about which way the wind is blowing. Genomic science carried the message that because

---

9 *New York Times* (20 December 2002); Sally L. Satel, "I Am a Racially Profiling Doctor," *New York Times* (5 May 2002).

10 Amy Harmon, "In DNA Era, New Worries about Prejudice" *New York Times* (11 November 2007); Richard A. Schweder, review of Carl Degler, *In Search of Human Nature, New York Times Book Review* (17 March 1991) 1.

human populations evolved in quite different environments, different races had different distributions of DNA. "There are clear differences between people of different continental ancestries," said Marcus W. Feldman, a professor of biological sciences at Stanford. Feldman was a racial egalitarian, but he nevertheless expected that researchers would establish the genetic origins of racial differences in IQ. "I can see it coming," Feldman said.[11]

To be sure, some egalitarians tried to suppress many of the scholars who were doing research on human bio-diversity. As a result, some research grants were canceled and some worthy scholars were marginalized. The strongest opposition came not from external forces of either the right or the left but from fellow scholars who were predisposed against research that challenged the conventional wisdom of the mainstream.[12]

Sometimes the censorship was self-imposed, as in the case of Bruce Lahn, a professor of human genetics at the University of Chicago. In 2006, Lahn presented evidence to show that mutations that affected the size of the human brain had occurred in Asia and Europe but not in Africa. Dr. Lahn, an immigrant from China, did not understand American political correctness and considered it "a triumphant moment" when he published two articles in a highly regarded journal, *Science*, maintaining that DNA changes had taken hold and spread widely in Europe and Asia but were not common in sub-Saharan Africa. One magazine described Lahn's research as "the moment anti-racists and egalitarians have dreaded," and the media department at the University of Chicago medical school feared the

---

11 Marcus Feldman, quoted by Amy Harmon, "In DNA Era, New Worries about Prejudice."

12 This suppression has been described in many good books. One of the best is *The Shadow University* (New York: The Free Press, 1999), by Alan Charles Kors and Harvey A. Silvergate.

work would be too controversial for the university. As one story in the *Wall Street Journal* noted, scientists were accustomed to dealing with many physical differences, but they "tensed up when it comes to dealing with the same sort of research on the brain."[13]

At first Lahn stood by his research, saying, "Society will have to grapple with some very difficult facts." But Lahn had second thoughts after he learned more about the extent to which his research had touched a raw nerve. The University of Chicago abandoned a patent application it had filed to develop a test that would draw on Lahn's work. And some of Lahn's co-authors were uncomfortable with the publicity their work was receiving. Lahn then turned to other projects, saying he had questions about "whether some knowledge might not be worth having." This statement predictably drew criticism on the World Wide Web. "Welcome to the new Dark Ages," one writer scoffed. Another wrote that Lahn had been made "to stand before the altar of equality and recant. The sun moves around the earth."[14]

Despite the suppression and self-censorship, genomic research continued. The medical discoveries were only the beginning of what the liberal journalist William Saletan called an "onslaught of genetic research." Saletan wrote regularly for *Slate*, a webzine affiliated with the *Washington Post*. In a series of columns in 2007, he compared genetic research to an "oncoming train." The first few cars, carrying medical discoveries, were "already in view" and right behind loomed additional research that showed that, compared with Whites, "blacks mature more quickly . . . and develop teeth, strength, and dexterity earlier. They sit, crawl, walk, and dress themselves earlier. They reach sexual maturity faster, and they have better eyesight." There were additional carloads of research that identified genes that

---

13   *Wall Street Journal* (16 June 2006).

14   *Ibid.*; E_Pluribus, comment at AmRen.com (18 December 2006).

varied among populations, and it seemed likely that some of these genes "affect mental traits."[15]

"How this happened isn't clear," Saletan wrote, but he thought it possible that "genes for cognitive complexity became so crucial in some places that nature favored them over genes for speed and vision." "Nature isn't stupid," Saletan wrote. "If Africans, Asians, and Europeans evolved different genes, the reason is that their respective genes were suited to their respective environments." Groups whose ancestors had evolved in frigid climes or high altitudes could be expected to differ from groups who traced their ancestry to the tropics or to sea level.[16]

Like most egalitarians, Saletan wished that the *New York Times* had been correct when it told its readers that James D. Watson did not have "a scientific leg to stand on." But this was not so. On the contrary, Saletan wrote, the time had come when egalitarians should "prepare for the possibility that equality of intelligence, in the sense of racial averages on tests, will turn out not to be true." To drive his point home, Saletan suggested a historical parallel. He said that modern egalitarians were facing a challenge similar to the one that evolution once posed for Christian fundamentalists. At first, many Christians had denounced Darwin's theory as, in the words of William Jennings Bryan, jeopardizing "the doctrine of brotherhood," undermining "the sympathetic activities of a civilized society," and "paralyzing the hope of reform." Saletan believed the same values were under attack in modern America. "But this time, the threat is racial genetics, and the people struggling with it are liberals."[17]

---

15 William Saletan, "Personal Best," Slate.com (5 May 2009); Saletan, "Created Equal," Slate.com (28 November 2007).

16 William Saletan, "Created Equal," Slate.com (28 November 2007).

17 *Ibid.*

Eventually, most Christians modified their understanding of Creation. In the 21st century, Saletan said, egalitarians faced a similar challenge. "You can try to reconcile evidence of racial differences with a more sophisticated understanding of equality and opportunity. Or you can fight the evidence." Saletan was "for reconciliation." He said that those who disputed the evidence would be regarded as "liberal creationists." He left readers with the impression that empirical disinterested science had established a hereditarian explanation for the IQ gap and that racial egalitarians were engaging in a sort of wishful, quasi-superstitious social scientism.[18]

Many of *Slate*'s readers rejected Saletan's assessment, just as many Christian fundamentalists once had rejected the views of Christian modernists. Readers flooded *Slate* with so many letters of complaint that the webzine's editor, Jacob Weisberg, felt compelled to offer an explanation, saying that that because Saletan was a senior writer his articles were not edited, "but these should have been—carefully." Within a week, *Slate* published a rejoinder by another columnist, Stephen Metcalf, who said the scientific argument was not yet settled. Far from being a conflict between science and superstition, Metcalf wrote, the debate over race, intelligence, and genetics was "a conflict between science and science." According to Metcalf, many years would pass before conclusions would be in order.[19]

In the face of criticism, Saletan backed down. "Last week," he noted in November 2007, "I wrote about the possibility of genetic IQ differences among races. I wanted to discuss whether egalitarianism

---

18 Ibid.

19 Jacob Weisberg, quoted by Gerald Bracey, "William Saletan, Race, Genes and Intelligence," *HuffingtonPost.com* (2 December 2007); Stephen Metcalf, "A Response to William Saletan's Series on Race and IQ," Slate.com (3 December 2007).

could survive if this scenario, raised last month by James Watson, turned out to be true." Saletan then explained that he now had misgivings. He was merely a journalist, he wrote. "I'm not an expert." "I don't want this role."[20]

Saletan also recognized that the new genetic research might reinforce views that anti-Black racists had traditionally put forward to justify segregation. Genetic researchers insisted that they were propelled by a desire to know the truth. But some of their findings—especially the ones that suggested that Blacks were, on average, less intelligent than Caucasians or Asians—offered new support for opinions that had once prevailed among White Americans. Saletan therefore came to wonder if the new research was subconsciously influenced by traditional racism. "We can't just be 'race realists,'" Saletan wrote. "We have to be realists about racism. No fact in human history is more pervasive than our tendency to prejudge, fear, despise, persecute, and fight each other based on even the shallowest observable differences."[21]

Saletan then made an about face. In 2007 he had urged egalitarians to come to terms with DNA. But in 2008 and 2009 he warned of the danger of believing that nature had endowed Blacks, on average, with traits that were problematical in terms of succeeding in school and thriving in a modern society. He feared that an anti-Black racism was simmering beneath the surface of White America and that old-fashioned bigotry might come to the fore if rank-and-file Whites were emboldened by genetic scientists. Saletan even feared that "racial framing"—reporting racial breakdowns on crime statistics or racial averages on standardized academic tests—would "promote differential treatment of people by race." "You have to beware," Saletan wrote, "the injustice this kind of grouping

---

20 William Saletan, "Created Equal," Slate.com (28 November 2007).

21 William Saletan, "Not Black and White," Slate.com (5 May 2008).

and averaging does to individuals." Saletan then developed a new definition of racism—"classifying and comparing by race, rather than using some other classification system or judging each person as an individual."[22]

Even for some egalitarians, this was too much. Writing for *The New Republic*, the Black linguist John McWhorter declared that Saletan had "learned his lesson too well. He was shot at like a varmint . . . after writing some columns on evidence that Black people are genetically less gifted mentally than Whites. Now, announcing that he 'learned his lesson the hard way,'" Saletan was inveighing against even tabulating crime statistics and test results by race. "What worries Saletan," McWhorter noted, "is that openly racist bloggers . . . are using the results as evidence that black people really are less intelligent than others."[23]

McWhorter thanked Saletan for "a lovely gesture of concern." But McWhorter insisted that the gesture was not necessary. While racially conscious bloggers were "chattering away year after year, we elected a black president," and the bloggers ("those bozos") "can't do a thing about it." McWhorter further noted that "when Saletan wrote about the evidence on Black intelligence, in a polite, informed way, it was a sign of our times that so many people were appalled at his having even brought up the topic." "Our public discourse is at a point where when Saletan even entertains the data that makes us so uncomfortable he is excoriated endlessly." In this context—one of "deeply rooted cultural revulsion towards open bigotry"—there was no need to suppress evidence. "We don't need [Saletan's] kind of protection," McWhorter concluded.[24]

---

22 Ibid.; William Saletan, "Mental Segregation," Slate.com (4 May 2009).

23 John McWhorter, "Why Saletan Thinks We Should Keep the Black-White Performance Gap Under Wraps," NewRepublic.com (1 May 2009).

24 Ibid; John McWhorter, "Saletan Responds," NewRepublic.com (5 May 2009).

The Race Realists

There is evidence to support McWhorter's view. Some examples have been cited already, among them: the furor that erupted when James D. Watson alluded to the average IQ of Black Africans; the controversy that engulfed Harvard's President Larry Summers after he mentioned that women have been less likely than men to make extremely high scores on standardized mathematics tests; the reprimand that student Stephanie Grace received for mentioning (in a private e-mail) the possibility (although not the likelihood, in Grace's opinion) that genetic inheritance might be partly responsible for the comparatively low scores that Blacks make on standardized academic tests.

Yet another example came to the fore in the Spring of 2013 when Jason Richwine, a Harvard-trained researcher then working for the Heritage Foundation, reported that immigrants from Mexico had an average IQ of only 89. This was not news. During the previous generation, many studies had made the same point and most knowledgeable social scientists accepted Richwine's estimate. Like Watson and Summers, however, Richwine was punished for saying something that well-informed scholars knew was true. He was forced to resign from his position at the Heritage Foundation, and he came in for severe criticism at Harvard. One group of graduate students said Richwine's Ph.D. degree should be rescinded on the ground that researchers in the social sciences were required to "take a course to ensure that we will not harm our research subjects." As interpreted by these graduate students, this requirement prohibited researchers from criticizing their subjects—or from mentioning any evidence that might be construed as criticism. Another 1,200 Harvard students—a group that apparently knew little about the persistence of racial and ethnic achievement gaps despite the expenditure of billions of dollars for school reforms—signed a petition that said, "If there are IQ differences across racial and ethnic groups, why didn't Richwine call for better education programs that would level out differences?" The petitioners acknowledged that "people differ in their biologically determined qualities," but nevertheless insisted that discovery of a correlation between some of these aptitudes and a group's success in school or the workplace was of no scientific interest and of no social significance, except to racists, sexists, and the like.[25]

At the same time, however, a growing number of scholars and writers embraced varieties of race realism. In 1978, Harvard Professor E. O. Wilson had been doused by students and ostracized by some colleagues, but eventually Wilson was widely celebrated as the pioneering founder of two new academic fields, evolutionary biology and evolutionary psychology. By the turn of the 21st century, these fields had come into vogue, despite their smacking of race realism. Meanwhile, the Internet was rife with realistic discussions of race, which sometimes was called "human bio-diversity" or simply "HBD." John McWhorter disparaged journalists and bloggers who ignored the taboos of the conventional mainstream. But many of these writers were people of superior intelligence.

Consider the case of John Derbyshire, who in addition to writing for various webzines also was a regular contributor to America's most influential conservative magazine, *National Review* (*NR*). By the time Derbyshire began to write for *NR*, the magazine had long-since moved away from its own youthful flirtation with hereditarianism. In 2007, *NR* expressed no support for James D. Watson, and in 2008 *NR* published a cover story entitled, "Escaping the Tyranny of Genes: The Fallacy of Genetic Determinism." The author of this article, Jim Manzi, denounced "the linkage of race and IQ," which Manzi associated with "the pretense to scientific knowledge." Like *NR*, most other conservative journals also steered clear of anything that smacked of race realism.[26]

---

25 Everette Dionne, "Harvard Students Petition," *ClutchMagazineonline.com*, 20 May 2013; Meghan E. Irons, "Harvard Students Erupt at Scholar Jason Richwine's Claim in Thesis," *Boston Globe*. 18 May 2013; "Harvard University Students Take a Stand," *TheSocietyPage.org*, 22 May 2013.

26 Jim Manzi, "Escaping the Tyranny of Genes," *National Review* (June 2, 2008).

Derbyshire was one of the leading writers at *National Review*, but he survived for several years despite occasional expressions of race realism. One instance occurred in 2010, when Derbyshire agreed to speak at the University of Pennsylvania Law School, where the Black Law Students Association (BLSA) assembled four members for a panel discussion of the question, "Should the government play a role in eliminating racial disparities in education and employment?" Derbyshire initially declined the invitation, saying, "perhaps, given my views—which I sketched for them clearly—I might not be a good 'fit' for the panel." But Derbyshire eventually accepted after the BLSA persisted with its invitation.[27]

Derbyshire began his remarks by saying that he thought the question before the panel was based on a false premise. He did not think racial disparities in education could be eliminated, and therefore a discussion about whether the government should play a greater or lesser role in eliminating them was beside the point. According to Derbyshire, these disparities were "facts in the natural world, like the orbits of the planets. They can't be legislated out of existence; nor can they be 'eliminated' by social or political action."[28]

Derbyshire offered both rational and empirical grounds for believing that there are "natural, intractable differences between the human races." His rational argument was Biology 101. "If a species is divided into separate populations, and those populations are left in reproductive isolation from each other for many generations, they will diverge. If you return after several hundred generations have passed, you will observe that the various traits that characterize individuals of the species are now distributed at different frequencies in the various populations. After a few *ten thousands* of generations, the divergence

---

27 "Remarks at a Panel Discussion," JohnDerbyshire.com/Opinions/HumanSciences/upennlaw.html.

28 *Ibid.*

of the populations will be so great they can no longer cross-breed; and that is the origin of species."[29]

Derbyshire proceeded to say that mankind "separated into two parts, 50, 60, or 70 thousand years ago, depending on which paleoanthropologist you ask. One part remained in Africa, the ancestral homeland. The other crossed into Southwest Asia, then split, and re-split, and re-split, until there were human populations living in near-total reproductive isolation from each other in all parts of the world. This went on for hundreds of generations, causing the divergences we see today. Different physical types, as well as differences in behavior, intelligence, and personality, are exactly what one would expect to observe when scrutinizing these divergent populations."[30]

Derbyshire then mentioned empirical evidence. There were, of course, racial differences in appearance. But there was much more. Derbyshire noted that over the course of seven Olympics "every one of the finalists in the men's 100 meters sprint was of West African ancestry—56 out of 56 finalists." Such an outcome was highly improbable if race was only skin deep. Derbyshire also noted that there was "a huge academic literature on the gaps in cognitive test results [i.e., IQ tests], practically all of it converging on the fact that African-American mean scores on cognitive tests fall below the white means by a tad more than one standard deviation." The gap did not disappear when Black and White subjects were matched in terms of social and economic factors. As Derbyshire saw it, the gap was so regular and persistent that it was extremely unlikely that heredity was not at least partly responsible for the disparities. Nor was it likely that the disparities could be eliminated by social engineering. Derbyshire also said there were substantial disparities in many other areas—including "the 'BIP' traits—behavior, intelligence, and personality."[31]

---

29 *Ibid.*

30 *Ibid.*

31 *Ibid.*

In a concluding comment, Derbyshire noted that racial disparities were statistical averages. He acknowledged that within each population there was much variation. Each race contained individuals who exceeded the group means. Given the difference between Black and White means on intelligence tests, however, one could deduce that only 15 percent of the African-American population would score higher on cognitive tests than the average White test-taker.[32]

Derbyshire spoke for only ten minutes. Had he been allotted more time, he could have mentioned that a substantial body of scholarship had also established a correlation between general intelligence and job performance. Industrial psychologists had conducted more than 500 studies that showed that cognitive tests were valid predictors of job performance. Another 500 studies by the U. S. Armed Forces yielded similar results. In military drills, for example, tank crews with higher average test scores made more *kills* than crews with lower average scores. Even when it came to the proverbial "kitchen patrol" (KP), there was a positive correlation between the scores servicemen made on the Army General Classification Test and the supervisors' assessments of their work. Researchers had also established that an IQ of at least 75 is required to master the subjects taught in elementary school; that high school students with an IQ below 105 are not likely to pass all the courses in a college prep curriculum; and that those with an IQ below 115 are not likely to succeed in graduate school. Research also indicates that the average IQ of high-level executives and of physicians is about 125, and that few people in these professions are found below IQ 115. For high school teachers, the minimum IQ is around 108, for fire fighters, 91, for truck drivers and butchers, 86.[33]

---

32 Ibid.

33 Linda S. Gottfredson, "Occupational Aptitude Patterns Map," *Journal of Vocational Behavior* 29 (1986) 254-91; Gottfredson, "Reconsidering Fairness," *Journal of Vocational Behavior*, 33 (1988) 293-319, especially 302-03.

Had Derbyshire been allotted yet more time, he might have mentioned more recent research that connected genetic developments with economic, educational, and cultural patterns. In the wake of *Sociobiology*, a landmark 1975 book by Harvard biologist E. O. Wilson, a growing number of scientists came to accept the hypothesis of group selection—the theory that Darwinian natural selection operated not only upon individuals but also on the groups to which the individuals belonged. There were critics, to be sure. As has been mentioned, on one occasion a group of detractors stormed a platform where Wilson was speaking, doused the professor with a pitcher of water, and chanted, "Wilson, you're all wet."

Nevertheless, *Sociobiology* appealed to many of the best minds in science. By the time a 25th anniversary edition of the book was published in 2000, Amazon.com listed 416 titles under "sociobiology" and 1,218 under "human evolution." Most mainstream media still gave their readers and listeners the impression that all groups have an equal distribution of potential talent—a view that Derbyshire derided as the Dogma of Zero Group Differences (or the DZGD, for short). But scientists increasingly acknowledged that different environments selected for different traits. Summarizing a view that had come to prevail among biologists and geneticists by the turn of the 21st century, *New York Times* science writer Nicholas Wade explained that racial differences arose "because after the ancestral human population in Africa spread throughout the world..., geographical barriers prevented interbreeding. Consequently, under the influence of natural selection . . . people . . . diverged away from the ancestral population, creating new races." In his 2014 book, *A Troublesome Inheritance: Genes, Race and Human History*, Wade summarized and discussed a large body of research that indicates that evolution in different environments has led to different distributions of genes that influence not just skin color but also behavior, intelligence, and personality. [34]

---

34 Edward O. Wilson, *Sociobiology: The New Synthesis* (Cambridge: Harvard

For some time it had been obvious that there were racial differences in skin pigmentation and in resistance to specific diseases. But in the 1950s and 1960s, informed opinion regarded these differences as relatively insignificant. Berkeley historian Kenneth M. Stampp reflected this view in 1956, when he asserted in memorable language, "Negroes *are*, after all, only white men with black skins, nothing more, nothing less."[35]

With the advance of research on DNA, however, many scientists came to think that the various races differed in significant ways. DNA researchers were no longer "talking about skin, eye, or hair color," wrote University of Iowa history professor Marshall Poe. They were "talking about intelligence, temperament, and a host of other traits." They were saying, "The races ... are differently abled in ways that really matter."[36]

This point was illustrated in 2006, when John Brockman, a literary agent for science writers, put a question to Steven Pinker, a Harvard cognitive scientist and popular science writer. Brockman noted that the history of science was replete with discoveries that were considered "socially, morally, or emotionally dangerous in their time: the Copernican and Darwinian revolutions are the most obvious." And he asked, "What is your dangerous idea? An idea you think about ... that is dangerous not because it is assumed to be false, but because it might be true?" In response, Pinker answered: "Groups of people may differ genetically in their average talents and temperaments." Marlene Zuk, an evolutionary biologist at the University of Massachusetts,

---

University Press, 1975); Steve Sailer, "Sociobiology at Age 25," *National Review* (19 June 2000); Nicholas Wade, "Two Scholarly Articles," *New York Times* (20 March 2003); Wade, *A Troublesome Inheritance* (New York: The Penguin Press, 2014).

35 Kenneth M. Stampp, *The Peculiar Institution* (New York: Alfred A. Knopf, 1956) vii.

36 Marshall Poe, "The Inconvenient Truth About Race," Azure.org.il /article.php?id=522, Autumn 5770/2009.

expressed the concern of many progressive egalitarians. Zuk noted that an increasing number of genetically-informed scholars believed that isolated groups of people, such as sub-Saharan Africans or American Indians, for example, were subject to differing selection. And that, Zuk noted, led "to the somewhat uncomfortable suggestion that such groups might be evolving in different directions—a controversial notion to say the least."[37]

However controversial the concept, Gregory Cochran and Henry Harpending expanded on this hypothesis in their book of 2009, *The 10,000 Year Explosion: How Civilization Accelerated Human Evolution*. Cochran was a physicist with a specialty in optics. He had worked in America's defense industry for years before turning his attention to evolutionary biology and genetic anthropology. Harpending was an anthropologist who helped to develop the Out-of-Africa Theory (the idea that *Homo sapiens* emerged in Africa more than a hundred thousand years ago and began to disperse elsewhere about 50,000 years ago). Harpending, like Cochran, also was a specialist in population genetics.[38]

In *The 10,000 Year Explosion*, Cochran and Harpending showed that people whose ancestors had a long experience living in agricultural communities eventually developed immunities to the diseases of domesticated livestock. And they also noted that descendants of farmers and herders were likely to have genes that fostered lactose tolerance. By way of contrast, people whose ancestors had lived in hunter-gatherer societies until quite recently were less likely to have such genes. They were more likely to possess genes that fostered running speed and quick bursts of energy.

---

37 John Brockman and Stevan Pinker, quoted by Steve Sailer, "It's the End of the World as We Know It," Vdare.com (15 January 2006); Marlene Zuk, "Misguided Nostalgia for Our Paleo Past," *Chronicle of Higher Education* (18 February 2013).

38 Gregory Cochran and Henry Harpending, *The 10,000 Year Explosion: How Civilization Accelerated Human Evolution* (New York: Basic Books, 2009).

The Race Realists

Cochran and Hapending also maintained that nature selected for traits of personality and character as well as differences in physique and resistance to pathogens. They said that because of natural selection, populations with longer exposure to agriculture or commerce were likely to have experienced genetic mutations that made them more industrious, future-oriented, and orderly than populations that survived by hunting and foraging. They said that descendants of foragers were genetically disposed to be impulsive. They said natural selection had shaped human nature somewhat differently, depending on whether one's long line of ancestors had lived in settled communities or as foragers. As psychologists Gregory Gorelick and Todd Shackelford noted in their review of *The 10,000 Year Explosion*, Cochran and Harpending speculated that "although impulsivity may have been adaptive in hunter-gatherer populations, selection pressures associated with agricultural living may have acted on some population gene pools by selecting for patience and the foregoing of immediate gratification."[39]

Some quotations may help to convey the theme and tone of *The 10,000 Year Explosion*.

> [T]he new pressure of an agricultural lifestyle allowed changes in the population's genetic makeup to take root and spread.

> [E]volution has taken a different course in different populations. Over time, we have become more and more unlike one another as differences have accumulated.

> [A]s the molecular revolution has unfolded..., we have learned a great deal more. . . . The obvious between-population differences that we knew of a few years ago were only the tip of the iceberg." "It's time to address the old chestnut that biological differences among human populations are 'superficial,' only skin-deep. It's not true.

> It's probable that the evolutionary response to farming also affected the distribution of cognitive and personality traits.

---

39 Gregory Gorelick and Todd K. Shackelford, "Why Genes Still Matter" *Evolutionary Psychology* 2010, 8:1, 113-118.

> People can learn new traditions, but genetic difference must make ... self-denial easier for some people than it is for others. It takes a certain type of personality—with traits including patience, self-control, and the ability to look to long-term benefits instead of short-term satisfaction—and natural selection must have gradually made such personalities more common among people that farmed for a long time.
>
> If the root cause of these differences [between those descended from several thousand years of settled farmers and those descended from nomadic hunters and foragers] are biological changes affecting cognitive and personality traits, changes that are the product of natural selection acting over millennia, conventional solutions to the problem of slow modernization among peoples with shallow experience of farming are highly problematic.
>
> [M]any who claim to accept the idea of natural selection reject most of the obvious implications of the theory when it is applied to humans.[40]

Cochran and Harpending were expressing a view that has come to be known as the theory of gene-culture co-evolution. This theory holds that human beings influence evolution by creating new ways of life that have an effect on which sort of people Mother Nature chooses to survive and multiply. Gene-culture co-evolution maintains that different groups develop different cultures, and those cultures, in turn, have some bearing on the distribution of genes in a society. Depending on the requirements of different environments, people with certain genes are selected for survival, while others are fated to decline. Over the course of millennia, different genes—including genes that influence behavior, intelligence, and personality (the BIP genes)—will blossom in some societies but not in others. The distribution and sequence of genes will vary, depending on whether a group lives in the tropics or the arctic; depending on whether a society is based on hunting, farming, commerce, or some other activity. The

---

40 Gregory Cochran and Henry Harpending, *The 10,000 Year Explosion*, x, 10, 19-20, 90, 67, 114, 122, 31, 170.

different populations still have much in common, since they had the same ancestors in the prehistoric past. But genetic adaptations through the ages are not insignificant.

By the first decade of the 21st century, this theory of gene-culture co-evolution had emerged as a new consensus among scholars who did research on human bio-diversity (although, to be sure, the theory was at odds with the egalitarianism that had prevailed in academic circles during the 1950s, 1960s, and 1970s, and continued to prevail in the mainstream media).

The recent scientific work on sociobiology and population genetics established the context for John Derbyshire's remarks at the University of Pennsylvania Law School. Limitations of time prevented Derbyshire from doing more than allude to the new science, but Derbyshire discussed Darwinism in several columns and the combination of natural selection and population genetics is key to understanding his assertion that racial and ethnic achievement gaps were "facts in the natural world, like the orbits of planets."

Writing on the World Wide Web, one critic characterized Derbyshire's remarks as "bunk," and another said, "I don't see how anyone didn't tackle this schmuck while he was giving this lecture." Yet another opined that mankind emerged in Africa and, as a result of this common origin, 95 percent of the genetic variation in the human genome was found in people all over the world. Therefore, this critic rejected the claim "that Black people are less intelligent because they chose to live in Africa while all the other races chose to migrate to other lands.... If Africa was the ancestral homeland, then everyone comes from the same genetical [sic] stock."[41]

Others, however, said the importance of race should not be

---

41 Adrian Holman, "John Derbyshire: A Racist Piece of Crap," AllVoices.com/contributed-news/5596713-john-derbyshire-a-racist-piece-of-crap.

discounted, even if 99 percent of human genes were shared among all people. Steve Sailer noted that humans shared "98 percent of our genes with chimpanzees (and, supposedly, 70 percent with yeast)." And Dr. Alan Bernstein, the president of the Canadian Institutes of Health Research, insisted that small genetic differences were far from insignificant. After mentioning that there was not much genetic distance between humans and gorillas, Bernstein said, "It's silly to try and be politically correct." Even when the same genes were shared, the frequencies of distribution often varied.[42]

Many of the 140 law students who heard Derbyshire were baffled and perplexed. They "had never heard anything like that before," one of their professors stated. But there were no confrontations. After his remarks, Derbyshire recalled, "people were pretty friendly, or else just ignored me in a way not (so far as I could tell) meant to be offensive." Derbyshire advised others who might be invited into a similar venue to "just be frank, honest, and polite . . . Nobody will set you on fire." One observer noted that the Black law students deserved some credit. "Derbyshire explained his views to them in advance, and they invited him anyway."[43]

As news of this panel discussion spread, Derbyshire acquired admirers. "The Derb is my new hero," wrote a tenured college professor who had previously kept what he called a "low profile" because he thought it "not worth the hassle of arguing with ideologues." "Wow!" wrote another correspondent. "Kudos to John Derbyshire for delivering a very difficult speech to that particular audience. Very brave effort to speak the truth about the existence of HBD [human bio-diversity]." "Now let's hope others, particularly those in academia, gain a spine."[44]

---

42 Ibid.; Steve Sailer, "It's All Relative," Vdare.com (2 August 2002); Alan Bernstein, quoted in *Toronto Globe and Mail* (18 June 2005).

43 Steve Sailer, "It's All Relative"; anonymous comments at iSteve.blogpot.com/2010/04/derbs-remarks-to-Penns-black-law.html.

44 Ibid.

Most writers at *National Review* continued to disdain race realism. Nevertheless, despite having expressed his views so candidly, Derbyshire continued to write for the magazine and, in addition, continued with a weekly radio broadcast, "Radio Derb," for *NR*'s online affiliate, *NRO* (*National Review Online*).

During the months after his talk at the Pennsylvania Law School, Derbyshire became even more outspoken. In *We Are Doomed*, a book of 2009, Derbyshire declared that a gulf separated most evolutionary theorists and genomic scientists from the mainstream media and most public leaders. The evolutionists and genomic scientists believed in the biological reality of race and also thought that racial and ethnic achievement gaps could not be eliminated, because these gaps were inevitable products of evolutionary adaptations. The evolutionary theorists and genomic scientists were, in Derbyshire's phrase, "Biologians." They recognized the importance of biology. They believed that human beings came into the world "with a good deal of our life course preordained in our genes." They thought that "roughly half"—"from one-quarter to three-quarters"—of the observed variation in human characteristics, "including cognitive and personality characteristics"—were "caused by biological differences."[45]

Most public leaders and mainstream journalists, on the other hand, were "Culturalists." According to Derbyshire, culturalists "insist[ed] that the ordinary rules of biological evolution ceased to apply to *Homo sapiens* when our species emerged from Africa to populate the rest of the world, around fifty thousand or sixty thousand years ago." They believed that the accidents of history and culture accounted for any variation in the distribution of human characteristics. In fact, culturalists believed this so deeply that, "while scoffing at God," they manifested "an almost religious hostility to any discussion of Homo Sap as belonging to the natural world and subject

---

45 John Derbyshire, *We Are Doomed* (New York: Three Rivers Press, 2009), 110, 144.

to the laws thereof." When it came to eliminating the achievement gaps, culturalists refused to entertain the possibility of impossibility.[46]

In 2011, Derbyshire speculated that deference to what might be called "racial correctness" threatened the primacy of the United States in world affairs. In commenting on the looming competition between the United States and China, Derbyshire conceded that each nation had strengths and weaknesses. But he recalled that in the past predominance had gone to countries that came up with major breakthroughs in technology. In the early decades of the 20th century, the United States was indebted to the likes of Thomas Edison and Henry Ford. More recently, the U.S. was indebted to the scientists and entrepreneurs who pioneered and developed transistors, computers, and the Internet. In the future, Derbyshire predicted, supremacy would go to the nation that made the next major breakthrough.

As Derbyshire saw it, during the next quarter century the most likely field for a major breakthrough was human genomics. The first sequencing of a human genome was completed in 2003, but, as Steve Sailer has written, that sequencing "only got us into the situation of the proverbial bear who went over the mountain to find himself confronted with another mountain." American researchers had been the pioneers in the early studies of the genome. Nevertheless, although continued research on genomics promised to yield information on many matters besides diseases and medical treatments, racial correctness was suppressing the funding of this research in the United States. It was doing so, Derbyshire said, because culturalists feared that the research would establish the importance of racial differences. The Chinese, however, had no such scruples. They were vastly increasing research on the genome and had, in fact, allocated some $1.5 billion for this work. One project at the Beijing Genomics

---

46   Ibid., 145, 146-47; John Derbyshire, "Republic of Hysteria," *Takimag. com* (12 January 2011); Dennis Mangan, "The Biological Reality of Race," *AlternativeRight.com* (3 December 2010).

Institute (BGI) was studying "the genetic basis for IQ's heritability." According to Derbyshire, the Chinese were "a competitor superpower with frankly race-realist attitudes," and this "uninhibited interest in the human genome" made it likely that China would "own the coming age's [next] killer technology."[47]

For some time, low-level eugenics had been tolerated in China, where there were very high rates of abortion for fetal abnormalities like Down Syndrome. The government's policy of restricting families to no more than two children also had eugenic consequences, for this policy disproportionately limited population growth among Chinese peasants, who as a group had lower IQs than their urban cousins. In addition, in Hong Kong a government-funded research program was deciphering 2,200 DNA samples from people, the majority of whom had IQs of 160 or higher. ("By way of comparison," one article in the *Wall Street Journal* noted, "the average Nobel laureate registers at about 145.") The goal of the Hong Kong researchers was to isolate the hereditary factors behind IQ. As Derbyshire saw it, "a race realist competitive superpower" was about to arise. While the United States and other Western nations were "fretting about the ethics" of genetic research, the Chinese were not agonizing over the rights and wrongs of genetic engineering. They were "just . . . doing it." And if the Chinese somehow managed to enhance their genome, the Chinese economy and military forces would become predominant within a few generations.

Only time will tell if this comes to pass. But at this stage one thing can be said with assurance. After his talk at the University of Pennsylvania, "the Derb" did not back down. He did not recant. Instead, in a radio broadcast in 2014, Derbyshire candidly summed up his views:

---

[47] John Derbyshire, "Genomics: China's New Killer App," *Takimag.com* (19 January 2011); Derbyshire, "The Future of Elite Attitudes on Race," at Vdare.com/articles/the-future-of-elite-attitudes-on-race (10 February 2012).

Different races have different averages and spreads of behavior, intelligence, and personality traits. That's biology 101. It happens in any widely distributed population of creatures under different selection pressures in different places. Those traits are all heritable: talk to dog breeders.

To succeed in American society as currently structured—and that includes most American schools—it helps if your individual traits of behavior, intelligence, and personality have certain patterns. It hurts if they have certain other patterns. To succeed in school, for instance, it helps a lot if you can sit still and take in what the teacher's saying, if you can grasp complicated ideas quickly, if you can concentrate for long spells on reading a textbook, if you cannot be over-concerned about socializing with your classmates, if you can defer gratification, and so on. If your traits go the opposite way, chances are you'll be less successful academically, though you might, of course, excel in other spheres.[48]

In one of his opinion columns, Derbysire also outlined his own program for school reform. Derbyshire's educational program came as a response to two sets of data. One set consisted of studies that reported that, despite all the efforts at school reform, the racial and ethnic achievement gaps had hardly budged. The overall disparities in 2011 were as great as they had been fifty years earlier. The other set included the international comparisons from the Programme for International Student Assessment (PISA). Despite all that had been written and said about the shortcomings of American education, Derbyshire wrote, "If you take the . . . PISA test scores and disaggregate USA students by race, we are up there near the top." "There is simply not much improvement to be made." "Our Asians are as good as Asia's Asians—actually, better than Koreans or Japanese. Our white kids beat everyone else's white kids except Finland's. Our Hispanics outscored all eight Latin American countries. Our black kids trounced Trinidad, the blackest nation on the PISA list."[49]

---

48 Transcript for Radio Derb, 17 May 2014, at JohnDerbyshire.com..

49 John Derbyshire, "What Should We Do with the Kids?" *Takimag.com* (21

Derbyshire acknowledged, "up to the age of 12, all kids need to be in school, learning to read, write and calculate, and hearing about basic civics." Beyond that point, however, Derbyshire thought formal education made sense only for "smart, studious kids." Unfortunately, there was another "large subgroup of adolescents"—Derbyshire estimated it "at about thirty percent overall though it cuts differently by race—for whom schooling [beyond 8th grade] is a complete waste of time." "In their boredom and irritation at being in an environment uncongenial to them," these non-academic teenagers often made life miserable for youngsters who were "bookish and willing to be educated." As Derbyshire saw it, "obliging [smart bookish kids] to share classrooms with uninterested, disruptive, ineducable peers is criminal."[50]

What, then, could be done to improve education? Derbyshire had a straightforward answer to this question. "The education of the educable would be improved if the ineducable were . . . sent home—in fact, barred from school premises." And then, to prevent the ineducable from roaming the streets, "making mischief," Derbyshire recommended a new style of school reform: reform schools. He would place the ineducable "under adult supervision . . . in some kind of work camps."[51]

Derbyshire's proposal to establish more reform schools smacked of satire, but during the years following his talk to the Black law students at the University of Pennsylvania, Derbyshire turned increasingly toward race realism. Some readers attributed this to Derbyshire's being diagnosed with a form of blood cancer. "A man's time on this earth is too short," one wrote. "In the end, what is remembered is courage, honor . . . Not much else." There was speculation that Derbyshire had decided, after years of being constrained by the conventional wisdom of the mainstream media, to

---

July 2011).

50 Ibid.

51 Ibid.

speak his mind while there was still time. Less sympathetic observers speculated that chemotherapy had either addled Derbyshire's brain or damaged his social radar.[52]

Whatever the reason, Derbyshire did not follow the examples of others who have been mentioned in this book. Unlike James D. Watson, Bruce Lahn, and William Saletan, Derbyshire did not apologize. Instead, he doubled down on race realism. In an address given at the 2012 meeting of the Conservative Political Action Committee (CPAC), Derbyshire recalled that in the 1960s he himself had believed that "group differences would surely melt away" once "well-known legal and social disabilities" were removed. But such optimism was no longer warranted. "Segregation and colonialism have long since been dismantled; trillions of dollars have been spent to rectify past wrongs; countless helping-hand policies have been enacted; yet the world, and our individual nations, are deeply stratified by race." The time had come for "'candor and realism' about race." As Derbyshire saw it, "group underachievement" was "a consequence of the laws of biology working on human populations." "The fact of group inequalities, even in societies that have striven mightily to remove them, is as natural and inevitable as individual inequality ... The only proper object of blame is Mother Nature." Derbyshire said that in the time that remained to him he intended "to do all I can to promote the idea that there is a sane path ... of 'candor and realism,' between phony egalitarianism and vicious neo-racism."[53]

Derbyshire was treading on thin ice. He was best known as a regular contributor to the flagship conservative magazine, *National Review*, the journal that William F. Buckley had established in 1955 with the avowed aim of refashioning conservatism. One of *NR*'s editors, Jeffrey Hart, has explained that *NR* was "directed at opinion makers" and the goal was "to change the mind of the American intellectual elite in a conservative direction." To that

---

52 Whisky, comment at iSteve.blogspot.com (8 April 2012).

53 John Derbyshire, "The Future of Elite Attitudes on Race."

end, during *NR*'s first decade Buckley severed all connections with two organizations whose political philosophy he considered less than respectable—the John Birch Society and the "objectivism" associated with Ayn Rand. Later, after the triumph of the civil rights movement, *NR* also embraced egalitarian racial views that were at odds with opinions that Buckley and others at *NR* had expressed in the 1950s and 1960s.[54]

Derbyshire understood all this. On one occasion, in response to a correspondent who had accused Derbyshire of pulling punches (!), Derbyshire explained: "Anyone running a mainstream conservative magazine has to continually demonstrate ideological purity in matters of race. They have to show repeatedly . . . that they are ideologically pure in this zone. Otherwise they won't be taken seriously by the cultural establishment. *National Review* wants to get certain ideas out to the public—ideas about economics, politics, law, religion, science, history, the arts, and more. To do that, the magazine needs standing in our broad cultural milieu. It needs status. That's hard at the best of times for a conservative publication. To lose status points—to lose standing . . . would be dumb."[55]

Derbyshire was one of *NR*'s most popular writers, but most of his gravitation toward race realism was expressed elsewhere—as in the talks at the University of Pennsylvania and at CPAC and in opinion columns at a feisty webzine, *Takimag*. It was a contribution to *Takimag* that led *NR*, in 2012, to part ways with Derbyshire.

To understand the provocative column, "The Talk: Non-black

---

[54] Jeffrey Hart, *The Making of the American Conservative Mind* (Wilmington: ISI Books, 2005), 241; Carl T. Bogus, *Buckley: William F. Buckley and the Rise of American Conservatism* (New York: Bloomsbury Press, 2012) *passim*; James Lubinskis, "The Decline of National Review," *American Renaissance* (September 2000).

[55] John Derbyshire, quoted by Anonymous, iSteve.blogspot.com (10 April 2012).

Version," one must take account of the context. Black journalists have written with dismay about "the talk" that many Black parents give their teenage sons—a talk in which the parents warn that, even if their boys have been behaving correctly, they will increase their problems if they sass, or even swagger, when questioned or confronted by police. Derbyshire, however, noted that "there is a talk that nonblack Americans have with their kids, too." He acknowledged that he had told his own children, aged 19 and 16, that they should use common sense. Given the statistics on inter-racial crime (which showed that Blacks were 13 times more likely to kill Whites than vice-versa), they should "avoid concentrations of blacks not all known to [them] personally." They should "stay out of heavily black neighborhoods." And if they were "at some public event at which the number of blacks suddenly swells, [they should] leave as quickly as possible." To this, Derbyshire added comments about group disparities in the distribution of intelligence and the importance of "always [being] attentive to the particular qualities of individuals."[56]

In response, *NR* fired Derbyshire. "There has to be a parting of the ways," editor Rich Lowry explained. "Derb has long danced around the line on these issues, but this column is so outlandish it constitutes a kind of letter of resignation. It's a free country, and Derb can write whatever he wants, wherever he wants. Just not in the pages of *NR* . . . or as someone associated with *NR* any longer."[57]

Lowry did not comment on Derbyshire's specific points but apparently feared that a continuation of Derbyshire's association would taint *National Review* and cause it to lose influence with America's elite opinion makers. Writing at *The American Conservative*, however, one of Derbyshire's friends, Noah Millman, raised a substantive point. Millman granted that the risk of associating with Blacks was greater

---

56 John Derbyshire, "The Talk: Nonblack Version," Takimag.com (5 April 2012).

57 Rich Lowry, "Parting Ways," nationalreview.com/content/parting-ways (7 April 2012).

than that of associating with Whites or Asians. But was the risk *so great* as to warrant the sort of dissociation that Derbyshire recommended? Millman did not think so, and he asked: "does [Derbyshire] take a similar attitude toward other risks? Toward . . . eating raw food, bicycling without a helmet, [or] traveling alone to a foreign country?" If not, Derbyshire could fairly be suspected of racism.[58]

Millman had made a good point, although one observer wondered if it was valid to "statistically nerd-out and pick apart something that's a somewhat exaggerated version of what every white person thinks." Still others said the controversy was about placing Derbyshire's comments in the proper context. Conventional liberals *and* conservatives viewed American race relations in the context of historic White oppression, while the views of race realists were influenced by current statistical disparities and recent developments in evolutionary science. Granting that Derbyshire may have exaggerated the danger of associating with Black strangers, several comments accused conventional conservatives at *National Review* of trying to crush "one thinker *pour encourager les autres*. This brouhaha is about silencing discussion, not improving it."[59]

L'affaire Derb gave rise to much discussion on the Internet. *Taki's Magazine* received 5,143 comments on Derbyshire's initial article, and thousands of additional comments were posted at other sites. The fervid correspondence mushroomed when Derbyshire penned additional articles, while other journalists weighed in with opinion pieces of their own. One of the best came from political philosopher Paul Gottfried. Gottfried said that, for him, it was not clear that "genetic disparities" were "critical for understanding key behavioral differences." Nevertheless,

---

58   Noah Millman, "A Quick Word on the Derb," *TheAmericanConservative.com* (9 April 2012).

59   RDE to *TheAmericanConservative.com* (9 April 2012); Steven Sailer, *ibid.*, (9 April 2012).

Gottfried maintained, it was "ridiculous to exclude [race realism] from public or scholarly discussion." Gottfried insisted that we should not regard racial differences as an "untouchable subject . . . that . . . we as a society agreed to turn into a 'stone cold, dead, closed question.'"[60]

---

60 Paul Gottfried, "Throwing People Under the Bus to Stop a Runaway Vehicle" *Takimag.com* (19 April 2012).

12

Robert Weissberg

In 2010, Robert Weissberg published an especially trenchant critique of school reform: *Bad Students, Not Bad Schools*. Because Weissberg emphasized that basic intelligence is a key to academic achievement, some readers might regard his book as another hereditarian work. Yet this would not be correct. Weissberg noted that science has not yet defined the boundaries between genetic and cultural influences, and he also emphasized the importance of motivation. He acknowledged that the academic work of weak students would improve if school reformers could convince those students that schoolwork was important. He did not dwell on IQ, DNA, or HBD.[1]

Bad Students grew out of personal experience as well as reading and thinking about American education. Weissberg was born in New York City in 1941. His family was satisfied with the education provided at their neighborhood elementary school, PS 75 (the Emily Dickinson School on Manhattan's Upper West Side). But there were problems at the Booker T. Washington Junior High School, which young Robert attended for a few weeks in 1953. This was a decade before many other New York schools "slipped into near disaster," but conditions at Booker T. had already deteriorated to the point that police had to be stationed on every floor. When Robert's mother heard stories of "mayhem bereft of any learning (other than skillfully avoiding schoolyard confrontations)," her response was *"genug est*

---

1   Robert Weissberg, *Bad Students, Not Bad Schools* (New Brunswick: Transaction Publishers, 2010).

genug' ('enough is enough' in Yiddish)." The Weissbergs became early participants in White flight when they moved to suburban New Jersey, where Robert eventually graduated from Teaneck High School. He went on to receive a liberal arts education at Bard College and graduate training in political science at the University of Wisconsin. Weissberg then became a professor at Cornell University and at the University of Illinois. Over the course of three decades, he published several books including, *The Politics of Empowerment* (1999), *Polling Policy and Public Opinion* (2002), *The Limits of Civic Activism* (2005), and *Pernicious Tolerance* (2008).²

In 2004, after being away from New York City for forty years, Weissberg returned to his hometown as a retired professor emeritus. When he described his experiences at Booker T. Washington JHS to a recent president of that school's PTA, he learned that conditions had become even worse. When he spoke to teachers from other schools, he heard similar reports. But "what finally instigated rethinking ... was actually meeting many of America's notable educators"—education professors and writers, high-ranking public officials, and wealthy philanthropists who were privately financing efforts at school reform. Most of these people were smart, and all were serious, but their opinions impressed Weissberg as "little more than heartfelt clichés."³

Thinking back to his days as a student at Booker T. Washington, Weissberg recalled that the school had been almost brand new in 1953 and there was nothing wrong with the teachers, save that they had to spend too much time trying "vainly ... to control miscreants." The problem had been with the students. Too many were "intellectually mediocre." Too many "disdain[ed] academic achievement." Too many were troublemakers. Yet when Weissberg discussed the state of public education with the leading experts and school reformers half a century

---

2   Ibid., ix.

3   Ibid., x.

later, "not a single pontificator put any blame on students themselves." Some experts on the left echoed Jonathan Kozol and said that schools were struggling because of inadequate funds; others followed Howard Gardner and Theodore Sizer and found fault with directive teaching that did not allow students to achieve deep understanding by constructing their own knowledge.

Meanwhile, many experts on the right agreed with E. D. Hirsch's critique of progressive education, while others said that things would be better if more veteran teachers followed the example of the young, hard-working rookies who enlisted in Teach for America. Experts from the left and right joined together in saying that schools and teachers should be held accountable for the scores their students made on standardized tests. None of the experts "put any blame on students themselves.. . . . The unpleasant possibility that students themselves hated school and their aversion was beyond remediation was ... unthinkable, and voicing it breached decorum."[4]

The conversations reinforced Weissberg's recognition that a sea change had occurred in the late 1960s. In the 1950s and early 1960s, against the background of the Cold War, most public schools had emphasized the importance of educating the brightest students. Grouping students by ability came into vogue, and many high schools added advanced placement courses to the curriculum. But the emphasis shifted after the post-Sputnik panic was replaced by concern about civil rights and race riots. Whether on the left or the right, mainstream educators no longer emphasized the importance of "helping a few Whiz Kids master quantum mechanics so as to protect us from Soviet rockets." Instead, educators shifted their emphasis to "moving the entire school population, but especially those at the very bottom, up a few notches." "Uplifting the bottom, not rewarding the smartest of the smart, became the new official policy." Eventually a

---

4   Ibid., vii, x.

Republican President, George W. Bush, appropriated the slogan of a Democratic activist, Marian Wright Edelman, and pointed the public schools toward a new goal: No Child Left Behind.[5]

The new emphasis was based on egalitarian assumptions. *New York Times* columnist Deborah Solomon summarized the underlying premise when she said, "Given the opportunity, most people could do most anything." Writing at *Diversity, Inc.*, columnist Luke Visconti asserted, "the solution for the disparities in education is not difficult when you accept that we are genetically all one human race." Summarizing the Dogma of Zero Group Differences, Visconti explained, "This doesn't mean everyone is of equal talent, but it does mean that every group of people has an equal percentage of talented people. Therefore, if education is managed correctly, every town—Black or white—SHOULD have the same outcome. . . ." In a popular textbook, Mary M. Frasier, a professor of educational psychology, affirmed, "There is no logical reason to expect that the number of minority students [in advanced classes] would not be proportional to their representation in the general population."[6]

Bad Students was a relentless critique of this "educational romanticism." Weissberg insisted that responsibility for learning should be shifted to students and their families, where most people had always recognized it belonged. With a combination of erudition and wit that is rare in scholarly analyses of public policy, Weissberg said "what everybody (or nearly everybody) knows to be true but

---

5   Ibid., 134, 137, vii-viii.

6   Visconti's article was reprinted at AmRen.com (24 December 2008); Deborah Solomon, interview with Charles Murray, as quoted by John Derbyshire, "The Straggler" (1 December 2008) at JohnDerbyshire.com/Opinions/Straggler/page.html; Mary M. Frasier, "Gifted Minority Students," in Nicholas Colangelo and Gary A. David, *Handbook of Gifted Education* (Boston: Allyn and, Bacon, 1997) 498.

is fearful of expressing in public—America's educational woes just reflect our current demographic mix of students."[7]

Weissberg posited that academic achievement (A) depends on a combination of intelligence (I), motivation (M), resources (R), pedagogy (P), and teaching (T). He recognized that even smart and motivated students do not learn algebra on their own. Teachers, textbooks, and other resources (T and R) are necessary. He acknowledged that the pedagogy or curriculum of a school (P) also matters. Even as he skewered E. D. Hirsch for demanding "a near Stalinist centralization of state authority over schooling" (because Hirsch would impose a one-size-fits-all system of national standards and national testing), Weissberg also indicated that he personally thought "core knowledge" was better than "constructivism." Yet while acknowledging the importance of resources, pedagogy, and teaching, Weissberg maintained that intelligence and motivation matter even more.[8]

To illustrate his main point, Weissberg developed the following formula as the key to understanding the current state of academic achievement (A) in the United States:

$$A = 8I \times 4M \times R \times P \times T$$

Weissberg presented this as a cooking recipe, with 8 portions for intelligence and 4 portions for motivation but only 1 portion for resources, pedagogy, and teaching. Unlike cooking recipes, however, Weissberg's formula was not additive. It was multiplicative. Its elements were multiplied, which meant that if any term was "0," the final result would be "0." If any element was very small, the overall result would also be small.[9]

---

[7] Robert Weissberg, *Bad Students, Not Bad Schools*, vii.

[8] Ibid., 148.

[9] Mathematicians would use exponents when expressing this equation. For a

Weissberg's formula could be adjusted for various levels of education. In the standard grades, K-12, greater emphasis might be placed on M (motivation), and perhaps this would also be the case in some college courses. In other fields, especially in the higher realms of mathematics and theoretical science, perhaps even greater emphasis should be placed on I (intelligence). But however the equation is rendered, it stresses the importance of what is sometimes called "human capital." Weissberg posited that student intellectual ability (I) had a huge impact on academic accomplishment (a value of 8), followed by motivation (M, a value of 4). Resources, pedagogy, and teaching were essential but had less force than intelligence and motivation. According to Weissberg, the basic problem with school reform was that most reformers were "in denial about why America's schools perform poorly." They focused on resources, pedagogy, and teaching. They proposed major investments in school facilities and in developing new curricula. They wanted to hire better teachers. But they neglected the formula's most important elements—brains and motivation.[10]

To support his formula, Weissberg mentioned a number of "natural experiments." He noted that the United States had recently experienced massive immigration, and most of the newcomers had settled in low-income neighborhoods with troubled public schools. But Weissberg also noted that "student performance in these oft-dreary, run-down, sometimes violence-plagued settings varies widely, and these dissimilarities are often so spectacular that the 'bad school did it' crime theory utterly collapses." On average, Hispanics from Central America, Mexico, and Puerto Rico had done poorly in these schools—and therefore seemed to offer "perfect smoking gun proof of the bad school-begets-bad-students hypothesis." But the children

---

similar view (*sans* the equation), see Tommy M. Tomlinson, "The Troubled Years: An Interpretive Analysis of Public Schooling since 1950," *Phi Beta Kappan* 62 (January 1981).

10   Robert Weissberg, *Bad Students, Not Bad Schools*, 2.

of the Vietnamese boat people had excelled in inner-city schools—despite suffering from years of trauma and family separations. In recent years, Chinese, Korean, and Russian immigrants had also excelled in inner-city schools—despite poverty and "the customary problems of learning a strange difficult language (with a confusing alphabet, to boot)."[11]

Most school reformers ignored the successes of the Chinese, Koreans, Russians, and Vietnamese. They refused to concede that "if new students arrive at a 'bad school' and excel it is implausible to insist that the school itself inherently destroys learning." Instead of acknowledging the importance of the students' intelligence and motivation—the human capital in Weissberg's equation—most reformers tried to improve urban education by dealing with the relatively less important points. Their emphasis was on the need for better teachers, smaller classes, reformed curricula, and high-tech innovations. "Bad schools are to be cured by more resources, more resources, and yet more resources."[12]

Racially balanced integration provided a second set of "natural experiments." Due to White flight, integration was usually a short-lived transitional period between the time when large numbers of African-Americans moved into a school and most Whites moved out. Nevertheless, there were exceptional instances where racially balanced integration persisted for a generation or more. In these instances of persisting integration, Black students enjoyed "every advantage imaginable in a 'good school' including learning side-by-side with smart white students." But this did not change academic outcomes. In 1984, when the National Institute of Education convened a panel of seven social scientists to review 157 studies of integration, only one of the panelists concluded that integration had boosted the achievement of

---

11   Ibid., 39, 44.

12   Ibid., 45, 39.

Black students substantially. Eleven years later, after reviewing another 250 studies, Janet Ward Schofield, a committed integrationist, reported that the reading skill of integrated Black students improved, but only slightly, while "mathematics skills . . . [were] generally unaffected by desegregation." In 2003, after the relation between racial mix and educational achievement had been studied by an army of social scientists, Abigail Thernstrom and Stephan Thernstrom reported that there still was "no scholarly consensus that a school's racial mix has a clear effect on how much children learn."[13]

For integrationists, the news from integrated upscale suburbs and college towns was especially bad. In Shaker Heights, Ohio, for example, African-American students lagged well behind their White fellow students and disproportionately chose not to enroll in academically advanced classes. On the national SAT exam, race-related differences in Shaker Heights were actually larger than the national average. And Shaker Heights was far from unique. The results were similar in several college towns—Berkeley, Chapel Hill, Evanston, Amherst. The racial achievement gap remained so large that the college towns created a National Task Force on Minority High Achievement to study the problem and develop a solution.[14]

Weissberg did more than highlight the failure of integration to boost the academic achievement of non-Asian minorities. He

---

13   James S. Coleman et al., "Recent Trends in School Integration," (April 1975) printed in *Educational Researcher* (June 1975); Raymond Wolters, *Race and Education*, 229; Robert Weissberg, *Bad Schools, Not Bad Students*, 46; National Institute of Education, *School Desegregation and Black Achievement* (Washington: Government Printing Office, 1984); Janet Ward Schofield, "Review of Research on School Desegregation's Impact," in J. A. Banks and C. A. McGee Banks, eds., *Handbook of Research on Multicultural Education* (New York: McMillan, 1995), 597, 610; Abigail Thernstrom and Stephan Thernstrom, *No Excuses*, 179-80.

14   Robert Weissberg, *Bad Students, Not Bad Schools*, 46-48; John U. Ogbu, *Black American Students in an Affluent Suburb*, passim.

also contended that integration depressed the achievement of White students. Although test scores and other statistics are not conclusive on this point, there are numerous descriptive accounts of the decline of education in the wake of integration, and Weissberg provided yet more descriptions. In one community near San Diego, for example, there were seven elementary schools, five of which were failing. When students from the five were allowed to transfer to the remaining two, "the influx of refugees ... outraged parents who paid a housing premium to enroll their offspring in the nearby superior school." They soon discovered that their high quality schools were "suddenly plagued by physical violence and 'purple language' thanks to these new arrivals." This should not have been a surprise, Weissberg wrote, and he asked: "Can one honestly insist that bullies and petty thieves will mend their ways if only sent to crime-free schools? A more likely scenario is that they will be energized by easy pickings."[15]

In their efforts to "make integration work," racially balanced schools also ceased grouping students by ability, relaxed standards of decorum, and placed more emphasis on remedial education and multiculturalism. As they did so, an increasing number of White families fled to private schools and distant suburbs. Weissberg devoted one chapter to what he called "the war on academic excellence." "The foolishness of the 'war' against America's most talented," he wrote, "is almost beyond belief, a relentless pursuit of an egalitarian fantasy at the expense of genuine educational accomplishment."[16]

School spending provided yet more natural experiments. Although readers of Jonathan Kozol's book *Savage Inequalities* (1991) might not know it, for several decades the expenditure in most predominantly Black inner-city school districts has exceeded the average expense for their state. In several areas—Kansas City, Hartford, and the "Abbott

---

15 Robert Weissberg, *Bad Students, Not Bad Schools*, 49.

16 Ibid., 113, 141-42.

districts" in New Jersey, for example—the expenditures in the inner-cities matched or exceeded the amounts spent in the states' wealthiest districts. Nevertheless, there was no substantial progress in closing the achievement gap. In Kansas City, the gap actually widened. According to Weissberg, "beliefs about the power of material resources, versus human capital (i.e., the students themselves) are . . . comparable to insisting that inept basketball teams could become champions if only given better practice facilities or nicer uniforms."[17]

Because of the natural experiments, Weissberg concluded that resources, pedagogy, and teaching (R, P, and T) were relatively insignificant. Because recent immigrants from China, Korea, Russia, and Vietnam did so well in inner-city schools, Weissberg stressed the importance of intelligence and motivation (I and M).

In emphasizing the importance of intelligence, Weissberg confronted what he called an "obvious truth" that most experts did not face. "Racial differences in cognitive ability" had become "great taboos," Weissberg wrote. "A straight-talking public conversation about education when it wanders into the racial/ethnic minefield is nearly impossible. Lying is endemic; explanations of why African-Americans do so poorly can be near mystical." In an egalitarian world, "hard-nosed realists" were "shunned or forced into silence," while "those skilled in manipulating statistics or flattering those desperate to hear good news ... rise to the top," "survival-of-the-fittest style." Weissberg, however, felt free to speak his mind because he was an independent academic, a retired professor who was not seeking grants from the government or from mainstream foundations. "I call them as I see them," Weissberg wrote, with a "let-the-chips-fall-where-they-may attitude"—"a great advantage in a field where nearly all research must ... not offend reigning check-issuing deities, liberal or conservative."[18]

---

17 Ibid., 103.

18 Ibid., 14, 95, xii.

Although Weissberg expressed his views candidly, he was also a careful scholar. He said it was "nonsense" to "just assume" that all groups have "equal proficiency." He noted that after publication of *The Bell Curve* (1994), fifty-two leading researchers affirmed that group-related variations in intelligence were real. He mentioned the "sizeable, scientifically-respectable literature [that] shows that IQ is substantially inheritable, and varies by demographic groups." He personally thought that the academic superiority of Caucasians and Asians was "likely to be at least partly genetic." Yet Weissberg also expressed touches of caution and uncertainty that befit a scholar who also recognized that modern social science had not yet developed methods to precisely determine the relative importance of heredity and culture. Weissberg recognized that motivation also was important.[19]

Because Weissberg emphasized that motivation mattered a great deal, he did not reject the possibility that school reformers might eventually persuade more students to take schoolwork seriously. In the current environment, however, the prospects were not good. Unlike the schools of yesteryear, which used competition and a variety of punishments to motivate students, the current fashion was to establish a "kinder, gentler educational atmosphere" that would instigate achievement by nurturing self-esteem. Weissberg disdained "these expert-supplied, 'culturally sensitive' strategies," which he described at some length. He contrasted them with the "old-fashioned methods" that many coaches still used "to instigate high performance from boys, especially black boys."[20]

Weissberg also lamented that high school students of every ethnicity were influenced by what he called "rampant cultural anti-intellectualism." This was manifest above all in peer pressure that valued popularity with the opposite sex and especially rewarded boys

---

19 Ibid., 15, 114-15.

20 Ibid., 56, 81-82.

who were athletes and girls who were stylish. Weissberg commended the work of psychologist Laurence Steinberg, who had shown "that commitment to schools is at an all-time low, and this indifference is not just centered in the notoriously under-performing inner-city schools." However, Weissberg went beyond Steinberg in suggesting that indifference to schoolwork often was a realistic adaptation to the facts of life. Many students simply were not capable of college work, or even of doing what once was required to pass high school algebra.[21]

Regardless of their ethnicity, Weissberg noted, students with low IQs eschewed study, tutors, libraries, and cram academies. For many students, this avoidance was a defense mechanism—a way to escape the travail of having to deal with material that was beyond their level of comprehension. Weissberg also mentioned that "dropping out" was nothing new. With a citation to Robert Hampel's "careful historical overview," Weissberg noted that in the past "motivation insufficiency was routinely 'solved' by mass exoduses [dropping out], not some now-forgotten pedagogical tricks. Nineteenth-century schools were under no pressure to retain malingerers."[22]

Weissberg thought modern America would be better off if more students followed the example of earlier generations. "Most of America's educational woes would vanish," he wrote, if "indifferent, troublesome students" dropped out of school "when they had absorbed as much as they were going to learn."

> In an instant, all the clamor for vouchers, smaller classes, additional social services, teaching the test, innovative pedagogy, recruiting better teachers, accountability, junking Progressive education, and all the rest would seem antiquated. . . .[23]

---

21 Ibid., 37.

22 Ibid., 80.

23 Ibid., vii.

Of course this view was anathema to school reformers. They said that America had to make do with the people who actually lived in the United States; and they predicted that if the number (or proportion) of college graduates declined, the U.S. would no longer be able to compete in an increasingly knowledge-based global economy. They said there would be trouble ahead "if the U.S. does not significantly improve college completion rates for African-Americans and Hispanics."[24]

Weissberg took aim at this "conventional wisdom"—the idea that America's "modern techno-society needs ever more well-trained people to survive." He noted that "cliché-mongering is not educational analysis," and he observed, "If anything, modern society does not require armies of highly-skilled workers." "A handful of very smart people may be able to compensate for thousands of dummies, and educating these smart people may be a far better strategy than imploring the latter to shape up." "Remember," Weissberg wrote, "if economic efficiency is paramount, the question is always the best investment." Weissberg believed that the money spent on school reform "could be better invested in, say, rebuilding America's deteriorating infrastructure or some other venture promoting economic growth (and construction workers could be those unable to get the high school diploma)."[25]

Weissberg also noted that the U.S. economy had prospered since the 1980s, even though the Japanese and some others exceeded the American average on academic tests. This led Weissberg to consider the possibility that conventional tests (the ones that showed Americans trailing Japanese students in solving quadratic equations, for example) may be less relevant to economic prosperity than untested skills in computer programming, Internet building, and graphics.

---

24 Stephen Klineberg, quoted by Ronald Brownstein, "The Gray and the Brown," *National Journal* (24 July 2010).

25 Robert Weissberg, *Bad Students, Not Bad Schools*, 273, 274, 252.

"Applying obsolete standards may explain the oft-noted paradox: our schooling's decline on traditional measures while we simultaneously lead the world in technological innovation."[26]

On a few points, Weissberg also differed from most "race realists." As has been mentioned, he was cautious in asserting that it was only probable that racial and ethnic achievement gaps were the inevitable result of human bio-diversity. He also differed from most realists with respect to immigration. Weissberg recognized that in the wake of massive Latino immigration to California, student scores on standardized tests plummeted from top to bottom. He noted that in the early 1960s California's public school system was ranked among the nation's best. But forty years later, because of the immigration from Central America and Mexico, California ranked 48th and 45th among the 50 states on NAEP tests of reading and math. Weisberg knew this was one of the reasons that most race realists were calling for a moratorium on immigration. Weissberg, on the other hand, favored a different approach. If improved academic performance was truly necessary for the United States, he wrote, "Just make immigration policy skill driven." Then academically-weak immigrant students would be replaced "by learning-hungry students from Korea, Japan, Vietnam, India, Russia, Africa, and the Caribbean."[27]

Style and substance are closely related, if not two aspects of the same thing. In its tone, *Bad Students, Not Bad Schools* conveyed sympathy for the weak students and harried teachers who had to deal with school reforms. Most students could be taught to read and compute at an elementary level. But Weissberg believed that "those unable to do college-level math or read complicated material cannot be upgraded by extra attention." When school reformers set high standards for all

---

26 Ibid., 272-73.

27 Ibid., 272; John Judis, "End State: Is California Finished?" *The New Republic* (26 October 2009); Robert Weissberg, *Bad Students, Not Bad Schools*, vii.

students—when they insisted that everyone should graduate from high school and go to college—the reformers succeeded only in making many young people miserable. The same would happen if those with a talent for music had insisted that all students must learn to sing *a cappella*, or if gifted athletes imposed a requirement that students must be able to sprint 100 yards in less than 11 seconds. Most people understood that it would be foolish to impose these requirements on students who are tone deaf or athletically challenged. So it was also, Weissberg believed, to require that those with low intelligence "devote untold painful hours to mastering algebra."[28]

While sympathizing with students and teachers, Weissberg showed scant regard for school reformers. He shared the opinion of erstwhile New York Senator Roscoe Conkling, who once said that Samuel Johnson knew nothing of the possibilities inherent in the word "reform" when Johnson said, "patriotism" was "the last refuge of a scoundrel." Although the reformers professed concern for weak students, Weissberg noted that they were feathering the nests of their own class. Instead of fostering blue-collar jobs where people of middling intelligence could earn decent wages, the reformers squandered billions to "make work" in education for white collar professionals. Weissberg noted that, after adjusting for inflation, spending per pupil had increased ten times over since 1940, and salaries for teachers were "just the tip of the iceberg." "Gone are the days when schools consisted of teachers, a few administrators, maybe a guidance counselor and a custodian or two. Today's facilities overflow with specialized staff catering to the complicated psycho-social needs of pupils who were, allegedly, ignored a generation back." Weissberg devoted one of his chapters to showing that, thanks to school reform, education had become "an anti-poverty program in sheep-skin clothing." Education had become a "job machine" for college graduates. It was "the New Great Society."[29]

---

28 Robert Weissberg, *Bad Students, Not Bad Schools*, 261, 109.

29 *Ibid.*, 241, 245, 233; Roscoe Conkling, quoted by Richard Hofstadter, *The American Political Tradition* (New York: Alfred A. Knopf, 1948), 174.

As Weissberg saw it, America's K-12 schools could be improved. The most sensible thing would be to group students into classes appropriate for their ability. But while Weissberg emphasized the importance of challenging the most gifted academic students, he also recognized the need for better vocational education. He also knew that different children take to different approaches to education. Some youngsters thrive in progressive schools, while others would do better with a structured, back-to-basics curriculum. It made good sense to offer choices. But Weissberg decried a favorite mantra of many reformers—that "everyone should go to college"; and he thought reformers were mistaken when they insisted that all high school students should take at least two years of algebra. Instead of uplifting the disadvantaged, this slogan and this policy damaged the confidence and self-image of weak students and increased the proportion that "dropped out" before graduating from high school.[30]

Yet sensible policies could not be implemented because America's most influential educators and school reformers refused to admit that some groups of students were smarter than others. They clung to egalitarian dogma, despite abundant evidence of differences in the distribution of academic aptitude and ability. They knew the truth, but they refused to discuss it. Meanwhile, the mainstream media fostered the mistaken belief that when it came to academic aptitude there were no inherent differences in the average capabilities of races, sexes, or classes.

---

30 Judge Richard Posner has expressed a similar view: "The challenge to American education is to provide a useful education to the large number of Americans who are unlikely to benefit from a college education or from high school courses aimed at preparing students for college. The need is for a different curriculum and for a greater investment in these children's preschool environment. We should recognize that we have different populations with different schooling needs and that curricula and teaching methods should be revised accordingly." "Rating Teachers," Becker-Posner-Blog.com/2012/09/rating-teachersposner.html (September 2012).

Weissberg, on the other hand, essentially attributed America's educational problems to the changing demographics of its public school students. The problem was not immigration *per se*, since immigrants from many foreign lands were thriving in America's public schools. The problem was that the proportion of African-American and Mestizo-Hispanic students was increasing rapidly, and these students—because of their cultural values or genetic inheritance (Weissberg wasn't sure which)—did not have what was needed to do well in school. Yet political correctness and the celebration of diversity barred reformers from speaking this truth. So the reformers focused instead on criticizing teachers and their unions.[31]

Weissberg thought most research and writing on education in modern America resembled astronomical research in 17th-century Italy. After Galileo's conviction, it became *de rigueur* to proclaim that the sun went around the earth. And in modern America, political correctness had made it socially obligatory for schools to ignore IQ and demography and to focus on eliminating racial and ethnic gaps. Weissberg found himself living in a country where, to hold a position of responsibility in education, one had to say that, when it came to public education, the goal was not to help individual students do as well as they could. It was to make sure that no group of children would be left behind.[32]

Weissberg was especially critical in assessing the role of social scientists. He described how standardized testing had been manipulated by ruses such as lowering the score required to

---

31 See Matthew Yglesias, "AFT Celebrates Teacher Appreciation Week," ThinkProgress.org/yglesias/2011/05/03/200838/american-federation-of-teacher-celebrates-teacher-appreciation-week-with-teacher-bashing/?mobile=nc; and Steve Sailer, "Why the Elite Bash Teachers," iSteve. blogspot.com/ 2011/05.

32 Steve Sailer, "Alchemists Can't Turn Lead Into Gold, Educrats Can't Eliminate IQ," Vdare.com (4 May 2008).

"pass" or increasing the number of students who were classified as "disabled" (and therefore exempt from testing). He showed how scholars "manufacture reality via including and excluding variables and choosing what to correlate with what." The racial and ethnic achievement gaps could be reduced (or even effaced) by making the questions so easy that almost everyone answered correctly, or by making the questions so difficult that almost nobody could answer correctly. If the questions were as easy as 2+2, there would be no gaps, since almost everyone would know the answer. Similarly, if the questions were so difficult as to require knowledge of the theory of relativity, the gaps would again disappear, since almost no one would answer correctly.[33]

Weissberg said the desire for good news about progress in reducing the achievement gaps had created a thriving market for mendacity. Philanthropists wanted to hear upbeat news, and educational "charlatans" were happy to supply it. When their ruses were exposed, they developed new proposals. Along the way, a great deal of money was wasted, but school reformers continued to insist that success was within reach, "just over the horizon."[34]

---

33 Robert Weissberg, *Bad Students, Not Bad Schools*, 35.

34 Ibid., vii.

Conclusion

When I began work on this book, a literary agent in New York told me he needed to know my "argument" because, he said, "today, all books about policy are 'argument' books." Nevertheless, I opted for the traditional form of historical writing, in which narration, evocation, and explanation are joined within a descriptive chronology. Instead of explicitly making an "argument," I have written biographies of prominent school reformers and some of their critics. Instead of marshaling evidence in support of a thesis or a particular policy, I have tried to tell interesting stories.

Perhaps I have gone too far in trying to be objective. I do have opinions—opinions that are at odds with views that prevail among most people who write about school reformers. It is time that I summarize these opinions, which are implicit and embedded throughout this book.

For much of the 20th century, traditional educators favored a back-to-basics curriculum that revolved around textbooks and direct instruction. "Progressive" educators, on the other hand, allowed students a great deal of freedom to learn on their own. Progressives called this "discovery learning," but traditionalists found fault with the progressives for "not teaching" and for not having a standard curriculum.

Despite these differences, before the 1960s, traditionalists and progressives agreed on one point. They both thought of students primarily as individuals, although they recognized that individual students belonged to different races, classes, and ethnic groups.

Eventually, a new approach came to the fore. As civil-rights activists increasingly demanded proportional representation for groups, and as multiculturalists encouraged members of minority groups to identify with their ethnic or racial roots, school reformers placed less emphasis on equality of opportunity for individual students. Instead, they demanded that no group should be left behind. A new generation of reformers then charged teachers and schools with responsibility for ensuring that the average test scores of Blacks and Hispanics would no longer lag behind the scores of Whites and Asians. To close the racial and ethnic "achievement gaps," school reformers recommended the reorganization of American education.

During the 1960s, 1970s, and 1980s, most egalitarian "gap closers" stuck to the playbook of progressive education. Since grouping students by ability had the effect of "resegregating" the pupils, with Whites disproportionately assigned to more advanced classes, progressives insisted that the full range of students should be placed in the same classroom. When the resulting mix included students who were reading or computing at markedly different levels, teachers discovered that they could no longer teach the class as a whole. Progressives then recommended that teachers adjust to heterogeneous classes by using new methods that were touted as especially appropriate for integrated classrooms—methods such as "peer tutoring" and "cooperative learning." Progressives urged schools to turn away from "teacher-centered instruction" and to embrace "student-centered learning." Teachers were encouraged to eschew the role of master or mistress of ceremonies and instead become facilitators of group projects. The ideal instructor was no longer a "sage on the stage" but a "guide on the side."

Inevitably, there was a backlash when the progressive approaches failed to close the racial achievement gap. A new variety of traditionalists then came to the fore in the 1990s. Like the traditionalists of yore, the neo-traditionalists emphasized direct

Conclusion

instruction and a standard curriculum. But the "neos" went beyond the "old timers" when they insisted that teachers should be rated (and paid) according to the progress their students made in closing the racial achievement gap on standardized tests.

I believe the egalitarian school reformers were well-intentioned but mistaken in important ways. They were naïve to think they could eliminate racial and ethnic achievement gaps that had endured despite the best efforts of previous generations of teachers and reformers. I further believe that neo-traditionalists propounded a false narrative of crisis; and that egalitarians, whether progressive or traditional, ignored the implications of evolution and subscribed to a mistaken belief that there are no inherent group differences.

The false narrative is that American schools are failing. I subscribed to this view at one time. I began to rethink this assumption when I learned that very poor immigrant students from China, Korea, Russia, and Vietnam have done well in America's inner-city schools. This called into question the idea that poverty caused low academic achievement, and the belief that inner-city teachers and schools were hopelessly bad.

I also learned that American students did well if their scores on international tests were disaggregated. The average scores for all American students were middling, but Americans were near the top when test scores were broken down by race and ethnicity, and when American students were compared with students in countries from which the Americans' ancestors came. White Americans did better than students in other predominantly-White nations (except Finland). African-American students did far better than Africans in African countries. America's Hispanic students outscored their counterparts in Latin America. And Asian-American students did as well as most students in Asia—and better than those in Korea or Japan. These test scores cast yet more doubt on the narrative of crisis.

In addition to doing well in international comparisons, the proportion of American youths who graduated from high school reached an all-time high in the 21st century, and on some tests, the average scores of modern American students were higher than the average scores of the past. These results were achieved, moreover, at a time when an increasing proportion of American students were being reared in single-parent families and a growing proportion of parents did not speak English.

Nevertheless, instead of praising American teachers and schools for succeeding despite difficult circumstances, egalitarian school reformers blamed teachers and schools for failing to eliminate differences in the average academic achievement of different racial and ethnic groups. The reformers lamented that on most tests the racial and ethnic achievement gaps were almost as large as they had been in 1954, when the U. S. Supreme Court handed down its landmark decision on school desegregation, *Brown v. Topeka Board of Education*. Eighty-five percent of Black students, and 75 percent of Latinos, still scored below the average White student. And because of this, reformers insisted that American teachers and schools had failed.

When it came to accounting for the disparities in the academic achievement of different groups, school reformers mentioned a number of factors that have been analyzed in the previous chapters. The reformers, however, paid scant attention to two important considerations. Only a few conceded that the largest lagging groups—African-Americans and Latino Americans—had developed attitudes that discourage academic achievement. Most reformers shied away from this sort of "cultural realism" because, some said, it smacked of "blaming the victim." The reformers also dismissed the idea that Nature had endowed different groups not only with different attitudes but different *aptitudes*. Some informed observers called this "race realism," but the leading school reformers insisted that group disparities were due to racial discrimination, to economic inequality,

Conclusion

to faulty teaching methods, to bad teachers or misguided parents, but not to differences in the attitudes or aptitudes of students.

I came of age when the civil-rights movement was at high tide, and for many years I subscribed to the egalitarian Dogma of Zero Group Differences, the DZGD. I thought that all important aptitudes, including the aptitude for school work, were distributed evenly among all sizeable groups of people. I was not dissuaded when most experts in the field of psychological measurement concluded that the IQ gap between Blacks and Whites was due, in part, to genetic inheritance. I wrote that the evidence on IQ was "not conclusive," that "it may be that the African-Americans' experience with slavery, segregation, and discrimination accounts for the fact that their IQ, on average, trails that of White Americans by about 15 points."[1]

That statement was technically correct, but it was also disingenuous and self-serving. I did not wish to alienate the academic establishment, but I knew that the gap between the test scores of Blacks and Whites did not disappear when subjects were paired in terms of social and economic factors. I knew that the differences were so large, so regular, and so persistent that it was not likely they were entirely due to discrimination, poverty, or bad schools.

While IQ studies presented one challenge to egalitarianism, another body of research also called the DZGD into question. Modern studies of DNA and evolution indicated that mankind separated into two parts about 50,000 years ago, with one part remaining in Africa, the ancestral homeland, and the other crossing into Southwest Asia. The second group separated again and again until there were human populations living in reproductive isolation from one another in almost all parts of the world. This continued

---

1 Mark Snyderman and Stanley Rothman, *The IQ Controversy* (New Brunswick: Transaction Publishers, 1988); Raymond Wolters, *Race and Education: 1954-2007* (Columbia: University of Missouri Press, 2008), x.

for hundreds of generations and, over time, there were numerous adaptations to differing climates and conditions. Opinions differ as to the full extent of these adaptations, but they went beyond changes in skin color. They included differences in musculature and brain size and different sequences in genes that influence behavior, intelligence, and personality. Contrary to an opinion that is fashionable in some academic circles, "race" is not simply "a social construct"; nor is it "skin deep." Races are biological realities—the result of Darwinian adaptations to different climates and environments. It is mistaken to assume that peoples who were geographically separated in their evolutions have developed the same distribution of aptitudes.

Although most school reformers did not pay heed to the good test scores or to the research on IQ and evolution, I believe these matters are important. I hold that any school reform not grounded in evolutionary reality will, in all likelihood, fail.

At the same time, I know that most students, professors, and academic presses will not countenance teachers, colleagues, or scholars who speak or write candidly about either IQ or the implications of evolution. Although the human genome has been decoded, scholars are expected to remain silent about the selection pressures that fostered ethnic disparities in the distribution of some traits. This expectation has been conveyed in many ways. One was the publicizing of a number of instances in which leading scholars were punished for expressing views that are considered taboo. At the University of California, Berkeley, Professor Arthur Jensen, the world's leading authority on IQ, was required to have police protection while teaching some of his classes. At the University of Minnesota, the nation's leading authority on identical twins reared apart, Thomas Bouchard, was maligned for emphasizing the importance of innate, hereditary factors. James D. Watson, a Harvard professor who had won a Nobel Prize as co-discoverer of the double-helix structure of DNA, was dismissed from his position at the Cold Spring Laboratory

Conclusion

after he commented on the average IQ of Black Africans. Meanwhile, Professor E. O. Wilson was doused by students and ostracized by some of his Harvard colleagues because of his work on evolutionary biology. And Lawrence Summers was forced out of the presidency of Harvard after he mentioned that fewer women than men have made extremely high scores on standardized mathematics tests. These scholars (and many others, some of whom are mentioned in the text of this book) suffered reprisals for questioning the reigning educational doctrine of our time—the DZGD.

By the last quarter of the 20th century, the United States had reached a point where most well-informed observers recognized the existence of group disparities but were loath to discuss these differences for fear of a backlash, or perhaps because it conflicted with a deeply held belief in the essential equality of mankind. They understood that they were expected to attribute any variations to the influence of discrimination or poverty. They knew that reprisals were in store for people who contended that America's achievement gaps were due, in part, to Mother Nature.

As egalitarianism became a pervasive orthodoxy, school reformers doubled down on their commitment to abolishing racial and ethnic achievement gaps. Instead of acknowledging that even capable teachers would fail if students were not motivated or lacked an aptitude for school work, reformers insisted that things would be better if the American educational system were re-fashioned. To that end, they proposed to change the way America's schools are organized and the way teachers are trained, hired, and fired.

I believe, on the other hand, that Americans would do well to appreciate the strengths of their nation's educational system and to try to fix what is wrong without declaring the whole system a failure. After the difficulties the United States has faced in the wake of "the Arab spring," and after experiencing the repercussions of deregulating

Wall Street, we should understand that breaking up large systems can have unintended consequences. We should be on guard, lest the effort to uplift weak students has the unintended effect of destroying an educational system that, when one takes everything into account, has worked reasonably well.

The reformers profiled in this book set out to change history: they perceived an unacceptable crisis or injustice in modern society, and they sought new educational paradigms to remedy it. They have now become a part of history. As we are distanced from them, it is incumbent on us to re-examine and rethink their most basic assumptions and prejudices.

Index

#

13-30 corporation 185, 187

A

Abecedarian Program 441–443, 460–461
ability grouping 91–92, 143–144, 159, 219, 251, 551, 564
accountability 9, 67–68, 77, 193, 274, 386, 395, 473–476, 481, 484, 486, 491, 560
achievement gap 7–9, 30, 103, 128, 179, 203, 209, 222, 244, 251–252, 257, 262–264, 268, 274, 288, 293–322, 324, 327, 330, 345–346, 350–351, 367, 371–372, 380–381, 384, 401, 407–408, 419, 439–440, 459, 462–466, 473, 483, 502, 508, 513, 525, 535, 538, 540, 556, 558, 562, 566, 570–575. See also standardized testing
Adams, Rich 114
adequacy lawsuits 49
adoption studies 438
Ahmanson Foundation 328
Ahnert, Edward 158

Alexander, Lamar 190
Allmendinger, David x
Alsup, William 29
Alter, Jonathan 416
Alvarado, Anthony 168, 175
Amazing Grace (Kozol) 35
American Association of University Professors ix
American Federation of Teachers 208
American Renaissance x
American Schools Development Corporation 124
Amherst, Massachusetts 118
Anderson, Nick 484
Annenberg Foundation 171, 175, 491
Annenberg National Institute for School Reform 151
Annenberg, Walter 151
apartheid 51–52, 61
Appleman, Deborah 310
applications for TFA 301–327
Appomattox Court House 242, 245
Armor, David J. 55, 454
Armstrong, Thomas 84
Arnold, Laura and John 304–328, 349
Associated Newspapers 192
"A Town Torn Apart" (NBC) 163
Auld, Janice 218
Austin Peay State University 27
authentic assessments 96, 100, 109
Ayers, William 26–27, 425–426

B

Bad Students, Not Bad Schools (Weissberg) 549–567
Ball, Harriet 334, 337
Baratz, Stephen S. and Joan C. 447–448
Barrell, Joseph 125
Barth, Richard 333, 349
Barton, Allen 164
Becker, Gary 437
Beck, Melinda 85
behavior and discipline, student 25, 56, 64
Bennett, William 51
Berkey, Margot 406
Berliner, David C. 258, 294–319
Bernstein, Alan 536
Bernstein, Richard 471
Besharov, Douglas J. 45
Betlach, Kilian 303–327
Biddle, Bruce J. 258
Biggs, Andrew G. 499
Big Picture Company 166
Bilentchuk, Luba 114
Bilentchuk, Michael 114
Bill & Melinda Gates Foundation, The 31, 152–157, 166, 349, 370, 484, 491–492, 506. *See also* Gates, Bill
Black Law School Association 290
Black Law Students Association 527
"blame the teachers" 9, 20, 32–33, 84–85, 120, 136, 138, 141, 149, 191, 196, 216, 265, 279, 296–321, 330, 360, 371–373, 382, 389–399, 400, 405, 413, 416, 424–425, 427, 435, 439, 480–484, 495, 496–497, 498, 502, 506, 565
Blind Side, The (book and film) 464
Bloomberg, Michael 376, 382–387, 475, 496
Bok, Derrick 515
Bolanos, Patricia J. 107–108
Bonnier Group 186
Boskin, Michael 456
Boston Globe 82, 150
Boston Herald 146
Bouchard, Thomas 438, 574
Braley, Troy 115
Bressler, Marvin 285
"bright person myth" 311
Brill, Steven 496–499
Broad, Edythe 416
Broad, Eli and Edythe 304–329, 411, 416, 496
Broad Foundation 398, 484, 491, 502
Brockman, John 531
Broder, David 151
Bronner, Ethan 46
Brook. David x
Brookings Institution, the 364
Brooklyn College 28
Brooks, David 343, 415–416, 450, 504
Brown Family Foundation 276
Brown v. Board of Education of Topeka 1, 252, 504, 572
Bruner, Jerome 80
Bryan, William Jennings 521
Buchanan, Patrick J. 434, 517
Buckley, William F. 542
Buffalo, New York 118
Buffet Early Childhood Fund 456
Buffett, Susan 456
Buffett, Warren 456
Bumpus, Janet 179
Buras, Kristin L. 259–260
Burgess-Harper, Kayrol 375
Burton, Roger 114
Bush, George H. W. 124, 472
Bush, George W. 120, 190, 303–328, 346, 472, 552

Index

Bush, Laura 303–328
Bush, Neil 120–121
Business Roundtable of Tennessee 189
busing for integration 3–7, 15, 53, 56, 473
Butz, Mary 505

C

California, Berkeley, University of 29, 30, 237, 348, 381, 457, 466, 467, 478, 479, 531
California, Los Angeles, University of 34
Cambridge, Massachusetts 44
Camden, New Jersey 44
Campbell, Donald 474
Campbell, Peter 194–195, 313, 316, 352
Campbell's Law 474–475
Canada, Geoffrey 450
Carabello, Tami 86
Cardinal Principles of Secondary Education (National Education Association) 133
Carey, Kevin 505
Carnahan, Ira 341
Carnegie, Andrew 141
Carnegie Corporation 328
Carter, C. Van 465
Cashin, Kathleen 387
Cashin, Sheryll 264
Catholic schools 69–70
Celebration School, Florida 107, 109–117
Central Park East Schools 167–176
Chagnon, Napoleon ix
Chall, Jeanne 243
Channel One 187–188, 192

Charen, Mona 460
charter schools 9, 33, 68–69, 71, 92, 107, 123, 178, 211, 270, 276, 333, 346–349, 354–355, 416, 419, 422–423, 473, 487–491, 498, 505
Cheating Our Kids (Williams) 356
child rearing 6–7, 61, 233, 438, 441, 444–448
Christian Science Monitor 471
Chubb, John 193, 199–201, 207–208
Cicero, Marcus Tullius 287
Civil Rights Act (1964) 2, 504
Claremont Graduate University 27
Clark, Kenneth 378
Clark, Percy 265
Clark, Russell 43
Clark, Stacy 312
Class Warfare (Steven) 498
Clinton, Bill 46, 303–328, 376, 472, 517
Clinton, Hillary 376, 461
Coalition of Essential Schools 150–151, 157–161, 180
Cochran, Gregory ix, 532–533
Cohen, David K. 130
Cohen, Lewis 180
Coleman, James S. 4, 38, 41–42, 53–56, 292–318, 359, 361–362
Collier, Peter 26
Columbia Teacher's College 21
Comer, James 124
Complex Justice (Dunn) 43
Compton, Bob 375, 437
Conant, James 38, 131, 133, 137, 143
Conkling, Roscoe 563
Conservative Political Action Committee 542
constructivism 92–93, 140, 252, 329, 510–511, 553
cooperative learning 85–86, 116, 118, 213, 219, 271

581

core knowledge 89, 472, 553
  criticism of 255–269
Core Knowledge Foundation 249, 275, 509
Corona, Sylvia 316
Corry, Michael 84
Coser, Lewis A. 257
Crain, William 353
"creative thinking" 100
CREDO (Center for Research on Education Outcomes) 325
Cremin, Lawrence 471
Crew, Rudy 175–176
crisis narrative, the 11, 571–572
critical thinking 90, 100
Cuban, Larry 34, 149, 298–322, 392, 408
Cubberly, Elwood P. 133
Curry, Ravenal Boykin IV 355

D

Daniels, Harvey 353
Daphtary, Ravina 309
Darling-Hammond, Linda 318–323, 366
Darwin, Charles 94–95, 521. See also evolution
Death and Life of the Great American School System, The (Ravitch) 402, 475, 483, 491
Death at an Early Age (Kozol) 37
Debunk TFA (website) 312. See also Teach For America, criticism of
"decoding" (learning strategy) 216, 223, 242–244, 247, 275. See also Slavin, Robert
Democrats for Education Reform 333, 355–362, 372–377, 382–389, 394, 404, 410, 415, 419, 422, 505
Derbyshire, John 1, 292, 526–545
desegregation, school 1–12, 473
  definition 2
  redefined 3
Devlin, F. Roger x
Dewey, John 5, 95, 133, 150, 250, 266, 425
"diasporic consciousness" 62
Dillon, Sam 432
direct instruction 63–65, 156, 232, 237, 243, 247, 266, 320, 380, 428, 459, 569–570
discipline. See behavior and discipline, student
discovery learning 93
disparate impact 426
diversity 4, 22, 28–29, 59, 82–83, 381, 433, 565. See also multiculturalism
Dogma of Zero Group Differences 291–292, 299–323, 453, 530, 552, 559, 564–565, 571, 573, 575. See also John Derbyshire
Dohrn, Bernadine 26
Dolan, Caleb 348–349
Dreams from My Father (Obama) 377
D'Souza, Dinesh 265
Dubner, Stephen 439
DuBois, W.E.B. 61, 254
Duncan, Arne 304, 413, 417–421, 484
Dunn, Joshua M. 43

E

Eagle Forum 162
Eagles, Charles W. x

Index

early childhood education 437–466
Eastern Michigan University 27
Eberstadt, Mary 82, 99, 102–103
Eddy, Elizabeth M. 20
Edelman, Marian Wright 552
Edison Schools 185, 191–211
 financing 202, 206–207
Edison, Thomas 189, 538
educational technology 211
Educational Testing Service (ETS) 432
Education Sector 505
egalitarianism 42, 82, 248, 251, 290,
 449, 507, 514, 519–524, 532,
 542, 552, 557–558, 564, 573
Eichmann, Adolf 25
Eisner, Michael 111–112
Eli Broad Prize for Urban
 Education 384
Eliot, Charles W. 132–133
empathy 15, 21, 67, 559
Equality of Educational Opportunity
 (Coleman) 359
Erikson, Erik 80
Espenshade, Thomas J. 451–452
Euclid 134
evolution 94–95, 288, 508–509, 516,
 521, 526–527, 530–536, 545,
 571, 574–575
evolutionary biology 288, 526,
 532, 575
Exxon Education Foundation 276

F

Farrar, Eleanor 130
Fee, Abby 309
Feinberg, Michael 295–319, 333–
 354, 391
Feldman, David 103

Feldman, Marcus W. 449, 519–524
Felker, Clay 186
feminism 28–29, 456
Fenty, Adrian 394–396, 407–413
Ferguson, Ronald 194, 451–452, 458
Ferrandino, John 153
Finn, Chester E. 45, 145, 148, 193,
 430, 452
Fisher, Donald and Doris 328,
 348–349, 411
Fliegel, Seymour 171
Florida Retirement System 207
Foote, Donna 306
Forbes 227
Forced Justice (Armor) 55
Ford Foundation, The 24, 491
Ford, Henry 538
for-profit schools 177, 185, 203,
 206–211.
 See also Whittle, Chris
Frames of Mind (Gardner) 81, 102
Francis W. Parker Charter School
 178–179
Frasier, Mary M. 552
Freedman, James O. 99
freedom-of-choice plans 54
Free Schools (Kozol) 24
Friedman, Milton 190
Fuller, Bruce 416, 457–461, 467
funding, education 97
 failure to improve achievement
 43–45

G

Galileo Galilei 565
Gallup polling 6, 50, 296
"gambler's fallacy," the 452
Garda, Robert A. 50

Gardner, Howard 1, 73–121, 123–124, 140, 180, 252, 258, 319, 329, 335, 395, 551
   personal life 78–81, 94
Garvey, Marcus 61
Gates, Bill 31, 152–156, 328, 364, 370, 416, 492, 500. *See also* Bill & Melinda Gates Foundation, The
Gates, Henry Louis 254
Gates, Melinda 370, 416. *See also* Gates, Bill; Bill & Melinda Gates Foundation, The
Gaziano, Todd F. 427
gene-culture co-evolution 534–535
General Electric 302–327, 497–498
general intelligence (*g*) 74, 77, 98
genome, human 517–523, 526, 530–535, 538–539, 545, 574
Georgetown University 264
Gergen, David 297
g factor, the. *See* general intelligence (*g*)
G.I. Bill, the 177
Gigot, Kalyn 329
Gladwell, Malcolm 370
Glassman, James 210
Glazer, Nathan 123
Goldman, Emma 141
Goodlad, John 34
Goodnough, Abby 238
Goodnough, Amy 346
Google, Inc. 90, 302
Gordon, Robert 364, 371
Gore, Albert 46
Gorelick, Gregory 533
Gottfredson, Linda 98
Gottfried, Paul 546
Grace, Stephanie 290–291, 525
Graham, S. Keith 39
Grannan, Caroline 210, 352
grants, financial 24, 31, 124, 130, 151, 154–156, 166, 171, 175, 202, 226, 230, 235, 239, 276, 285, 299–332, 349, 374, 398, 411, 421–422, 455, 459, 506, 558
Grant, Ulysses S. 242
Gray, Vincent 406–407
Greene, Jay 156
Green, Elizabeth 355
Greene, Maxine 26
Greenhut, Steven 499
Green v. New Kent County 3
Guggenheim Foundation 24

H

Hale-Benson, Janice 104–105
Hall, G. Stanley 133
Hampel, Robert L. 33, 130, 560
Hancock, John Lee 464
Hanushek, Eric 360, 363, 371–372, 435
Hanus, Jerome 270
Harlem Children's Zone 450
Harpending, Henry ix, 532–533
Harris, Irving B. 455
Hart, Betty 243, 315, 444–445
Harte, Lori 312
Hartford, Connecticut 44
Hart, Jeffrey 543
Harvard Education Review 447
Haycock, Kati 393
HBD. *See* human bio-diversity (HBD)
Head Start 40, 221, 447, 455, 460, 462, 465, 467
  Early Head Start 455
Head Start Impact Study (Department of Health and Human Services) 463
Head, Stephan M. 28–29
Hechinger, Nancy 193
Heckman, James J. 440, 446, 460

Index

Hegel, Georg Wilhelm Friedrich 242
Hemp, Paul 123
Herbert, Bob 348
heredity 74, 288, 290, 292, 392, 433, 438–439, 443–444, 449, 465, 507, 513–546, 549, 559, 571, 574
Heritage Foundation, The 162, 525
Herrnstein, Richard 288–290, 507, 514
Hess, Frederick 324, 361
Higher Order Thinking Skills (HOTS) 232–235
High Tech High 156
Hirsch, E. D. 1, 89, 97–98, 148, 171, 174, 241–279, 387, 395, 471, 509, 551, 553
Hochschild, Jennifer 5
Holder, Eric 426, 428
Holt, Jim 449
Holt, John 20
homeschooling 58, 211
Hone, Brian 127
Hood, John 372
Hoover Institution, The 472
Horace's Compromise (Sizer) 123, 130, 150, 151
Horace's Hope (Sizer) 123, 130
Horace's School (Sizer) 123, 130
Horowitz, David 26
Houston Independent School District 325
Howell, Cynthia 346
Hoxby, Caroline M. 489
Hughes, Langston 23
human bio-diversity (HBD) 433, 437–439, 526, 549, 562
Humboldt State University 27
Huntington, Samuel P. 62

I

Illinois at Chicago, University of 27, 425
Immig, David 311
"inadequate mother" thesis 448, 450
individualized education plans 85
inequality 47, 48. *See also* integration, racial
inner-city schools 63
integration, racial 3–6, 49–62, 262, 473, 555–557
  effect on performance 54
  "re-segregation" 51–52, 65
intelligence. *See* IQ
Intelligence and How to Get It (Nisbet) 443, 449
interdisciplinary learning 90
Internal Revenue Service 492
International Reading Association 231
IQ 42, 73–76, 88, 98, 101, 115, 237, 263–264, 277, 288–292, 314, 360–362, 368, 381–382, 392, 433, 435, 438–439, 443–449, 461, 464, 466, 499, 507–508, 513–515, 519, 522, 525–530, 539–540, 549, 559–560, 565, 573–574
Ithaca, New York 117
It Takes a Village (Clinton) 461

J

Jannarone, Thomas 226
Jay Mathews 339
Jensen, Arthur 237, 292–318, 381, 439, 508, 574
Jobs, Steve 496–497, 500

Johanningsmeier, Edward x
John Birch Society, The 543
Johnson, Bil 317
Johnson, Elmer 162
Johnson, Lyndon B. 127, 460, 509
Johnson, Samuel 563
Johnston, Michael 477
Jones, Robert 153
J. P. Morgan 302
J. Sargent Reynolds Community College 242, 245

Klineberg, Stephen 8
Kohl, Herbert 260, 447
Kohn, Alfie 118–120, 353
Kopp, Wendy 283–330, 333, 335, 349, 371, 380, 389–396, 414, 416
Koufax, Sandy 400
Kozol, Jonathan 1, 15–71, 235–239, 318, 329, 357, 487, 551, 557
  criticism of 66
  hunger strike 66
  personal life 46
Kramer, Rita 21–22, 27–28
Kristof, Nicholas 9–10, 196, 370, 449

K

Kahlenberg, Richard 262
Kaiser, George 456
Kane, Thomas 364, 371
Kansas City, Missouri 43
Kanu, Adaobi 339
Kaplowitz, Joshua 307–308
Kennedy, Edward 270
Keppel, Francis 127
Key Schools (Indianapolis) 107–109
Kilpatrick, William Heard 266
kinesthetic intelligence 86, 104, 105
King J., Martin Luther 25, 254
KIPP
  Bridge College Preparatory 352
  KIPP Academy 333, 337–355, 371
  Knowledge is Power Program 304–328
Kirp, David L. 456–459, 466
Klagholz, Leo 226
Klein, David 511
Klein, Ezra 395
Klein, Joe 463
Klein, Joel 31, 295, 375–376, 382, 387–388, 394–395, 416–418, 475, 499, 500, 505

L

Labaree, David 33–35, 437
Lahn, Bruce 519–520, 542
Lam, Diana 387
Lareau, Anette 445
Leaf, Jonathan 71
Lee, Robert E. 242
Left Back (Ravitch) 472
Lemann, Nicholas 219
Levin, David 333–354, 391
Levine, Arthur 375
Levin, Harry 201
Levitt, Steven 439
Liberty Partners 207
Liebman, James 5
Limbaugh, Rush 118
Lincoln, Abraham 25
Littky, Dennis 159–166, 173, 175
Locke High School 286, 306, 313
Los Angeles Times 369, 416, 421
Loury, Glenn 49
Lowry, Rich 544

Index

M

MacArthur Foundation 171
MacDonald, Heather 460
Madden, Nancy 213, 226–229
magnet schools 68
Malcolm X 49, 61
Mandel, Steve and Sue 304–328
Mangone, Gerard x
Manias, George 164
Manual High School 154–155
Manzi, Jim 526–529
Marino, Peter 187
Marquette University 27
Marshall Plan for Teaching 322
Martin, Gerald x
Massachusetts Comprehensive Assessment System 178
Mathematica Policy Research 325
Mathews, Jay 46, 171, 326, 335, 337, 346, 402, 471
"Matthew Effect," the 244, 466
Mayflower, the 255
McCain, John 376
McCarthy, Colman 323
McClay, Wilfred M. 270
McIngvale, Jim 338
McMurray, John 117
McWalters, Peter 165
McWhorter, John 524–525
Meaningful Differences in the Everyday Experience of Young American Children (Hart and Risley) 444
Meier, Deborah 167–177, 492, 507
Menand, Louis 255
Metcalf, Stephen 522
Met School, the 166
Michigan State University 22
Milk, Harvey 163
Millman, Noah 545

Milwaukee Journal Sentinel 153
mimetic education 89
Minnesota, University of 30–31
Minow, Martha 291
Mintz, Susan 310
misbehavior. *See* behavior and discipline, student
Mission Hill School 177
Moe, Michael 202
Moen, Francesca 86
Moffitt, Philip 186
Mooney, Tony 86
Moreno, Paul D. x
Morgan, Dan 149
Mosle, Sara 148, 171, 296–321
Mosteller, Frederick 127
Moynihan, Daniel Patrick 127
Mozart, Wolfgang Amadeus 94
MSNBC 430
multiculturalism 62, 104, 570
multiple intelligences 73–121, 140.
See also Gardner, Howard
multiple-intelligences schools 107–116
Muncey, Donna 158
Murdoch, Rupert 411
Murphy, Jerome 170
Murray, Charles 45, 98, 173, 237, 264, 490, 507, 514

N

NAACP. *See* National Association of the Advancement of Colored People (NAACP)
NAEP. *See* National Assessment of Educational Progress (NAEP)
Nathanson, Robert 218
National Assessment of Educational

Progress (NAEP) 221, 278, 384–386, 401, 428–429, 432, 436, 476, 489, 562
National Association of Scholars (NAS) 30
National Association of the Advancement of Colored People (NAACP) 5
National Council for Accreditation of Teacher Education (NCATE) 34
National Council of Teachers of Mathematics (NCTM) 272, 510
National Education Association 133, 485
National Endowment for the Humanities (NEA) 276
National History Standards 272, 510
National Institute of Education 55, 555
National Review 526–529, 542, 544
National Science Foundation 272
National Task Force on Minority High Achievement 556
National Teacher Project 389–396, 394
Nations Academies 211
natural experiments 554
NBC 163
neighborhood schools 2
Ness, Molly 309
Nevels, James 206
Newsweek 163, 165, 492
New York Times 217, 218, 225, 238
Nisbett, Richard 443–447, 461
No Child Left Behind Act 9, 62, 132, 180, 210, 273–275, 322, 368, 370, 383, 429, 431, 451, 472–473, 487, 507, 552
Noddings, Nel 49
No Excuses (Thernstrom) 350
non-directive teaching 100, 252

O

Obama, Barack 322, 376, 379, 388, 410, 413–421, 454, 484
obedience. *See* behavior and discipline, student
Occidental Quarterly, The x
Oher, Michael 464
Oklahoman, The 402
Oldham, Dustin 293–318
Olin Foundation 276
On Being a Teacher (Kozol) 25
Onorato, Katherine 306
Ordinary Resurrections (Kozol) 35
O'Reilly, Brian 206
Orfield, Gary 53, 57
Ounce of Prevention Fund 455

P

Packard Foundation 456
Palacios, Joseph 115
Palmer, John 311
Parker, George 406
Parks, Rosa 254
patriotism 25
Patterson, Orlando 254
Perlstein, Linda 403
Pernicious Tolerance (Weissberg) 550
Perot, Ross 285
Perry, Bruce 452
Perry Preschool 441, 443, 460–462
Peterson, Paul E. 361, 428
Petrilli, Michael J. 64, 506
Pettus, Peter x
Pew Charitable Trusts 455
Phelps, Scott 265
Philadelphia, PA 205–206

Index

Phillips Academy 128–129
Phillips Electronics 191
phonics 214–217, 223, 229, 243, 247, 253, 274, 386, 387, 428
Piaget, Jean 458
Pinker, Steven 531
pluralism 61. *See also* multiculturalism
Poe, Marshall 531
Pogrow, Stanley 227–228, 231–235
politicization of education 25–34
Politics of Empowerment, The (Weissberg) 550
Pomfret School 124–125, 129
Porter, Andrew 152
"portfolio method," the 95–97, 109, 112, 142, 172
Portland Oregonian 154
Posner, Richard 434, 440, 500
Postman, Neil 261
poverty 35–38, 48
Powell, Arthur 130
Powell, Lewis 7
pre-K education 454–456, 466, 484
pre-kindergarten education. *See* pre-K education
Primedia Corporation 188
private schools, elite 101–103
problem-based learning 100
Programme for International Student Assessment (PISA) 430–435, 440, 540, 571
progressive education 33–35, 81, 89, 108, 112, 118–119, 125, 129, 138–150, 160, 168–178, 196, 213–216, 223, 231, 250–254, 258–259, 265–267, 275, 318–319, 386, 425, 472, 560, 569
property taxes and education 47–48
Providence Journal-Bulletin 150, 158
Prugh, David 316
Pusey, Nathan 127
Pyati, Nick 310

R

race. *See* heredity; integration, racial; race differences in intelligence; racism
race differences in intelligence 237, 292, 433, 513–546. *See also* heredity;
Race to the Top Program 322, 420
Rachel and Her Children (Kozol) 35
racial identity 61
racial integration. *See* integration, racial
racial non-discrimination. *See* integration, racial
racism 18–19, 345, 358, 392. *See also* integration, racial
Rand, Ayn 543
Rand Corporation, the 209
Raspberry, William 105
Ravitch, Diane x, 1, 31–32, 133–134, 147, 155–156, 196, 211, 273, 354, 363–364, 366–367, 371–372, 383–387, 402–403, 408, 424, 471–511, 513
Raymond, Margaret 489
Reeves, Richard 186
Regnery, William x
Rehnquist, William H. 3
Reign of Error (Ravitch) 504
Reilly, Cathy 406
Reinoso, Alberto 221
research and development 189–191, 193
"re-segregation". *See* integration, racial
Resnick, Lauren 343
Rhee, Eric 389–395
Rhee, Inza 405
Rhee, Michelle 333, 388–410
Rhodes Scholarship 16
Richwine, Jason 499, 525

Rickets, Glenn 29
Ridge, Tom 190
Riessman, Frank 447–448
Rifkin, Taylor 317
Riley, Richard 146
Risley, Todd 243, 315, 444–445
Rivken, Steven 371
Rivken, Steven G. 363
Rizzo, Judith 218
Roberts, John 4, 58
Robertson, Julian 304–328
Robertson, Pat 118
Robinson, Michael 115
Rockefeller Foundation, the 24
Rockoff, Jonah 10, 400
Romney, Mitt 376
Roosevelt, Eleanor 255
Roosevelt, Franklin D. 267
Roosevelt, Theodore 132
Roots and Wings 223
Ross, Andrew 112–113, 116–117
Rothman, Stanley 514
Rothstein, Jesse 478
Rothstein, Richard 225, 262, 351–353, 502
Roy, Priya 296–321
Rubenstein, Edwin 432
Ruenzel, David 123
Ruffini, S. J. 228
Russell, James 133
Russo, Alexander 424
Ruth, George "Babe" 400
Ryan, James E. 43, 45, 59
Rye, New York 51

S

Sacks, Peter 474
Sailer, Steve ix, 58, 264, 330, 368, 400, 427, 433, 453, 506–507, 536, 538
Saletan, William 520–524, 542
Saltman, Kenneth 424
Sanandaji, Tino 433
Sanders, William 362, 371
San Jose State University 28–29
Sarason, Seymour 85
SAT (Scholastic Aptitude Test) 249, 294, 301, 360–361, 429, 494, 499, 508, 556
Savage Inequalities (Kozol) 15, 41, 46, 50, 557
Saving Schools (Peterson) 428
Scarr, Sandra 98
Schanzenbach, Diane Whitmore 424
Schiller, Friedrich 241
Schlafly, Phyllis 162
Schmidt, Benno 192–193, 207, 211
Schofield, Janet Ward 556
Scholastic Aptitude Test. *See* SAT
school choice 2, 9, 67–70, 174, 196, 222, 270, 473, 486–493
Schrag, Peter 471
Schwarzenegger, Arnold 421
Schweder, Richard A. 518
scripted lessons 218, 224, 226
Secord, Robert 163
segregation. *See* integration, racial
self-esteem 21
Seligman, Daniel 263–264
Sentilles, Sarah 308
Shackelford, Todd 533
Shaker Heights, Ohio 556
Shakespeare, William 134
Shame of the Nation, The (Kozol) 21, 52
Shanker, Albert 87, 144, 174
Shaw, Linda 53
Shteir, Rachel 323
Simon, Neil 285
Simons, William 379
Sirota, David 435

Index

site-based management 222, 271
Sizer, Nancy 128
Sizer, Theodore 1, 20, 123–180, 201, 222, 258, 318, 329, 395, 551
size, school 143–144, 152–156, 175
Slavin, Robert 1, 213–239, 243
Smith, Lydia A. H. 322
Snyderman, Mark 514
Snyder, Rachelle 295–319
social capital 55
social justice 26–34
social pathology rationale 448
Sociobiology (Wilson) 288
Solomon, Deborah 552
Southern California, University of 29, 305
Sowell, Thomas 428
Spearman, Charles 73
Spencer, Richard x
spending for education 38–51
Spiegel, Gabrielle M. 255
"Sputnik Moment," the 431, 551
Staiger, Douglas 10, 364, 371, 400
Stampp, Kenneth M. 531
standardized testing 4, 6, 9, 33, 40, 42, 44, 53, 55, 59, 62–65, 68, 82, 95, 108, 137, 145–146, 155, 160, 173–180, 190, 193, 195, 197, 200, 203, 206, 207–208, 220, 223, 225, 235–236, 238, 250, 263, 271, 273–278, 297–325, 337, 345, 350–354, 359–371, 373–375, 379, 382–386, 383, 390–399, 407–408, 413–415, 418, 421, 422–425, 430–433, 442, 458, 473–485, 489–492, 498, 500, 507–511, 528–529, 540, 551, 557, 562, 571–572. *See also* SAT (Scholastic Aptitude Test)
State University of New York, Plattsburgh 22
Steinberg, Laurence 560
Stephan, Walter G. 58
Sternberg, Robert 98
Stern, Sol 24, 26–28, 32, 67, 176, 278–279, 386–387
Stevens, Robert 255
Stipek, Deborah 89
St. John, Nancy 58
St. Louis Post Dispatch 32, 86, 104
Stone, Frank 114
Stone, Janette 114
Strauss, Valerie 403
Stringfield, Samuel 158, 277
Strom, Bill 316
Students First organization 410
Success for All (SFA) 213–239, 304
Summers, Lawrence 289–290, 525, 575
Sumner, William Graham 95
Sunday Telegraph 163
Symonds, William C. 156

T

Taki's Magazine (Takimag) 539, 541, 544
Taylor, Jared 427
Teachers College, Columbia University 251
Teach For America 1, 9–10, 239, 283–330, 333–335, 349, 355, 360, 389–390, 394–396, 411–414, 477–479, 551
  criticism of 305–318
"teaching to the test" 274, 317, 337, 480. *See also* direct instruction
TEACH program 389–396
technology and education 199–201
Tested (Perlstein) 403
testing. *See* standardized testing

Texas Assessment of Academic Skills 336, 337
Thayer High School 158–167
The Big Picture: Education Is Everyone's Business (Littky) 166
The Burden of Brown (Wolters) xi
The Culturally Deprived Child (Riessman) 447
The Night is Dark and I am Far from Home (Kozol) 24
The Revisionists Revised (Ravitch) 472
Thernstrom, Abigail and Stephen 7, 45, 55, 56–57, 67, 172, 194, 344–350, 426, 556
The Shopping Mall High School (Farrar) 130
Thomas B. Fordham Institute 472
Thomas, Clarence 49, 61
Thomas, Evan 393, 481–482
Tilson, Whitney 66, 71, 327, 333, 343, 354, 355–360, 373–380, 385–388, 404, 409, 415–416, 477, 499, 505, 509
Time 19, 20, 304
Time Warner 187, 192
Title I programs 221–224
Tough, Paul 340
traditional education 34, 84–86, 106, 119, 169, 179, 569–571
transformational education 89, 100
Traub, James 98–99, 102, 123, 450, 452
Trends in International Math and Science Studies (test) 278
twin studies 438, 443
Two Million Minutes (Compton) 375, 436

U

Urban Institute 325
USA Today 403
U.S. News & World Reports 149

V

Vallas, Paul 218, 418
value-added model (VAM) 362–372, 400, 422, 473, 476–480, 483, 486, 491, 495, 497–499
Vander Ark, Tom 152
Venezky, Richard L. 228–229
Visconti, Luke 552
vouchers 9, 33, 69–70, 92, 177, 270, 459, 473, 560

W

Wade, Nicholas ix, 530
Walberg, Herbert J. 172, 230–231
Walker, J. Samuel x
Wall Street Journal 39, 45, 99, 114, 150, 157, 173, 368, 402, 409, 500, 520–521, 539
Walton Family Foundation 276, 398, 491
Washington, George 22, 255
Washington State University 28
Washington Teachers Union 396–399
Wasley, Patricia 311
Watson, James D. 515–517, 521, 525–530, 542, 574
Way, Patricia 86
wealth redistribution. *See* inequality
We Are Doomed (Derbyshire) 537

Index

Weil, Sandy 153
Weingarten, Randi 379, 393–399
Weisberg, Jacob 522
Weissberg, Robert 1, 262, 350, 452–453, 460, 466, 549–567
Welch, Jack 385, 478, 497–498
Weld, William 190
Wells, Amy Stuart 57
"white flight" 4, 56–57, 68, 262–265, 555
Whitmire, Richard 392–401, 410
Whitney High School, Cerritos, California 119–121
Whittle, Chris 1, 185–211, 213
whole school reform 223
Williams, Joseph 355–356, 374, 388, 419
Wilson, Edward O. 288–291, 508, 526, 575
Winerip, Michael 476–477
Winfrey, Oprah 410
Wingert, Pat 85, 481–482
Winter, Susan 164
Wise, Arthur E. 311, 322
Wolters, Mary xi
Wong, Kristen 303–327
Wood, Peter 29
word recognition 214
Wordsworth, William 241

Y

Yale University 5, 21, 29, 30, 34, 148, 192, 196, 243, 301, 305, 307, 308, 324, 334, 479, 486, 511

Z

Zuk, Marlene 531

About the Author

Raymond Wolters is the Thomas Muncy Keith Professor of History Emeritus at the University of Delaware. He was born in Kansas City, Missouri, in 1938 and educated at St. Francis High School near Pasadena, California, at Stanford University, and at the University of California, Berkeley. In 1965, he joined the faculty of the Department of History at the University of Delaware, where he taught American history for 49 years. Wolters is the author of seven books that deal with various aspects of American race relations: *Negroes and the Great Depression* (1970), *The New Negro on Campus* (1975), *The Burden of Brown* (1984), *Right Turn* (1996), *Du Bois and His Rivals* (2002), and *Race and Education, 1954-2007* (2009). He has also published essays, articles, and reviews of more than one hundred volumes.

In 1960, when he was a student at Berkeley, Wolters met another Berkeley student, Mary McCullough. Mary and Ray were married in 1962, and from 1965 until 2014, they lived in or near Newark, Delaware, where they reared three sons. Professor Wolters retired from the University of Delaware in 2014, and since then, he and Mary have divided their time between Delaware and Florida. They attend St. Rose of Lima Catholic Church in Chesapeake City, Maryland, and St. Peter the Apostle Church in Naples, Florida.

More books from . . .

Washington Summit Publishers
WashSummit.com

The Chosen People: A Study of Jewish Intelligence and Achievement
    Richard Lynn

The Global Bell Curve
    Richard Lynn

IQ and Global Inequality
    Richard Lynn and Tatu Vanhannen

The Limits of Democratization: Climate, Intelligence, and Resource Distribution
    Tatu Vanhannen

The Newton Awards: A History of Genius in Science and Technology
    Michael H. Hart & Claire L. Parkinson

The Perils of Diversity: Immigration and Human Nature
    Byron Roth

Race Differences in Intelligence: An Evolutionary Analysis
    Richard Lynn

Understanding Human History
    Michael H. Hart

www.ingramcontent.com/pod-product-compliance
Lightning Source LLC
Chambersburg PA
CBHW061922220426
43662CB00012B/1773